A History of
European Printing

Un livre sans faute est une chimère aussi
rare que les centaures et les hippogriphes.

G. CRAPELET *Etudes pratiques et littéraires*
sur la typographie   Paris 1837

A History of European Printing

Colin Clair

1976

Academic Press

London · New York · San Francisco

A Subsidiary of Harcourt Brace Jovanovich, Publishers

ACADEMIC PRESS INC. (LONDON) LTD
24–28 Oval Road
London NW1 7DX

U.S. Edition published by
ACADEMIC PRESS INC.
111 Fifth Avenue
New York, New York 10003

Library of Congress Catalog Card Number: 74–10333

ISBN: 0–12–174850–2

Typeset by W. S. Cowell Ltd, Ipswich and
Printed in England by J. W. Arrowsmith Ltd, Bristol

To the memory of Hedy Clair

Introduction

To write a History of Printing in Europe in a single volume is an attempt to squeeze not a quart but a gallon into a pint pot. But with the economic situation as it is the prospect of a multi-volume history which the subject deserves must be somewhat remote. In the present volume an attempt has been made to trace the main outlines in the development of the craft of printing in Europe from the time of Gutenberg to the present day. Some may consider that a disproportionate amount of space has been allotted to the fifteenth and sixteenth centuries, but after all this was the period during which printing was steadily overcoming its early difficulties and gradually surmounting the technical problems which beset its cradle days. If printing in Britain has been somewhat cursorily dealt with, it is because the present author has already treated the subject in detail in his *History of Printing in Britain*.

In writing a history of this sort the author must acknowledge the help received from his precursors in this field. But since bibliographical research is continually unearthing new facts, any pilfering from earlier writers is beset with pitfalls. A further difficulty which confronts the author is the fact that finds which invalidate preconceived notions are often to be found tucked away in a variety of learned journals.

My more immediate thanks are due to Dr Desmond Flower, who first suggested that I should undertake this work, and to Mr George D. Painter, O.B.E., and Dr Dennis Rhodes for their encouragement and unselfish help. Very special thanks, also, to Mr J. S. G. Simmons of All Souls College, Oxford, for placing his unrivalled knowledge of early Russian printing at my disposal.

The name of an author between brackets, viz. (Carter, 1962), means that the relevant book on the subject can be found in the bibliography provided, thus dispensing with an accumulation of footnotes. The location of some books is still, in this work, spoken of as the British Museum Library, because its new title of British Library (Reference Division) might be unknown to many readers.

In dealing with a vast subject in limited space much must perforce be omitted. Nevertheless the author hopes that this work will prove useful to all who are interested in the history of the only art which can record all others.

Contents

Introduction vii

1. The Birth and Infancy of Printing 1
2. First Fruits of the Invention 15
3. The Spread of Printing in Germany 23
4. Printing crosses the Alps 37
5. Early Printing in France 59
6. Fifteenth Century Printing in the Netherlands 73
7. Beyond the Pyrenees: early Printing in the Iberian Peninsula . . 78
8. Switzerland's first Printers 87
9. Printing comes to England 94
10. Early Typography and Technical Innovations 107
11. Renaissance and Reformation 120
12. Germany in the Sixteenth Century 127
13. The Aldine Press and others 143
14. Printing in Sixteenth Century France 159
15. Swiss Printing in the Sixteenth Century 179
16. Sixteenth Century Printing in Spain 185
17. Christopher Plantin and his times 195
18. Early Jewish Printing 204
19. The first Music Printers 207
20. The Book Fairs 219
21. Early Printing in Scandinavia 224
22. Evolution of Printing in Central Europe 232
23. Eastern Europe: Russia and Poland 246
24. Successors of Caxton: Sixteenth Century Printing in England . . 254
25. The Seventeenth Century 272
26. Around the Mediterranean 305
27. The Eighteenth Century 312
28. Dawn of the Machine Age 355
29. A Chapter of Inventions 368
30. Nineteenth Century Printing in Europe 384
31. Some Private Presses 406
32. Art Nouveau (Jugendstil) and After 415
33. Modern Trends in Printing 426

Appendix I – Establishment of Early Presses in Europe –
    15th Century 431
Appendix II – When and Where the first Books were Printed . . 435
Bibliography 447
Index 465

I

The Birth and Infancy of Printing

THE invention of printing from movable type in Western Europe* was the result of a pressing need occasioned by the growth of literacy. From the sixth to the twelfth century the manuscript copies of religious and secular writings turned out in the scriptoria of the monasteries sufficed for the relatively small demand. The twelfth century, however, saw Europe emerging gradually from what history books used to call the 'Dark Ages', and a burgeoning of intense intellectual activity led to the founding of the first universities in Europe: Montpellier (before 1137), Vicenza (1204), Toulouse (1229), Padua (1222), followed by scores of others, including Bologna, Paris and Salerno, during the next hundred years. Furthermore the pilgrimages and crusades of the Middle Ages led to fruitful cultural exchanges.

This intellectual activity inevitably led to an increasing demand for books, the more so since the study of those days was almost entirely book study. The number of manuscript works available soon proved inadequate; books such as were turned out by the monks with unhurried care were all very well for the monastic library, but for student use there had to be rapid multiplication of texts in portable form and relatively inexpensive. Thus there grew up in each university city an organized system of supplying students with texts for the subjects comprised in the scholastic curriculum. To do this effectively the manuscript was separated into gatherings and distributed among the university scribes, each of whom copied what was termed the *pecia*, and the complete text was copied onto as many *peciae* as were necessary to make up the complete *exemplar*. This *exemplar* was then deposited with the authorized book dealer of the medieval university, who was known as a *stationarius*, probably because he had a fixed booth or stall assigned to him in or near the university. Students or copyists could then hire an *exemplar* and copy it *pecia* by *pecia*. The charges were based on a unit made up of a folded sheet of eight pages, with sixteen columns of sixty-two lines each. In this manner texts could be copied fairly rapidly.

---

* It was known in China in the eleventh century, but no development was possible at that time owing to the peculiar characteristics of the Chinese language.

Although the original regulations of the universities forbade the selling of books, the basis of the stationer's activity was gradually widened until in intellectual centres such as Florence and Paris it had grown into a bookselling business with the opening of shops where manuscripts could be purchased by the general public. This trade rapidly increased, especially during the first half of the fifteenth century, as new mental concepts in art, religion, literature and science spread through Europe and man's horizons widened. Reading and writing became, more than ever before, a necessity for the man who wished to make his way in the world. There can be little doubt that more than one mind must have been conscious of the wealth of business which awaited the man who could find a speedier method of producing books.

Of one thing we may be certain, that the invention of printing was not the work of any one man unaided by outside influence. It must have occurred to more than one thoughtful mind that the reproduction of texts by some mechanical means rather than having them copied laboriously by innumerable scribes was only rational. It is no denigration of Gutenberg to realise that others besides himself were tackling the same problem. To him there remains the inalienable title of being the first to resolve the problem in practical terms.

'But why,' the reader may ask, 'were no attempts made to solve the problem before the middle of the fifteenth century? Universities were already in existence during the thirteenth century.' The answer is simple. The price of parchment or vellum, on which manuscripts were written, would have been too high to serve economically as a printing surface, if copies were to be produced on a large scale. Thus the invention of printing had to wait until paper, which had first appeared in Europe in the twelfth century, became sufficiently common and of a reasonable price. As Dr Bühler has pointed out* the use of paper was being increasingly frequent for the production of manuscript volumes during the first half of the fifteenth century. Thus

> 'the reading public had become accustomed to a physical material suitable for books which was at once cheaper than vellum and whose source of supply was not dependent upon the whims of Mother Nature. Paper production could be increased rapidly; the production of calves could not.'

That there was printing of a kind in Holland very early is now a well established fact, though the identity of the printer (or printers) is even today as much a mystery as is the place and date of printing of the surviving fragments.

Although some eight distinct types, all based upon contemporary Dutch handwriting, have been noted in these early fragments, all are rude and clumsy and show no trace of any development.† For all we know this printing may

* Curt F. Bühler, *The Fifteenth-Century Book*. Philadelphia, 1960. p. 41.
† Six of these types are now thought to have come from one press, and the subject is still under investigation by Dutch bibliographers.

have preceded that of Gutenberg, but whether Holland or Germany is entitled to the honour of being first in the field, there is no doubt that to Mainz and Johann Gutenberg we are indebted for the practical method of typographic printing still in use today.

Before dealing with the work of Gutenberg and others perhaps it would be as well to say a few words about the so-called 'block books', since it was once thought, erroneously, that they were the forerunners of typography, and that the earliest of them dated from around 1420. In fact they are mainly dateable from about 1460 onwards, and despite the discovery of printing from movable characters, persisted for the next twenty years or so, pursuing their independent course.

One should bear in mind that the purpose of the block-book had nothing to do with the dissemination of literature. It was merely an extension of the single leaf block print aimed at providing the illiterate with visual concepts of the Christian religion. These early block-books are therefore either Biblical in subject or moralizing discourses, with titles in keeping, such as the *Biblia Pauperum*, the *Canticum Canticorum*, and the *Ars Moriendi*. The one exception to this general rule seems to have been the Latin grammar of Donatus which, being in constant demand and of no great length, could economically be printed by the method described below, and indeed continued to be so printed for some time after the invention of printing from movable type.

Block-books are so-called because each page was hand cut on a single block of wood in high relief. This block could be engraved with letters only, as in the case of the Donatus; with pictures only; or with a combination of both letters and pictures. The feature which distinguishes xylography (engraving on wood) from typography is the fixity of the characters or designs on the block. Printing from the engraved block was done by means of a frotton or burnisher, the block having first been covered with a thin water-based ink and a sheet of damp paper applied to it. The back of the paper was then rubbed with the frotton until an impression from the raised surfaces of the block had been transferred to the paper. Block-books were normally printed on one side only of the leaf, since rubbing the verso would cause blemishes to the image on the recto. Such a method of printing, in which the subject matter is printed on one side only of the leaf is termed 'anopistographic'. Late examples of block-books, however, were occasionally printed on both sides in a press, once the use of oil-based printer's ink became normal.

The illustrated block-books may be divided into two groups: in the one the pictures are without text, a simple description being engraved at the bottom of the page or in cartouches issuing from the mouths of the principal personages, not unlike the strip cartoons of the present day; the other group has a full page explanation or commentary printed on the page opposite the picture. The only

FIGURE I. A leaf from the block-book known as *Ars Moriendi* (*The Art of Dying*). It is thought to have been printed in the Netherlands about 1466.

> ·veɔ̃ cõtinere ſe vel incõtinere ſe nõ eſt
> ſimplias incõtinenae ſed eius que eſt p̃
> ſimilitudinem vt et is qui arca iram eo
> dem modo ſe habet incõtimens nõ eſt di
> cendus· Omnis enim ſupereꝗcœſſiua pra
> uitas ꝗ amenaa ꝗ timiditas ꝗ intemperã
> aa ꝗ crudelitas · aut immanitas eſt aut
> morbi. Nam qui talis nacura exiſtit vt

FIGURE 2. The only block-book known to us without illustration is the Latin grammar of Ælius Donatus which was fairly short and so could be economically printed by this method. Note the many contractions.

block-book known to us without illustration is the grammar of Ælius Donatus.

Since the aim of the early block-books was to make the teachings of the Church plain and profitable to the illiterate, illustrations were the main feature. Many block-books, therefore, consist of pictures only; and even when text is added it is minimal. The principal block-books, of which there were many different editions, are the *Apocalypse*, the *Ars Moriendi*, the *Biblia Pauperum*, the *Speculum Humanae Salvationis*, and the *Canticum Canticorum*. But there are various others, often known in but a single edition, or even from a surviving fragment. Among these are the *Historia Davidis*, the *Oracula Sybillina*, the *Decalogus*, the *Septimia Poenalis*, and the Heidelberg *Dance of Death*.

Eminent scholars have for long sought to assign dates to these books, and until comparatively recently they were believed on account of their somewhat rudimentary appearance and from the style of the woodcuts to have preceded printing from movable type. The chief obstacle in the way of establishing any date for them was the fact that the block-books themselves afforded no evidence apart from wear or cracks on the block, which would at most give an order of precedence to the various editions.

However, reliable evidence has recently been furnished by scientific examination of the paper on which these block-books were printed. The late Dr Allan Stevenson devoted much time, patience and expertise to the examination of watermarks, aided by modern technological inventions such as β-radiographic prints from high-intensity Carbon 14 sources, and he was able to date a number of these early block-books. The date of the British Museum copy of the *Biblia Pauperum* is given by him as 1465, and the *Canticum Canticorum* and *Ars Moriendi* have been assigned the date 1466.

The printing of block-books continued for some time after printing from movable type had become common, and some of the later ones bear the printer's name. One of the most popular guide books of the Middle Ages, known in various manuscript versions from the thirteenth century onwards, was the *Mirabilia Romae*, the first printed edition of which appeared as a block-book, printed about 1475 in a German version called *Wie Rome gepauet ward*. It is one of the longest of the block-books since it contains ninety-two leaves printed on both sides. Its unknown printer is thought to have been a German working in Rome, and the name of Ulric Han has been suggested.

Block-books did not therefore go out of fashion as soon as printing from movable type was invented. Indeed an Italian adaptation of the *Biblia Pauperum* called *Opera nova contemplativa* was printed as a block-book at Venice as late as around 1512. Most of the block-books originated in the Low Countries, though a few came from Germany, such as the Heidelberg *Biblia Pauperum* and a rather surprising late specimen on the art of wrestling, printed at Landshut by Hans Wurm during the first decade of the sixteenth century. This book, of which typographic editions were printed at Augsburg by Hans Sittich (1511) and at Strassburg by M. Hupfuff (1512), is known only from a single copy in Berlin. Whereas the earliest block-books dealt mainly with the teaching of the Scriptures, some of the later ones, such as the one just mentioned, dealt also with secular subjects. A similar book was Johann Hartlieb, *Die Kunst Chiromantia*, containing forty-four cuts of hands preceded by a page of text. It appeared about 1475.

Only one recorded specimen of xylography comes from France, and is known as *Les Neuf Preux*. It consists of only three sheets of paper, each of which has a block print of three figures: three classical champions – Julius Caesar, Hector and Alexander the Great; three champions of the Old Testament – Joshua, David and Judas Maccabaeus; and three champions of medieval history – Charlemagne, Arthur, and Godfrey of Boulogne. Beneath each picture is a six-line stanza in rhyme, cut in bold lettering. The work is thought to have been printed in Paris about 1455.

Those who bought the early block-books were not the unlettered laity but mainly the clergy, who sought by their means to instruct their flock in the eternal verities. The *Ars Moriendi*, for example, is concerned with the passing from life to death in a manner befitting a true Christian. The illustrations show how the angels help him to remain steadfast in his beliefs and to resist and overcome all the wiles of evil spirits. Seldom afterwards do we find a stronger unity between picture and text. Never again, it seems, has the book formed such a homogeneous entity as in these inexpensive productions of the woodcutter's art.

Other xylographica include woodcut single sheets, often in the form of calendars which usually listed a table of the lucky and unlucky days for letting blood! The *Temptationes Vitae* (*c.* 1470) enumerates the seven deadly sins, whilst the *Arbor duorum mandatorum*, originating in Germany about 1480 has a diagram in the form of a tree, illustrating Matthew xxii, 37–40.

Provided they did not run to an excessive number of pages block-printed pamphlets, once they had been cut, could be produced cheaply and fairly rapidly. But the method was a crude one and the only reason such books survived was by reason of their cheapness, and thus they survived for a time in the form of the ABC with the Lord's Prayer, the Ave Maria, moral saws, and the inevitable grammar of Ælius Donatus, the only extant complete xylographic edition of which was issued by Conrad Dinckmut, a book binder and later printer at Ulm.

JOHANN GUTENBERG

It is remarkable that although circumstantial evidence is sufficient to show that Gutenberg was the inventor of the first practical method of printing from

IEAN GVTTEMBERG

FIGURE 3. One of the many imaginary portraits of Gutenberg, of whom no authenticated portrait is known.

movable type, there is not one single book or piece of printing in existence which bears his name.

Johann Gensfleisch zur Laden, known as Gutenberg from the house in which his family, one of the patrician clans of Mainz, then lived, left his native town in 1428 and settled at Strassburg. The date of his birth is unknown, but it probably lies between 1394 and 1399. It is worth while noting that several members of the family, including Gutenberg's father, were closely associated with the archiepiscopal mint at Mainz; from which it may be assumed that Johann had some knowledge of the goldsmith's craft.

About the year 1436 Gutenberg was busily occupied at Strassburg with certain experiments bearing on the art of printing. For historical evidence concerning his activities we are obliged to rely largely on two incomplete sources –

the records of a lawsuit of 1439, termed the 'Strassburg Documents' and the record of another court action in which Gutenberg figured in 1455, and known as the 'Helmasperger Notarial Instrument'. Save for these rather meagre records original documentary evidence regarding the invention of printing is regrettably lacking, if it ever existed. This is not entirely to be wondered at, for apart from time's wanton wastage, the Rhine valley was at that period the scene of frequent warfare and Mainz itself was pillaged and burned on 27/28 October, 1462, during the armed conflict between the rival archbishops, Adolf von Nassau and Diether von Isenburg. The Thirty Years' War inflicted further damage as did the plundering mobs of the French Revolution in 1792–93.

The Strassburg Documents, unfortunately incomplete, are of considerable interest because they contain the first known references to tools, implements and material 'pertaining to printing.' The main part of these documents is the record of a lawsuit brought against Johann Gutenberg in 1439. From the evidence it appears★ that a few years before, a certain Andreas Dritzehen of Strassburg had been taught certain crafts by Gutenberg, which included gem cutting and polishing. Sometime after, Gutenberg made a contract with Hans Riffe, Andreas Dritzehn and Andreas Heilmann for making mirrors by a process known to Gutenberg, which they expected to sell in large numbers during the course of a great pilgrimage to Aachen (Aix-la-Chapelle) which was expected to take place in 1439. When the pilgrimage was postponed for a whole year, the two Andreases asked Gutenberg to teach them something of 'all the other arts and crafts' which he was said to practice, but of which they knew nothing. To this Gutenberg finally agreed and a fresh contract was drawn up by which Dritzehn and Heilmann were to pay together 250 guilders, of which 100 guilders were due immediately, the balance to be paid to Gutenberg in three instalments. The contract was to run from 1438 to 1443, and contained a clause providing that in the event of a partner dying 'all his tools and finished work and the art' (namely the knowledge) should remain the property of the firm. His heirs were not allowed to replace him but would receive 100 guilders in compensation.

This clause came into effect almost at once, for Andreas Dritzehn died at the end of 1438. His brothers Georg and Klaus asked to be taken into partnership in his place. Gutenberg naturally refused, and the brothers took him to court, which decided in Gutenberg's favour. Although the depositions in this case reveal little as to what work Gutenberg was actually engaged in, they show that

---

★ All the documents about Gutenberg were collected and published by K. Schorbach in *Festschrift zum 500 jahrigen Geburtstag Gutenbergs*. Leipzig, 1900. Text in German with notes. See also O. W. Fuhrmann, *Gutenberg and the Strasbourg Documents of 1439*, New York, 1940. Text in original German, modern German, French and English, together with useful and important notes.

his expenses were heavy and that he had borrowed large sums of money to finance his experiments.

He was shown to possess a press built by the joiner Konrad Saspach, had need of lead and other metals for his experiments, and made what were described as 'formen' (type?) which could be melted down. A goldsmith named Hans Dünne testified that in 1436 he had received 100 guilders from Gutenberg 'allein das zu dem trücken gehöret' (just for that which appertains to printing).

The need for secrecy in whatever work Gutenberg was engaged upon is shown by the fact that when Andreas Dritzehn was dying the inventor sent for all the existing 'formen' and had them melted down in his presence. He also instructed Klaus Dritzehn to dismantle an object with two screws which held together 'four pieces'; but these, according to Klaus, were nowhere to be found. What these 'four pieces' were has been the subject of much conjecture. Perhaps a forme, but more likely something in the nature of a mould for casting type.

'Only this is certain,' writes Dr Scholderer,* 'that if Gutenberg did succeed in producing any printed matter while he was at Strassburg no trace of it survives, and although this may possibly be due to the ravages of time, yet his results were not significant enough to justify the renewal of the five-year contract, which lapsed in 1443.' Gutenberg's name appears in the Strassburg tax books for the last time on 12 March 1444. His name has not been found in any archives between that date and 17 October 1448, by which time he had returned to Mainz. What would we not give to know what exactly he was doing during those four and a half mute years? What significance, if any, can be found in the fact that contemporaneously with Gutenberg's experiments at Strassburg some form of printing appears to have been attempted at Avignon in France by a goldsmith named Procope Waldfoghel, who with his wife Anna arrived there from Lucerne about the beginning of 1444? Waldfoghel was a wanderer – we hear of him in Prague, in Lucerne, and in Avignon – and it is not beyond the realm of possibility that he had worked in Strassburg, or that he had even met Gutenberg and knew something (but not the essentials) of his work. Unfortunately the enigma is never likely to be solved.

On his arrival at Avignon Waldfoghel made it known that he had discovered a method of writing by mechanical means, but being without sufficient money to pursue his researches he needed backers. To this end he approached a Jew named Davin de Caderousse to whom he is said to have taught, in return for money advanced, the secrets of his method. This took place before 10 March 1444. At about the same time he joined forces with a locksmith named Girard Ferrose, who helped him in his experiments. A third person to be initiated into the great project was a student named Manaud Vitalis, to whom, on 4 July 1444,

* Victor Scholderer, *Johann Gutenberg*. London, 1963. p. 12.

Waldfoghel promised to deliver 'duo abecedaria calibis, et duas formas ferreas, unum instrumentum calibis vocatum vitis, quadraginta octo formas stangni, necnon diversas alias formas ad artem scribendi pertinentes'.* Whether or not the word *forma* here means type, as it did later, the tools mentioned in the Avignon contracts seem to include almost everything needed for printing.

Two years later Vitalis returned the 'instruments . . . of iron, steel, copper, brass, lead, tin, and wood', and acknowledged that he had been taught what was a practical and useful art when diligently practised. This art (whatever it was) was also taught to others on payment of a fee, on condition that they were not to reveal its secret without permission, nor to practice it within a certain distance of Avignon.

Waldfoghel's name does not turn up elsewhere after he and Ferrose had left Avignon in May 1446, to avoid their creditors. Whether he and Gutenberg were working along the same lines it is impossible to say, but he would appear to have encountered the stumbling block which besets the path of so many inventors, Gutenberg himself included, namely the lack of sufficient funds to realise his full intentions.

Back in Mainz Gutenberg again sought funds for his experiments and in October 1448, borrowed 150 guilders for which a relative of his acted as surety. But this sum was insufficient for his purposes and in or about 1449 he began to borrow large sums from a lawyer of Mainz named Johann Fust.

In the first instance he borrowed, in 1450, 800 guilders at interest, on the security of his equipment. This sum was quickly swallowed up, and Gutenberg asked the lawyer for a further loan. By this time Fust was most probably fully aware of the prime importance of the work upon which Gutenberg was engaged, and consented to a further loan of 800 guilders only if he were taken into partnership in 'the work of the books' (das werck der bücher), and given a share of the profits.

On 6 November 1455, Fust sued Gutenberg for the repayment of both loans, together with accrued interest, amounting in all to 2,026 guilders. Such documentary evidence as exists relating to the court action which resulted from the quarrel between the two men is contained in the report of the notary Helmasperger and referred to as the Helmasperger Instrument. It has often been assumed that Gutenberg was quite unable to pay and that, in the words of Dr Steinberg, 'he seems to have saved very little from the wreck of his fortune'.†

But, as George D. Painter has convincingly pointed out,‡ the court ordered

---

* Two steel alphabets and two iron forms, one steel instrument called a *vitis* (vice or press?) forty-eight tin forms, and also various other forms appertaining to the art of writing.
† S. H. Steinberg, *Five Hundred Years of Printing*. 1961 edn. p. 18.
‡ George D. Painter, *Gutenberg and the B36 group. A re-consideration*, in 'Essays in honour of Victor Scholderer', Mainz. 1970.

Gutenberg to repay only the first 800 guilders, together with such of the second loan as was spent otherwise than for the purpose of their partnership. That amount cannot have been very large since a considerable portion must have been spent on the partnership project – 'the work of the books' – which was, in effect, the Latin Bible of which we shall speak later. The total sum was probably in the region of 1,200 guilders; a large sum but only about half of Fust's original claim.

Gutenberg acknowledged that the first loan was not intended for the work which was the aim of the partnership – namely the Bible – but for his own purposes. What exactly those were we must consider later. The Helmasperger Instrument is concerned only with the legal aspect of Fust's claim, and Fust himself was, during the course of the action, reduced to demanding only principal and interest on such part of the money that had not been used for their common work.

After the lawsuit and at the liquidation of the partnership Mr Painter estimates that with his half-share in the Bible sales and profits on other pieces of printing, Gutenberg was enabled to repay Fust and to regain possession of the equipment which Fust had received as surety for the first loan. 'The old view,' he writes, 'that Gutenberg was left bankrupt and deprived of his equipment is erroneous and gratuitous.'

Did Fust foreclose because the business of book-printing was now clearly seen to be a going concern with a richly profitable future which he intended to pursue to his own advantage? With the help of the accomplished Peter Schöffer, whose services he had acquired, and who appeared as a witness on his behalf, he set up the eminently successful firm of Fust & Schöffer. Gutenberg, for his part was not idle, as we shall see. A man who after years of patient experiment had brought to a successful conclusion an invention of outstanding importance was hardly likely to refrain from putting it to further commercial use. Although Schöffer continued in partnership with Fust, two other workmen, Berthold Ruppel and Heinrich Kefer, who had been among the witnesses for Gutenberg are known to have become well-known printers after the death of Gutenberg, and probably continued to work for him until his retirement in 1465.

Although twenty-eight documents of unquestionable authenticity have been discovered with contemporary references to Gutenberg, only three contain any reference to printing, and then only in the most guarded terms. This is meagre evidence on its own to substantiate the claim that Gutenberg was the inventor of printing from movable type. It is, however, supplemented by a large body of testimony from contemporary writers in support of the claim.

Of great importance in this respect is the *Cronica van der hilliger Stat van Coellen*, a history of Cologne published in 1499 by Johann Kölhoff the Younger. It contains a chapter on the origins of the art of printing which states that the invention took place at Mainz about 1440, and states definitely that 'the first inventor of printing was a citizen of Mainz and was a native of Strassburg and was named John Gutenberg'. (Spelt 'Gudenburch' in the original.)

Of the many early statements concerning the origins of printing this is one of the most interesting since the author tells us that his information was obtained from Ulrich Zell, who had introduced printing into Cologne during Gutenberg's lifetime, and had himself learned his trade with Peter Schöffer. Even though this information comes at second hand, it is important in view of the source, and also because it states clearly that Mainz printing differed from the much cruder Dutch 'prefigurations'.

Of twenty-seven books published before 1500 containing references to the invention of printing, eight mention Gutenberg by name as the inventor. Twelve statements give Mainz as the place where the invention first saw the light, while four say Germany without mentioning any specific place. In fact, whatever experiments had been taking place in Holland in connection with printing, they remained abortive and it was at Mainz that the practical solution was first found.

What was the problem facing Gutenberg which took him so long to solve? Not the press, certainly, because that could be adapted from the wine press so commonly employed in the vineyards surrounding Mainz. Nor was the cutting of punches a matter of insuperable difficulty, for the technique of engraving dies for coins and medals was part of the goldsmith's craft, and Gutenberg came from a family whose members were active at the Mainz mint. As late as 1444 Gutenberg was enrolled among the goldsmiths in the Strassburg militia.

Many of the early printers had been goldsmiths in their time. Nicolas Jenson was a master of the mint at Tours, and Peter Drach, who worked at Speyer around 1476 was also a mint master. Other printers who had at one time or another been goldsmiths included Anton Koberger of Nuremberg, Johann Rymann of Augsburg, Georg Husner of Strassburg, and Nicolaus Goetz of Cologne.

The really important inventions were the adjustable mould for casting type and the composition of a suitable alloy as type metal. It is true that nothing definite is said in the course of the law suit about a mould, and only vague references are made to such things as 'four pieces' and 'two screws'. This is only to be expected, as neither party would have been willing to disclose trade secrets. But as De Vinne pointed out, 'the mould was the only implement connected with typography which would at once lay open to an intelligent observer the secret of making types'.* Small wonder, then, that Gutenberg should observe the utmost secrecy over this essential instrument. Another reason for the vagueness of the terms employed in these and other documents

* T. L. De Vinne, *The Invention of Printing*. New York, 1876. p. 399.

of the time is that the craft was too new to possess a vocabulary of generally accepted technical terms.

The conditions of secrecy under which Gutenberg and his initiates worked have unfortunately left us with no detailed explanation of how the work of typefounding and printing was carried on, nor do we know much about the experiments which led to the eventual discovery of a practical *modus operandi*. The colophon to the *Catholicon* of 1460, of which more later, merely tells us that its successful printing was due to the 'marvellous consistency in size and proportion between patterns and moulds'.

In former times historians of printing often assumed that the earliest types were cut from wood, and this misconception was no doubt responsible for the Coster legend. If the main reason for the invention was the economic one of being able to turn out hundreds of identical copies of a text in less time than a scribe could produce one, wooden type was not the answer. To produce a complete fount of wooden characters would have taken the most experienced wood-carver a great deal of time, and after a very short period of use it would need to be replaced.

To quote De Vinne once again: 'He was the inventor of typography, and the founder of modern printing, who made the first adjustable type-mould.' The outstanding feature which distinguishes the typefounder's mould is the fact that it is adjustable for width of opening – a necessity if some letters are not to stand too far away from others. The problem which faced Gutenberg and which he eventually solved was that of making letters of the same body and height-to-paper, but different in width, and this could only be done by making the mould in two halves adjustable in their distance one from the other so as to allow the casting of letters of different width.

We have no means of knowing what Gutenberg's mould looked like, but given the conservatism of the printing industry, in which few changes of equipment were made for four hundred years, it was probably no different in essentials from that depicted in the French *Encyclopédie* of the eighteenth century. The oldest known drawing of a typefounder's mould is in Cornelius van der Heyden, *Corte instruccye ende onderwys*, printed by Joos Lambrecht (himself a punchcutter and typefounder) at Ghent in 1545. The mould held by the caster would have been recognisable by his nineteenth-century counterpart.

Another problem which Gutenberg had to solve, and which must have meant the expenditure of much time and money, was the composition of a suitable typemetal, for on this depends both the sharpness and the durability of the type. The basis of the alloy from which type is cast seems, at least from the sixteenth century, to have been lead. According to Harry Carter* analysis of

---

* H. Carter, *A View of Early Typography*. Oxford, 1969. p. 21.

samples from the workshop of Christopher Plantin dating from about 1580, gives 82 per cent lead, 9 per cent tin, and 6 per cent antimony, with a trace of copper. Early documents seem to suggest that up to the middle of the sixteenth century tin was the main ingredient. The first printed book to contain a description of typecasting, the *Pirotechnia* of Vannoccio Biringuccio, first printed at Venice by Venturino Roffinello in 1540, says that 'the letters for printing books are made of a composition of three parts of fine tin, an eighth part of lead, and another eighth part of fused marcasite of antimony'. Many early printers mentioned tin, to the exclusion of other metals, in the colophons of their books, which often stated 'stanneis characteribus excepti sunt' or 'libros stanneis typis imprimendi'. But tin could hardly have been the sole ingredient; possibly the term 'stannum' was used as the general term for typemetal. The colophon to a book printed at Augsburg by Anton Sorg in 1476 declares that it was printed 'in letters of tin'. It may well be that the practice of using tin as the chief ingredient was abandoned during the sixteenth century, for the verses beneath the cut of a typecaster in Jost Amman's *Ständebuch* of 1568 run:

'Ich geuss die Schrift zu der Druckerey
gemacht aus Wissmut, Zinn und Bley.'

which seems to indicate that the printers of Nuremberg had found an alloy approximating more nearly to that used today, which is, for letterpress, about 70 per cent lead, 25 per cent antimony and 5 per cent tin. For composing machines the amount of lead is about 10 per cent more, with a corresponding reduction in the amount of antimony.

2

First Fruits of the Invention

THE earliest products of the printing press are known only by surviving frag-ments, often owing their survival simply to the fact that bookbinders of the period found them useful for stiffening their bindings. They bear no indication of their printer's name, nor of the place and date of their origin. In all proba-bility there were others which the passage of time and the indifference of former centuries have swept out of existence.

Possibly the oldest piece of printing in Europe made from separate movable cast metal types is the fragment of a German poem on the Last Judgment, sometimes referred to as the *Sibyllenbuch*. This small portion of a single leaf, printed on both sides, was discovered in 1892 in an old binding at Mainz, and now reposes in the Gutenberg Museum in that city.

The alignment of the type, which is similar to that used in the 36-line Bible (see p. 17), is not perfectly straight and the lines are not justified (i.e. are of irregular length). From variations in the inking we can see that there is a lack of uniformity in the type-height; some letters were slightly too high, showing an over-inked spread, others were too low and printed more faintly. It is thought that the complete book was made up of thirty-seven leaves with twenty-eight lines to the page, and the date of printing has been variously conjectured as from 1442 onwards. Professor Zedler concluded that it was printed between 1444 and 1447, just at the end of Gutenberg's sojourn in Strassburg. Professor Ruppel places the date at around 1446, but other authorities are inclined to date it around 1454.

In that same year came the earliest dated documents printed from movable type, in the shape of two editions of an Indulgence granted by Pope Nicolas V in aid of Cyprus in its struggle against the Turks. One is set in thirty lines, the other in thirty-one, and each edition is found in a number of variants. Some copies are dated 1454 and others 1455, so that the Indulgence could be sold in two successive years. The 30-line Indulgence can be attributed to the press of Gutenberg, Fust and Schöffer, because the large type used in the headings is the same as that used in the 42-line Bible (see p. 17). The headings in the 31-line Indulgence are in the B36 type (i.e. 36-line Bible). In his closely reasoned article on *Gutenberg and the B36 group*,★ George D. Painter makes what appears to be an unassailable case for the identification of the B36 printer with Gutenberg himself.

An early state of the B36 type is found in the *Türkenkalender* (a propaganda calendar directed against the Turks), for the year 1455, printed presumably at the end of 1454. Progressive modifications of the type are found in various works of this period, including other calendars and several editions of the popular Latin grammar of Donatus. These latter are all fragmentary, for the *Türkenkalender* is the only one of Gutenberg's small printings known in complete form in a copy now preserved at Munich.

One fragmentary broadside has in the past caused a certain amount of confusion among bibliographers; namely the so-called *Astronomical Calendar*. This fragment, discovered by Dr Zedler at Wiesbaden in 1901, was sent by him to the Berlin Observatory, which reported that it was calculated for the year 1448. It was therefore assumed to have been printed at the end of 1447. But there were those who could not reconcile so early a date with the appearance of the type and press-work, which seemed of a standard hardly credible for so early a date. The mystery was eventually solved by Dr Carl Wehmer, who first pointed out that this fragment, printed on vellum, was not a calendar but a table of the planets indicating their position in the zodiac at the new and full moons of the year 1448.† Its purpose was to enable amateur astrologers to calculate horoscopes without recourse to a professional. The significant fact is that it could still be used for two or three decades after the year for which it had been drawn up, and would therefore still be worth printing – and on vellum for durability – for many years to come. On typographical grounds it must have been printed not earlier than 1457, just before the commencement of the 36-line Bible.

Also printed in this type, around 1454 or 1455 was a Donatus, *De octo partibus orationis*. Fragments on vellum of three different editions in this type are known, two of which were found in the binding of a book printed at Strassburg in 1488. These small pieces may have been trial runs before more important work, but at the same time, and particularly in the case of the Donatus, they were texts which were in continuous demand and could be sure of a ready sale. When we consider that most of these pieces are now known only by fragments discovered by chance, such as the *Provinciale Romanum* found at Kiev, it is probable that there were others, now either irretrievably lost or awaiting belated discovery. Printing of this kind, in addition to giving the printer useful experience in his new craft, was probably financially rewarding and free from the risk inherent in producing for the first time a large and expensive book.

★ George D. Painter. *Op. cit.* pp. 301 *et seq.*
† *Mainzer Probedrucke* . . . Munich, 1948.

But such a book had to come, for that was the incentive for all this laborious preparation – the attempt to prove that by mechanical means the work of the scribe could be accomplished in a much shorter time and with the additional advantage that no matter how many copies were made the text would be identical in each. 'It was Gutenberg,' writes Victor Scholderer, 'who set going the movement towards universal literacy which is one of the main conditions of the Western way of life.'

The first actual book to come from the printing press was a Latin Bible – the very first printed edition of the Scriptures. This Bible, sometimes called the Mazarin Bible because a copy belonging to the cardinal of that name was the first to attract the attention of scholars, is a monumental work printed for use in church. It is not dated, but was probably completed at the end of 1455 or the beginning of 1456; certainly not later than that year since the rubricator's date in the Mazarin copy was 15 August 1456. It was, however, not by chance that the first printed book was a Bible, for in those days, when the majority of those who could read were clerics, no book could have been more saleable, which accounts for the fact that during the remaining years of the sixteenth century around 150 different Bibles were printed.

This Biblia Latina from the press of Fust and Schöffer is a handsome book, printed in the gothic textura already used for headings in the 30-line Indulgence of 1454. This Bible is also known as the 42-line Bible because most of the copies known have forty-two lines to the column. In some copies, however, the first nine pages have only forty lines to the column and the tenth page has forty-one. For in fact there were two settings, in the earlier of which the type used in composing the first few pages must have been cast on a slightly larger body, which was then filed down to get more lines on the page.

Whether Gutenberg himself had a hand in it is not known. He may have worked on it during the early stages, but it was certainly printed in the main by Fust and Schöffer. It must have been costly to produce, for the two folio volumes contain 1,282 leaves, and a number of copies were printed on vellum. The privately-printed pamphlet of Edward Lazare, *Die Gutenberg – Ein Census* (1951) lists forty-six known surviving copies: twelve on vellum and thirty-four on paper.* But some of these are imperfect and the number of complete copies is four vellum and seventeen paper.

A few years after the publication of this Bible there came another, known as the 36-line Bible, the origin of which is still a matter for speculation. It is printed throughout in the third state of the type used in the Table of Planets, in several editions of Donatus, and later on in a few books printed at Bamberg by Albrecht Pfister (see p. 25). It is a much rarer book than the 42-line Bible,

* The Shuckburgh-Scribner copy raises the total to 47.

who its printer was is uncertain (though most probably Gutenberg to judge from the type), and opinions vary as to whether it was printed at Mainz or at Bamberg, though the evidence for Bamberg seems all but conclusive. The fact that several fragments of the book have been found in the neighbourhood of Bamberg suggest that it may have been printed there; on the other hand Pfister may have bought up the remaining stock when he bought the type with which it had been printed.

Most of the text seems to have been set up from a copy of the 42-line Bible, for it repeats several errors in that work. It is hardly likely that Pfister printed it, for although he made use of the type his first books show him to have been quite a novice at the art. As A. W. Pollard remarks (*Fine Books*, 1912), 'Gutenberg has certainly a better claim to have printed this volume than any one else who can be suggested.' Dr Zedler's ascription to Johann Neumeister, working at Bamberg (Z.f.B. 1941, pp. 176 *et seq.*) is not generally accepted.

The date of printing of the 36-line Bible would seem to lie between 1458 and 1461, the earlier date being the more probable. It contains 884 leaves printed in double column. Dr Ferdinand Geldner has suggested that the Prince-Bishop of Bamberg had it printed for distribution among religious houses, and that a sum of '523 pfund 4 pfennige' paid out by the Cathedral treasury in December 1459, defrayed the cost (Geldner, 1964).

On 29 June 1456, Pope Calixtus III (Alonso Borgia) issued a Bull concerning the defence of Christendom against the threatened danger from the Turks. This was printed, shortly afterwards, by the printer of the 36-line Bible. The first edition, of which only one copy is known, is in Latin; another edition, in German, is known also by one surviving copy, which bears the rubricator's date, 1456. (A facsimile, with notes, was published at Berlin, 1911.)

Towards the end of the same year was printed a calendar commonly referred to as the Purging or Blood-letting calendar (Laxierkalender) for the year 1456. This form of calendar, much in vogue during the Middle Ages, gave the favourable and unfavourable days for blood-letting or purging. The type used is similar to that employed in the Table of Planets referred to earlier. The only known copy of this calendar was found in 1803 in the binding of an account book for the year 1457 in the Mainz archives.

And now we come to a book which is not only the first printed book to state clearly the names of its printers, as well as the place and date of printing, but is also one of the most beautiful books ever printed. The colophon reads: 'Per Iohannem fust Civem maguntinum. Et Petrum Schoffer de Gernszheim. Anno domini Millesimo. cccc. lvij. In vigilia Assumpcionis' (i.e. 14 August 1457). It is a Latin *Psalter*, printed in large textura of two sizes – twenty lines to the page for the Psalms, Canticles and Creed, and twenty-four lines to the page for the Prayers and liturgical matter. The most striking features of the book are the magnificent lombardic capitals in red, light purple and blue. So beautiful is the ornamentation of these decorated initials that the page closely resembles an illuminated manuscript, which was, at that time, the very effect the printers wanted to create.

Normally coloured printing would be made by printing the colours separately, but in the case of the *Psalter* the letters and coloured decoration must have been printed simultaneously, for in every copy known there is always absolutely perfect register. Again, the impression could not have been made from a single block inked in more than one colour, for even by making use of stencils the colouring could not have been made so perfectly sharp, even had that method been practicable, which is doubtful. In fact, as Heinrich Wallau, himself a master printer, pointed out in 1900, the printing must have been made from engraved metal plates in two separate parts which fitted together. Each part was inked separately, the plates were reassembled and printed together at one pull of the press. (In Otto Hartwig, *Festschrift*. Mainz, 1900.)

The *Psalter* was published in two forms, the one consisting of 143 leaves, the other having an additional thirty-two leaves containing the Vigils for the dead and other prayers. Only ten copies of the *Psalter* are now known, five of each issue and all on vellum. Among these the only perfect copy of the 143-leaved issue is in the John Rylands Library, Manchester; and the only perfect copy of the issue with 175 leaves is in the Vienna State Library. Another edition of the *Psalter*, with 136 leaves, was printed in the same style by Fust and Schöffer and completed on 29 August 1459, the chief alteration being in the arrangement of hymns.

Fust and Schöffer realised that the types, both of the 42-line Bible and of the *Psalter*, so eminently suitable for a large service book, would not be practical for every kind of book. Without type of smaller size it would have been impossible to print volumes containing a large amount of text while keeping the number of pages within reasonable bounds. The solution was to design a type which would give sixty or more lines per column on a double-column page. As a result the partners completed on 6 October 1459, Gulielmus Duranti, *Rationale divinorum officiorum*, a folio of 160 leaves printed in a small type which became known as the 'Durandus' type. Its large capitals were printed in red and a dull grey-blue and the small capitals mostly in red. The rubrics were also in red (hence the name).

The cutter of this type remains unknown, but in all probability it was designed by Peter Schöffer, who had been a skilled calligrapher before becoming a printer. We know little about Schöffer's early days, beyond the fact that in 1449 he was studying in Paris and was a copier of manuscripts. By 1455 he had returned to his native Germany and was working with Gutenberg. In two editions of Cicero (1465, 1466) Fust states that these books were produced 'manu Petri de Gernsheim pueri mei', the word *puer* in that context meaning an employee. After Fust's death in 1466 Schöffer married his daughter Christina and by her had four sons, three of whom, Gratian, Johann, and Peter, became printers in their turn.

Johann Fust died in Paris during a business trip to that city at the end of 1466. His widow, Margarete, then married a bookseller named Conrad Henkis, and Peter Schöffer took over the sole management of the press until his own death in 1502. His output was considerable, and for the years when he worked alone Hellmut Lehmann-Haupt (*Peter Schoeffer of Gernsheim and Mainz*) lists no fewer than 228 books and broadsides – a number which probably falls far short of the actual number, for in the course of five centuries many items, particularly broadsides, are bound to have disappeared. Towards the end of 1469 or early in 1470 Peter Schöffer issued his first book list, of which one copy only has survived, and on 7 September 1470 he completed one of his most beautiful books, a two-volume folio edition of the Letters of Saint Jerome.

Meanwhile, at Mainz there appeared in 1460, without name of printer, the large Latin grammar and dictionary of Johannes Balbus known as the *Catholicon*, a work written in the thirteenth century by a Dominican of Genoa. The problem of the printer's identity still remains. The *Catholicon* is printed, two columns to a page, in a small and undistinguished type which later turns up at Eltvil. Dr Zedler (*Das Mainzer Catholicon*) confidently attributes the book to Gutenberg, but conclusive evidence as to the printer is still lacking. Dr Aloys Ruppel (*Die Technik Gutenbergs und ihre Vorstufen*) thinks it came from the press of Fust and Schöffer. Another candidate put forward in some quarters is Heinrich Keffer, who had formerly worked with Gutenberg at Mainz and later became a printer at Nuremberg, where he worked with Hans Sensenschmidt. In the colophon of their first book, *Codex egregius comestorii viciorum* (1470) occurs the formula 'Nuremberge anno . . . patronarum formarumque concordia et proporcione impressus', the words being exactly the same as those used in the colophon of the *Catholicon*.

This book appears on Schöffer's book list of 1470, but as he was a bookseller as well as a printer he may well have simply bought up what was left of the stock. He seems hardly likely to have printed it in an earlier type inferior to the 'Durandus' type which he already possessed. On 26 February 1468 a certain Dr Konrad Humery acknowledged the receipt, from the estate of Johann Gutenberg deceased, of 'certain forms, letters, instruments, tools, and other things belonging to the work of printing . . . which were, and still are, mine'. From this we may deduce that Dr Homery was for some reason the legal owner of Gutenberg's remaining material.

Whoever did print the *Catholicon* was, on the basis of type, also responsible for two other books produced at about the same time: the *Tractatus rationis* of

Mattheus de Cracovia, and the *Summa* of Aquinas, both undated. Dr Zedler believes that the *Summa* preceded the *Catholicon*, and that the *Tractatus* was printed when the *Catholicon* was half completed.

Only a few miles from Mainz is the small town of **Eltvil,** where in 1467 one Heinrich Bechtermüntze began to print a Latin–German vocabulary known as *Vocabularius Ex Quo.* He died while the book was in the press and it was completed on 4 November of that year by his brother Nicholas and a certain Wygand Spiess of Orthenberg. A second edition was printed by Nicholas Bechtermüntze alone on 5 June 1469. In both cases the type used was, apart from a few modifications, that of the first edition of the *Catholicon.* No satisfactory explanation is forthcoming as to how these types came into the possession of the Eltvil printers while Gutenberg was still alive, for his death did not occur until 3 February 1468. Are the brothers Bechtermüntze also to be placed among the contenders for the title of having printed the *Catholicon,* as Bernard suggested? (A. Bernard, 1853.) This is hardly likely unless they had printed the book in Mainz, for there it was printed according to the colophon in the book itself, and also according to Schöffer's catalogue.*

Not far from Mainz is the village of **Marienthal.** There, in the Kogelherrenhaus, the religious body known as the Brothers of the Common Life printed a few service books and indulgences between the years 1474 and 1476, the chief product of their press being a *Breviarium Moguntinense.* The two type-faces found in this Breviary are a heavy Gothic letter similar to that found in the books of Ther Hoernen at Cologne.

Not long after Schöffer had parted from Gutenberg and had begun to employ the new craft in an impressive manner, the number of printers increased. A widening of the field of activity for this new invention was imminent. In itself inevitable, this process was hastened by the sacking of Mainz in October 1462, although by now presses were at work in at least two other German towns, Strassburg and Bamberg. Indubitably the economic stresses which this disaster inflicted upon Mainz must have led to the departure of many workmen formerly employed by Gutenberg, Fust and Schöffer.

Little of importance came from the press of Fust and Schöffer between the Bible, completed just over two months before the sacking of the city, and the Cicero, *De Officiis,* of 1465. But once Schöffer was in sole charge, his business acumen, shown by the important sales organisation which he built up, made him an important figure who made of printing and bookselling a major industry.

When printing spread from Germany to other countries, the printers still clung to the idea that their books must resemble as closely as possible the manuscripts of the national scribes, and it took nearly a century for printed books to

* Gutenberg probably stopped printing around 1461–2 having sold the B46 type to Pfister and the *Catholicon* type to Bechtermüntze.

free themselves from this influence and establish a style of their own. Thus when the North Germans Sweynheim and Pannartz became the first to introduce printing into Italy at Subiaco (p. 37) they had, although more familiar with gothic forms, to fashion their types in accordance with the contemporary Italian scribal hand, which we now call 'roman'. At first they made use of a semi-gothic type, which they later replaced by one more roman in character.

Nevertheless there was one fundamental difference between the printed book and the manuscript it strove initially to copy. However neat and regular the handwriting of the scribe might be, no two instances of the same letter would be exactly alike, and it was these slight variations which gave vivacity to the well-written book and added to the aesthetic pleasure it provided. The punch-cutter, however, had to choose one model for each character, and one only. He might, if his taste were good and his technical skill adequate, produce letters whose appearance on the printed page would be, perhaps, neater than the manuscript, but lacking in liveliness. On the other hand, if he were a poor designer or copied clumsily the result could be disastrous, for any defects would, by repetition, become painfully obvious.

3

The Spread of Printing in Germany

THE new art soon spread far beyond the bounds of Mainz. By the end of 1470 presses had been set up in seven German towns, and by 1499 there were no fewer than fifty localities in Germany where printing was known. But Mainz was never, after 1470, the chief centre of printing in Germany and for several years Peter Schöffer was its only printer. For one thing the struggle between Dieter of Isenberg and Adolf of Nassau, rivals for the archbishopric of Mainz, led to the sacking of the city by Adolf's troops on 27 October 1462. This crippled trade for some years and many craftsmen, including printers, moved from the city. Moreover, it is likely that some ambitious journeymen, having learned something of the new craft in Mainz were anxious to set up as master printers on their own account.

Without financial backing this was no easy task. A printer had to rent a dwelling capable of housing his press and material, and because the early presses printed only a single page at a time, to do business on any but the meanest scale would necessitate a minimum of two presses. Also, if he decided to try his fortune in a foreign land, he had either to be acquainted with the language or to find a native scholar who could supervise the editorial side of the business. Many did emigrate, which accounts for the many German names to be found among the earliest printers in other European countries. The master printers of these printing offices were likely to be former workmen of Gutenberg or of Fust and Schöffer, or men who had learned their trade from this source.

Some became veritable nomads, trusting to luck to find a backer who would enable them to settle and establish themselves. Such a one was Marcus Ayrer who, between 1483 and 1506, is known to have printed at Nuremberg, Regensberg, Bamberg, Ingolstadt, Erfurt, and Frankfurt-on-the-Oder.

Strassburg, where Gutenberg had conducted his early experiments, was an important city in the fifteenth century. Its burgesses were rich and cultivated, and according to that learned Italian traveller Aeneas Sylvius some of the houses of the wealthier citizens of Strassburg were so proud and costly that no king would have disdained to live in them. Its cathedral rises in majesty over a conglomeration of gabled roofs in Hartmann Schedel's *Liber Chronicarum*. In 1388 the councillors of the city ordered a bridge to be built over the Rhine to link up with Kehl, thus putting Strassburg more directly in touch with German commerce and culture in Swabia.

In view of the city's growing importance it is not surprising that around 1460 the first press was established there, under the direction of Johann Mentelin, a native of Schelestadt, and at the time a scribe and episcopal notary. For a long time it was not known how many books he printed, for it was not until he had been active for at least thirteen years that he printed either his name or a date in any of the works which came from his press. But evidence provided by such things as dates of purchase, rubrication, and so on, enable us to form a fairly good idea of their sequence. His active career as a printer spanned nearly twenty years, from *c.* 1460 to 1478, the year of his death.

Mentelin was a sound business man if a somewhat careless printer. His first important publication was a Latin Bible issued in 1460–61, and whereas the 42-line Bible occupied 1,286 pages, Mentelin saved a great deal on the cost of printing by squeezing his Bible into 850 pages. An even more lucrative venture was his printing of the first edition of the Bible in German (and for that matter in any modern language), a folio of 406 leaves which appeared in 1466. Despite the inaccuracy of much of the translation, it remained the standard text for all German Bibles before Luther.

This was further proof of Mentelin's sound business instincts, for obviously a Bible in the vernacular was assured of a good sale. He was also one of the first printers to advertise his wares, for about 1470 he issued a catalogue containing the titles of nine books; though in this field he may have been preceded by Peter Schöffer, who printed his first known list of titles late in 1469 or early in 1470. Mentelin also issued the first printed edition of *Parsifal* (1477), the famous epic of Wolfram von Eschenbach.

Mentelin died on 12 December 1478, leaving two daughters, one of whom married his successor, Adolf Rusch of Ingwiller, and the other Martin Schott, also a printer. It was Rusch who first introduced roman types into Germany. For a long time he remained unidentified and was referred to as the R-printer from the peculiar form of that majuscule in his roman fount. Rusch's type is a pure roman and the first known use of it occurs in Hrabanus Maurus, *De Universo* (1467). This was about the same time as Sweynheim and Pannartz were using their first true roman in Italy.

Among other early Strassburg printers were Heinrich Eggestein, who printed the second Bible in German (1470) and the first German Psalter (*c.* 1473); Georg Husner, who printed in partnership with Johann Beckenhub in 1473, and struck a new note in providing roman capitals for a text in round gothic; Heinrich Knoblochtzer, who after working at Strassburg from 1476 to 1484, later went to Heidelberg; Martin Schott, Mentelin's son-in-law; Johann Prüss, whose undated *Buch der heiligen drei Könige* contains fifty-eight woodcuts of considerable merit; Martin Flach, whose first book appeared in 1487, but who had worked at Strassburg, presumably as a journeyman, as early as 1472; and Johann Grüninger, who printed several medical works by Hieronymus Braunschweig.

The earliest incunabula were not illustrated. The first printer to add illustrations to his books was Albrecht Pfister of **Bamberg**, who began printing about 1460. Like many other early printers he had previously been a cleric, and he is recorded in 1448 as being secretary and procurator to the precentor Georg von Schaumberg, who later became Prince-Bishop of Bamberg. Nine editions are known to have come from his press up to the time of his death, which took place not later than 13 April 1466. But since of the extant Pfister-printed books none have survived in more than three copies we cannot rule out the possibility of other books having been printed and subsequently lost.

In addition to being the first printer of illustrated books, Pfister was also the first to print books in the vernacular. Only two of his books are dated and only two contain the name of the printer. They were printed in the following order according to Dr Zedler:

Der Ackermann von Böhmen (of which only one copy survives).
Ulrich Boner, Der Edelstein (February 1461).
Buch der vier Historien (May 1462).
Biblia Pauperum (two editions: Latin and German).
Second issue of Der Ackermann.
A second German Biblia Pauperum.
A second issue of the Edelstein.
Belial in German (the only book not illustrated).

In Pfister's first book he did not attempt to print text and blocks simultaneously, but printed text first and left spaces for the woodcuts. This we know because the only surviving copy of Der Ackermann in the library at Wolfenbüttel lacks the woodcuts which are found in the second edition. In choosing the work of Johannes von Schüttwa (d. 1414) as his first book, he sought out a work which Gustav Ehrismann described as 'das Meisterstück der deutschen Prosadichtung bis zur Reformation', and one which was to be reprinted at Basel, Esslingen, Strassburg, Ulm, Augsburg, Leipzig and Heidelberg during the course of the fifteenth century.

The second book, Ulrich Boner's Edelstein, is a collection of fables gathered together from the works of Æsop, Avian, Petrus Alfonsi and others by the Dominican from Berne, who flourished about the middle of the fourteenth century. The two issues from Pfister's press were the only ones to be printed in the fifteenth century. The 'four histories' comprised in the next book are those of Joseph, Daniel, Judith and Esther, and since such collections of biblical tales were compulsive reading in those days for the semi-literate public which later was to feed avidly on chap-books the work probably sold well. The Biblia

Pauperum, known in manuscript and xylographic form, was for the first time printed by Pfister in a booklet of thirty-four pages, and, unlike the *Ackermann,* pictures and text were printed together in one forme.

With the printing of *Belial,* a story of the struggle between Christ and Satan for the souls of men, written in the fourteenth century by Jacobus of Theramo, Bishop of Spoleto, Pfister's press closed down. There may have been other books now lost, for there was time enough between the printing of the *Edelstein,* completed 14 February 1461, and the publication of the *Vier Historien* at the beginning of May 1462, to have allowed for other work. Pfister himself died before 13 April 1466. Of his family we know practically nothing. The supposition that he had a son Sebastian who printed around 1470 finds no confirmation.

As stated earlier, the books of Pfister are printed in the types used for the 36-line Bible, most probably printed by Gutenberg. How did he acquire them? Probably by purchase from the printer who may have been quite willing to dispose of material for which he had no immediate use, or which was unsuitable for his future plans. Not unnaturally, seeing that his books were printed in the type used for the 36-line Bible, Pfister was at one time thought to have been the printer of this work, and it was for long known as the Pfister Bible. But this is disproved by the typography of Pfister's first book, which, although printed later than the 36-line Bible shows plainly the novice hand.

For fifteen years after the death of Albrecht Pfister, Bamberg was without a printer, until in 1481 Johann Sensenschmidt from Eger set up a press there and printed the *Missale Ordinis S. Benedicti,* commonly known as the Bamberg Missal. Sensenschmidt, who had previously had a press at Nuremberg, completed the Missal on 31 July 1481. From 1482 until May 1491 he was in partnership with Heinrich Petzenheimer, but died soon after the latter date, whereupon Petzenheimer went into partnership with Laurentius Sensenschmidt and Johann Pfeyl. During his stay at Bamberg, Johann Sensenschmidt was called to Regensburg to print a Missal there with Johann Beckenhub in 1485, and two years later he made a journey to Freising where he printed, this time alone, another Missal. The only other printers at Bamberg during the fifteenth century were Hans Spörer and Marcus Ayrer, both of whom were wandering printers, working wherever they could find business.

Cologne, on the Rhine, and within easy reach of Mainz, must have been one of the first cities in Germany to hear of the new art of printing, and by the end of 1465 a printer was working there, one Ulrich Zel of Hanau, a clerk of the diocese of Mainz. Where he learned to print is not known but it was probably in the workshop of Fust and Schöffer at Mainz. He was active until the end of the century and died around 1507, with some 200 books to his credit. Unlike many of his colleagues he seldom produced large folio volumes, but made a speciality of small quartos dealing in the main with minor theological works and volumes of sermons. In this respect it should be noted that of more than 1,300 titles printed at Cologne before the end of the century, more than half were theological writings, and almost all were in Latin. Zel became a burgess of Cologne and married the daughter of a patrician, Katharina Spangenberg.

Arnold ther Hoernen, who began to print at Cologne in or before 1470, is said to have learned his craft with Zel, and was active until 1482, about a year before his death. The earliest editions of that most popular of epitomes of history, the *Fasciculus Temporum* of Werner Rolewinck, were published in Cologne in 1474 – one by Arnold ther Hoernen and the other by Nicolaus Götz. The second printer's mark used in Germany, following that of Fust and Schöffer, was that of ther Hoernen, whose device was a shield bearing his housemark and the initials *a.h.* The *Sermo ad populum predicabilis* which he printed in 1470 has the leaves numbered in the centre of the right-hand margin, an innovation which was not followed up. After his death his widow married the Cologne printer Conrad Welker, a native of Boppard, who carried on the business, aided possibly by his step-son, Diederich Molner.

Johann Kölhoff, a native of Lübeck who had learned his trade with Wendelin of Spira at Venice (see p. 40), settled at Cologne about 1472 as merchant and bookseller as well as a printer-publisher. Beginning his career by printing a dozen tracts by Thomas Aquinas, he was active up to the time of his death in 1493. He was the first to introduce printed signatures at the foot of the page in his edition of Johannes Nider, *Praeceptorium divinae legis* (1472). Kölhoff's device featured the arms of Cologne. The business was carried on after his death by his son Johann Kölhoff II, who in addition to being printer to the Town Council, was also a merchant, dealing in a wide variety of goods. In 1499 he printed the *Cronica van der hilliger Stat van Coellen*, a book of value to historians of printing because of its reference to Gutenberg and the origins of printing. Its value to the printer was negative, for the book was banned and confiscated, and Kölhoff was banished from the city.

A very important printer-publisher was Heinrich Quentell from Strassburg, who settled in Cologne about 1478, working there for the remainder of the century. Between 1478 and 1480 he printed two vernacular Bibles, one in the dialect of Lower Saxony and the other in the Rhenish-Westphalian dialect prevalent along the lower Rhine. This Cologne Bible exerted a considerable influence on Bible illustration for many years. It had more than a hundred woodcuts running the full width of the double-columned page, all of which were obviously the work of a skilled artist, though his identity is unknown. Koberger, who knew the sales value of good illustrations better than most, did not hesitate to make use of them at Nuremberg in 1483 for his own High German Bible.

Other Cologne printers who were active about this time include Nicolaus

Götz, Conrad Winters, Bartholomaeus von Unkel and Hans Schilling (Johannes Solidi). But one should not leave fifteenth-century Cologne without recalling that it was in that city that William Caxton learned the art of printing, and that Theodoric Rood – the first Oxford printer – was a native of Cologne.

Founded by the Roman emperor Augustus, **Augsburg**, thanks to the rich and powerful Fuggers and the Welser shipping interests, was in the fifteenth century a city of great importance. The first printing press was established there in 1468 by Günther Zainer, who came there from Strassburg, where he had possibly gained his knowledge of printing as an employee of Johann Mentelin.

His total output consisted of around 120 books, which to begin with he printed in a gothic type of the variety known as fere-humanistica, common also to the books of other Augsburg printers. But in 1472 he used for an edition of the *Etymologiae* of Isidore a roman face which is among the earliest roman cut in Germany. In the subscription to a 'bleeding calendar' for 1472 he states that the type was cut 'lest we should seem to yield precedence to the Italian' (*ne italo cedere videamur*). For Augsburg was far enough south to feel a strong Italian influence, and Zainer was anxious for his work to be able to stand comparison with that emanating from Venice and elsewhere in Italy. It is thought that he based the design for his roman type on the hand of the Augsburg calligrapher Heinrich Molitor. Nevertheless, some of his later books are printed in a fairly large textura.

Zainer's German edition of the Golden Legend – *Leben der Heiligen* – came out in 1472 and was the first illustrated book printed at Augsburg, containing 120 woodcuts. The text was evidently printed first and space left for the cuts, some of which overlap the text. About twenty books from Zainer's press were illustrated and this led to a dispute with the woodcutters of the town, for long one of the chief centres in Germany for the production of playing cards and for wood engraving of all kinds. It was finally decided that Zainer could print illustrated books only on condition that he employed members of the woodworkers' guild to cut his blocks. Zainer was also the first printer (if we except the solitary example of Schöffer in the 1457 *Psalter*) to make use of specially designed initials instead of leaving blanks to be filled in later by the rubricator.

Zainer died in 1478, by which time other printers were at work in Augsburg. In 1472 Johann Bämler printed the first German edition of the well-loved priests' handbook called the *Summa confessorum* in a new letter form in which one can see a foreshadowing of the later Schwabacher.

Bämler worked at Augsburg from 1472 until 1495. Like many of the early printers he had started life as a scribe and illuminator, appearing as 'schreiber' in the Augsburg archives as early as 1453. Like Zainer, he seems to have learned to print at Strassburg. One of Bämler's most successful books was the *Buch der Natur* of Konrad von Megenberg (1475) which contains the earliest known botanical wood engravings. He also printed the earliest illustrated book on the Crusades – *Historie wie die Türken die christlichen Kirchen angefochten* by R. de Sancto Remigio (1482) in which one of the larger cuts shows the Pope preaching to a crowd of pilgrims.

Anton Sorg, originally a 'briefmaler' and 'kartenmaler', began his career as a printer in 1475, and between that year and 1493 became the most prolific of Augsburg's fifteenth-century printers. He published a number of travel books, including the first German translation of the travels of John de Mandeville (1481), Breydenbach's *Reise ins heilige Land* (1488) and Hans Tucher, *Reise in das gelobte Land* (1486). But his best work was a history of the Council of Constance by Ulrich von Reichenthal (1483) profusely illustrated with woodcuts, chiefly of the armorial bearings of the dignitaries present, drawn in outline and intended to be hand-coloured. There are also coats of arms of all countries of the known world (including many mythical ones). This was the first armorial to be printed.

Towards the end of the century a number of printers began working at Augsburg, for by the turn of the fifteenth and sixteenth centuries the great commercial activity of both Augsburg and Nuremberg went hand in hand with a leading position in the intellectual life of the time. One of the most important of these printers was Hans Schönsperger, celebrated as the printer of the *Teuerdanck* of 1517, of which more will be said later. He began to work there about 1481 and became known as a prolific printer of illustrated books, though most of the cuts he used were based on work previously produced by other printers. Thus his German *Hortus Sanitatis*, which he brought out in August 1485, has cuts copied from the edition issued by Schöffer at Mainz in March of the same year. In the botanical drawings of his edition, Schönsperger made use of stencils for colouring, as he did also in the 1488 edition. Both editions can be seen in the British Museum.

Among the Augsburg printers of the latter part of the fifteenth century, Erhard Ratdolt holds a rather special place, for his active life as a printer was divided between Germany and Italy. Of his work in Venice between 1476 and 1486 something is said in a later chapter. In 1486 he returned to his native Augsburg at the solicitation of the bishop Friedrich von Hohenzollern, and printed a number of works there between 1487 and 1516. He specialised mainly in liturgical books, but also printed, as he had done in Venice, mathematical and astronomical works.

The first book he printed on his return to Augsburg was an *Obsequiale* for Bishop Friedrich von Hohenzollern, completed in February 1487, and containing a woodcut portrait of his patron printed in black, red, yellow and olive-brown – the first German printing in four colours. So highly considered was his printing of service books that many sees in Southern Germany and Austria called upon him to reprint their church books, so that we find him printing *Breviaries* and *Missals* for Freising, Brixen, Passau, Regensburg, Constance, Melk and Salzburg, as well as *Directories, Antiphoners, Obsequials* and *Vigils* to booksellers' commissions. One can understand why this should be so when one looks at such a specimen as Ratdolt's Augsburg Missal of 1496, with its immaculate red and black printing.

Apart from these liturgical books mention may be made of the Johannes de Thwrocz, *Chronica Hungarorum* (1488), the cuts in which, though not originals, comprise some very lively battle scenes. (First edition, see p. 235.)

If in **Nuremberg** nothing flourished quite so luxuriantly as commerce, this does not mean that literature or the arts generally suffered in consequence. The central position of the city made it a meeting place for scholars and artists from various countries, and like Augsburg it was famous throughout the Middle Ages for its woodcutters. The city's patrician government and stable social order allowed artists and printers to work with an agreeable sense of security, though the conservative nature of that government had a somewhat stultifying effect upon the adventurous mind and made of Nuremberg a rather unintellectual society which served to emphasise the more the scholarship of men like Willibald Pirckheimer and Conrad Celtis.

Two printing offices introduced the new art into Nuremberg within a short time of each other. The first was that of Johann Sensenschmidt, financed by Heinrich Rumel, the second that of Anton Koberger. Sensenschmidt's first book, Retza, *Comestorium*, appeared in 1470. A copy, now in the University Library at Erlangen, was donated to the Nuremberg Carthusians in 1472 from 'Henricus Rumel und magister Sensenschmidt puchtrucker', but Rumel's name does not appear in any book printed by Sensenschmidt. Towards the end of 1472 we find Sensenschmidt on his own, but about April 1473 he entered into a partnership with Heinrich Kefer and on the eighth of that month they signed the completed *Pantheologia* of Rainerius de Pisis, the only book at Nuremberg to bear the name of Kefer, who had been one of Gutenberg's servants and testified in the law suit with Fust. After a year's interval we find Sensenschmidt with a new partner, Andreas Frisner, described as 'imprimendorum librorum corrector'. Sensenschmidt continued to print at Nuremberg until 1478 when, unable to face the competition from Koberger, he went to Bamberg.

Were there printers at Nuremberg before Sensenschmidt? The names of Conrad Zeninger of Mainz and a certain Franz Vestenberger have been mentioned as printing there in the 1460s. If this were so, no vestige now remains of their work. The greatest name connected with early Nuremberg printing is certainly that of Anton Koberger, who came from an old Nuremberg family of craftsmen. For a man with the business acumen of Koberger, Nuremberg at that time offered almost unlimited scope, for the city had by then acceded to the first position in the goods trade of Germany, thanks largely to the foresighted policy of the ruling classes in abolishing all existing restrictions on foreign merchants in Nuremberg and permitting trade association with aliens, so that the city became a trading mart visited by and almost indispensable to foreign merchants. Here Koberger set up in business in 1470 as printer, publisher and bookseller and made of his firm the most enterprising publishing house of the century. He worked on a large scale and at the height of his activities is said to have owned twenty-four presses and to have employed more than a hundred workmen. His energy and efficiency as a publisher was so great (he printed no fewer than thirty-three Bibles) that his presses could not sustain the whole of his publishing programme and he was obliged to farm out work to other printers, notably to Johann Amerbach at Basel. Their correspondence forms an important source of bookselling history in the fifteenth century.

Koberger was undoubtedly able to call upon ample funds, for his outlay on paper alone must have been tremendous, since he was no printer of meagre tracts and pamphlets but went in for large folio volumes of many pages. His Rainerius de Pisis, *Pantheologia* of 1474 (which he seems to have pirated from Sensenschmidt's edition of 1473) runs to 865 leaves, and the Nicolaus de Lyra, *Postillae super Biblia* (1481) comprises 939 leaves in its two volumes. His Bibles, too, called for a vast amount of paper.

Undoubtedly the best-known of Koberger's publications is the *Liber cronicarum* of Hartmann Schedel, better known perhaps as the Nuremberg Chronicle. This sumptuous folio was printed in 1493 in both a Latin and a German version, and was the happy result of a combined effort of scholar, artist, printer and business-man. It contains 1,809 woodcuts by Michel Wohlgemuth and Wilhelm Pleyden-wurff, of which 1,164 are repeats. The Latin version runs to 326 leaves, but the German translation (by Georg Alt) is of 297 leaves only, because Aeneas Sylvius's description of Europe was abbreviated in the German version and the account of Italy omitted.

Koberger, who had already been successful with illustrated Bibles and lives of the saints, favoured the idea of a lavishly illustrated history to appeal to a popular market, but the expense entailed was so heavy that he had to obtain financial backing from two rich citizens of Nuremberg, Sebald Schreyer and Sebastian Kammermeister, who entered into a profit-sharing contract with the publisher. Hartmann Schedel, who compiled the text, was a physician, humanist and polyhistor, and owner of what in those days was a vast personal library.

Another finely illustrated book from Koberger's press was the *Schatzbehalter* of Stefan Fridolin, which appeared in 1491 with ninety-six full-page illustrations, mostly of Biblical subjects, cut by Wohlgemuth. Bibles were always a staple of the early printing trade, and Koberger published his first Latin Bible in 1475. But whereas most of the Bibles printed in Germany up to that date had been in plain text, Koberger was convinced that the layman, as distinct from the scholar, who needed no such stimulus, would welcome the Scriptures in an illustrated edition. The success of his German Bible of 1483 (for which he used blocks from the Cologne Bible of Heinrich Quentell) amply vindicated his judgment.

He undoubtedly received encouragement from Michel Wohlgemuth, who was not only a painter and engraver but also the proprietor of a busy artistic workshop. He settled at Nuremberg in the 1480s, married the widow of the artist Hans Pleydenwurff, and took over his workshop which he made into a thriving business, in which his stepson Wilhelm Pleydenwurff assisted him. When Dürer published his *Apocalypse* in 1498 he could count on a market for which Koberger and Wohlgemuth had prepared the ground.

Koberger's list was, on the whole, made up of familiar and established works such as Pliny's *Natural History* and the *Catena aurea* of Thomas Aquinas. He was not a venturer into untried paths, but depended largely on the mass appeal of the works he published. He became a publisher on a grand scale by virtue of an efficient sales organisation with agents and factors in various parts of Europe. He also invested capital in the businesses of other publishers. But as so often happens his heirs possessed little of the founder's business acumen and after his death in 1513, the firm closed down in 1526.

In 1471 the astronomer Johann Müller of Königsberg (Johannes Regiomontanus), with the help of Bernhard Wetter, set up a press at Nuremberg for the publication of scientific works. He issued a list of mathematical texts and scientific works which he intended to print, but would-be purchasers must have been disappointed when the press closed within a year, after Müller had been appointed Bishop of Regensburg. Among the books which came from his press during its short life was his own *Tractatus contra Cremonensia*, but although he was the author of the first systematic treatise on trigonometry, *De triangulis*, it was not printed until half a century after its author's death, by Johann Petri at Nuremberg in 1533.

Friedrich Creussner, active in Nuremberg from 1472 until the last decade of the century, claims our attention as being the printer of the first edition (albeit in German) of the Travels of Marco Polo. Although this work was written in French at the end of the thirteenth century, the original French text was not printed until 1824, by the Société Géographique. An incomplete French version was printed by E. Groulleau in 1556. Creussner also published in 1489 a Bertholdus, *Horologium Devotionis*, the woodcuts in which are said to have been the prentice work of Albrecht Dürer, who had entered the workshop of Michel Wohlgemuth at the end of 1486.

Other Nuremberg printers of the incunabula period include Conrad Zeninger, who later moved to Venice; Peter Wagner, whose *Küchenmeisterei* was one of the earliest books on culinary matters; Georg Stuchs, a printer of liturgical books, whose *Obsequial* for Regensburg use shows early use of music notation; and Caspar Hochfeder who, after printing at Nuremberg from 1491 to 1498 or 1499, moved first to Metz and then to Cracow, where we shall meet him in a later chapter.

Nuremberg was the city in which we first come across a style of letter, a variety of bastarda, which ultimately became known, though nobody seems to know why, as 'schwabacher'. First used by Creussner in 1485 it became very popular down to the middle of the sixteenth century, when it was supplanted by Fraktur, though remaining in type-founders' catalogues until the eighteenth century. 'Of the three German bastardas which preceded Fraktur,' writes A. F. Johnson, 'Schwabacher was easily the most widespread. In Nuremberg, where it originated, it is all but universal.' Despite the name given to it, there is nothing to connect this particular letter-form with the little town of Schwabach in Franconia. (A. F. Johnson, 1934.)

For a century before the invention of Gutenberg **Ulm** was one of the most important centres in Europe for the production of playing cards, so that one would expect the early printers at Ulm to have had no difficulty in finding qualified wood cutters to illustrate their books. That would be true up to a point, for Ulm did have engravers as good as those at Augsburg, but they were few in number, especially in the second half of the fifteenth century when the town of Ulm was so often visited by the plague that those who could sought their living elsewhere.

As the B.M.C. remarks: 'Owing doubtless to a commercial crisis in the 1470s and continual plague in the following decade, Ulm's typographical history is rather a gloomy one, as Johann Zainer, Dinckmut, Holle and Reger, all of whom started doing very good work, seem in every case to have lost their capital and been obliged to give up their presses, so that by the beginning of the sixteenth century printing in Ulm had almost entirely stopped.'

Under the circumstances it is not surprising that Johann Zainer, the town's first printer, should choose to open his printing office with the *Regimen wider die Pestilenz* of Heinrich Steinhöwel – a book which bears the date of 11 January 1473, a year in which the plague was particularly severe. This was the first treatise on the plague to be printed. Johann, like that other member of the family, Günther Zainer of Augsburg, had learned to print at Strassburg, and probably settled at Ulm around 1472.

Zainer published several well-illustrated books, including a Boccaccio, *De Claris Mulieribus* (1473) with some eighty woodcuts. On the first page a delightful half border of Adam and Eve shows Eve being tempted by the serpent whose scaly coils are looped to form an initial S. And in one amusing cut Sappho is shown playing a lute, surrounded by various other musical instruments. Some excellent woodcuts are also found in Zainer's edition of Æsop, *Vita et Fabulae* (*c.* 1477). At about the same time as he published this Latin Æsop, Zainer also brought out a German version which proved so popular that no fewer than eleven editions were printed in various German towns before the end of the century, with illustrations for the most part copied from the 200 woodcuts in the original Ulm edition. The original blocks were used by Günther Zainer in his Augsburg edition. Whether the two men were brothers is not known, but both came from Reutlingen and used the same printer's mark.

Unfortunately Johann Zainer encountered financial difficulties and is said to have left Ulm in 1493 on account of his debts, but he returned three years later and printed a few books; although his career lasted until 1523, his latter years were devoted mainly to book-selling.

Conrad Dinckmut published several illustrated books, such as the *Schwabischer Chronik* of 1486, and, like Zainer, printed Steinhöwel's treatise on the plague. Like Zainer, too, he got into financial difficulties and left Ulm in 1499. In 1482 Lienhart Holle printed at Ulm an edition of Ptolemy's *Cosmographia*, translated by Jacobus Angelus. The type in which it was printed is said to have been based on the handwriting of Nicolaus Germanus, the editor of the text, and centuries later it served as a model for the 'Ptolemy' type used in 1894 by St John Hornby at the Ashendene Press. In 1483 Holle brought out the first of several editions of the *Buch der Weisheit der alten Weisen*,* a version of the *Kalila Wa-Dimna* of the Brahmin Bidpai. It was so successful that his competitor Dinckmut printed it in 1485. But, like the other Ulm printers, Holle could not make his business pay. He printed a few books at intervals until 1492, when he departed for Nuremberg, but no longer as his own master. Johann Reger acquired some of Holle's type, but left Ulm for good in 1499. It was not a lucky town for printers.

Not far from Ulm is the town of **Esslingen,** which had its first printer, Conrad Fyner, in 1473 or maybe earlier. He has a place in printing history as the printer of J. Charlier de Gerson, *Collectorium super Magnificat*, containing the earliest known attempt at music printing. This consists of five descending square notes in imitation of Roman notation representing sol, fa, mi, re, ut. There is no stave, but in some copies the lines have been drawn in.

At **Reutlingen**, the home of the two Zainers, a press was first set up by Michel Greyff at the end of 1476. In 1489 he printed a book about witches, *Von den Unholden oder Hexen* by Ulricus Molitoris. Strangely enough his colleague at Reutlingen, Johann Otmar, who had begun to print there in 1479, brought out another book on the same subject, *De Lamiis*, shortly afterwards. Otmar was responsible for the first proper title-page in Germany when he printed Gruner, *Officii Missae sacrique Canonis expositio* in 1483. Otmar worked at Reutlingen until 1495, and afterwards had a press at Tübingen.

* A collection of animal fables, at that time as familiar as Aesop.

Although it was later to become one of the most important publishing centres in Germany, **Leipzig** saw comparatively little printing during the fifteenth century. Here, as in Ulm, the plague, that scourge of the Middle Ages, caused heavy mortality, and in 1450 no fewer than 8,000 had died of the pest. Enough to scare off any would-be settlers in the city.

In fact there is some doubt as to who was the first printer in Leipzig. It is generally thought to have been Marcus Brandis, whose edition of Johannes Annius, *Glossa super Apocalypsim*, was completed on 28 September 1481. Brandis printed there until about 1490, but his output was small. However, another claimant for the honour of being Leipzig's first printer is Conrad Kachelofen, who is said to have printed two broadside manifestos by the Town Council of Erfurt in December 1480. But the first conclusive evidence of his activity as a printer is the Latin *Psalter* of 1485, a copy of which is in the University Library at Leipzig. Whether or not Kachelofen was Leipzig's first printer, his was certainly the most important of the early Leipzig presses. He printed Latin and German editions of the *Ars Moriendi* (printed so many times towards the end of the fifteenth century) in movable type with copies of the blocks used

Grammatica Noua

FIGURE 4. Title-page of Nicolaus Perrottus, *Grammatica Nova*. Hagenau: Heinrich Gran. c. 1491.

in the older xylographic versions. Kachelofen worked on his own until 1498, after which he printed a few books together with his son-in-law, Melchior Lotter. Although most of Kachelofen's books were small quartos of around sixty leaves, he printed in 1498 a *Missale Pragense,* a folio of 355 leaves, with rubrics and music staves red printed. In 1495, when the plague again struck at Leipzig, Kachelofen went to Freiburg, where he was able to complete the Meissen Missal which he had begun at Leipzig. He died in 1528 or 1529, and his business was carried on by Melchior Lotter. Other Leipzig printers of the fifteenth century were Martin Landsberg (Martinus Herbipolensis), Arnoldus de Colonia, Gregorius Böttiger and Jacobus Thanner.

The year 1480 saw the first press set up in **Magdeburg** by Bartholomaeus Ghotan, probably a native of the town seeing that two of his brothers became burgesses of that city in 1500. Ghotan, like so many early printers, had previously been a cleric, and he seems to have worked with the help of the printer Lucas Brandis, whose types he used. In 1484 Ghotan moved to Lübeck, where we shall meet him again.

He was followed at Magdeburg by two partners, Albert Ravenstein and Joachim Westval, whose activity was short-lived. Then came Simon Koch from Weilburg, near Mainz, who was active in Magdeburg from 1486 until the beginning of the sixteenth century. Contemporary with him was Moritz Brandis, whose printing career extended over much the same period, and who twice printed a Magdeburg *Missal.*

4

Printing crosses the Alps

THE art of printing was introduced into Italy by two Germans, Conrad Sweynheim and Arnold Pannartz, in 1465. After the sack of Mainz they set out for Rome with the intention of setting up a press in that city. On the way they stopped at the monastery of St Scholastica (for both were clerics) in the village of Subiaco, north of Rome. This was a house of the Benedictines ruled over by the future Cardinal Torquemada (in the Italian form Turrecremata). There they set up a press and produced the first book printed on Italian soil, a *Donatus*, of which, unfortunately, no copy is now known. This was followed by an undated Cicero, *De Oratore*, completed before the end of September 1465. This large quarto of 109 leaves betrays no sign of the novice hand, and shows that its printers had received a thorough training. Moreover, the book was printed two pages at a time when other printers were still dealing with their quartos page by page.

Only two more books were printed by the Germans at Subiaco: the first edition of Lactantius, *De divinis institutionibus*,* and an edition of St Augustine, *De civitate Dei*. The type in which these books are set is interesting because the letters show a stage midway between the gothic style to which the printers would have been accustomed in Germany and the hand favoured by the Italian humanists, which became known as 'roman' or 'antiqua', and which in consequence has been termed 'gotico-antiqua'. In modern times the types of the Lactantius served as a model for C. H. St John Hornby's edition of Dante's *Inferno*, printed at his Ashendene Press (1909).

The two printers did not stay long at Subiaco. Foreseeing no great future in a prolonged stay at the monastery, they resumed their journey to Rome, which, only thirty miles away, had as yet no printer. There, in the home of the brothers Piero and Francesco de' Massimi, they set up their press.

ROME

By the end of 1467 they had completed their first book at Rome: the ever-popular Cicero, *Epistolae ad familiares*, which succeeding generations of printers

---

* The Lactantius contained the first Greek type used in Italy.

were to issue time and again. But now the fount which they had used at Subiaco was discarded in favour of a purer roman with full serifs and, though perhaps less pleasing to the eye than the Subiaco type, it approached more nearly to what is today considered a true roman letter.

They printed regularly until 1473, but by the beginning of 1472 they were in financial difficulties as a result of over-production. In Rome the printers depended almost entirely upon the patronage of the Curia, and when the initial interest shown by cardinals and other high dignitaries of the Church began to wane, there was no wealthy merchant class, as in Venice and Milan, on whose custom they could rely. Their editor, the Bishop of Aleria, wrote to Pope Sixtus IV on their behalf, pointing out the difficulties the printers were beset with and asking for assistance. A printed version of this letter was prefixed to the fifth volume of their edition of Nicolaus de Lyra, *Postilla super Bibliam* (1472). Its main interest today is that in it the printers gave a list of what they had so far printed, and how many copies of each title.

The printers also addressed themselves personally to the Pope, pointing out that they were clerics (Sweynheim of the diocese of Mainz and Pannartz of the diocese of Cologne) and petitioning to be granted a canonry each in a cathedral church, with the stipends appertaining to it, and secondly one or two benefices each in no matter what diocese. Sixtus IV met their demands and enabled them to carry on for another year.

But after the completion of an edition of Pliny's *Natural History* on 7 May 1473 the partnership was dissolved. Conrad Sweynheim gave up printing altogether and became a map engraver. Pannartz resumed printing by himself after an interval of some eighteen months, and on 2 December 1474, issued a Perottus, *Rudimenta grammaticae*. His last, uncompleted work, was a new edition of the *Letters* of Saint Jerome, of which Vol. I bears the date 28 March 1476. The work was not finished until 1479, when Georg Lauer brought out Vol. II. As far as can be ascertained, Sweynheim and Pannartz together produced four books at Subiaco and forty-eight at Rome. Pannartz, working alone, issued a further dozen books. Sweynheim, who had been working for three years on maps for an edition of Ptolemy's *Geography*, died in 1477 before they were finished. The Ptolemy was eventually issued in 1478 by Arnold Buckinck: the only known book by this printer.

Disputing the title of Rome's first printer is Ulrich Han, a native of Ingolstadt, whose first authenticated book is the *Meditationes* of Cardinal Turrecremata, dated 31 December 1467. But it is thought that he may have printed in Vienna in 1462. His Cicero, *Tusculanae quaestiones* of 1 April 1469, has the imprint 'Rome per Mgrm Vlricvm han de wienna'.

Han worked in Rome until 1478, and from 1471 until 1474 took as partner a merchant of Lucca named Simon Nicolai Chardella, in an attempt to weather the crisis in the book trade which had hit Sweynheim and Pannartz. The partners left aside classical literature and concentrated on law books. But Han is also known for one particular liturgical book, a *Missal* for Rome use which he printed in 1476, and which contains one of the earliest examples of real music printing, though probably not the first, as is sometimes stated.* In any case, the Han *Missal* is a handsomely printed book, and its use of a five-line stave for the music is unusual in an Italian service book of the period, and was not often followed by later printers. From 1474 until 1478 Han worked alone, ending his active career in Rome with another edition of the work with which he had started, namely the *Meditationes* of Turrecremata. His erstwhile partner set up a press of his own in conjunction with a cousin.

Sixtus Riessinger was working in Rome at least as early as 1468, but went to Naples in 1471 to become the first printer in that city, where he was active until 1479. Another Rome printer was Georg Lauer from Würzburg, the man who completed the *Letters* of St Jerome begun by Pannartz. He was active from 1470 until 1481, and for a time was partnered by Leonhard Pflugel.

The Sicilian Giovanni Filippo di Legname from Messina, a scholar and frequenter of the papal court, set up a press which, writes Dr Scholderer, 'seems to have corresponded to the private press of modern times mainly for the purpose of printing the writings of the Pope himself and of others in authority, and providing them with suitable dedications, directed where they might fructify' (*Fifty Essays*, p. 204). Although sometimes termed the first native printer in Italy, he was probably only the publisher and financial backer of the press, and the title of the first native printer in Italy should more properly go to the priest Clement of Padua, who completed a book at Venice in May 1471 and was a self-taught working printer. The press of Legname functioned regularly, though on a small scale, from 1470 until 1476, after which there is a gap of several years. At the end of 1481 he established a second press which was in operation until 1483 or 1484.

Among other fifteenth-century printers working at Rome, Stephan Plannck from Passau was one of the most prolific, with some 300 editions to his credit, but much of his output was ephemeral and without importance. He began his Rome career in 1479 or 1480 and was active until the end of the century. He must have set up his press in Ulrich Han's former quarters, for one of his books bears the imprint 'in domo quondam Magistri Udalrici Galli barbati'.

Like Lauer, Eucharius Silber, who worked at Rome from 1480 until 1509, was a native of Würzburg, and on account of his origin was sometimes called Franck Alemanus, Würzburg being in Franconia. At first Silber printed mainly

---

* The earliest known is the Gradual of *c.* 1473 – the work of the unlocated Printer of the Constance Breviary.

humanistic works, but later his output included guide books for pilgrims to the Holy City, manuals of ecclesiastical law, and indulgences. He was the first printer to obtain a privilege from the Roman Curia, and the costs of his *Summa de ecclesia contra impugnatores potestatis Summi Pontificis* (1489) were borne by the Holy See. At a time when editions rarely exceeded three or four hundred it is surprising to find that he printed no fewer than 1,500 copies of Aristotle, *Politica* (1492).

VENICE

It was yet another German, John of Speyer (Johannes de Spira) who first introduced printing into Venice, where it immediately took root and flourished, unlike Rome where neither from a literary or typographic standpoint was fifteenth-century printing what one might have expected from that great city. The first book printed at Venice was, following the examples of Subiaco and Rome, an edition of the ever-popular Cicero, *Epistolae ad familiares* (1469), which Johannes de Spira reprinted almost immediately. On 18 September 1469 this native of Speyer was granted by the Signoria a monopoly of printing in Venice for a term of five years. Such a privilege, enforceable by fine and confiscation of any contraband books, could have had a most hampering effect upon the immediate future of printing in that locality, but this was a problem which efficaciously solved itself when John of Speyer died only a year after he had set up his press. Although the business was continued by his brother Wendelin, the authorities, petitioned perhaps by business interests or other intending printers, refused to grant another such extensive monopoly and confined their future privileges to cover specific books. As a result, within about two years of John of Speyer's death Venice had a dozen or so printers.

Wendelin de Spira completed an edition of St Augustine, *De civitate Dei*, which his brother had left unfinished and thereafter books came swiftly from his press, and by the end of 1472 he had issued between fifty and sixty books. But by this time he had rivals. Even before the end of 1470 a most formidable competitor had entered the field in the person of the Frenchman Nicolas Jenson.

Jenson, a native of Sommevoire, some thirty-five miles east of Troyes, had been an official in the royal mint at Tours and a skilled engraver ('homme adextre en tailles et de caractères de poinçons'). In October 1458 he had been sent by Charles VII of France to Mainz to learn what he could about the newly-discovered art of printing. What he did there, or whether he met Gutenberg, no one now knows, but the fact remains that in his very first book at Venice, Cicero, *Epistolae ad Brutum* (1470), his knowledge and skill as an engraver was manifested in his handsome roman type, less bold than that of John of Spira, but more neatly engraved and more carefully cast. 'It remains unsurpassed as a type for quartos and small folios' (Carter, 1969).

From 1470 to 1480 Jenson printed continuously, producing some 160 editions.

After Wendelin de Spira had adopted a small rounded gothic known as 'rotunda' to economise space when printing law books, Jenson cut a similar but more expertly designed face which he first used in 1474.

The rivalry between Wendelin de Spira and Nicolas Jenson had caused each of them to seek to outstrip the other in production, and during the years 1471 and 1472 the two presses were between them responsible for some sixty-four editions, or almost three a month. By this time, however, other printers were settling in Venice. Paper was cheap and of good quality, workmen were not lacking, and above all there was a varied and fairly rich clientèle.

Christopher Valdarfer, a native of Regensburg, brought out fourteen books in 1471, Clement of Padua began to print in the same year, and 1472 saw the first book printed by a native Venetian when Gabriele and Filippo Piero brought out the *Philocolo* of Boccaccio. All in all, a total of 134 editions came from the Venetian presses in 1471–72, and the total was more than the market could at that time absorb, with the result that there was a sudden recession in the book market, and in the following year only twenty-five books in all were printed at Venice.

From this time onwards we hear little of Wendelin, whose business was taken over by John of Cologne (Johannes de Colonia) and Johann Manthen. John of Cologne had married the widow of John of Speyer, and in 1471 had financed the printing by Wendelin of Cicero, *De finibus*. Manthen, who came from the neighbourhood of Düsseldorf, was a businessman rather than a printer. This new partnership began in 1474 and during the course of the year printed eighteen works.

Faced with rich competitors, Jenson, to protect his own interests, went into partnership with two financial backers, Johannes Rauchfas and Peter Uglheimer, the firm operating under the style of Nicolas Jenson and Partners (Nicolaus Jenson et Socii). In this way the printing–publishing market in Venice around 1474 was dominated by these two firms. The last-named firm relied essentially upon the technical expertise of Jenson himself allied to the commercial acumen of Uglheimer; Wendelin's successors, whose production was technically inferior to that of their rivals, relied largely on the business abilities of John of Cologne. By 1476 the two firms between them accounted for half of all the books published in Venice during that year.

The years during which these two syndicates operated were years of growing prosperity for the Venetian book trade. In 1476 another famous partnership began when Erhard Ratdolt from Augsburg arrived in Venice and joined forces with two other Germans, Bernhard Maler and Peter Löslein. Maler, always named first in the colophons, was almost certainly the head of the firm. Ratdolt was in charge of the printing with Löslein (who had proceeded B.A. at Paris in 1461) as corrector of the press.

Their first production was the *Kalendarium* of Johann Müller of Königsberg (Regiomontanus), in which occurs the first *displayed* title-page.* For the first time since the invention of printing the title was set out on a separate page at the beginning of the volume, accompanied by the imprint giving place, date and name of printer. It took several years before the practice of having a separate title-page became general. The *Kalendarium* was printed in Latin and in Italian during 1476 and in German in 1478, the two versions of 1476 being the first books dated with Arabic numerals. Again, in this book, for the first time in Italy we have woodcut initials printed with the text instead of a vacant space left to be filled by the illuminator.

FIGURE 5. Title-page, with woodcut border, of a Calendar with dissertations by Johannes Müller, called Regiomontanus. Venice: Erhard Ratdolt, 1482. The first edition was 1476.

* The first title-page occurs in the Bull against the Turks printed by Peter Schöffer in 1463.

But perhaps the most remarkable of Ratdolt's Venetian books is his *Euclid*, with its 420 woodcuts and some 200 diagrams fashioned from brass or type-metal rules. Ratdolt, for his time, was more interested than most in technical innovations, but the credit for the artistic borders and capitals seen in the firm's publications of 1476–78 may well belong to Bernhard Maler, a painter by profession as his name implies.

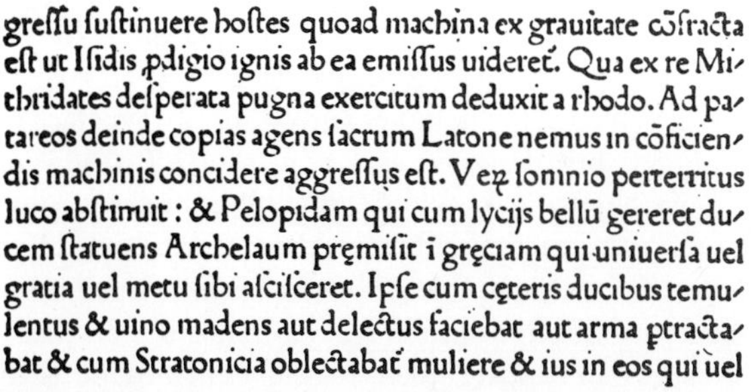

greſſu ſuſtinuere hoſtes quoad machina ex grauitate cōſracta
eſt ut Iſidis ꝓdigio ignis ab ea emiſſus uideret. Qua ex re Mi-
thridates deſperata pugna exercitum deduxit a rhodo. Ad pa-
tareos deinde copias agens ſacrum Latone nemus in cōficien-
dis machinis concidere aggreſſus eſt. Ver̄ ſomnio perterritus
luco abſtinuit : & Pelopidam qui cum lycijs bellū gereret du-
cem ſtatuens Archelaum prēmiſit i grēciam qui uniuerſa uel
gratia uel metu ſibi aſciſceret. Ipſe cum cēteris ducibus temu-
lentus & uino madens aut delectus faciebat aut arma ptracta-
bat & cum Stratonicia oblectabat muliere & ius in eos qui uel

FIGURE 6. Specimen of type used by Erhard Ratdolt for his edition of Appian's *Historia Romana*, Venice, 1477.

Unfortunately the partnership came to an end in 1478, being one of the many casualties among printing businesses brought about by a virulent outbreak of the plague in that year. Of twenty-two firms who were working in Venice at the beginning of that year, eleven disappeared either for good or temporarily. Many printers left the city and moved to other towns in Italy. No more is heard of Ratdolt until April 1480, when he completed on his own a Benedictine *Breviary*. He continued printing until 1486, when, at the instigation of the Bishop of Augsburg, he decided to remove his presses to his native town.

Jacques Le Rouge (Jacobus Rubeus), who worked in Venice from 1473 onwards, seems to have been a member of the Le Rouge family of Chablis (see p. 66), and was a friend of Jenson, who left sums of money both to him and his wife, Pierrette. Although his press was modest compared with that of Jenson, he printed books of fine quality, and of his total output, not large in itself, a great proportion are first editions of the text. His types bear a close resemblance to those of his fellow Champenois, and it is quite likely that he bought type or matrices from his compatriot. Le Rouge was one of those who left Venice at the time of the plague, and he transferred his press to Pinerolo.

When things returned more or less to normal, the rival firms of Jenson and John of Cologne decided to amalgamate, especially as Rauchfas had died in 1478 and the death of John of Cologne seems to have taken place early in 1480. On 29 May of that year the new company was formally established with the style of 'Giovanni da Colon, Nicoló Jenson e Compagni'. On 7 September of the same year Jenson made his will,* which provides us with a valuable record, and he is thought to have died soon afterwards.

But although the company had been set up for an initial period of five years, it lasted for only eighteen months, at least as a printing house. After Jenson's death a German, Hans Herbort, became printer to the company, making use of Jenson's types, and from November 1481 we find him printing for himself. The company had, in fact, abandoned printing for bookselling, building up an extensive business with branches all over north and central Italy.

If the names of his partners are long since forgotten by all save bibliographers, that of Jenson has survived as the designer and cutter of a typeface owing nothing to manuscript models but designed as a new tool for a new medium, with legibility as its main object. Indeed Florentine bibliophiles would have none of it, deeming it unworthy of their libraries. But as Johannes Herbort, Jenson's successor, pointed out in a catalogue of books for sale issued around 1482, 'the characters are so methodically finished by that famous man that the letters are not smaller or larger or thicker than reason demands or than may afford pleasure'.

Certainly Jenson's roman, which was first used in the Eusebius, *De evangelica praeparatione* of 1470, has been subjected to the sincerest form of flattery in modern times, for among the founts based upon it are the 'Golden Type' of William Morris, the Doves Press roman of Cobden-Sanderson and the Riverside Press 'Montaigne' of Bruce Rogers. The one flaw in Jenson's fount as a whole is the excessive height of the capitals which tend to catch the eye in defiance of the principle that the perfect type should be invisible.

From 1481 onwards printing at Venice gradually passed out of the hands of foreigners into those of the Italians themselves. Prior to that date the Germans had had practically a monopoly of printing in the city; yet the last twenty years of the century saw almost a hundred presses installed in the city, all but fifteen of which were controlled by Italians.

Boneto Locatelli is the printer whose name appears most often in Venetian books towards the end of the fifteenth century, with a total of 144 editions to his credit. He began printing in 1487 and became the printer to the publishing firm of Ottaviano Scotto. Of considerable importance, too, were the brothers Joannes and Gregorius de Gregoriis of Forli, who established themselves in Venice in 1482. A certain Jacobus Britannicus was associated with them until 1484, after which date the brothers continued to print alone until well into the sixteenth century. The first authenticated production of this firm is Valerius Maximus, *Facta et dicta memorabilia*, dated 18 June 1482.

---

* The will has been printed more than once. It is given in full, with a translation into French by Henri Nonceaux in the Bulletin de la Société des Sciences de l'Yonne, Vol. 48, p. 267.

Joannes Vercellensis, after printing in Treviso from 1480 to 1485 and momentarily in Venice in 1482, finally settled in Venice in 1486, where he continued to print alone until 1499, when he was joined by his brother Albertinus. The firm was active until well into the sixteenth century, printing mainly classics interspersed with a few Italian literary texts.

A name of considerable importance in the history of Venetian printing is that of Andrea Torresano, who eventually became the father-in-law of Aldo Manuzio. Torresano was born at Asola, in Lombardy, in 1451. According to his own account he had been active as a printer in Venice since 1475 or earlier but the first known work to bear his name is a Roman Breviary dated 12 October 1479. From August 1480 until January 1481 he worked in partnership with Bartholomaeus de Blavis and P. de Plasiis, after which date he formed a new partnership with de Blavis and Maphaeus de Paterbonus. From 1486, or perhaps earlier, he worked on his own.

Dr Scholderer has paid tribute to the skill with which he made use of one and the same setting for producing two editions of different format. This was a Latin version of Aristotle's works printed by Torresano in 1483, which was first completed in six parts, large folio, with sixty-six lines to the page. Two of these parts were then printed as smaller folios with forty-nine and fifty lines to the page, the necessary alterations having been made to headlines and signatures. 'The success with which these delicate manipulations were carried through,' writes Dr Scholderer, 'is a testimony to the skill and enterprise of Torresanus, whose office was of course one of the leading establishments in Venice at the height of that city's typographical primacy.' According to Bernoni, Torresano learned his trade from Nicholas Jenson.

A great deal of printing was done in Venice at this time for the territories now comprised in Yugoslavia, mainly in the field of service books, and in 1493 Torresano printed a Roman Breviary (*Brvijal po zakonu rimskoga dvora*) in Glagolitic characters. The editor of this edition, of which copies are extant at Munich and Zagreb, was Blaž Baromić (*c.* 1450–*c.* 1507), canon of Senj. The knowledge of printing which he acquired in Venice later enabled him to set up a printing office at Senj in Croatia, where he was assisted by Silvester Bedričić and Gaspar Turčić.

Torresano made use of Jenson types, having probably bought matrices from the Frenchman. But he did not confine himself to these, for Proctor identified twenty-two distinct faces in books bearing his imprint. His 1487 edition of Sabellico, *Rerum Venetarum Decades IV*, is a typographical masterpiece. His work carries over into the sixteenth century, and in 1508 he entered into partnership with Aldo Manuzio, who had married his daughter in 1505 (see p. 143).

It is impossible here to mention all the printers who worked in Venice towards the end of the fifteenth century. Aldo Manuzio, who moved from La Mirandola to Venice about 1490, is treated at length in Chapter 13. We have spoken of the printing carried out in Venice for territories on the eastern shore of the Adriatic. The first Croatian printer to work in Venice was Andrija Paltašić of Kotor (Andreas de Paltasichis Cattarensis), who set up his press in 1476, and seems to have used types of Jacob de Fivizanno. Little is known of him. He is thought to have been born around 1440 and died after 1492. Thirty-one books are recorded from his press, but his output may well have been larger. He worked alone for a time, but later went into partnership with Bonino de Boninis, a compatriot of his who came from Dubrovnik and is also known as Dobruško Dobrić. He is later found at Verona and Brescia.

Ottaviano Petrucci was born at Fossombrone in 1466 and went to Venice about 1490. He devoted his time to perfecting a method of printing music from movable types, and in 1498 was granted a patent by the Signoria of Venice giving him the exclusive right of printing music for voices, organ and lute. He was the first to design a music type for mensural notation which fitted together sufficiently well to allow of perfect registration of the notes on the stave. He worked in Venice until 1511, when he returned to Fossombrone. (See p. 209.)

Founder of one of the earliest large-scale publishing businesses in Italy was Ottaviano Scotto, who was born at Monza around 1440. When he was about thirty-five he went to Venice, attracted by the commercial possibilities afforded by the new art of printing. There he was responsible for establishing a press in his house, employing among other printers Battista Denti di Bellano. From 1479, the earliest recorded date of books published by Scotto, until 1484, he was himself occupied with printing as well as with the marketing of his books, but from that time until his death fourteen years later, he contented himself with publishing, although he is still recorded in a document of 1492 as 'librorum impressor'. His regular printer was Boneto Locatelli from Bergamo, who printed for the firm until well into the sixteenth century, when the business had passed to the heirs of Scotto. So busy and so successful did the firm become that in due course Locatelli was able to add his name to that of Ottaviano Scotto as partner. But Locatelli himself could not on his own turn out the large and varied production which the growing business called for, and many other printers worked for Scotto, among them Matteo Capcasa, Giovanni and Gregorio de Gregori, Johannes Hamman, or Hertzog, Andrea di Paltascichi, Albertino Rosso and Bartolomeo de Zanis de Portesio.

Scotto's production was eclectic, for it comprised theological works, service books, ancient classics and Italian literature, legal works, philosophy, and science. He was one of the first Italians to issue liturgical books, which were printed for him by Giovanni Emerico, Johannes Hamman and Lucantonio de Giunta.

Ottaviano Scotto died on 23 December 1498, after which the business was carried on by the 'Heirs of Ottaviano Scotto', who were his brother Bernardino and his nephews Amadeo, Paolo, Ottaviano and Giovanni-Battista. In 1507 Amadeo, who may be considered the head of the firm, went into partnership with the brothers Battista and Silvestro Torti, Lucantonio de Giunta, Giorgio Arrivabene (called Parente) and Antonio Moreto.

Greek printing at Venice was undertaken by a Cretan named Zacharias Callierges, who printed for a wealthy fellow countryman, the bookseller Nicolaus Blastus. He is said to have spent five years perfecting the Greek type which first appeared in the *Etymologicum* completed on 8 July 1499. Blastus had already applied for a privilege for all books printed with this Greek type, which was cast in one piece with its accents, whereas the Aldine type needed separate accentuation. Callierges printed four books before the end of the century, and then nothing until 1509. Later he removed his press to Rome.

Printing was indeed a flourishing industry during the thirty years which preceded the end of the century, with the impressive figure of 4,500 editions, almost one seventh of the total number of editions produced in the whole of Europe during the same period (Scholderer, 1966, p. 205).

FLORENCE

Printing was introduced into the city of Florence by one of her famous sons, the goldsmith Bernardo di Cenni del Fora, called Cennini, who among other works was responsible for some of the finest reliefs on the reredos of the Baptistery at Florence. He was assisted at the press by his son, the nineteen-year-old Domenico. Yet they are known by one book only, the Commentary on Virgil by Servius Maurus Honoratus, which was issued in three parts during the years 1471 and 1472. However, Cennini may, as Duff suggests (E.P.B., p. 74), have cut type for other printers.

A printer from Mainz, Johannes Petri, who is thought to have worked for Peter Schöffer, came to Florence about 1471, and we find his name recorded for the first time in the *editio princeps* of Boccaccio's *Filocolo*, dated 12 November 1472.

One of the most interesting of the early presses working in Florence was surely that known as the Ripoli Press, at which nuns are said to have worked as compositors. In 1300 the Dominican nuns who dwelt in a convent at Piano di Ripoli, on the outskirts of Florence, built a new convent inside the city, in the Strada della Scala, to which they gave the name of Sant' Jacopo di Ripoli. For about eight years, from 1476 until 1484, the building housed a printing press which was run by the conventual procurator Fra Domenico da Pistoia, assisted by the confessor Fra Piero da Pisa. The first book from this conventual press was a *Donatus*, every copy of which has now disappeared, completed on 14 November 1476. Until the death of Fra Domenico in 1484 the press was very active, for according to B.M.C. some seventy editions were issued during this time, not counting a considerable number of single sheets which, like the *Donatus*, have now vanished. The earliest surviving book from the Ripoli press is the *Legenda di S. Catarina* (24 March 1477). The still extant Diary of the press, written almost entirely in Fra Domenico's own hand, is a valuable source of information regarding the activities of this unusual printing house, from which we may learn the prices paid for such things as ink, paper and type-metal.*

The first known book to be issued with copperplate engravings was printed at Florence in 1477. This work, *Monte santo di Dio* by Antonio Bettini of Siena, was printed by Nicoló di Lorenzo, also known as Nicoló Tedesco since he came from Breslau. In 1481 the same printer brought out a Dante, *Divina commedia*, with engravings by Baccio Baldini after Botticelli; but the printer seems to have found difficulty in printing text and engraving together on the page, with the result that only the first three plates are so treated, the remainder being printed on separate slips of paper and pasted in.

A native of Florence who returned to his home town after printing at Naples was Francesco di Dino, who worked in Florence from 1481 until 1497. His printing house was close to the Ripoli convent and it is thought that he may have received some help from the conventual press in setting his edition of Luigi Pulci, *Morgante Maggiore*, a reworking of an earlier poem on Orlando, for the accounts of the Ripoli press show that they received payment 'per parte dello aiutarci comporre il Morgante' in July 1481 and again in February 1481–82.

To Florence belongs the honour of being the first city to print the works of Homer in Greek; the printer was the Cretan Demetrius Chalcondylas, who produced it at the expense of the brothers Bernardo and Nero Nerlii. Dedicated to Lorenzo de' Medici, it was published in two folio volumes in 1488–89. Twelve years earlier the Cretan had printed at Milan the first all-Greek text (see p. 53). Incidentally, as a sidelight on the steep ascent in the market prices for incunabula, a copy of the Homer now in the British Museum was bought by George III's librarian, Mr Barnard, for seven shillings!

A dominant figure in the life of Florence from 1489 until his execution in 1498 was the friar Girolamo Savonarola, whose virulent exhortations and sermons were set up in print almost as soon as they were delivered. These tracts, though for the greater part badly printed, are redeemed by their wood-cuts, often quite charming and all of distinctively Florentine workmanship, the special characteristic of which was the enclosing of the illustration by a narrow border cut on the block itself, giving the cut the appearance of a framed picture.†

* See E. Nessi, *Diario della stamperia di Ripoli*. 1903.
† See Gustave Gruyer, *Les illustrations des écrits de Savonarole*. Paris, 1879.

Most of the Savonarola tracts were printed by Lorenzo Morgiani and Johannes Petri, Antonio Miscomini, and Bartolommeo di Libri.

It was Miscomini who printed in 1493 the *Libro di Giuocho delli Scacchi*, an Italian version of the Latin *De Ludo Scaccorum* by Jacobus de Cassolis, with a large cut at the beginning showing courtiers playing chess in the presence of the king, and thirteen smaller cuts personifying the various pieces, the *populari*, or pawns, being shown as members of different trades. Caxton had already translated the work from the French version of Jean de Vignay, and published it at Bruges in 1475 as *The Game and Playe of the Chesse*.* Miscomini, who had previously worked at Venice and at Nonantola, was active in Florence from 1481 until about 1498.

For a quarter of a century the press of Bartolommeo di Libri was busy in Florence, yet until he was rescued from oblivion by Robert Proctor his name was almost unknown, even to historians of printing. For he was, writes A. W. Pollard (1912) 'an example of a man who, though he did excellent work, hardly ever troubled himself to take credit for it.' Out of more than 120 editions which are now credited to him, only eight bear his name. His earliest dated (but unsigned) book is Leonardo Dati, *La Sfera*, completed on 9 November 1482, and he was printing until 1508 at least. Proctor considered that Bartolommeo di Libri was the actual printer of the magnificent Homer attributed to Demetrius Chalcondylas (Damilas), who was probably the designer of the Greek fount, which is similar to the Lascaris printed at Milan in 1476 (see p. 53). But nowhere in the colophon to the Homer does the name of di Libri occur.

The *Arithmetica* of Filippo Calandri is not only one of the first but also one of the most charming books on the subject. It was printed in 1491 by Lorenzo di Morgiani and Johannes Petri, with some delightful illustrations drawn in outline, as were most of the early Florentine illustrations. During their partnership from 1490 until 1496 these two printers brought out several important illustrated books, including the *Epistole e Evangelii* (1495) which Arthur Hind (1935) considered to be 'the most considerable achievement of XV-century Florentine book illustration.' It contains 144 illustrations, as well as twenty-five small half-lengths of prophets, evangelists and epistle writers and there are fourteen varieties of border design. The aim of the printers seems to have been to surpass the two Venetian editions of the book which were printed by Anima Mia in 1492 and 1494.

The printer Francesco Bonaccorsi worked in Florence from 1486 until 1497 with material largely inherited from Miscomini. In 1495 he printed an edition of Æsop's *Fables* for Piero Pacini da Pescia, who published many of the best Florentine illustrated books including the *Epistole e Evangelii* mentioned above. Like many early printers Bonaccorsi had been a cleric.

* This is a moral allegory – not a treatise on the actual game.

One should perhaps mention Vespasiano da Bisticci (1421–98), a bibliophile and the most famous bookseller of his time in Florence, who, on behalf of Cosimo de' Medici got together in the space of twenty-two months, with the help of forty-five scribes, some 200 volumes of all that was best in Humanist literature for the library at Fiesole. He was also responsible for furnishing with manuscripts the library of Federigo da Montefeltro at Urbino, which, according to Bisticci, contained no printed books,* these being too plebeian for the ducal taste.

BOLOGNA

The immediate and sustained success of the printing trade in Emilia stems from the flourishing life and growing fame of the university of Bologna. Already in the thirteenth century the city had its master scribes, a school of calligraphy, and workshops for the preparation of codices. Already, also, there were well-known libraries – those of the Stazionari, of the religious Orders, of the Capitol, and of the Collegio Gregoriano. During the second half of the fifteenth century Giovanni II Bentivoglio, overlord of Bologna, not only embellished the city, but was never slow to call upon talent and reward it.

No fewer than 47 known presses were at work in Bologna before the end of the century; but competition was fierce and half of these firms went out of business after having printed one, or at most two books. It was the large firms with capital resources which stayed the course, and Dr Bühler has shown that over fifty per cent of the 268 Bolognese incunables came from the presses of the five largest firms (Bühler 1960). Seventy-nine of them were printed by Ugo Rugerius, sixty-nine by Franciscus de Benedictis, and sixty-one by Benedictus Hectoris. But whereas the seventy-nine of Rugerius were spread over twenty-one years, Franciscus de Benedictis took only half that time to produce his sixty-nine.

The products of the Bolognese presses between 1470 and 1500 show remarkable diversity. The Faculty of Law at Bologna was world-renowned, so it is not surprising that law books, both civil and canon law, predominated. But books on medicine and the Greek and Latin classics did not lag far behind. And when it became increasingly evident that the day of the scribe was over, the *feneratores librorum* and the *petiarii* themselves became either printers or associates in some publishing enterprise.

No printing press appeared in Bologna before 1470, probably owing to the opposition of the scribes. The first to set up a press in the city was Baldassare Azzoguidi, as he himself affirms at the end of the first large work which he issued, the *editio princeps* of the works of Ovid. With him were associated Francesco dal Pozzo of Parma and Annibale Malpigli of Padua. The last-named

---

* 'e non v'è ignuno a stampa.'

was the technical manager of the press, the premises and capital for which were provided by Azzoguidi. Francesco dal Pozzo was a writer and humanist who acted as editor and proof-reader. Although the first dated book from this press is the *Ovid* of 1471, the partners may have published a few pieces in 1470. However, the partnership did not last long, and Annibale soon started his own press aided by his brother Scipione.

The three men who were the first to introduce printing into Bologna were all in some degree connected with the university. Malpigli, the printer, a Doctor of both Arts and Medicine taught logic and moral philosophy, whilst two of Baldassare Azzoguidi's brothers, Pietro and Alberto, were teachers.

Francesco dei Benedetti came to Bologna from Venice around 1482 and printed there until 1495, the year before his death. He printed first editions of several of the works of the once celebrated Latin poet, Baptista Mantuanus who was for long the poet of school-rooms, and it is more than likely that his Eclogues was one of the schoolbooks used by Shakespeare, who quotes and praises the 'good old Mantuan' in *Love's Labours Lost*.

Andreas Portilia, who had previously worked in Parma came to Bologna and completed a Tartagnus, *Lectura* at the end of 1472 or beginning of 1473. But finding things too difficult in Bologna he soon went back to Parma. A far more active printer was Ugo Ruggeri, already mentioned, who divided his time between Reggio Emilia, Pisa, and Bologna.

Certainly one of the most active among the printers of Bologna was Ugo Ruggeri, who came to the city before 1473 and was for a time Governor of the Collegio Reggiano in the University. Like so many of the early printers, he was a cleric in minor orders. Some of the fourscore books to his credit were printed in association with Donnino Bertocchi, who was for a time active in Reggio Emilia, to which town Ruggeri himself removed in 1500 for what was to be the final stage of his career as a printer.

Among other Bolognese printers were Dominico de' Lapi, Caligula de Bazaleri (who began printing in 1480 when only 19), Benedetto di Ettore (1493–1523), Ercole Nani (1492–*c.* 1504), and Johannes de Nördlingen, who was at times partnered by Henricus de Haarlem. One peculiar fact about Bolognese printing in the fifteenth century is the complete lack of Bibles, liturgical books and the great theological writers.

MILAN

In view of the prosperity of Milan in the middle of the fifteenth century coupled with the fact that its ruler, Duke Galeazzo Maria Sforza, was a liberal patron of the arts, it seems rather surprising that the city had no printer until 1471 – two years after John of Speyer had begun to print in Venice. It is true that earlier at least two abortive attempts had been made to introduce the new art into the capital of Lombardy. One Galeazzo de Crivelli intended to set up a press in 1469, and in 1470 a physician named Antonio Planella was considering, if a ten years' privilege were forthcoming from the Grand Council, leaving Venice for Milan and starting a printing office there. Nothing came of these early attempts, and the honour of establishing the first press in Milan went to another physician, Pamfilo Castaldi from Feltre, a man already over seventy years of age. He was, in fact, the proprietor of the press, but the actual printers employed by him were the brothers Antonio and Fortunato Zarotto.

Only three books are known from this press, the earliest of which is an edition of Festus, *De verborum significatione*, dated 3 August 1471. Castaldi, however, returned to Venice, whence he had come, in 1473. Perhaps, at his age, for he was born in 1398, he found the strain of managing a printing-office too great for him. The exclusive privilege he had been accorded expired with his departure, and so left the almost unexploited field open to others. The void was immediately filled by two printing offices, the one being set up by Philippus de Lavagna and the other by Antonio Zarotto, who had been in charge of Castaldi's press. Lavagna certainly lost no time in stepping into Castaldi's shoes, for he completed on 25 March 1472 an edition of Cicero, *Epistolae ad familiares*, and this may even have been preceded by an unsigned Phalaris of 1471 printed in a type similar to that of the Cicero. Indeed, in his Avicenna, *Canon de medicina* (12 February 1473), he formally claimed to be 'the first introducer and inventor of this art of printing in this city'. Although the owner of a press, it is doubtful if Lavagna was the actual printer of the books he published, which were probably the work of his first foreman, Giovanni de Sidriano.

Lavagna's chief rival in Milan at that time was Antonio Zarotto who, in May 1472, signed a contract as partner in a syndicate which included another former employee of Castaldi, Gabriel Orsoni as corrector, the humanists Cola Montano and Gabriel Paveri-Fontana as editors, with Pietro Antonio de Burgo de Castilliono as financial backer. Zarotto was the technical manager, charged with maintaining four presses and supplying the necessary type and material.* The first work produced by Zarotto was a grammar by that calumniator of Plato, George of Trebizond. As far as is known the syndicate was dissolved at the expiration of the three years mentioned in the contract, but Zarotto continued to print with unabated vigour until the first decade of the sixteenth century, with a particularly productive period during his first decade, for by the end of 1486 he had issued more than a hundred editions, mostly of works by the humanists.

Christopher Valdarfer, who had previously worked in Venice, moved to Milan about this time and in addition to his own output worked probably for

---

* The contract is printed in Sassi, *Historia literario-typographica Mediolanensis.* 1745.

both Lavagna and Zarotto. Lavagna had two workmen in his office who in 1477 set up in business on their own. They were the Bavarians Leonhard Pachel and Ulrich Scinzenzeler, whose first book, an edition of Virgil, was completed on 1 December 1477. They worked together in partnership for ten years, but after 1487 each worked independently of the other though maintaining a common stock of material. Ulrich was the more prolific of the two, and after 1500 his business was continued by his son Johannes Angelus.

The output of the two firms was considerable and more than half the Milanese production of books from 1478 until 1496 was directly attributable to these two establishments, and there is little doubt that they were also responsible for books issued by several Milanese publishing firms. With Zarotto they monopolised the greater part of Milanese printing up to the end of the century. Another Milanese printer, Giovanni Antonio de Honate, unable to sustain the competition, removed his press to Pavia.

Dionigi da Paravicino, after introducing printing into Como with Ambrogio degli Orchi, moved to Milan where in 1476 he printed the first book wholly in Greek – the Greek grammar of Constantine Lascaris, the Greek fount for which was probably designed by the Cretan, Demetrius, called Damilas because he was born in Milan of Cretan parents. From 1478 until 1481 Paravicino worked mainly for the Pisan publisher Bonaccorsi who issued a remarkable series of Greek and Greek-Latin texts, including the first printed edition of Theocritus.

OTHER ITALIAN TOWNS

The year 1470 saw printing introduced into two small Umbrian towns, **Foligno** and **Trevi.** Of the two Trevi claims priority, for a contract dated 5 July 1470 shows that work had already begun on a large folio edition of Bartholus de Saxoferrato, *Lectura super prima parte Infortiati*, completed in the following year. This may well have been antedated by a small pamphlet dealing with the 'Perdono d'Assisi'. In each case the printer was Johann Reynhard (Reinhardi), who in 1473 was working in Rome.

At Foligno the first press was set up by the wandering printer Johann Neumeister of Mainz, who was invited to work in the house of the papal mint-master Emiliano de' Orsini. Here he printed the *editio princeps* of Leonard Aretino, *De bello Italico adversus Gothos* in 1470 and two years later gave the world the first printed edition of Dante's *Divina commedia*. This was followed in the same year by two more editions, one printed at Mantua, the other at Venice.

Parma first received the art of printing from a native of Turin, Andrea Portilia, who completed his first book, the Plutarch *De liberis educandis* on 23 September 1472. His type suggests that Venice was his training ground. In 1473 he moved to Bologna, remaining in that city until 1478, when he went to

Parma, where he continued to print until 1482, when he transferred his press to Reggio Emilia.

The second press at Parma was that of a printer from Lyons named Etienne Coralle, whose first known work, a Statius, *Achilleis*, was finished on 23 March 1473. The remarkable colophon is thus translated by A. W. Pollard in his *Essay on Colophons*:

> 'Should you find any blots in this work, excellent reader, lay scorn aside, for Stephanus Corallus of Lyons, provoked by the ill will of certain envious folk who tried to print the same book, finished it more quickly than asparagus is cooked, corrected it with the utmost zeal, and published it for students of literature to read, at Parma, 23 March, 1473.'

Dr Scholderer points out that the phrase 'more quickly than asparagus is cooked' (citius quam asparagi coquuntur) was a classical reminiscence, and that Suetonius recorded it as being one of the favourite expressions of the Emperor Augustus. Coralle left Parma in 1478 to become a bookseller at Mantua.

Of the later fifteenth-century printers at Parma, Angelo Ugoleto, a native of the city, worked there until 1501, when he was succeeded by Francesco Ugolete, who worked mainly in partnership with Ottaviano Salado. Little printing, however, was done at Parma between 1495 and 1499 owing to the wars which over-ran this region.

Ferrara had in those days a Court which rivalled in splendour those of Milan and Florence. For long the domain of the Este family, this city was the venue of artists and writers from all over Europe. In 1471, the year in which Ercole I succeeded to the dukedom, Ferrara was endowed with a printing press; a fact which might appear strange to those who knew Ercole, for the duke, although a patron of the arts, belonged to a class of self-styled connoisseurs who felt that to own a printed book rather than a handsomely illuminated manuscript was beneath their dignity. For this reason possibly, and owing to the fact that Ferrara was of small commercial importance, few printers found a lengthy sojourn there at all lucrative. In fact the first on the scene, a Frenchman named André Beaufort (Andrea Belforte) from Picardy was himself responsible for almost half the total number of books printed at Ferrara during the fifteenth century.

Beaufort's first period of activity in Ferrara was from 1471 until 1475, after which his press ceased to function until about 1479. Similar interruptions occurred after the end of 1481, when the press closed down for two years or more, and after the latter part of 1489 for about a year and a half. We know that Beaufort had been a scribe, and possibly during the periods when his press was inactive he was penning manuscripts for the duke and his courtiers. From 1485 until 1489 he printed mainly medical works, meant to cater for the needs of the medical faculty at the university, which reopened in 1485 after having been closed for three years owing to the war between Ferrara and Venice.

Ferrara's second printer was Agostino Carnerio, son of the bookseller Bernardo Carnerio for whom Beaufort had in 1473 printed an edition of the *Institutes* of Justinian. Another early printer was Lorenzo de' Rossi of Valenza, on the river Po. The Latinized form of his name was Laurentius de Rubeis de Valentia. He printed an Averroes, *Colliget*, in 1482 at Ferrara, but his main period of activity began in 1489 and continued well into the sixteenth century. Among the few illustrated books to come from Ferrara in the incunable period was his edition of Foresti, *De Claris Mulieribus* (1497), containing 172 portraits of women famous in history and fable, though several of the blocks served to represent more than one character.

We have seen that Sixtus Riessinger left Rome in 1469 to become the first printer at **Naples.** His first book there was the *Bulla anni jubilei* of Pope Paul II which, although undated, must have been printed before 19 April 1470. After 1479 he returned to Rome, where in 1481 we find him partnered by Georg Herolt. Riessinger had gone to Naples under the patronage of the King of Naples, Ferdinand I, who is said to have offered the printer (who was formerly a cleric) a bishopric, which Riessinger, however, declined.

Piedmont saw few printers during the fifteenth century, for during much of this period the territory had been ravaged by the Franco-Italian wars, with plague, poverty and suffering everywhere. It was not until the middle of the next century that France restored Savoy and Piedmont to the exceptionally able prince, Duke Emanuele Filiberto. It is small wonder that few printers tried to make a living there. Nevertheless, printing was introduced into **Turin** in 1474 by Giovanni Fabri, a native of Langres in Burgundy, whose original name was presumably Jean Fabre. His first book, printed in partnership with another Frenchman, known in Italy as Giovannino di Pietro, was a Roman Breviary (possibly the earliest printed). Apart from a two-year interval at Caselle, Fabri worked in Turin until 1491. His usual roman type betrays a Venetian origin, and we know that one of his books, a Cicero, *De Officiis*, was printed as a commission for the Venice syndicate of Jenson and De Colonia.

Other printers to work at Turin before the close of the century were Francesco de Silva (1485–1513) and Nicolaus de Benedictis (1490–1519). Nicolaus, who described himself as a Catalan, had already printed in Venice in 1481. At Turin he printed for a time in partnership with Jacopo Suigo.

On 11 May 1484, three citizens of **Siena** – Laurentius Canizarius and Jacobus Germonia, doctors of law, together with Lucas de Martinis, submitted a petition to the authorities claiming exemption from import duty of paper and export duty on books to be published by the press they had just established. With certain reservations their claim was granted, and their first book saw the light that same year, printed for them, since they had not the technical ability, by Heinrich Dalen of Cologne, known as Henricus de Colonia, who had begun his career at Brescia in 1474, and subsequently printed in several places, including Bologna. For the next few years he alternated between Bologna and Siena, but in 1490 we find him at Lucca and in 1493 at Urbino. He retained a bookselling business at Siena until his death shortly after the end of the century. Another printer from Bologna, Henricus de Haarlem, also printed at Siena, for a time in association with Johannes Walbeck.

Modena, a stronghold of the Este family, and from 1452 capital of the Duchy of Modena, welcomed Hans Wurster, a Bavarian from Kempten, as its first printer. His first dated work was a fine quarto *Virgil* completed on 23 January 1475. Wurster had already printed at Bologna in 1473 and 1474 and in 1479 moved on to Basel. Baldassare de Struzzi printed two books at Modena in 1476 and 1477, but the first regular press in that city was established in 1481 by Domenico Rococciola, who printed there until 1506, being succeeded by his nephew Antonio, who kept the printing office going until 1521.

Leonardo Acate (Leonardus Achates de Basilea), after having worked at Padua and Sant'Orso, became the first printer at **Vicenza** in 1474, working there until 1491. Hermann Liechtenstein of Cologne completed his first book at Vicenza, an undated Orosius, *Historiae*, probably at the beginning of 1475. He is best remembered as printer of the *editio princeps* of Ptolemy, *Cosmographia*, in a Latin version issued in September 1475. Editions soon came from Bologna (1477), Rome (1478), and Florence (1482). Liechtenstein's edition had no maps. The first to include them was the Bologna edition of 1477 (with the erroneous date 1462). Among the early presses at Vicenza was that of the Viennese, Stephan Koblinger, who printed three books there in 1479 and 1480 before returning to his native city, where he is thought to have been the unnamed printer who introduced printing to Vienna (see p. 141).

The first book to be printed at **Brescia** was a *Virgil* of 1473, but the name of the printer is unknown. The type used suggests Georgius de Butzbach who had already printed at Mantua. Later in the same year a native of Brescia, Tommaso Ferrando, who had previously printed at Mantua, returned to his native city and printed *Statuta Communis Brixiae*. He issued several books between 1473 and 1493. Also working in Brescia were the brothers Angelus and Jacobus de Britannicis. The latter, after working in Venice since 1481, began printing at Brescia in 1485 in partnership with his brother, who was apparently the business manager of the printing office. The last printer to work in Brescia before the end of the century was Bernardinus de Misintis who began to print there in 1492 in association with Caesar Parmensis.

Printing arrived at **Pavia** in 1473 with an edition of Angelus de Aretio, *Lectura super Institutionum*, from the printing house of Joannes de Sidriano. The first printer at **Padua** was Laurenzo Canozio da Lendinara who printed there a Mesue, *Opera*, dated 9 June 1471, a book which was for long assigned to

Florence. But more important was Matthaeus Cerdonis who printed some sixty books at Padua between 1482 and 1487. At **Cremona** Dionigi Paravicino, in partnership with Stefano dei Merlini and Dr Francesco Granelli established the first press in 1471, but the only work from this firm now known is the *Lectura super primam partem digesti novi* of Angelo da Perugia.

It is impossible to date precisely the first book printed at **Perugia,** but it must have been before the end of 1471, after Braccio de' Baglioni and Matteo, son of the jurist Baldo degli Ubaldi had arranged for the printing of Ubaldi's works by the German printers Petrus Petri of Cologne and Johannes Nicolai from Bamberg. Their books are all undated, but the original contract between the parties is dated 1 May 1471. Other printers in Perugia during the fifteenth century were Johannes Vydenast and, for a while, Stephan Arndes, who later went to Schleswig.

A Fleming named Gerard van der Leye (Gerardus de Lisa), settled at **Treviso** and became the first printer there. A scholar, recorded as 'grammaticae professor', he printed about twenty books at Treviso between 1471 and 1476. In 1477 he printed at Venice, and in 1479 was known as a bookseller at Udine. In October 1480, an edition of Platina, *De honesta voluptate*, the earliest known printing at **Cividale,** was printed 'impensis et expensis Gerardi de Flandria'. Other early presses at Treviso were those of Michele Manzolo (1476–80) and Johannes de Hassia (1476).

The first, as it was the most noteworthy, book printed at **Verona** during the fifteenth century was Robertus Valturius, *De Re Militari.* It appeared in 1472, embellished with eighty-two woodcuts depicting various engines of war, but of its printer we know little save that in the colophon he describes himself as John of Verona, son of Nicolai. It has been conjectured, though without any documentary proof, that the designer of the woodcuts was Matteo de' Pasti, who painted the Triumphs of Petrarch for Piero di Cosimo de' Medici at Venice in 1441. On the other hand there is the possibility that the illustrations were by Valturius himself, who had written the book about nine years earlier.

Apart from the Valturius the only other early Verona book with illustrations is the Latin–Italian edition of *Aesop*, with the Italian version by Accio Zucco. The printer was Giovanni Alvise, assisted by his brother Alberto, and the illustrations seem to be by the same hand which designed the Valturius. A Frenchman named Petrus Maufer from Padua printed a *Josephus* at Verona in 1480, but this appears to be the only book he issued in that town. Another temporary printer was Boninus de Boninis, who printed the second Latin and first Italian editions of Valturius (1483) before moving to Brescia.

A group of five books, all in the same type, including a Mesue, *Opera*, and printed in 1471, were at one time attributed to a Florentine press, but are now known to have been printed at **Padua** by Lorenzo Canozio da Lendinara

(Ridolfi, 1958) who thus becomes the city's first printer. The family were wood carvers and Lorenzo is recorded as having worked with his brother Cristoforo at Ferrara, Modena and Padua as carvers of the cathedral stalls. He printed at Padua for some three years and died in 1477. The next printer at Padua was a native of the town, Bartolommeo de Valdezoccho, whose first book, dated 21 March 1472, was an edition of Boccaccio, *Fiammetta*. He was partnered at first by a German, Martin von Siebenbäumen, but from 1474 until 1476 he printed alone. Matthaeus Cerdonis printed some sixty works at Padua between 1482 and 1487, mostly small books on medicine, mathematics and astronomy.

After 1472 printing spread quickly throughout Italy, being introduced into seventy-two towns before the end of the fifteenth century. But many of these were small places to which a printer had come and gone, leaving behind just one or perhaps two books before seeking a locality with better prospects. In such cases the town in question had often to wait for years before a new press was established. Nevertheless the seventy-two Italian towns which possessed presses by the end of the century compares favourably with Germany's fifty and France's thirty-nine.

5

Early Printing in France

SURPRISINGLY, printing was not introduced into France until 1470, and even then not as a business venture but as a service to the cause of learning by two professors of the Sorbonne. In view of the fact that Strassburg was endowed with a press around 1460 (perhaps as early as 1458) it seems strange that **Paris** should have remained aloof from the new art for yet another decade.

The main reason was intense opposition from vested interests. Paris was a centre for the dissemination of manuscripts, both in connection with the university and for private patrons, and it has been estimated that there were in the city at that time no fewer than six thousand copyists, scriveners and illuminators who were far from enthusiastic over Gutenberg's invention. Already in 1465 they had managed to confiscate a load of books brought into Paris for sale by Fust, who was forced to return to Germany without having sold any of them (Chauvet, 1959).

The two men who installed the first press in France were Guillaume Fichet and Jean Heynlin, both men of standing in the University of Paris. The former was born in 1433, probably at Petit-Bornand, in what is now Haute Savoie; Jean Heynlin was born at Stein, in the Grand Duchy of Baden about 1430. After they had received permission from the authorities to set up a press in the buildings of the Sorbonne, they brought to Paris three men to run it: Ulrich Gering, Martin Crantz, and Michael Friburger, all three Germans, who arrived in Paris probably at the end of 1469. Gering came from Munster, in the canton of Lucerne, and had been a student at Basel University where he took his B.A. in 1467. Friburger was from Colmar, and Martin Crantz, who seems to have been a typefounder, was from Stein, Heynlin's birthplace. In the summer of 1470 they finished the first book printed in France – an edition of the letters of Gasparinus Barzizus, in the manifesto of which Fichet states the aim of the press, which was to provide sound texts of the ancient authors.

If one can attach any credence to a manuscript preserved in the Bibliothèque de l'Arsenal at Paris, Charles VII sent to Mainz, in October 1458, one of the best engravers of the Tours Mint, Nicholas Jenson, to find out what he could concerning Gutenberg's invention, news of which had reached the king's ears. Jenson went to Mainz, where he stayed for some time. Meanwhile Charles VII had died and the new king, Louis XI, was opposed to almost anything which had been promulgated by his father. Whether Jenson returned to France is a moot point. If he did, it was not for long, for as we know, he went to Italy some time before 1470, the year in which the first Paris press went into operation.

The type chosen (probably by Fichet) for the books produced at the Sorbonne was not, as might have been expected, a gothic of the type used in French manuscripts of the period, but a very legible roman, modelled on the type which Sweynheim and Pannartz were then using at Rome.

To Guillaume Fichet we owe the earliest document of undisputed authenticity which specifically credits Gutenberg with the invention of printing. This is a letter which Fichet addressed to Robert Gaguin; a letter which was printed and included in a dedicatory copy of Gasparino's *Orthographia* which Fichet sent to Gaguin. The relevant part of the letter runs:

'It is of the restoration of humane studies that I now speak. Upon these (so far as I gather by conjecture) great light has been thrown by the breed of new makers of books whom, within our memory, Germany (as did once upon a time the Trojan Horse) has sent broadcast into every quarter. For they say that there, not far from the city of Mainz, there appeared a certain John, whose surname was Gutenberg, who, first of all men, devised the art of printing, whereby books are made, not by a reed, as did the ancients, nor with a quill pen, as do we, but with metal letters, and that swiftly, neatly, beautifully.'*

Thirty books are known to have come from the Sorbonne press of Guillaume Fichet and Jean Heynlin before the end of 1472.† In September of that year Fichet left Paris for Rome with his patron Cardinal Bessarion, and Heynlin, who had acted as corrector, retired from that position and was replaced by Erhard Winsberg. Possibly his eyesight, always weak, had further deteriorated; it was on account of bad eyesight that he had had to relinquish the post of Prior of the Sorbonne in 1470. Jacobus Magni, *Sophologium*, was probably the last volume issued from the Sorbonne press, and in 1473 the printers now left to their own devices moved to the sign of the Golden Sun in the rue Saint-Jacques.

The type used by them at the Sorbonne had become very worn and unfit for further use, so that the first thing they did after their removal was to renew their material, and they cut a new face, a gothic of the type known as *fere-humanistica*. On 21 May 1473, appeared the first book in the new fount, the *Manipulus Curatorum* of Guy de Montrocher.

In 1474 a certain Hermann Statboen, who was Schöffer's representative in

---

* Translation by Walter A. Montgomery, Ph.D. in Douglas McMurtrie.
† The press printed Cicero's *Orator* and a Valerius Maximus, but no copies of these are now known.

Paris, died before he had taken out naturalization papers, and since he was therefore a foreigner his goods and stock, both in Paris and at his depots in Angers and elsewhere, were seized by the fiscal authorities and publicly sold for the ultimate benefit of the royal treasury; though Peter Schöffer did eventually receive some indemnity for the loss of his books. But with this example before them, Gering, Friburger and Crantz applied for and were granted letters of naturalization in February 1474–75.

In the meantime two workmen who had been trained at the Sorbonne press, Peter Kaiser and Johann Stoll had set up in partnership, also in the rue Saint-Jacques, at the sign of the Green Ball. The name of Kaiser (or as he was known in France, Pierre César) appears for the first time in an edition of the *Manipulus Curatorum*, which their former employers had already published. Stoll's name is not mentioned in this book, but the names of both are to be found in the undated Zamora, *Speculum vitae humanae*, printed probably in 1473.

By January 1478 Gering, Friburger and Crantz had printed some thirty books, among them the first Bible printed in France. After this date we hear no more of Friburger and Crantz, and Gering continued the business alone until around 1479–80, when for a short time he went into partnership with Guillaume Meynial. Towards the end of 1483 or beginning of 1484, Gering moved his printing office to the rue de Sorbonne, where he printed in conjunction with Berthold Rembolt.

Other printers had by this time decided that it was worth while setting up shop in the French capital, and by 1480 about ten presses were working in Paris. Booksellers began to realise that they could sell printed books more easily now than manuscripts, the price of which had fallen considerably, and since they were not competent to print themselves, sought the services of the best printers.

In 1475 Louis Symonel of Bourges, in partnership with Richard Blandin of Evreux, Russangis, a goldsmith of Paris, and two journeymen named Simon and Gaspar set up another printing office in the rue Saint-Jacob known as 'Au Soufflet Vert', a business which was active for some ten years and produced thirty-three recorded editions. The two earliest works from this press were a grammar and a rhetoric from the pen of Guillaume Tardif, a colleague of Fichet and Gaguin at the Sorbonne.

The earliest printed books to appear in Paris were all in Latin, and it was not until January 1477 that the first work in the vernacular was printed there. This was a three-volume work the *Grandes Chroniques de France* published by Pasquier Bonhomme, one of the four principal booksellers of the University of Paris. Printed in a 'lettre bâtarde' of medium size, it is the only known book signed by him, though some legal tracts, unsigned, but in the same type, are probably his.

Three years after Gering and his partners had issued their first book in Paris, a native of Liège named Gillaume Le Roy brought the art of printing to **Lyons**, where on 17 September 1473, he completed Innocentius III, *Compendium breve*. The press was financed by a wealthy merchant of Lyons named Barthelémy Buyer, was set up in his house, and it is his name, rather than that of Le Roy, which generally figures in the colophons. Indeed, during Buyer's lifetime, which ended in July 1483, the printer's name is mentioned only on three occasions, once each in 1473, 1477, and 1482.

Contrary to the practice in Paris, nearly all the books from this press are in French, for whereas in the capital books were produced largely to meet the demands of the students and teachers at the University, in Lyons they were meant to appeal to the general reading public, rather than to scholars. Lyons proved to be a good market for printed books and before the end of the fifteenth century more than 160 printers had worked there, among whom Germans were predominant to such an extent that printers as a class became known in that city as 'les allemands'.

Lyons was at this time one of the most prosperous cities in France, thanks largely to its proximity to Germany and Lombardy on the great commercial route between the Ile-de-France, Burgundy, and the Mediterranean countries. Moreover, the Lyons Fair, held four times yearly between 1463 and 1484, was a cosmopolitan rendezvous attracting merchants from far and wide. Each fair lasted for a fortnight and all merchants were admitted except the English, 'nos ennemis anciens'. The fair was suppressed in 1484, when several provinces, notably Languedoc, accused Lyons of securing the lion's share of French commerce. The ostensible reason given by the authorities in Paris was that Lyons was too near the frontier, 'à cause de laquelle extremité plusieurs fraudes y sont commises'. However, the four fairs with all their privileges were re-established by Louis XII in 1498. They reached their apogee in the first half of the sixteenth century (see p. 219).

The second press to function in Lyons was run by two Germans, Marcus Reinhard of Strassburg, and Nicolaus, the son of Philip Müller of Bensheim, who called himself Nicolaus Philippi. On the latter's death in 1488 one of his workmen, Johann Trechsel, married the widow and took over the press, which he ran until 1498, printing mostly works of theology and medicine, including an Avicenna in three large folio volumes. Josse Bade became reader for him until he himself set up as a printer in Paris. It was he who persuaded Trechsel to branch out into a new field with his illustrated *Terence* of 1493.

After the two large commercial cities of Paris and Lyons came the turn of the French provinces, in which a number of printing offices were established before the close of the century. **Toulouse** was possibly the first, for there Heinrich Turner, a printer from Basel, completed on 20 June 1476, the *Repetitio rubricae*,

FIGURE 7. Two charming woodcuts from the *Comoediae* of Terence, printed by Johann Trechsel at Lyons in 1493.

etc. of Andreas Barbata. Toulouse would have been a natural stopping place for German workmen on the road from their native country to Spain by way of Lyons. Whether **Albi** should take precedence over Toulouse is still a matter of conjecture, for an anonymous printer, whom some have identified with Johann Neumeister, printed at Albi the undated tract by Aeneas Silvius, *De* *amoris remedio*, perhaps as early as 1475. There followed in rapid succession presses at Angers (1477), Vienne (1478), Chablis (1478), Poitiers (1479), and Caen (1479). That **Angers,** where printing was introduced by Jean de la Tour and Jean Morel, should have been one of the first provincial towns to welcome the new art is explained by the fact that it had a university which was in constant touch with that of Paris and whose needs were, on a smaller scale, very similar. That **Chambéry** should have had a press as early as 1484 was due to the fact that it was the seat of the Dukes of Savoy, and therefore would provide a market for such books as the treatise on hunting, *Livre du Roy Modus* (1486), with which Antoine Neyret attracted his clientèle of country nobles.

In many places the Church provided an incentive for a printer to make at least a short stay, and this accounts for the fact that in many towns the first book printed was a service book. Breviaries, Missals, and Diurnals for local use were a source of livelihood to a large number of early printers. Thus Pierre Metlinger, the first printer at **Dôle** (1490) left that town at the instigation of the abbot of Cïteaux to go to **Dijon,** where he printed for this rich abbey, his first book there, completed 4 July 1491, being *Privilegia ordinis Cisterciensis*. In a similar fashion **Cluny** sought the printer Michael Wenssler to print for them, in 1492, a *Breviarium Cluniacense*. Jean Le Rouge of Chablis introduced printing into **Troyes** with a *Breviarium Trecense* (25 September 1483); at **Châlons-sur-Marne,** the first printed work was the *Diurnale Catalaunense* issued by Arnauld Bocquillon with the obviously inaccurate date of 1403; while at **Chartres** Jean du Pré completed a *Missale Carnotense*, the first work to be printed in that town, on 31 July 1482.

Jean du Pré is one of the great names in the early history of French printing. From his printing office, where he was at the time partnered by Didier Huym, came a folio *Missel de Paris* completed 22 September 1481, which was not only his first dated book, but also the first Paris book to contain native woodcuts. This was followed, two months later, by a *Missel de Verdun* with new and better executed illustrations. In the colophon of this work he describes himself, without any false modesty, as 'imprimeur très expert', which he undoubtedly was; so much so that his reputation was widespread and not only was he called to Chartres, as we have seen, to print there a Missal and a Breviary, but he also printed service books for use at Limoges, Angers, Besançon, Nevers and Rheims.

It was du Pré who assisted Pierre Gérard, the prototypographer of Abbeville (1486), and Jean le Bourgeois, one of the first printers of Rouen, by providing type and blocks as well as workmen, and these were undoubtedly branch offices of his Paris establishment. The Saint Augustine *La Cité de Dieu* in the French translation of Raoul de Presles was issued at **Abbeville** in two volumes (1486 and 1487) and bears the joint imprint of Jean du Pré and Pierre Gérard. Each of the twenty books comprised in the work is headed by a woodcut of considerable artistic merit, inspired, says Arthur Hind, by a Turin manuscript of 1466 executed for the Grand Bastard Antoine of Burgundy. The cuts are not signed, but it is thought that Pierre Le Rouge of Chablis, who was a calligrapher and engraver as well as a printer, may have been the cutter. It is certainly one of the finest of the early French illustrated books.

Jean du Pré worked for many of the leading booksellers and publishers, amont them Vérard, Tréperel, Caillaut, and Denis Meslier. One of his finest books was the romance of *Lancelot du Lac*, of which the first volume, in Dupré's types, was issued at Rouen, and the second by Dupré himself at Paris. Both were completed in 1488, but the second volume came out before the first, which may have been due to du Pré's greater experience. The book opens with a magnificent woodcut of King Arthur and his Knights at the Round Table, within a four-piece ornamental border of birds and foliage.

From the time of du Pré onwards the illustrated book became increasingly popular. Between July 1488 and February 1489 Pierre Le Rouge, the native of Chablis mentioned above, produced in two large folio volumes one of the marvels of early typography, a universal chronicle entitled *La Mer des Hystoires*, which he printed for Vincent Commin. This was a translation from *Rudimentum Noviciorum*, first printed by Lucas Brandis at Lübeck in 1475. For the French version the chronicle was extended to 1483, the coronation year of Charles VIII. Some of the illustrations derive from the Lübeck edition, but there are many new ones and a wealth of decorative border pieces. Particularly fine is the full page cut in volume two showing a two-fold subject – the Baptism of Clovis and the Battle of Tolbiac, with a massing of lances and spears reminiscent of Ucello.

Together with Jean du Pré, Guy Marchant was one of the Paris printers who played a great part in the development of the illustrated book in France. In 1485 he issued his first illustrated book, a *Danse Macabre*, the first edition of which was a small folio of ten leaves with seventeen woodcuts, the text being printed in *lettres de forme* similar to the type used by Jean du Pré in his Missals. A second edition was augments to sixteen leaves with six additional cuts. The figures in these two editions being all male, Marchant later brought out a *Danse macabre des femmes*.

Altogether Guy Marchant printed about a hundred books, but his fame rests mainly on five editions of the *Danse macabre* and seven editions of the *Kalendrier des Bergers*, an almanac for country folk the first edition of which appeared in 1491. This book (of which two copies only are known) is a small folio of only thirty leaves, and with far fewer woodcuts than appear in later editions. In 1493 came an entirely new edition, considerably augmented, with the title *Compost et Kalendrier des Bergiers* which had a striking success and was followed by another edition within three months, again enlarged in figures and text. It is a curious compilation both as regards text and illustrations, being a mixture of elementary astrology, agricultural precepts, and elementary hygiene.

The first book printed at **Chablis** was *Le Livre de bonnes moeurs* of the Augustinian monk Jacques Legrant. This was the work of Pierre Le Rouge, member of a large family of printers, engravers and miniaturists, prominent among whom was Jacques Le Rouge, the friend of Nicolas Jenson (see p. 43). Pierre, after introducing the new art into his native town of Chablis, went to Paris, where he worked from 1479 until 1493, becoming King's Printer in 1488. His most important book was *La Mer des Hystoires* mentioned above. Other members of the Chablis family of Le Rouge were Jean, who printed the first book at Troyes, a Breviary for local use, in 1483; Guillaume, who printed at Chablis, Troyes and Paris until his death in 1517; and Nicholas, who worked at Paris around 1490 and then at Troyes, after the departure of Guillaume, from 1494 until 1531.

During the early days of printing in France Bibles and Books of Hours provided the most remunerative work, and in this branch of printing the tradition of the illuminated manuscript lasted longer than in any other. Before the invention of printing books of prayers were hand-written on vellum and decorated with initials illuminated in gold and colours. Frequently they were enlivened with skilfully executed borders depicting flowers, birds and insects or human scenes of an edifying nature. Such books, inevitably costly, were a family's treasured possession, handed down from one generation to another.

The rich, who alone could afford such luxuries would have looked askance at a Book of Hours in unadorned typography, accustomed as they were to the rich ornamentation of the hand-written books of prayers and meditations. Printers felt bound to follow suit, and while Venice became the chief centre for the production of illustrated Missals, the printers and publishers of Paris developed and exploited the Book of Hours, and the period between the death of Louis XI, 1483, and the accession of Francois I in 1515, was, in France, its Golden Age.

The first booksellers in France to publish printed Books of Hours illustrated with engravings were Simon Vostre and Antoine Vérard. The latter, calligrapher and miniaturist by profession, became one of the most successful publishers of the late fifteenth century. Whether he was himself a printer is doubtful, despite the occasional colophon which states 'imprimé par Antoine Vérard'. This was often no more than a formula and many printers worked for him. During the first phase of his activity, until around 1492, the style of woodcut illustration varied according to the printer he employed. After that date there is a unity of style in the figures which suggests that he had some permanent artist working for him.

The earliest books in which Vérard's name occurs are the *Horae B.V.M.*

dated 2 September 1485, and the *Decameron* of 22 November 1485, which was almost certainly printed for him by Jean du Pré. Among other printers who worked for him were Pierre Le Rouge, Pierre Levet, Jean Tréperel, Jean Ménard, le Petit Laurens and Pierre le Caron. The great majority of the types used in Vérard's books are peculiar to him, so that it is possible, as Macfarlane suggests,* that although he employed various printers, Vérard's books were produced in an establishment of his own.

Before the end of 1486 he brought out a copiously illustrated edition of *Les Cent Nouvelles Nouvelles*, the printing of which is usually assigned to Pierre Levet. It has a frontispiece showing Louis XI and the Duke of Burgundy together with their courtiers. But the large illustrated books by which he is best known began to appear regularly from 1491. The quality of the illustrations in Vérard's books varies considerably, for, as Pollard says: 'illustrations originally made for other men gravitated into his possession and were used occasionally for new editions of the book for which they had been made; much more often as stock cuts in books with which they had nothing to do, while if another firm brought out a successful picture book Vérard imitated the cuts in it with unscrupulous and unblushing closeness.' In fact little is known of the sources of Vérard's illustrations. Some were copied, as Pollard has said, but we know also that cuts frequently passed from one printer to another, and even from one country to another. Macfarlane points out that cuts from one of Vérard's most successful books, the *Art de bien vivre et de bien mourir* (1492) later went over to England, some of them being found as late as 1568 in *The Booke of Nurture*, printed by T. Este.

Between 1485 and 1512 at least 286 books were published by Antoine Vérard, of which Books of Hours formed a considerable part. The remainder were made up mainly of books of chivalry, translations from the classics, together with lighter reading such as Boccaccio and the *Cent Nouvelles Nouvelles*. It is worth while remarking that with the exception of the Books of Hours and the Paris Missal and Paris Manual of 1496 and 1497, all Vérard's texts are in the vernacular and printed in a *lettre bâtarde* which gives them the appearance of a manuscript copy.

Vérard seems to have been the first publisher of Hours, for he brought out an edition dated 6 February 1485 (probably 1485–86). By the end of the century he had issued some thirty editions.

Unlike Vérard, Simon Vostre, who was a Paris bookseller-publisher from 1486 until 1520, published little save Books of Hours, of which some ninety in all are recorded as his. Most of them were printed for him by Philippe Pigouchet. His earliest production was an edition of the Roman Hours for

---

* J. Macfarlane, *Antoine Vérard*. London, Bibliographical Society, 1900.

Ere ypd i the gof
pel of fant ioon
in the. rij. che=
ptur that the
Sayterday Be
foz palme foon Day the. Bj .

day/Befoz Befterday cowntant
the fayd faytterday (z Befterday
Wyth other .iiij.dapes in put.
That owr falwpour iefu cryft
com in Bethany in the Bowf of
ocn man callyt leprowe .The
f iiij

FIGURE 8. Woodcut from *The Art of Good Lyvyng and Good Dyeng*, printed by Antoine Vérard at Paris in 1503. It shows Jesus at Bethany (S. John, chap. XII).

Vostre, completed 16 September 1488, but of this work, recorded by Brunet, no copy can now be traced. In 1491 he printed a fine edition of the Paris Hours and with it began a series for which he became famous. Books of Hours occupied his press almost exclusively for the next six or seven years, but from 1498 he did other work as well, such as Pierre Gringoire, *Le château de labeur* (31 March 1500–1), and Christine de Pisan, *Les cent histoires de Troie* (n.d.). Besides Hours in the Roman use, Pigouchet printed a large number of local Hours, for the use of Paris, Auxerre, Arras, Mons and Sarum. Very few of the French *Horae*, whoever the publisher, are alike in every copy. This was probably due to various factors: they were sometimes made up to the wishes of private customers, or special issues were arranged for the many dioceses which ordered them.

The British Museum has a copy of an interesting Book of Hours for Sarum

FIGURE 9. Rouen was an important centre of the trade with England in liturgical books during the 16th century. Here are two pages from a Sarum Book of Hours printed for the Rouen bookseller Jean Richard by Philippe Pigouchet at Paris.

use which the S.T.C. ascribes to Jean Philippe *c.* 1495, and H. Thomas to J. Poitevin, *c.* 1499.* This copy contains at the end the autograph of Arthur, Henry VII's eldest son, who inscribed it as a gift to Sir Thomas Poyntz.

Scarcely less prolific than Vostre and Vérard as publisher of Hours, of which he himself was the printer, was Thielmann Kerver, but the quality of his work is not comparable with that of his precursors in the field.

If Lyons was three years behind Paris in setting up its first printing press, it was nevertheless before Paris in printing the first book in French. This was Jean de Vignay's translation of the *Legenda aurea* of Jacobus de Voragine, which Guillaume Le Roy completed on 18 April 1476, and this was soon followed by Chauliac, *Le Guidon*, which for many years remained a classic for surgeons. Its author was physician and chaplain to Pope Clement VI at Avignon. And some seven years before Paris the printers of Lyons were engraving decorated initials to replace those which had previously been inserted by rubricators.

With type from Basel, Martin Huss printed the *Mirouer de la Redemption* (26 August 1478), the first Lyons illustrated book. Its 257 woodcuts were made from the blocks used by Bernhard Richel at Basel in his German edition of 1476. This was evidently a popular work, for Huss re-issued it in 1479 and 1482, and it was later reprinted more than once by Matthias Huss. The translator was Julien Macho. Before Paris, too, Lyons published three editions of that celebrated classic the *Roman de la Rose*. The earliest illustrated edition of this work came from the Lyons firm of Gaspard Ortuin and Peter Schenck about 1480, and contains eighty-six woodcuts. Jean Syber's edition appeared about 1485 and that of Guillaume Le Roy about 1487. The work was first printed in Paris by Jean du Pré about 1494.

From Lyons comes the earliest drawing of the interior of a printing office, in *La grāt danse macabre*, issued by Matthias Huss in 1499. It shows the pressman defending himself against Death with his ink-balls, the compositor seated before his case, and the bookseller at his counter. Although partly based on cuts in the Paris edition of Guy Marchant, the chief interest in this particular edition is this representation of Death and the Printers, which is not in the Paris edition.

By the end of the century some fifty printing houses were active in Lyons, and for the number of master printers at that time, Lyons comes immediately after Venice and Paris. But few of them seemed to make any money if one may judge from their frequent removals and the difficulties they had in paying their taxes. Some stayed the course by a careful evaluation of the market. Jacques Maillet, whose first book was the evergreen *Valentin et Orson* (30 May 1489) made a speciality of romances of chivalry, for, he said, 'le commun entendement écoute plus volontiers des paraboles que des préceptes'.

* B.M.C. lists it among "books printed in unassigned types". The Gesamtkatalog favours Jean du Pré.

Jean Fabri brought out a fine *Missal* for Geneva use, and Antoine Lambillion wooed the scholars with editions of Virgil and Seneca. And since Lyons was above all a mercantile city Pierre Mareschal could not but succeed with a little manual of accountancy for merchants who still counted by means of jetons.

At Toulouse Heinrich Turner was followed by Johann Parix from Heidelberg, who printed a number of legal works as well as some books in Spanish printed in partnership with Esteban Clebat. These included the first known edition of a Spanish translation of Æsop's *Fables* (1488), a Spanish version of the *Mélusine* of Jean d'Arras (1489) and a Catalan version *La Visió delectable* of the famous treatise of Alfonso de la Torre.

Something should be said of Pasquier Bonhomme, who, as a *libraire-juré* of the University of Paris specialised in the sale of manuscripts, but when he realised that printing was the art of the future he set up a press in his house, and although no printer himself he nevertheless signed the first book with French text to be issued in Paris: the *Chroniques de France* (3 vols. folio, 1476). It was printed in an excellent specimen of the transitional type which still retained some of the characteristics of the manuscript. After his retirement in 1484 the business passed to his son Jean, who produced a number of well-illustrated books such as *La Destruction de Troye* (1484) and *Le Livre des ruraulx prouffitz* (1486).

Although **Rouen** had no press until about 1487, it was not long before it became important in the history of French printing. Its location on the Seine proved advantageous both for despatching books to Paris or for exporting them to England. In fact both Paris and Rouen were important centres of the trade with England in liturgical books. Not only had the French printers greater experience in this form of printing, and far more attractive illustrations, but they could supply service books at a price with which the English printer could not compete, for both vellum and paper cost far less in France than in England. For one thing, there were paper mills in many of the towns and villages of Normandy, at Fervaques, Valognes, Pont-Audemer, Maromme and other places. Duff tells us how, before setting up a press in Edinburgh, the merchant Walter Chepman sent Andrew Myllar to Rouen to learn the art of printing and to bring back material.

The man who first began to print at Rouen was a native of the town named Guillaume le Talleur, whose first dated work, *Les Chroniques de Normandie* was published in May 1487. He may have started work earlier, for he printed an *Entrée du roi Charles VIII à Rouen*, an event which took place in April 1485. It seems very probable that the London printer Richard Pynson, who was also a native of Normandy, learned his trade from Le Talleur, whose device he later adopted and who printed at least two law books issued by Pynson soon after he came to England. Other Rouen printers who worked for the English market between 1490 and 1556 were Martin Morin, Pierre Olivier, Pierre Violette, Richard Hamillon, Robert and Florent Valentin, Nicolas Le Roux, and Jean Le Prest.

Lantenac was provided with a printing press in 1487, when Jean Crès brought out Mandeville, *Voyage en terre sainte*. **Rennes** was even earlier, for Pierre Bellescullée completed there, on 26 March 1484, a *Coutumes de Bretagne*. Later that same year another Breton press was functioning at **Bréhan-Loudéac**, where Jean Crès together with Robin Foucquet issued in December *Le Trepassement de Notre-Dame*.

6

Fifteenth Century Printing in the Netherlands

THAT printing was practised in the Low Countries at an early date is clear from actual specimens of early Dutch printing (sometimes referred to as 'Costeriana') which are still extant, mainly in the form of numerous undated fragments, though where and by whom they were made remains unknown.

Among these early Dutch printings is a series of different editions of the Latin grammar of Donatus, several of which seem to have been printed on one side of the leaf only, and appear extremely primitive. There exist also fragments of the *Doctrinale* of Alexander Gallus, an edition of *De salute corporis* by Gulielmus de Saliceto, the *Singularia Juris* of Ludovicus Pontanus, four editions of the *Speculum* and a treatise by Aeneas Sylvius. The last-named work alludes to Sylvius as 'Pius Secundus Pontifex Maximus', and since Pius II did not become Pope until August 1458, the work cannot have been printed before that date. There is no evidence for dating any of these works earlier than 1460.

The first press in Holland to which a printer's name can be assigned is that set up at **Utrecht** by Nicolaus Ketelaer and Gerardus de Leempt, who signed a Petrus Comestor, *Historia scholastica super Novum Testamentum* in 1473. This was possibly preceded by two other books, an Aquinas, *Liber de rege et regno* and by Augustinus, *De mirabilibus Sacrae Scripturae*, for of all the books issued by this press only three are dated – two in 1473 and one in 1474. A formerly unassigned copy of the *Gesta Romanorum* (unsigned and undated) is now thought to have come from this press.

Almost simultaneously with Utrecht, printing started at **Alost** in 1473 with two unsigned Latin tracts – Aeneas Sylvius, *De duobus amantibus*: and Dionysius Carthusiensis, *Speculum conversionis peccatorum*. A third book printed at Alost in the same type, the *Textus sunnularum* of Petrus Hispanus, bears the names of Thierry Martens and Johann of Westphalia. Johann, known also as Johann of Paderborn, and a former scribe, moved to Louvain at the end of 1474, leaving Thierry Martens to print alone in that town until he, too, moved on, at first to Antwerp in 1493, and then to Louvain 1498. He left Louvain in 1502 and returned to Antwerp, where he remained for a further ten years, only to settle finally at Louvain in 1512.

The first printer at **Louvain** was Johann Veldener, whose first known book was the *Belial* of Jacobus de Theramo, issued in August 1474. Not long after came Johann of Westphalia, whose first book at Louvain appeared in December 1474. Unlike Veldener, who soon moved on, he remained at work in Louvain for twenty-two years, and produced nearly 200 books. The small oval portrait of the printer, which he used as his device, first appeared in his edition of Justinian, *Institutiones* (21 November 1475). It is the earliest known cut in books printed from movable type in the Netherlands.

Veldener worked in Louvain until 1477 or 1478, and during this time became the first in the Netherlands to print a book illustrated with woodcuts. This was the *Fasciculus temporum* of Werner Rolewinck (1476) containing nine blocks copied from the Cologne edition of 1474. In 1477 Veldener, having moved from Louvain to Utrecht, printed there *Epistelen en Evangelien*, which he completed on 4 November 1478. He stayed in Utrecht for three years and his last book in that city was another edition of the same work, dated 9 October 1481. In 1483 he was working at Kuilenberg. Veldener is thought to have been the printer from whom Caxton learned the craft, for the former is considered, from typographical evidence, to have been the unnamed printer at Cologne of the *Flores S. Augustini* (*c.* 1472) on which, according to Wynkyn de Worde, Caxton had worked.

In his last Utrecht book Veldener made use of the two halves of one of the double compartment woodcuts used in the Dutch editions of the *Speculum*. In 1483, when he was in Kuilenberg, he used several of the *Speculum* blocks divided to fit a smaller book. Where Veldener acquired these blocks we do not know; perhaps while he was working at Utrecht.

In the very year which saw the establishment of a press at Alost, the Englishman William Caxton began to print at **Bruges.** He printed six books there, all of them undated, but the first book, the *Recuyell of the Historyes of Troye* was completed either at the end of 1473 or the beginning of 1474. Until comparatively recently it was thought that Caxton had learned the art of printing from Colard Mansion at Bruges, but the claims that Mansion was the first to print at Bruges and was wholly or in great part responsible for the six books now known to have been printed by Caxton alone, were successfully refuted by L. A. Sheppard,* who has shown that there is no evidence of a partnership between Mansion and Caxton, that their two presses were in all probability independent one of the other, and that, contrary to what had previously been believed, it was from Caxton that Colard Mansion learned to print.

Caxton printed four other books at Bruges with the fount he used for the *Recuyell*, but the sixth book, a French translation of *Cordiale quattuor novissimorum* (Les quatre derrenieres choses) is printed in a different type and one may

* L. A. Sheppard, 'A new light on Caxton and Colard Mansion' in *Signature*. N.S. No. 15, 1952.

therefore presume that it was the last of his Bruges books to be printed before his first press closed down, which must have been before 29 September 1476, when his tenancy of premises at Westminster began.

Colard Mansion was a calligrapher before he began to print. His first printed book was a treatise by Petrus de Alliaco called *Le jardin de dévotion*. It bears no date, but the colophon describes it as 'primum opus impressum per Collardum Mansion'. It was completed towards the end of 1474 or early in 1475, a year or more after Caxton had started working at Bruges. The first dated book issued by Mansion, *De la ruyne des nobles hommes et femmes* by Boccaccio, has, Duff tells us, a curious history. 'It was issued first without any woodcuts, and no spaces were left for them. Then the first leaf containing the prologue was cancelled, and reprinted so as to leave a space for a cut of the author presenting his book. At a later date the first leaves of all the books, excepting books i and vi, were cancelled, and reissued with spaces for engravings.' (Duff 1893.)

The third Bruges press was that of Jean Brito, from Pipriac in Brittany. He printed at least half a dozen books at Bruges, some of which have survived only in fragmentary form. None bears the date of printing, but one, *Deffense de M. le Duc et Mme. la Duchesse d'Austriche et de Bourgogne* can, from internal evidence, be assigned to the beginning of 1478 or slightly earlier. The bastarda text type used by Brito bears a marked resemblance to that which was used by Veldener at Utrecht and later by William de Machlinia in London. The type may indeed have been supplied by the former, for De Vinne states that 'it would seem that Veldener was not only working as a printer, but that . . . he was doing business to some extent as a manufacturer of types for the trade' (De Vinne, 1876).

The year 1477 saw the introduction of more presses into the Netherlands. At **Delft** Jacob Jacobszoon van der Meer began to print in partnership with Mauritz Yemantszoon van Middelborch, and on 10 January 1477 they completed a *Biblia Neerlandica*. This was the first time that the Old Testament had been printed in Dutch, but although the work was styled a Bible, it included neither the Psalms nor the New Testament.

About the same time a German from Cologne named Richard Pafraet started printing at **Deventer,** the first two books appearing in 1477. Pafraet produced a large number of books during an active career in Deventer which lasted until 1511. The second printer at Deventer was Jacobus de Breda, who flourished from 1485 until around 1518. Between them these two printers were responsible for a quarter of the total number of books printed in the Netherlands during the fifteenth century.

Another early Dutch printer was Pieter van Os who worked at **Zwolle** from 1479 until about 1510, though since so many of his books are undated a precise chronology of his publications is difficult to establish. He was preceded

FIGURE 10. A handsome woodcut from S. Bernardus, *Sermones*, printed at Zwolle by Pieter van Os in 1495.

by Johannes de Vollenhoe, known by one book only – an edition of Petrus Hispanus, *Summulae logicales*, printed in 1479, which states in its colophon 'per impressuram dni Iohannis de vollenhoe presbiteri in Zwollis'. His press was presumably taken over by Van Os.*

One of the outstanding printers of the Netherlands during the fifteenth century was Gerard Leeu, who began to print at **Gouda** in 1477 and worked at

* For the rediscovery of this book see L. & W. Hellinga in *Beiträge zur Inkunabelkunde*, Folg. 3, No. 1, 1965.

Gouda until 1484, when he moved to Antwerp, feeling that that important city offered a greater field for his talents than did the small town of Gouda. On leaving Gouda, Leeu took with him material he had acquired from the Haarlem printer Jacob Bellaert who died in 1486. He also engaged the artist who had worked for Bellaert, known only as the 'Graveur de Haarlem', and took him to Antwerp, where he illustrated many of Leeu's later books, including a Ludolphus, *Vita Christi*, of 1488, with its superb 'Salvator Mundi', one of the finest woodcuts made in the Netherlands during the fifteenth century.

Among the many books printed by Leeu at Gouda and Antwerp are several in English issued at Antwerp between 1486 and 1493. One of these is called *Cronycles of the londe of Englõd* (1493), the last book he printed before his untimely death at the hands of one of his workmen, Henric van Symmen, in the course of a quarrel.

Because of its importance in the world of commerce more printers settled in **Antwerp** during the fifteenth century than in any other Netherlands town. First to do so was Mathias van der Goes, whose first book was completed on 8 June 1481. He continued to print there until his death in 1492, and was succeeded by Govaert Bac, who married his widow and was active in Antwerp until 1511. Thierry Martens, setting up his third press at Antwerp, worked there from 1493 until 1497, but in the following year moved to Louvain.

In 1483 Jacob Bellaert set up a press at **Haarlem**. The same year saw the establishment of presses at **Leiden**, by Heynricus Heynrici; at **Kuilenberg** by Jan Veldener; and at **Ghent** by Arend de Keysere, who had already introduced printing into **Audenarde** in 1480. He remained in Ghent until his death in 1489, and although his widow, Beatrice, carried on the business for a short time, no copy is known of anything printed by her. At a later date she married Henrik vanden Dale, who is mentioned as a printer at Bruges in 1505.

Brussels had only one press during the fifteenth century. It belonged to the religious association known as the Brothers of the Common Life, who set up a press in their house known as Nazareth and printed their earliest recorded book, a Gerson, *Opuscula*, in March 1475. Their second dated book, and the first to bear the Brussels imprint (elaboratùm bruxelle opido brabancie) was the *Gnotosolitos* of Arnoldus de Geilhoven, completed on 25 May 1476. They continued to print regularly until 1485, the last known work to come from their Brussels press being a *Breviary* dated 15 June 1485. In 1484 the Brothers produced the only illustrated book printed at Brussels during the fifteenth century – a quarto volume entitled *Legende sanctorum Henrici imperatoris et Kunigundis imperatricis*. This work is the only one of some thirty-five books printed at this press to bear the name of the printers (impresse . . . per fratres communis vite in nazareth). After the closing down of this press Brussels remained without a printer until the following century.

7

Beyond the Pyrenees:
early Printing in the Iberian Peninsula

THE first introduction of the art of printing into Spain coincided with the accession to the throne of Isabella of Castile in 1474, for the first known book printed in Spain appeared at the end of 1473. Not, however, the first book in Spanish, for it was in Latin. The first printers in Spain were Germans who, coming from their country by way of the Mediterranean to avoid the barrier of the Pyrenees, settled around what is now known as the Costa Brava, and set up their presses at Barcelona, Gerona, Lerida, Tarragona, Tortosa, and further inland at Saragossa. For several years, not knowing much of the language of their adopted country, they printed mainly Latin books. Of books in the Castilian tongue they printed none at all, and when they undertook to print a book in the vernacular of their locality, in Catalan or Valencian, they were careful either to print in partnership with a native, as the German Peter Brun did with the Spaniard Pedro Posa, or to employ correctors with a sound knowledge of the language.

Juan Cristiano Seiz, in his book *Annus tertius saecularis inventae Artis Typographicae*, printed at Haarlem in 1741, stated that the art of printing was introduced into Spain in the year 1473: and that the first book was an Aristotle printed at Barcelona. Until recently most historians of printing have considered this statement to be erroneous, but more recent investigations have shown that Seiz was correct as to the date, though more by luck than anything else, for the book he mentions was the Bonetus, *Metaphysica* printed at Barcelona by Pere Miquel in 1493.

The early history of printing in Spain is more obscure than elsewhere in Europe. Indeed, until comparatively recently the small volume of poems by Bernardo Fenollar called *Obres e trobes daual scrites en laors de la Sacratissima Verge María*, printed by Lambert Palmart (after 25 March 1474) was considered to be the first book printed in Spain. It was described in the catalogue of the Exposicion Historico del Libro, 1952, as 'the first indubitable printing in Spain so far known'.

However, in 1959 and 1960 there appeared two articles, written independently, which shed new light on the origins of printing in Spain and transferred the site of the first press from Valencia to Barcelona. One was Laurence Witten, 'The Earliest Books printed in Spain' in *Papers of the Bibliographical Society of America*, Vol. 53, 1959; the other was Prof. Jordi Rubió, 'Wurden die ersten Pressen in Barcelona und Zaragoza von einem Mann geleitet?' in *Gutenberg-Jahrbuch*, 1960. The arguments put forward were later reinterpreted by George D. Painter in 'The First Press at Barcelona' in *Gutenberg-Jahrbuch*, 1962.

From the evidence of these experts in the field of incunabula it now appears fairly certain that printing was introduced into Spain at **Barcelona**★ and that the first press in that city was not, as had hitherto been thought, that of Johannes de Salsburga and Paulus de Constantia, but was run by three other Germans, namely Heinrich Botel, Georg von Holz, and Johann Planck. On 5 January 1473 Botel, also known as Henricus de Saxonia, entered into an agreement by which he was to teach the other two the art of printing, in return for which they would provide capital for the enterprise. The first book from this press was an undated Aristotle, *Ethica, Oeconomica et Politica*, which, seeing that the company was formed in January 1473, could hardly be later than towards the end of that year, and probably preceded by a month or so the undated edition of the same work produced at Valencia by Lambert Palmart.

The press of Lambart Palmart, another German printer, at **Valencia,** thus becomes the second to function in Spain. His *Obres e trobes*, for long considered his first work, was probably preceded, according to Mr Witten by four undated pieces which included the second printing of the Aristotle and a Phalaris, *Epistolae*. It seems rather remarkable that two editions of the same work by Aristotle should follow so closely on the heels one of the other at two different Spanish towns. It must have been either pure coincidence or commercial rivalry. Mr Painter is of the opinion that Palmart's reasoning took the line that where there was enough profit for one man there might be enough for two.

At **Saragossa** the first printer was Mateo Flandro (Matthew of Flanders) who completed there a *Manipulus curatorum* on 15 October 1475. This is the earliest book printed in Spain to have a complete imprint, although the Johannes, *Comprehensorium* printed at Valencia by Palmart 23 February 1475, is the first with printed date and place. Mateo Flandro may possibly have been the Matthew Vendrell who printed at Barcelona in 1482 and at Gerona in 1483. After this solitary production by Mateo Flandro, no further printing seems to have taken place at Saragossa until 1480, when Paul Hurus, a native of Constance, set up a press there which was active till almost the end of the century.

First to introduce printing into **Seville,** and the first Spaniards to print in their native land, were Antón Martínez, Bartolomé Segura, and Alfonso del Puerto,

---

★ The suggestion that the *Synodal* of Segovia (*sine nota*) was printed in that town by Johannes Parix at an earlier date lacks conclusive evidence.

La philofofia moral del Ariftotel: es afaber Æthi
cas: Politbicas: y Economicas: En Romançe.

FIGURE 11. First Spanish edition of Aristotle's *Politica* and *Economica*. Saragossa, Jorge Coci, 1509.

whose first production was Diaz de Montalvo, *Repertorium quaestionum super Nicolaeum de Tudeschis*, 1477. At the end of the book is a quatrain in Latin which, translated, reads: 'If you wish to know who were the first printers who at that time lived in Seville, knowledgeable and experienced in their craft, showing it in its full ingeniousness, they were three men called Antonius Martini, Alphonsus de Portu, and Bartolomeus Segura.'

They printed two editions of the *Sacramental* of Clemente Sánchez de Vercial, the first dated 1 August 1477, and the second 28 May 1478; and after this Antón Martínez disappears and the remaining two issued two or three books in 1480, including the popular *Fasciculus temporum* of Werner Rolewinck. This was the first dated book with illustrations to come from Spain, and the cuts seem to have been copied from a Venice edition of the work, printed in 1479 by Georg Walch. By 1482 Alfonso del Puerto was printing on his own.

In 1490 the first of a line of officially sponsored national dictionaries appeared at Seville. This *Vocabulario universal en latin y en romance*, commissioned by Queen Isabella of Spain, was printed at Seville by 'Paulo de Colonia y socios'. A handsome book, it was the first production of a syndicate of German printers who had settled in Seville at the invitation of Ferdinand and Isabella, and called themselves the 'Cuatro Compañeros Alemanes'. The company consisted of Pablo de Colonia (whose name always comes first, and who was the director of the company), Hans Pegnizer of Nuremberg, Magno Herbst and Tomas Glockner. Their antecedents are unknown, but from typographical evidence Häbler concluded that they had worked previously in Venice.

The last known book printed by the four in association was Diego de San Pedro, *Carzel de amor*, completed on 3 March 1492. In that year they also produced the first book with music printed in Spain, the *Lux Bella* of Domingo Marcos Durän. From 1493, after the death of Pablo de Colonia, the firm was known as the 'Tres Compañeros Alemanes'.

Hans Pegnitzer, whom we have mentioned as one of the partners in this Seville venture, was associated in 1496 with Meinard Ungut, when they established the first printing press in **Granada** where they issued Francisco Jiménez, *Vita Christi*. Ungut worked in Seville from 1491 until the end of the century, mostly in partnership with Stanislaus Polonus. Their first dated book was Didacus de Deza, *Defensiones sancti Thomas Aquinatis*, 4 February 1491, and they continued to print together until 1499, after which Stanislaus Polonus worked alone. Their decorative work was stylish and remarkably good is the title cut of the King enthroned from Colonna, *Regimiento de los principes*, 1494.

Although some early histories of printing give 1480 as the date when printing was first introduced into **Toledo**, it is now generally conceded that the first printer there was Juan Vázquez, who at the end of 1483 or beginning of 1484 began to print a series of indulgences, the first of which was probably a *Bula de indulgencias de la Santa Cruzada*. He is known also as the printer of Pedro Jiménez de Prexamo, *Confutatorium errorum* dated July 1486. Antonio Tellez, the second printer, worked at Toledo from 1494 until around 1497, but produced nothing of particular value.

Then, in 1498, Toledo received the press of Peter Hagenbach, who had previously worked at Valencia, and came to Toledo probably at the invitation of Melchior Gorricio, who provided the capital for Hagenbach's two surviving books of 1498. Hagenbach was also favoured by the patronage of the arch-bishop of Toledo, the future Cardinal Jiménez, for in 1499 he brought out a Mozarabic Missal at the archbishop's demand and at Gorricio's expense. On 9 January 1500, he brought out an enlarged edition of this *Missale mixtum*. This Missal had been first printed at Venice in 1488, but the errors in it were so numerous that it never received Papal approval, and the copy printed by Hagenbach was corrected by order of Cardinal Jiménez. It remains a superb example of sumptuous liturgical printing, with a Canon cut of Christ on the cross with the Virgin Mary and St John. Among other books printed by Hagenbach at Toledo, where he printed until 1502, was Caesar's *Commentaries* in a Spanish translation (1498) the title-page of which bears the arms of Ferdinand and Isabella. Among his works is a recently discovered *Celestina* in its earlier recension, with a rhyming colophon of 1500.

The early history of printing in **Salamanca** remains somewhat obscure due to the anonymity of the printers there. Norton tells us that of well over 100 books in the fifteenth century, only four have any printer's name. Three are signed by Leonardus Alemanus and Lupus Sanz; the fourth was the first work of a press established by Hans Gysser in 1500. The first dated, but unsigned, book printed at Salamanca was the original edition of the Latin grammar of Antonio de Nebrija, a work which remained in favour for nearly three centuries. The printer remains unidentified.

Pamplona had as its first printer Arñao Guillén de Brocar, who was to become famous during the next century for his printing of the great Complutensian Polyglot Bible, of which we shall speak later. His first known work is a Manual for Pamplona use dated 15 December 1490; a book which, incidentally, is not recorded by Haebler. His last dated work at Pamplona is an edition of the Synodal Constitutions of that town. He then moved to Logroño, where he printed some fifty books.

From 1480 until the end of the century printing at Saragossa was entirely in the hands of Pablo Hurus or of his brother Juan, who deputised for him during the period from 1488 to 1490. From that year onwards the Hurus press was among the most active in Spain. In 1498 Pablo Hurus issued a Spanish translation of Breydenbach's *Peregrinationes* under the title *Viaje de la tierra sancta*. On the last page is his device, which first appeared in Diaz de Montalvo's *Ordenanzes Reales* which he completed on 3 June 1490. This was probably the first printer's mark used in Spain, though it may possibly have been preceded by that of the Compañeros Alemanes. Hurus' device consists of two triangles, each with a letter *h* inside (for the brothers and partners Pablo and Juan) separated by a cross. In the Breydenbach the device is flanked on the left by St James of Compostella and on the right by St Sebastian.

In **Burgos** the first printer was Fadrique Alemán de Basilea, generally accepted as being the Friedrich Biel who had printed at Basel in partnership with Michael Wenssler around 1472. He began to print at Burgos in 1485* and the first two devices of which he made use in that city include the initials *f. b.* His first dated work is the *Grammatica* of A. Guttierez, completed 12 March 1485. He printed about sixty books during the fifteenth century and became one of the best printers in Spain. His edition of *Celestina* (1499 or early 1500) is the earliest surviving edition of the oldest known form of this work.

Murcia's first printers were Lope de la Roca and Gabriel Luis de Arinyo who completed the *Oracional* of Fernán Pérez de Guzmán on 26 March 1487. Montserrat secures a foothold in the fifteenth century through the press of Johann Leuschner, who used a metal-cut of the 'Seated Madonna of Montserrat' as his device. His first recorded printing is an edition of Bonaventura, *Meditationes vitae Christi*, dated 16 April 1499, and he followed it with the same author's *De instructione novitiorum*. Leuschner had previously printed at Barcelona from 1495 onwards, in partnership at first with Gerhard Preuss and later with Johann Rosembach. In 1498 he printed alone Aegidius Columna, *De regimine principum* in Catalan and Pontanus, *De divinis Laudibus*.

Mateo Vendrell, whom we have mentioned in connection with Saragossa, printed at **Gerona** Felipe de Malla, *Memorial del pecador remut*, dated 17 November 1483, being the first to print in that town.† Zamora was endowed with a press in the previous year when Antonio de Centenera printed a *Vita Christi per coplas* by Iñigo Lopez de Mendoza, dated 25 January 1482. In the following year he printed Enrique de Villena, *Doze Trabajos de Hércules*, with some interesting cuts displaying, in the words of Arthur M. Hind, 'a combination of decorative and bizarre qualities which characterise much Spanish work' (Hind, 1935).

At the outset Spain had adopted a fashion of printing which was little more than an imitation of French and Italian models, but it was not long before the new techniques had been assimilated and adapted to the characteristics of the Spanish temperament. The main centres of printing were at Valencia, Seville, Burgos, Barcelona, Salamanca, Saragossa and Toledo. There is no question yet of Madrid, which has no place in the history of printing until 1566. Although the early printers of Spain were for the most part Germans, it was not long before they adopted a style suitable to the taste of their Spanish customers, and by the last decade of the fifteenth century Spanish books could hold their own with those of other European countries.

* He was commissioned by the cathedral authorities to print 2000 copies of a broadsheet in 1482, but no known work of his can be dated prior to 1485.
† He is recorded as a 'merchant and citizen of Barcelona'.

A few other Spanish presses of the fifteenth century remain to be dealt with. At Barcelona, following that sole production of Botel, Georg vom Holtz, and Johan Planck in 1473, we find the partners Juan de Salsburga and Pablo Hurus at work in 1475, followed about three years later by Nicolaus Spindeler, who printed partly with Pedro Brun, who also partnered Pere Posa in that city in 1481. From then until the end of the century Pere Posa printed on his own, after which he was succeeded by his nephew and namesake. Posa was a Catalan, and thus signed himself Pere rather than Pedro.

Pere Miquel, another Catalan, worked at Barcelona from 1491 until at least 1495, his death occurring two years later. His last known work was the *Usatges de Barcelona e Constitucions de Catalunya*, unsigned, but printed with his types, though perhaps by Diego de Gumiel, who completed in 1497 an edition of *Tirant lo Blanch* (by Juan Martorell?) which Miquel had begun. The next Barcelona press was that of Hans Rosenbach, who had previously worked at Valencia, and after printing at Barcelona from 1492 until 1498, when he moved to Tarragona. Diego de Gumiel printed a few books towards the end of the century before moving to Valladolid about 1502.

The successor to Lambert Palmart at Valencia was Alfonso Fernández de Córdoba, who worked at times in partnership with Gabriel Luis de Arinyo, and was active at intervals between 1477 and 1485. Nicolaus Spindeler, who worked off and on at Valencia, was a wandering printer, for he is known to have worked also at Tortosa, Barcelona and Tarragona. His main period of activity at Valencia was between 1494 and the end of the century.

Only one printer seems to have worked at **Zamora** during the fifteenth century, and that was Antonio de Centenera, who introduced printing into that town in January 1482, with an edition of Inigo de Mendoza, *Vita Christi per coplas*, and produced a small number of books there during the ensuing ten years.

At **Huete**, in the province of Cuenca, Alvaro de Castro printed Alfonso Diaz de Montalvo, *Ordenanzas reales*, completed on 11 November 1484, and followed this with another edition in August 1485. This work was handsomely decorated with metal-cut border pieces partly executed in punch-work and decorative initials, which from their subjects seem to have been made specially for the book. Several Indulgences were printed in De Castro's types in 1486, 1487, and 1490, but there is no evidence to show whether or not they were printed at Huete. Previous to his arrival in that town, De Castro had printed at Santiago in 1483, in association with Juan de Bobadilla, a *Brevarium Compostellanum* for the cathedral of that city.

PORTUGAL

The first book printed in Portugal of whose existence there is conclusive proof was a Pentateuch in Hebrew completed at **Faro** on the press of Don Samuel

Porteira, 30 June 1487. The press was financed by Don Samuel Gacon. Only one copy of this work is known to exist, the vellum copy in the British Museum, for Häbler was in error when he mentioned a copy in the Bodleian Library.

The first incunable in the Portuguese language is a Portuguese translation of Ludolphus de Saxonia, *Vita Christi*, which was printed at **Lisbon** in four volumes during the year 1495 by the partners Valentim Fernandez (sometimes known as Valentinus de Moravia) and Nicolau de Saxonia. The translation, undertaken at the command of the Infanta Isabel, Duchess of Coimbra, was begun by Fr Nicolau Vieira and completed by Fr Bernardo de Alcobaza. The translation of this work, which was popular all over the Iberian peninsula, was not very good, many passages of the original text were missing, and either the work had not been very well edited or the manuscript from which it was printed was a poor one. The 1502 Spanish version of Ambrosio Montesino was much better.

This is the only work known to have been produced by the partnership, and the press was continued by Fernandez working on his own, and continuing to print rather spasmodically until 1518. Nicolau de Saxonia worked independently until 1498, the date of the Braga Missal which was his last known production.

Despite the poor translation, the *Vita Christi* was nevertheless a fine piece of printing which Häbler described as 'one of the most beautiful incunables ever

FIGURE 12. Woodcut of a King and Queen at prayer from Ludolphus de Saxonia, *Vita Christi*, printed at Lisbon in 1495 by Valentin Fernandez and Nicolao de Saxonia.

executed in the whole of the Peninsula'. Its four volumes have some fine wood-cuts, that of the Crucifixion, a close copy of a copper engraving by the Master E.S. of 1466 being specially notable.

At **Leira** a Hebrew press was set up in 1492 by Abraham ben Samuel D'Ortas, though only four works from this press seem to have survived. Three Hebrew books are known for the years 1492, 1494 and 1495, and nothing further is known of the press after 1496, when it produced three variant editions of Abraham ben Samuel Zacuto, *Almanach perpetuum coelestium motuum*, the only Portuguese incunable to be issued from a Hebrew press printed in latin in a gothic type. The book, which is a translation of the Canons from Hebrew into Latin by José Vizinho, is said to have been that used by Columbus to predict the eclipse of the moon to the terrified natives of Jamaica.

A press was set up at **Oporto** in 1497, and on 25 October of that year Rodrigo Alvares completed the *Constitutions* of the bishopric of Oporto in Portuguese.

The third town in Portugal to possess a printing press, and the first to print in other than the Hebrew tongue, was the small town of **Chaves** in northern Portugal. This press is known only from a recently discovered *Confessionale*, dated 8 August 1489, printed 'na vila de chaves' by an anonymous printer. The text is in Latin with a colophon in Portuguese.* The B.M.C. Vol. X hazards a guess that the printer may be Johann Gherlinc, who printed at Barcelona from 1486 until 1489 or later, and in 1494 set up a press at Braga, in northern Portugal.

* S. Cornil, *Un évènement bibliographique* in 'Revue des langues vivantes'. Vol. 32, No. 5, 1966.

8

Switzerland's first Printers

It is now generally accepted that Berthold Ruppel was the first printer at Basel, although uncontrovertible evidence to substantiate the claim is lacking. Of the books he printed there only one is signed (with the Christian name only) and none are dated save the 1477 Nicolaus Panormitanus, *Super libros Decretalium*, which he signed jointly with Wenssler and Richel. Ruppel had learnt his craft in Mainz from Gutenberg himself and is identified with the 'Bertolff von Hannauwe' who testified on Gutenberg's behalf in the 1455 lawsuit against Fust. He was probably working at Basel before 1470.

In the middle of the fifteenth century **Basel** was a town with about 15,000 inhabitants, but though small its geographical position made it an important commercial centre, and the University founded there in 1460 made of the town a gateway through which the stream of humanistic studies flowed from Italy to Germany and France. Although Basel did not become a member of the Swiss Federation until 1501, it was recognised as an outstanding centre of learning long before that, and by the end of the 1460s prospects for a printer were sufficiently favourable for Ruppel to set up his press, closely followed by others. Ruppel's first work seems to have been an undated Latin Bible, after which came Nicolaus de Lyra, *Postilla super Evangelia* and Gregorius, *Moralia in Job*. Dr Kurt Ohly suggests that Ruppel began his preparations as early as 1468. This seems a valid suggestion, since there is documentary evidence concerning a strike of printers' journeymen in the city in 1471, and since the settlement of the dispute mentions master printers in the plural, we must assume that at least two printers were working in Basel. One of these would have been Michael Wenssler from Strassburg, who was a student at Basel University in 1462.

Although the first dated book of Wenssler, an edition of Barzizius, *Epistolae*, which he printed in partnership with one Friedrich Biel, came out at the end of 1472, he may have been printing before then. For the first few years his press seems to have been active and prosperous, judging by the still extant records of the city tax collections. In 1475 he collaborated with Bernhard Richel, active as a Basel printer 1474–82, in an edition of Caracciolus, *Quadragesimale*, after which he began a series of legal works which kept him busy for several years. In 1477 he was associated with Ruppel and Richel in the printing of Nicolaus

Panormitanus, *Super libros Decretalium*, a massive work in five volumes, which involved the partners in heavy financial loss, since it chanced that in the very same year two editions of this work were published in Venice, one by Jenson and the other by Johannes de Colonia and Manthen, and this unwelcome and unexpected competition militated against the sale of the Basel edition.

From this time onward Wenssler was constantly in financial trouble over the repayment of loans, though he continued to print quite large works, such as the *Summa* of Thomas Aquinas, mainly on borrowed money. But eventually he fell foul of the law over certain dubious transactions and about the middle of May 1491, he fled from Basel, leaving his debts and his wife behind. Later he turned up at Lyons, where he rented a press from Matthias Huss and confined himself more or less to the printing of local service-books whenever he got a commission. In this way he printed at Cluny a Breviary and a Missal in 1492 and 1493 respectively, and a *Diurnale Matisconense* at Mâcon in 1494. But this business cannot have been very remunerative, for in the colophon of the Cluny Missal he states that it was produced 'plus affectu devotionis quam lucrandi causa'.

However, his fortunes revived a little when, back at Lyons, he undertook once more the printing of large legal works. He continued to work at Lyons until 1498, when he was involved in an unsavoury quarrel during the course of which a man was killed. Wenssler thought it best to flee and he managed to secure from the authorities at Basel a safe conduct for his return to that city providing he came to terms with his creditors there.

Not for long were Berchtold Ruppel and Michael Wenssler the only printers in Basel. Among those who sought their living by the press in this university town were Bernhard Richel, Martin Flach, Johann von Amerbach, Hans Grüninger, and Johann Froben, to name but the best-known. Bernhard Richel of Ehewiler became a burgess of Basel in 1474 and celebrated the fact by bringing out in that same year his first dated book *Sachsenspiegel*. He signed in all some twenty-two works before his death in 1482. One of his most important productions was the *Spiegel menschlicher Behältnis* (1476), a German version of the *Speculum Humanae Salvationis*, with 278 woodcuts. Richel also printed a German version of the popular *Fasciculus temporum* of Werner Rolewinck entitled *Bürdin der Zyt*, with a colophon telling the reader that the book had been printed by 'Bernhart Richel Burger right clear and neat' in 1481.

Johann Amerbach was born near Reutlingen in Swabia in the year 1444. He took his degree at Paris where he studied under Heylin, and later went to Nuremberg, where he entered the printing-office of Anton Koberger as corrector. Having thus gained some experience of the printing trade, he settled in Basel in 1475 and set up his own business. He began to print around 1478, but the first work he signed is a collection of tracts by Vincent de Beauvais dated

13 December 1481. He worked in Basel for nearly forty years and became one of the most famous and skilful printers of his day, and, himself a scholar, was the friend of the leading scholars of the time, men like Wimpheling and Reuchlin.

Amerbach was the first of the Basel printers to make use of a roman fount. He had a long business association with Adolf Rusch of Strassburg, whose advice he sought in 1485 as to the feasibility of printing an edition of St Augustine, *De Civitate Dei*, a work which he actually printed four years later. The success of this and other writings of St Augustine led him eventually to undertake his most costly enterprise, the printing of the complete works of St Augustine for the first time. He began in 1491 by engaging Augustinus Dodo to prepare the manuscripts for the press but it was not until 1506 that the work was completed, and in the meantime he had printed the works of St Ambrose in three volumes (1492). The collected edition of St Augustine was printed in about 2,000 copies, most of which were taken over for sale by Koberger, who found them difficult to dispose of, for two years later Froben mentioned in a letter that the Nuremberg publisher still had about 1,000 copies left. Yet today only four perfect copies are known, three of which are in the University Library at Basel and the other in the library of Wadham College, Oxford. A generous benefactor to the Charterhouse at Basel, Amerbach was buried there after his death on 25 December 1513.

Martin Flach, 'native and citizen of Basel' is first mentioned in the signed Rodericus Zamorensis, *Speculum vitae humanae* of 1475, and although he was still alive in 1514 most of his printing was done well before the end of the century. As he became a member of the City Council, civic affairs may have taken up much of his time. Johann Besicken may have worked for him as a journeyman, for although Besicken is mentioned in the city records as a printer in 1477 ('in der St Alban-Vorstadt beim Bridenthor') the only books he is known to have printed on his own account are dated 1482 and 1483. He is presumably the Besicken who was printing at Rome in the 1490s.

Nicolaus Kesler, of Bottwar, was probably at one time employed by Richel, and began to print on his own account about 1483 in the house 'zum Blumen' once occupied by Richel. He is thought to have been Richel's son-in-law. In 1485 he printed a Basel Missal, was still printing in 1510, and was alive as late as 1519.

Michael Furter from Augsburg is mentioned as a printer in January 1483, but does not seem to have been a master printer until the 1490s. He was active almost up to the time of his death in 1517. His best-known works are La Tour Landry, *Der Ritter von Thurn*, and Johannes Meder, *Quadragesimale*, both with interesting woodcuts. He also printed in 1496 one of the earliest books on music, the *Lilium musicae planae* of Michael Keinspeck, with musical notes.

FIGURE 13. From S. Augustine: *De Civitate Dei*. Basel: Johann Amerbach, 1481. The woodcut shows S. Augustine and the Cities of God and Satan.

Johann Froben, who became one of the most famous Basel printers by the beginning of the sixteenth century (see page 121), began his career as a journeyman and then foreman for Amerbach. He became a citizen of Basel on 13 November 1490, and his first signed and dated book is a Latin Bible of 27 June 1491. He issued a few books in partnership with Johann Petri and jointly with Amerbach printed a large Latin Bible at the close of the century. Not yet was he 'omnium chalcographorum princeps' as Martin Dorp called him; that still lay ahead.

Johann Bergmann von Olpe, priest and chaplain of the Cathedral at Basel printed from 1494 until 1499. He printed several of the works of Sebastian Brant including the celebrated *Stultifera navis* both in Latin and German, as well as Reuchlin, *Scenica progymnasmata*. One of his last works, issued in 1499, was a *Diurnale Basiliense*.

Another Basel printer of these early days was Jakob von Pforzheim who was active there from 1488 until 1509 and whose output included the works of Chrysostomus. He is also known (though not in his books) as Jakob Wolff. About 1493 he issued Christoforus Columbus, *Epistola de insulis nuper inventis*, with illustrations interesting in view of their subject matter. They were used again in another edition of the same work by Bergmann von Olpe published at Basel in 1495.

When we consider Basel, a free city of the Holy Roman Empire, with its many and excellent printers, it comes as a surprise to learn that the first dated Swiss printing known to us was the work of a clerical printer, Canon Helyas Helyae (von Lauffen) of the small abbey at Beromünster, near Lake Baldeggen and remote from the main streams of traffic. The book in question was Joannes Marchesinus, *Mammotrectus super Bibliam*, bearing the date of completion 10 November 1470. And by pure coincidence this work was finished on exactly the same day as the edition of that book printed by Peter Schöffer at Mainz! The canon printed in all six works in a not unpleasing type transitional between gothic and roman, before his death in 1475. The undated *De officio missae*, a tract by Nicolaus Andreae, was probably his last work.

Whether the canon, already an elderly man when the *Mammotrectus* was printed, himself did the printing is open to doubt. As a Syndic of the Abbey of Münster he visited Basel in 1466 on ecclesiastic business and it may be that he first became acquainted with the new art at that time, for Ruppel might well have been printing by then. The strike of pressmen in 1471 would seem to indicate that printing had already become an established trade there for some time. If so, might not the canon have persuaded some journeyman printer to work for him at Beromünster?

In 1478 printing was introduced into **Geneva** by Adam Steinschaber of Schweinfurt, who completed Francisco Jiménez, *Le Livre des saints anges* on 24

March of that year. 'Genevan printing' writes Dr Scholderer, 'makes an impressive start with no fewer than four *editiones principes* of French texts all in the course of the year 1478.' The other three were Pierre d'Arras, *Histoire de la belle Mélusine*; the *Doctrinale de sapience*; and the romance of *Fierabras*. A facsimile edition of the *Mélusine* with an Introduction by Dr W. J. Meyer was issued by the Schweizer Bibliophilen Gesellschaft in 1923.

Steinschaber does not appear to have worked for very long at Geneva, for his name does not occur in any book after 1480. His type seems to have been used later for an undated edition of *Fierabras*, printed by one Simon du Jardin, known only from this signed book. The most important of the early Genevan printers was Aloys (or Louis) Cruse, otherwise known as Louis Guerbin, said to have been the son of a doctor named Guerbin de la Cruse, who had come to Geneva from Germany, having gallicized his name from what was possibly Krause. His first work, a *Breviarium* for Geneva use commissioned by the Bishop Jean de Savoie, bears the date 30 August 1479. At the request of the same prelate he printed in June 1480, *Les Constitutions synodales de l'Eglise de Genève*. In the summer of 1482 Louis Cruse moved to Promenthoux, near Nyon, probably to escape the plague, which was causing great mortality in Geneva at the time. There he printed a *Doctrinal de sapience* dated 2 August 1482, but seems to have returned to Geneva by the end of the year, for he signed another edition of *Fierabras* in that city at the end of March 1483. He continued to print fairly regularly, with the exception of the years from 1489 to 1492, when no printing at all was done in Geneva, until 1509, when his name occurs for the last time in a Breviary for Lausanne use.

Jean Belot, from Rouen, became a citizen of Geneva in 1494, and set up a press there towards the end of 1497, during the earlier part of which year he had printed at Grenoble. He had already printed at Lausanne in 1493 a Missal for local use. He was active in Geneva until the beginning of the sixteenth century, and died in 1512.

The first book to be printed at **Zürich** was the *Laus et commendatio . . . cantici Salve regina* by the Dominican Albert von Weissenstein (Albertus de Albo Lapide). Issued *sine nota* it is thought to have been printed about 1479, probably by Sigmund Rot, a printer from Bitsche in Lorraine, who became a citizen of Zürich in that year. The place where it was printed we may assume to have been the Dominican monastery at Zürich. The printer was also responsible for a pamphlet commemorating the jubilee of Pope Sixtus IV. Although we cannot be certain that Rot was the printer, it was almost certainly printed in Zürich, for the watermark shows a bull's head with a Z for Zürich above it. However, there seems to have been no further printing at Zürich until the beginning of the sixteenth century.

Although regular printing in **Lausanne** did not take place until the middle of the sixteenth century, the town can lay claim to one incunable, for in 1493 Jean Belot from Rouen printed there a *Missale in usum Lausannensem*, before going on to Geneva.

9

Printing comes to England

IT was a quarter of a century after the art of printing had been put to practical use that the first press was established in England; and by that time presses were functioning in nearly fifty towns in Italy and more than a score of towns in Germany. Strangely enough, with the exception of Germany, England was the only country in Western Europe where the pioneer of the new art was a native of the country. Perhaps even more strange is the fact that England's first printer, William Caxton, was a man past middle age, whose whole life previously had been spent almost entirely in connection with the wool trade.

Moreover the press which Caxton set up at Westminster at the end of 1476 was his second press, for he had already printed at Bruges (see p. 74). After thirty years' residence abroad, Caxton returned to England in 1476. He chose Westminster rather than the City of London for the site of his press, probably on account of its proximity to the Court, where he had influential patrons. The exact date when he took up his residence at Westminster is unknown, but it must have been before the end of 1476, because an Indulgence of Pope Sixtus IV which he printed there was discovered at the Public Record Office in 1928, and this is hand-dated 13 December 1476. His printing house was not, as depicted in some fanciful paintings, in a side-chapel of the Abbey, but in a house close to or adjoining the Chapter House.*

There Caxton brought out the first dated book printed in England, *The Dictes or Sayengs of the Philosophres*, completed on 18 November 1477. It had been translated from the French by Caxton's friend and patron Earl Rivers. Caxton's press turned out at least thirty books within the first three years – possibly more, because a number of these were quite small and it is not unlikely that some others have disappeared in the course of time. But even though some of his books were but 'small storyes and pamfletes', others were substantial folios, such as the first printed edition of Chaucer, *The Canterbury Tales* (372 leaves), which is undated but probably finished in 1478. As an instance of the printer's conscientiousness, when he learned that this edition had been made

---

* See Lawrence Tanner, *William Caxton's houses at Westminster* in 'The Library', September 1957.

FIGURE 14. Spread from Aesop's *Fables*, printed by William Caxton in 1484 in his own translation from the French. The many woodcuts are derived from Johann Zainer's Ulm edition of *c*. 1476.

from a very corrupt text, he printed the whole work again (1484), this time with woodcut illustrations and from a different manuscript.

In connection with his printing of the *Sarum Ordinale*, Caxton issued the only known example of a printer's advertisement in England in the fifteenth century. It reads:

> If it plese ony man spirituel or temporel to bye ony pyes of two and thre comemoracions of salisburi use, enpryntid after the forme of this present lettre whiche ben wel and truly correct, late hym come to westmonester in to the almonesrye at the reed pale and he shal have them good chepe.

Underneath was an appeal in Latin, *Supplico stet cedula*, or 'Don't tear down this advertisement.' The term 'pye' is the French version of pica, the old Latin name for the *Ordinale*, and was probably so-called because the black-letter type on white paper or vellum gave the book a magpie appearance. The 'Red Pale'

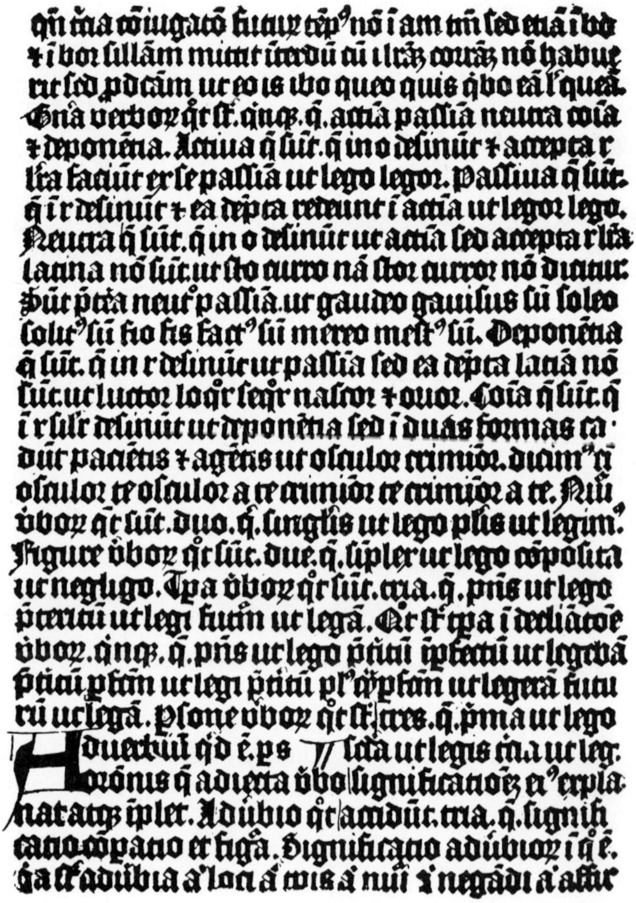

FIGURE 15. A page from *Textus ethicorum Aristotelis* (trans. Leonardus Aretinus) printed at Oxford, 1479, and ascribed to Theodore Rood of Cologne.

mentioned was probably a personal trade-mark hung outside his printing office.

The largest book which Caxton printed was an edition of that very popular work *The Golden Legend* by Jacobus de Voragine. For this work, which had already been translated from the original Latin of the *Legenda Aurea* into both English and French, Caxton himself made a new translation by collating manuscripts in all three languages. It was a tremendous task, and he has left on record in his prologue that he was at one time 'in maner halfe desperate to have acomplissed it' and 'was in purpose to have left it'. But the Earl of Arundel urged him to complete it, promising to take a reasonable quantity of the printed book. This book has seventeen woodcuts the full width of the page in size as well as 50 column-width cuts of Old Testament scenes and Saints with their emblems, some of which are repeated. At the beginning is a cut of the Saints in Glory, the largest block that Caxton ever used.

Among the best-known of Caxton's productions in England are *The Historie of Jason* (1477), Boethius, *The Consolacion of Philosophie* (1478), *The Mirrour of the World* (1481), the *Fables* of Æsop (1484) and *Reynart the Foxe* (1481), the first edition in English of the famous German classic *Reineke Fuchs*. Caxton himself translated this from the Dutch edition printed at Gouda by Gheraert Leeu in 1479. A two-way traffic this, for the *History of Jason* was reprinted by Leeu from Caxton's edition. Caxton must have been one of the most industrious of printers for he translated no fewer than twenty-two of the books he published. Two of these books were printed by royal command: one at the desire of Henry VII, and the other at the express wish of the King's mother, the Lady Margaret Beaufort. They were respectively the *Faytts of Arms* (1489) from the French of Christine de Pisan (itself a French version of Vegetius, *Epitome Rei Militaris*) and *Blanchardyn and Eglantine* (1489), the latter from a French manuscript which he himself had long before sold to the Lady Margaret.

Caxton died after completing a translation of the *Lives of the Fathers*, which was later published by his successor Wynkyn de Worde. The exact date of his death is not known, but it was some time in 1491. England's debt to her first printer includes more than the introduction of the printing press; he was the first disseminator of good literature in the vernacular. His greatness lies in what he printed rather than how he printed. His output included books on education, classics, encyclopaedias, morality and religion, allegory, chivalry, romance, history and poetry. Had he lived a little longer he would have added travel to that list, for he intended to print Sir John Mandeville's *Travels*, and it was left to Wynkyn de Worde to bring out an edition of that work in 1499.

Not for long did Caxton remain the sole printer in England. A native of Cologne, Theodore Rood, set up a press at Oxford in 1478, and two years later another alien, known as Johannes Lettou, probably because he was a native of Lithuania, introduced the art of printing into the City of London. The first

FIGURE 16. From *De proprietatibus rerum*, printed by Wynkyn de Worde in 1495, shortly after Caxton's death.

piece of printing we can associate with his press is an Indulgence for aid against the Turks, an edition of which had recently been printed by Caxton. It was at once obvious that Lettou's small neat type was much better suited to this kind of jobbing printing than was Caxton's. The hint was not lost and it was probably this fact that induced Caxton to make his small type No. 4, which he thereafter used for such work. Two books followed from Lettou's press in 1480 and 1481 respectively – *Quaestiones Antonii Andreae super XII libros metaphysice Aristotelis* and *Thomas Wallensis Expositiones super Psalterium*. Lettou's work was more technically advanced than that of Caxton, and he was the first in England to make use of quire signatures and to set his page in double column.

About 1482 he was joined by William de Machlinia, a native of Mechlin (Malines) in Flanders. The two men printed in partnership five law books, none of which are dated, and one only, *Tenores Novelli* has a colophon, which tells us that their printing office was 'juxta ecclesiam omnium sanctorum'; but since there were at that time several churches to which the term All Saints was applied the address is too vague to identify. Lettou now disappears from printing history as mysteriously as he entered it, and Machlinia continued to print alone after moving to new premises by the Fleet Bridge. None of his books are dated, but two of the types which he used appear to be identical with those used by Jean Brito of Bruges. One item of historical interest printed by Machlinia is the Bull of Pope Innocent VIII granting dispensation for the marriage of Henry VII and Elizabeth of York, a union which put an end to the long hostility between the rival houses of York and Lancaster.

Meanwhile printing was being carried on at Oxford, and the first book printed there gave rise to the erroneous belief that English printing had originated in that city. An edition of Rufinus, *Exposicio Sancti Ieronimi Apostolorum*, was dated MCCCCLXVIII, and the omission of one X by the printer led to the publication in 1664 of a book which invented the tale of one Frederick Corsellis having been privily taken from Haarlem to Oxford to introduce the art of printing into England. The date is now generally accepted as being 1478.

Not until the fourth book came from this press was the name of the printer divulged as Theodore Rood of Cologne, whose previous history has not been traced. About 1483 Rood went into partnership with an Oxford stationer Thomas Hunte, and in all fourteen books came from this press between 1478 and 1486, the last being the *Liber Festivalis* of John Mirk (1486), which was signed by Hunte alone, Rood having apparently left England in 1485. After that there was no printing at Oxford until 1517, when a second press was established there by John Scolar.

In London, Caxton's business was, after his death, taken over by his assistant, Wynkyn de Worde, a native of Lorraine, who probably came to England with Caxton in 1476 as his foreman. He used Caxton's material and continued to

FIGURE 17. Woodcut of an angler from *The Book of St. Albans*, printed at Westminster by Wynkyn de Worde in 1496.

print at Westminster until 1500, first of all finishing some of the work upon which Caxton had been engaged at the time of his death, and later reprinting some of his former editions. The first book he printed on his own account is generally thought to be *Chastysing of goddes chyldern*, which is undated, but was probably printed in 1492. The first book in which we find his name is the *Liber Festivalis* printed in 1493. Although Samuel Palmer, in his *General History of Printing*, tells us that De Worde cut a new set of punches on taking over the business, there is no evidence that he was a punch-cutter and most of the types he used, apart from Caxton's old material, were from matrices imported from France and the Low Countries.

In 1495 Wynkyn de Worde printed the *Vitas Patrum* which Caxton had translated in the last year of his life, and, probably in the same year he brought out an English translation by John of Trevisa of Bartholomaeus Anglicanus, *De proprietatibus rerum*, which embodied in the colophon the fact of Caxton's having worked on the undated Cologne edition. The colophon also reveals the fact that the paper was made by John Tate the Younger and the book is probably the first, therefore, to have been printed on paper made in England by John Tate of Hertford, the first English papermaker, who had a mill at Sele in that county.

In 1499, just before he left Westminster for the City of London De Worde printed the edition of Mandeville's *Travels* which Caxton would have printed had he lived. Although Pynson's edition of this work (of which only one copy is known) probably appeared in 1496 that of De Worde is the first illustrated edition to appear in England. In 1500, having printed at least a hundred books at Westminster, Wynkyn de Worde moved his press to Fleet Street, at the sign of the Sun, probably in order to be nearer the booksellers and the new clientèle for whom he intended to work.

When William de Machlinia either retired from business or died around 1490, his premises and some of his material were taken over by Richard Pynson, a native of Normandy, who probably learned his craft from the Rouen printer Guillaume le Talleur, who printed at least two books for him and whose device Pynson later adopted. The first dated book from Pynson's press, which was then situated in the parish of St Clement Danes, was the *Doctrinale* of Alexander Grammaticus, issued in 1492. It may have been preceded, however, by various undated books, among them an illustrated folio edition of *The Canterbury Tales* printed in types of French origin. At the end of the century, after he had printed almost ninety books, he moved his press to the sign of the George, next to the church of St Dunstan-in-the-West, Fleet Street. He may have been prompted to move for reasons of safety, for in that year he was attacked by a mob led by one Henry Squires. It was the culmination of a series of hostile moves against him and his workmen, occasioned by a general hostility towards foreign craftsmen. Within the jurisdiction of the City he may have felt safer. Among the books Pynson printed during this first period of his career the finest was undoubtedly the splendid *Sarum Missal* printed at the expense of Cardinal John Morton and finished on 10 January 1500. It remains one of the finest specimens of early printing in England, and for it special borders and ornaments were cut, including a full-page cut of the prelate's coat of arms.

The second English provincial press was set up at St Albans, about twenty miles from London, and there eight books were printed by a man of whom we know next to nothing, but who was referred to by Wynkyn de Worde as 'sometyme scole master of Saynt Albons'. He used three bastarda types and one text, all very similar to those used by Caxton. The first book to come from the press of this schoolmaster-printer was an edition of Augustinus Datus, *Super*

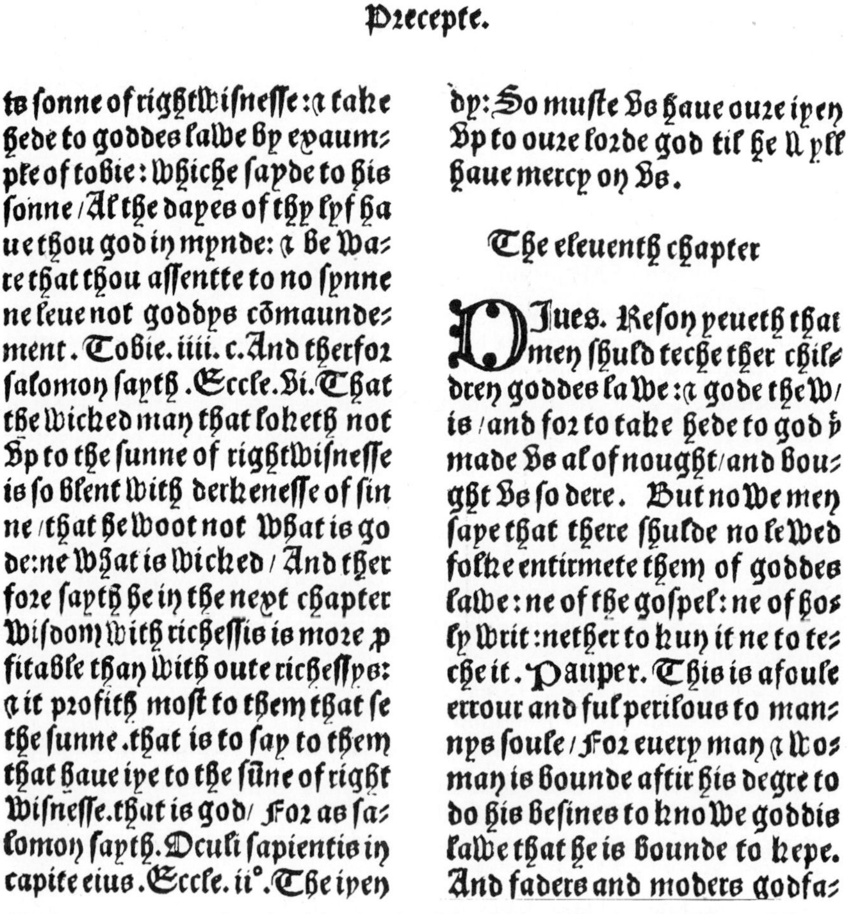

Precepte.

te ſonne of rightwiſneſſe :ɑ take hede to goddes lawe by exaum-ple of tobie: whiche ſayde to his ſonne / Al the dayes of thy lyf ha ue thou god in mynde: ɑ be wa-re that thou aſſentte to no ſynne ne leue not goddys cōmaunde-ment. Tobie. iiii. c. And therfor ſalomon ſayth. Eccle. vi. That the wicked man that loketh not up to the ſunne of rightwiſneſſe is ſo blent with derkeneſſe of ſin ne /that he woot not what is go de: ne what is wicked / And ther fore ſayth he in the next chapter Wiſdom with richeſſis is more p fitable than with oute richeſſys: ɑ it profits moſt to them that ſe the ſunne. that is to ſay to them that haue iye to the ſune of right Wiſneſſe. that is god/ For as ſa-lomon ſayth. Oculi ſapientis in capite eius. Eccle. ii°. The iyen

up: So muſte we haue oure iyen up to oure lorde god til he u pll haue mercy on us.

The eleuenth chapter

Diues. Reſon peueth that men ſhuld teche ther chil-dren goddes lawe :ɑ gode the w/ is /and for to take hede to god p made us al of nought/and bou-ght us ſo dere. But now we men ſaye that there ſhulde no lewed folke entirmete them of goddes lawe: ne of the goſpel: ne of hos ly writ :nether to kun it ne to te-che it. Pauper. This is a foule errour and ful perilous to man-nys ſoule /For euery man ɑ wo-man is bounde aftir his degre to do his beſines to knowe goddis lawe that he is bounde to kepe. And faders and moders godfa-

FIGURE 18. From the first dated book printed by Richard Pynson, the *Dives and Pauper* finished on 5 July 1493 in premises near Temple Bar, London. The type probably came from France, where Pynson, a Frenchman by birth, had business connections.

Eleganciis Tullianis, undated, and with a colophon which merely says 'Apud Sanctum Albanum'. It was probably printed in 1479 or 1480.

The first dated book from the St Albans press was the *Rhetorica Nova* of Laurentius de Savona (which Caxton was also printing about the same time). The colophon states: 'Impressum fuit hoc presens opus Rethorice facultatis apud villa sancti Albani. Anno domini M.CCCC.Lxxx.' This was followed by four other scholastic works, printed presumably for the Abbey school, and finally two works of more general interest, the *Chronicles of England* and

FIGURE 19. Woodcut and ornamental borders from Chaucer's *Canterbury Tales*; the first attempt at a collection of Chaucer's writings. The book, printed by Richard Pynson in 1526, was issued in various parts, of which the *Canterbury Tales* is one.

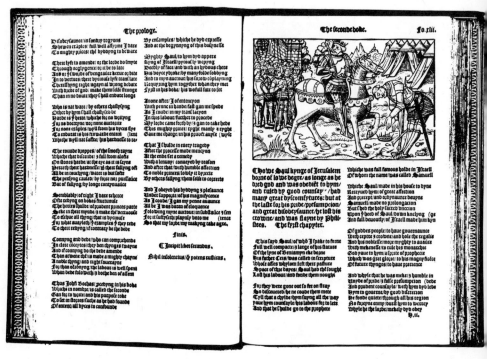

FIGURE 20. Boccaccio, *The Fall of Princis*, translated by John Lydgate. Richard Pynson, 1527.

treatises on hawking, hunting, and coat armour, known collectively as the *Book of St Albans*.

The second treatise ends 'Explicit Dam Julyan Barnes in her boke of Hun-tyng', and this has often led to all three treatises being ascribed to a certain Dame Juliana Berners, Prioress of the Nunnery of Sopwell, a dependency of St Albans. Most of the hawking and hunting treatises seems to derive from Twici's *L'Art de Vénerie* and the *Livre de Chasse* of Gaston, Comte de Foix. The treatise on coat armour contains the earliest specimens of colour work in English printing. Red, blue and brown were used, apart from the normal black, and the yellow which appears on some of the shields was probably added by hand. This *Book of St Albans* is dated 1486, and was, as far as we know, the last book printed at St Albans until 1534, when John Herford worked there for about five years.

The last of the fifteenth-century printers to work in England was Julian Notary, a native of Vannes in Brittany. He began work about 1496 with an edition of *Quaestiones Alberti de modis significandi* issued in partnership with two stationers who, though known only by their initials, are thought to have been

FIGURE 21. A spread from John Rastell, *The pastyme of people*, 1529. It contains 18 full-page cuts of English kings.

Jean Huvin of Rouen, who dealt in books for the English market, and John Barbour of Coventry.

The partners issued a second book in 1497, a Sarum Hours of which only a fragment of four leaves remains, though luckily these include the colophon, which shows that the book was printed for Wynkyn de Worde. In 1498 Notary and Barbour (Huvin having left the partnership) brought out a Sarum Missal, the first edition printed in England, again for Wynkyn de Worde, who may have had some interest in the press. In 1499 Barbour in turn disappeared and Notary continued to print alone. In 1500 he printed one of the earliest miniature books, a 64-mo Sarum Hours, of which only sixteen pages are known, in the form of a half-sheet (i–k) now in the Public Library at Victoria, Australia. The printed page measures 1 inch by $1\frac{3}{8}$ inches. The last book which Notary printed at his premises in King Street, Westminster, was an edition of Chaucer, *Love and complaintes between Mars and Venus.* Then, following the example of Wynkyn de Worde, he left Westminster and set up his press just outside Temple Bar, possibly in the premises which Pynson had just vacated.

Towards the end of the fifteenth century certain changes came over the incipient book trade in England. Foreign competition had been negligible up to the time of Caxton's death, but during the last decade of the century both France and Italy printed books for the English market. We have already seen that Gerard Leeu printed a number of books in English at Antwerp. Johannes Herzog in Venice as well as several French printers began to print and export service books for Sarum use, and a number of foreign stationers settled in England with a view to marketing these wares.

10

Early Typography and Technical Innovations

ONE of the most remarkable features in the history of printing is its initial perfection. The 42-line Bible, the first sizeable book to be printed from movable type, remains one of the finest, whilst the Mainz Psalter of 1457 is unexcelled for the beauty of its type. Yet of the designers and the cutters of the letters used by the fifteenth-century printers we know hardly anything.

It has been stated that the early printers all made their own type, but this is very unlikely, except perhaps for those printers who had had previous training as goldsmiths, with experience of cutting various dies or engraving seals. Also there were probably men with these qualifications, not printers themselves, but who could adapt their skills to the new craft. Such a one was the seal-engraver Joost Burnhart of Basel, who made some type for the Swiss printer Bernhard Richel in 1472. Tradition has it that Peter Schöffer was a punch-cutter, though possibly he was merely a designer of type, having been a skilled calligrapher.* Nicholas Jenson was much admired for the beauty of his types, but although we know that he possessed punches and matrices for them, there is no proof that he was a punch-cutter.

In fact, as Mr Harry Carter has pointed out (Carter, 1969) the earliest punch-cutter of whom there are satisfactory records is Henric Pieterszoon de Letter-snijder of Rotterdam, one of whose founts was being used at Antwerp by Mathias ven der Goes in 1492. Henric Pieterszoon has been credited with five typefaces, some of which appeared in books which he himself printed, and which were used in Netherlands books until 1580. In Italy, contemporaneously with Henric of Rotterdam, Francesco Griffo of Bologna was cutting type for the famous house of Aldo Manuzio.

Many of the early printers in London used type which originated in Flanders, and we find that certain faces used by Caxton, De Worde, Lettou and Machlinia are identical with those being used in the Netherlands by Veldener, from whose workshop they probably came. But although the colophon of one of Veldener's books praises his skill at engraving in relief, it is as well to remember that the colophons of the early printers were frequently no more than advertising 'puffs'.

* His son, Peter Schöffer II was a punch-cutter.

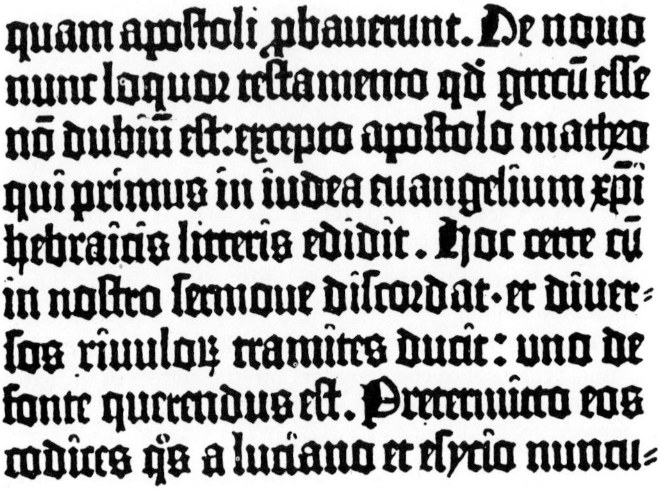

quam apostoli pbauerunt. De nouo
nunc loquor testamento qd grecu esse
nō dubiū est:excepto apostolo matheo
qui primus in iudea euangelium xp̄i
hebraicis litteris edidit. Hoc certe cū
in nostro sermoue discordat·et diuer=
sos riuuloy tramites ducit: uno de
fonte querendus est. Preterquicto eos
codices qs a luciano et esycio nuncu=

FIGURE 22. The pointed gothic type known as textura used by Gutenberg in the 42-line Bible printed at Mainz before August 1456. In England it was known as black-letter.

We have to wait for the sixteenth century before punch-cutters and typefounders can be identified by name.

Because printing was at first intended as a process for the more rapid reproduction of manuscripts, it follows that the first printers modelled their typefaces on the local book-script of the time. From the many idiosyncratic hands of the eighth century Charlemagne and his advisors – among them Alcuin of York – decided upon a radical reform of writing, and a standard style, known thereafter as the Carlovingian, was ordered to be observed by a decree of 789. This style remained for centuries the leading book-script all over Western Europe. From the eleventh century onwards various changes became noticeable as national characteristics developed, and in the northern parts of Western Europe especially there was a marked tendency towards condensation, an increase in vertical effect, and all curves began to disappear. These modifications changed the morphology of the caroline minuscule and gave rise to the style known as gothic, a form which is presented at its most formal in sepulchral brasses of the fifteenth and sixteenth centuries. The name 'textura' has been given to this formal style because of the woven effect given by the balance of black and white upon the page. This was the style of letter chosen for the famous 42-line Bible, and on account of the solemnity of its appearance (which so fitted it for sepulchral brasses) it had a long life as the most suitable letter for liturgical printing.

But such majestic type as that used in the 42-line Bible, although suited to Missals and other service books would have been too severe and heavy for the

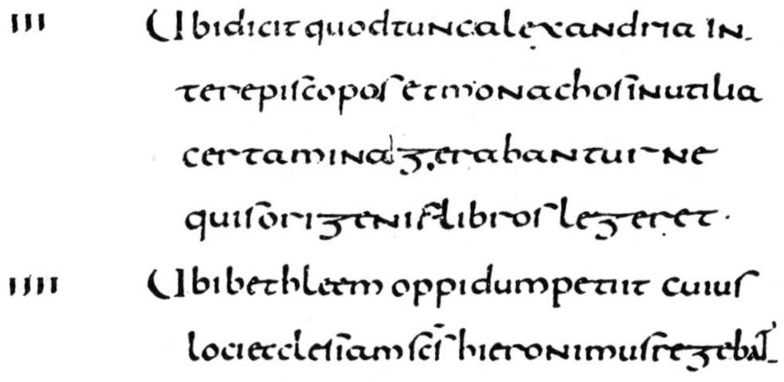

III   Ubidicit quodtuncalexandria in.
terepiſcopoſ et monachoſinutilia
certaminaʒ.erabantur ne
quiſorigenislibroſlegeret·

IIII   Ubibethleem oppidumpetit cuiuſ
locieccleſiam ſci hieronimuſregebat_

FIGURE 23. The Carolingian minuscule, illustrated here from a 9th century manuscript, represents the first attempt, after the fall of the Roman empire to formulate a standard hand throughout western Europe.

majority of secular works as well as being space-consuming. So for Latin texts the early printers cut a less formal letter, though still adhering to manuscript form: a small gothic of slightly rounded form, deriving from the book hands of the fourteenth century or earlier. Known as 'lettre de somme' by French bibliographers in contrast to the 'lettre de forme' of the more formal textura, it is sometime referred to as gotico-antiqua or 'gothique bâtarde'. As the main influence upon the early typefaces was the kind of writing habitual in the locality where the printer worked, and which he sought to imitate with varying degrees of skill, it is not surprising that there should be considerable variation in the cutting of founts.

However, there was a reaction against the gothic character in the humanist circles of Italy, where it was considered difficult to read with ease. The young especially preferred the neo-Caroline minuscules, a book hand which began to establish itself soon after the beginning of the fifteenth century, probably in Florence. According to Professor Ullman★ this humanistic script 'was inspired by Coluccio Salutati, invented by Poggio Bracciolini, encouraged by Niccoló Niccoli, preferred by the Medici and their imitators among the book collectors, even in far-off Britain, sold and promoted by canny book dealers such as Vespasiano da Bisticci. It was inevitable that it should be preferred by the early Italian printers.'

It followed that those among the early printers who went to Italy from their native Germany had to adapt their printing to the taste of their new customers, and many of the early printers of Italy stocked two varieties of typeface: the traditional gothic for the more conservative professions, such as the Church and the Law, and the humanistic letter which eventually developed into the 'roman'

★ B. L. Ullman, *The Origin and Development of Humanistic Script.* Rome, 1960.

Ale dye tzyt des leues wyrt in vierē ge deilt · als in die tzit d' dwalinge ynd in dye tzyt d' wederropynge off der vernut wynge ynd in dye tzyt der soenyn/ ge ynd der pilgrym gie Dye tzyt der dwalynge ys vā Ada tzyt dae he van gode dwaeld durch dye sun den docrēde tzo moyses tzo· ynd de se tzyt helt dye kyrche vā septuage/ sima bys pasche·Glosa Septuage sima ys als men leecht Alleluya voer vastauent · want dan so leest men dat begynsel vāder bybel daer beschreue ys der cirster vader dwa lynge· Dye tzyt der wederzoe/ pynge off der vernuwinge begynd van moyses yñ duerde bys dat cris tus gheboren was In wylcher tzyt dye mynsche worden tzo dem ghelo ue gheroefen durch die propheten yñ

vernuwet Inde desse tzyt helt dye hylge kyrch vā dē Aduēt bys kers dach tzo · wāt dā so leest men ysay am den propheten der vā dysser ver nuwynge clerlych spzycht Dye tzyt der versoenynge ·ys dye tzyt da twyr durch xpūs versonet wor den·ynd dysse tzyt helt dye heylige kyrch vā paysche bys pynstē ·wat dan leest mē Apocalipsis .dat ys dat boych d' verhoelenheyt dat vol komlich spzycht vā der versoenin ge Dye tzyt der pylgremacie ys die tzyt des leues·da wyr synt pyl grym yñ altzyt in strydē·ynd dese tzyt helt dye hylge kyrch acht dach na pinxtē bys tzo dē Aduēt·want dā leest mē d' konyngē boiche daer men yn leest vā menigerhāde stry dē·yñ dye machabeusche · daer onse geystliche stryt myt wyrt betzeichet Mer die tzyt dy da is vā kyrstdach bys septuagesima.eyn deyl ys be/ grepen vnder der tzyt der versoe nynge ynde dye ys van vreuden als vā kyrstdach bys tzo dem achte dach na dē druytzehē dach ·ynd eyn deyl is begrepē vnder d' tzyt der pyl gremagie. dat ys vāder octaue vā druytzē dache tzo der septuagesima Ind die vier verwādelynge vā dys sen tzyde machmē neme na dē vier deile van dē iair·so datmē dē wyn ter reche off schicke by dē eirstē· ynd den lentzē tzo dē anderē · den somer tzo dē derdē·yñ dye kerfst tzo dē vier den Tzo dē anderen, mail so mach men sy rechē gegē dye vier tzyden vā dem daghē·soe dat mē dye nacht rechē tzo dē eirsten·den morghēn tzo dem anderen ·den middach tzo dem tyrdē·dye vesper tzyt tzo dē vierdē· wāt alt was dat dye dwalyng eer

FIGURE 24. A form of gothic Bastarda known as Upper-Rhine type, as exemplified in this *Passional* by Jacobus de Voragine, printed at Cologne in 1485 by Ludwig Renchen.

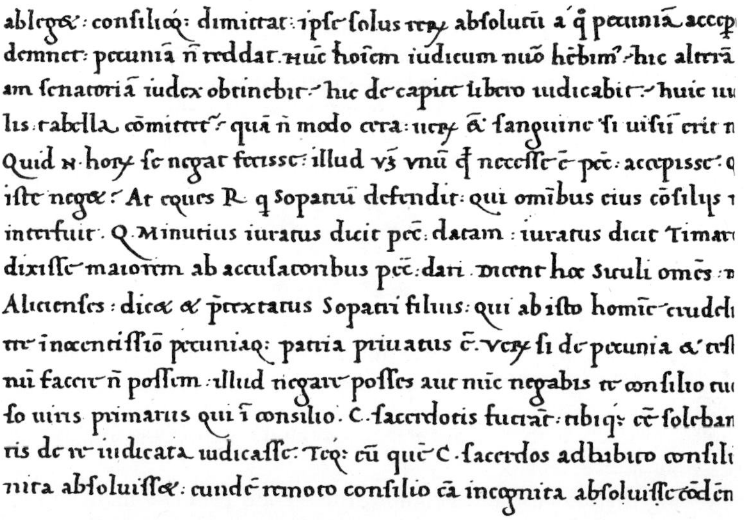

FIGURE 25. An example of the so-called humanistic manuscript hand of the fifteenth century which served as a model for many of the early Italian types.

(or 'antiqua' as the Germans call it), for classical texts. Not that this was a hard and fast rule, for some classics were still printed in gothic and some law books were produced in roman, but the trend was established. In fact the first Italian printers, Sweynheim and Pannartz, when they left Subiaco for Rome, abandoned their semi-gothic Subiaco type and opted for a pure roman letter in their Cicero of 1467.

The fact that printing began in the Rhineland and soon spread through other parts of Germany before crossing the frontiers to other parts of Europe meant that German printers were first off the mark in introducing certain innovations in their methods of printing.

In 1457 Fust and Schöffer began to replace the rubricator's initials by woodcut letters, they improved upon the red printing with which they had experimented in the 42-line Bible, and they hit upon the device of the printer's mark to single out their books from the products of other presses.

This printer's mark was first cut for the 1462 Bible printed at Mainz, for although it is known in a copy of the 1457 Psalter now in Vienna, this is thought to have been added to the book at a later date. The device of two shields hanging from the bough of a tree represents the partnership of Fust and Schöffer, and the shields bear their respective housemarks. The design was imitated by several other early printers, the earliest being in a tract printed at Rome around 1470 by Ulrich Han. Bernard Richel and Nicolaus Kesler at Basel, Gerard Leeu at Gouda, Conrad Winters at Cologne, and Martin Landsberg at Leipzig, were

Pñs boc opufculuȝ finitũ ac cõpletũ·et ad
eufebiaȝ ȝei mduſtrie in ciutate Ⓜaguntñ
per Johannē fuſt ciuē·et Ꝑetrũ ſcbꝛiffxer ȝe
gernPᴇ̄ym clericũ ȝioteꝓ ciuſdeȝ eſt confu̾
matũ. Anno incarnacõis ȝñice·Ⓜ·cccc·lxij·
Jn vigilia aſſump cõis gᴆoſe virgims marie.

<small>FIGURE 26. Colophon and printers' device from the Latin Bible printed at Mainz in 1462 by Johann Fust and Peter Schöffer.</small>

among the printers who used as their mark the device of two shields supported from a bough.

Following that of Fust and Schöffer, the second printer's mark in Germany was used by Arnold Ter Hoernen at Cologne and appeared in Adrianus Carthusiensis, *De remediis utriusque fortunae* (8 February 1471). The device is a single shield with his housemark and the initials a. h.

The first printer's mark used in Italy was that of Ulrich Han at Rome, which first appeared in Paulus II, *Regulae cancellariae apostolicae* (after 20 September 1470) and was, as we have said, a copy of the Fust and Schöffer device. In Belgium the first printer's mark was also the first appearance in any book of the portrait of the printer, for it is in the form of a small medallion with the head of Johannes de Westfalia and occurs in his Louvain edition of *Justianiani Institutiones* (21 November 1475). It was used as his device in seven books printed by Johannes de Westfalia between 1475 and 1484. In Switzerland the first printer's mark was that used by Michael Wenssler at Basel in Clement V, *Constitutiones*, dated 2 May 1476. It shows two shields hung from two horns; the one on the left has an incomplete cross – that on the right a brook with two stars, arms of the Wenzel family of Sternbach.

In France the first printer's mark to appear was used by Nicolas Philippi at Lyons, and consists of an orb and cross together with a monogram which can be read as either NM or MN, and the exact significance of which is not known. It can be seen in his *Vitae sanctorum patrum*.

The first printer to make use of a *registrum*, or index, was the Roman printer of the Epistolae Hieronymi, unsigned, but probably Sixtus Riessinger, which was published not later than 1470. It was not called a registrum in this work, but under the title *Inchoationes quinternorum* the printer gave a list of the first words of each of the eighty or more gatherings. Ulrich Han was the first to employ a more normal register in his Turrecremata, *Expositio Psalterii* (4

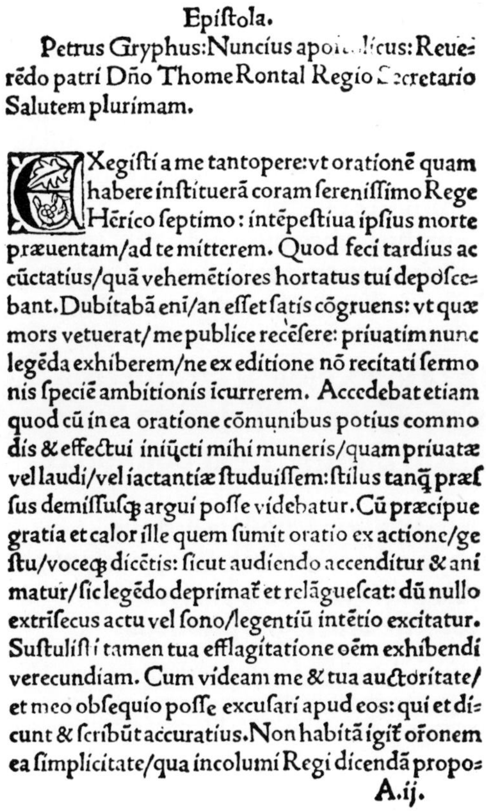

Epiſtola.
Petrus Gryphus:Nuncius apoſ..lícus:Reuez
rédo patrí Dño ThomeRontal Regio Sxretario
Salutem plurimam.

Xegiſti a me tantopere:vt oratíonē quam
habere inſtituerā coram fereniſſimo Rege
Hérico feptimo : íntēpeſtiua ípſius morte
præuentam/ad te mítterem. Quod fecí tardíus ac
cūctatíus/quā vehemētiores hortatus tuí depóſcez
bant.Dubítabā ení/an eſſet fatís cōgruens: vt quæ
mors vetuerat/ me publíce recéſere: priuatím nunc
legēda exhíberem/ne ex edítione nō recítatí fermo
nis fpecíē ambítionis icurrerem. Accedebat etiam
quod cū ín ea oratíone cōmunibus potíus commo
dis & effeɗui iniūcti míhí muneris/quam priuatæ
vel laudí/vel íactantíæ ſtuduiſſem:ſtilus tanꝗ præſ
ſus demiſſuſꝗ argui poſſe vídebatur.Cū præcípue
gratía et calor ílle quem fumit oratio ex actíonc/ge
ſtu/voceꝗ dicētis: ficut audíendo accendítur & aní
matur/fíc legēdo deprímař et rclāgueſcat: dū nullo
extrífecus actu vel fono/legentíū íntētio excitatur.
Suſtuliſſ í tamen tua efflagitatione oēm exhíbendí
verecundiam. Cum vídeam me & tua auɗóritate/
et meo obfequío poſſe excufari apud eos: qui et díz
cunt & fcríbūt accuratíus.Non habítā ígiř ořonem
ea ſímplícitate/qua incolumí Regi dícendā propoz

A.ij.

FIGURE 27. The first book printed in England entirely in roman type – the *Oratio* of Petrus
Gryphus. Richard Pynson, 1509. The fount is one common to several Paris printers.

October 1470), giving not only the catchwords of the gatherings but also those
of the double sheets.

The separate title-page, as we know it today, came into being some years
after the invention of printing. The first printers followed slavishly the form of
the manuscript book, and the manuscripts taken for copy had no title-pages.

Cſar in orbe decus:doctorũ
gloria vatum
Dux tribuis meritis pre/
mia digna ſuis
Cinge pcor viridi mereor
ſi forte corona.
Tempora: ptingat lau/
rea ſancta comas
Tũc ego pro tanto ſemper
tibi munere vinctus
Cantabo laudes dum mihi vita tuas
Dũ mihi vita manet tollã ſuper aſtra nepotes
Ceſaris ethereos:inclita facta canens.

Ode Monocolos Tetrametros Choriã
bicos Conradi Celtis ad diuum Fride
ricum paranetice et palinodice:

Ceſar magnificis laudibus inclitus
Rex regum dominus maxime principum
Si quis priſca tuis tempora ſeculis
Vel conferre velit regna prioribus

FIGURE 28. A Bastarda much employed by Friedrich Creussner at Nuremberg from 1485 is known as Schwabacher, though for what reason no one can now say. This example is from Conrad Celtes, *Proseuticum ad divum Fridericum* III, printed by Creussner about 1487.

The parchment on which manuscripts were written was costly and to use a whole sheet of it merely to inscribe a title would have been unnecessarily expensive. Sufficient information to identify the book was given in the opening lines of the work, which normally began with *Incipit* in Latin, or other words meaning 'Here begins . . .' in whatever language the book was written in. So early printed books began in similar fashion.

Scribes rarely named themselves, and many splendid early manuscripts are without name, date, or place. If any name were mentioned it was usually that of the rubricator who decorated the manuscript with initial letters and coloured ornamental borders. He usually added a paragraph at the end of the book giving his name and the date on which he completed the book. Some of the early printers followed suit. They printed a paragraph at the end, called the colophon, giving their names, and occasionally the place and date of printing. Unfortunately it took some time before this became common practice, and even after

the end of the fifteenth century one finds many instances of unsigned and undated books. This is regrettable; we could date the famous 42-line Bible more
definitely if its printers had added a full and informative colophon. All we know
is that the rubricator, one Henry Cremer, finished his work on the Paris copy
known as the Mazarin Bible on 15 August 1456.

The first printed colophon appeared at the end of the famous *Psalter* of 1457
(the first book with a printed date) in which Fust and Schöffer advertised themselves as makers of books by a new process. The printer of the *Catholicon* of 1460
affixed to the book a long colophon in which he tells us it was printed in Mainz
in 1460, but with an excess of modesty which bibliographers have not really
appreciated has omitted to tell us who he was.

The earliest known example of a printed title is found in Pope Pius II's Bull
against the Turks, printed in 1463 and consists of two short lines:

> Bulla cruciata sanctissimi do-
> mini nostri Pape cŏtra turchos

But it took many years before the use of a title-page became common, and at
first took the form of a brief mention of book and author placed at the top of an
otherwise blank page and known as a 'label title'. Later, the blank space on the
title-page beneath this label was often filled with a woodcut illustration.

In 1500, at Leipzig, Wolfgang Stöckel, who printed in that city from 1495
to 1526, was the first to issue a book with a complete title-page giving subject
title, name of publisher, name of printer, and date and place of printing. This
was an edition of *Textus Summularum Petri Hispani* printed for Johann Haller
of Cracow.

Erhard Ratdolt, the Augsburg printer who worked for some years in Venice
was responsible for the first displayed title-page with a decorative border. The
book was the *Calendar* of Johannes Regiomontanus, printed by Ratdolt at
Venice in 1476. The decorations are in pure outline, a laborious task for the
block cutter since it meant cutting away the larger part of the surface of the
block to get the necessary lines in high relief. But the effect is most graceful.

The fashion for decorating the title-page with a woodcut border spread
rapidly throughout the whole of Europe, but the Venetian practice of cutting
the block to show black lines upon a white ground was reversed by some
printers who found that white designs on a black ground were more easily, and
thus more cheaply, produced.

PRINTERS' ADVERTISEMENTS IN THE FIFTEENTH CENTURY

Once the new art of printing had got into its stride, printers needed to make
their products known to potential buyers, and the advertisements drawn up by
the early printers are now priceless rarities, and a fruitful source of information
concerning the history of bookselling. Books were merchandise, often heavy

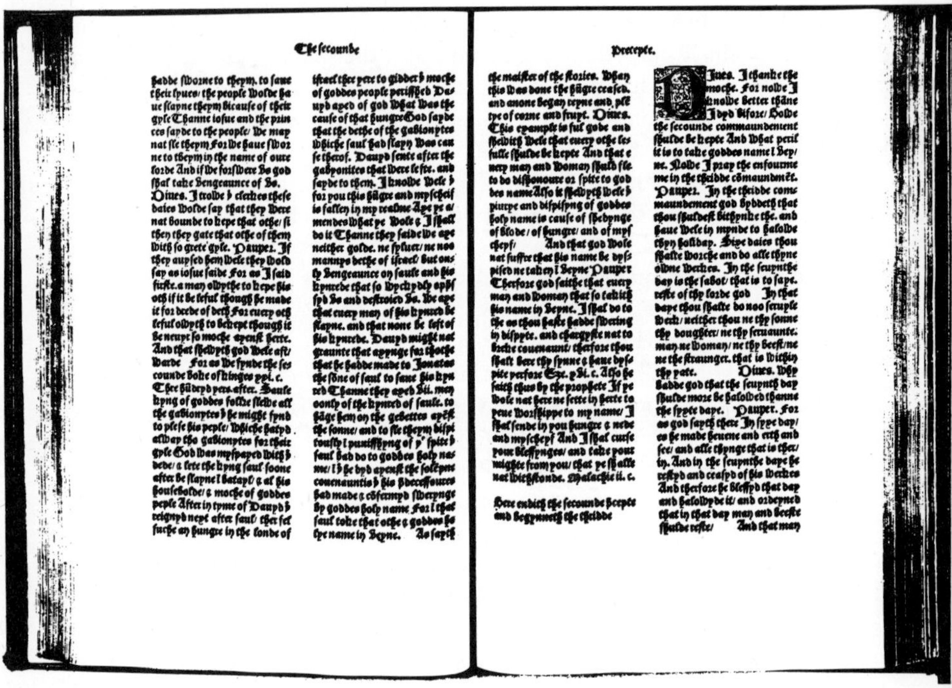

FIGURE 29. Henry Parker's *Dives and Pauper*. London: Richard Pynson, 1493. The type was based on a French model and resembles some used in the books published by Vérard.

and voluminous, and were handled like other goods. Among the waggons laden with wares which trundled between various market towns, many would carry books carefully packed in barrels; but whilst other sellers of merchandise hung up or called out their wares, the printer was able to make use of his own trade. He printed bills listing his books and distributed them in each town where they were on sale. Very few of these early advertisements have survived in view of their ephemeral nature, and thus it would be wrong to cite any specimen as a certain 'first'.

The first extant book advertisement is that issued by Mentelin at Strasburg, probably in 1469, and of which there is a copy in the British Museum. It is a broadside folio of forty-two lines advertising the *Summa de casibus* of Astesanus de Ast, of which Mentelin printed several editions, the first appearing in 1469. A long eulogy of the book ends with the words 'Veniant ad hospicium . . . Et habebunt largum venditorem'. The space after 'hospicium' and before 'Et' was left to enable the inn where the seller could be found to be inserted. At the foot of the B.M. copy is written 'Zum Wilhelmum Sautroiber', he being a bookseller (and also a city councillor) of Landshut.

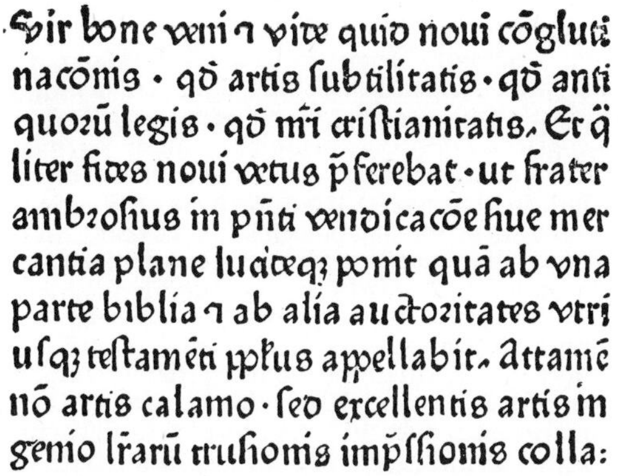

·Sir bone veni ꝗ vite quid noui cōgluti
nacōnis · qō artis fubtilitatis · qō anti
quozū legis · qō mī criſtianitatis. Et ꝗ
liter fites noui vetus p̄ferebat · ut frater
ambzofius in pūti vendicacōe fiue mer
cantia plane luditeꝗꝫ pomit quā ab vna
parte biblia ꝗ ab alia auctozitates vtri
ufꝗꝫ teſtaméti pplus appellabit. Attamé
nō artis calamo · ſed excellentis artis in
genio lrarū truſiomis impſſionis colla:

FIGURE 30. Part of an advertisement by the Strassburg printer Heinrich Eggestein. About
1466.

The second example was printed by another Strassburg printer, Heinrich
Eggestein about 1470 and is a bombastic and almost unintelligible advertisement
for a Bible – not the 45-line Bible which he brought out in 1466, but the
undated edition of 41-lines probably completed in 1470.

At some date prior to September 1470 Peter Schöffer of Mainz issued a single
leaf folio of forty-six lines forming a prospectus of his edition of the Letters of
St Jerome which was completed on 7 September 1470. Even at that date
printer–publishers were fully alive to the dangers of competition and Schöffer
warns the reader not to buy any inferior edition (i.e. Mentelin's), but to wait
until Michaelmas for his own edition.

About 1469 or 1470 Peter Schöffer printed a list of the books he had in stock.
Of the twenty-one titles shown, some three or four, such as the Petrarch,
Historia Griselidis, are today unknown as Schöffer imprints.* After the list of
books offered for sale there is a specimen of the large Psalter type spelling 'hec
est littera psalterii'. At the foot of the only surviving specimen, at Munich, is
the written information 'Venditor librorum reperibilis est in hospicio date Zum
Willden mann'. (The book salesman is to be found at the inn The Wild Man.)
As this prospectus was found pasted into a manuscript which had once belonged
to Hartman Schedel, compiler of the famous 'Nuremberg Chronicle' it seems
plausible that the inn in question was the well-known 'Gasthaus zum Wilden
Mann' situated in the Weinmarkt at Nuremberg.

Advertisements then, as now, did not always state nothing but the truth. The
prospectus states that all the books listed 'are set in the same Mainz type as this
announcement', whereas in fact many books listed were not printed in the 1462

* Unless it is the undated edition printed at Cologne by Ulrich Zell, which Schöffer may
have accepted on a sale or return basis.

> Ls ich vormals. In zweyen meinen schrifften. Die ich aus meiner erenn nod/
> turfft/hab aufgehen laffen/angezeigt.wy der hochgeborn furst herr Heinrich
> hertzog zu Sachssen zc. Off gehalten tag zu Molhawsen/mir in rucken vn/
> verschuldt.das ich vnwarheit solle geret vnd damit wider mein pflicht gehan/
> delt habe.hat zumessen lassen.wie ich dargege mein entschuldung getan/auch
> der vnd ander vnrechten beswerung halben.so mir vo gemeltem hertzog Hein
> richen manigfeltiglich begegent/den vffrichtigste weg ordenlichs rechten zu/
> gebrauchen vorgenomenn. Hab ich hertzog Heinrich montags nach Letare
> nechstuerschinnen/mit zweien meiner frunde Hugolot vnnd Wolffgang von
> Miltitz/sampt einem offenbaren schreiber/mein offen brieff geschickt/des in/
> halt hirnach volget.   Dem hochgebornen furste vn hern.hern Heinrichen
> hertzoge zu Sachssen zc. Thue ich Heinrich von Sleinitz obermarschal/mit
> diesem meinem offenbriue ersuchen. Nachdem ewer furstliche wird/mich mit
> worttens vn schrifften/an mein Eren vnd gelympff/wider recht vn alle billickeit

FIGURE 31. Here is a form of Bastarda known as the Wittenberg letter because its use was confined mainly to that town and its neighbourhood. This specimen is from a letter by H. von Schleinitz printed at Leipzig by Melchior Lotter in 1510.

Bible type of the prospectus, but in the Psalter type, the Catholicon type, and the Durandus type.

Other printers soon followed suit – Bämler and Zainer in Augsburg, and Creussner in Nuremberg were among the first. They were followed by book-sellers who by the 1470s were issuing lists of the productions of a number of printers. And as printing spread to countries outside Germany, there too we find the printers' wares being advertised at an early date.

Sweynheim and Pannartz, Italy's first printers, once they had moved from Subiaco to Rome, began to advertise their wares, listing nineteen titles in 1470 and twenty-eight in 1472. Furthermore, they added useful information by giving the prices of the books and the number of copies printed of each edition, though the fact that with four exceptions the size of the edition is in every case given as 275 makes one wonder whether this was no more than a generalization. It seems rather unlikely that they would have printed their editions in unvarying numbers irrespective of the fact that some were small quartos and others ponderous folios, and that some would obviously be better selling lines than others. The highest priced book listed by them was the two-volume Bible, which they sold at twenty ducats.

It is hardly likely that the first printers would have run off large editions, for it must have taken some time, in the case of this new art, to estimate the potential market. It is said that the earliest record of an edition of 1,000 copies is provided by the *Pars secunda super librum secundum decretalium* of Gregory IX by Panormitanus, printed at Venice in 1471 by Wendelin de Spira. But statistics regarding the size of editions in the fifteenth century cannot be taken as gospel, for in the majority of cases we have only the printer's word for it, and it would have been to his advantage to exaggerate in the hope of warding off competition in those non-copyright days.

One printer–publisher of the fifteenth century who made the fullest use of advertising was that great entrepreneur Anton Koberger of Nuremberg, who had factors in all the important cities of Europe and boosted his books with all the publicity he could muster, in advertisements which touched upon every good reason why scholars and the reading public in general should buy his wares, whether by reason of their cheapness, their comprehensiveness, their textual fidelity, or the excellence of their presswork.

Even in England our first printer made use of the printed handbill in advertising his *Sarum Ordinale*. This is the only known example of a printer's advertisement in England during the fifteenth century, and ends with the plea 'Supplico stet cedula', or 'Please don't tear down this notice' (see p. 95).

Renaissance and Reformation

THE GROWTH OF THE PRINTING TRADE IN THE SIXTEENTH CENTURY

THE opening years of the sixteenth century found the book established in its modern form and provided with a constantly growing market. In the forty or so years which had passed since the invention of printing, presses had been set up in almost 250 towns in Western Europe. In some of these, it is true, printers had come and gone, leaving in their wake a few books only, printed perhaps as a commission from some individual patron.

But the printer, who was still for the most part the seller and publisher of his own wares, needed a stable market to recompense him for his capital outlay and the recurring expense of large quantities of paper. It is not surprising, therefore, to find that printers tended to establish themselves in the large commercial centres, in university towns, or in the proximity of a Court. Economic, social, and political forces hindered the establishment of large-scale and durable businesses away from these centres – a state of affairs which lasted, by and large, until the nineteenth century, when means of rapid communication offset the disadvantages under which smaller communities had suffered. As an instance of the contrast between the centralised markets and those on the periphery, whereas Nuremberg had sixty-two printers between 1470 and 1600, Lübeck during the same period, although one of the leading Hanseatic towns with a population of 80,000 (as against 48,000 in the late nineteenth century) had only eleven printers. Hamburg employed nineteen printers between 1491 and 1600, but Cologne, between 1464 and 1600 had no fewer than ninety-three (Benzing, 1963).

The printing press was called into being by the growth of literacy, and it was upon the continuing growth of the reading public that the prosperity of the printers depended. Only vague generalisations can be made about the extent of literacy during the sixteenth century. In England, the estimate by Sir Thomas More, made in 1533, that more than half the population could read English is at most a guess, and may well have been exaggerated to sustain his arguments. Nevertheless there is little doubt that there existed a reading public which grew as educational facilities developed. The increase in the number of printers during the last twenty years of the fifteenth century is an indication of the growing demand for their wares. During the sixteenth century, not only was there a tremendous widening of the intellectual, aesthetic and social horizons, brought about by the Revival of Learning, but a notable increase in trade, leading to an increase in wealth, created a larger demand for instruction.

During the first decade of the printing industry the number of copies printed of almost any book was small, for the earlier printers were feeling their way and it was important not to print more copies than the market could absorb. From the available evidence we find that the average edition printed during the infancy of the art varied between 150 and 200 copies. Although, when working in Rome, Sweynheim and Pannartz normally printed about 275 copies of a book, they found themselves left with quite a number of unsold copies.

But from 1480 onwards, when the printing trade had become better organised, the average number of copies steadily mounted, and by the end of the century a figure of 1,000 copies was not uncommon. In fact Koberger, who had agents in many countries and might be termed the first international publisher, brought out editions of 1,500 copies. In 1515 Froben at Basel printed 1,800 copies of the first edition of Erasmus, *Moriae encomium*. During the second half of the sixteenth century Christopher Plantin, a publisher with customers in every European country, normally printed editions of between 1,250 and 1,500. Occasionally the run would be larger. His 16mo *Virgil* was printed in an edition of 2,500 copies, for the demand was there. However, it must be borne in mind that one of the difficulties which confronted a publisher in the sixteenth century was a scarcity of books, apart from the classics and the Bible, which could be printed to show a profit. For this reason many of the books published by Plantin were partly or wholly subsidised by their authors, who either paid for the paper or undertook to buy a stipulated number of copies. Occasionally, for an important work which was expensive to produce, Plantin would arrange for another publisher to take part of the edition.

At the beginning of the sixteenth century the average edition of a book was between 1,000 and 1,500 copies, and this figure became more or less stabilised throughout the century. In England the ordinary edition of books, except for Bibles and some other religious and educational works, was limited to 1,500 copies or less by an order of the Stationers' Company in 1588.* 'This was in order to protect the workmen,' writes Mr H. S. Bennett, 'and was made at a time when the demand for books was far greater than it had been say fifty years before' (Bennett, 1952).

Bibles, liturgical books and school grammars were in a class on their own. Plantin printed 3,000 copies of his Hebrew Bible of 1566 of which he sold large quantities to the Jews of North Africa through the intermediary of Jan Rade-maker, agent on the Barbary Coast for the rich Antwerp ship-owner Gilles

* *A Copie of certen orders concerning printing.*

Hooftman.* The first printing of Luther's Bible is said to have been in an edition of 4,000 copies (Febvre & Martin, 1958). Up to the year 1501 the Bible had appeared in more than ninety Latin editions as well as some thirty vernacular editions in six languages. The demand for Bibles has seldom slackened so that in spite of the necessary outlay on large quantities of paper, Bible printing was, and always has been lucrative for the printer, with few exceptions.† Church service books were also in great demand. During the six years 1571–76 the Antwerp printer Christopher Plantin despatched to Spain alone a total of more than 52,000 service books, and had twelve presses working solely on this export business (Rooses, 1882). Indeed, during the first century following the invention of printing there was a considerable export trade in missals and breviaries. Paris and Rouen supplied the English market and Venice furnished countries east of the Adriatic with liturgical books in the slavonic tongues.

Although the introduction of printing meant that all literature previously in manuscript, whatever its category, could now be made available in quantity, the works most in demand were those on religious themes, and almost half the books printed before the end of the fifteenth century were of a religious nature: Bibles, theology, patristics, controversial treatises and books of piety. Producing complete works of the Fathers of the Church, especially when it was a case of an *editio princeps*, must have been a colossal task for the early printers. Apart from the great expense of the printing, there was the wearisome hunt for acceptable manuscripts, followed by their collation and the final establishment of a text. No wonder that Johann Amerbach wrote to Koberger, after the completion of the *Opera* of St Augustine in eleven parts: 'Est mihi maximus labor in Augustino'.

Another field which lay open to the printer was the provision of educational books. The need for text-books, already great in the time of Gutenberg, grew steadily greater during the sixteenth century. Latin was then a universal language, essential for the professional classes, and the writing and speaking of Latin was one of the aims of education. 'All men,' wrote the famous school-master Roger Ascham, 'covet to have their children speak Latin.'

One elementary Latin grammar which held widespread sway for a thousand years and more was the fourth-century grammar compiled by Aelius Donatus (*Donatus de Octibus Partibus Orationis*) and which was the most widely used of all the medieval text-books. In fact the name of its author became the general term for a grammar text-book, and both Chaucer and Langland speak of 'learning a donat'. The first edition of this work printed from movable type was issued at Mainz around 1454 or 1455 by an unnamed printer (probably Gutenberg), and it was many times produced by xylography. Its influence

---

* J. Denucé, *L'Afrique au 16e siècle et le commerce anversois.*
† Plantin's eight-volume Polyglot brought him fame, but left him burdened with debt.

began to wane during the Renaissance, and it was derided by Rabelais,* but it was a source of profit to many early printers. The *Doctrinale* of Alexander de Villa Dei was another important school book of the later Middle Ages, and it continued to be used well into the sixteenth century.

After the Bible, the book which has the best claim to be considered the most widely read book in the world is the *Imitatio Christi* of Thomas à Kempis. Not withstanding the enormous number of manuscripts available the Imitation was one of the earliest books to be printed. In 1471, two years after the author's death, Günther Zainer of Augsburg brought out the first printed edition of this much loved book, of which well over 3,000 editions, in many languages, have since been published. Primarily written for the monasteries of the Brothers of the Common Life, it became so highly prized throughout the Western world that it was considered worthy by Cardinal Richelieu to inaugurate his newly founded Imprimerie Royale in a folio volume printed in 1640.

The first half of the sixteenth century saw the emergence of two 'best-sellers': the German, Martin Luther, and the Dutchman, Erasmus of Rotterdam. Luther's treatise, *An den christlichen Adel deutscher Nation*, a tract which helped to set in motion the Reformation, sold 4,000 copies within five days when it was published in 1520. All of Luther's tracts sold well, but their sales were exceeded by his German translation of the New Testament. The first edition, in September 1522, was quickly sold out and a second edition appeared three months later. Altogether fourteen authorized and sixty-six pirated editions appeared within the next two years. The first whole Bible in Luther's translation appeared in 1534, and no fewer than 430 editions of the complete Bible or parts of it were issued in Luther's lifetime.

In 1500 the *Adagia* of Erasmus was first published at Paris by Johann Philipp, and within twenty years thirty-four editions were called for. His other writings sold equally well, especially the *Moriae encomium*, a brilliant satire on universal folly, which Gilles de Gourmont first brought out at Paris in 1511. It was written during Erasmus's stay in England, at the house of Sir Thomas More.

Apart from the works of Luther and Erasmus the best-selling book of the sixteenth century was the *Orlando Furioso* of Ludovico Ariosto, which first appeared at Ferrara in 1516. This edition, however, like all those before 1532, has only forty cantos. The first definitive version, with forty-six cantos, was printed at Ferrara in 1532, and was one of the main instruments for the victory of Tuscan as the Italian language. More editions of this work have been published to date than of any other Italian book.

It was during the sixteenth century that the printed classics began to come into their own. Some fine editions of ancient texts had already, during the

---

* *Gargantua*. The First Book, Chap. XIV.

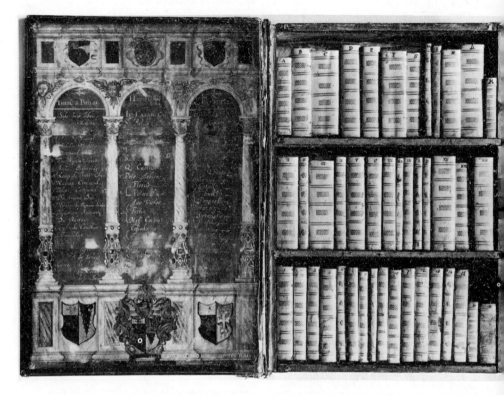

FIGURE 32. A "Travelling Library" now in the Brotherton Collection, the University Library, Leeds. The books, comprising Theology, Philosophy, History and Poetry were printed, mainly in the Netherlands, between 1557 and 1616.

previous century, come from the presses of Italy, but after 1501 the demand for these examples of the civilisation of Greece and Rome became more widespread as the influence of the Renaissance spread from Italy to other countries. In France, in the Netherlands, and elsewhere printers began to turn out in considerable numbers learned editions of the classics and of the works of the humanists.

The enthusiasm for antiquity which is one of the characteristics of the Italian Quattrocento sought in the realm of literature one aspect of the magnificence of Roman culture which Italians regarded as their heritage, but which had been almost forgotten during the Middle Ages when it existed only in the form of manuscript copies not readily accessible to the majority of people. With the advent of printing the renewal of these past glories became possible at the very time when the minds of men were awakening to new mental concepts in all branches of learning.

Little by little all the essential works of the Latin authors were committed to print. Tacitus, infrequently printed before 1500, went into many editions in the succeeding years. The vogue of the plays of Terence spread, and the illustrated version of the *Comoediae* printed by Johann Trechsel at Lyons in 1493 was reprinted thirty-one times in the space of twenty-five years. The works of Virgil, printed 161 times in the fifteenth century, were reprinted 263 times in the sixteenth (not counting the numerous translations). Among the poets who received the honours of the press were Catullus, Tibullus and Propertius (usually united in one volume), Horace, and Persius. The favoured historians were Livy, Suetonius, Sallust, Caesar, and Valerius Maximus.

After the Romans the Greeks. But here the printers encountered a technical problem – the cutting of a Greek fount; a problem rendered the more difficult in that the Greek alphabet contains accents and breathing signs. The first printers had some difficulties when it came to interpolating quotations from the Greek, especially in the works of Cicero. The earliest solution was either to translate the quotations into Latin or to leave a blank space into which the Greek words could be written by hand. Efforts were then made to cut a few letters of the Greek alphabet, and a limited use of Greek types with no, or imperfect, accents was made in books printed at Rome and Venice. Then came the first complete Greek text – an edition of the pseudo-Homeric *Batrachomyomachia* published by Tomaso Ferrando at Brescia, undated, but probably printed in 1474. The first signed and dated book printed wholly in Greek was the Greek grammar of Constantine Lascaris, printed at Milan in 1476 by Diogini da Paravicino with a fount (the first to contain Greek capitals) designed by the Cretan Demetrius Damilas.

But Greek printing did not really get under way until the sixteenth century, after Aldo Manuzio had decided to make the editing of Greek authors one of his principal aims. Unfortunately the types he chose, based upon the cursive Greek hand of his day, were not only unattractive, but made difficult to read on account of the various contractions and ligatures. However, there came from his press the *editiones principes* of a score or more Greek authors (see Chapter 13).

Nevertheless, although the Greek fount employed by Arnao Guillén de Brocar in 1514 for the Complutensian Bible of Cardinal Jiménez (see p. 188) and modelled on a manuscript lent by Pope Leo X was well designed, it was never employed elsewhere, possibly because it was too large to be economical. And so the founts used by Aldo established a vogue for cursive Greek types and even the celebrated 'Grecs du Roi' of Garamond (see p. 174) contained far too many contractions and ligatures, although beautifully designed and well cut.

The first printers had to combine the functions of printer, editor, publisher and bookseller, but by the beginning of the sixteenth century a gradual separation of these various functions was taking place, and the most financially rewarding of these diverse aspects of the book trade was that of publisher. Possibly the first man to make publishing his sole occupation was Hans Rynmann of Augsburg, whose imprint is found on almost 200 books, not one of which he had printed himself, but which were supplied from places as far apart as Basel, Hagenau, Venice, Nuremberg and elsewhere. He called himself 'the most famous archibibliopola of the German nation'.

But to be a successful publisher necessitated the outlay of considerable sums in advance against a problematical profit at an indeterminate date. Some were successful: Koberger, Froben, Amerbach, and at a later date the Plantin Press, the Giunta family, and at Lyons, Guillaume Rouillé or Roville.

By 1520 the book had at last become completely emancipated from the manuscript and had become a typographical entity with its own characters, format and decoration. Roman type gradually and almost everywhere supplanted gothic. In France decoration of books, especially Books of Hours and romances of chivalry, remained for a time faithful to the characteristics of gothic art, but by the middle of the century the influence of Geoffroy Tory had rejuvenated the French book, which found new life at the hands of printers like Simon de Colines and Robert Estienne.

12

Germany in the Sixteenth Century

IN the early sixteenth century Germany was becoming the centre of the European economic system. The growth in population was paralleled by a growth in industry which in the large towns was organised in powerful craft guilds. The money market in Germany was particularly vigorous, and the Augsburg firms of Hochstetter, Welser, and above all Fugger, had agents in every city in Europe and interests which extended to the New World. In fact the Germany of Luther was at the beginning of the sixteenth century the most flourishing territory in Europe, despite the fact that it was in no sense a political entity and lacking a strong central authority.

Growth in population, growth in literacy and growth in economic activity all favoured the printing trade, now securely on its feet after a half century of experiment. Those cities which had been of importance in the early days of printing – Mainz, Cologne, Strassburg, Augsburg and Nuremberg – were still in the forefront of German book production. In the second half of the century Frankfurt-am-Main became the leading city in this field, mainly on account of the activity of the publisher Sigmund Feyerabend. And the comparatively small town of Wittenberg was to achieve a measure of fame as the chief disseminator of Reformation tracts.

Mainz, the cradle of printing, could never regain the lustre of its infancy. Fust's former partner, Peter Schöffer I, died at the end of 1502 or beginning of 1503, his last book being a Mainz Psalter completed on 20 December 1502. And with his passing there passed also the great epoch of Mainz printing. Four sons survived him, the eldest, Gratian, becoming a printer at the small town of Oestrich on the Rhine. Johannes took over the management of the Mainz firm, Peter II became a printer at Mainz and elsewhere, but of the subsequent career of Ludwig there is no record. Peter Schöffer II had a varied career which has, so far, been insufficiently recorded. He printed one or two books at Mainz in 1512 and 1513, and then moved to Worms, where in 1526 he printed Tyndale's first completed New Testament in English, and in 1529 a German Bible for the Mennonites. Expelled from Worms for his religious convictions he went to Strassburg, where he printed several books during the next decade. Later he went to Venice, where he again printed a few books. He died at Basel in January

1547, having acquired a considerable reputation as a punch-cutter (Carter, 1969). His son, Ivo, was a printer at Mainz from 1531 until 1555, and during the course of his career was appointed University printer as well as printer to the Cathedral Chapter.

Prominent among other printers at Mainz during the sixteenth century were the two Behem – Franz (1540–82) and his son Kaspar (1563–92). From 1555 Franz Behem ran a publishing firm jointly with the Mainz bookseller Theobald Spengel, who was later joined by his son-in-law Nikolaus Geyer and the Cologne publishers Birckmann and Quentel to form a syndicate known as the 'Grosse Kompagnie'.

Two families of printers were busy in Cologne during the sixteenth century – Birckmann and Gymnich. The firm of Birckmann was founded by Franz Birckmann, who began as a bookseller in 1511 and turned to publishing two years later. He soon built up an extensive business and was one of the best-known figures at the Frankfurt Fair (see p. 219). After his death in 1530 the business was in the hands of his brother, Arnold Birckmann the Elder, active as a printer-publisher until 1542, both at Cologne and Antwerp, where he had a branch of his business. His successor was one of his sons, Arnold Birckmann II, and another Birckmann – Francis – acted as agent for the firm in England.

The founder of the Gymnich family was Johann Gymnich I, who printed at Cologne from 1520 until 1544. His son Martin was active there from 1542 to 1551, and another son, Johann II, from 1550 until 1556. Martin's son Johann printed from 1572 until 1596, so that the activity of this dynasty of printers covered almost the whole century. Like the Birckmann, the Gymnich family also had a branch office at Antwerp.

Another well-known Cologne printer was Materne Cholin, a Belgian from Arlon, a friend and business associate of Christopher Plantin, with whom he had extensive dealings. It was to Cholin that Plantin sent his merchandise for the Frankfurt Fairs, and the Cologne printer saw to their dispatch down the Rhine. Cholin, who died in 1588, became a member of the city Council and official printer to the city. Among other printers at Cologne were Walther Fabritius (1553–72) and Gottfried von Kempen (1576–98), who from 1583 onwards was the publisher of the *Relationes historicae*, later called the *Mess-relationen*, which appeared regularly. Hermann Bungart, who had begun to print in 1493 at Cologne, was active right up to 1521.

Among the major figures of the early part of the century were Eucharius Hirtzhorn (Cervicornus), Johann Soter and Peter Quentel. Cervicornus was a native of Cologne who worked there from 1516 until 1547 with the exception of three years, 1535–38, when he was at Marburg. In 1547 he went to Coblenz and set up the first press in that town. In addition to printing the works of the humanists, Cervicornus also printed for Quentel and Johann Gymnich.

Johann Soter, who worked at Cologne from 1518 to 1543, was also the proprietor of a paper-mill at Solingen. He came from a family of paper-makers and eventually became the first printer at Solingen, where he worked during the latter part of his career. His press was adjoining the mill on the river Wupper, just outside the town, and his imprint stated 'Salingaci apud molam chartaceam cis Viperam'.

The *editio princeps* of the printed English Bible, the work of Myles Coverdale, appeared in 1535 – a small folio volume with no indication of either printer or place of publication. For long it was thought to have been printed by Christopher Froschauer at Zürich; modern research, however, is inclined to attribute it to the two Cologne printers, Cervicornus and Johann Soter. The initials used in this Bible are found in books issued by these two printers, the former of whom established a press at Marburg, where the Bible was probably printed, in 1535.

Peter Quentel, son of Heinrich Quentel, played an important part in the civic life of Cologne and was a Councillor from 1515 to 1543. Under him the business begun by his father in the previous century prospered. To the English he is best known as printer of the earliest (though possibly unfinished) edition of the New Testament printed at Cologne from the translation made by William Tyndale. The first ten sheets had been secretly printed when the editors had to flee to Worms, where the work was begun afresh. Of Quentel's edition only a fragment now survives, in the Grenville Library at the British Museum.

At Nuremberg the firm of Koberger was still flourishing at the beginning of the century, but after the death of its founder in 1513 the business rapidly declined and in 1526 it finally closed down. Hieronymus Höltzel (1500–25) and Friedrich Peypus (1512–34) were among the printers at the beginning of the century, but after the death of the latter in 1534 Johann Petri became Nuremberg's chief printer. In 1525, shortly after opening his printing house, Petri issued a type specimen sheet showing his stock of types, which included three romans, two italics, Greek, Hebrew and two Frakturs. According to his brother-in-law, Johann Neudörffer (in his *Nachrichten*), these types were actually cut by Petri, but Mr Carter thinks they were more likely the work of Peter Schöffer II.

Wittenberg owed its importance as a centre of printing in the six-teenth century to two factors: the foundation of a university in 1502; but more important still the arrival there of Martin Luther. What had previously been no more than a small provincial township where the first two printers, Nikolaus Marschalk (1502–04) and Wolfgang Stöckel (1504) could only manage to produce about nine books between them, suddenly took its place in the foremost rank of book-producing centres.

Wittenberg's fourth printer, Johann Rhau (called Grunenberg), who worked there from 1508 until 1525, found a lucrative market in printing school books for the recently opened university, and when Martin Luther began to write with a view to publication, it was natural that the only printer in Wittenberg should print them. But so great was the demand for Luther's writings that the local printer was not always able to cope with it, and some of the work was farmed out to the prominent Leipzig printer Melchior Lotter. But this procedure became dangerous for Lotter after George, Duke of Saxony, an ardent Catholic, had forbidden the dissemination of writings by the Reformers under the severest penalties.

And so Melchior Lotter, an astute businessman, sent his son (also named Melchior) to Wittenberg to open a branch of his business there around 1519, while four years later the youngest son, Michael Lotter, also went there. In 1520 Luther took a decisive step towards his break with Rome when he published his tract, *An der christlichen Adel deutscher Nation*, which Melchior Lotter printed. Two years later Melchior Lotter the Younger printed at Wittenberg Luther's translation of the New Testament, with woodcuts by Lucas Cranach the Elder. This edition is sometimes called the 'September Testament' because another edition was published in December of the same year.

Yet another press opened at Wittenberg in 1523 – that of Hans Lufft, who printed there until shortly before his death in 1584. For a few years he also had a branch office at Königsberg. He was soon turning out editions of Luther's writings at a rate which made his business a spectacular success. In addition to Lutheran tracts, Lufft also printed editions of the classics, school books and dissertations for the university. But Luther was far and away his best seller, yet great as were the sales of his sermons and tracts, they were surpassed by the enormous sales of Luther's translation into German of the whole Bible, which Hans Lufft completed in 1534. Small wonder that he became known as 'the Bible printer', for between 1534 and 1574 he printed more than 100,000 Bibles. Luther's Bible became almost at once the most widely read book in Germany and influenced decisively the development of the German language.

Since the writings of Luther and other German Reformists were intended to appeal to the masses, they were printed for the most part in the vernacular rather than in Latin, with the result that the proportion of works printed in the German language grew steadily, and the works of Luther in particular represented more than a third of all the writings in German published between 1518 and 1525. Printers and publishers profited by the obsession with theological controversy, and both Melchior Lotter and Hans Lufft became rich and esteemed members of the community, and the latter eventually became burgomaster of Wittenberg.

But while profits accumulated for printers able and willing to produce Lutheran propaganda, there were parts of Germany where the picture was otherwise. As we have already seen, the Elector George of Saxony would not tolerate the dissemination of Reformist tracts, and Leipzig, to mention one important city, was soon bereft of a number of printers who found that the printing of Catholic works at that time hardly sufficed for a living. More shrewdly Wolfgang Stöckel set up a branch office outside the jurisdiction of the Elector, where he could print Lutheran writings with impunity.

Tübingen, where a university had been founded in 1477, had its first printing press in 1498, when Hans Otmar came there from Reutlingen, where he had printed from about 1482. He printed mainly theological works, both on his own account as well as for the first Tübingen publisher, Friedrich Meyenberger. After three years, however, he removed to Augsburg, where he was active from 1502 until 1514.

He was succeeded by Thomas Anshelm, who had previously worked at Strassburg and Pforzheim until in 1511 he was invited to settle at Tübingen, possibly by Johann Reuchlin, who furthered his interests and introduced him to Philip Melanchthon, Michael Hummelberger and other Tübingen humanists who treated him on terms of equality and induced him to place his press almost exclusively at the service of humanism.

Rather surprisingly there was no regular printer at **Frankfurt-am-Main** until 1530, for although Beatus Murner can claim to have been the city's first printer, he only worked there between 1511 and 1512, issuing about nine books which were printed at the monastery of the Discalced Carmelites and edited by his brother Thomas, who was a member of the Order.

But in 1530 there came from Strassburg the printer Christian Egenolff, who worked at Frankfurt for a quarter of a century and during that time printed more than 500 books embracing a wide variety of subjects. Born at Hadamar, Egenolff became one of the most famous printers of the first half of the sixteenth century and developed a business which was carried on by his heirs until 1605 and which developed into an important type foundry.

Egenolff's first press was at Strassburg, where he worked for three years and seems also to have acted as type-founder for the printer Wolfgang Köpfel. His earliest fully dated book at Frankfurt came out in December 1530 and most of his types appear to have originated in Basel, though the 110-mm roman used, for instance, in Dorstenius, *Botanicum* (1540), may, according to Mr A. F. Johnson, have been cut by Egenolff himself, though there would appear to be no recorded evidence that he was a punch-cutter.

After Egenolff's death in 1555 his widow engaged Jacques Sabon of Lyons to take over the management of the foundry. In 1563 he went to Antwerp and worked for a time in Plantin's establishment. Later he returned to Frankfurt and in July 1571 married Egenolff's grand-daughter Judith. In the following year the typefoundry was settled on her as her share in the inheritance, so that Sabon became the master of the foundry. In the meantime the printing office

Der Apotecker.

Erfte teil des Confectbüch
lins oder Hauß Apoteck/ Von
gemeinen breuchlichen Latwergen vnd
Confecten/künftlich vnd recht zu
bereyten/behalten vnd nütz
lich zugebrauchen.

Vorred.
Jeweil nach dem gemeynen
ſprichwort/der honig vñ zucker

Jch hab in meiner Apotecken
Viel Matery die lieblich ſchmecken/
Zucker mit Würtzen ich conficier
Mach auch Purgatzen vnd Cliſtier/
Auch zu ſtercken den krancken ſchwachit
Kan ich mancherley Labung machn/
Das alles nach der Artzte raht
Der ſeinen Brunn geſetzen hat.

FIGURE 33. Two pages from the *Confectbuch und Hauss Apotek* by Walther Hermann Ryff. Frankfurt-am-Main: Christian Egenolff's heirs. 1567. The cuts are by Jost Amman, one of the best-known German book illustrators of the 16th century.

had lost a certain amount of business owing to the advent of competition, but it was still of major importance and was eventually handed over by Egenolff's widow to her three sons-in-law. By a contract concluded among the heirs the foundry was separated from the printing and publishing business, and on 24 December 1572 it became the first independent typefoundry in Germany. After the death of Egenolff's widow in 1577 the foundry was moved to a separate and larger building, the printing office remaining in the old building.

Before his death in 1580 Sabon had accumulated a large stock of matrices from the best punch-cutters. He himself cut a score of typefaces, and he is credited with being the first to cut the unaccustomed large sizes from pica upwards. But his smaller type – the 'kleinen Fraktürlein Sabons' – was no less popular.

After Sabon's death his widow married Conrad Berner from Hechingen, who in 1592 brought out the oldest known Frankfurt type specimen sheet. It included all the types which Sabon had got together; a fine array of roman, italic and Greek from the punches of Garamond, Granjon, Haultin and Sabon himself, together with ornaments and arabesque borders. The specimen does not include samples of all the stock, for an advertisement at the foot of the sheet states: 'Because German and Hebrew types are not so much sought after they, and some of the Latin types, are not shown here, although the best of them are readily available.'

As to the subsequent history of the foundry, which was one of the main suppliers of type to Central and Northern Europe during the seventeenth and much of the eighteenth century, Conrad Berner died in 1606. His widow then married Paulus Egenolff, who was University Printer at Marburg, and the management of the foundry was taken over by Johann Berner, who died in 1626. One of his daughters, Katharina, married the typefounder Johann Luther, who became the proprietor of the business, which was carried on by his descendants until 1780. By this time the fortunes of the foundry had declined and it was sold by Dr Johann Nikolaus Luther to the typefounder Carl Berner, who was probably a descendant of Conrad Berner, and it became the Bernersche Schriftgiesserei, which closed down about 1810.

The place of Frankfurt in the book trade was greatly enhanced by the activity of the famous publisher Sigmund Feyerabend (1560–90), who employed many of the best Frankfurt printers and invited the leading German artists of his day to decorate his books, among them the Nuremberg artists Virgil Solis and his pupil, Jost Amman. The best-known work of the latter is *Eygentliche Beschreibung aller Stände*, referred to more often as *Das Ständebuch*, which Feyerabend published in 1568 with 114 cuts above rhymes by Hans Sachs, depicting various trades and professions. Among the works of Virgil Solis we might single out his illustrations to the folio Lutheran Bible which Feyerabend published in association with David Zöpfel and Johann Rasch in 1560, for these illustrations were copied in the first edition of the Bishops' Bible published by Jugge at London in 1568, and in many other Bibles printed around this time.*

André Wechel, son of the Paris printer Chrestien Wechel, worked at Frankfurt between 1572 and 1581 and was succeeded by his sons-in-law Claude de Marne and Jean Aubry, whose business was of considerable importance during the last twenty years of the century. Although the printing trade was comparatively late in gaining a foothold in Frankfurt, Benzing lists no fewer than eighty-eight printers at work in that city between 1511 and 1726 (Benzing, 1963).

At **Augsburg** Hans Schönsperger the Elder, who had begun to print there

---

* See Colin Clair, *The Bishops' Bible 1568* in the Gutenberg Jahrbuch, 1962.

in 1481, held an important place in the city's life during the first twenty years of the sixteenth century, and in 1508 he was appointed Printer to the Emperor Maximilian I for life. He was given the task of printing Maximilian's *Gebetbuch* (Prayerbook) which the emperor had compiled for the use of the Order of Saint George formed in 1469 by his father, Friedrich III, and Pope Paul II for the defence of Christendom against the Turks.

This book of prayers was set in a new type cut by an Antwerp craftsman, Joost De Neger, brought to Augsburg by Maximilian. It was a bastarda of large size, possibly based on the hand of the Augsburg calligrapher Leonhard Wagner. Ten copies of this book were printed on vellum in 1513, of which five copies only are now known. A year or so after publication a copy was sent to Dürer, who ornamented its margins with a series of fanciful designs brilliantly executed in coloured inks. This unique copy is now in the State Library at Munich.

The bastarda in which this book was set is of the form to which the name of Fraktur is now applied, and which is historically important in that it became in Germany the rival of roman type and could claim to be the German national letter. Between 1513 and 1524 eight varieties of Fraktur were cut, one of the earliest being that used in *Der Teuerdank*, the first edition of which Hans Schönsperger printed at Nuremberg, though for the second edition in 1519 he returned to Augsburg. *Der Teuerdank* is a fantasy woven about Maximilian's honeymoon with Marie of Burgundy – a marriage thanks to which he was able to secure the major portion of the Duke of Burgundy's lands. It is a rhyming chronicle in the style of the 'Ritterromane' of the Middle Ages, and just as boring, planned and edited by Maximilian's secretary, Melchior Pfinzing. It was first circulated in manuscript about 1505.

The printed version contains 118 woodcuts from various hands: seventy-seven by Leonhard Beck, twenty by Hans Schäufelein, thirteen by Hans Burgkmair and eight others by four unidentified artists. The type is said to have been modelled on the hand of Vincenz Rockner, the court secretary at Vienna, and cut by Hieronymus Andreae. *Der Teuerdank*, by its type and illustrations, is significant in that it gave an impetus towards independent development in German typography, for since the beginning of the century German type design had been strongly influenced by Italy.

In 1522 appeared a Fraktur of the type which became traditional in Germany, first seen in the captions to Dürer's engravings in the *Triumphwagen Kaiser Maximilians*. The type was designed by the Nuremberg 'rechenmeister' Johann Neudörfer and was cut by Hieronymus Andreae who, wrote Neudörfer, 'cut it in wood and after that made steel punches and varied the same script in several sizes' (Faulmann, 1882).

The *Triumphs of Maximilian* was commanded by the emperor as a pictorial

FIGURE 34. A page from the famous *Teurdanck*, a poetical paraphrase of the life of the Emperor Maximilian, edited by Melchior Pfintzing. The work was first printed with the imprint Nuremberg) by Hans Schönsperger the elder in 1517.

record for posterity of the splendour of his court and the magnificence of his own achievements. The whole project consists of three sets of designs: 'The Triumphal Arch, or Gate of Honour'; 'The Triumphal Car'; and 'The Triumphal Procession'. The designs for the first two were by Albrecht Dürer, the third by Hans Burgkmair. 'No ruler,' writes J. R. Hale,★ 'used the woodcut to such various ends as did Maximilian, from crude and cheap broadsheets justifying particular political moves to the elaborate "Triumphal Arch" and the massive illustrated books "Freydahl" and "Teurdank", which gave, under the gauziest of disguises, a vision of Maximilian as a multi-talented superman.'

★ J. R. Hale, *Renaissance Europe 1480–1520*. 1971.

No fewer than ninety-two blocks were cut for the 'Triumphal Arch' by eleven different engravers. The design was drawn in the main by Albrecht Dürer, though it seems that Hans Dürer and Hans Springinklee had a share in its composition. The laudatory verses were by Hans Stabius, the emperor's historiographer. The 'Triumphal Car' was also designed by Albrecht Dürer, though not completed until after Maximilian's death. But the most important of these 'Triumphs' is the 'Procession', consisting of a series of 135 large woodcuts which, joined together, would extend to a length of 175 feet! If the series had been finished according to the original drawings, now in the State Library at Vienna, the number of woodcuts would have exceeded 200. A badly edited version of the 'Triumphal Procession' was printed at Vienna in 1796, forty of the original blocks having been found at Ambras, in the Tyrol, where they had probably been deposited at the time of the emperor's death, while the remaining ninety-five were discovered in the Jesuits' College at Graz, in Styria. The original drawings from which the blocks were engraved are thought to have been by the Augsburg artist Hans Burgkmair.

At Augsburg Hans Schönsperger, who had begun to print there in 1481, was still active at the beginning of the sixteenth century, but about 1510 he handed over the business to his son, Hans Schönsperger the Younger. But in 1517 he went to Nuremberg to print the *Teuerdank* (see p. 134). In printing, as in many other spheres of activity a father's outstanding talents are not always manifested in the son, and the role of the younger Schönsperger was a very modest one compared with that of his father. In 1523 he set up a press and paper mill at Zwickau, but ran into debt and in 1525 was arrested at the Leipzig Fair. On account of his creditors he was unable to return to Augsburg and from 1532 until 1549 he lived at Schwabmünchen.

Sylvan Otmar, who printed at Augsburg from 1513 to 1533, was the son of the fifteenth-century printer Hans Otmar. Just as his father had printed editions of Tauler, Seuse and Geiler, the German mystics, so the son began his career by printing works which were derived from the devotional mysticism of the late Middle Ages. In 1518 he printed one of the classic books of mystical literature, the *Theologica Germanica*, which Luther rated immediately after the Bible and St Augustine. Its author is unknown, for he practised strictly what he taught, namely the hiding the 'creature' that no glory might fall upon him who held the pen. In the same year, 1518, Sylvan Otmar followed the thirteen pre-Lutheran Bible translations which his father had printed with a fourteenth. Soon after Luther had taken his stand against the Papacy, Otmar became one of the staunchest supporters of the Reformation. After his death the business was carried on by his son Valentin, but was no longer as important as it had been.

Erhardt Öglin, from Reutlingen, learned to print at Basel. In 1502 he settled in Augsburg, where he printed at first with Hans Otmar but from about 1510 began to print on his own. He was the first Augsburg printer to produce works in Hebrew and was also known as a music printer (see p. 209).

During the sixteenth century **Berlin** was merely the courtly residence of the Electors of Brandenburg and had not yet attained the importance which it was to acquire later as the capital of the German Reich. So perhaps it is not surprising that printing bypassed Berlin for nearly a century until Hans Weiss arrived from Wittenberg in 1540, bringing his press and material with him. He printed mainly official documents, until 1547, and Berlin was once more without a printer until 1574, when a colourful character named Leonhard Thurneysser arrived. He was a man of choleric disposition and many talents. Originally a goldsmith, he became successively a founder, court physician, astrologer, alchemist and printer, and for thirteen years was private physician to the Elector Johann Georg von Brandenburg and his wife. He began to print in 1574, turning out calendars, prognostications, works from his own pen and official documents for the Electoral Court. He owned many founts, especially Oriental ones, and is said at one time to have employed as many as 200 workmen. But owing to a series of misfortunes he was obliged, in 1577, to sell his business to his chief compositor, Michael Hentzke, who carried on the printing office until he died in 1580. A printer named Nikolaus Voltz then married Hentzke's widow and continued the business until 1591, when he moved to Frankfurt-on-the-Oder, where he was active until 1619.

At **Breslau** (now Wrocslaw) was founded a 'Stadtbuchdruckerei' which became widely known and has flourished through the centuries. Its founder, Andreas Winkler, received permission from the authorities in December 1538, to open a printing office in the city, where he was active until 1553. He was followed by Crispin Scharffenberg (1553–76), whose son Johann succeeded him and ran the business until 1586. The last owner of the press during the sixteenth century was Georg Baumann the Elder, who died in 1607.

Printing at **Lübeck** during the period under review was dominated by the Richolff, father and son. Georg Richolff the Elder, who had learned his trade with Lucas Brandis, worked at Lübeck from 1500 until 1516, with a brief interlude at Münster around 1508–9. After his death his widow continued the business for a time. The son Georg Richolff II, though continuing the Lübeck business was often called upon to print elsewhere; thus we find him at Uppsala and Stockholm (see Chapter 21) as well as at Hamburg. In 1540 he was summoned from Lübeck to Uppsala where he printed the Vasa Bible (see p. 225) after which he returned to Lübeck, where he died in 1573.

A mention should be made of the Johann Balhorn printing house which flourished between 1528 and 1603. The firm was run until about 1597 by two men of the name of Johann Balhorn, presumably father and son. The former printed from 1528 to 1573 and was succeeded by Johann Balhorn II who ran the business until around 1597, after which it was continued by the bookseller Laurentz Albrecht. The 'Balhornsche Druckerei' is remembered as having added a new word to the German language. The verb 'verbalhoren' means to alter something so that it no longer makes sense, and stems from the habit of Johann Balhorn II in 'improving' his text in subsequent editions.

The only other printer of importance in Lübeck during the sixteenth century was Aswer Kröger (1562–*c.* 1595) who took over the Richolff press after the death of Georg Richolff the Younger.

The Brothers of the Common Life, who had introduced printing into **Rostock** in 1476, continued to print there until 1530, and in 1526 they printed an edition of the New Testament in Danish and Latin. Of the remaining printers in Rostock, Ludwig Dietz, from Speyer, worked there for half a century, from 1509 to 1559, apart from a visit to Copenhagen in 1548–50 when he was called upon to print the Danish Bible. In 1558 he was appointed University Printer. The second half of the century saw the establishment of the printing house of Stephan Möllemann, who in turn became University Printer, and was active from 1561 until 1610.

At the beginning of the sixteenth century the majority of printers in Germany were still using mainly gothic types, and that remained the case, at least for books printed in the vernacular. 'The fact that Germany alone resisted the invasion of the Renaissance types of Italy,' writes A. F. Johnson, 'was probably due to nationalist pride.' Even Latin texts were usually set in *rotunda*, a rounded form of gothic which had taken the place of the old *textura*, reserved principally for church service books. Books in the vernacular were generally set in that form of bastarda known as Schwabacher first introduced by Friedrich Kreussner at Nuremberg in 1485. However, Schwabacher gradually declined in favour and was eventually replaced by Fraktur, although it appeared in German type specimens for some time to come.

An outstanding feature of the decoration of German books during the first half of the century was the wealth of woodcut illustrations and title-borders. Of the latter something like a thousand blocks were produced within a quarter of a century. At Augsburg, Daniel Hopfer designed some striking borders for the printer Sylvan Otmar, used for (*inter alia*) the title-page border of the Old Testament in German (1523). Hans Weiditz, another Augsburg woodcutter, was responsible for some forty title-borders as well as a great number of book illustrations. Georg Lemberger worked for the main Lutheran printers, Melchior Lotter, Hans Lufft, and Johann Grüninger. Some borders, such as that specially designed for the *Hortus Sanitatis* published at Strassburg by Mathias Apiarius in 1536, are by artists whose identity is now unknown. At Nuremberg Hans Springinklee and Erhard Schön were employed by Friedrich Paypus and by the famous firm of Koberger. At Frankfurt-am-Main, Hans Sebald Beham

Balſami   cinamomi   Piperis nigri
croci   coſti   Semis petroſelini
Squinanti   Zinziberis   Ozimi
Malabarri   Mirre   anagodani
Terpentine   Folij aquatici
Olibani/ideſt thuris maſculi   carthami/ideſt ſeminis croci ortulani·
caſſie lignee   Agarici   Pentaphilonis/ana. Ɔ.j
Spice celtice   Reupontici   Baccarum lauri· Ɔ.ſem.
Yreos   Diptam   Vini venuſtiſſimi.ʒ.j.
Praſſij/ideſt marubij albi   Mellis quod ſufficit
coloquintide   Sticados arab·   Werd gemacht als ich hernach daruon
Artimiſie   calamenti   ſchreiben vnd leren wil.

Zů dem vierden wie men die compoſita vnd ſimplicia zůſam
men vermiſchen ſoll/nach rechter kunſt vnd art/vff das ſie yr vollkommende würckung
vollbringen mögen nach dem die alten Philoſophi daruon ſchreiben·

FIGURE 35. Woodcut from Hieronymus Braunschweig, *Das buch zu distillieren*, an early trade book printed at Strassburg in 1519 by J. Grüninger.

did some excellent work for Egenolff as designer of the illustrations and title-border of the *Biblicae Historiae* (1534), a series of illustrations which were copied by publishers in Paris and Antwerp.

Printing began at **Munich** with a German edition of the popular *Mirabilia Urbis Romae* from the press of Hans Schauer, which appeared in 1482 under the title *Püchlin wie Rom gepaut war*. It has survived in one copy only, now in the Bayerischen Staatsbibliothek. The second known printer in this Bavarian city was Benedict Buchpinder, who printed Balthasar Mansfeld, *Almanach für München auf das Jahr 1491*, a single sheet wall calendar.

But the first regular printer in Munich was Hans Schobser, who came there from Augsburg, where he had printed from 1487 until 1498, though whether he was a native of that city is not known. He probably set up his press in Munich some time in 1500, for he is known to have printed there a Mansfeld *Almanach* for the year 1501. His first book was possibly the undated Paulus Wann, *Quadragesimale*, which appeared in 1501.

At the beginning of the sixteenth century Munich did not rate among the great German cities, for the business activity of the town could not compare with the rich centres of industry of nearby Augsburg and Nuremberg; Ingolstadt, with its university founded in 1472, was the nearest centre of learning, and the nearest centres of religious life were Freising and Salzburg. Thus the chances of a printer making a successful career out of books seemed rather remote. Nevertheless Schobser, who had learned his trade with Anton Sorg, was active there for thirty years, and his son Andreas for another thirty-four. His mainstay was in the printing of official documents for the ducal chancery and the Court as well as municipal decrees and statutes. He printed books as well and was the printer, *inter alia*, of some of the few Munich Luther reprints.

In 1564, after the death or the retirement of Andreas Schobser, the business was taken over by Adam Berg the Elder at the instigation of Duke Albrecht V, who was his patron. He was active from 1564 until 1610, so that these three printers between them spanned the whole of the fifteenth century. Apart from his official printing Berg produced more than 300 works, and became an important music printer. He also printed the first sizeable book with copper engravings to come from Munich. This was the first edition, 1568, of Hans Wagner, *Beschreibung Wilhelms Herzogs und der Renata gehaltenen hochzeitlichen Ehrenfestes*.

It has been impossible so far to establish with any certainty the identity of the first printer in **Vienna**. The suggestion has been made that Ulrich Hahn printed at Vienna some time in the 1460s, but if so, nothing of his work in that city has survived. Seven books were printed at Vienna in 1482, with no mention of the printer's name. Among them was a *Vocabolista Italico-Tedesco* with a colophon: 'Stampada in Viena: Gedruckt zu wienn'; and an edition of *Guidonis* *de Monte Rotherii, Manipulus Curatorum,* 'finit feliciter Impressum Wienne Anno Dni. MCCCCLXXXII'.

The BMC does not commit itself and merely says that 'the printer of the 1482 *Vocabolista* appears to have started work in 1482 when he produced at least seven books all mentioning Vienna as the place of printing and the date 1482'. It goes on to say that the printer may possibly be identified with Stephan Koblinger who had printed at Vicenza 1479–80 and may well have been the 'Steffan Koglinger' who acquired citizenship of Vienna in 1481. Certainly the type in which these books are printed is an Italian text type similar to that used in Vicenza printing of the period. But a case has also been made for Johann Petri, the 'Johann Wiener' who had printed a Virgil at Vicenza in 1476 and later set up as bookseller and publisher at Passau.

The first identifiable printer at Vienna is Hans Winterburg, who began to print there in 1492, acquired citizenship of Vienna in 1496 and continued his active career until his death in 1519. He probably learned his trade at Mainz and states in the colophon to *Lucii Apulii Platonice et Aristotelici philosophi Epitoma,* which he completed in November 1497, 'Impressus per Ioannem de hibernia arce haud procul a ripis Rhenanis et urbe inventrice et parente impressorie Artis Mogunciaco feliciter'.

After the death of Winterburg his material was acquired by Hans Singriener, from Ötting in Bavaria. He began to print in 1510 in partnership with Hieronymus Vietor, a printer from Liebenthal in Silesia whose family name was Büttner (i.e. 'Cooper'), and who styled himself at various times Philovallis (i.e. Liebenthal), Vietoris, Dolarius, and sometimes merely Hieronymus. Singriener's partnership with Vietor lasted until 1514, after which he printed alone. He died in 1545, having printed over 400 editions, and left behind him a well-equipped printing office which was taken over by his son Matthaeus, who from 1547 to 1549 was partnered by his brother Johann II Singriener. From then on Johann the younger printed alone until his death in 1562. It is interesting to note that of the nineteen master printers at work in Vienna during the century following the invention of printing, Johann II Singriener was the only born Viennese. Two came from Poland and the others were mainly German.

One of these Germans, Stephan Kreuzer, who worked in Vienna from 1572 until 1594, was appointed the first official University printer in 1575. His output was extremely varied and he issued books printed in German, Latin, Italian, Hungarian, and Hebrew.

Raphael Hoffhalter was a Pole, whose family name was Skrzetuski. After a period in the Netherlands, and later at Zürich, Hoffhalter went to Vienna in 1555 and joined with Kaspar Kraft, from Ellwangen, who had been formerly with the firm of Adler and Zimmerman as type designer and founder. Hoffhalter himself, in addition to being a printer and bookseller was also an engraver and type-founder. He was active in Vienna from 1556 until 1562, when, because he was a Protestant, he had to leave that city and went to Debreczin, where he died at the beginning of 1568.

The first book to come from an Austrian printing office was not, however, printed in Vienna, but at Trent, in South Tyrol, where a German, Albrecht Kunne, perhaps on his way to or from Venice, printed *Geschichte des zu Trient ermordeten kindes*, dated 6 September 1475. But when he left Trent shortly afterwards his type remained there and passed into the ownership of Hermann Schindeleyp, who published in February 1476, the *Historia completa de passione et obitu pueri Simonis* of Johann Mathias Tuberinus, another work of local interest. An unsigned *L'aspra crudeltà del Turco a quegli di Caffa*, printed after 7 June 1475, may well have been the work of Albrecht Kunne, but we know nothing further of his work in South Tyrol where in 1479 a priest from Bergamo, Giovanni Leonardo Longo, had a press which he worked for a short while.

At **Graz**, in Styria, there seems to have been no printing until Alexander Leopold set up a press there in 1559. Only three books from this press are now known, and the printer is thought to have died in 1562. As was customary in those days, one of his apprentices, Andreas Franck, married Leopold's widow, and carried on the business from 1563 until 1575, when he left Graz for religious reasons. But the best-known printer at Graz during the latter part of the six-teenth century was Georg Widmanstetter, who worked there from 1587 until 1618, and after his death the printing office was carried on by his heirs.

A wandering printer from Regensburg named Hans Kohl (in its Latinised form Johannes Carbo) was working in Vienna between 1548 and 1552, when he either died or returned to Regensburg. His printing office in Vienna was taken over by Michael Zimmermann from Zürich, who was active in the Austrian capital from 1553 until 1565, and who printed works in Italian, Spanish, Arabic, Hebrew and Syriac, for which the exotic characters, at any rate the Syriac, were cut by Kaspar Kraft, who was also responsible for the Cyrillic types used by Raphael Hoffhalter.

Also active from 1559 until 1565 was the printing office of the Jesuits in their premises 'Am Hof', under the direction of the Rector Johann Victoria, a native of Spain. Twenty-five books are known from this particular press, which ceased in 1565 and was sold in 1577 to Nikolaus Telegdi, the head of the order at Gran, who used the material to start a printing office at Tyrnau.

Other printers at work in Austria during the latter part of the sixteenth century include Kaspar Stainhofer (1565–75), Stephan Kreutzer (1572–94), Michael Apffel (1576–88), Leonhard Nassinger (1579–88), David and Hercules Denecker (1576–85) and Leonhard Formica (1588–1605).

13

The Aldine Press and others

AT the beginning of the sixteenth century, the most illustrious among the many printers of Italy was Aldo Manuzio, though less perhaps for his skill as a printer than for his scholarship and his technical innovations. He was born around 1449 at Bassiano, near Sermoneta, and while still a youth went to Rome, where he studied under Gaspare da Verona and Domizio Calderini. Later he studied Greek at Ferrara with Battista Guarino, the son of the famous humanist Guarino Veronese. Not long after this he settled at Mirandola under the patronage of the extraordinarily gifted Pico, that admirable Crichton who died at the early age of thirty-one. Pico obtained for Aldo the post of tutor to his two young nephews, Alberto and Leonello, the sons of his sister, Caterina Pio, and at their palace at Carpi, not far from Modena, he stayed for about six years.

About 1488 Aldo settled in Venice, where he edited and prepared for the press the writings of the Greek authors, probably for the printer-publisher Andrea Torresano of Asola, who had come to Venice about 1470, and worked for Nicolas Jenson before setting up in business on his own account, around 1479, the year in which he printed a Roman Breviary. From Andrea Aldo Manuzio learned the rudiments of printing and publishing, though from the technical point of view, seeing that he had served no apprenticeship to the craft, it is hardly likely that he was at first a practising printer. He then set up as an independent publisher, his first book, the Greek grammar of Constantine Lascaris, being completed in March 1495. This marked the beginning of a long series of scholarly publications which have made the name of the Aldine Press famous.

Manuzio's main interest was in the publishing of the Greek classics. Although not the earliest publisher to issue books in that language, he soon surpassed all others in the number of his editions. Of the forty-nine first editions of Greek authors printed up to the time of Manuzio's death, no fewer than thirty came from his press.

In 1495, after the *Erotemata* or Greek grammar of Lascaris, he issued the first editions in Greek of Musaeus, *Hero and Leander*, and Prodromus, *Galeomyomachia*. The *editio princeps* of Theocritus followed in February 1496, and that of Aristophanes in 1498. But the most remarkable work of these early years was his first edition of Aristotle in Greek, brought out between the years 1495 and 1498 in five large volumes dedicated to his former pupil, Prince Alberto Pio. In these works and the various Greek grammars and dictionaries which he printed, Aldo was assisted as editor by Marcus Musurus, a Greek who taught at nearby Padua.

It was unfortunate, however, that Aldo Manuzio should have based the design for his Greek type on the handwriting of Musurus, which, however well suited with its ligatures and contractions for rapid note-taking, had not the simplicity essential for a readable type. It was cut by Francesco Griffo, if that punch-cutter's claim to have cut 'all the types with which Aldus has ever printed' is correct. Considerable skill was employed in the cutting of the punches, but the resulting fount does not compare in legibility with the lower-case Greek which had already been used by Jenson.

Aldo's new roman, however, was quite another matter. Unlike the Greek it was designed for purely typographic needs, free from the slavish imitation of manuscript sources. Until 1496 Aldo had obtained what roman he needed for prefaces, colophons and the like, from common trade sources. In February 1496, however, he printed a Latin dialogue called *De Aetna*, the work of the Venetian nobleman and scholar Pietro Bembo (1470–1547), for which he used a new roman face which the late Stanley Morison described as 'the origin of all old-faces'. In its first state it was somewhat marred by imperfections in the cutting and too thick capitals. It was later recut and in its final and perfected form, as seen in the Perottus, *Cornucopia*, of 1499, and in the *Hypnerotomachia Poliphili* of the same year, it stands out as a face of great beauty.

hominum negligentia deperierint : nos
enim ;dum Romaceſſemus;unam ,quae
in ima ripa ſpeculi eſt Dianae Aricinae,
pro miraculo uidimus. Sed nihil eſt pro
fecto (mihi crede), nihil eſt fili (ut ego
ſemper diccre ſoleo) ; quod effici ab ho-
minc cura , diligentiáq; non poſſit : nos
enim (ut de me ipſo loquar) ;quibus tamen ; ex quo hanc uillam exaedificaui -
mus, iam inde ánte, q̃ tu ẽs natus, conſu

Figure 36. The Aldine roman as used in Pietro Bembo, *De Ætna*, printed at Venice in 1496 by Aldo Manuzio. This is the first state of this fount, which was later perfected in cutting, and soon superseded the Jenson roman.

Hora quale animale che per la dolce efca, lo occulto dolo non perpen
de, poftponendo el naturale bifogno, retro ad quella inhumana nota fen
cia mora cum uehementia feftinante la uia, io andai. Alla quale quando
effere uenuto ragioneuolmente arbitraua, in altra parte la udiua, Oue &
quando a quello loco properante era giunto, altronde apparea effere affir
mata. Et cufi como gli lochi mutaua, fimilmente piu fuaue & delecteuo-
le uoce mutaua cum cœlefti concenti . Dunque per quefta inane fatica,
& tanto cum molefta fete corfo hauendo, me debilitai tanto , che apena
poteua io el laffo corpo fuftentare. Et gli affannati fpiriti habili non effen
do el corpo grauemente affaticato hogi mai foftenire, fi per el tranfacto pa
uore, fi per la urgente fete, quale per el longo peruagabondo indagare,
& etiam per le graue anxietate, & per la calda hora , difefo , & relicto
dalle proprie uirtute, altro unquantulo defiderando ne appetendo , fe
non ad le debilitate membra quieto ripofo . Mirabondo dellaccidente
cafo, ftupido della melliflua uoce, & molto piu per ritrouarme in regione incognita & inculta , ma affai amœno paefe. Oltra de quefto, forte
me doleua, che el liquente fonte laboriofamente trouato, & cum tanto
folerte inquifito fuffe fublato & perdito da gliochii mei. Per lequale tu-
te cofe, io ftetti cum lanimo intricato de ambiguitate, & molto trapen-
fofo. Finalmente per tanta laffitudine correpto, tutto el corpo frigefcen-

FIGURE 37. A page from the superb edition of Francesco Colonna, *Hypnerotomachia Poliphili*, printed at Venice by Aldo Manuzio, 1499. The artist remains unidentified.

As an example of fine printing the latter book forms the high water mark of Aldo's career. None of his other books was outstanding from the point of view of typography, yet no one can gainsay that the *Hypnerotomachia* is a masterpiece of the printer's art in which beauty of type and of illustration are enhanced by the excellence of the press-work. Perhaps the reason is to be found in the fact that of all Aldo's major works this book alone was printed on commission and

the financial aid thus provided may have enabled the printer to devote exceptional time and care to this magnificent product of his press. Strangely enough
the creator of its hauntingly beautiful illustrations remains unknown. Whoever
he was, he was certainly, as Arthur Hind declares, 'an artist of charming invention and sensitive genius'. This dream-allegory, once dismissed as a farrago of
precious nonsense, is today the subject of reassessment in the light of modern
research into the workings of the unconscious mind.* Its author was a Dominican
monk, Francesco Colonna, who died in 1527 at the age of ninety-four, leaving
the world this enigmatic love story.

Despite the beauty of this particular book, Aldo's reputation rests not on his
ability as a printer, but as a publisher, and more especially as the publisher of a
series of classical texts in small octavo editions. It was a great departure from
tradition, for up to that time the classics had generally been issued in large folio
editions, well suited to a rich man's library and purse, but beyond the means
of the growing numbers of students at the universities who badly needed carefully edited editions of the classics in both durable and portable form at a
reasonable price.

For this series of 'pocket classics', which combined compactness with scholarship, Manuzio needed a new type in order to compress what normally filled a
folio volume into the smaller page area of a pocketable octavo. His solution of
the problem lay in a complete innovation, for he called upon Francesco Griffo
to cut a face based on the current Chancery hand termed *cancelleresca*. It was a
slightly sloped letter, in imitation of the cursive hand, cut for Small Pica and in
effect both legible and good looking. For some reason this design became known
among English-speaking nations as 'italic', but the Italians themselves refer to
it as 'cursive' (*corsivo*), as do the Germans (*Kursiv*), whilst the Spaniards com-
memmorate the cutter by calling it *letra grifa*.

The Aldine italic suffered from the same disadvantage as did the Aldine
Greek; it followed too slavishly the habit of the scribes in employing ligatures,
a device totally unsuited to typography. Nearly seventy ligatures are found in
the early texts of the Aldine pocket classics. Nevertheless, the low price and
scholarly editing of this series of classics, which began in 1501 with an edition
of *Virgil*, ensured for the new cursive type a wide distribution and at the same
time a reputation it did not rightly deserve. Its chief claim to fame is that it was
the first of its kind, but it cannot be denied that the Vicentino italics designed
by Lodovico degli Arrighi were vastly superior to Manuzio's both in design
and practicality.

However, so popular was it for a considerable time that despite all his efforts
to protect his invention by persuading the Senate of Venice to grant him an

* E. P. Goldschmidt was blunter. He said it was written by a lunatic. (*The Printed Book of
the Renaissance*. 1950.)

exclusive privilege for the use of this character, Manuzio had the mortification of seeing it impudently counterfeited, in particular by the printers of Lyons. Imitations of the Aldine classics began to appear with increasing frequency, and although Aldo issued a broadside warning, *Aldi Monitum in Lugdunenses Typographos*, dated 16 March 1503, in which many of the counterfeits are named, the piracy continued. The chief counterfeiter was Balthazar da Gabiano, a native of Asti in Piedmont, who was the representative in Lyons of the Venetian firm known as 'La Compagnie d'Ivry'.

In 1512 Gabiano was partnered by Barthélemy Trot, who introduced the fleur-de-lys found on many of the Lyons counterfeits. Although Manuzio's patent was subsequently renewed by Julius II for fifteen years from January 1513 and confirmed by Leo X in 1514, it was of little avail to the patentee, and before long most printers in Italy had acquired imitations of the Aldine italic. 'The Italic became a symbol of learned humanism,' writes Mr Carter, 'and in Italy, and to a less extent in western Europe as a whole, it made great inroads on the Roman' (H. Carter, 1969).

Early in March 1505 Aldo Manuzio married Maria, daughter of the printer Andrea Torresano of Asola. He was then a man of fifty-six – his bride barely twenty. From this marriage came five children – two daughters and three sons, one of whom, Paolo, succeeded to his father's business.

Manuzio's career was beset with many difficulties, for although Venice was a city of wealth and culture, it was not immune from the effects of the constant wars and foreign invasions of Italy. The League of Cambrai (1508) was motivated in Pope Julius II's hatred of Venice, which led him to court the aid of foreign powers in invading the territory of the Venetians, who were defeated at Agnadello on 14 May 1509. The subsequent treaty imposed harsh terms upon the Republic from which it never quite recovered.

During this difficult period Aldo's business slumped considerably and he himself had to make long absences from Venice between 1506 and 1512, during which time his press turned out only eleven books. His home life, too, was troubled, for his brothers-in-law were ne'er-do-wells and his son Antonio had to flee from justice. In 1512 Manuzio returned to Venice for good, and from that time until his death on 6 February 1515 he issued a further thirty-two books. During his active life as a publisher he had issued a series of classics notable for the accuracy of their texts, due largely to the unremitting care exercised by himself and a select team of editors who were among the greatest scholars of their day.

Antonio Blado was also among the most important printers in Italy during the sixteenth century. He settled in Rome as a printer around 1516, in which year he brought out an edition of the *Mirabilia Urbis* and also ten sermons of Saint Paul: *Decalogus de Sancto Paulo primo heremita*.

The first phase of Blado's activity came to an end in 1539, the year in which he became printer to the Camera Apostolica. His predecessors in this post had been, since the beginning of the century, Marcello Silber, Jacopo Mazzochi and the humanist and traveller Francesco Minicio Calvo. Calvo printed at Rome from 1523 to 1534, and was printer to the Camera Apostolica at least from 1527. In 1534 he went to Milan. These three were licensed to print for the Camera Apostolica but, unlike Blado, they did not have an exclusive privilege.

At first Blado was paid at piece-work rates, but from 1539 he was in receipt of a regular salary. In addition, he frequently received extra payment for special work. Thus, in September 1539, the Camera paid him ten scudi d'oro 'pro impressione bullarum decimarum in tota Italia impositarum'. This piece of printing mentions Blado for the first time as *Camerae Apostolicae Impressor*.

In 1539 Blado was instructed by Cardinal Marcello Cervini to begin the printing of the Greek manuscripts in the Vatican library, and the first of these to appear was the famous commentary of Eustazio upon *Homer*, the first volume of which came out in 1542. Publication of the second volume was held up, possibly for financial reasons, until 1545 when it appeared, not in the fount used for Volume I, but in a smaller and more handsome type.

Like many other Italian printers in the first half of the sixteenth century, Blado had his founts of Aldine italic. A. F. Johnson cites three well-known editions as examples of the popularity of the letter: the *Decameron* printed in 1516 by Filippo Giunta at Florence, the first editions of Machiavelli's works printed at Rome by Antonio Blado in 1531 and 1532, and Marcolini's *Dante* of 1544. 'These types,' he writes, 'depart from the original chiefly by cutting down the enormous number of ligatures at first used by Aldus. The design remains the same and the model is adhered to in the consistent use of upright capitals' (Johnson, 1934).

The *Machiavelli* was Blado's most important work to date and the text was based on the author's own manuscript made available to the printer by Cardinal Gaddi, to whom the work is dedicated. This edition was quickly copied (line for line) by Bernardo Giunta, and issued only a few days after Blado's in an attempt to pass it off as the original edition.

In addition to the *editio princeps* of Machiavelli, Blado also printed another important first edition, the *Repubblica dei Veneziani* of Donato Giannotti. Almost simultaneously another edition was produced by Tommaso Giunta, and so popular was this work that eight editions were published during the author's lifetime as well as a German translation.

Another italic type of distinction made use of by Blado was the second fount of Lodovico degli Arrighi (see p. 156), which can be seen to advantage in Camillo Agrippa, *Trattato de scientia d'arme* (1533). The superiority of Arrighi's cursives over those of Aldo Manuzio both in design and practicality soon

PARTE XIII

perſeueraſſe con animo di volere pur' ferire col taglio,di man-
dritto,o di riuerſo:Queſto potrebbe riparar' di croce,et ſpinge-
re cõ la punta verſo lui,ouero riparar' di coperta uenẽdo in Pri-
ma, & ſpinger' di ſotto,& di ſopra ſecondo le forze ſue: et ſe
pur' in quel tempo il detto auerſario tentaſſe pur d'offenderlo
con detti colpi di taglio dal mezʒo in giù': Queſto andarebbe,
contra eſſo ſpingendo ſubito per hauer minor' colpo da lui,et per
farli maggior la riſpoſta. Sono diuerſe altre vie ancora per in
trar per forza d'arme,perche ritrouandoſi vno pur ne la mede-
ſima Terza Guardia larga, & contraſtando à mezʒa ſpada
col nemico, quãdo cercaſſe intrarli per forza di fore ſopra la
ſpada per darli nel petto,ritornarebbe di quella Terza ne la Se
conda ſtretta,& ſubito paſſato il ſuo colpo,di nouo ſpingerebbe

FIGURE 38. Italic type used by Antonio Blado for his edition of Camillo Agrippa, *Trattato de scientia d'arme.* Rome, 1553.

ousted the latter and enjoyed the inevitable sequel of being extensively copied and used all over Europe.

On account of his special relationship with the Camera, the bulk of Blado's work was made up of such items as Bulls, Briefs, Edicts of the Church, Indulgences, etc., and he was responsible for printing the first *Index Expurgatorius* in 1557. His business was continued by his heirs until 1593.

Whilst Aldo Manuzio was concerned mainly with the classics and Lucantonio Giunta with liturgical books, the Venetian printer Francesco Marcolini threw himself whole-heartedly into the production of Italian literature. He arrived in Venice from Forli in 1534 and between 1535 and 1559 he issued around 100 books, starting with *La Cortigiana* by Pietro Aretino, many of whose works he printed. Aretino had fled to Venice from Rome after the election to the papacy of Adrian VI, whom he had savagely derided.

Marcolini printed much Italian literature in a fine italic type, and his books are notable for their handsome initials (many decorated with views of cities) and ornaments. Among his finest productions were an excellent edition of Dante (1544) and the architectural works of Serlio. In July 1536 Marcolini acquired a privilege for printing music and in that year brought out an *Intabolatura di Liuto* and five books of the Masses of Adrian Williaert. A portrait of the printer appears in his edition of A. F. Doni, *I Marmi*, which he printed at Venice in 1552.

A justly celebrated family of printers were the Gioliti de' Ferrari, who, as printers and booksellers, flourished without interruption from 1483 until 1606, mainly in Trino and Venice.

The first of the family to print called himself Bernardino Stagnino, but his family name appears in the colophon of an edition of Calepinus, *Dictionarium*, which he printed in his native Trino in 1521, and in which his name is given as 'Bernardinus Jolitus alias de Ferrariis dictus Stagninus'. He began to print in 1483 at Venice and continued well into the next century.

Next, chronologically, was Giovanni il Vecchio, who introduced the printing press into Trino in 1508 and specialised in legal books. He worked for a while in partnership with the publisher Gerardo de Zeis. Some time after 1531 he was working a press at Turin, perhaps as owner, in conjunction with Martin Cravoto and Francesco Robi, but after the French occupation of the city in 1536 he went back to Venice where he was active until 1539. But by far the most important member of the Gioliti was Giovanni Gabriele, called Gabriel, the son of Giovanni the Elder. Not only was he one of the outstanding Venetian printers of his time, but also one of the first large-scale commercial publishers. His shop in Venice, the Libreria della Fenice, soon had branches in Naples, Bologna, Ferrara and elsewhere. From 1536 to 1540 he worked in partnership with his father, but after his father's death he began to print on his own account. His name is important in the history of Italian literature since he was the publisher of most of the Italian writers then in vogue, including Aretino, Bembo, Bentivoglio, Tasso, Muzio, Parabosco, Cavalcanti and many others. He published twenty-two editions of Petrarch's *Rime* between 1542 and 1560, and no fewer than twenty-eight editions of Ariosto, *Orlando Furioso*, during the same period. Nine editions of the *Decameron* also came from his press.

Later he began a new and prosperous venture with his translations of Greek and Latin authors, and became the first publisher in Italy to bring out collections of various authors in separate volumes, printed in uniform style and dealing with a specified subject. He began the series with *Collana degli istorici greci e latini*. Gabriele Giolito died in 1578, but the firm was carried on by his sons until 1606.

At Rome one of the most prolific printer-publishers of the early sixteenth century was Giacomo Mazzocchi, though it is difficult to say how many of the books bearing his imprint were actually printed by him. His first dated book, Vibius Sequester, *De Fluminibus* (10 May 1505), was printed for him by Joannes Besicken, and Isaac has shown that many books with his name as printer are in the types of Joannes Beplin. Publishing was doubtless his main occupation. According to Fumagalli his press was destroyed during the sack of Rome in 1527, which would explain the appearance of his imprint at Zürich in 1527–28, in *Libri de re rustica*, the last known of his books.

We have already seen that Francesco Griffo of Bologna was the designer and cutter of types for Aldo Manuzio, and the creator of his italic and his cursive Greek. He was also himself a printer, having founded a press in his native city around 1516. In September of that year he issued Petrarch's *Canzoniere et triomphi* as the first of a series of Italian and Latin classics in a 24mo format printed in a very small italic. Only six of these books are known to have been published and in 1518 the printer was involved in a quarrel with his son-in-law, who was killed. Griffo's fate is unknown, but he may have been executed, for he is mentioned as deceased in 1519. In addition to the types which he cut for Manuzio and for his own use, he is thought to have been responsible for the types used by Bernardino Stagnino in his 1512 edition of Dante.

In Florence a good standard of printing was maintained throughout the sixteenth century. In 1503 came the first book known to be from the press of Filippo Giunta – an octavo edition of Catullus, Propertius, and Tibullus. This heralded a long series of octavo classics printed in italic which Filippo issued in competition with those of Aldo Manuzio. The Giunta, like the Gioliti, were a family of printer–publishers. Filippo's brother Lucantonio had a press at Venice, Giàcomo worked at Lyons, and other members of the family were established in Spain, at Burgos and Salamanca. They were publishers more than printers, though they had their own types and presses, but other printers worked for them.

After Filippo di Giunta's death in 1517 the press passed to his heirs and until 1531 the imprint of the firm was 'Haeredes Philippi de Giunta', though Filippo's son Barbardo seems to have been the man in charge. He was active in Florence until 1550. Bartolomeo Zanetti, a native of Brescia, who was one of those who worked for Filippo Giunta, printed a number of books in Florence before moving to Venice some time after 1525. About 1545 he was again in Florence in partnership with Antonfrancesco Doni until they eventually quarrelled. Zanetti printed one book at Fontebuono in 1520, a commission from the monks of Camaldoli. Another Florentine printer, the Fleming Laurentio Torrentino was responsible for a very fine edition of *Pandette* (1531).

The fine traditions of the fifteenth century lingered awhile in Naples, where the German, Sigismund Mayr brought out a number of humanistic works, including a handsome edition of the works of Gioviano Pontano between 1505 and 1508. He died in 1517 and his press was carried on for a few years by his widow Caterina. Jean Pasquet printed, *inter alia*, the works of Belisario Acquaviva and of Agostino Nifo, and worked in Naples from about 1517 until 1526. He had originally worked as an assistant to Mayr. Around 1550 a few fine books appeared in Naples, among them Federico Grisone, *Gli Ordini di Cavalcare* and Antonio Mariconda, *Le Favole di Aganippe*.

The printer Petrus Porrus, who had a press at Turin, was summoned to Genoa in 1516 to print the polyglot Psalter edited by Agostino Giustiniano, Bishop of Nebbio. This was printed in Hebrew, Greek, Arabic and roman types. But the most important printer in that city from 1533 until 1573 was Antonio

FIGURE 39. In 1511 Ottaviano de' Petrucci set up a press in his native town of Fossombrone at the request of the bishop of the diocese, Paulus de Middelburgo. In 1513 he printed the prelate's *De recta Paschae celebratione* from which this page is taken.

Bellone, who in 1557 styled himself 'tipografo ducale'. His grandson Marcantonio ran the press from 1573 until 1581, when he moved to Turin, and later to Carmagnola.

At Milan the Fleming, Gotardus de Ponte, probably a native of Bruges, was active from 1500 until 1538, printing not only on his own account, but also for various publishers, among them the brothers De Lignano. During the years 1520–21 he also printed at Como. The firm of Rocho & Da Valle Brothers worked at Milan during the first thirty years of the century, with Rocho printing alone from 1524 until 1530.

Other Milanese printers active during the sixteenth century include Francesco and Simone Moscheni (1541–66), Gerolamo de Meda (1544–74) and Antonio degli Antoni (1544–1600).

The famous printer of Hebrew books, Girolamo Soncino, worked at Rimini from 1520 until 1527 when he moved to Cesena, where he remained for the next three years. Bernardino Vitali, a well known printer of Venice, went to Rimini in 1521 and printed there the *Venetias* of Publius Modestus, worthy of note for its delightful title-page.

Turin had a busy printer in Martino Cravoto, who worked there from 1535 to 1573 with a break of several years during the French occupation of Piedmont, when he moved to Venice. He worked for several publishers including the famous Giovanni Giolito. Nicoló Bevilacqua, a native of Trento who printed at Venice between 1554 and 1572, went to Turin in 1573. He was summoned there by the reigning duchess, Marguerite of France, to take charge of the newly founded Compagnia della Stampa. Unfortunately he did not long enjoy his new office, for he died in 1574. The printing house was continued by his heirs and managed by his son Giovanni Battista, who seems to have been active in Turin until 1599, specialising in works of jurisprudence.

Lucca makes no great show in the history of printing during this century, nevertheless it produced a literary landmark in the vast *Novelliere* of Matteo Bandello, the first three parts of which were printed at Lucca by Vincenzo Busdraghi in 1554. (The fourth part was published at Lyons in 1573.) Here we find the sources of Shakespeare's *Much Ado* and *Twelfth Night*, as well as Webster's *Duchess of Malfi*, and some of the stories were incorporated into Painter's *Palace of Pleasure* (1565–66).

The idea of establishing at Rome a press serving the purpose of the Holy See came from Pope Paul IV, but was not put into effect until two years after his death, which took place in 1559. The proposal was implemented by his successor, Pope Pius IV, and the press was opened in 1561. At the suggestion of Cardinal Seripando the technical management of the new printing office was confided to Paolo Manuzio, the son of Aldo Manuzio, who was summoned from Venice for that purpose, leaving his son Aldo to look after the business in that city. Paolo was given the task of superintending the printing of a projected series of sacred writings such as the patristic books in addition to the various decrees and ordinances promulgated by the Holy See. His salary was to be 720 gold *scudi* a year.

The contract was confirmed by a *motu proprio* of the Pope dated 8 August 1561, and Manuzio received the 'cittadinanza Romana' on the 16 September following. The papal press was known as the Stamperia del Popolo Romano because although under ecclesiastical control the printing house was partly supported by the commune of Rome. For this reason the editions produced by Paolo Manuzio, such as the *Canones et Decreta Concilii Tridentini* (1564), bear the imprint 'In aedibus Populi Romani. Apud Paulum Manutium'. However, various difficulties which cropped up in the exercise of his functions, and notably those raised by the magistrates 'del Popolo', who looked upon him with less favour than did the Pope, all combined to render his stay in Rome far less satisfactory than he had anticipated and in 1570 he relinquished his post, which he ceded to Fabrizio Galletti.

Three years later, and one year before the death of Paolo Manuzio, Rome saw the establishment of another famous press, the Stamperia Medicea, by Ferdinando de' Medici, one of three cardinals charged with the task of endeavouring to reconcile the dissident Eastern churches, for the victories of the Turks coupled with the schism among the Christians of the Orient was a growing cause of concern to the Holy See, already combating the spread of the Reformation. The press was to specialise in Oriental languages in order to print sacred writings and theological works in Arabic, Chaldean, Syriac, Persian, Ethiopic and other tongues. The cost was borne mainly by Cardinal Ferdinando de' Medici, and the press was placed under the superintendance of Giovanni Battista Raimondi, son of a rich citizen of Cremona. Raimondi had studied Oriental languages during a long stay in Asia, and on his return to Italy had translated from Arabic into Latin the *De Conis* of Apollonius Pergeus. He presided for a number of years over the new printing house, for which Robert Granjon worked as a punch-cutter (see p. 177).

There was little printing at Verona until the middle of the century. According to Dr Rhodes not more than thirty-eight books were printed in that city in the thirty-eight years from 1491 to 1529,* in which year Stefano Nicolini da Sabbio and brothers set up a press which lasted for no more than three years, after which Stefano moved first to Venice and then to Rome. After a gap of eight years Antonio Putelletto printed a few books between 1540 and 1546. But printing did not become a regular industry in Verona until in 1570 Sebastiano dalle Donne started a press which flourished until the end of the century and

---

* D. E. Rhodes, *An outline of Veronese Bibliography, 1472–1600*, in 'Annali', Series I. Vol. V, 1971 of Padua University.

had as his competitor Girolamo Discepolo, who printed there from 1584 until 1598, when he moved to Viterbo. Discepolo printed a fair number of books, among them the statutes and privileges of Verona in two folio volumes (1588) commissioned by the publisher Marc'Antonio Palazzolo.

No mention of printing in sixteenth-century Italy would be complete without some reference to the Italian writing-books of the period. Soon after 1520 we find a new kind of italic appearing at Rome, based not on the cursive humanistic script such as the Aldine type and its imitators, but on the more elaborate hand of the Papal chancery – the 'corsiva cancellaresca'. The propagators of this new form of cursive were the professional scribes in the Vatican chancery, among them Lodovico degli Arrighi of Vicenza, commonly known as Vicentino, and Giovanantonio Tagliente.

Ludovico Vicentino was calligrapher, type designer and printer as well as being the publisher of the first important writing book, *La Operina . . . da*

FIGURE 40. Title-page of *Il modo de temperare le Penne,* by the Vatican scribe Ludovico degli Arrighi, also called Vicentino. It was published at Rome in 1523.

imparare di scrivere littera cancellarescha, printed at Rome in 1522. The cursive letters were cut by the goldsmith Lautizio Perusino (or to give him his full name, Lautizio di Bartolomeo dei Rotelli) and printed from wood blocks. Two years later Giovanni Antonio Tagliente published his writing book *Lo presente libro insegna la vera arte delo excelléte scrivere de diverse varie sorti de litere*, which was printed at Venice by Stephano de Sabio.

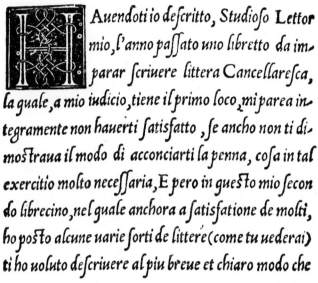

FIGURE 41. Arrighi's chancery italic as shown in his writing book *Il modo de temperare le Penne*. His punch-cutter was the medallist Lautizio di Bartolomeo dei Rotelli.

In *La Operina* Arrighi describes himself as a 'scrittore de' brevi apostolici'. Two years later he became also a printer, and in July 1524 brought out a collection of Latin poems called *Coryciana*, the colophon to which reads: 'Impressum Rome apud Ludovicum Vicentinum et Lautitium Perusinum.' This book, like all Arrighi's books, was a quarto and printed in one single size of a very beautiful cursive, with, for the first time, what are known as 'swash' capitals. He printed several books of Gian Giorgio Trissino, a wealthy aristocrat from Arrighi's own home town of Vicenza, and in his tragedy *Sophonisba* Trissino pays tribute to the beauty of the printer's italic. A tribute well deserved, for in the opinion of A. F. Johnson Arrighi 'produced the finest italic of his day and, at any rate in Rome, was unrivalled as a printer'.

The book of Tagliente mentioned above contains examples of various hands and also examples of the Hebrew, Persian and Chaldee alphabets. The calligraphic part of the book, like Arrighi's, is engraved, but there are a number of leaves printed from type, a calligraphic italic not unlike Arrighi's larger type. The same fount was used on the title-page and in the colophon of another book by Tagliente – *Luminario di arithmetica* (1525).

Another Renaissance scribe who brought out his own writing book was Giovanni Battista Palatino, a native of Rossano in Calabria, who later acquired Roman citizenship. Secretary of the Accademia degli Sdegnati, and one of the most versatile calligraphers of his time, he brought out in 1540 *Libro Nuovo d'Imparare a Scrivere Tutte Sorte Lettere* . . . printed at Rome by Baldassare di Francesco. Another edition was printed in the same year by Antonio Blado. Incidentally, in the dedicatory address Palatino assigns the invention of printing to Gutenberg in 1452, and mentions Jenson as bringing the art to perfection.

Ferdinando Ruano, a Spaniard employed as a scribe at the Vatican Library issued his *Sette Alphabeti* at Rome in 1554, published by Valerio Dorico and Luigi fratelli Bressani. Another scribe employed in the Vatican Library, Giovanni Francesco Cresci had his *Essemplare di piu sorti Lettere* printed by Antonio Blado in 1560. It went through several editions and was followed by the same author's *Il Perfetto Scrittore* (1570), the examples in which were cut by Francesco Aureri.

The writing master Vespasiano Amphiareo, a Franciscan, published *Uno Novo Modo a Scrivere*, printed at Venice by Gabriel Giolito, and Giuliantonio Hercolani, a cleric and doctor of law, published his *Essemplare utile di tutte le sorti di lettere cancellaresche* about 1572, and his *Scrittor' Utile* in 1574.

THE VATICAN PRESS

In Rome, the growing use made by the papacy of printing, both for the spiritual mission of the Church and for the temporal government of the city, led to the nomination of official printers, and eventually to the foundation of the first Vatican Press under the style of Tipografia Camerale in 1559.

During the first quarter of the century Marcello Silber was printer for the Curia of Bulls, Chancery regulations and publications of an administrative nature. Antonio Blado of Asola, active from 1516 until 1567, and one of the most productive of Roman printers during the sixteenth century, brought out a variety of books in most branches of learning; nevertheless the majority of Blado's publications were of an official character. Upon the inauguration of the Tipografia Camerale he became its technical director; at this time the press was not installed within the precincts of the Vatican, but the move took place on 27 April 1587 in accordance with the Bull *Eam semper* of Pope Sixtus V. In 1589 Antonio's son Paolo Blado was offered the directorship for life, but gave up the post in 1593.

But whereas the Tipografia Camerale had confined itself to official publications, the need was felt to bring out correct editions of the patristic writings and ecclesiastical history in general. It was for this reason that Pope Sixtus V instituted the Vatican Press within the palace in 1587. The management of this press, which was governed by a body of cardinals, was entrusted to Domenico Basa. Among the important works issued were the twelve volumes of Baronius, *Annales Ecclesiastici* (1588–1607); seven volumes of the works of Saint Bonaventura (1588–96); the Sistine Bible of 1590, and the Clementine Bible of 1592. Several well-known printers like Giacomo Tornieri and Luigi Zanetti worked for the Tipographia Vaticana while at the same time issuing their own productions.

THE INDEX

Throughout Western Europe governments were becoming increasingly concerned at the growing number of books with possibly dangerous implications, such as the implied threat to constituted authority, and nowhere more so than in Italy. In 1527 Pope Clement VII had issued the Bull *In coena domini*, which condemned heretical books and their readers, and even earlier, in 1487 Pope Innocent VIII had issued a Bull *Contra impressores librorum reprobatorum* which was printed at Rome.

Various early lists of censored books, known as Catalogues, were published during the first part of the sixteenth century, but although Cardinal Carafa, as Inquisitor-General, had issued in 1543 a general indictment of those books and printers of which he disapproved, it was not until his pontificate that, as Paul IV, he was able to bring out the first full and official *Index Librorum Prohibitorum*. The first edition of this Index was printed in 1557 by Antonio Blado, but was found to be so full of errors and solecisms that it was suppressed before publication, and a second edition was brought out in 1559. It was never published in Paris, nor in Spain, and even in Italy it was received with some misgivings.

In 1564 came the Tridentine Index, which appears to have been recognised at once as the authoritative utterance of the Roman Catholic Church on the subject of books, and was widely circulated. First printed at Venice by the Aldine Press it was reprinted ten times between 1564 and 1593. The last Index of the sixteenth century was the Clementine Index of 1596 promulgated by Pope Clement VIII.

The effects of the Index were felt throughout Europe by the bookselling and publishing trades, for booksellers became disinclined to take the risk of importing books which might eventually be banned, and often they were prevented even from selling books they already had in stock.

14

Printing in Sixteenth Century France

AT the beginning of the century France was still producing books in a style which made no attempt to free itself from slavish imitation of the manuscript. Vérard continued to publish Books of Hours and popular literature in the traditional 'lettre bâtarde'. Large initials with grotesque masks recalled the conceits of the calligrapher. Several of the printers who had made a name for themselves during the fifteenth century were still active and producing books, often beautiful indeed, but in a style which was soon to look archaic when the new generation of printers, inspired by the spirit of the Renaissance, began to adopt a completely new style. By the middle of the century only works of jurisprudence, in the main, were still being set in gothic types, though naturally here and there in the provinces one comes across printers with neither the inclination nor perhaps the capital to renovate their material.

However, in Paris by 1530 most of the leading printers had adopted roman and italic types and the book was now becoming a typographic entity in its own right instead of an imitation manuscript. Under the influence of Italy, French printers began to evolve a new style of decoration. Even more important, there sprang up in France, as in Italy, a number of scholar printers whose books were aimed at a steadily growing academic clientele and who themselves were men of letters, capable of furnishing critical editions of a learned text.

The Bible being the keystone of medieval scholarship, it is not surprising that theology and patristics provided the first printers with the bulk of their work to which they added service books and canon law. But once the Renaissance had spread to France it found there, in the domain of the printed book, a new generation of printer–publishers, imbued with the spirit of Humanism and who had, in their own craft, an ideal means for its diffusion. The new learning brought about a reappraisal of the classics, and this led to the publication of many Latin and Greek texts. And since a ponderous folio would have found little sale among students, astute printers followed the example of Aldo in Italy and began to print their classics in small octavo volumes. But the new studies were not confined solely to a reassessment of the past. It was an age of discovery which enlarged not only the horizons of the natural world, but man's mental horizons also. Curiosity became a besetting virtue and both natural and applied science benefited from it.

The first of these scholar-printers in France was a Fleming, Josse Bade (1462–1535), known also by the Latinised form of his name, Jodocus Badius Ascensius, namely from Aasche, near Brussels, though it is now thought he was born at Ghent. At all events, it was in that city that he studied under the Brothers of the Common Life, afterwards going to Louvain University. He finished his studies in Italy, at Ferrara and Mantua, and then settled at Lyons as a schoolmaster. He became the friend and later the son-in-law of the printer Johann Trechsel, whose daughter Thalia he married and in whose printing house he became a corrector.

Bade went to Paris in 1499 and himself became a practising printer in 1503, possibly with the financial help of Jean Petit, one of the four important sworn booksellers of the University of Paris. Bade's printing office and bookshop became widely known under the name *Praelum Ascensianum* when he transferred his business in 1507 from the rue de Carmes to the rue Saint-Jacques, then the main publishing centre of Paris where, among his colleagues, were the Petits, the Marnefs, the Kervers, Jean de Gourmont, François Regnault and many others. The competition must have been enormous. He used as his mark a printing press, this being its earliest representation. It is to be seen on the title-page of the first printed edition of Ausonius, which Bade issued in 1513, but first appeared in 1507 in the *Secunda pars operum Baptistae Mantuani*.

Josse Bade carried on the work begun by Trechsel and published and annotated himself a great number of Latin classics. He was also the first publisher of the great Greek scholar Guillaume Budé.

A press of even greater fame than that of Josse Bade for the dissemination of the classics was the office of Henri Estienne (Henricus Stephanus), the founder of a famous dynasty of printers. Wolfgang Hopyl, who had succeeded to the business of his former partner, Johann Hygman, in 1498, took as his new partner in 1502 Henri Estienne, who had married Guyone Viart, Hygman's widow. The two men separated in the following year and Henri Estienne remained the sole proprietor of the business, the craft of which he had possibly learnt as an assistant to either Hygman or Hopyl. He was never a prolific printer and during his active career from 1502 until 1520 produced on the average only seven books a year, but those which he did produce were important both by reason of their literary value and the quality of the printing. He was associated with Jacques Lefèvre d'Etaples, the friend of Erasmus, and published many of his writings and those of his disciple, Josse Clichtove. Apart from these, Henri d'Estienne's publications consisted mainly of medical, mathematical and liturgical works. He died in 1520, leaving a daughter and three sons, François, Robert and Charles.

FIGURE 42. From Cebes, *La Table*, translated by Geoffroy Tory and figuring his device of the broken pot. Printed at Paris for G. Tory & J. Petit, 1529.

At his death Henri Estienne left his already celebrated business to Simon de Colines, with whom he had business connections, and the latter not only became the third husband of Guyone, but also continued in a worthy manner the traditions of the firm until Robert Estienne became old enough to enter the business in 1525. In the following year Simon de Colines set up his own press at the sign of the Soleil d'Or in the rue Saint-Jean-de-Beauvais, where he worked with tremendous industry for fourteen years before moving in 1539 to the rue Saint-Marcel. Although not a scholar like the Estiennes, he nevertheless printed a great number of learned and scientific works amongst a total output of some 750 books. As a printer he ranks high, and his edition of Jean Ruel, *De Natura Stirpium* (1536), is one of the handsomest folios of the period, with an elaborate title-border which has been attributed to Oronce Fine. Tradition, supported by an epigram addressed to Sebastien Gryphe by the poet Visagier (Vulteius), asserts that Simon de Colines was a punch-cutter as well as a printer.* Speaking of the Jean Ruel book, Updike writes: 'I know few books more satisfying throughout than this noble folio volume – one of the finest of sixteenth-century French books.' The fine criblé initials in this work are attributed to Tory (Updike, 1922).

For books in smaller format, such as his editions of Horace and Martial, Colines used italic, of which he had several varieties. In addition to a couple of founts in the Aldine manner he also had two cursives derived from Arrighi, the larger of which can be seen in his *Raison d'architecture antique* (1539), a French translation of Vitruvius.

Robert Estienne and his son Henri II were the two most eminent scholar-printers of sixteenth-century France. Robert Estienne was a biblical as well as a classical scholar, and is as famous for his multiple editions of the Bible as for the beauty of his reprints of the classics or his assiduity as a lexicographer. He enjoyed the patronage of François I, who appointed him Royal Printer in Hebrew and Latin in 1539 and Royal Printer in Greek the following year, after the death of Conrad Néobar. He was renowned for the scrupulous attention he paid to the accuracy of classical texts. A Calvinist in his religious views, he was compelled by the hostility of the Sorbonne, once the death of the king had deprived him of royal protection, to leave Paris and in 1550 he settled in Geneva.

'These two men (Robert Estienne and Simon de Colines),' writes A. F. Johnson, 'together with Geoffroy Tory the book decorator and Claude Garamond the engraver of types, transformed the French book.'

Geoffroy Tory (c. 1480–1533) has a two-fold claim to distinction. As artist he was mainly responsible for the French Renaissance style of book decoration; at the same time he is honoured as one of the precursors of French philological study. Tory was born at Bourges and his first studies were made at the university of that town. At the beginning of the sixteenth century he pursued his studies first in Rome and then at Bologna under Filippo Beroaldo, who later became librarian of the Vatican. It was undoubtedly this contact with Italian humanism which made its mark on his subsequent career.

After his return to Paris, where he settled around 1507, he spent several years teaching, while devoting much of his spare time to editing and correcting Latin classics for Paris booksellers. During this period he became interested in drawing and engraving and to further his studies in this direction he again visited Rome,

* Le Bé, in his *Memorandum*, attributed three sets of matrices in his typefoundry to De Colines.

returning to Paris in 1518 after an absence of a year or more, and there setting up as a bookseller at the sign of the *Pot Cassé*. Most writers state that he was also a printer, but this is by no means certain. Weiss writes in the *Biographie Universelle*: 'Lottin certainly does not include him among the Paris printers of the sixteenth century. From this one must conclude that he was never more than *libraire*, as he describes himself at the end of all his own books.'

In 1525 Simon de Colines printed a Book of Hours which can claim to be one of the finest examples of this class of printing for which Paris was so famous. There are thirteen large woodcuts by Tory and the borders which surround each page are also from his hand. These borders, of which there are sixteen varieties repeated, are so sharp and delicate that they were probably cut on metal rather than wood.

The book by which Tory is best known is his own *Champ Fleury*, which was probably printed for him by Gilles Gourmont, and is one of the outstanding French books of the sixteenth century. First published in 1529, it deals, as the subtitle proclaims, with 'the art and science of due and true proportion of attic letters, otherwise known as antique letters, and commonly Roman letters, proportioned according to the human body and countenance'. The book, the text of which is today almost unreadable, is in three parts. The first is a plea for the regularisation of the French language; the second deals with the design of the Latin alphabet and the relation of the letters to the proportions of the human body and face; the last has to do with the pronunciation of individual letters and finishes with a treatise on the Hebrew, Greek and Latin languages and their alphabets. In addition to an alphabet of roman capitals meticulously drawn, the book also shows alphabets of four kinds of letter: 'Cadeaulx, Forme, Bastarde ou De Somme, Tourneaure.' The last-named was a very formal writing which served for inscriptions on tapestries and stained-glass windows.

On his return from his second visit to Italy Tory introduced into French printing woodcut decoration in the Italian manner, and the lightness and delicacy of this style imposed itself on Parisian printing to the extent of modifying completely the existing method of layout and decoration. But from the purely typographical angle Tory's influence was slight. The types in which the books bearing his imprint are set look old-fashioned for their date, and there is no evidence that he was ever a punch-cutter, as Bernard suggested. Although from 1531 onwards his imprint suggests that he printed as well as sold books, any such claim is frequently contradicted by typographical evidence. Nevertheless he was honoured in 1531 with the title of 'Imprimeur du Roi', but this was probably due less to the typographical quality of his publications than to his advocacy of French as a literary language.

On Christmas Eve 1534 the printer and punch-cutter Antoine Augereau was hanged and burned in the Place Maubert, Paris, for his part in the 'affaire des placards'.* His printing office in the rue Saint-Jacques had been in existence for only three years, but he was nevertheless an important figure in the history of French type design if only for the reason that he was the tutor of the more famous Claude Garamond.

Augereau was a native of Poitou, related probably to two Augereau who are known to have been working in Poitiers at that time – Michel Augereau, a printer and his son Guy, a 'graveur de lettres d'impression'. About 1608 Guillaume Le Bé II drew up an inventory of the foundry which he had inherited from his father. Among the material he noted down a 'vieu Cicero Romain Augereau'. About 1643 Le Bé wrote a 'Mémoire sur l'imprimerie', from which one may infer that the roman lower-case used at Venice by Aldo Manuzio was being imitated by the French soon afterwards and cites Augereau among those who did so. He writes that Manuzio's roman 'fut incontinant suivie et imitée en France et particulièrement à Lion et Paris dez les années de 1480 et 1500 par un nommé Augereau et Me. Constantin et mieux par Simon de Colines'.

Le Bé also tells us that Claude Garamond served his apprenticeship with Augereau before going to work first with Pierre Haultin and then with Claude Chavallon. La Caille, writing in 1689, considered Augereau to have been, along with Simon de Colines, one of the first in France to have cut punches for roman type. The Greek type used by Augereau shows a close resemblance to one of the three Greek founts used by Simon de Colines, and it may well be, as Mme Veyrin-Forrer suggests,† that the part played by Augereau in the foundry of Simon de Colines was a large one.

Simon de Colines was among the first in France to adopt the Aldine letter and Le Bé mentions the type cut by him and used by Robert Estienne – in particular a Saint-Augustin which Estienne named 'Sylvius' – because he first used it in January 1531 for the *Isagωge* of Jacques Sylvius (Dubois). This handsome quarto is of importance both from the philological and typographical viewpoints. Since the fount had been cut with accents and small superimposed letters to convey the author's etymological and phonetic ideas, it was responsible in no small measure for the spreading of the use of accents in French writing. To the student of printing it is important in that this lower-case became for two centuries the traditional European roman, later named 'Garamond'.

Another instance of intermarriage among printers' families in order to further business interests is that of Michel de Vascosan, whose first wife was Catherine, daughter of Josse Bade. Their own daughter Jeanne married another printer, Frédéric I Morel. Vascosan was admitted as a printer in 1530 and 'libraire juré'

* In October 1534 the walls of Paris and other French cities were plastered with posters virulently attacking the doctrines of the Mass and the Eucharist.
† 'Antoine Augereau', in *Paris et Ile-de-France*, Vol. 8, 1956.

the same year. He was appointed 'Imprimeur du roi' in 1561, and died in 1577.

Vascosan printed in a simple and straightforward style and his folios, such as the *Quintilian* of 1567, show to advantage the excellent use he made of the Garamond romans. In 1559 he printed the first folio edition of Amyot's translation of Plutarch's *Lives* and in 1574 a seven-volume Amyot version of *Les Oeuvres morales et meslées de Plutarque*. He worked in the rue Saint-Jacques at the sign of the Fountain, and until 1539 signed his books 'in aedibus Ascencianis'.

Among the initials he used in the later years of his career were many of the large letters designed by Oronce Fine, which first appeared in his *Protomathesis*, published by Gerhard Morrhé in 1532, a work in which all the illustrations are by the author himself. Fine, or Finé as his name is often spelt (although the *Nouvelle Biographie Générale* insists that it is Fine and *not* Finé), was a well-known mathematician and astronomer who also dabbled in book illustration and published several maps. The ornamental borders which he designed for the scientific works printed by Simon de Colines show a considerable mastery in this art. He came from the Dauphiné and adopted the dolphin as a decorative motive. He wrote many books, mainly on mathematical subjects.

After the death of Vascosan, Fédéric Morel became the most important printer in Paris since most of those who were prominent during the reigns of François I and Henri III were dead and had not been replaced by men of equal merit. Fédéric Morel, however, proved himself to be the worthy successor of his father-in-law (he had married Jeanne de Vascosan). He practised from 1557 to 1581, and was appointed in 1571 Royal Printer in Hebrew, Greek and Latin, as well as French. It was in that year that he printed the celebrated edict *Sur la Réformation de l'Imprimerie*, promulgated from Gaillon by Charles IX in May 1571. This edict, which contained twenty-four clauses, made apprenticeship obligatory in order to become a journeyman printer. The term of apprenticeship was qualified simply as 'un temps suffisant', but the minimum period from then onwards was three years, increased in 1615 to four years. The edict also required a master printer to be certified as capable by two sworn booksellers and two other master printers. Prior to this enactment anyone could set up as a master printer in France.

Fédéric Morel printed some 300 books, in addition to official acts, and at his death in 1583 was succeeded by his son, who had taken over the royal printership when his father retired in 1581. A scholar, like his father, he ranked among the finest printers of his time in France, and carried on the family business until his death in 1602, when he was succeeded by his son, who was also royal printer from 1602 until 1624. Fédéric II Morel had a younger brother, Claude, who was also a printer.

The Paris printer and bookseller Jamet Mettayer worked in that city from

1573 to 1588, and after an interval at Tours, from 1589 to 1594, he returned to Paris where he was active until 1605. He was Royal Printer in Mathematics, but also produced some handsome liturgical books as well as the first edition (1594) of the celebrated *Satyre Ménippée*, a political pamphlet, the work of seven collaborators, which recognised Henri IV as the man most likely to restore peace to a land rent by religious struggles. Mr A. F. Johnson goes so far as to say that Mettayer was 'perhaps the best printer in Europe in his day' (Johnson, 1928).

Rheims is not a town one would normally connect with early printing, but it has its place in the history of the English Bible, for it was there, in 1582, that the first Roman Catholic version of the New Testament in English was printed by Jean de Foigny, a local printer. It was printed there because political upheavals had compelled a temporary removal of the English seminary from Douai, where it had been founded by William (afterwards Cardinal) Allen in 1568. In 1593 the college returned to Douai, and there the complete Bible was printed in two volumes (1609–10) by Laurence Kellam. Though the work shows evidence of much sound scholarship, the frequent obscurity of its language detracted from its popularity. Nevertheless it was reprinted at Rouen in 1635.

The end of the sixteenth century marked a decline in the standard of book printing in France. The wars of religion and the economic difficulties which sprang from them made it difficult for printers to engage upon any long-term projects or works which called for a considerable outlay of capital. And, secondly, the great printers of the first half of the century, who had combined excellence of book design with scholarship of no mean order, were dead, leaving no worthy successors.

After 1572, when the most violent phase of the religious struggles between Catholics and Huguenots opened, the number of significant books published in France showed a marked decline. The increasing severity of the laws of censorship and the regulations of the guilds hampered all attempts at improvement. After the occupation of Lyons by the 'Ligue' in 1573 many Protestant printers began to move to Geneva.

The middle years of the century showed French printing at its best; it was a period of great activity in the book world and both quantity and quality were equally high.

PRINTING AT LYONS

As we have already seen, from the fifteenth century onwards Lyons was one of the great centres of printing. From 1473 until 1500 a succession of printers from Guillaume Le Roy onwards made that city a formidable rival to Paris in the book world. At the beginning of the sixteenth century a notable array of printers were continuing the work of their precursors: Bonnin, Huguetan,

Jacques Moderne, Claude Nourry, Janot des Champs, Devilliers, Etienne Baland, François Juste, Jacques and Olivier Arnoullet, Jean Crespin, Jean and Francois Frellon, and above all Sébastien Gryphe (1525–66) and Jean de Tournes (1504–64). Not far behind the last-named were Macé Bonhomme and Guillaume de Roville.

During the whole of the sixteenth century Lyons maintained its reputation as a centre of printing and publishing, and the middle of the century was a period of intense activity, when we encounter such names as Melchior and Gaspard Trechsel, Denis de Harsy and Thibaud Payen; then, a little later, Balthasar and François Arnoullet, François Gryphe, Philibert Rollet, Benoît Rigaud, Jean Cauteret, Thomas Guérin, Jean d'Ogerolles, Pierre and Jacques Roussin, Bathélemy Vincent and a number of others who successfully continued the traditions of Lyonnese printing.

In 1532 (though undated) appeared the first book of Rabelais, treating of Pantagruel. It was published by Claude Nourry (called le Prince) and probably put on sale at the Lyons Fair of 3 November 1532, under the title of *Les Horribles et épouvantables faits et prouesses du très renommé Pantagruel, roi des Dipsodes*. Since Rabelais considered it unwise, as the recently appointed physician to the Hôtel-Dieu de Notre-Dame de Pitié du Pont-du-Rhône, to publish so frivolous a work under his own name, he disguised it under the anagram Alcofribas Nasier.

Rabelais also acted as editor for the Lyons printer Sébastien Gryphe (a native of Reutlingen whose born name was Greiff) when he printed certain apocryphal fragments of Cuspidius and the Greek text with a revised translation of the *Aphorisms* of Hippocrates.

The son of a printer, Michel Greiff, Sebastian learned his trade in Germany and in Venice before settling in Lyons. He specialised in small format editions of the classics, imitating in this the Aldine editions, and was also a printer of such humanists of the day as Erasmus and Budé. His house became the meeting place of many of the finest writers and scholars of that time, among them Clément Marot, Maurice and Guillaume Scève, the jurist Alciato, Sadolet bishop of Carpentras, Hubert Susanneau and François Rabelais. He printed at Lyons for thirty-four years, until his death in 1556. Unfortunately his business declined in the hands of his natural son François Gryphe, who died at the end of 1599 burdened with debts.

It was Sebastian Gryphe who, far from feeling jealous of a rival, gave every assistance to Etienne Dolet when the latter began to print in 1538. Some of the early books bearing Dolet's name were printed by Gryphe, who seems also to have provided the younger printer with some of his type. It was Gryphe, too, who did not hesitate to shelter Dolet when in 1534 he was liberated from the prison of Toulouse, and to offer him a post as corrector.

Etienne Dolet, who was executed as a heretic in Paris on 3 August 1546, was a complex personality whose character was thus summed up by the Abbé Niceron: 'He was excessive in everything, doting on some and hating others with fury; pouring praise upon some, tearing others to pieces mercilessly, always attacking, always being attacked, of a scholarship beyond his years, a tireless worker, and with it all proud, disdainful, vindictive and an uneasy and troubled man.'* In short, a *déséquilibré*.

On 6 March 1538 Dolet obtained a royal privilege to set up a printing office and the first book to come from his press in that year was his *Cato Christianus* of forty pages. Two other books bearing his mark which are also dated 1538 were printed for him by Gryphe. From then until 1541 he printed editions of the Latin classics as well as works on the French language and the art of translation.

But although Dolet was befriended by Sebastian Gryphe, he was looked upon in less friendly fashion by many of the other printers in Lyons, probably because Dolet was less than tactful in the manner in which he referred in his *Commentaries* to negligent and careless printers, often blinded and rendered careless by drink, seldom without any vestige of learning, who could hardly print a book without innumerable faults! And when the printing trade at Lyons was affected in 1538 and 1539 by very serious strikes among the journeymen, Dolet, although himself a master printer, supported the claims of the workmen, which did not, of course, endear him to his colleagues. Moreover, as he himself had never served an apprenticeship, he was considered an interloper.

In 1542 Dolet enlarged his workshop, moved to new premises and during his rather short career printed some eighty works, among which were a number of theological works by authors of reformist tendencies, as well as a New Testament in French which was ordered to be burned by decree of the Parlement de Paris. No copy of this work is known, since it was never actually published, but was seized on Dolet's premises and burned in front of Nôtre Dame in February 1543. These works, together with his own heretical writings, eventually led him to the stake. His trial was long, the main charges were blasphemy, sedition and exposing for sale prohibited and condemned books, and the outcome was never in doubt.

It was not a good time for the unwary printer. Augereau was hanged and burned in 1534; Dolet was burned at the stake in 1546. In 1560 the Paris printer Martin l'Homme was hanged for printing a pamphlet against the Guises, and in particular the Cardinal de Lorraine. Its title was *Epistre envoyée au Tigre de France*. In 1572 the well-known printer Andreas Wechel narrowly escaped death during the massacre of Saint Barthlomew. He fled from Paris and settled at Frankfurt-am-Main.

* *Mémoires pour servir à l'Histoire des Hommes Illustres.* Vol. xxi, p. 118.

Among the most celebrated printers of France during the second half of the sixteenth century were the two Jean de Tournes, father and son. The father began to work as a master printer at Lyons in 1542. Whether or not he was apprenticed to the Trechsels, as some say, he certainly worked for a time with Sebastian Gryphe. His first book was *Le Chevalier Chrestien*, a translation by Louis de Berquin of Erasmus, *Enchiridion militis christiani*, a small octavo volume of 317 pages. A rare work today, for only three copies are known, this first-fruit of his press was already a good example of its printer's technical skill. From the very beginning it became apparent that the books from the printing house of Jean de Tournes were to be of outstanding quality.

About 1547 Jean de Tournes took as a partner in his business Guillaume Gazeau, who had married his daughter Nicole in 1545, and their partnership lasted until 1563. In 1559 de Tournes was recompensed for his fine craftsmanship by being appointed Royal Printer at Lyons. His active career lasted from 1542 until 1564, when he died of the plague, which is said to have claimed between forty and fifty thousand victims in Lyons.

The elder Jean de Tournes was a great believer in the sales value of illustration as well as in their efficacy in helping to understand and remember the text. His chief illustrator was an artist called Bernard Salomon, known as 'le petit Bernard', who first worked for him in 1547 and continued to do so until 1561. Two of the most celebrated books printed by Jean de Tournes with engravings by Salomon were the Bible of 1553 and the Ovid, *La Metamorphose figurée*, of 1557; this latter work, with 178 charming woodcuts, was so popular that five further editions were published during the century. No wonder his employer termed him, not unjustly, 'le plus excellent ouvrier qui fust en France'.

An even more delightful book is the *Illustratione de gli epitaffi et medaglie antiche* of the Florentine, Gabriele Symeoni, which was published by Jean de Tournes in 1558, with woodcuts and medallions by Bernard Salomon, whose first important work for the printer had been a collection of 113 woodcuts to illustrate the very popular *Emblems* of Andrea Alciati, first published in 1547 and often reprinted. The *Quadrins historiques de la Bible* (1553) exhibits no fewer than 199 of Salomon's graceful vignettes.

The stamp of a good printer can usually be found on his title-pages. One of Jean de Tourne's most characteristic is the very fine title-page to Erasmus, *De Duplici Copia Verborum* (1558), with its setting of title in a double reversed pyramid and a striking medallion of the head of Erasmus, engraved, without a doubt, by Bernard Salomon. Moreover, it is followed by a splendid opening page set in condensed italic with a perfectly placed foliated seven-line drop initial.

Through the work of both Tory and Jean de Tournes we are constantly aware of an Italian influence. In the case of Tory this was the result of his first-hand acquaintance with the country. In Lyons, where Jean de Tournes worked, the influence of Italy had been at work since the fourteenth century when many Italian merchants settled in that city. Long before the campaigns of Charles VIII the number of bankers, artists, engravers and merchants of Italian origin at Lyons was very large, and it is only natural that these foreigners should bring to their adopted country their native ideas and customs. For the Renaissance to pass completely into France it needed only a more frequent and more direct contact, and one result of the Italian campaigns from 1494 to 1559 was a greater awareness of what Italian civilisation had to offer. Jean de Tournes, who in his early days with Gryphe had helped to print the *Opere Toscane* of Luigi Alamanni, tells in his preface to the *Triumphs* of Petrarch how much pleasure he found in the Tuscan tongue. Like many of the early printers he was a scholar, a man on friendly terms with the intellectual élite of Lyons, and one who was highly respected by his colleagues.

After his death in 1564 he was succeeded by his son Jean de Tournes II, who in October of that year was appointed to the office of King's Printer enjoyed by his father. But Jean II lived in troubled times, when France was plagued by religious wars. In 1567 trouble came to a head in Lyons when the Protestant forces tried to capture the city but were defeated by the Catholic army. As a result, many Protestant sympathisers, among whom was de Tournes, were imprisoned. The printer spent more than two months in prison before he was released, only to find his house pillaged and his workshop stripped of material. Often harassed he nevertheless continued to print, and in 1569 published what might have been a fine *Suetonius* had he been able to procure paper as good as that used by his father.

Towards the end of 1584 he became so uneasy about his future that he drew up his will; but though his life was not endangered he was forced to leave friends and country and went, as did so many other printers of similar religious persuasion, to Geneva, where he died in 1615. It was not until 1728 that the firm of de Tournes returned to Lyons in the persons of Jean-Jacques and Jacques de Tournes, who set up as booksellers in that city.

Born about 1518 at Dolus, near Loches in Touraine, Guillaume Roville or Rouillé* was for almost half a century one of the leading bookseller-publishers in Lyons. He had been trained in that business at Venice with Giovanni Giolito and his son Gabriele, with whom he continued business relations. Soon after his arrival in Lyons he married Madeleine de Portonariis, daughter of Domenico and niece of Giovanni Giolito's some-time partner Vicento de Portonariis.

Unlike Gryphe, Roville did not specialise, but published anything that promised a substantial profit. His apprenticeship in Venice, and the establishment

---

* Baudrier favours Rouillé. The *Nouvelle Biographie Générale* says Roville, *not* Rouillé.

of his brothers-in-law in Spain, gave him an outlet for his books both in Spain and Italy. Although forced to compete with Jean de Tournes, he never produced work of comparable quality, being more concerned with quick production; nevertheless the printers who worked for him, such as Etienne Roussin, Jean Ausoult, Philippe Rollet and Berthélemy Frein, were all excellent printers if not of the standard of Jean de Tournes. Roville was, above all, an astute man of business and to defray costs he shared many of his publications with his colleagues.

One member of the Giunta family, famous at Venice and Florence, settled in Lyons and he and his heirs were prominent there throughout the sixteenth century. This was Giacomo or Jacques Giunta, who was born at Florence in 1486 and learned the trade of bookseller-publisher at Venice with his uncle, Luc-Antonio Giunta. Provided with ample funds, he established a publishing house and for twenty-seven years, from 1520 until his death in 1547, he employed a score of printers and published a great number of books, mainly in the fields of theology, jurisprudence and medicine. He became head of the important 'Compagnie des Libraires lyonnais', and had agents and depôts all over Europe. Moreover, since there were members of the Giunta family working not only in Venice and Florence but also at Genoa, Burgos, Salamanca and Madrid, a profitable marketing network was assured over a large part of Europe. Under the circumstances it is not surprising that Jacques Giunta was able, in 1537, to lend Cardinal de Tournon the sum of 50,000 *livres tournois* to be employed on royal business. The firm he founded at Lyons was carried on by his heirs until 1599, and after that by Horace Cardon and his successors up to the time of the French Revolution.

In a work of this nature it is not possible to devote space to all the Lyons printers of the sixteenth century, for Baudrier in his great work on the subject gives a 'Liste générale des imprimeurs et libraires de Lyon aux XVe et XVIe siècles' which contains some 160 names! Among the most important were the following: Jean Barbou, called 'Le Normand', active at Lyons 1524-42, was the founder of the celebrated family of printer-publishers of that name. In 1539 he printed in a neat italic an edition of the works of Clément Marot for François Juste, himself a printer and publisher. Claude Nourry comes into the limelight as the first publisher of *Pantagruel* by 'Alcofrybas Nasier', otherwise François Rabelais. Undated, it was probably on sale at the Lyons Fair in November 1532. An edition was published in the following year by the above-mentioned François Juste. The brothers Jean and François Frellon were among the prominent printer-publishers of Lyons, where they worked between 1530 and 1570. François Frellon is justly remembered for having published at Lyons in 1538 *Les simulachres et historiees faces de la mort*, the Dance of Death, with woodcuts generally thought to have been cut by Hans Lützelburger after the designs of

171

Hans Holbein. The printers of this book were Melchoir and Gaspard Trechsel, the sons of Johann. Gaspard was one of the printers who moved to Vienne in 1541 owing to the serious journeymen's strike in Lyons, but he returned there in 1544.

Denis de Harsy and his son Antoine between them were active printers for half a century, from 1523 until 1574. Benoist Rigaud, a rather neglected printer who could at times rival the best, had a lengthy business career, from 1550 until the end of the century. The best-known and most skilful of four Rigaud brothers (the others were Simon, Pierre and Claude), he specialised in romances of chivalry, including three editions of *Amadis de Gaule*.

The Arnoullets were another famous family of Lyons printers and publishers. Altogether no fewer than ten members of the Arnoullet family were printers or booksellers at Lyons between 1485 and the beginning of the seventeenth century. The founder of the dynasty was Jacques Arnoullet, who died in 1504. His son Olivier, as we have seen, printed many works of popular literature, but Balthazar, the eldest of his grandsons, deserves a place among the great printers of his day. Born about 1517, he presumably learned his trade from his father, and when he was about twenty years old he entered the printing house of Jean Barbou as a journeyman. Not long afterwards he became that printer's son-in-law by marrying Denise Barbou in 1541.

Jean Barbou died the following year and Balthazar Arnoullet took over the business under the style of 'Balthazar Arnoullet et les héritiers de Jean Barbou'. His talents were recognised by one of the leading Lyons booksellers, Hughes de la Porte, for whom he printed several volumes of jurisprudence. In 1546 he explored a new field with his *Epitomes des Rois de France*, which was the first French book to be illustrated with copper engraved portraits done by Claude Corneille, known as Corneille de la Haye.

Among the books by which Balthazar Arnoullet is best known are his editions of Fuchs, *De historia stirpium* (1549), the *Décades* of B. Aneau (1549), Guillaume Guéroult, *Chroniques des Empereurs* (1552), and the *Epitome de la Corographie d'Europe* (1553) containing plans of various cities. He is also known as the clandestine printer of the treatise on the doctrine of the Trinity by Michael Servetus called *Christianismi Restitutio*. This book, printed at Vienne in Dauphiné in 1553, formed one of the main charges brought by Calvin against Servetus, who was burned at the stake together with his book, on 27 October of that year. All copies of the book which could be found were destroyed and the first disclosure to the world at large of the existence of this book was made in Dr William Wotton, *Reflections upon Learning, Ancient and Modern*, published at London in 1694.

The first known book to have been printed at **Bordeaux** was *La Traité contre la peste . . . par maistre Gabriel Tarague, docteur en medicine*. This small quarto of ten leaves, printed in gothic type, appeared in 1519 and was the work of Gaspard Philippe, who settled at Bordeaux in 1518, having previously worked in Paris from 1499. Only one copy of this work is recorded and is in the Bibliothèque Mazarine, Paris.

Philippe printed little at Bordeaux, for he died in 1520, the business being taken over by his chief workman Jehan Guyart, who married his patron's widow, Gillette, and was an active printer in Bordeaux for twenty years. About thirty works from his press have survived.

The first recorded printer at **Clermont-Ferrand** was Jacques Mareschal, who in 1523 brought out *Les Ordonnances royales*, which has the colophon 'Nouvellement imprimé à Clermont par Jacques Mareschal'. But whether the book was actually printed at Clermont is doubtful. Mareschal, who was a printer-publisher at Lyons from 1498 until 1529, had depôts for the sale of books both in Paris and at Clermont-Ferrand, and it is quite possible that the book mentioned was actually printed at Lyons.

Still further south, printing was introduced into **Aix-en-Provence** in 1552 with the *Reiglement des advocats* from the press of Vas Cavallis, and in the same year Jean de Vingle and Pierre Poivre became the first printers at **Pau**, their first book being *Los Fors et Costumas de Béarn*, written in the dialect of Béarn.

Guyon Boudeville worked at Toulouse from 1541 until 1562. Previously a journeyman, he set up as a master printer in the rue Villeneuve, occupying the premises of Nicolas Vieillard, whose press and material he took over and from whom he had perhaps learned his craft. There he printed Pierre Merchadier, *Blason de la Perle*, and possibly the *Alphabetum seu Instructio Sacerdotum* which bears no imprint. Later he moved to premises near the Collège de Foix, as we see from his imprint 'e regione Fuxi'. A book of local interest was the *Histoire tolosaine* of Antoine Noguier, which he printed in 1556. His most elaborate production was the *Epitome . . . des dix livres de Vitruve* compiled by Jean Gardet and illustrated with thirty-five copper-plate engravings by the architect Dominique Bertin – the fourth in date (1559) of books with copper-plate engravings printed in France.

Almost nothing is known of the designers and cutters of letters who worked for the printers of the fifteenth century. Indeed it is not until around 1530 that we may begin to identify typefaces with a known punch-cutter. France, in particular, can claim some of the finest punch-cutters of the sixteenth century, with names like Augereau, Garamond, Granjon, Haultin and Le Bé, together with the somewhat lesser figures of Simon de Colines and Jacques Sabon.

One of the most celebrated of French punch-cutters was Claude Garamond (c. 1480–1561). We spell his name nowadays with a final 'd', but he himself spelt his name Garamont, a spelling we find in the colophons of some books he published, on his portrait engraved by Léonard Gaultier, and on official acts during his lifetime. Only in the manuscript notes of Guillaume I Le Bé, his pupil, do we find for the first time the 'd' instead of 't'. Even Lottin, in his *Catalogue* of 1789,* spells the name 'Garramont'. But the 'd' spelling has now become universal.

Garamond was not himself a printer, but he published a few books in partnership with Pierre Gaultier, a printer whose daughter Guillemette he married. As a punch-cutter he worked in close collaboration with the printer Robert Estienne, and the fount which Estienne used for his superb *Biblia Sacra* of 1532, a fount based on the Aldine roman of 1495, was probably cut by Garamond. Others of his series of roman types appeared at intervals in the books issued by Rober Estienne. 'By the time of his death in 1561,' writes Mr Carter, 'there was in general use a range of roman types of uniform design distinguished by their graceful proportions and brilliance of cut that was attributed to this artist by such trustworthy authorities as Christophe Plantin and Jacob Sabon' (Carter, 1969).

But the name of Garamond is especially associated with the celebrated Royal Greek types, some of which were shown for the first time in the exceedingly rare *Alphabetum Graecum*, an octavo pamphlet of sixteen leaves printed and published at Paris by Robert Estienne in 1543.

Until 1540 Robert Estienne used Greek type similar to that employed by Conrad Néobar, the King's Printer in Greek. Néobar (who, unlike Estienne, was not a printer by profession) died in 1540 and his official title passed to Estienne, who was already King's Printer in Hebrew and Latin. On 1 October 1541 the king, François Ier, granted his royal printer an order on the Treasury for the sum of 225 *livres tournois* to be paid through him to Claude Garamond to defray the cost of cutting punches for special Greek founts known afterwards as the 'Grecs du Roi'.

The designs for these types were based on the handwriting of Angelos Vergetios, a scribe and cataloguer in charge of the royal collection of Greek manuscripts at Fontainebleau. The exceptional beauty of his calligraphy is shown to advantage in his manuscript of Aristotle's *Politics* preserved at the Imprimerie Nationale and which served as a model for Garamond.

These Greek types were cut in three sizes: *gros parangon* (which approximated to the English double pica); *gros romain* (English great primer); and *cicéro* (English long primer). The three sizes are shown in the handsome Greek edition of *Appiani Alexandrini Romanarum Historiarum* published in 1551, 'one of the most exquisite books printed from these founts' according to Updike (*Printing Types*, 1922). Apart from the *Greek Alphabet* of 1543 already mentioned, the first full-length book to make use of one of these founts was the

---

* Lottin, A.M. *Catalogue chronologique des Libraires et les Libraires – Imprimeurs de Paris.*

Praeparatio Evangelica of Eusebius (1544), a folio set in the second size of type, the *gros romain*. Two years later the *cicéro* was used for a 16mo *New Testament*, whilst the *gros parangon* made its first appearance in a folio edition of the same work, published in 1550.

These founts, although undeniably beautiful, would not be practical for use in the majority of books today, for the number of ligatures would be found excessive, and indeed called for the cutting of an almost incredible number of punches, and setting from these types cannot have been easy.*

Among the most prolific type-designers and punch-cutters of the sixteenth century was Robert Granjon, born in Paris about 1513 and possibly the son of Jean Granjon, a bookseller in Paris from 1504 to 1522. We know next to nothing of his early years, but he had his own business in Paris by 1545, in which year he took as his apprentice a certain Hubert d'Armilliers (according to Renouard's spelling).† This must surely be the 'Hubertus Danvillier, fondeur de lettres' who arrived in London in 1551 and obtained his denisation on 28 January 1553. The 'Anthony Danvillier, fusor typographus' who received letters of denisation on 30 May 1567 was presumably his younger brother.

In 1549 Robert Granjon began to publish books, at first by himself and later in partnership with Michel Fezendat until 1551. His output of punches and matrices over a period of more than forty years was extremely large, beginning with the italic he supplied to Jean de Tournes and to Sebastien Gryphe about 1543 (the first face which can be attributed with some certainty to him). Granjon was without doubt a highly skilled craftsman and A. F. Johnson has described him as 'without a rival in that age as a designer of the cursive family of types'.

The earliest known publication of Robert Granjon is a New Testament in Greek and Latin dated 1549 which bears the address: *Apud Robertum Granion, in taberna Gryphiana* – the former dwelling of François Gryphe, brother of Sébastien, who worked there from 1532 to 1545. Whether Granjon himself cut the type for this book it is hard to say, for copies of the same publication are known bearing the imprint of Jacques du Puys and also of Michel Fézendat.

Shortly before 1557 Granjon moved to Lyons, where he married Antoinette, the daughter of the famous engraver and illustrator Bernard Salomon. In 1557 he made typographic history by publishing I. Ringhieri, *Dialogue de la vie et de la mort*, set in a new script type of his own design, which he termed *lettre françoise* and which later became known as *Civilité* from the fact that it was frequently used for setting the courtesy books for children, of which the most widely circulated was the *De civilitate morum puerorum libellus* by Erasmus,

---

* The subsequent curious history of the matrices and punches of the 'Grecs du Roi' is related by Raymond Blanchot in the *Gutenberg Jahrbuch*, 1957.
† Ph. Renouard, *Imprimeurs et Libraires Parisiens du XVIe siècle*. Paris, 1964.

FIGURE 43. Title-page of *Dialogue de la vie et de la mort*, by Innocenzio Ringhieri, printed by Robert Granjon in the type which he called 'lettre françoise' and was later known as Civilité type. Lyons, 1558. This is the second edition, the first having been published in 1557.

together with its numerous adaptations, which were known in France as *La Civilité puérile*. The history of these early script types has been dealt with at length in H. Carter and H. D. L. Vervliet, *Civilité Types* (Oxford, 1966).

Although Granjon was, as Bernard Salomon termed him in his will, 'maistre imprimeur, citoyen de Lyon', after about 1562 he was to be found in a number of cities – Antwerp, Frankfurt, Paris and Rome. He seems to have spent a considerable time in Antwerp between 1563 and 1570, and while there he cut type for Willem Silvius and Christopher Plantin. From 1572 to about 1575 he was in Paris, after which he returned to Lyons for a couple of years. In 1578 he went to Rome where he was working until his death on 16 November 1589.

'Probably his most distinguished work,' writes A. F. Johnson, 'was done as a designer of italic types,' and that authority has enumerated them in an article, *The Italic Types of Robert Granjon.** He also cut some romans, one of which was used by Paolo Manuzio, as well as Greek and the oriental types which occupied his long stay in Rome, where he was employed by Domenica Basa, technical director of the Stamperia Vaticana and by the celebrated orientalist Giambattista Raimondi, scientific director of the renowned Stamperia Medicea.

In 1579 he cut an Armenian type, a specimen of which he presented to Pope Gregory XIII at a special audience. 'This,' writes Dr Vervliet, 'is a superb letter, superior by far to that produced by contemporaries like Leonhard Thurneyser zum Thurn a few years later, in 1583, in his oriental printing-office at Berlin.' It was used in the Armenian calendar printed by Domenico Basa in 1584. It also appears in the *Hydragiologia* of Marco Colonna, bishop of Salerno, printed at Rome by Bonfadini in 1586.

Although there is no explicit proof, it is practically certain that the syriac type used in the *Catechism* of 1580 printed for presentation to the Lebanese Synod was the work of Granjon, for there was no other punch-cutter then working in Rome who could have done it so well. This was followed by a Cyrillic alphabet shown in Roccha, *Bibliotheca Apostolica Vaticana* (Rome, 1591).

In 1582 appeared the only known volume bearing the imprint of Granjon at Rome, the *Directorium Chori ad usum sacrosanctae Basilice Vaticanae*, etc., 'Rome. Apud Robertum GranIon Parisien'. This is a rare work, but it must be confessed that the printing, as shown by the copy in the Music Library at the British Museum, is not of a very high standard. Although Granjon's name is on the title-page, there is no proof that he was responsible for the music type.

In addition to the exotic types already mentioned, Granjon also cut, during his residence in Rome, several sizes of arabic and possibly the Hebrew used by the Stamperia Medicea.

At an earlier stage in his career Granjon was for a short time a music publisher, but his activities in that field were limited to little over a year, during which he brought out four music books: *Chansons Nouvelles* of Beaulaigue (1558–59); *Motets* by the same composer (1559); and the *Premier* and *Second Trophée de Musique* (1559). In December 1557 he had formed a partnership with Guillaume Guéroult and Jehan Hiesse with a view to publishing music, but a dispute

* *The Library*. XXI. 3 & 4. Dec. 1940–March 1941. pp. 291 ff.

between the partners, followed by a law suit, brought the association to an end by the beginning of 1560.

Granjon was renowned particularly as a designer of italic types and the Granjon italic became as widespread among European printers as was the roman of Garamond. Generally speaking, the slope of his cursive types is much more pronounced than we find in the italics of Aldus and Arrighi and their imitators. A. F. Johnson lists fourteen italic types cut by Granjon 'among the best of the sixteenth century'.

15

Swiss Printing in the Sixteenth Century

IN the year 1537 Matthias Biener, better known perhaps by the Latinised form of his name, Matthias Apiarius, set up the first press at **Bern**. He came from Bavaria – his birthplace the little town of Berchingen – and he is first heard of as a bookbinder at Nuremberg. After his arrival in Switzerland around 1525 he is said to have learned how to print at Basel, and then went to Strassburg, where he printed from 1533 to 1537, in which year he settled at Bern. A short time previously he had printed a series of musical works in collaboration with Peter Schöffer II. Why he broke off his partnership with Schöffer and went to Bern no one knows.

His first book at Bern was a *Compendium Musices* by the Lüneburg cantor Lampadius. Among the larger works which came from the press of Apiarius were the Chronicles of Sebastian Franck, a history of the Milan wars and a *Catalogus*, a compendium of world history by Valerius Anshelm. From 1543 onwards he printed for other publishers, notably for Johann Oporin at Basel and for his brother-in-law Rupprecht Winter. A large part of Apiarius's work as a printer is known to us solely because he made use of waste pages from them in his bindings, for he still carried on his original trade as a binder.

Matthias Apiarius died towards the end of 1554 and was succeeded in the business by his sons Samuel and Sigfrid, the former looking after the printing office whilst the latter took charge of the bookbinding. As his printer's mark, Apiarius made use of a punning device on his own name – a common practice among many early printers. It shows a bear seeking honey in the trunk of a tree from which issues a swarm of bees (*Biene* in German). Samuel Apiarius became known as a printer of not only religious songs, but also songs of battle or 'Schlachtlieder', such as *Das Lied von der Schlacht beschähen vor Sempach* (1555). He was at one time in trouble with the authorities and banished from the district. During his absence his brother Sigfrid, the bookbinder, took over the printing office and printed, *inter alia*, *Ein hüpsch Lied vom Ursprung der Eydgnoschafft*, which has on its title-page a cut of William Tell shooting at the apple on his son's head. Sigfrid (who was also the town piper) died in 1565; his brother died in Basel in 1590, and the business was carried on for a while under the style of 'the Heirs of Samuel Apiarius'.

Another printer who worked in Bern during the latter half of the sixteenth century was Bendicht Ulman, active from 1561 until 1593. He had probably been at one time apprenticed to Mathias Apiarius, and both he and his step-son Vinzenz Im Hof, in partnership with whom he printed from 1574 until 1593, were also book-binders.

Basel became a most important centre of printing at the beginning of the sixteenth century, for Amerbach, Froben and Johann Petri were all at work there. Especially so during the period which witnessed the collaboration between Erasmus and his friend Johann Froben, for whom he produced his edition of the *New Testament* in Greek and Latin, published in 1516. This was the first attempt to produce a correct version of the Greek text, and although it had its defects it proved immediately successful and served as a basis for the translations of Luther (1522) and Tyndale (*c.* 1525). Froben, who specialised in the publication of Greek books, was the publisher of most of Erasmus's work, and saw himself as the propagator of the humanist ideals. One of the most erudite of the early scholar-printers, Froben soon made his printing office the meeting place of the literary world of his day.

In 1527, Johann Froben died as the result of a fall from a book-ladder. Before his death he had printed more than 250 works, mainly in Latin and Greek, and made of Basel one of the great centres of the book trade in editions of the classics, a number of which he edited himself. Many of his books were decorated with title-pages, borders and illustrations designed by artists of the calibre of Urs Graf and Hans Holbein.

Froben worked with a maximum of seven presses, a large number for that time, and among his many publications the most noteworthy include, apart from his Bibles and the works of Erasmus, the writings of the Church Fathers, such as the ten-volume folio edition of Saint Augustine.

Adam Petri, who worked at Basel from 1507 until 1527 was a nephew of Johannes Petri of Langendorf. He did not encroach on Froben's domain but devoted himself in the main to printing books in the German tongue, and from about 1518 he turned to printing the writings of the Reformers, especially those of Martin Luther. Luther's New Testament made its first appearance at Wittenberg in September 1522, and three months later Adam Petri brought out an edition at Basel. After his death in 1528 the business was continued by his son Heinrich (Henricpetri) who published chiefly editions of the Greek and Latin classics. He also brought out several editions of the famous *Cosmography* of Sebastian Münster.

Johann Oporin, active from 1541 until 1566, was another Basel printer of importance, who had been for a while a Corrector for Froben. Probably the most important book to come from his office was Andreas Vesalius, *De humani corporis fabrica*, issued in 1543. This work is a landmark in the history of medicine and marks the beginning of modern anatomical studies. Its merit was enhanced by the truly remarkable illustrations, by an unknown artist, once thought to have been John of Calcar, a pupil of Titian. After some initial trouble with the magistrature, Oporin was eventually allowed to print the Koran in a Latin version by the Zürich theologian, Theodor Bibliander, and this appeared in folio in December 1542, with the editor's 'pro Alcorani editione apologia'.

From another Basel printing office, that of Michael Isengrin, came two works of considerable importance. In 1542 appeared Leonhard Fuchs, *De historia stirpium commentarii*, one of the most famous of early herbals, with its 512 superb woodcuts. In 1556 Isengrin published Georgius Agricola, *De re metallica*, the author's most widely known work and the first systematic treatise on metallurgy and mining. Illustrated with splendid woodcuts by Hans Rudolf Deutsch, it was for long the standard work on the subject. Incidentally, an English translation was made in 1912 by Herbert Hoover, who later became President of the United States.

The most famous Zürich printer of the sixteenth century was Christoph Froschauer, a native of Ottingen in Bavaria. He was probably the son of the printer Hans Froschauer who worked at Augsburg from 1494 to 1507. In 1519 Cristoph became a citizen of Zürich and set up his press there in 1521. His first known work, printed in that year, consisted of two German translations of Erasmus: *Ein Klag des Frydens* and *Ein nützliche ynderwysung.* . . .

Froschauer was quick to print Luther's Bible, and his first edition (with the Apocrypha translated by Leo Juda) came out in three folio volumes, 1524–29. In the following year he brought out a second edition in a single volume, octavo, and in 1531, the third edition, revised, in one folio volume embellished with many woodcuts. Though the major part of the text was that of Luther, some parts were newly translated by the preachers of Zürich. A fourth edition, quarto, without illustrations, appeared in 1534.

In 1545 Froschauer printed the *Bibliotheca universalis* of Conrad Gesner (1516–65), the earliest alphabetical general bibliography. A folio of 631 leaves, it lists some 12,000 works in Latin, Greek and Hebrew. In 1548–49 there followed the Subject Index in twenty volumes. In 1548 Froschauer printed the *Swiss Chronicle* of Hans Stumpf, in the first volume of which is an interesting woodcut of a press at work, showing the forme run out after an impression and the pressman removing the freshly printed sheet.

Froschauer was for many years a regular visitor to the twice-yearly Frankfurt Fair where he did profitable business. On such occasions his printing office was left in the capable hands of his brother Eusebius and the latter's two sons Eusebius and Christoph. When the elder Froschauer died in 1564 he left the business, since he himself was childless, to his nephew Christoph Froschauer II, who never married and at his death in 1585 the business came to an end. Eventually the printing office itself was acquired by Johann Wolf.

One must not forget another work of Gesner, which was also published by

Froschauer, for the *Historia animalium* of that author really marks the starting point of modern zoology. The first of the five volumes was published at Zürich in 1551, the last appearing in 1587, twenty-two years after the author's death. Its excellent illustrations, some by Gesner himself, were frequently copied.

FIGURE 44. A page from Conrad Gesner, *Historia Animalium* printed by Froschauer in Zurich in five folio volumes between 1551 and 1587. The animals shown are the Lynx (top) and what Gesner describes as the Patagonian Su.

Geneva was, of course, the great centre of the Reformation during the sixteenth century, and with the outbreak of the Wars of Religion many Protestant printers from France found it wise to transfer their activities to Geneva and other Swiss cities, so that the number of printers working in Geneva grew steadily. What Basel was to Germany as a production centre of Reformation writings, so Geneva was to France. Conrad Badius arrived there in 1549 and Robert Estienne in the following year. In 1551 came Jean Crespin. These were but three of many. 'The number of printers and booksellers officially admitted as residents during 1550–57 exceeded sixty,' writes Mrs Elizabeth Armstrong, 'ranging from established merchant printers to journeymen.'

Among the Geneva printers of the second half of the sixteenth century we find Henri Estienne, Eustace Vignon, François and Jean Le Preux, Thomas Courteau, Jacon Stoer, Abel Rivery, Jean Bonnefoy, François Perrin, and Antoine Blanc. In 1557 Conrad Badius printed for the Marian exiles in Geneva an English version of the Scriptures in a twelvemo edition, easily pocketable, and in 1560 appeared a fine quarto edition of the whole Bible in English, translated by William Whittingham and his colleagues, and printed by Rowland Hall at the press set up in Geneva by the English refugees. The popularity of this Geneva Bible was so great that by 1644 no fewer than 140 editions had been printed.

Robert Estienne, after his arrival in Geneva lost no time in settling down to work. Apart from the works of the Reformers such as Calvin, Théodore de Bèze and Martin Bucer, he printed in 1554 a revised *Alphabetum hebraicum* following the pattern of his Paris edition of 1554, and in 1557 he brought out his improved edition of the 1545 Bible in three folio volumes with a new translation by Théodore de Bèze, which was immediately pirated by Oporin at Basel, and Nicholas Barbier at Zürich. After the death of Robert Estienne in 1559, the printing office was managed by Henri II Estienne, the most gifted of his sons. The latter's greatest achievement was the *Thesaurus linguae graecae* completed in 1572, a worthy parallel to his father's Latin *Thesaurus*.

Another refugee from France for religious reasons was Pierre de Vingle,* a native of Lyons, where he first worked as a journeyman and later foreman for Claude Nourry, called Le Prince, whose only daughter Catherine he married in 1525. He went into partnership with his father-in-law in 1526, but five years later he had to leave Lyons for having printed *Unio dissidentium* by the Lutheran Hermann Badius. He fled to Switzerland, but being refused permission to set up a press in Geneva, he printed clandestinely. Later he removed to Neuchâtel and the first book he printed there was *Le Livre des marchans* a violent satire against the papacy by Antoine Marcour, which was completed on 22 August

* He was also known as 'Pirot Picard'.

1533 and published with the fictitious imprint 'Imprimé à Corinthe . . .'. A number of his publications were printed with false names and addresses.

Pierre de Vingle printed many of the writings of the Reformers, and in 1534 he brought out the first French Protestant version of the Bible, translated by Pierre Robert Olivetan. This is often referred to as the *Bible de Serrières* from the name of the village close to Neuchâtel where de Vingle had his printing office.

One of the most important works ever printed in Switzerland was the *Christianiae religionis institutio* of Jean Calvin (1509–64), published at Basel in 1536 by Thomas Platter and B. Lasius. This, the first published statement of the fundamental doctrine of Calvinism, was a work of tremendous influence, afterwards published in almost innumerable editions and translations.

Yet another refugee from religious persecution was Thomas Guarin, who in 1557 arrived at Basel from Tournai. He later married the daughter of Michael Isingrin, to whose business he succeeded. He had a long career as a printer–publisher and among those who worked for him was the artist Tobias Stimmer.

Prominent among Genevan printers after the middle of the sixteenth century was Thomas Courteau (Curteus), once an agent for Robert Estienne when the latter was still in Paris. Courteau's name is first found on the books he printed in 1557 in partnership with Nicolas Barbier. In 1563 he was working with two presses, but in the following year he obtained permission to install a third press. His work must therefore have seemed important to the authorities, for according to the Genevan Council Register of 25 June 1563, only three printers were allowed four presses: Henri II Estienne, Antoine Vincent, and Jean Crespin. After the death of his partner, Courteau printed on his own account until 1567, the year of his death.

There were, of course, a host of other printers in Geneva at this time, and the city became for France as important as was Basel for Germany in the field of book exports.

16

Sixteenth Century Printing in Spain

THE typography of Spanish books during the sixteenth century shows no marked change from that of the incunabula period until well after the middle of the century. The isolated position of Spain together with the innate conservatism of the Spanish people precluded any rapid changes of fashion. Printers remained faithful to the manuscript tradition long after it had been abandoned elsewhere. Until the middle of the century a heavy black letter was customary for the text and roman type did not come into general use in Spain until fairly late. The title was often cut on wood, and the imprint was usually to be found in the colophon, as in the earliest printed books.

Spanish printing was shared by a number of cities and not, as in England, confined mainly to the capital. For one thing, there was no fixed capital in Spain until 1560, and even then there was no printing in Madrid until 1566. The total number of books printed in Spain in the course of the century was by no means large, for it was less than the output of the town of Lyons alone during the same period.

At the beginning of the century Seville had a press which ranks high in Spain's printing history, for Jacobo and Juan Cromberger made Seville a centre of good printing in the Spanish style. It is generally accepted that they were father and son. Jacobo was a German and says so in some of his colophons; but Juan is never so described, possibly because his mother was Spanish.

For a time Jacobo worked in partnership with Ladislao Polono and their first production was, according to Don Joaquín Hazanas y la Rúa,* *Passiones quas beatissimi apostoli*, completed in March 1503. In the same year they printed *El Libro de Marco polo veneciano*, the first edition in Spanish of that famous work.

On 12 June 1539, a contract was concluded between Juan Cromberger and another Seville printer Juan Pablos (Giovanni Paoli, a native of Brescia), by which the latter, accompanied by his wife and Gil Barbero, his pressman, were to go to Mexico and set up a press in Mexico City, which they were to manage for Cromberger. They arrived in Mexico City in September of that year and the first known imprint from this printing-office, the first in Mexico, was a *Manual de Adultos*, completed by Juan Pablos on 13 December 1540. He is

* *La imprenta en Sevilla.* Seville, 1892.

thought to have printed earlier *Breve y mas compendiosa doctrina christiana*, but no trace of this book can now be found.

Despite the rather onerous terms of the contract, Pablos worked for Cromberger the stipulated ten years, after which he purchased the business, and from then onward his name appears in the colophon of the books he printed. He obtained from the Viceroy a privilege giving him the exclusive right to print in Mexico. This brought a protest from a number of other printers, among them Antonio de Espinosa, who had thought of emigrating to this New World. However, in 1550 Espinosa signed a contract with Juan Pablos to go to America and work in the latter's establishment as punch-cutter and founder. In 1558, when the profession of printer in Mexico was thrown open to all, Espinosa set up a press on his own account and in 1559 published the *Gramática* of Maturini. His printing did not differ much from that of Pablos, for whom he probably continued to cast type.

Juan Cromberger was active for a shorter period than his father and in consequence he printed fewer books. He specialised in religious works and editions of the classics, and made use of some elaborate borders to be seen for example in his editions of Josephus (1532) and Marcus Aurelius (1533). He died in 1540 and the firm continued until 1557 under the style of Juan y Jácobo Cromberger.

Apart from the large printing offices in Salamanca, Seville, Saragossa and Valladolid, Spanish printing as a whole presented at the outset of the century a somewhat heterogeneous mixture of borders and woodcuts combined with a heavy, but in its way impressive, gothic type. During the first part of the sixteenth century we find the German Peter Hagenbach turning out a Mozarabic Breviary and Missal at Toledo in 1502 in the style of manuscripts, and Jorge Coci at Saragossa, who took over the Hurus establishment in 1506, also printed some elaborate liturgical books, including a *Missale Romanum* in 1510. The second half of the century ushered in a more restrained style, influenced in its classical sobriety by the Spanish books imported from France and the Netherlands.

During the course of the century new printing offices sprang up in various Spanish towns, but towards the end of the century the standards of Spanish printing began to decline, partly owing to the numerous wars in which the country became involved under Philip II, which resulted in a drain upon the financial resources of the country. This had its effect upon the printing industry, which also had to contend with a decline in standards of workmanship and a deterioration in the quality of paper, as well as in artistic taste.

As soon as the *Corte* was established in permanent fashion in Madrid in 1561 and the city had become the new capital, its population began to grow at an extraordinary rate. The increased demand for books, which had previously been met by Toledo and Alcalá, led to the setting up of the first press in **Madrid** itself.

Until 1566 the chief distributors of books in Madrid were Francisco López the elder, a bookseller of Valladolid who published a number of books printed for him at Alcalá by Andrés de Angulo, and Alonso Gómez, 'librero en Corte', for whom books were printed, also at Alcalá, chiefly by Juan de Villanueva. It was Gómez who established the first printing office in Madrid during the second half of 1566 in partnership with Pierres Cosín. Their first printing was a royal decree concerning the price of bread, but their first book was Inigo López de Mendoza, *Proverbios y Sentencias*, a 12mo of 108 leaves, dated 1566.

The partnership did not last long, for by the end of 1567 Gómez was printing on his own and in 1568 Cosín had his own business. Until his death in 1584 Alonso Gómez was the chief printer in Madrid and from 1567 was granted the title of 'Impresor del Rey' – a title which was continued by his widow, who carried on the business until she died in 1595.

None of the Madrid printers of the sixteenth century were very proficient technically. One of the best was Pedro Madrigal who began to print there in 1586 and died in 1594. He printed a number of books both in Spanish and Latin, including a Spanish translation of Tasso, *Ierusalem libertada*, 1587, and in 1589 the first edition of Antonio de Herrera, *Historia de lo sucedido en Escocia é Inglaterra en quarenta y quatro años que bivio Maria Estuarda, Reyna de Escocia*.

In keeping with the status of the new capital, Philip II inaugurated an *Imprenta Real*, with Tomás Junti as its first printer. Junti began his new office in 1594, but in the books he printed up to 1596 there is no mention of his title of 'Impresor del Rey' or of the 'Imprenta Real', which may have been out of deference to the widow of Alonso Gómez, who still used the title of 'Impresora del Rey'. She died at the end of 1595 or beginning of 1596, and several works printed by Junti in the latter year bear the words 'En la Imprenta Real', but with no mention of the printer's name. Tomás Junti was active until the year of his death, 1624.

Printing was introduced into **Alcalá de Henares**, birthplace of Catherine of Aragon and Miguel Cervantes, in the year 1502 by Stanislao Polono, who had previously worked at Seville with Meinhardt Ungut. In 1502 he migrated to Alcalá, attracted no doubt by the growing importance of the town, which six years later had its own university, founded by the famous Cardinal Ximinez de Cisneros. The first work printed in Alcalá was a handsome four-volume edition of Ludolphus de Saxonia, *Vita Christi*, in the Spanish translation of Montesino. The title-page bears the royal arms and a woodcut showing the author presenting a volume of his work to Ferdinand and Isabella.

Alcalá's most famous printer during this century was Arnao Guillén de Brocar, who first printed there in 1511, having previously worked at Pamplona and at Logroño. During the years 1514 to 1517 he successfully carried through the task of printing the first complete polyglot Bible. This six-volume folio Bible was produced under the patronage and at the expense of Cardinal Francisco Ximenez de Cisneros, Archbishop of Toledo. The languages employed in this Bible, often referred to as the 'Complutensian Polyglot' from the Roman name for the city, were Latin, Greek, Hebrew and Chaldee.

Brocar was a prolific printer, and some fifty books are known to have been printed by him at Logroño, where he maintained a press for many years. Among the books he issued there was a fine edition of Fernando Perez de Guzman, *Cronica del rey don Juan el Segundo* (1517) which was printed by command of the Emperor Charles V. From 1503 onwards Brocar printed the Latin grammars of Antonio de Nebrija, the famous humanist of Salamanca University. Brocar also printed at Valladolid, Burgos and Toledo.

Another renowned Spanish press of the period was that of Jorge Coci at Saragossa. Like many other early printers in Spain he was of German origin, and the original form of his name was probably Georg Koch. He took over the press previously run by the brothers Pablo and Juan Hurus, and in September 1499, signed a *Breviary* of the Hieronymite Order in conjunction with Leonhard Hutz and Wolf Appentegger (a nephew of Pablo Hurus). From 1506 he printed alone, and since there was at the time no other press in Aragon proper, Coci had the monopoly of certain classes of official printing. Hieronymus Roman, in his *Republicas del Mundo* (1575) says of Coci that he did more than any other printer for the spread of printing in Spain. After his death the press at Saragossa was continued by his son-in-law Bartolomé de Nagera, at first in association with Pedro Bernuz. But after a short time the partnership was dissolved and each worked independently at Saragossa for some years, though they probably came to some mutual arrangement for we find the first edition of Juan de Yciar, *Recopilacion subtilissima intitulada Orthographia practica* was printed in 1548 by Bartolomé de Nagera, while the second edition, retitled *Arte subtilissima por la qual se ensenar a escrivir perfectamente*, was printed in 1550 by Pedro Bernuz.

This famous writing book was the work of the young Biscayan, Juan de Yciar, who had settled in Saragossa as a calligrapher and writing-master, and the engraver Jean de Vingles, a native of Lyons who had for long worked in Spain. The 1550 edition was an enlarged version of the *Orthographia* of 1548, with surrounds of ornamental woodcut borders instead of the fleurons used in the first edition. So popular was this work that it went through at least eight editions between 1548 and 1566. A facsimile of the 1550 edition was published in 1960 by the Oxford University Press, with an English translation of the text by Evelyn Shuckburgh.

At Burgos Fadriqué Aleman, the first printer in that city (see p. 83) continued to work there well into the sixteenth century, and although only eight dated books are known to have come from his press between 1501 and 1508, from then on until the end of his career in 1517 another fifty or more books may be added, including the earliest known edition of the *Historia de la bendita Magdalena* (1514) written at the behest of Queen Isabella. In that year he also printed a verse translation of Dante's *Inferno* by the Archdeacon of Burgos, Pedro Fernandez de Villegas.

Alonso de Melgar was his successor at Burgos, working there from 1519 to 1525, after which there appeared a more important printer in Juan de Junta, a member of the celebrated Florentine family of printers, who took over the business of Alonso de Melgar in 1526. He set up another press at Salamanca in 1532, and other members of the Junta or Giunta family continued printing in Salamanca until the end of the century.

In Valencia the only press which survived from the fourteenth century was that of Cristóbal Cosman, whose last known work was a *Floretus* of December 1517. The work by which he is best known is the *Cancionero general* of 1511, the first edition of this collection of poems compiled by Fernando del Castillo. Although protected by privilege, it was nevertheless pirated, under a different title, by Jacobo Cromberger.

One of the chief printers of Valencia during the first quarter of the century was Juan Joffre, who was a native of Briançon. He began printing at Valencia in 1502 and his last recorded work was dated 22 March 1530. He specialised in books of a local character, often in the Valencian vernacular. He was succeeded by Francisco Diaz Romano, who printed in 1538 a *Historia de Valencia* by P. A. Beuter.

During the second half of the sixteenth century many new presses were established in Spain, for printing made a very late start in many cities; thus Cordoba had no press until 1566, Bilbao waited until 1578, Cadiz had no printing office until 1595, and Málaga not until 1599. These towns were not then as important as they became later, and depended for books on neighbouring cities which possessed a press. The main centres of printing were Seville, Salamanca, Saragossa, Valencia and Barcelona, and towards the end of the century Madrid.

At Granada, where printing was first started by Meinard Ungut and Johann Pegnitzer in 1496, Sancho de Nebrija printed a number of books between 1533 and 1552, including several works by his father, the celebrated grammarian Antonio de Nebrija, whose full name was Antonio Martinez de Xaravia. Sancho was one of the earliest printers in Spain to make use of roman type.

A much finer fount of roman was used by Andres de Angulo at Alcalá for a life of Cardinal Ximenez written by Alvar Gomez de Castro and published in 1569. Updike shows an illustration of this type (*Printing Types*. Ex. 230) and

FIGURE 45. Title-page of the Life of Saint Amaro, by Alfonso Diaz de Osma. Burgos. Juan de Junta 1552.

says of the book 'its simple text-pages are almost Jensonian in their reliance upon pure typography for beauty'.

The three Spanish towns most actively engaged in printing at this time were Seville, Barcelona and Salamanca. In the last-named town A. de Portonariis, a printer related to the Italian family of that name who were publishers at Lyons, brought out in 1550 a Spanish translation of the *Odyssey* which owes nothing to Spanish influence for it is set in the Basel italic then widely used by contemporary printers in Switzerland, France and Italy. A more important Salamanca printer at that time was Juan de Porras, most of whose output was of an academic nature for use by teachers and scholars at the Salamanca University. For much of his later career he was principal printer for the Franciscan Order in Spain.

In 1547 Andrea de Portonariis (like Juan de Junta of Italian origin) settled at Salamanca where he was active for some twenty years, and his press was continued for a further twenty years by members of his family. In 1550 he printed a Homer wholly in italic type, a most unusual style for Spanish literary texts at that period. The text is in Spanish, with the title *De la Ulyxea XIII libros*, and the type probably came from Lyons where he had previously worked.

During the sixteenth century the vihuela, strung and played like a lute, but with a body resembling a guitar, was a favourite solo instrument in Spain, and one 'vihuelista' named Pisador printed or had printed for him at his own house in Salamanca a *Libro de musica de vihuela* (1552), which gives the voice part and the vihuela accompaniment in elaborate but rather crude music printing.

In Barcelona one of the longest established printers of the sixteenth century was Carlos Amoros who printed in that city from 1509 until 1554. In 1534 he printed Father Tomich, *Historias e conquestas dels excellentissims e catholics Reys de Arago*, which bears the arms of Aragon on the title-page. Hans Rosenbach, who had worked in Barcelona since 1492, had a long career which lasted well into the sixteenth century, and during which he printed books not only in Barcelona, but also in Tarragona, Perpignan, and Montserrat.

Diego de Gumiel was among the first native Spaniards to practice the art in his own country, where so many of the early printers were foreigners, mainly German. He began to work at Barcelona in 1494, but later went to Valladolid, and thence to Valencia, where in 1513 he printed a romance called *Question de amor* in which we find some handsome woodcut capitals. The title-page of his *Aurem opus regalium privilegiorum* (1515) shows a very fine crest with the arms of the kingdom of Valencia.

The most active among the printers of Toledo was Juan de Ayala, who worked there from 1530 onwards and produced some eighty known works of various categories. The woodcuts in his books are technically more advanced than those appearing in most Spanish books of that period. Unlike most of his contemporaries, Juan de Ayala did not use gothic type exclusively, for he occasionally made use of roman, particularly for his titling.

The first known printing at Medina del Campo was carried out by the wandering printer Nicolas Gazini of Piedmont who completed on 10 April 1511 an edition of Diego Rodríguez de Almela, *Valerio de las istorias escolasticas*, which he printed for the Salamanca bookseller Josquin Lecaron. However, the most important printer at Medina during the first half of the sixteenth century was Pedro de Castro, who worked for a time in Seville before settling definitely in Medina, where he had already printed in 1538, and from 1541 until about 1550 he printed there a variety of books, mostly in gothic type, although his edition of *Las Obras de Boscán y Garcilaso* (1544) was set in roman.

During the years when the Crombergers were working in Seville, another printer was busy there, one Juan Varela who printed a number of works at Seville between 1514 and 1539, after having previously worked at Toledo. His production comprised romances of chivalry, the works of Spanish authors, and religious and liturgical books, including a *Missale Hispalense* which he printed in 1529, 1530, and 1537.

Other well-known Seville printers of the sixteenth century include Domenico de Robertis (1534-49) and Sebastian Trujillo (1543-67) known principally for his printing of the treatises (nine in all) in favour of the Caribbean Indians by Fr Bartolomé de las Casas.

For the first thirty years of the century, printing at Valencia showed little advance technically, the books produced being mainly in the gothic style of the preceding century. A typical example of Valentian printing at that period is the *Aureum opus regalium privilegiorum et regni Valentiae* printed in 1515 by Cristóbal Kofman. Juan Joffre, a native of Briançon, brought out a number of works interesting mainly for their woodcuts. In 1514 he printed an edition of the well-known *Celestina* or *Tragicomedia de Calisto y Melibea*. Francisco Díaz Romano, from Guadalupe worked in Valencia between 1531 and 1541 in much the same style as his predecessors. When he returned to his native land, his printing office was taken over by Juan Navarro (Juan de Oces).

But printing in Valencia showed a marked change in style with the arrival of Juan Mey, who started to print there about 1536. Mey was a Fleming who came from Opprech, and the authorities of Valencia were so impressed with his work that they allowed him a grant for three years, which was increased in 1551 and 1552. Juan Mey died in 1555 and his business was continued first by his widow and then by his son Pedro Patricio Mey.

Although Mey printed a few books in gothic type, his normal work was executed in roman and italic, and while some of his founts were rather poor, others were quite good. He printed the *Apologia* of the Valentian humanist Juan Battista Agnés (1543) in which the author commends Mey and his partner Juan Baldovino, who were jointly responsible for the work, for their knowledge of languages and writes that they were the first printers in Valencia to set books in Latin, Greek and Hebrew types. One of Mey's most notable works is the *Fori regni Valentiae* (1547-48), a folio with a typical Renaissance border enclosing a large shield on the title-page bearing the imperial arms of Spain, and on the verso a similar border with the arms of Valencia.

During the course of the sixteenth century an enormous number of books were printed in the Spanish language in countries outside Spain – in Italy, in

France, in Portugal, and above all in the Netherlands. From about 1530 onwards Antwerp was a great centre of Spanish printing and books in that language came from the presses of Jan Steels, Martin Nucio, Jean Bellère, Jan Waesberghe, Christopher Plantin, and others.* In the following century Amsterdam, which had supplanted Antwerp in the commercial world, exported a great quantity of books in Spanish, and in Belgium Brussels did likewise.

For the first half of the sixteenth century Spanish typography showed little

FIGURE 46. Title-page of 'Don Quixote', published in Madrid in 1605 by Juan de la Cuesta.

* See further in J. Peeters-Fontainas, *Bibliographie des Impressions Espagnoles des Pays-Bas.* Louvain, 1933.

development, and as Updike has pointed out, books printed in Spain, even after 1550, are almost indistinguishable from incunabula. Books were still designed as folios or large quartos, set in a massive black letter, rather more rounded in form than the early German gothic types. The introduction of roman type, which was at first confined mainly to scholarly texts printed in the university towns such as Salamanca and Alcalá de Henares, received some impetus from printers of Italian origin, like the Juntas and the Portonariis, but its use did not become widespread until after the middle of the century, and when it did the founts employed were not particularly distinguished. But under the influence of books in the vernacular imported from the Netherlands, the style of Spanish printing began to change, especially when the massive volumes of an early day were replaced by smaller sizes, for which the roman letter was both more suitable and more economic. Spanish books printed in the Netherlands were almost always in roman type, and the Spanish printers tried to copy them, but aesthetically without much success, for not only was the gothic style in the Spanish tradition, which was always conservative, but there were difficulties, as the Flemish printer Matthieu Gast found, when he settled in Salamanca, in procuring satisfactory founts of type.

17

Christopher Plantin and his times

In the Netherlands the first part of the sixteenth century was remarkable for a large output of devotional works, many of a mystical nature: a profusion of edifying treatises with titles such as *Hortulus animae*, *Rosarium mysticum*, *Gheestelicke boomgaard*, *Vergier spirituel*, *Evangelishe peerlen* and *Troost der Siele*. Among the works with a mystical tendency which proved most remunerative for the printers were those of Saint Bernard; for instance the *Boecxken van verduldich Lyden* (Michel Hillen van Hoochstraten, 1518 and 1520), *Onser Liever Vrouwen Souter* (Eckert van Homberch, 1503 and 1520) and *Een Boecxken van den hemelschen Wyngaert* (W. Vorsterman, 1537). Just as popular were the works of St Bonaventura, who became general of the Franciscans in 1256 and was later cardinal and bishop of Alba. The works of the 'Seraphic Doctor' were frequently printed in the Netherlands, both in Latin and Dutch.

Lives of Jesus Christ, notably those by Ludolphus de Saxonia and St Bonaventura, were even more popular in the Netherlands than elsewhere in Europe. The original Latin text, printed for the first time at Strassburg in 1474, and a translation of which was the first incunable in the Portuguese language, appeared at Antwerp in a Flemish version in 1487 (G. de Leeu). In that same city, at the beginning of the sixteenth century, six editions of this work were printed before 1536, shared between Eckert van Homberch, Adrien van Berghen and Claes de Grave. Numerous, also, were the Netherlands editions of Jean Charlier de Gerson and of Thomas à Kempis.

Some 4,000 books were produced in the Netherlands during the first forty years of the sixteenth century and more than half of these were produced in the city of Antwerp alone. The reason is simple. Antwerp, during the first half of the century was a city of extraordinary prosperity, having inherited the departed glories of Bruges, then but a shadow of the great mart it had been in the thirteenth and fourteenth centuries. 'No city except Paris,' wrote Motley, 'surpassed it in population; none approached it in commercial splendour.' Small wonder then that of the 133 printers who set up in business in the Netherlands between 1500 and 1540 no fewer than sixty-six had elected to try their fortune in Antwerp, for there they could find not only greater freedom than elsewhere, but also a unique combination of conditions favourable to success:

an intellectual climate, a reservoir of artistic talent, a supply of credit, and a market organisation not available in any other trading centre' (Motley: *Rise of the Dutch Republic*, 1855).

At this time Antwerp played an important part in the diffusion of the Bible, more especially in the vernacular. From Nyhoff we learn that no fewer than fifty-seven Bibles or parts of the Bible were printed at Antwerp between 1500 and 1540, of which forty-two were in Flemish. The earliest Dutch version of the Bible had been printed at Delft in 1477 by Jacob van der Meer and Maurizius Yementszoon, and the sixteenth century witnessed an extensive output, not only of complete Bibles, but also works paraphrasing the Gospel teachings, such as the *Bibel in 't Corte*, or abridged Bible (Claes de Grave, 1513), which was in essence a Flemish version of Petrus Comestor, *Historia scolastica*. In view of the popularity of this work the printer brought out new editions in 1516 and 1518, this time with woodcut illustrations.

When, in 1522, Martin Luther had completed his German translation of the New Testament, Flemish versions began to appear almost at once. In 1524 Adrien van Berghen printed the *Epistelen van Paulus, Catholycke Epistelen*, etc., after Luther's own translation, and in the same year he brought out a Flemish edition of the New Testament based on the Luther translation, with an introduction by Erasmus. Jan van Ghelen, Hans van Ruremonde and Martin de Keysere followed suit.

It was more than the Catholic Church could stomach to see the presses turning out Bibles in a translation due to the very man who had published the famous theses which were at the base of the Reformation. Charles V dealt with the matter by issuing decrees which provided the severest penalties against the printing, writing or reading of the works of those looked upon as heretics. The only Bible permitted was the Vulgate, which was declared authentic by the Council of Trent at its fourth sitting in 1546.

As a result of the decrees promulgated by Charles V between 1521 and 1550 in an attempt to stem the progress of Lutheran doctrines, at least three Antwerp printers were executed: Adrien van Berghen in 1542, Jacob van Liesvelt in 1545, and Niclaes van Oldenborch in 1555. The last-named had published in 1526, even before the complete Luther Bible had appeared, an *Oude en Nieuwe Testament* which made use of part of Luther's translation, and immediately after the publication at Wittemberg in 1534 of the first complete edition of Luther's translation into German of the Bible, Liesvelt issued in 1535 a new edition of his Bible, this time entirely based on Luther's version. In 1540 he brought out a new edition of the Bible with marginal notes of so marked a Lutheran tendency that they could hardly fail to attract the attention of the Inquisitors. The exact grounds upon which Jacob van Liesvelt was condemned to death are unknown, but his Lutheran activities had for some years made him suspect in the eyes of the authorities. After his death, his widow and his son brought out a new edition of the Bible, but this time without marginal notes, and in an edition corrected in accordance with the Vulgate.

'Of all the printers whose works have ever adorned the literary republic, none, I think, stand upon so broad and lofty a pedestal as Christopher Plantin.' These words of Dibdin★ are high praise, but not unjustified. In his day he was the biggest industrial printer in Europe, but although he turned what had been a hand-craft into an industry, commercial considerations were never allowed to lower the high typographical standard of the books sent out from 'The Golden Compasses' to all the cities of Europe and beyond the seas.

He was born in the vicinity of Tours around 1520. In his youth he became apprenticed to Robert Macé II, a well-known printer of Caen, and in that town he met his future wife, Jeanne Rivière. They moved to Paris about 1547, and it is likely that Plantin found employment with the printer Jacques Bogard. After less than three years in Paris Plantin left France for good, this time to settle in Antwerp, where he worked for a time as a book-binder, though it was clearly his intention to become a master printer, since in 1550 he was entered in the register of the Antwerp Guild of Saint Luke as 'boeckprinter'.

He probably lacked at first the necessary capital to set up as a master printer, and he may possibly have worked for a time for Jean Bellère. It was not until 1555 that he managed to set up his own press. The first years were far from easy, and accusations of having printed a heretical book threatened in 1562 to cut short his new career and for a time he was obliged to leave Antwerp.

By June 1563 he was able to return to Antwerp and a four-year period of partnership with some rich merchants of the city placed his business on a sound financial basis. Despite the competition of the many printers then working in Antwerp, among whom were Jean Bellère, Jan Steelsius, Jan de Laet, Gillis Coppens van Diest, Martin Nuyts, Jan Withage, and Ameet Tavernier, the Plantin press soon became, not only the most important in Antwerp, but one of the most important in Europe. At the same time the printer made many friends among the notables of the city and secured a decided advantage by gaining the good-will of two powerful protectors – Cardinal Granvelle and the secretary to King Philip II of Spain, Gabriel de Zayas.

By 1565, within ten years of setting up his business, Plantin had seven presses working; in 1576, at the height of his prosperity he had twenty-two. Just what this meant, in relation to his epoch, may be judged from the fact that such famous printers as the Estiennes and Manuzio normally used from two to four

★ Dibdin, Rev. T. F. *The Bibliographical Decameron*. 1817.

and only exceptionally five or six. But then Plantin was not merely a fine craftsman; he was the first great industrialist in the field of printing.

In 1566 Plantin successfully weathered a second crisis. In that year a great political and religious storm broke out in the Netherlands culminating in the iconoclastic fury which led to the general desecration by the Reformers of hundreds of churches throughout Flanders and Brabant. This Calvinist revolt was quelled by the authorities during the first months of 1567, but having openly espoused the cause of the Reformation, Plantin's partners found it prudent to disappear. Plantin himself had reason to fear, for he and many of his intimate friends were suspected of heresy. His colleague, the printer Willem Silvius, had that very year been imprisoned, accused of having taken part in the revolt of the iconoclasts.

It was at this moment of crisis that Plantin put forward his idea of a magnificent polyglot Bible. Through the intermediary of powerful protectors, in particular Gabriel de Zayas, he managed to secure the patronage of Philip II, King of Spain and of the Netherlands. The danger passed; one did not trouble a royal protégé. If the magnificent polyglot Bible, in eight massive folio volumes, brought him fame, it also left him with a burden of debts covered neither by the sales, nor by the King of Spain.

All previous Bibles and service books were surpassed by this Bible and the splendid series of liturgical books which followed. Between 1571 and 1576 Plantin's output of liturgical books for Spain was so enormous that no fewer than twelve presses were kept busy on orders from the King of Spain. During those six years he despatched to Spain 18,370 Breviaries (from small 16mo to folio), 16,755 Missals, 9,120 Books of Hours, and 3,200 Hymnals, in addition to other service books (Rooses, 1882).

Plantin did not specialise in one type of book, yet almost without exception his publications fell within the domain of erudition. He became the accredited publisher of the greatest botanists of his time, and his herbals did full justice to the work of Rembert Dodoens, Matthias de l'Obel and Charles de l'Ecluse. Cartography was represented by the atlases of Abraham Ortelius; topography by the superb Description of the Low Countries from the pen of the Florentine, Giucciardini. Dictionaries for the student, such as the *Promptuarium latinae linguae*, and for the philologist, as exemplified in the *Thesaurus theutonicae linguae*, met with deserved success. Compact editions of the classics earned their printer the gratitude of students, and even Church music was represented in the Plantinian catalogue.

His period of greatest prosperity was the decade from 1567 to 1576, when he moved to a site on the Friday Market at Antwerp still in existence as the Plantin–Moretus Museum. But on 4 November 1576, when he had barely settled down in his new premises, came catastrophe in the shape of 'The Spanish

CHRISTOPHORVS PLANTINVS
TVRONENSIS   E · de Boulonois fecit

FIGURE 47. Portrait of Christopher Plantin engraved by the Flemish engraver Edmé de Boulonois.

Fury', when the Spanish garrison plundered and sacked the rich city during three days of carnage and pillage – an orgy of destruction in which between six and seven thousand people perished.

The enormous ransom Plantin was forced to pay meant that he had to give up half of his new premises to cut down expenses. Yet so truly did he live up to his device 'By Labour and Constancy' that within two years his printing house, the Golden Compasses, was once again a going concern.

In 1578, when the States-General had for the time being gained the upper hand against the Spanish and established themselves in Antwerp, Plantin became the official printer to the new authorities, and in that capacity found himself obliged to print many anti-Spanish pamphlets, a fact which led, not unnaturally, to accusations of time-serving. He probably thought, wrongly as it happened, that the Spaniards would never regain the upper hand in Brabant. He did all he could to gain the favour of William the Silent, to whom he dedicated his 1581 edition of the *Kruydtboeck*, or Herbal, of Matthias de l'Obel.

When the advance of Alexander of Parma foreshadowed the imminent siege of Antwerp he left his Antwerp business in the hands of his sons-in-law Jan Moerentorf (Moretus) and François Raphelenghien, and went to Leyden, where he set up a printing office in 1583, and on the death of Willem Silvius became printer to the recently founded university. But although he was well treated in Leyden he never felt really at home there and in 1585 returned to Antwerp, a city he loved and from which he had always been loth to move, despite the attractive offers made to him from other countries.

But the Antwerp to which he returned after its capture by Alexander Farnese was no longer the great commercial centre it had been. The mass emigration of both artists and scholars had deprived him of his most valued collaborators, and he had to renounce the idea of printing any more of the scholarly works which had made his name. Moreover he had to pay enormous interest yearly on loans contracted for printing the Polyglot Bible, and extensive orders for liturgical books for Spain, which were later cancelled, involved him in immense sums which he could not recover. He died on 1 July 1589. He left five daughters, and though he had two capable sons-in-law it must have been a bitter blow to him that his only son had died while still a boy, so that no one of the name of Plantin remained to carry on the firm which his business acumen and great industry had raised to such heights.

★　★　★　★　★　★　★

The first recorded reference to a punch-cutter in the Netherlands is in connection with the tragic death of the printer Gheraert Leeu, who was stabbed to death during a quarrel by one of his workmen, Henric van Symmen, who is described in the documents as a 'letterstekere' or cutter of letters. This event took place in 1493.

The best-known of the early Netherlands punch-cutters is probably Henric Pieterszoon, known as Henric Lettersnijder, who worked at Rotterdam, his native town, as well as at Delft and Antwerp. As a printer he was active from 1496 until about 1511, but he printed few books, for his main occupation was that of punch-cutter and type-founder, and founts which he cut were used by sixty per cent of Low Countries printers during the first half of the sixteenth century (Carter, 1969). His son Cornelis, who worked at Delft from 1517 onwards was also a punch-cutter.

In 1536 Joos Lambrecht, a native of Ghent, began work in that town. He was a printer, punch-cutter and engraver, and in what leisure time he had, a poet and philologist. He engraved his own printer's mark, an oak tree with the motto *Satis quercus*. His earliest book was probably the *Epistolae Erasmi* of 1536, and for his printing he used black-letter, roman and italic which he cut himself, as well as some French type (Vervliet, 1968). He had four founts of roman and was the first to print Dutch books in roman type rather than the more usual black-letter.

In 1553 he left his native land for religious reasons, as a convert to the Reformation, and settled at Wesel in Germany. He had already got into serious trouble for printing the *Corte instruccye ende onderwys . . .* of Cornelis van der Heyden (1545), which was declared heretical by the religious authorities. A scholar as well as being an excellent printer, he published one of the earliest grammars of the Dutch–Flemish language – his own *Nederlandsche Spellijnghe*, which appeared at Ghent in 1550. At Wesel he printed a few small pieces and died there in 1556.

In 1567 Plantin published a specimen of his types: *Index, sive Specimen Characterum Christophori Plantini*, of which there were two issues, one showing forty-one and the other forty-two types. Proofs of a later specimen, compiled about 1579, show sixty-six type faces.

One of the first punch-cutters to supply him with type was his compatriot François Guyot, who had come to Antwerp from Paris, where his brother-in-law Alexandre Beaujon was also a letter founder. On 22 August 1539 he became a citizen of Antwerp, and probably cut some of the type which first made its appearance in Antwerp printing about 1540. His types were very popular and were used not only by Netherlands printers, but also in England, Scandinavia, Germany, Spain, Portugal and South America. Guyot was made free of the Guild of St Luke in 1561 under the designation of 'Francoys de lettergieter' and until shortly before his death in 1570 cast type regularly for Plantin. He also justified the strikes that Plantin bought in France. A broadside specimen sheet in the Fölger Library at Washington, D.C., has been identified as his, and is the oldest specimen known by a man who was not himself a printer. Of his sons, François II carried on his father's business until after 1597; Christoffel Guyot, after serving as compositor for Plantin from 1582 to 1585 later became a master printer at Leyden. Gabriel Guyot was more of a wanderer, for we find him working for John Day in London in 1576; at Antwerp in 1579; at Middelburg from 1580 to 1581; and again in London from 1583 to 1588.

During the year 1566 Robert Granjon (see also p. 175) was in the Netherlands, staying in Antwerp for a time, during which Plantin contracted with him for the supply of punches and matrices of his script type, the *lettre françoise d'art de main* as its designer termed it. This was not Plantin's first contract with the French punch-cutter, for he had on 5 July 1565, ordered two italics, shown on Plantin's specimen of 1579. Always on the lookout for new developments in typography, Plantin was using Granjon's script type not long after Granjon himself had first made use of it in 1557, for in 1558 Plantin printed an *A.B.C.*, eight pages of which were set in Granjon's *lettre françoise*.

Working in Antwerp at about the same time as Guyot was the punch-cutter Ameet Tavernier, who, unlike Guyot, was also a printer. He was a native of Bailleul who had learned the art of cutting punches from Joos Lambrecht at Ghent. He was the first to introduce into the Netherlands the types imitating handwriting (later known as Civilité types). He first used it in *Goede manierlikje seden*, a Flemish version of Erasmus, *De Civilitate*. Although the book is unsigned, it was probably printed by Tavernier himself at Antwerp in 1559. Later books in this and also a second civilité type bore his imprint.

Curiously enough, although this kind of typographic script was invented in France (see p. 176) its use was far more widespread and lasted longer in the Low Countries. It served for jobbing, for the printing of government edicts, and also to some extent for book work, though in this field it was used mainly for moral tracts and courtesy books for the young.

Like Joos Lambrecht, the punch-cutter Hendrik van den Keere the Younger came from Ghent. When the former left the country in 1553 his house and material were acquired by Peter van den Keere, Hendrik's grandfather, who does not, however, seem to have published anything under his own name. His son, Hendrik van den Keere the Elder, was a well-known Ghent printer. The younger Hendrik was a punch-cutter and typefounder and from 1569 until his death in 1580 he undertook the typefounding for Plantin, in succession to François Guyot, and also cut some thirty new type faces for him. Until recently comparatively little was known of Hendrik van den Keere and his work, but the systematic cataloguing of printing material at the Plantin-Moretus Museum in Antwerp has led to a revaluation of his position among the punch-cutters of the Low Countries. 'It may safely be said,' writes Dr. Vervliet, 'that the collection of his work in the Museum Plantin-Moretus – some 40 sets of his punches and matrices – the bills from him, correspondence, account books and posthumous inventories, amount to the earliest detailed picture that we have of a working typefoundry. That in itself should earn him a conspicuous place in typographical history.'*

After his death the greater part of Van den Keere's material was sold to Plantin, though some of the matrices were acquired by Thomas de Vechter,

---

* *Sixteenth century printing types of the Low Countries*. Amsterdam, 1968.

who had been the foreman caster to Van den Keere. De Vechter settled in Leyden as a typefounder in 1584, and from him many of the Dutch printers of the time received faces cut by his former employer. Van den Keere cut nine roman and twelve gothic faces, one rotunda, several alphabets of Lombardic initials and a 'Mediane gheschreven letter', a civilité type more pleasant to the eye than that of Tavernier.

Of other Netherlands punch-cutters during the sixteenth century we know little. Judocus Hondius, the son-in-law of Hendrik van den Keere, is reputed to have been a punch-cutter and Dr. H. F. Wijnman claims that he cut three exotic faces (Arabic, Samaritan and Ethiopic) for the Raphelengian office at Leyden in 1595.

18

Early Jewish Printing

SOME twenty years elapsed after the invention of printing before the Jews began to print books in Hebrew, and during the fifteenth century, because of unfavourable conditions in Germany, printing in Hebrew was confined mainly to Italy, Spain and Portugal. The first printed book in Hebrew was a *Pentateuch* printed by Abraham Garton at Reggio Calabria, in Italy, and completed on 5 February 1475. The second book came from Piove di Sacco, and was printed by Meshullam Cusi; but although there was Hebrew printing soon afterwards at Ferrara and Bologna, Jewish printing in general centered upon Mantua.

The chief printer family engaged in the production of Hebrew books were the Soncinos, a family which derived its name from the town of Soncino in the duchy of Milan. The first member of the family to become a printer was Israel Nathan ben Salomo, who set up a Hebrew press at Soncino in 1483 and published his first work, the treatise *Berakot*, on 2 February 1484. His son Joshua brought out the first complete Hebrew Bible at Soncino in 1488.

The press was a travelling one, being found at Soncino, 1483–86; Casal Maggiore, 1486; at Soncino again, 1488–90; Naples, 1490–92; Brescia, 1492–94; Barco, 1494–97; Fano, 1503–06; Pesaro, 1507–20 (with intervals at Fano, 1516, and Ortona, 1519); and finally at Rimini, 1521–26.

The first half of the sixteenth century saw the spread of Jewish presses into Turkey and into Bohemia. About the year 1503 the Jew David Nahmias and his son Samuel left Spain for Constantinople, where they set up a press and in 1505 printed an edition of the *Pentateuch*. They were soon followed by other Jewish printers, including Gershon Soncino, the grandson of Israel Nathan ben Samuel. Gershon Soncino died around 1530 and his work was continued by the last of the Soncinos, his son Eleazar, who worked at Constantinople from 1534–47. There was also a Hebrew press at Salonica, where Don Judah Gedaliah printed some thirty works in Hebrew from about 1512 onwards.

In Central Europe the first Jewish press was set up in Prague by Gershon ben Solomon Cohen, who founded in that city a dynasty of Hebrew printers known as 'the Gersonides'. He began printing in 1513 with a book of prayers, and during his career as a printer supplied Jewish communities in Germany and Poland. About 1518 he was joined for a time by Hayyim ben David Schwartz, a wandering printer who, after working in Prague from 1514 to 1526, is found at Oels in Silesia, at Augsburg, at Ichenhausen and, finally, in 1546 at Heddernheim.

Another famous printer of books in Hebrew was Daniel Bomberg, born at Antwerp (c. 1483). The Jewish Encyclopedia says that he learned the art of printing and type-founding from his father Cornelius, which seems unlikely, for Cornelius Bomberg (or Van Bomberghen) was a rich merchant and financier, and friend of Sir Thomas Gresham. He had fruitful business connections with Venice, and it was probably on his father's advice that Daniel Bomberg settled in the Italian city, at what date is uncertain. In 1495 Cornelius Bomberg had commissioned the printer Johannes Hamman, called Herzog, who had printed in Venice since 1482 to bring out at his expense a revised edition of the Breviary for the Cathedral of Antwerp.

In 1515 the Augustine monk Félix de Prato, with whom Daniel was on friendly terms, received from Pope Leo X the authorisation to publish a new translation of the Bible. He began with the *Psalms*, the editing of which he confided to Daniel Bomberg, and it was printed in September 1515 by Hamman's partner, Petrus Liechtenstein. The colophon states that it was printed 'Impensis ac sumptibus egregii viri do. Danielis Bombergi Antverpiensis'.

Daniel Bomberg, who possessed his father's business acumen, decided that a Hebrew press would be a lucrative affair, and in 1515 he obtained from the Venetian Senate a privilege for printing books in Hebrew, and his activity for the next thirty-three years made of Venice the centre of Hebrew publishing. The first recorded work from the press of Daniel Bomberg was an edition of the Pentateuch, together with portions of works by the Prophets, dated 30 November 1516 and printed entirely in Hebrew characters. He issued (1516–17) the first rabbinic Bible, edited by Félix de Prato, a converted Jew.

In 1518 all printing privileges were revoked by the Senate, and to secure the right to continue the printing of Hebrew books Daniel Bomberg had to pay the large sum of 500 ducats for a renewal of his privilege for ten years. But it was money well spent in view of the success his press enjoyed. Whether Bomberg himself was ever a printer is doubtful; his main activities were those of publisher and bookseller. His first edition of the Talmud, edited by Rabbi Chiyyah Meir ben David, was printed by the German-Jewish printer Cornelius Adelkind. It appeared between the years 1519 and 1523.

Daniel Bomberg was active in Venice until 1549, his output including Bibles, grammatical and lexicographical works, ethical treatises, together with the first complete editions of the Babylonian Talmud and the Jerusalem Talmud, and he is said to have employed a very large staff of Jewish scholars as correctors. He returned to Antwerp some time after 1549 and died there on 21 December 1553. The Venetian press was carried on by his son David.

The first real competition experienced by Bomberg came from Marcantonio Giustiniani, who opened a Hebrew press near the Rialto bridge. The first book from this press, a *Commentary on the Pentateuch* by Moses Nachmanides, appeared in 1545, but this press closed in 1552. Two other Hebrew presses started up in Venice around the middle of the sixteenth century, those of the brothers Dei Farri and of Francesco Brucioli, but neither was very successful.

For more than twenty years, until 1544, the Jewish printer Cornelius ben Baruch Adelkind worked for Daniel Bomberg. In 1544 he worked for Giovanni di Gara, and in the following year his name appeared on the title-pages of Hebrew books published in Venice by Giustiniani. From 1546 to 1553 he printed and published on his own account. Then in 1553 he moved from Venice to Sabbionetta, where he was employed by Tomaso Foa. Cornelius had a son, Daniel, who was with Giustiniani in 1550 and from 1551–52 printed on his own account, but little is known of his life.

Giovanni di Gara, who acquired most of Bomberg's type and described himself as the 'heir of Bomberg', issued a series of notable Hebrew publications between the years 1565 and 1609; thus we find that the activity of Bomberg and Di Gara spans almost the entire sixteenth century.

Most of the Hebrew type faces used in Venice at this time were cut by the celebrated Parisian punch-cutter Guillaume Le Bé, who visited Venice in 1545 and stayed there until 1550, cutting Hebrew type and making matrices and moulds for Marcantonio Giustiniani, Daniel Bomberg and Mazo dei Parenza. He also cut Greek type for Christoforo Zanetti, who was di Gara's chief printer.

In 1485, when the first Hebrew press was established in Naples by Joseph ben Jacob Ashkenazi of Gunzenhausen, there was a large Jewish community, augmented by arrivals from Spain and Portugal. By 1490 there were several Hebrew presses in the city, but all Hebrew printing came to a standstill in 1494 with the destruction of the Jewish community and the confiscation of their property. Three Italian cities share the credit of having produced between them the first printed Hebrew text of the Bible: Bologna, *The Pentateuch* (1482); Soncino, the *Early and Later Prophets* (1485–86); and Naples, the *Wisdom Books* (1486–91).

19

The first Music Printers

THE printing of musical notation set the early printers a problem which at first they found almost insoluble, and which baffled them for more than half a century. Once the principle had been discovered letterpress printing was relatively simple. But for musical notation there has to be a staff of four or five continuous horizontal lines on or between which the notes have to be accurately placed at varying heights. The notes themselves needed heads of various shapes in order to indicate time values.

Although for the printing of church music (plainsong) only a small number of note shapes were needed, for mensural music six or seven different shapes as well as a number of signs indicating rests were necessary, and the difficulties of setting must have appeared overwhelming to the first printers. And so, when a book on music theory needed a musical quotation, one way of overcoming the difficulty was by avoiding it altogether and leaving a blank space to be filled in later by hand. An example of this is seen in the 1480 Gafurius, *Theoricum opus*.

In 1473 Conrad Fyner of Esslingen printed Gerson, *Collectorium superMagnificat* and to show readers a descending scale of five notes he merely printed a descending row of five black squares preceded by a letter F to indicate an F-clef. In England Wynkyn de Worde made an attempt to insert a musical illustration in a printed text in somewhat similar fashion, by combining rules and raised quads to form a staff and notes in an attempt to show the consonances of Pythagoras mentioned in Worde's edition of Ranulph Higden's *Polycronicon*. But this could hardly be called music printing.

The first effective method was to have the notes printed from wood or metal blocks and the lines drawn by hand. Subsequently both staves and notes were printed from blocks. In the earliest German secular song *Von sant Ursulen schifflin*, printed at Strassburg in 1498, notes, staves and text were all cut on wood.

The earliest known music printing is thought to have been a Gradual (that part of the Mass sung by the choir), the only complete copy of which is now in the British Museum (IB 6883). It bears no date and there is no mention of the printer, but the text type is the same as that used in the 'Constance Breviary', which was printed not later than 1473. The Gradual is assumed to belong to the same period. It was printed from type with notes in Gothic notation by double impression.

On October 12 1476, Ulric Han completed his Missal for Rome use and in the colophon claimed to have invented music printing. Han's Missal is certainly the earliest book of printed music to bear a date, and unlike the Gradual mentioned above it was printed in Roman notation, namely with square notes. German printers favoured the Gothic notation, sometimes called Hufnagel-schrift', or 'horse-shoe nail' from the shape of the predominant single note.

Han's Missal, besides being a beautifully printed book, was unusual in its use of a five-line stave in a liturgical work, when a four-line stave was more usual. In 1480 the Venice printer Theodor of Würzburg brought out the *Grammatica* of Franciscus Niger which contains the earliest known mensural music printed from type, though without the lines of the staves, which were intended to be added by hand. But this early use of movable type for mensural music had no successor until the end of the century, and in fact music was being printed from wood blocks right through the sixteenth century and even beyond.

Under the circumstances the work done by Ottaviano dei Petrucci in printing from movable types at the beginning of the sixteenth century is in many ways most remarkable.

Born at Fossombrone in 1466, Ottaviano de' Petrucci went to Venice about the year 1490, and whilst there he was encouraged by two of his compatriots, Bartolomeo da Fossombrone and Francesco Spinaccino, a teacher of the lute, to seek a practical method of printing music. Eventually, on 25 May 1498, he received an exclusive privilege to print music from the government of the Republic of Venice. But it was not until 14 May 1501, that his first book made its appearance. It was a collection of musical compositions mainly by Flemish masters entitled *Harmonice Musices Odhecaton*. It was reprinted in 1502 and again in 1504. Of the *editio princeps* only one copy is now known, in the Biblioteca del Conservatorio at Bologna. This volume was the first of a set of three, the second and third being published in 1502 and 1503 respectively.

Between 1504 and 1508 he undertook the printing and publication of *Frottole* (lit. 'trifles'), works by contemporary Italian masters, of considerable historic and artistic value. In 1508 he began printing music for the lute, and was the first printer to do so, with the *Intabulatura de Lauto* of Joan Ambrosio Dalza.

What is striking about the work of Petrucci is its technical mastery in an entirely new field. In the words of Mr Hyatt King: 'He combined notes, rests and directs of an elegant design with a well-aligned text and beautiful but unobtrusive initial letters. The registration of notes on the stave is as perfect as is the spacing of the parts, which are usually laid out separately on open pages, in the manner of a choir-book.'* Of him Friedrich Chrysander writes: 'He is the only one connected with music whom we could in any sense put by the side of Gutenberg.' Even if we think such a statement rather too extravagant, since he was not the inventor of printing from movable type, he was the first to design a type for mensural notation which fitted together more accurately than anything previously attempted and thus facilitated perfect registration of notes on the staves. He is said to have printed by triple impression: first the staves, next the text, and finally the notes – a lengthy and costly process.

It was a period during which the lute had attained its highest pitch of perfection, and its place in the musical life of Western Europe was unrivalled. The earliest printed lute books were Italian, and Italy remained the most prolific producer of such books throughout the sixteenth century. The privilege which Petrucci was accorded in 1498 related not only to 'canto figurado' but also to the printing of 'intabuladure d'organo e de liuto'.

Petrucci printed at least forty-three musical works at Venice, before transferring his press to his birthplace, Fossombrone, in 1511. There he continued to print musical works, in addition to other books, until about 1520. He died in 1539. After Petrucci had left Venice, the chief music printers there were Andrea Antico of Montana, himself a musician, and Bernardinus Vercellensis. Antico is said to have printed the first organ tablature, printed by means of wood-blocks, in 1517. He printed several collections of motets and songs for Andrea Torresano, the father-in-law of Aldo Manuzio. Bernardinus Vercellensis printed, among other things, *Ricerchari, Motetti e Canzoni* by Marco Antonio Cavazzoni, published at Venice in 1523. Printed possibly from metal blocks, this organ tablature is the earliest known example of printing notes above each other to form chords. Metal blocks were probably used also by Petrus Sambonettus of Siena for printing the musical setting of *Canzone, sonetti, strambotti et frottole* (1515) though the accompanying text was type-set. This is the only work known of this printer, who was a Neapolitan by birth.

The first German printer to follow and profit by the invention of Ottaviano Petrucci was Erhard Öglin of Augsburg, who himself cut types in imitation of the Italian's but lacking their elegance. Under the direction of the famous humanist Conrad Celtis he printed in 1507 Petrus Titonius, *Melopoeiae*, consisting of twenty-two pieces for four voices. The book has two splendid woodcuts: 'Apollo on Parnassus' and 'Apollo and the Muses'.

Öglin, a native of Reutlingen, was a journeyman printer at Basel during the last decade of the fifteenth century, and in 1505 went to Augsburg where he printed at first in partnership with Hans Otmar and later with Jörg Nadler. From 1508 until 1518 he worked alone, and was, incidentally, the first Augsburg printer to use Hebrew characters.

* A. Hyatt King, *Four Hundred Years of Music Printing*. London, 1964.

The second German printer of music was Peter Schöffer the younger who began music printing about 1512 with Arnold Schlick's *Tabulaturen etlicher Lobgesang und Liedlein auf die Orgel und Lauten*. Thereafter he either bought or made a set of mensural music types which resemble those of Petrucci. His printing was more refined than that of Öglin. At Strassburg in 1535 he printed in collaboration with Matthias Apiarius the *Rerum Musicarum* of Johann Frosch – a treatise in which are sixteen pages of musical examples in four or six parts, printed on facing pages.

Other music printers followed Öglin and Schöffer in Germany. In 1520, at Augsburg, Sigismund Grimm and Marcus Wirsung made a handsome job of the *Liber Selectarum Cantionum*, a volume, edited by the composer Ludwig Senfl, containing a series of motets by various composers including Josquin, Pierre de la Rue and Senfl himself.

The first German printer to use music types similar to those of Pierre Haultin (see p. 212) was Christian Egenolff, who published a setting of the *Odes* of Horace in 1532 at Frankfurt. But the lead in German music publishing during the fifteenth century was taken over by Nuremberg, where the publisher and bookseller Hans Otto and the printers Johann Petri, Johann vom Berg (Montanus) and Ulrich Neuber all printed collections of both sacred and profane music. In Munich Adam Berg printed several sets of the works of Orlando di Lasso and at Heidelberg Johann Kohlen published in 1558 the lute *Tabulaturbuch* of Sebastian Ochsenkuhn – a collection of works by various composers arranged for the lute.

Georg Rhau, who printed at Wittenberg from 1508 until 1525 was, as well as being the first of Luther's printers, the publisher of the first Protestant hymnbook in 1524, and issued the *Choralbüchlein* of Spangenberg in 1536. He also printed Martin Agricola, *Musica instrumentalis*, which, in addition to the woodcut illustrations in the text contains also folding plates which have examples in Gothic notation and German lute tablature. From Leipzig came one of the most delightful little woodblock music books of the sixteenth century – Martin Luther's *Geystliche Lieder* printed by Valentin Babst in 1545. The tunes and text of each page are enclosed in ornamental borders.

A very popular work during the first part of the sixteenth century was Gregorius Reisch, *Margarita Philosophica*, a sort of encyclopedia dealing with a variety of subjects. The section on music has an interesting frontispiece, the central figure in which is a woman shown holding a piece of music in both gothic and mensural notations. Around her are musicians playing harp, lute, recorder, and portable organ. The first edition of this work, which was frequently reprinted, came from the Freiburg press of Johann Schott in 1503. Another edition, with woodcut music examples was printed at Strassburg in 1512 by Johann Grüninger, who had earlier printed Johannes Reuchlin, *Scenica*

Progymnasmata (1498) considered to be the earliest printed play with printed music.

FRANCE

The printing of mensural music by two impressions was both costly and time-consuming and in France little use was made of this method except by Etienne Briard, a printer of Avignon, who produced the sacred compositions of Elzéar Genêt, known as Carpentras from his birthplace. The composer paid for the cutting by Briard of a special type in which the music notes had round heads. Not only did Briard abandon the traditional square and lozenge form for the breves, semibreves and minims, replacing them by round-headed notes, but he replaced the complicated system of ligatures by a simple and rational notation representing the real duration of the notes. The first work of Genêt to appear in this new style was issued by Jean de Channay, an Avignon bookseller – a *Liber Missarum* dated 15 May 1532.

The first Paris printer to print music by single impression was Pierre Attaignant, who was active from 1514 until about 1552. He served his apprenticeship with Pigouchet, whose daughter he married, and until 1525 was in partnership with Poncet le Preux. From 1528 Attaignant who, according to Ph. Renouard, now cut and cast his own material, devoted himself mainly to music-printing.

For the double (or maybe triple) impression of Petrucci he substituted printing in one pull of the press by utilising type carrying both notes and a portion of the stave; these portions joined together to print as the straight lines of the stave. For long it was thought that Attaignant's music type was supplied by the punch cutter Pierre Haultin, but there is now some doubt about this attribution, which was made by Fournier le jeune in his *Traité de l'imprimerie musicale*, 1763.

Pierre Attaignant dated the first of his many music publications – *Chansons nouvelles en musique* – 4 April 1527. On 18 June 1531, François I granted him a privilege for six years to print and sell music 'en choses faictes et Tabulature des jeux de lutz, flustes et orgues'. From 1537 to 1545 he worked in partnership with the bookseller Hubert Jullet, who had married his daughter Germaine. In 1538 he subscribed himself 'imprimeur de musique du Roi'.

On account of the large number of his publications Attaignant played a large part in the diffusion of French music. His collection of twenty Masses, published in 1532, included works by Mouton, Haurteur, Gombert, Gascoigne, Manchecourt, and Sermisy. Four years previously he had printed the *Chansons* of Clément Jannequin, one of the originators of 'programme' music, for many of his choral pieces bear such titles as 'The Battle of Marignan', 'The Siege of Metz', 'The Chattering Women' and so on.

Attaignant was the sole printer of music in Paris until 1549, when Nicolas Duchemin set up in competition, followed by Le Roy and Ballard in 1551. Three different styles of music type are found in Attaignant's publications, but

FIGURE 48. This Missal for Würzburg use is the earliest dated book with printed music to appear in Germany. It was printed at Würzburg by Georg Reyser in 1481.

who cut them is still uncertain. The attribution to Pierre Haultin is based on a tradition that he cut a single-impression music-type about 1525, recorded, as stated, by Fournier le jeune. Whether he cut Attaignant's music type or not, he was an excellent punch cutter, in addition to being a very good printer.* Born at Villaine-sous-la-Flèche (Sarthe) probably at the end of the fifteenth century, he is known to have been working in Paris in 1523 and during his long career

* He cut music type for Attaignant's competitor, Nicolas Du Chemin.

cut a large number of distinguished type faces, including music type. One of the sets of matrices for music type in the Plantinian collection at Antwerp is thought to have been by him.

Attaignant claimed to have cut his music type himself, and this was never denied by Pierre Haultin. The privilege which Attaignant received from François I, dated 18 June 1531, declares that 'ledit suppliant par longue excogitation et travail desperit et a tresgrans fraiz, labeurs, mises et despens ait invente et mis en lumiere la maniere et industrie de graver, fondre et imprimer les dictes nottes et caracteres.'

After Attaignant, the most important music publisher in France was Robert Ballard. On 15 February 1552, Henri II granted to Ballard and his cousin Adrian Le Roy a privilege appointing them sole printers of 'la musique de chambre, chapelle, et menus plaisirs du roi'. This privilege, periodically renewed by successive kings, gave Ballard and his heirs a virtual monopoly which lasted until 1788. Most of the music type used by Robert Ballard was cut by Guillaume Le Bé (1525–98), who was one of the most famous punch-cutters of the sixteenth century.

Robert Ballard married in 1559 Lucrèce Dugué daughter of Jean Dugué, the king's organist;* and through this marriage Ballard made many useful contacts both at Court and in the world of music.

The first publication of Ballard and his partner was the *Premier Livre de Tabulature de Luth . . . composé par Adrian Le Roy*, dated 29 August 1551, and followed on 12 September by the *Premier Livre de Tablature de Guiterre*. One of the most interesting among the vast number of publications issued by this firm was the *Balet comique de la Royne* devised by Baltasar de Beaujoyeulx, with music by Beaulieu and Salmon, and published by Le Roy and Ballard in association with Mamert Patisson in 1582. This ballet had been given in 1581 to celebrate the marriage of Margaret of Lorraine, sister of Henri III, to the Duc de Joyeuse, and is sometimes called the first modern ballet.

Robert Ballard, who had at least seven children, died in July 1588, and was succeeded in the business by his son Pierre. Adrian Le Roy died in 1598 and left no descendants. In the forty-seven years of activity between 1551 and the death of Le Roy, the firm had become one of the notable in Europe for music printing and publishing, and in a bibliography Lesure and Thibault list 319 publications to their credit.

The only inroad made upon the Ballard family's exclusive privilege was in 1639, when Jacques de Sanlecque (see p. 300) was granted a ten-year privilege for printing plainsong with his new type.

At Lyons the printer Jacques Moderne, whose first signed and dated book

* Many writers, following Ph. Renouard and others, have erroneously stated that Ballard married the daughter of Guillaume Le Bé.

appeared in 1529, began to print music books in 1532, beginning with a *Liber decem missarum*, which is signed 'impressum per Iacobum Modernum de Pinguento' after his native town Pinguente, on the Istrian peninsula, then a part of the Venetian Republic, and now called Buzet, in Jugoslavia. In 1538 he published *Le Parangon des Chansons*, and this is perhaps the earliest example of facing pages of music being printed *tête-bêche* (head to tail) so that singers on opposite sides of a table could read from the same book.

The Paris printer Nicolas du Chemin, a native of Sens, in addition to printing books on medicine, grammar, arithmetic, and Latin classics, printed books of music between 1549 and 1576 with music type supplied by Pierre Haultin. His first volume of music was *Premier Livre, contenant xxviii Pseaulmes de David* (1549), and during his career he published around a hundred editions of music books.* He himself was not a musician but relied on a succession of editors for this branch of his work.

In Belgium the printing of music by woodblock continued into the sixteenth century. The first printer to set music from type was Cristoffel van Remunde who specialised in church service books. In addition to liturgical works for local use, such as his Utrecht Missal of 1527, this Antwerp printer produced service books for the English market including a Manual for Sarum use (1523) and a Manual and Processional also 'ad usum Sarum' (1528). These were printed for Peter Kaetz and Francis Birckman, London booksellers.

The first Belgian printer of non-liturgical music was the Antwerp printer Symon Cock, who in 1538 produced *Een devoot en profitelijck boecxken* by double impression in two colours – black for the notes and red for the staves. Cock obtained from the Emperor Charles V a privilege for six years for the printing with musical notation of the Dutch translation of the Psalms rhymed by Willem van Zuylen van Nyevelt. This *Souter Liedekens* appeared in 1540, and was so successful that up to 1613 it had been reprinted thirty times. The four-line staves are printed in red and the notes (still neumes, with no indication of time) in black.

The first Antwerp printer to use movable music type was Tielman Susato, a musician who settled in that city about 1529 as instrumentalist and music copier. In 1542 he went into partnership with the bookseller Henrik ter Bruggen and the printer Willem van Vissenaecken as a music publisher. The partnership soon broke up and Susato went into business on his own. From 1543 until 1561 he printed a quantity of music, both sacred and profane.

His chief rival, who eventually surpassed him in importance, was Pierre

* See F. Lesure & G. Thibault, *Bibliographie des éditions musicales publiées par Nicolas du Chemin* in 'Annales Musicologiques', I. 1963.

Phalèse, a bookseller of Louvain, who in January 1551 obtained permission to set up a music-printing office and in the following year brought out a collection of songs in four parts by Jehan de Lattre. He was born Pieter vander Phalizen, but printed and published under the French form of his name. He made a reputation as a music printer which extended far beyond the Netherlands. In addition to collections of songs, Phalèse published a good deal of instrumental music, notably a precious collection of music for lute called *Luculentum theatrum musicum* (1568). After his death in 1573 the business was continued by his sons Corneille and Pierre II. The last-named transferred the establishment to Antwerp around 1581 and printed at various addresses in that city until his death in 1609. For a number of his more important publications he went into partnership with the Antwerp printer Jean Bellère, and in 1590 they issued a very fine edition of the *Symphonia Angelica* of H. Waelrant. Hubert Waelrant, a Belgian-born and Italian-trained musician, himself went into the music publishing business in partnership with the printer Hans de Laet until the latter's death around 1567. He edited a number of important collections of music, including nine volumes of *Sacrae cantiones* and three volumes of the *Jardin musiqual*.

The most celebrated of Antwerp printers, Christopher Plantin, made a speciality, especially during the second half of his career, of liturgical books; apart from this remunerative work, he did not attempt music publishing in a big way, probably thinking that it would be imprudent to compete with a specialist like Pierre Phalèse, among whose composers figured all the great names of the period. Nevertheless his *Octo Missae* of Georges de la Hèle was a magnificent production, well worthy of the reputation of the press which printed it. Not expecting to make much profit from the few musical works he published, Plantin insured himself against loss by getting the composers to assume part of the expenses. His work in this field was remarkable for quality rather than quantity, and the main reason which induced him to enter this highly specalised branch of the printing industry appears to have been purely fortuitous, and due in some measure to the vast amount of material he had accumulated for his ill-fated Royal Antiphoner. When he found himself unable to recover from Philip II the debts he had incurred in purchasing no fewer than 1,800 reams of special paper and in having a series of decorative alphabets designed by the finest artists and engravers in Antwerp, Plantin found himself obliged to sell some of the paper and to use the rest for printing Masses by De Kerle, De la Hèle and Filippo di Monte. His music types were for the most part the work of the punch-cutter Hendrik van den Keere.

Apart from Antwerp and Louvain, Gent was the only Belgian town in which music printing was carried on, the printer being Gislain Manilius, son of the well-known Gent printer Corneille Manilius. In 1565 he printed, together with the music, the Flemish translation of the *Psaumes* of Clément Marot, which had been made by the painter-poet Lucas d'Heere. Although it had been sanctioned by the Dean of Sainte-Gudule, the work was placed on the Index and for that reason is very rare. Rarer still is another edition of the Psalms translated by the Reformer, Pierre Dathenus, and printed *sub rosa* by Manilius. Only one copy is known, now in the library of Gent University. Manilius also printed the music of Mathias de Castelyn, *Diversche Liedekens* (1573).

Although no complete editions of musical works were engraved in Belgium during the sixteenth century, there exist a number of prints by Belgian engravers which incorporate a musical text. The best known is that engraved by Jan Sadeler after Martin de Vos and published at Antwerp in 1584. It shows the Virgin and Child with St Anne. The principal subject is surmounted by a group of six angels holding open a music book which shows a four-part *Ave Maria* by the Antwerp musician Corneille Verdonck. This is the earliest known musical composition printed by engraving. It preceded by two years the two earliest books of engraved music printed at Rome by Simon Verovio.

In England the first pieces of music and text to be printed by single impression were contained in *A New Interlude and a mery of the Nature of the iiii Elements*, printed at London by John Rastell without a date, but thought to have been published around 1525. In 1530 a book was printed in London bearing the title *In this boke ar cōteynyd xx sōges*. It was for long attributed to Wynkyn de Worde, but later, in the binding of a book at Westminster Abbey, was found the title leaf of the Medius part of this music book, and conjugate with it part of a leaf with a blank recto and a colophon on the verso. Unfortunately the binder had cut off part of the colophon, which appears to read 'Imprynted in Londō at the signe of the black Morēs'. The type in which the music is printed seems to have been copied from that used by the Augsburg printer Erhard Öglin, but has not been found in any other work and the printer remains unidentified.

In 1550 Richard Grafton printed *The Booke of Common praier noted*, which contained John Merbecke's simple musical setting devised to supply a chant for the new Protestant services less ornate in character than the chant which had been used in the Latin Sarum rites. The music is in square notation on red four-line staves. About 1560 John Daye printed the first edition of the Psalms in the settings of Sternhold and Hopkins to be printed in England. The original edition had been printed at Geneva in 1556, probably by Jean Crespin.

In 1575 Queen Elizabeth I granted to Thomas Tallis and William Byrd the sole privilege for the publication of music books (apart from metrical psalters) and the first work to be printed under that patent was their *Cantiones* in six parts (1575), the printing of which they entrusted to Thomas Vautrollier, the Huguenot printer from Troyes who had settled in England in 1562. There is no record as to the provenance of his music-types, but some of them are thought to have come from Johann Petreius of Nuremberg.

FIGURE 49. Title-page of *Orphenica lyra,* music for the vihuela compiled by Miguel de Fuenllana and printed at Seville in 1554 by Martin de Montesdoca. Note the dedication to Philip of Spain as 'Rey de Ynglaterra'.

One of the best-known printers of music in England at the end of the six-teenth century was Thomas East, and in 1588, after some twenty years of general printing, he became the first regular English music printer and publisher. In that year he printed the *Psalmes, Sonets and songs of sadnes and pietie* by William Byrd and introduced into England the work of the Italian madrigal school with the *Musica Transalpina* compiled by Nicolas Yonge. It contained, translated into

English, fifty-seven madrigals by composers such as Palestrina, Lasso and Ferrabosco, as well as two by Byrd. Again, the music type is thought to have been imported from Johann Petreius of Nuremberg.

In 1598 a fresh patent was granted to Byrd's pupil, Thomas Morley, who assigned licences to Thomas East, Peter Short, and a publisher named William Barley. The last few years of the sixteenth century and the beginning of the seventeenth saw the publication of many of the masterpieces of the English madrigalists, such as *The Triumphes of Oriana* by Thomas Morley, Morley's *First Booke of Balletts to Five Voices*, and the first set of John Wilbye's *Madrigals*, all printed by Thomas East, as well as compositions by John Dowland and Thomas Weelkes.

Music printing in Spain during the sixteenth century was rather rudimentary, the earliest examples being found in liturgical books, such as the Processional printed at Seville by Meinard Ungut and Stanislaus Polonus in 1494, or that issued by Jorge Coci at Saragossa in 1526.

The secular music printed in Spain during the sixteenth century was frequently rather crude and often in the form of illustrations to theoretical works on music such as *El libro llamado declaración de instrumentos musicales* by Juan Bermudo printed at Ossuna by Juan de León in 1555.

The popularity of the lute in other countries of Europe was equalled in Spain by that of the vihuela, a species of guitar with six courses instead of the four on the latter instrument. In 1554 Martin de Montesdoca printed at Seville Miguel de Fuenllama, *Libro de musica para Vihuela, intitulado Orphenica lyra*. From Valladolid in 1538 came the *Libro del delphin de musica para tañer vihuela*, printed by Hernandez de Cordova.

Even earlier, in 1535, the press of Diaz Romano at Valencia had issued Luys Milan, *Libro de musica de vihuela de mano intitulada El Maestro*. The vihuela de mano was, as its name suggests, played by the fingers of the hand, as opposed to the *vihuela de arco*, played with a bow, and the forerunner of the viol.

20

The Book Fairs

AT an early date in the history of bookselling it had become customary to buy and sell books at fairs. The towns in which these fairs were held enjoyed certain privileges which they extended to the merchants who traded at them, money changers were on hand to facilitate the transactions, and carters arranged the transport of merchandise. They were the meeting places of printers, booksellers and publishers from all over Europe, who were intent on examining the latest publications, replenishing their stocks, buying (in the case of printers) strikes or matrices or other material for their printing offices. During the centuries immediately following the introduction of printing, the main fairs at which commercial dealings in books were carried on were Antwerp, Lyons, Frankfurt and Leipzig.

Early on, one of the most important was the Lyons fair, which came into existence in 1420. This city had become an important centre of printing at an early date, largely owing to its proximity to Germany and Lombardy, on the great commercial route which linked the Ile-de-France, Burgundy and the countries of the Mediterranean. From 1446 until 1484 the Lyons fair was an accepted cosmopolitan rendezvous for merchants of all categories. In 1463 Louis XI granted *lettres de franchise* for four fairs yearly of a fortnight's duration each; previously there had been three fairs of twenty days' duration. During the reign of Louis XI merchants of all nationalities were admitted with the exception of the English, 'noz ennemis anciens'.

But in March 1484 the fairs were suppressed, allegedly on account of the nearness of Lyons to the frontier, 'à cause de laquelle extremité plusieurs fraudes y sont commises'. However in 1498 Louis XII confirmed the four fairs with all their privileges, and this confirmation was repeated in 1514, 1547 and 1559. The Lyons fair reached its apogee in the first half of the sixteenth century, when the great Italian publishers, the Giunta family, the Gabiani and the Portonarii established important branches of their business there.

During the course of the sixteenth century other fairs grew in importance and gradually eclipsed the fame of Lyons. The two most important were those of Frankfurt and Leipzig. Frankfurt was famous for its trade in cloth and manufactured goods long before the advent of the printed book. In fact, unlike

Lyons, printing at Frankfurt got off to a rather slow start, and did not become of importance until around 1530, when Christian Egenolff went there from Strassburg and was a major printer for a quarter of a century (see p. 131). Nevertheless the Frankfurt fair had attracted the attention of well-known printers long before that; men like Peter Schöffer, Michael Wenssler and Johann Amerbach, and it was not long before this 'shop-window of the Muses', as Henri Estienne termed it,* became the Mecca of the book trade. Its twice-yearly fair, held in spring and autumn, was attended by printers and booksellers from all over Europe, as well as by scholars of all nations, who came to Frankfurt to meet their colleagues and to inspect and buy the latest books.

From 1495 onwards Anton Koberger was a constant visitor to the Frankfurt fair, taking with him bales of books. In 1506 he had a warehouse there so that he could leave his unsold stock from one fair to the next. Thenceforward the number of booksellers attending the fair grew from year to year. The great printer–publisher Christopher Plantin visited the fair regularly until infirmity made the journey too exhausting; when he could no longer go personally, he sent his son-in-law Jan Moerentorf. Like Koberger before him he had a shop and warehouse for the storage of his wares. After the Lenten fair of 1579 there remained in this *pachuis* 11,617 books representing some 240 different titles, and at the time of Plantin's death books to the value of 8,024 florins were in store there, as well as punches, strikes and matrices. He also had a Frankfurt agent, Jan Dresseler.

Besides looking after the interests of his own extensive business at the fair, Plantin would represent other publishers on a commission basis, their goods – books, atlases, maps, and engravings – being despatched to him on sale or return. As an instance of this practice we may take the following entry in Plantin's *Grand Livre*:

> 11 August, 1558. Received from Hubert Golz to take to Frankfurt the following books, on the understanding that I will pay him 55 patards for each book, or return them to him. Received 44 *Vitae imperatorum imagines*.

When it was first inaugurated as a book mart, business at the Frankfurt fair was conducted on a cash basis, but later it became customary to give credit from fair to fair, i.e. six months' credit, accounts being reckoned in Rhenish *goldgulden*; but customers with large accounts would frequently be given a year's credit. The entries in the Plantinian account books of the transactions which took place at the Frankfurt fair would provide a wealth of material for the cambist. The various European currencies accepted by Plantin, *florins d'or*, *pistolets*, *doubles ducats*, *angelots*, *ducats d'Hongrie*, *daldres d'Hollande*, *longues croix*, etc. are given with their equivalents in Flemish currency.

---

* *Francofordiense Emporium, sive Francofordienses Nundinae*, 1574.

Many booksellers relied on the fair for a major portion of their sales. The Zürich publisher Christoph Froschauer records that he took to the Frankfurt fair in 1534 2,000 copies, folio and octavo, of the *Epitome trium terrae partium*, and managed to sell half of them, with the expectation of selling the remainder at the following fair. The fair was also a market for the sale of printers' stock-in-trade, both founts of type and matrices.

During the sixteenth century, when the publishing business was still in its infancy, and printers were still booksellers, the book-dealer or *buchhändler* came into being. Although not the correct dictionary translation of the word, he was nevertheless a 'book handler', making the rounds of the printers and visiting the fairs with his stock. At the beginning he was merely a pedlar, but the more efficient became wholesale dealers, ignoring the small local fairs and setting up their booths only in the larger ones.

At Frankfurt the growing distinction between printer and publisher was first emphasised by a protocol of the Town Council in 1569, which reads: 'dass obenzehlte Personen nit allein Buchtrucker, sondern mehreren Theils zum Theill Buchhaendler zum Theill Buchfuehrer seint.'*

Our knowledge of the products of early presses is derived in part from catalogues, for from the start printers found it advantageous, indeed necessary, to issue a list of what they had for sale. Mentelin issued a list of books, pasted in his *Summa Astexana* (1469), and in 1500 the bookseller Albrecht de Memmingen published a list of some 200 titles under the heading *Libri venales Venetiis, Nurembergae et Basiliae*. In the sixteenth century it became increasingly necessary for publishers to issue catalogues of their stock and this practice was followed by publishers from widely separated countries: Manuzio in Venice, Simon de Colines in Paris, Christopher Froschauer in Zürich, Sébastien Gryphe in Lyons, Johann Froben in Basel, and Christopher Plantin in Antwerp. Such catalogues were distributed by publishers or their factors at the Frankfurt fairs, but eventually it was found necessary to issue a general catalogue listing the new books on sale at the fair. The initiative for this came from the Augsburg book dealer Georg Willer who had an extensive clientèle and was a regular visitor to the fair.

The first catalogue of the fair was issued by him in 1564, and his catalogue appeared twice yearly until 1592. The first issue was only a small quarto of twenty-two pages, mentioning 252 books. The Willer catalogue remained without a rival until in 1577 a similar catalogue was issued by another Augsburg firm, Johann Portenbach and Thibaus Lutz, and continued by them and their successors until 1616.

In 1569, following the diffusion of seditious literature and a considerable

---

* The persons enumerated above are not printers only but more often partly booksellers or partly publishers.

counterfeiting of the imperial privileges, an Imperial Book Commission was set up and the Frankfurt magistrature was ordered to examine the privileges of all booksellers visiting the fair to see what they had printed during the last five years. This Imperial Commission exercised an influence over all the book trade of which Frankfurt was the centre, and its too rigorous censorship after it had been established in the city by Rudolf II in 1579 led ultimately to the decline and decay of the Frankfurt book trade. Its operations were largely controlled by the Jesuits who made of it an instrument for the furtherance of the Counter-Reformation. Its arbitrary and partisan censorship in a city where there were, at that time, four times as many Protestants as Catholics, led to unsuccessful remonstrations.

After the Thirty Years' War many dealers who had ceased to attend the fair during those troubled years did not resume their business relations after the Treaty of Westphalia in 1648, and as the restrictions imposed by the Imperial Book Commission increased, this, together with the absence of foreign merchants, proved a blow from which Frankfurt was unable to recover. Fewer books were exhibited from year to year and in 1749 the fair ceased entirely.

From the fifteenth until the seventeenth century Frankfurt had been the centre of the trade in Catholic literature in Latin. That part of the trade grew gradually less with the increase in the use of the vernacular and the decline of Latin as a European *lingua franca*. Protestants, who mainly used the vernacular, became the most prolific writers, both in theology and science, and publishing enterprise and the wholesale marketing of books passed from Frankfurt to Leipzig.

The Leipzig fair was also an ancient one, going back to 1165. In 1268 the Margrave Dietrich von Lansberg issued a decree which assured protection to all merchants coming to the fair, even if Saxony were at war with the sovereigns of these merchants. During the ensuing centuries Leipzig became a magnet for traders, attracting visitors from many countries, including Poland and Russia, many of whom remained to settle in the city.

During the fifteenth century the fair developed rapidly and was held three times yearly – at Easter, Michaelmas, and the New Year. During the sixteenth century, as printing grew in importance foreign booksellers in increasing numbers visited the fair. But if the development was rapid during the sixteenth century, that of the seventeenth, despite the Thirty Years' War, was still more remarkable, whilst the eighteenth, especially after the cessation of the Frankfurt fair, was better still. During the first decade of the eighteenth century four times as many publications were listed in the catalogue of the Leipzig fair as in that of its rival at Frankfurt.

Goethe, who visited the city in 1765, has recorded his impressions of the town and the fair in his *Dichtung und Wahrheit*, recounting with what interest he wandered through the market and past the stalls, where, in the year of his visit, some 6,000 merchants were assembled.

There came a recession during the Napoleonic wars, but after 1820 prosperity returned, and in 1840 no fewer than 23,000 merchants were trading at the fair. The city's total population at that time was under 50,000. Much of the success of the Leipzig fair was undoubtedly due to its intermediate position between Western and Eastern Europe.

Like Frankfurt, Leipzig had its catalogue of the fair, the first *Leipziger Messkatalog* appearing at the time of the Michaelmas fair of 1594, printed by Henning Gross. From 1598 until 1619 a second catalogue was issued by Abraham Lamberg, and from 1620 the catalogue was published jointly by the two firms.

In modern times the Frankfurt Book Fair was revived just after the Second World War and in 1969 there were no fewer than 3,131 exhibitors showing some 208,000 titles, of which about 68,000 were new publications.

Transport of merchandise to the fairs was either by boat or by wagon. Whether loaded on to boats or carts, or on pack-horses or mules, the goods were usually well wrapped in coarse canvas tied with ropes. For the carriage of books, bales and casks were the containers most used. When Plantin visited the Frankfurt fair, or in later years his son-in-law Jan Moerentorf (Moretus), they went by wagon from Antwerp as far as Cologne, and from there by boat up the Rhine, though it is on record that Moerentorf in 1566 made the journey from Antwerp to Cologne on foot! The books intended for the fair were normally sent to Plantin's colleague Materne Cholin of Cologne, who saw to their despatch down the Rhine. For the Lenten fair of 1579, for example, six barrels filled with books were sent in this manner to Frankfurt, containing 5,212 copies of sixty-seven different titles.

The journey to Frankfurt was not always uneventful. In 1586 Plantin's factor, Jan Dresseler was seized, robbed, and taken prisoner by a band of unpaid mercenaries when travelling between Brussels and Namur. As a consequence of this form of occupational risk he had an additional clause inserted into his contract with Plantin stipulating that if he fell into the hands of enemies the printer was to pay half his ransom.* In the same year a similar misfortune overtook Jean Bellère's son Lucas, who, while on his way to Frankfurt was seized by brigands and held to ransom. Writing to the geographer Ortelius from Rome in 1578, Hermannus Hortenbergus Noviomagus tells him: 'I have received from Muret three books of *Variarum Lectionum* so that I can send them to Trent and thence to Plantin's agents at the Frankfurt Fair, so that they shall not fall into the hands of the soldiers who prowl about the roads.'†

* *Correspondance de Plantin.* Vol. 7, p. 286.
† J. Hessels, *Ecclesiae Londino-Batavae Archivum.* Vol. 1, p. 172.

21

Early Printing in Scandinavia

LÜBECK, that powerful Hanseatic city, was Germany's great outlet for trade with Scandinavia. Almost half a century before the spread of the Reformation into these northern lands German printers had brought the new art and even at the time of Sweden's greatest political might under Gustavus Adolfus, German printers were the only ones working in Stockholm. 'Lübeck,' wrote Aeneas Sylvius in 1458, 'possesses such wealth and such power that Denmark, Sweden and Norway are accustomed to elect and depose kings upon a sign from her.' Such an immense influence upon the Swedish economy was exercised by this Hansa stronghold that the first of the Vasa kings, Gustavus I (1523–60) was chosen king on Lübeck's insistence.

The first to print in **Stockholm** was a travelling German printer named Johann Snell, who was called from Lübeck to print there a Missal for the diocese of Uppsala, which he completed in 1484. It was preceded by the collection of fables called *Dialogus Creaturarum*, a quarto bearing the date of 20 December 1483.

Snell was followed by Bartholomaeus Ghotan from Magdeburg, who printed some books, mainly liturgical, in 1487, and after him came Johann Fabri who printed a few books, including Breviaries for Stregness and Uppsala. But the first properly established press in Sweden was that set up at Uppsala in 1510 by Pawel Grijs, the first printer of Swedish birth. His first book was a Psalter for the diocese of Uppsala.

Georg (Jürgen) Richolff the Younger, in addition to continuing his father's business at Lübeck (see p. 137), was often called upon to print elsewhere, and we find him at Uppsala in 1526, when he printed the *editio princeps* of the New Testament in Swedish. In 1526 King Gustav I commissioned him to establish a Royal Printing House. Appointed the first King's Printer in Sweden, Richolff brought from Lübeck his own type foundry, matrices from which were used by later royal printers.

The first Swedish printers, such as Snell and Ghotan, used mainly textura faces interspersed with gothic *lettre bâtarde*. When Richolff printed the New Testament in 1526 and other writings occasioned by Gustav Vasa's espousal of the Reformation, he began to make use of Schwabacher types, then being commonly used in Germany. These types came, it seems, from Stephen Arndes in Lübeck and Melchior Lotter at Wittenberg (Bengt Bengtsson, 1956). In 1541 Richolff printed the first edition of the Bible in Swedish, known as 'Gustav Vasa's Bible', the cost of which was met by a special contribution of corn from each parish. For this Bible Richolff used a newer Schwabacher as well as two founts of Fraktur. Roman type did not come into general use in Sweden until half way through the sixteenth century, and most of the roman and italic faces of that period came from Basel.

Meanwhile, another press was established in Sweden at **Söderköping** in 1523 by Bishop Johann Brask, the actual press work being in the hands of one Olaus Ulrici whose first book was *Historia S.Nicolai Lincopensis*, while at Uppsala in 1525 Bartholomaeus Fabri (possibly the son of Johann Fabri) did some printing in partnership with Georg Richolff.

In 1543 Stockholm welcomed a printer, Amund Laurentsson, who worked there for more than thirty years, until 1575. His first book, the Finnish Primer of Bishop Michael Agricola, was also the first book printed in Finnish (see p. 229). He was succeeded by Torbjörn Tidemansson, who only seems to have printed during the years 1576–77, and after him came Anders Torstenson, active from 1578 until 1582.

In 1582 came Stockholm's last sixteenth-century printer, Andreas Gutterwitz, who had been a printer at Rostock and Copenhagen during the previous ten years. He was also a typefounder and cast the runic types used in an alphabet book of runes by the Swedish antiquary Johannes Bureus (1611). Gutterwitz died in 1610, and two years later the contents of his foundry were inventoried. We know, therefore, that he was well provided with matrices, which included a Basel italic, founts of Fraktur and roman, as well as what were described in the inventory as 'Muncka matrizer'. These monk matrices were probably some form of gothic type used in liturgical printing, and may have come originally either from the Lübeck firm of Richolff, or maybe from the stock of Bartholomew Ghotan. The runes in the *Runa A.B.C. Boken* of Bureus were designed by the antiquary and are said to have been cut at the expense of the Swedish king. A second edition was printed at Uppsala in 1624 by E. Mattsson, the successor of Gutterwitz, whose material, after his death, was purchased by the Crown (which had previously owned half of the Gutterwitz printing office) and transferred to Uppsala, where Eskil Mattsson had been appointed Printer to Uppsala University.

DENMARK

At the beginning of the sixteenth century Denmark was, in the field of printing, merely an appendage of North Germany, and for a considerable period Danish book production was deeply marked by German influence. However, the century witnessed a considerable extension of the printing trade, the Lutheran Reformation leading to the establishment of a number of presses.

Strangely enough the first book printed in Denmark, *De obsidione et bello Rhodiano* by Gulielmus Caorsin, was the work of Johann Snell, who also introduced the art of printing into Sweden. Completed at Odense in 1482, it preceded Snell's work at Stockholm, and so was the first book to be printed in any part of Scandinavia, though Snell also printed in the same year a *Breviarium Ottoniense* which may have preceded the Caorsin.

He was followed by Gotfred of Ghemen, who worked in Copenhagen from about 1489 until around 1510, and was the first to print a book in the Danish tongue, a rhymed chronicle called the *Danske Rimkronike*, which this Dutchman from Gouda printed in a quarto edition in 1495 and reprinted in octavo in 1504 and 1508.

From Lübeck came Matthaeus Brandis who in 1510 printed at Copenhagen a fine *Missale Hafniense*. Later his press was taken over by Canon Poul Raeff, the first Dane to print (1513), who in 1519 printed a *Missale Nidrosiense* at the request of the Archbishop of Trondhjem in Norway, Erik Valkendorf. At a time when the Reformation was splitting the country, Raeff was a pillar of Roman Catholicism, printing liturgical books as well as Catholic propaganda. He was active as a printer until 1533, working also in the towns of Aarhus and Nyborg.

Other presses were established at **Malmö**, where Johann Hoochstraten and Oluf Ulrickson were the printers; at **Roskilde**, where Hans Barth had his printing office from 1534 and 1540; and at **Viborg**, where Hans Vingaard, a native of Stuttgart, set up the first press. Vingaard was the printer most active in the cause of the Reformation, and in 1531 he moved to Copenhagen, where he remained until his death in 1559. He was the printer of many Reformation tracts by Peder Palladius, and for some years was printer to the university at Copenhagen.

Malmö, which at that time was Danish, was another centre of the Reformation, and Oluf Ulrickson, who had previously worked for Bishop Hans Brask at Söderköping, worked in Malmö from 1528 to the middle of the century. The other Malmö press was established around 1530 by the Danish writer Christiern Pedersen, another staunch supporter of the new religion, for whom the press was managed by the Dutch printer Jan Hoochstraten. This press lasted only until 1535, during which time it issued a number of religious and political tracts, a psalm book, and several of Pedersen's own works. Pedersen, who had worked in Paris and Antwerp as an itinerant printer, was the first to introduce the Renaissance style into Danish books, and his Malmö press was the first in Denmark to make use of italic types. After leaving Malmö he took over the business of Hans Vingaard.

The first printer to use roman type in Denmark was Hans Barth at his

FIGURE 50. Title-page of the first Danish edition of *Reynard the Fox*, translated into Danish verse by Hermen Weigere. Lübeck: Georg Richolff.

Roskilde press, not far from Copenhagen. This was in his edition of Melanchthon, *Instructio visitationis Saxonicae* (1538). In 1540 Barth printed the first edition of the New Testament in Icelandic, the first book printed in that language.

By the middle of the sixteenth century the style of Danish books began to show a marked change in make-up and typography due to the work of two printers of outstanding ability, Lorenz Benedicht and Matz Vingaard. But before these two had established their presses a German from Rostock, Ludwig Dietz, had been called to Copenhagen to print a Bible, no local printer being at that time capable of so considerable a task. This was the first printed Bible in Danish, known as Christian III's Bible because the king had ordered it to be translated from Luther's version. This well-printed folio which appeared in 1550 with many woodcut illustrations was similar in style to a Low German Bible which Dietz had already printed, and since he was a German his Danish Bible was typically German in style, both in respect of its initials and the use of Schwabacher as the text type. The second Danish Bible, known as Frederick II's Bible, was printed at Copenhagen by Matz Vingaard in 1589, with illustrations similar to those used in the English 'Bishops' Bible' of 1568.

One of the most competent sixteenth-century printers in Denmark was Lorenz Benedicht, who worked in Copenhagen from about 1560 until 1601. He was the first printer in Denmark to make Fraktur his principal type, and he also introduced music printing into that country with the *Danske Salmebog* of Hans Thomesen in 1569. This was followed in 1573 by Nils Jespersen's *Gradual* (Hammerich, A. *Dansk Musikhistorie*. 1921).

The famous astronomer Tycho Brahe, when he mounted his observatory at the castle of Uranienborg, on the little island of Hven, also set up a small printing office. Even when he was living in exile at Wandsbeck, in Holstein, he took with him his press and there printed the first edition of his *Astronomiae instauratae mechanica* in 1598.

NORWAY

It may seem strange that there was no printing in Norway until the middle of the seventeenth century, but just as Finland was supplied with books from Sweden, so Norway obtained them from Denmark. Up to 1814 the countries were politically united, and for a long time the centre of the literary life of both countries was Copenhagen, and there the earlier Norwegian literature was printed.

Not until 1643 did Norway get its first press, when the Danish printer Tyge Nielsen was called to Christiania (now Oslo) to print there the *Postilla catechetica* of the priest Christen Bang. His visit was a brief one, and his successo·s were Melchior Martzan (1647–50) and Valentin Kuhn (1650–54).

FINLAND

The origins and development of printing in the Finnish language are linked with the spread of the Lutheran doctrine in the northern lands, more especially following Sweden's break with the Church of Rome during the reign of Gustavus Vasa, for Finland had been part of Sweden since the fourteenth century, and from 1556 had been administered directly from Stockholm, which supplied Finland with printed matter.

Chiefly responsible for the initial spread of Lutheran ideas in Sweden was the

Finnish reformer Mikael Agricola, the son of a poor fisherman in the south of Finland, who had studied theology under Luther at the university of Wittenberg, and later became Bishop of Åbo (Turku). In 1542 appeared Agricola's Catechism, *Abckiria Michael Agricola Christiano Salutem*, which was the first book to appear in the Finnish tongue and was followed by others printed at Stockholm by Amund Laurentsson. In 1548 appeared Agricola's translation of the New Testament into Finnish, again printed at Stockholm.

But the first press in Finland itself was not established until 1642, two years after the foundation of the University of Åbo. The first printer was the Swede Peder Eriksson Wald from Vasteras, who was active there until 1653. His first work, and thus the first printing in Finland, was a Latin dissertation of Michael Wexionius, *Discursus politicus de prudentia* (1642). During the following year he printed the first Swedish and Finnish books to be published in Finland. The first was Isak Rothovius, *Nagra christeliga boot prediknigar* (Christian Penitental Sermons), followed by *Ylimmäisen Keisaren Jesuxen Christuxen mandati eli käsky* (The Mandates or Commandments of the Highest King, Jesus Christ).

In 1642, the same year as the founding of Wald's press, was published the first Bible in Finnish; but this came from Stockholm, where it was printed by Henrich Keisarilda, under the patronage of Queen Christina, whose engraved portrait appears in some copies.

The production from the first Finnish press was scanty, and after Wald's death in 1653, the university press was run by various Swedish printers, but it proved inadequate to meet demands, and in 1669 another press was established at Åbo by the bishop, Johann Gezelius, and managed by Johann Winter, who had previously worked at Dorpat, and who showed far greater activity than his colleagues of the university press. In addition to the printing of Gezelius's own works, he issued a variety of school books and official publications, and in 1680 was appointed royal printer for Finland. In 1685 there came from his press the first Bible in Finnish to be printed in Finland itself. There is a copy of it in the British Museum. Winter died in 1706 and the press soon afterwards came under the management of Henrik Christofer Merckel.

The only other town in Finland to possess a printing press during the seventeenth century was Viborg, where it was established by Bishop Petrus Bang in 1689 and run by Daniel Medelplan, who left Viborg, however, in 1693 and went to Pälkäne. During the Northern War, which broke out in 1700, the press at Viborg was destroyed and the two at Åbo were removed to Sweden. It was nine years before Finland had another press.

ICELAND

Although there were no printing presses in Norway and Finland until near the middle of the seventeenth century, Iceland's first press was set up at Hólar about

1530. The first known book to have come from this press was a *Breviarium Holense*, printed by Jón Matthiasson, known as 'Svenski' (the Swede) in 1534, under the patronage of Jón Arason, the last Catholic bishop of Hólar. Unfortunately the last known complete copy of this book disappeared when the library in which it was kept was destroyed by fire in 1728, but two leaves were later found in the binding of a book in the Royal Library at Stockholm. The type is a rather clumsy Schwabacher almost certainly not new when first brought to Iceland.

Two other books, known only by imperfect copies, are clearly from the press of Matthiasson, who accepted the Lutheran reforms inaugurated by Christian III and remained in his living at Breidabólsstadur until his death in 1567. One, of which a single copy remains in the University Library at Copenhagen, is an Icelandic translation of the Passion sermons of Antonius Corvinus; the other, again in a unique copy at the Royal Library, Copenhagen, is known as the *Gudspjallabók*. The respective dates of printing have been attributed to 1559 for the former and 1562 for the latter.

After the death of Matthiasson, he was succeeded in his benefice by Gudbrandur Thorláksson, who was later made bishop of Hólar. He made use of Jón Matthiasson's old press and sent Matthiasson's son, Jón Jónsson, to Copen-

FIGURE 51. Verso of the title-page of Arngrimur Jónsson, *Anatome Blefkeniana*, printed in Iceland at the first Hólar press by Jón Jónsson in 1612. Jónsson learned to print in Denmark.

hagen to learn the art of printing and to bring back further equipment. From 1577 until 1624 Bishop Gudbrandur, with Jón Jónsson as his first printer (d. 1616) and then with the latter's son, Brandur, carried on a considerable amount of printing, mainly consisting of religious books. Among these pride of place must certainly go the first edition of the complete Bible in Icelandic, printed under the auspices of Frederick II of Denmark. This great folio of 622 leaves was completed in 1584 and has many illustrations and decorative initials. 'In no subsequent book of the Hólar press,' writes Benedikt S. Benedikz, 'was so much and so devoted attention given to proof-reading, even to the insertion of corrections by hand.' (*Spread of Printing: Iceland.* 1969).

In 1589 the press was moved to Núpufell, where Jón Jónsson printed Summaries of the Old and New Testaments, but later was brought back again to Hólar, where in 1594 he printed a *Graduale*. He continued to manage the press until his death in 1616, when he was succeeded by his son Brandur. The first Hólar press, though it continued to function until 1685, lost much of its impetus with the death of Bishop Gudbrandur Thorláksson in 1627. Until about 1773 the press at Hólar was the only one in Iceland, save for the years 1685–1697, when a press was working at Skálholt.

22

Evolution of Printing in Central Europe

In dealing with printing in Central Europe one is frequently baffled by the varying nomenclature of towns and cities due to the ebb and flow during the centuries of its constituent countries. This table is intended as a help to puzzled readers.

G stands for German, C for Czechoslovak, H for Hungarian and R for Romanian.

In accordance with the expressed wish of the government of Romania, that country is spelled with an 'o' and not Rumania as at one time.

Alba Julia (R) = Gyulafehérvàr (H) = Karlsburg, and earlier Weissenburg (G)
Cluj (R) = Kolosvǎr (H) = Clausenburg (G)
Brno (C) = Brünn (G) = Brinnium (Latin)
Bratislava (C) = Pozsony (H) = Pressburg (G)
Brasov (R) = Brassó (H) = Kronstadt (G) = Corona (Latin)
Sibiu (R) = Nagy-Szeben (H) = Hermannstadt (G)
Usti (C) = Aussig (G)
Plzen (C) = Pilsen (G)
Orastie (R) = Szászváros (H) = Broos (G)
Olomouc (C) = Olmütz (G)
Oradea (R) = Varad (H) = Grosswardein (G)
Bardejov (C) = Bartfa (H)
Trrava (C) = Nagyszombat (H)
Levoca (C) = Leutschau (G)
Kosice (C) = Kassa (H)
Karlovy Vary (C) = Karlsbad (G)
Bistrita (R) = Beszterce (H) = Nösen; Bistritz (G)
Sebesul sasesc (R) = Szászsebes (H) = Mühlbach (G)
Sighisoara (R) = Segesvár (H) = Schassburg (G)
Abrud (R) = Abrudbanya (H) = Altenburg (G)
Gyakos (H) = Jakobsdorf (G)
Cris (R) = Keresd (H) = Kreisch (G)
Selimbar (R) = Sellemberk (H) = Schellenberg (G)
Harina (R) = Harina (H) = Mönchsdorf
Mukacevo (C) = Munkács

BOHEMIA

Until recently it was generally accepted that the first book printed in Bohemia and the first printed book in the Czech language was the *Trojánská Kronika*, printed probably at Pilsen (Plzeň) by an unknown printer. This historical romance about the destruction of Troy was written in the thirteenth century by Guido della Colonna, and a manuscript now in the library of the monastery of Osek may well have been the source of the printed version, which bears the date 1468. As the manuscript is similarly dated it may well be that the printer gave in his colophon the date of the written text. Recent research has brought to light the fact that some of the letters of this Trojan Chronicle were adopted from an *Agenda Pragensis*, printed in Pilsen at a later date. The date of printing of the Chronicle may therefore have to be advanced by as much as ten years.

Were the date of printing of the Trojan Chronicle proved to be later than 1475, then the Bohemian *New Testament* of that year might well be the oldest book printed in that country. Unfortunately neither of these two incunabula mentions the place of printing, and whereas Dobrowsky suggests Pilsen as the town, Darlow and Moule (2175) incline towards Nuremberg as the possible place of origin of what is the *editio princeps* of the New Testament in Bohemian. In favour of Pilsen is the fact that there are shared characteristics in the types of the two books. To make matters more confused František Horak considers that the 1475 New Testament may have been printed in Prague (Horák, 1968).

The first Bohemian book of which we can be reasonably certain both of the date and place of printing is a Latin handbook for the clergy, *Statuta provincialia Arnesti*, the colophon of which states that it was printed at New Pilsen on 26 April 1476. The unknown printer was probably a Czech, for the type, a bastarda based on the local manuscript hand, bears a family likeness to that used in the Trojan Chronicle.

The early printers in Bohemia were singularly loath to disclose their names. The first recorded name is that of the German itinerant printer Johann Alakraw, who in 1484 made his appearance in the little town of Vimperk (Winterberg), having come from Passau. In Vimperk he printed three books, two in Latin and one in Czech, after which all trace of him is lost. The Latin works were *Soliloquia animae ad Deum*, mistakenly attributed to the philosopher Aurelius Augustinus, and Albertus Magnus, *Summa de eucharistiae sacramento*. Both these works bear his name, but the third work, a Calendar for the year 1485 – the oldest Czech wall calendar – has no mention of the printer. It is, however, printed in the same type as the two Latin works – not in gothic, as might have been expected, but in an Italian rotunda.

Of the thirty-one Czech incunabula recorded (of which four are now missing), Prague printers were responsible for fifteen, of which thirteen now exist. Once again we are confronted with anonymity; not a single book produced at Prague during the fifteenth century contains a printer's name. The earliest dated book from Prague is a *Psalterium Bohemicum* of 1487, thought to have been printed by Jonata z Vysoké Mýto, whose name appears in the city archives. He is often referred to by the German form of his name, Jonathan von Hohenmauth. An earlier Prague book, the *Statuum utraquistorum articuli* of 1478 [Hain, 1879], cannot now be traced.

In 1488 the first regular press was established at Prague by Jan Kamp in association with a merchant named Severýn, and the first substantial work of this press was the *Biblia Bohemica* of August 1488, the *editio princeps* of the complete Bible in Czech, a folio of 609 printed leaves (Darlow and Moule, 2177). A corrected reprint of this Bible came the following year from the press of Martin z Tišňova at Kutná Hora (Kuttenberg), about forty miles south-east of Prague. The Kamp-Severýn press at Prague, although its output was relatively small, continued to function well into the sixteenth century, and after the death of Severýn in 1520, his son Pavel Severýn, who had worked for some time as a journeyman printer, took over the business.

Another Prague press of the fifteenth century was that of a printer referred to simply as Beneda in the city's archives. Between 1492 and 1496 he printed five works in Schwabacher type, none of which were of particular importance, but one treatise, upon the Sacrament, by Václav Koranda, has the first printed Czech title-page. This was the only Czech press of the fifteenth century to employ none of the diacritical marks introduced by Jan Hus, and normally a characteristic of Czech printing. Of Beneda's blood-letting calendar for 1496 only a single mutilated copy is known and of the Aesop printed at Prague by Kamp only a few leaves are extant.

Whereas Pilsen had always been the centre of Catholic resistance to the Hussites, Prague was a stronghold of Reform. 'The University of Prague, founded in 1348, at a time when there was no comparable institution in any German land,' writes H. A. L. Fisher, 'gave to the movement of religious reform in Bohemia a force and consistency which would otherwise have been lacking to it.' *

All three known presses at work in Prague during the fifteenth century belonged to Czechs, and from the very beginning we find that in Bohemia the introduction of printing manifested itself not in Latin but in the vernacular. The types used were generally a bastarda of local design, and gothic founts from other countries are seldom found.

The first to print at Prague in the sixteenth century was Mikuláš Konáč, who, in partnership with Jan Wolf, produced a number of books in Czech and Latin between 1507 and 1530. Meanwhile the earliest version of the Bible in Russian was being printed in the 'Byelorussian' dialect by Franciska Skorina, a native of Polotsk. He set out to translate the whole Bible. This he may have done, but today a few portions only are known, mostly printed at Prague between 1517 and 1519, but at least two parts – Acts and Epistles – were printed at Wilno in 1525 (Darlow and Moule, 7777–80). They were printed in Church Slavonic ('Tserkovni'). At Wilno he printed in 1522 a prayer book for travellers called *Malaia podoroznaia Knizica.*†

* H. A. L. Fisher, *A History of Europe.* 1936, p. 355.
† See Alexander Nadson, *Skaryna's Prayer Book*, in the Journal of Byelow Russian Studies, Vol. 2, No. 4, 1972.

Other Prague printers of that period include Jan Severyn the Younger, who printed for a time in partnership with Bartholomew Netolicky, Jan Kosorsky and Jiří Cerny Rozdalovsky, known as Melantrich. (*see infra*)

From the technical point of view the work done by Skorina in Prague is exceptional when compared with contemporary Czech printing. The high standard of the press work and ornamentation, which reveals a West European influence, might lead one to assume that Prague was not the real place of origin, save that there is no evidence to the contrary. But was Skorina himself the printer? He had studied at two universities – Philosophy at Cracow and Medicine and Science at Padua – and was a Doctor 'artium bonarum' as well as Doctor of Medicine. He himself was responsible for the translation of the Bible, but these various scholarly qualifications scarcely presuppose a technical ability as a printer. On the other hand, there is no evidence to connect the work of Skorina with any known printer.

The first-named printer at Pilsen was Mikuláš Bakalář, or Nicholas the Bachelor, whose press was active from 1488 until 1513. As might have been expected in that town, known as 'Pilsna christianissima semperque fidelis', he was a Roman Catholic. Among the books he is known to have printed are the popular *Peregrinations* of Bernhard von Breydenbach, the first Czech Psalter (1499) and the first Czech dictionary (1511). All his books are printed in Schwabacher type and all are in Czech.

MORAVIA

Early printing in Moravia showed one marked difference from Bohemia in that the printers were German, most of their books were in Latin, and their types were all gothic emanating from Germany and Venice. Printing was first introduced into Moravia by Conrad Stahel, a German from Blaubeuren who had previously worked in Venice, where in partnership with Andreas Corvus he had produced a Breviary for the diocese of Olomouc (Olmütz) in Moravia. In 1481 he printed at Passau a Breviary for local use in association with Benedict Mayr, and in 1486 he set up a press at Brno (Brünn) together with a printer from Ulm named Matthias Prünlein.

The earliest book they are known to have printed at Brno is a quarto *Agenda* for the diocese of Olomouc, unsigned but dated 7 October 1486. The first book signed by the printers, who incidentally called themselves 'impressores veneti', was a *Missale Strigoniense*, for the diocese of Esztergom, dated 21 November 1491. Their most important work was the *Chronica Hungarorum* of Johannes de Thwrocz (1488), a history of Hungary with woodcut illustrations, reprinted less than three months later at Augsburg by Erhard Ratdolt. The type used by Stahel and Prünlein was of Venetian origin, and may possibly have

FIGURE 52. This woodcut, from Johannes de Thwrocz, *Chronica Hungarorum*, printed at Brno by Conrad Stahel and Mathias Preunlein in 1488, shows Hungarian peasants being driven into captivity by the Mongols in 1241 A.D.

come from Ratdolt, with whom they may have had a working arrangement, but the illustrations in the *Chronica* are not those in Ratdolt's edition.

Among the smaller works from the Brno press was a pamphlet, *Von allen paden* ... (1495), a tract in German about the medicinal value of bathing in natural hot springs. But although it bears the name of Clement von Graz as its author, it is in fact a plagiarised version of *Gute Lehre von allen Wildbädern* by the Nuremberg printer–poet and mastersinger Hans Folz. The copy of the first-named book in the British Museum (IA 51720) is the only one now known, but a facsimile reprint was issued at Brno in 1929.

After printing a *Statuta synodalia* for Olomouc the partners separated in 1498. Stahel printed a Psalter on his own in the following year and then returned to Venice. Prünlein moved to Olomouc, where he is known to have printed two small tracts in 1499, after which he disappears, his place being taken by Conrad Baumgarten, who had previously worked at Danzig. He arrived at Olomouc in 1500, but by 1503 he had moved to Breslau (now Wroclaw), and three years later was to be found at Frankfurt an der Oder. His output was mainly religious and he is not known to have printed in any language other than Latin.

Another printing office was established at Olomouc in 1538 by Jan Olivetsky, called Hlaváč, who worked there until his death in 1547. He had obtained from Ferdinand I a privilege for printing governmental regulations, almanacs and similar official publications. After the death of Jan Olivetsky, the business was carried on by his son Sebastian, save during his minority, when it was managed for him by Johann Günther, who also had his own printing office in Olomouc from 1551 to 1571, and prior to that had printed at Prostějov (Prossnitz). Günther had learned his trade at Nuremberg, where he printed a few books around 1541.

The first Czech book to be printed in Moravia was produced at Prostějov by a native of that town, the printer Kaspar Neděle, sometimes known, from his birthplace, as Kaspar Prostějovsky. This book, of which no copy has survived, dealt with the correspondence carried on between John Dubčansky, protector of the sect called the Habrowaners, and the members of that sect. In 1530 Neděle moved to Lultsch and worked there until his employer, Dubčansky, was imprisoned in 1537. But the first regular printing office in Prostějov was that of the above-mentioned Johann Günther, who printed there a few books, among which a *Pentateuch* of 1541, before going to Olomouc.

Some of the best printing in Moravia during the sixteenth century was done by the press of the Bohemian Brethren, founded around 1557 at Ivančice by Alexander Oujezdsky. The press published a number of religious works including several editions of the sect's Hymn-books, splendidly printed and ornamented. In 1578 the press was forced to move to Kralice, near Willimowitz in Moravia, a castle which belonged to Jan of Zerotin, a member of the sect who bore most of the cost of the press, including the financing of the celebrated six-volume Bible, known as the Kralice Bible (Darlow and Moule, 2186), issued between 1579 and 1593. The press continued to operate in Kralice until after the battle of the White Mountain in 1620 when its work was interrupted for a time. In 1629 it was moved to Prerov and later to Lesno in Poland.

After the battle of the White Mountain, when Frederick of Bohemia was defeated by the League under Tilly, printing in both Bohemia and Moravia received a setback from which it did not completely recover for the next two hundred years.

Although there were a considerable number of Slovak printers at work at the outset of the sixteenth century, most of them were working abroad, in Austria, Italy, Switzerland, Poland and elsewhere. Of those who worked in their homeland, Pavel Kyrmezet printed *Komedia česká* at Prague in 1566, *Komedia nová o vdově* at Litomyšl in 1573, and the play *Tobias* at Olomouc in 1581. The first native Slovak printing office was at Presov in 1573, followed by others at Šintava (1574), Bardejov and Banská Bystrica (1578), Trnava (1579), Hlohovce and Plavecky Štvrtek (1581) and Bratislava (1594). These were not, for the greater part, permanent presses, but itinerant businesses making use, as a rule, of type that was primitive and badly worn.

The Slovak printer David Gutgesel set up his press at Bardejov in 1578, and in the following year printed Kulczar's *Postille* in Magyar. In 1581 he brought out a Czech translation of Luther's *Catechism*. Books in Latin also came from this press, many of them polemical works on theology. At Banská Bystrica the printer was Kristofer Scholtz, from whose press came a number of religious tracts, including the *Confessio verae religionis* of Rehor Melcer.

One of the outstanding printers in Prague during the second half of the sixteenth century was Jiří Melantrich, a friend of many of the humanists, among them Zikmund Hruby, a corrector at the Froben press in Basel. It is thought that Melantrich acquired some of his printing experience in that city before returning to his homeland about 1540. After a short period at Prostějov, Melantrich went to Prague where as a young man he had studied at the university, and became the partner of the printer Bartoloměj Netolický. In 1549 he printed for Netolický an edition of the Czech Bible, and by 1552 had himself become the owner of the press, which he built up into a flourishing business, producing more than 200 publications. His portrait appears, kneeling before a cross on a hill overlooking the town, in the Bible of 1570.

HUNGARY

It was during the reign of Matthias Corvinus, King of Hungary, that the first printed book made its appearance in that country. Matthias, who for a soldier showed a highly commendable attitude towards the arts of peace, not only founded the university of Pozsony (Pressburg) but possessed one of the finest libraries of the time, destined, alas, to be pillaged in 1526 when the Turkish Sultan Suleiman entered Buda after the battle of Mohács in 1526. Matthias, who had a great passion for ancient manuscripts, many of which he had acquired from Greek refugees after the fall of Constantinople, had no similar regard for the products of the printing press to judge by his harsh treatment of the printers during his occupation of Vienna from June 1485 to his death in 1490. It is therefore the more surprising that he was initially responsible for the setting up of the first press in Hungary.

On 5 June 1473, the first book from this press was completed at Buda by Andreas Hess. It was the *Chronica Hungarorum*, sometimes called 'Chronicon Budense', written by Simon Kézai at the end of the thirteenth century. Of the printer we know little more than the statements contained in the dedication of the *Chronica*, from which we learn that he had recently come from Rome, where he had had the opportunity of learning the new art of printing. His master was probably Georg Lauer, who printed at Rome from 1470 until 1481, for the types of the *Chronica* resemble those used by Lauer. In fact the work may well have been begun in Rome and finished at Buda. In any case, Hess's activity in that city was short-lived. After printing one more book – Basilius Magnus, *De legendis poetis*, he disappears without trace.

The arrival of Hess in Buda seems to have come about as the result of a visit to Rome of the Provost Ladislaus Karai, Vice-chancellor of Matthias Corvinus, during which he had an interview with Cardinal Caraffa, the head of the monastery of Saint Eusebius, in which for a time Lauer had his workshop. It seems possible that Lauer was asked to print the *Chronica* at Buda and being too busy despatched his pupil with the necessary material in his place.

A second press seems to have functioned in Hungary from 1477 to 1480, though neither place nor printer has yet been ascertained. From this press came a *Confessionale* of Antoninus Florentinus, with the date 1477, and for this reason the anonymous printer is merely known as the 'Printer of the Confessionale'. The types are almost certainly those used by Mathias Moravus, who worked at Genoa in 1474 and printed at Naples from 1475 to 1491. However, a blood-letting calendar originating from this Hungarian press in 1480 was printed in the name of a priest of Pozsony (now Bratislava). As the only known copy was found in that town, there is the possibility that the printing office may have been situated there.

No further books were printed in Hungary itself for another half century, for after the death of Matthias Corvinus the country lapsed into feudal anarchy and later the Turkish domination retarded all cultural manifestations. Books were still printed in the Magyar tongue, but in other countries. Thus Erhardt Ratdolt printed a Hungarian Missal at Verona in 1480 with the inscription 'impensis Joannes Cassis dicti librarii ex Ratisspona'. And in the same year he printed for the same bookseller a Breviary for Esztergom (Gran), but this time at Venice. Later, when he returned to Augsburg, Ratdolt printed in 1488 the *Chronica* of John Turóczi. An example of this work, printed on vellum and formerly belonging to the library of Matthias Corvinus is now in the British Museum.

Some early works on the history of printing credit Anthoni Koberger of Nuremberg with having printed the first book in Magyar, a life of St Stephen. This claim, however, cannot be substantiated.

After Hess's press had closed down, Hungarian booksellers were obliged to import the books of foreign printers. From Cracow, in 1533 came the first text printed in Hungarian, a translation by Benedek Komjati of the Letters of St Paul, for the spread of printing within Hungary was greatly hindered by the incursions of the Turks, who destroyed many towns.

Such printing as occurred during the sixteenth century was due mainly to the efforts of the Protestant Reformers, who set up the first Protestant press in Hungary at Szeben (now Sibiu, Romania) in 1529, under the direction of Lucas Trapoldner. No books, however, have survived from this press which seems to have functioned only for about a year, but a Gemmarius, *Libellus grammaticus*, has been recorded.

The most important of the early sixteenth-century presses was that of Johann Honter, pedagogue and reformer (1498–1549). In 1533 he returned from Basel to his native city of Brassó (now Brasov, Romania), where he recruited trained pressmen and printers for a press which printed educational, moral, religious and legal books, including some of the works of Honter himself, who became a parish priest in 1544. Two years later he started a paper mill for the use of his press. After Honter's death the press was continued by another pastor named Valentin Wagner, who in 1550 printed Luther's *Catechism* in Cyrillic characters for the use of Greeks. In 1555 he added an engraving press and in 1557 brought out an edition of *Imagines Mortis* with illustrations after Holbein. After Wagner's death at the end of that year the printing office ceased work for a time, until it was taken over in 1580 by János Nyirö, who was succeeded in 1583 by the printer Georg Greus from Hermannstadt.

In 1536 a press was established at Sárvár-Újsziget, in the Transdanubian provinces, by Tamás Nádasdy. From this printing office came in 1539 the *Grammatica Hungarolatina* of János Erdösi (Sylvester), and in 1541 Sylvester's translation of the *New Testament*.

The year 1550 saw the beginning of Gaspar Heltai's press at Kolozsvár (now Cluj, Romania) which he worked in partnership with György Hoffgreff until 1552, when Hoffgreff departed after a quarrel, but returned in 1554 to take charge of the press. Between them they produced some thirty-three books. Then Hoffgreff disappears and Heltai continued the press from 1559 to 1574, in which time he brought out sixty-three titles. After his death the widow carried on the printing office until 1584, and from then until the end of the century it was efficiently managed by the son, Gaspar Heltai II. Gaspar Heltai I printed a number of Hungarian works, such as Tinódi's *Cronica* (1554) and his own *Szás fabula* (Hundred Fables) in 1566. Among other things he endeavoured to systematise the Hungarian spelling.

During the second half of the sixteenth century many itinerant printers visited the small towns of Hungary, taking with them their primitive equipment. One of them, Bálint Mantskovit, eventually settled in Vizsoly, where he is known to have printed at least twelve books, including the first complete Hungarian Protestant Bible in the translation of Gáspár Károlyi (1590, Darlow and Moule, 5406).

At about the same time as the *Typographia Honteriana*, there flourished at Brassó, independently of that press, a printing office which made use exclusively of Cyrillic characters and worked in the main for the church in Romania. The printer was Oprea Logofatul, but the undertaking was directed by his partner, the Deacon Coresi. After the completion of a few works for the Orthodox Church, Coresi moved for a while to Tirgoviste in Wallachia. After his return from that town in 1560 Coresi found in Johann Benkner, a magistrate of Brassó (Kronstadt) and owner of a paper mill there, a zealous supporter. From 1563 to 1579 Coresi ran the press on his own. At the end of 1579 he went to Szászváros (Mühlbach) but returned to Brassó within a year and carried on the press until around 1583, which was probably the year of his death. His son Serban succeeded him and printed mainly liturgical books until 1588. In printing the Gospels of 1579 and 1583, Coresi was aided by a colleague named Manaila, whose name appears in the colophon.

Yet another printing house employing Cyrillic letters was functioning at Brassó from 1567 until about 1578, run by one Lorint, who later worked at Gyulafehérvár (Karlsburg).

At Debrecen the famous Polish printer Rafael Hoffhalter was active between 1563 and 1565, when he moved to Várad (now Oradea, Romania), where his son Rudolf also worked, from 1567 to 1568. Rudolf later also went to Debrecen, where he printed a number of Protestant books.

Another well-known Hungarian printer of the sixteenth century was Gál Huszár, a zealous Reformer, who worked at Ovar, Kassa, Debrecen and Komjati before moving to Papa, where he died in 1574, and where his son David, who was a pastor at the Reformed Church in that town, took over his father's press. Nothing from that press is known later than 1577.

The second and third quarters of the sixteenth century had seen the Reformation triumphant in Hungary, but during the last decades of the century the Counter-Reformation took the offensive, and for that purpose a printing office was most necessary. So Miklós Telegdi, Administrator of the Archdiocese of Esztergom (Gran), set up a printing establishment which he bought from the Viennese Jesuits in 1577 and installed in his home at Nagyszombat (now Trnava, Czechoslovakia). It was known as the 'Typographia Telegdiniana' and functioned from 1578 until 1587. (During the Turkish occupation the residence of the Primate of Hungary was moved from Esztergom to Nagyszombat.) The name of only one printer employed at the Typographia Telegdiniana has come down to us. He was Valentin Otmar, who worked there in 1584. Could he have been a relative of the former Augsburg printer Valentin Otmar (fl. 1542–63)? Possibly his son?

The town of Szeben (now Sibiu, Romania) had a number of printers during the course of the sixteenth century, none of whom were active for more than a few years. The most important seems to have been Johann Heinrich Crato, who printed eleven books between 1591 and 1594, and may possibly have been related to the Wittenberg family of printers named Krafft (Crato). After his death in 1595 the business was taken over by Johann Fabritius, who died in 1601.

Johannes Manlius was another wandering printer, whom we find working in a number of small towns of Hungary between the years 1582 and 1604, printing Protestant treatises. He died at Keresztur (now Deutschkreutz, Austria) in 1604.

Towards the end of the century printers in Hungary began at last to find outlets for their work in other than religious fields, and the first Hungarian textbook on botany, *Herbarium* by Peter Juhász, appeared in 1578, printed at Kolozsvár by Gaspar Heltar.

ROMANIA

The origins of printing in that part of Europe which we now know as Romania, and which in Gutenberg's day comprised the states of Wallachia and Moldavia, are as difficult to elucidate as are those of printing in Jugoslavia. It is generally acknowledged that the first book actually printed in Romania was a *Liturghier*, or Orthodox Missal, printed at Tirgoviste in 1508, 'by the labour of the humble monk and Priest Makarie' at the command of 'the Grand Voivode of all the land of Hongro-Wallachia and of Podunavia', to quote from the colophon.

But who was this Makarie? Some authorities say he was that very monk Makarie who had printed at Cetinje and who, at the advance of the Turks, transferred his press to Wallachia, a country which, together with Moldavia, offered some protection to the Orthodox believers oppressed by the infidel. But, according to P. Alanasov,* such an affirmation is categorically weakened both by the typographic appearance of the books printed at Tirgoviste and the language in which the texts are written, when compared with the Montenegrin books.

The printer of the former, Alanasov says, was of Bulgarian origin, born in Romania, the son of Bulgarian parents who had fled from the Turks. For, as Professor Bogdan tells us,† 'at this period the Romanian lands became the Italy of the Bulgars, and just as the Greeks who fled into Italy after the collapse of the Byzantine Empire resuscitated there a renaissance of the classics in art and science, so the Bulgars who had fled to Romania laid the foundations of the Bulgaro-Romanian literature which dominated Romania from the fourteenth to the seventeenth centuries'.

The Romanian Makarie may have learned to print, thinks Alanasov, in Cracow, where he may have had a hand in the production of the books in Cyrillic characters produced by Swietopek Fiol (see p. 247). The use of Bulgarian originals for these editions leads one to suppose that Bulgars had been engaged as editors, correctors and possibly printers.

Makarie's *Liturghier* of 1508 was followed by an *Octoich* in 1510 and an *Evangheliar* in 1512, all of them in Church Slavonic. The first book to be printed in the Romanian language was a *Catechism*, showing a Protestant tendency, printed at Sibiu in 1544. Later, a number of books in Romanian were printed at Brasov (then Brassó, Hungary) by the deacon Coresi (see also p. 240). Among these was an edition of the *Gospels* in Romanian, published in 1561.

The liturgical works printed in Romania may have been printed at the request of the Moldo-Wallachian voivodes, but possibly the main instigator was the Moldavian king, Stephen III (the Great), who resisted for long the advances of

---

* 'L'Imprimerie en Roumanie' in *Etudes Balkaniques*, No. 6, 1967.
† Cultura veche romina. Bucharest, 1891.

the Turks and Poles, and who was known as a protector and patron of letters in his kingdom.

The town of Tirgoviste saw the production of a second *Octoich* in 1535, without a printer's name, and in 1545 one Dmitri Logofetul printed there a Slavonic *Molitvennik* (Prayer Book) and an *Apostol* (1547).

Between 1559 and 1581 nine books in Romanian came from Coresi's press at Brassó in Hungary, and a tenth, a translation by Deacon Serban of *Genesis* and *Exodus*, was printed at Orastie at the instance of the Calvinists (1582).

The town of Belgrad in Transylvania (Alba Julia, Gyulafehérvár, Weissen-burg) had its first press in 1567, the printer being Raphael Skrzetuski, called Hoffhalter, who remained there for two years and received the title of royal printer to the Prince of Transylvania, Jan Sigismund Zapolya. He died there about 1569 and his son Rudolf printed at various places in Hungary. He himself did not print in Belgrad, where, after his father's death, the royal printing office came under the inspectorate of the minister Stephen Császmai and was run by a schoolmaster named Gregor Wagner.

The Romanian and Slavo-Romanian books printed at Brasov at the expense of the merchant Hans Benkner are now exceedingly rare, and many may have been later destroyed by the Orthodox clergy as being tainted with heresy. For the *Catechism* of Sibiu, the Romanian *Four Gospels* printed at Brasov (1560–61), as well as the series of Romanian and Slavo-Romanian printings put out by Coresi and his successors, all reflect the progress made by the doctrines of the Reform in Transylvania.

JUGOSLAVIA

In the year 1483 a Glagolitic Missal* in the Croatian tongue appeared without mention of place or printer. The type is without doubt of Venetian origin, and it is known that Croatian and Serbian printers had been working for some time in Venice. The first known Croatian printer was Andrija Paltašić from Kotor, who was active in Venice from 1476, having, it seems, taken over material from the printing office of Jacob de Fivizzano. In 1478 he was partnered by a fellow-countryman Bonino de Boninis, the Latinised name of a native of Dubrovnic called Dobruško Dobrić. Boninis did not remain long in Venice, for he was in Brescia in 1480, Verona in 1481–82, again in Brescia from 1483 until 1491, and was in Lyons in 1500.

Among other South Slav printers working in Italy during the fifteenth century were Grgur Dalmatin and the Slovene Mattheus Cerdonis of Slovenj-

---

* Glagolitic is the name given to the alphabet (said to have been invented by St Cyril of Thessalonika in the ninth century A.D.) in which some of the earliest extant manuscripts of Old Church Slavonic were written.

gradec (Windischgratz), who worked with Ratdolt at Padua before the latter returned to Augsburg. One of the earliest books printed in Glagolitic characters was a Breviary in the Croatian tongue published at Venice by the famous printer Andrea Torresano, and edited by a Croat, Blaz Baromić. It was completed on 13 March 1493. The Serbian printers Božidar Vuković, from Podgorica, and Jerolim Zagurović, from Kotor, also printed at Venice during the sixteenth century, as did Božidar Ljubavić and his sons Djuradi and Theodor.

To return now to the Glagolitic Missal published *sine nota* in 1483. Recent research by Croatian specialists has tried to show that the Missal may have been printed in Croatia, but no conclusive evidence has yet been offered and the matter is still a subject of controversy. Valentin Putanec argues from an inscription found in the Zagreb copy of the Missal that Abbot Nicola of the monastery at Mordruš founded there the press which was responsible for the book. Two other researchers, Zvonimir Kulundzić and Josip Badalić, are in favour of Kosinj as the site of the press. If either of these conjectures prove correct, the date of the first printing on Jugoslav soil will have to be advanced by a decade, since the Makarije *Oktoich* of 1494 was previously considered as such. That book was in the Serbian tongue and printed in Cyrillic characters, probably at Cetinje. This, again, has now been antedated by a Breviary in Glagolitic characters printed at Kosinj in 1491, and thought to have been printed by Grgur Dalmatin, who at one time worked at Venice in partnership with Jacobus Britannicus (Badalić, 1966).

Until recently it was assumed that the first known presses in South Slav territory were founded in 1493 – one on the South Adriatic coast at Centinje (or Obod) and the second in the north, at Senj, on the coast of Croatia. But now it appears that a press was in operation eleven years earlier if indeed the Missal of 1483 was printed at either Modrus or Kosinj.

Towards the end of the fifteenth century a Serbian press was established at Cetinje in Montenegro in the province of Zetska, the last remaining portion of the once mighty Serbian empire. The earliest book to come from this press was the first half of an *Oktoich* (Parts I–IV) in the Serbian tongue and printed in Cyrillic characters. This folio volume was printed between the beginning of 1493 and 4 January 1494 under the supervision of the monk Makarije, who had at one time worked at Venice, though our knowledge of his activities there are negligible. Although most Serbian liturgical books were printed in Venice, some xylographic printing seems to have been carried out in a monastery at Rujno, near Titovo Užice.

A printing office for Serbian books was established in Venice by a refugee Montenegrin noble, Božidar Vuković, who was active there from 1519 to 1538. He printed a number of liturgical books in Cyrillic characters, the first to appear being a *Liturgiarion* dated 1519. He died shortly before 1540 and his business

as printer and publisher was carried on by his son Vinzenz until around 1561.*
The printing office of one Jakob from Herzgovina printed a *Molitvoslov* or
Horologium in 1556 and another publisher of Serbian liturgical books was
Hieronymus Zagurovic from Kotor. Later these small printing offices were
taken over by the Venetian printers Rampazetto and Ginami, who were active
from 1597 until 1538.

In 1552 printing was introduced into Belgrade at the press founded by
Radiša Dimitrović, whence was issued the *Cetveroblagovestije* (Four Gospels)
in Serbian-Cyrillic, a folio volume on stout paper, printed in red and black,
with twenty-four lines to the page. There is a perfect copy in the University
Library at Zagreb.

Some mention should be made of the printing office at Rijeka (Fiume)
belonging to Simon Begna-Kožičić, Bishop of Modrus, who had a press installed
in his private residence in 1530, the printing being carried out by a wandering
printer known as Bartolomeo da Brescia. The first book turned out by this
press was a Book of Hours – *Oficii blazenie devi marie* – dated 1530. This was
followed by a Missal – *Misal Hrvacki* – in Croatian-Glagolitic characters. The
title-page bears a rather charming cut of St Jerome, and the book contains, in
addition to a full-page woodcut of the Annunciation of Matthew of Treviso,
several smaller cuts. The date of publication is 1531, and in the same year the
press produced a Ritual and a book of the lives of the Popes and Emperors
from the Bishop's own pen.

* The Vuković, father and son, were the chief patrons of Cyrillic printing in Venice, and
they financed at least thirteen liturgical books, all extremely rare today.

23

Eastern Europe: Russia and Poland

Despite the growing expansion of Poland in the fifteenth century after the defeat of the Teutonic Order in 1410 and more especially the second Treaty of Thorn (1466) which consolidated the Polish-Lithuanian empire, Cracow was the only Polish city, during that century, to possess a printing house. It was since 1364 a university town and a cosmopolitan city which had already felt the influence of humanism. But although, even in the fifteenth century, Polish master printers were at work in Italy, Spain and elsewhere, the first printers in Poland were all foreigners. From Bavaria came Florian Ungler and Caspar Hochfeder, as well as the bookseller Melchior Frank and his uncle Peter Reismoller from Augsburg. From Franconia came Johann Haller from Rothenburg and Georg Stuchs of Sulzbach. From Würtemburg came the bookseller Georg Fenig, who settled in Poznan (Posen) and from Alsace came the paper-maker Frederic Schilling.

As far as we know the first piece of printing in Poland was a Calendar for 1474, printed at the end of 1473 at Cracow by a printer thought to have been Kaspar Straube, who was also the printer of Franciscus de Platea, *Tractatus restitutionum* (1475), the first book printed in Poland unless that honour is due to the Turrecremata, *Explanatio in Psalterium*, which was printed not later than 1476, when a copy was rubricated. The printer of this latter book is thought to have been Caspar Hochfeder (sometimes called Gaspard of Bavaria), who also issued, about the same time, Saint Augustine, *Omnes libri*. Hochfeder came from Heiligbrunn, near Nuremberg, and worked for the industrialist Johannes Haller of Rothenberg, who towards the end of the fifteenth century set up a book-selling business in Cracow and dealt in books printed for him in Nuremberg, Leipzig and Venice for sale in Poland. Many well-known printers, among them Ungler and Vietor, worked for him. To the business of publishing and book-selling he added that of a wine merchant and paper-maker. Around 1528 his widow still rented a mill 'in quo papyrus conficitur'.

But these printings of Straube and Hochfeder were in Latin, and the story of vernacular printing in the East Slav countries does not really begin until 1491 in that same city of Cracow, when the bookseller Johann Haller financed the printing of a number of liturgical books which he hoped to sell to the clergy of the Orthodox Church in Poland and Russia. He engaged as printer Swietopek Fiol (Sweybold Veyl, Szwaipolt Fieol), who came from a German family long established in Poland. He printed five works in Cyrillic characters, the punches for which were cut by a Brunswick engraver, Rudolf Borsdorf. These books were a Choral book for eight voices (*Oktoich*), a Psalter, a Mass book for the great feasts (*Triod' Postnaja*), a Mass book for the period from Easter to Pentecost (*Triod' Cvetnaja*) and a Book of Hours (*Časoslovec*). The *Oktoich* and the Book of Hours are dated 1491, the Psalter is no longer extant and the two Mass books are undated. Since it is unlikely that all five fairly large works were printed in the same year, it is possible that the actual date of the first Cyrillic printing may be before 1491.

The experiment was not a success. In January 1492 the Catholic clergy, who, incidentally, received their liturgical books from German printers established in Venice, such as Nicolas of Frankfurt and Peter Lichtenstein of Cologne, forbade the printing of books in Cyrillic destined for a rival Church. Fiol himself, accused of heresy, had to leave Cracow hurriedly. But his work in that city, although of short duration, was the first step in the development of Cyrillic printing. After his expulsion from Cracow, Fiol went to Lócse (Levoca), where he died in 1525.

Next came Florian Ungler from Bavaria, who did some good work around 1514, but the first printer in Poland fully to recognise the value of good typography was Hieronymus Vietor, who had previously worked in Vienna. He arrived in Cracow in 1517, and worked at first in partnership with Marcus Scharffenberg and later with Ungler.

By the beginning of the sixteenth century, Poland was able to supply most of the paper needed from her own paper mills, the first of which had been established at Pradnik Czerwony, near Cracow, in 1491. The finest paper in Poland was turned out by the Alsatian Frederic Schilling, the Polish form of whose name was Szyling. He had charge of the mill at Pradnik Duchacki from about 1495. By the middle of the sixteenth century there were no fewer than thirty-five paper mills in Poland.

The prime factor in the development of printing at Cracow was the University, with its thousands of students from all the surrounding countries. The local booksellers, unable to obtain a sufficient quantity of books from abroad, were forced to rely on local printers; Haller furnished at least 200 titles by 1528, probably a much greater number, since text books are the least likely to survive. Vietor and Ungler between them must have issued many hundreds of books, most of which have now disappeared. Of the forty works mentioned in the will of Ungler's widow in 1551, only a handful are now extant.

Florian Ungler, who simply signed himself 'Florian Bawar' (i.e. Florian the

Bavarian), began to print in Cracow about the end of 1510, when he produced an Almanach for 1511, and the *Algorithmus* of Johann de Sacrobusto. His printing press was set up in the house of the Humanist, Erasmus Ciolek, and on it he printed many academic text books. Above all he was the printer of the first book to be printed in the Polish language, *Zywot Pana Jezusa Krysta* (The Life of Jesus Christ). This work was translated from the German by Baltasar Opeć of Cracow at the command of the queen, Elisabeth.* Two editions of this work appeared in 1522, one from the press of Johann Haller and the other printed by Vietor; but this is unquestionably not the first, and although the actual date of the original edition is not known, it is probable that Florian Ungler printed it towards the end of 1515. It may have been preceded, or perhaps followed, in the same year by *Raj duszny*, a Polish version of the *Hortulus animae* translated by Biernat of Lublin and printed by Ungler in partnership with Wolfgang Lern.

Vietor also printed books in the Polish language, other than the *Life of Christ* already mentioned. They included an edition of *Ecclesiastes* in the Polish translation of Hieronymus of Wielun – the earliest edition of a book of the Bible printed in Polish. Vietor's edition of Sebaldus Heyden, *Puerilium Colloquiorum Formulae* (1527), is printed in Latin, German, Polish and Hungarian.

Another important name in Polish book production was that of Matthäus Scharffenberg, one of a family of printers, the best-known of whom are Crispin and Johann, both printers at Breslau. Crispin Scharffenberg was active in that city from 1553 until 1576, and his son Johann ran the business from his father's death about 1577 until 1586, when he, too, died. Three years later his widow married the merchant Georg Baumann, who ran the printing office until 1607. The widow carried on the business until 1618, when Baumann's son Georg Baumann II was old enough to take charge himself. He in turn printed from 1618 until 1650, and the printing office remained with his heirs until about 1730. Thus it remained a family business for nearly two centuries.

The first printer known to have worked in Breslau (now Wroclaw) was the canon of the cathedral of that town, one Caspar Elyan, who ran a press from 1475 to 1480, from which came the first piece of text printed in Polish: the Pater, *Ave Maria and Credo* in the *Statutà Synodalia Vratislava* of October 1475.

A long succession of books in Polish came from the press of Hieronymus Vietor, who was the first to introduce the Aldine italic into Poland. The second half of the sixteenth century saw an increase in the number of Polish presses. Cracow was no longer the sole town in which printing was practised, for presses were set up in Poznań, Toruń, Wilno and Zamość. Even a small town such as Brześć Litewski (Brest-Litovsk) had its press, on which was printed in 1563 the first complete Bible in Polish.

* Daughter of King Casimir Jagiello.

Much of the impetus given to printing came from the Reformation which had the services of the Cracow printer Maciej Wirzbieta, who published the works of the eminent Polish writer Mikolaj Rej, whose *Mirror or Portrait of an upright man* appeared at Cracow (1567–68), printed, as were most of the Polish books of that period, in Schwabacher type. But perhaps the most important printer of the period was Jan Janusowski, who owned the printing house called 'Lazarzowa', formerly owned by Vietor. Janusowski attempted to rationalise Polish orthography by publishing in 1594 a specimen of letter-forms designed by himself, which he called 'Novy karakter polski', and used them in the prefaces of the two volumes of *Statutes, Laws and Constitutions of the Polish Kingdom* which he published in 1600. Janusowski was the first to introduce into Polish typography copper engraving, though he seldom made use of it, and based his aesthetic ideas almost totally upon a well-balanced layout. Himself an erudite man, he was the chief publisher of the works of Jan Kochanowski, the most famous Polish poet before Adam Mickiewicz.

As in most other European countries, the standard of printing declined noticeably during the seventeenth century. In the case of Poland this was due largely to the incessant wars which impoverished the country. Nevertheless the end of the century saw some books of considerable interest issuing from Danzig such as the *Selenographia* or description of the moon by the astronomer Jan Hevelius (1647) and the *Exoticarum plantarum centuria prima* by the botanist Jacob Breyn (1678).

Towards the middle of the eighteenth century there was a noticeable resurgence in the intellectual life of Poland, and Warsaw became the chief centre of publishing in the country, due in large part to the activities of Michal Gröll and Piotr Dufour. But unfortunately the cultural life of the country was towards the end of the century rudely shattered by the partition of the country and the loss of its independence in 1795.

RUSSIA

Printing came to Russia relatively late, for the country was separated from the cradle of the art in Western Europe not only by distance, but also by religion and by cultural – and especially by graphic – traditions.

We know that the printer Bartholomaeus Ghotan went to Russia in the fifteenth century and visited the city of Novgorod in 1494. But what happened to him is a mystery. He was certainly dead by 1496 and there is no evidence that he printed whilst in Russia. The documented history of printing in Cyrillic types in the Eastern Slavonic lands really begins at Cracow in Poland, where in the year 1491 Schweipolt Fiol is said to have printed some liturgical books for the publisher Johann Haller, as related on page 246.

For printing in Muscovy itself we have to wait until the middle of the sixteenth century. Tsar Ivan IV (1533–84), known to us as Ivan the Terrible, who for all his pathological outbursts of cruelty was an intelligent and astute man, was anxious to gain some knowledge of Western technical and military skills. To this end a Saxon named Hans Schlitte began in 1547 to recruit men for service in Muscovy. Among the party that set out for Russia were a papermaker, a book-binder and a printer, but apparently they never reached their destination for the men were intercepted at the instigation of the Hansa, which looked on such developments as threatening its interests.

Five years later King Christian III of Denmark – anxious to spread the Lutheran faith in Muscovy – offered to send an ambassador named Hans Missen-heim Bogbinder★ to Moscow carrying Bibles and two other religious works. The Danish king undertook to have them printed if the Tsar would arrange to have them translated into Russian, but nothing positive seems to have emerged from this proposal.

Nevertheless, the idea of printing was already abroad in Moscow about this time, for examples of the art had probably reached Muscovy by way of the market city of Novgorod. In 1551 the copyists of manuscripts had been criticized by the Church for their inaccuracies; and Ivan's expansionist policies, which led to the conquest of Kazan in 1552 and of Astrakhan in 1556, meant that there was an urgent need for liturgical books for the churches newly established in the conquered lands. The Tsar and the Metropolitan Macarius of Moscow supported the setting-up of a press in the capital, and during the second half of the 1550s and the first half of the 1560s a number of books were printed which, although they lack any mention of place or date of printing, can be confidently assigned to Moscow.

Seven of these so-called 'anonymous' editions are known to have been printed, though copies of only six of them survive. All are small folios and con-sist of three Gospels, two Psalters, and one Lenten Triodion. They share four typefaces and five of them have woodcut headpieces in common. Technically they show all the signs of being pioneer efforts: line endings are not invariably justified, signing and foliation are uncertain, and a primitive single-pull method of red printing is used in some of the volumes. On the other hand three of the four typefaces employed are well-cut founts based on contemporary book hands. The ornamental headpieces also show close connections with contempor-ary Moscow manuscript decoration. The printer or printers of these volumes are, of course, unknown, but a Marusha Nefedev and a Vasyuk Nikiforov are mentioned in a Moscow document of 1556 in terms which indicate that they were a printer and a block-cutter respectively. It is also possible that the printers of the first Moscow dated book – the *Apostol* (Liturgical Acts and Epistles) of 1564 – may have been at some time connected with this anonymous press.

★ Bogbinder was a family name, not an occupational one.

The *Apostol* was printed, states the colophon, by Ivan Fedorov and Petr Timofeev Mstislavets in Moscow between 19 April, 1563, and 1 March, 1564. A small folio of 268 leaves, this book is set in a fine new fount (about 24-point) which is based on the book-hand of the period. Its headpieces are splendid white-line woodcuts incorporating flower and foliage motifs based on Moscow manuscript decorations which have themselves been shown to derive ultimately from an ornamental alphabet cut by the German master Israhel van Meckenem in the 1480s (Angermann, 1972). The book is unsigned and has no title-page, but is foliated. None of the typographical materials which appear in the anonymous printings are to be found in the *Apostol*. A frontispiece depicting St Luke is copied from a woodcut by Erhard Schön, which first appeared in a German Old Testament printed at Nuremberg in 1524.

The second book issued by the two printers was a *Chasovnik*, an octavo of which the first edition was printed between 7 August and 29 September, and the second between 2 September and 29 October, 1565. Soon after the completion of the second edition of this *Chasovnik*, or Book of Hours, the two printers, who had fallen foul of certain powerful authorities in Moscow, were forced to leave the country. Giles Fletcher the Elder, who led an English embassy to Moscow in 1588, reported that "Some yeres past, the house was set on fire in the night time, and the presse and letters quite burnt up, as was thought, by the procurement of the cleargy men."*

In 1568 Ivan Federov and Petr Timofeev Mstislavets were at Zabludov in Byelorussia, where, under the patronage of Prince Georgii Khodkevich, Hetman of Lithuania, they published a Didactic Gospels in 1569. This work, like Fedorov's later products at Lvov and Ostrog, is printed in his Moscow type and has his Moscow woodcut ornaments. After the completion of the Gospels, Mstislavets left Fedorov and went to Vilna, where he set up a press financed by the merchants Kuzma and Luke Mamonich. Cyrillic printing continued in Vilna until the middle of the seventeenth century.

Ivan Fedorov himself soon left Zabludov and printed a Primer and a second edition of the *Apostol* at Lvov in 1574.† By 1578 he was to be found on the estate of Prince Constantine Ostrozhskii at Ostrog in Volhynia, and there he printed a small bilingual Greek and Slavonic reading book for the local school.‡ In 1580 he printed a combined Psalter and New Testament, and during the following years he published the first printed edition of the Slavonic Bible, known from its place of printing as the 'Ostrog Bible' (1580–81; most copies

---

* *Of the Russe Common Wealth.* Hakluyt Soc., 1861.
† Jakobson, R. *Ivan Fedorov's Primer*, in Harvard Library Bulletin IX (1955/6).
‡ Grasshoff, H. & Simmons, J. S. G. *Ivan Fedorovs griechisch-russisch kirchenslavisches Lesebuch von 1578* in Abhandlungen der deutschen Akademie der Wissenschaften, Klasse für Sprachen, Literatur und Kunst, 1969, No. 2. Berlin.

have a cancel colophon dated 1581). This impressive folio formed a fitting climax to its printer's career. Although he did not die until December, 1583 (in Lvov), he is not known to have printed anything subsequent to this Bible.

Meanwhile printing had been revived in Moscow by Nikifor Tarasiev and Andronik Timofeev Nevezha, who printed a Psalter there in 1568. Nevezha later moved the press to the Aleksandrovskaya sloboda (60 miles NE of Moscow) where he printed a Psalter in 1577 and an undated Book of Hours, but printing in Moscow did not recommence until 1589. Between that year and the end of the century Nevezha produced fewer than a dozen books – all of them liturgical.

Three printers were active in Moscow during the first decade of the seventeenth century – Ivan Andronikov Nevezhin (possibly Nevezha's son), Anisim Mikhailov Radishevskii, and Nikita Fedorov Fofanov (Luppov, 1970). They worked in the official Printing House and produced ten books between 1603 and 1611, including Radishevskii's fine folio Gospels of 1606. Their efforts were interrupted by the upheavals which took place during the period known as the 'Time of Troubles'. The Printing House was destroyed in 1611, but Fofanov managed to evacuate his press to Nizhnii Novgorod, where in 1613 he printed a six-leaf colophon to a work which has not survived.

With the accession of the first Romanov Tsar, Mikhail Fedorovich (1613–45) conditions became more propitious, and the unbroken tradition of the rebuilt Moscow Printing House starts in 1614. The products of the press continued to be liturgical books, which still attempted to look like manuscripts. The first formal title-page in a Moscow book dates from 1641, the first illustration from 1637, and the first Moscow book which was not specifically liturgical or religious (it was a Primer) from 1634. All three books were printed by an independent entrepreneur, Vasilii Fedorov Burtsov-Protopopov, who rented a couple of presses in the Printing House in the 1630s.

The first genuinely secular book to be issued by the Printing House itself was a Russian translation of Jacobi von Wallhausen's *Kriegskunst zu Fuss*, the text of which was printed in Moscow in 1647, but the engravings, imported from Amsterdam, were not received until two years later. The year 1649 also saw the publication of the *Ulozhenie* or Legal Code of Tsar Aleksei Mikhailovich.

The 1650s were marked by religious controversies which arose partly from Patriarch Nikon's attempt to remedy the incorrectness of the existing liturgical texts, in which he aroused the conservative opposition of the clergy and people. But eventually the first Moscow edition of the Slavonic Bible appeared in 1663, based largely on the Ostrog Bible.

During the years 1679–83 a number of works were printed by Simeon Polotskii, who had been tutor to the Tsar's children, at a press specially established for him by the Tsar's command in the Kremlin. Four of these books contain engravings by Afanasii Trukhmenskii based on drawings by Simon

Ushakov, and these were the first engraved book illustrations to be printed in Muscovy. An engraved primer for use by members of the Tsar's family and court was printed in a small edition in 1694 by the director of the Moscow Printing House, Karion Istomin.

By 1700 not much more than 500 books had been printed in Moscow during almost a century and a half, and of these only seven (or fifteen if we include primers) were secular in character. Moreover typographical standards were, if anything, worse than they had been in 1564.

Printing in Russia during the seventeenth century was confined almost entirely to Moscow itself, but three books were printed between 1658 and 1661 at a press which Patriarch Nikon caused to be transferred from Kuteino in Byelorussia to the Iverskii Monastery near Novgorod. A wandering printer, Spiridon Sobol, printed at Kiev in the 1620s and at Kuteino, Buinichi, and Mogilev in Byelorussia during the 1630s and 1640s. In the Ukraine, at Kiev (which became part of Muscovy in 1654) a press had been at work in the Monastery of the Caves from 1616 onwards, and Lazar Baranovich, bishop of Chernigov (also in the Ukraine) established a press at Novgorod-Severskii in 1674 which he moved to his episcopal seat in 1679 (Titov, 1916, and Kameneva, 1959). The products of these Byelorussian and Ukrainian presses were far more varied than those of the Moscow Printing House, and, being more exposed to influences from the West were technically more adventurous, especially with regard to ornaments and illustration. But for any major changes in the content and style of the Russian book one has to await the impact of Peter the Great in the early years of the eighteenth century.

24

Successors of Caxton:
Sixteenth Century Printing in England

LAWYERS, doctors, schoolmasters and priests were the people for whom the early printers mainly catered, and one of their biggest markets was that of service books for the churches. At the beginning of the sixteenth century there was no liturgical unity in England. Although the Roman Rite was in use throughout the land, it was modified in certain respects following the accepted usage of the great cathedral churches. The five chief 'uses' were those of Salisbury (which differed least from the Roman use), York, Hereford, Bangor and Lincoln. Of lesser importance were those of Aberdeen, Abingdon, Croyland and London. Canterbury adopted the Sarum Use, which lasted until 1534, and was revived during the few years of Mary Tudor's reign.

Compared with France and Germany, England had comparatively few printers, and they were unable to meet the demands of the church for service books. In 1500 there were only five printers in London and the number increased very slowly, so that English booksellers and publishers had to call on foreign printers to augment the supply. Moreover, French printers had greater experience in this form of printing and could also supply the books at a price with which the English printer could not compete. During the first half of the sixteenth century, therefore, we find service books being printed for the English market at Rouen and Paris, though Missals for Salisbury use were also printed by Michael Wenssler of Basel, Johannes Herzog of Venice and Christopher Ruremond of Antwerp. At that time there was no law preventing the importation of such books.

Among the most important printers at the beginning of the century were Thomas Berthelet and John Byddell. Like several other early printers in England, the former was of French descent. He was a busy printer for a quarter of a century, from 1524 until around 1549, when his nephew Thomas Powell took over the business. Berthelet became King's Printer in 1530 and in 1531 he printed Sir Thomas Elyot's *Boke named the Governour*, a treatise on education and politics which he reprinted several times and which remained a popular book throughout the century. He also printed other works by the same author,

by the hanbe.   134

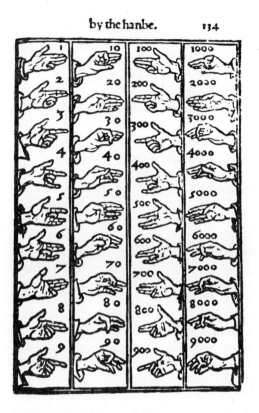

FIGURE 53. A method of expressing numbers by the hand as given in Robert Record, *The Ground of Artes*, printed by Reyner Wolfe, 1543. The author was a physician and mathematician, and the first writer on arithmetic and geometry in English.

including the *Castel of helth* (1539) and his large *Dictionary* (1538). In 1540 Berthelet printed the first complete edition of William Lily's Latin grammar, which became the standard Latin grammar used by most of the English public schools until well into the nineteenth century. Berthelet's edition is said to have been produced for the young Prince Edward and it is sometimes called 'King Edward's Grammar'. Another notable work from this printer was *The Institution of a Christian Man*, a treatise on various articles of religious belief compiled by the bishops and issued under the king's authority. It was printed in both quarto and octavo editions, the former being a very handsome piece of work. Berthelet's funeral is quaintly described by Henry Machyn in his *Diary*, published by the Camden Society.

John Byddell had been an assistant to Wynkyn de Worde, of whose will he was one of the executors, and into whose premises – the Sun in Fleet Street – he moved after de Worde's death. Most of Byddell's books were of a theological nature, but among the books of a miscellaneous nature which he printed is the earliest botanical work of William Turner, the 'Father of English Botany' – a small quarto called *Libellus de re herbaria novus* (1538).

Although before the end of the fifteenth century Bibles had been printed in German, Italian, Dutch, French, Danish, Bohemian and Spanish, England was still without a printed Bible in the tongue of the people. Caxton could not have printed one, for in 1414 a law was enacted that all persons found reading the Scriptures in the mother tongue should 'forfeit land, catel, lif, and goods from their heyres for ever'. It was because the dissemination of the Scriptures in English was prohibited by the ecclesiastical authorities that Tyndale was obliged to take refuge in Germany to complete his translation of the New Testament, the first to be printed in the English language, which was issued by Peter Schöffer at Worms in 1525 or 1526. The completion of the English Bible was due to Miles Coverdale, and this first English Bible ever to be printed was published in 1535. Even today it is not known for certain where or by whom it was printed, but it is now generally considered to have been printed at Marburg by E. Cervicornus and J. Soter.

In 1537 an English Bible was printed at Antwerp by Matthew Crom. It received the commendation of Archbishop Cranmer, who, through the intermediary of Thomas Cromwell, obtained from the king a licence for this Bible (known as the 'Matthew' Bible) to be bought and read in England. Since it had been printed abroad it could only be sold complete in sheets to some English printer, and in this case the expense was borne by Richard Grafton (a member of the Grocers' Company) and Edward Whitchurch (a member of the Haberdashers' Company), who regarded the transaction as an ordinary piece of merchandising, since neither were printers. Since, as J. F. Mozley writes: 'the publisher of scripture, particularly of a complete Bible, in those days gave heavy hostages to fortune',* Grafton, in return for his heavy outlay requested a privilege from the king forbidding the reprinting of this Bible until he had sold all his copies.

Since the 'Matthew' Bible gave offence in certain quarters owing to the controversial nature of some of its references to the Church of Rome, Cromwell decided to replace it by a new version without any polemical annotations. Coverdale was entrusted with the revised translation, and Grafton and Whitchurch were once again employed as publishers, probably because as merchants of standing they were better able to bear the enormous cost of financing the printing of a Bible than were the London printers of the time.

* *Coverdale and his Bibles*. 1953.

For technical reasons Cromwell decided to have the book printed in Paris by François Regnault, who had already printed service books for the English market. But in December 1538 the Inquisitor-General for France seized the sheets that had already been printed. So Grafton and Whitchurch, in the words of John Foxe, 'became printers themselves (which before they never intended) and printed out the said Bible in London'. The 'Great Bible', as it was called, was completed by April 1539, and by December 1541 they had printed seven editions of this work, for which they had the sole publishing rights. Petit and Redman printed a Bible for Berthelet in 1540, but this was by comparison poorly printed.

On the accession of Edward VI, Grafton was appointed King's Printer in succession to Berthelet, which gave him the sole right to print all Acts and Statutes. He held the appointment for six years only, for on the king's death he foolishly printed a proclamation of the accession of Lady Jane Grey, in which he signed himself 'Printer to the Queen'. For this indiscretion he forfeited his office, which Queen Mary gave to John Cawood. Grafton had already been imprisoned and fined for having printed the 'Great Bible', for he could not escape the consequences of his patron Cromwell's fall from favour and subsequent execution.*

Whitchurch, who had been a friend of the martyr John Rogers, Tyndale's disciple and editor of the 'Matthew' Bible, was in disgrace during Mary's reign and ceased to print until after her death.

Grafton was replaced as Royal Printer by John Cawood in 1553. Upon his appointment Cawood was given a writ of aid addressed to mayors, sheriffs, bailiffs and other officers of the Crown to enable him to take up, during one year, 'as many prynters, composytours, and founders, as well householders as prentyces and jornymen as others' for his work. As Queen's Printer to Mary, Cawood was responsible for printing the proclamations and acts promulgated during her reign, but on the accession of Elizabeth I the proclamation of 17 November 1558 to that effect was printed by Richard Jugge. On 25 January 1559 Cawood's name was coupled with Jugge's in the printing of *An Acte whereby certayne offences be made Treason*, and from that time they continued jointly to print the State Papers.

In 1551 Jugge was granted a licence to print the New Testament in English because, says the licence, 'printing by strangers has led to errors of translation'. This testament was handsomely printed and illustrated with eighty-six competently executed woodcuts, probably of Flemish origin. Jugge published many editions of the New Testament, but the highlight of his career was his printing of the so-called 'Bishops' Bible', a revision of the 'Great Bible' planned by

---

* In 1542 Convocation pronounced that the 'Great Bible' must not be read in church. A year later all private reading of the English Bible was forbidden.

❡The excellent Tryumphe of Chastitie.

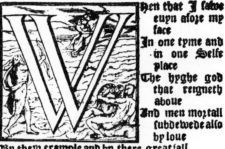

Hen that I sawe eupn afoze mp face
In one tyme and in one Selfe place
The hyghe god that reigneth aboue
And men moztall subdewede also bp loue
By they: example and bp there great fall
Some profpte to mp felfe then dpd I call
And fome comefozte it was alfo to me
Euen as other were I foz to be
When Phebus a god was taken in that lure
And the ponge Leader a man pure
Both twapne ftrpcken wpth loues darte
And Juno and Dpdo lafpd with that parte
Not that Dpdo that men doth wzpte
That foz Eneas wpth death was dpte
But that noble Lady true and iufte
foz Spchen her lope and hartes lufte
I ought not to mozne thoughe that bnware
I were taken in loues craftie fnare
Being but a bery ponge man of age
foz to be banquifhed wpth fuch a rage
And pf that mp Lady that I loue beft
Wpll not with loue in no wpfe be oppzeft
f.   But

FIGURE 54. A page from *The Tryumphes of Fraunces Petrarcke*, printed by John Cawood *c.* 1565. The initial is one of a series cut by the Flemish artist Arnold Nicolai.

Matthew Parker, Archbishop of Canterbury, and carried out by a panel of translators from among the bishops. Hence the name.

The first edition of the Bishops' Bible appeared in the autumn of 1568. The engravings with which it is illustrated are copies of those originally drawn by Virgil Solis for the folio Lutheran Bible published at Frankfurt in 1560. The blocks may have been borrowed especially for this first edition, for they do not appear in any subsequent edition. The second folio edition (1572), to compensate for this lack of illustration, makes a profuse display of decorated initials. One of these was not happily chosen, for when the handsome initial beginning

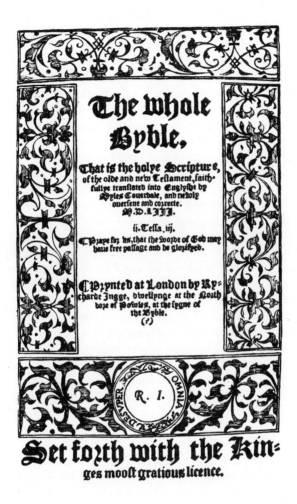

FIGURE 55. Title-page of the Coverdale Bible issued by Richard Jugge in 1553. This was a reissue of the remainder of Andrew Hester's edition, bought up by Jugge.

the Epistle to the Hebrews was seen to represent Leda and the Swan, such incongruity was severely censured.

Although Jugge's work, in his later years, was almost exclusively confined to the printing of Bibles, Prayer Books, Homilies, Injunctions, Proclamations and all the official work that fell to the lot of a royal printer, he issued in 1565 one celebrated medical work, *The birth of mankynde*, by the physician Thomas Raynalde. This work, the first on obstetrics in English, had originally been printed in 1540 by one Thomas Raynald, thus arousing conjecture as to whether printer and physician were one and the same person.

Richard Tottel worked for forty years in Fleet Street and specialised in law books, for the printing of which he held a monopoly. Of all the monopolies this was possibly the least obnoxious, for the work was highly specialised and unsuited to the average printer. But although law books were his staple, he is perhaps better known to the student of English literature for *Tottel's Miscellany*, of which he printed seven editions between 1557 and 1574, and which preserves all the original verse of the Earl of Surrey and of Sir Thomas Wyatt known to be extant. The correct title of this work is *Songes and Sonettes, written by the ryght honorable Lorde Henry Haward late Earle of Surrey, and other*. Among Tottel's other publications were Gerard Legh's *Accedens of Armory* (1562, 1576 and 1591), Lydgate's *Fall of Princis* (1554) and Tusser's *A hundreth good poyntes of Husbandrie* (1557).

One of the finest English printers of the sixteenth century was John Day. He probably started his career as a bookseller and his earliest publications, in which he was partnered by William Seres, seem from internal evidence to have been the work of a Flemish printer, possibly Steven Mierdman. His best work came after the accession of Elizabeth and he was fortunate in securing the patronage of Archbishop Matthew Parker, under whose direction he printed in 1567 a Saxon homily entitled *A Testimonie of Antiquitie* which Parker edited, and for which Day used the first Anglo-Saxon fount. Carter and Ricks, in their foreword to Mores's *Dissertation*,* doubt the assertion contained in the preface to Asser's *Ælfredi regis res gestae* that Day himself cut the Anglo-Saxon types in that book, and think it likely that the roman letters were of Flemish origin and the runes mixed with them were made in London by one of Day's foreign journeymen.

In 1563 Day printed the first edition of *Acts and Monuments of these latter and perilous days* . . . better known to us as Foxe's *Book of Martyrs*. This folio volume of some two thousand pages printed in double column was illustrated with more than fifty woodcuts which, though often crude, were vigorous and calculated to appeal to the unlearned reader. The book met with such approval (on the part of Protestants) that three editions were sold out during Day's lifetime.

One of the first books to call attention to John Day's excellent workmanship was *The Cosmographicall Glasse* by the Norwich physician William Cunningham (1559). 'As a piece of printing nothing better had hitherto appeared in England'

---

* Edward Rowe Mores, *A Dissertation upon English typographical founders and founderies*, (1778) Oxford Bibliographical Society, 1961.

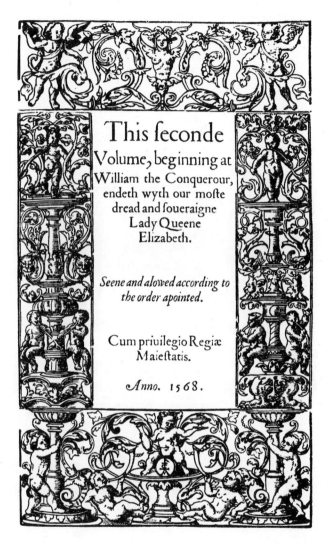

This seconde
Volume, beginning at
William the Conquerour,
endeth wyth our moste
dread and foueraigne
Lady Queene
Elizabeth.

Seene and alowed according to
the order apointed.

Cum priuilegio Regiæ
Maieftatis.

Anno. 1568.

FIGURE 56. Title-page of the second volume of Richard Grafton's *Chronicle at Large*, 1568–69.

(Updike, 1922). The text is set in a handsome italic, cut probably by François Guyot, and the book contains, in addition to diagrams and maps, a number of large woodcut pictorial initials. Day printed the first English translation of Euclid in 1570, and in the same year issued the most famous of Roger Ascham's books, *The Scholemaster*.

---

the creation · Genesis. · I.

The firſt booke of Moyſes, called in

Hebrue of the firſt worde of the booke *Bereſchith*, and
in Greke * Geneſis.

☙ The firſt Chapter.

2 The earth and the deapethes. 3 Lyght. 6 The firmament oʒ heauen.
10 The earth, and the ſea. 14 The ſunne, the moone, and the ſtarres.
21 Fiſhes. 24 The beaſtes of the earth. 26 The creation of man. 29
God geueth vnto man the power of procreation, and ſubdueth all
thyngs vnto hym. 30 Gods prouiſion foʒ lyuelode.

IN the begin-
nyng * GOD
created the hea-
uen and the
earth.
2 And the earth
was without
fourme, and
was voyde : &
darkneſ [was]
vpon the face of the (c) deepe, and the (d)
ſpirite of God moued vpon the face of
the waters.
3 And God ſayde, let there be light: and
there was light.
4 And God ſawe the lyght that it was
good : and God deuided the lyght from
the darknes.
5 And God called the light day, and the
darknes night : "and the euenyng & the
moʒnyng were the "firſt day.

6 And God ſaid : "let there be a "firmament betwene the waters, and let it
make a diuiſion betwene waters and
waters.
7 And God made the (c) firmament, and
ſet the diuiſion betwene the waters
which [were] vnder the firmament, and
the waters that [were] * aboue (h) the
firmament : and it was ſo.
8 And God called the firmament the
heauen : and the euenyng and the moʒnyng were the ſeconde day.
9 And God ſawe: "let the (c) waters vnder the heauen be gathered together into one place, and let the dʒye lande ap-
peare : and it was ſo.
10 And God called the dʒie lande the earth,
and the gatheryng together of waters
called he the ſeas : and God ſawe that it
was good.
11 And God ſayde : (l) let the earth bʒyng
A j forth

FIGURE 57. The first chapter of *Genesis* from the 'Bishops' Bible'. London: Richard Jugge,
1568.

Day held some very lucrative privileges, and in 1577 he and his son Richard
were granted a patent for life with survivorship to print the Psalms in Metre,
the A.B.C. with the little Catechism and the Catechism in Latin and English.

These were some of the most rewarding monopolies in the trade, and later became the subject of numerous complaints from the poorer printers. Day died on 23 July 1584 after an active career of almost forty years.

Contemporary with Day and Jugge was Steven Mierdman, who printed in Antwerp, London and Emden and was among the most important printers of Reformation books. On the accession of Mary Tudor Mierdman left England and eventually settled at Emden. During his career he worked for a number of stationers and printed many books bearing fictitious names and addresses.

Other well known printers of the later part of the sixteenth century were Reyner Wolfe, Henry Bynneman, Henry Denham, Thomas Vautrollier and Thomas East. Wolfe was the first printer in England to possess a large stock of

FIGURE 58. From the John de Beau Chesne and John Baildon's *A Booke containing divers sortes of hands*. London: Thomas Vautrollier, 1571. Page showing the Text Hand.

Greek type and held a patent for printing in Greek. In 1543 he printed the *Homilies* of Saint John Chrysostom in Latin and Greek – a book notable for some fine pictorial initials possibly of Italian origin. Like John Day he became one of the select group of printers favoured with the patronage of Archbishop Parker, whose editions of Bishop Jewel's *Apologia* (1562) and of Matthew Paris, *Historia Major* (1571) he printed.

Of Bynneman we can say with Plomer that 'he printed good literature and printed it well' during a career which lasted from 1566 until 1583. He worked with three presses and had a varied stock of type, including Greek and Hebrew, for after Wolfe's death Bynneman had acquired much of his material. He obtained a privilege to print 'all Dictionaries in all tongues, all Chronicles and histories whatsoever'. This enabled him to print the famous book known as Holinshed's *Chronicles*, which appeared in 1577. The second edition, the one which Shakespeare probably used, revised and augmented by Raphael Holinshed, William Harrison and others, was printed by Henry Denham. Bynneman, who died on 15 April 1583, was the first printer in England to use a script type of the kind known as 'secretary'. It appears in the colophon of the 1576 edition of A. Guarna, *Bellum grammaticale*.

Henry Denham, an apprentice of Richard Tottel, set up his own business in 1564. He was a printer for the trade and during his industrious career worked for many London stationers. In 1566 he printed William Painter's *Palace of Pleasure* for his old master Tottel and for William Jones, who shared the edition. In 1563 a Bill was passed by Parliament allowing the Bible to be translated into Welsh and the first part to be printed was the New Testament, translated by W. Salesbury and R. Davies, and printed by Denham in 1567 for Humphrey Toy. Among the many books printed by Denham were Reynold Scot, *A perfite platforme of a Hoppe Garden* (the first book published in England entirely on the subject of hop-growing) 1574; a quarto edition of Castiglione, *The Courtier* (1577) and John Baret, *An Alvearie* (1573 and 1580). The first edition of this last-named work was a dictionary in English, French and Latin, to which Greek was added for the 1580 edition. In that same year Denham printed another pedagogic book – a curious volume by William Bullokar called *Bullokars booke at large for the amendment of orthographie for English speech*.

Around 1583 a syndicate of four – Edmund Bollifant, Arnold Hatfield, John Jackson and Ninian Newton – set up as printers to the trade under the style of the Eliot's Court Press. Jackson was the only member of the press who was not a printer, and he probably provided the initial capital for the partnership. For more than a decade leading London stationers employed the Eliot's Court Press, which took as its device the caduceus.

Among the many craftsmen who, persecuted for their religious opinions, fled from France and Flanders during the sixteenth century and sought refuge in England was a Frenchman named Thomas Vautrollier, a Huguenot by conviction, who was granted letters of denization on 9 March 1562. From 1569 until 1587 Vautrollier worked as a printer in London, with two brief interludes in Edinburgh, and during that time he built up a substantial business.

One of his most lucrative ventures was a tutor compiled by Claude de Sainliens (Claudius Holyband) and called *The French Littleton* to show that it was as essential to the student of French as the original 'Littleton' had been for students of law. It went into many editions from 1576 onwards and was several times reprinted by Vautrollier's successor, Richard Field.

A work with which Vautrollier was particularly associated was Calvin's

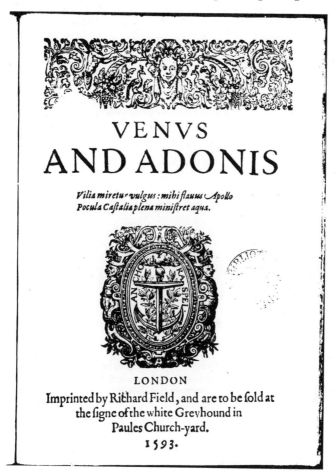

VENVS
AND ADONIS

Vilia miretur vulgus: mihi flauus Apollo
Pocula Castalia plena ministret aqua.

LONDON
Imprinted by Richard Field, and are to be sold at
the signe of the white Greyhound in
Paules Church-yard.
1593.

FIGURE 59. Title-page of the unique copy of the first edition of Shakespeare's *Venus and Adonis*, now in the Bodleian Library, Oxford. London: Richard Field 1593.

Institutes, of which he printed both the Latin version and an English translation by Thomas Norton (1578). The great Latin edition of 1576 was edited by Vautrollier himself with the assistance of Edmund Bunney, who was also responsible for the Latin *Compendium* published in the same year as the complete work. In 1583 Vautrollier also printed the Latin *Epitome* of the *Institutes* made by the preacher William de Lawne, whose son Gideon became apothecary to James I. The frequency with which the *Institutes* was printed shows how popular this work was at the time and how lucrative for the printer.

In July 1580, at the instance of the General Assembly of the Church of

r· 741·

A N

APOLOGIE

for Poetrie.

Written by the right noble, vertu-
ous , and learned , Sir Phillip
Sidney, *Knight.*

Odi profanum vulgus,et arceo.

AT LONDON,
Printed for *Henry Olney,* and are to be fold at
his fhop in Paules Church-yard, at the figne
of the George, neere to Cheap-gate.
Anno, 1595.

FIGURE 60. Title-page of *An Apologie for Poetrie* by Sir Philip Sidney. London, 1595. It was printed for Henry Olney by James Roberts.

Scotland, he was invited to set up a press in Edinburgh, for although Alexander Arbuthnot was working in that city, his slowness in providing Bibles seems to have annoyed the Assembly. In 1583 Vautrollier went to the Scottish capital and there printed about eight books before returning to England, one of which was the first of King James's published works, *Essayes of a Prentise in the Divine Art of Poesie* (1584). But strangely enough, no edition of the Book of Common Order (the authorised manual for public worship in the Church of Scotland from 1556 until 1644) came from his Edinburgh press, the two editions of 1587 being printed in London after his return.

Vautrollier printed a few music part-books, but a better-known music printer of the Elizabethan period was Thomas East, yet he had been printing for twenty years before he struck out in that line. In 1588 he began to print music and became the first English music printer and publisher, although during the period between 1566 and 1587 almost every category of literature was represented in the list of his printings. The last few years of the sixteenth century and the beginning of the seventeenth saw the publication of most of the masterpieces of the English madrigalists, such as the *Triumphes of Oriana* by Thomas Morley, Morley's *First Booke of Balletts*, and the first set of John Wilbye's *Madrigals*, all printed by Thomas East, as well as compositions by John Dowland

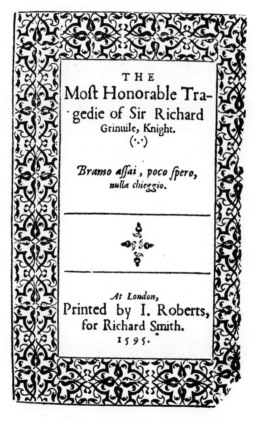

THE
Moſt Honorable Tra-
gedie of Sir Richard
Grinuile, Knight.
(∴)

Bramo aſſai, poco ſpero,
nulla chieggio.

At London,
Printed by I. Roberts,
for Richard Smith.
1595.

FIGURE 61. Title-page of *The Most Honorable Tragedie of Sir Richard Grinvile,* a poem by Gervase Markham. Printed, 1595, by James Roberts, a printer to the trade.

and Thomas Weelkes. In fact from the time he began printing music until his death at the beginning of 1609, hardly a year went by without several volumes of sacred or secular music coming from East's press. Of the printer's origins we know nothing. In his books he spells his name East, Est, and Este, and may possibly have been of Italian extraction.

An outstanding figure in the printing trade towards the end of the sixteenth century was Christopher Barker, a wealthy member of the Drapers' Company and a shrewd business man who managed to acquire the most lucrative of all patents for a man with sufficient capital to exploit it – namely the Bible patent.

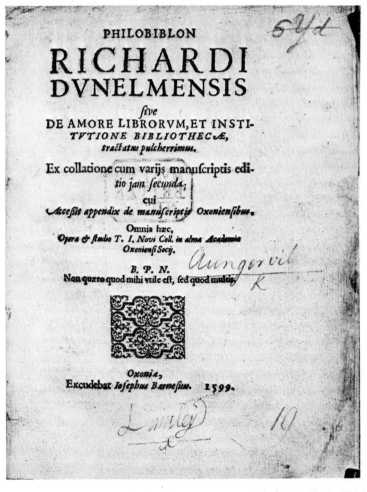

FIGURE 62. Title-page of the first edition in England of Richard de Bury's *Philobiblon*, printed at Oxford in 1599 by Joseph Barnes. It was edited by Bodley's first librarian, Thomas James.

He became a publisher around 1569 and took as his device the Tiger's Head, badge of the Walsingham family, with which he was closely connected.

Although in August 1577, Christopher Barker had been one of the stationers who signed the petition against privileges (see Lansdowne MS 48) this did not prevent him from obtaining a patent (*Patent Roll*, 19 *Eliz. Part 8*) which granted him the office of royal printer of all statutes, books, bills, Acts of Parliament, proclamations, injunctions, Bibles and New Testaments. . . . Also of all service books to be used in churches, and all other volumes ordered to be printed by the Queen or Parliament. He had already shown his business acumen in obtaining a privilege for printing the *Geneva Bible*, of which he and his assigns and deputies had brought out more than fifty editions between 1576 and 1600.

THE STATIONERS' COMPANY

On 4 May 1557, the Stationers' Company was granted a royal charter – an event of great importance in the history of English printing. While the Stationers saw in the charter a means of protecting their craft from unregulated competition, the Crown saw in it a means of controlling the increasingly powerful printing press from which came so many seditious and heretical books.

By the Charter of 1557 no one was allowed to print unless he belonged to the Company or held a licence under royal letters patent. This had the effect of restricting printing to London, for the only outside body empowered to print by royal licence was the University of Cambridge, and there printing had lapsed since 1522. The University of Oxford had no legal warrant for printing until 1586. Although printing had earlier been practised in a few provincial towns, most of these presses no longer functioned.

By the time Queen Elizabeth I came to the throne foreign competition in the printing trade at home had been virtually eliminated. An order restricting aliens had been promulgated by the Mayor and Commonalty of London in 1555 whereby no citizen was allowed to employ a foreigner except in certain trades, which did not include printing and bookselling. This elimination of foreign competition, although welcomed by English printers, was a hindrance to technical improvement, and for many years the quality of English printing was poor in comparison with that of France, Holland, Switzerland and Italy. In effect all printing and bookselling in England was controlled by the hundred-odd men who comprised the Stationers' Company at the time of its incorporation.

Membership of the Stationers' Company was by servitude, patrimony, redemption or translation. An apprentice had to serve for at least seven years before he was made free of the Company, and in no case could he become a freeman before the age of twenty-four. Freedom by purchase was the only way in which aliens could become members, and even so, very few were admitted. Reyner Wolfe was made a freeman of the Company, possibly owing to the

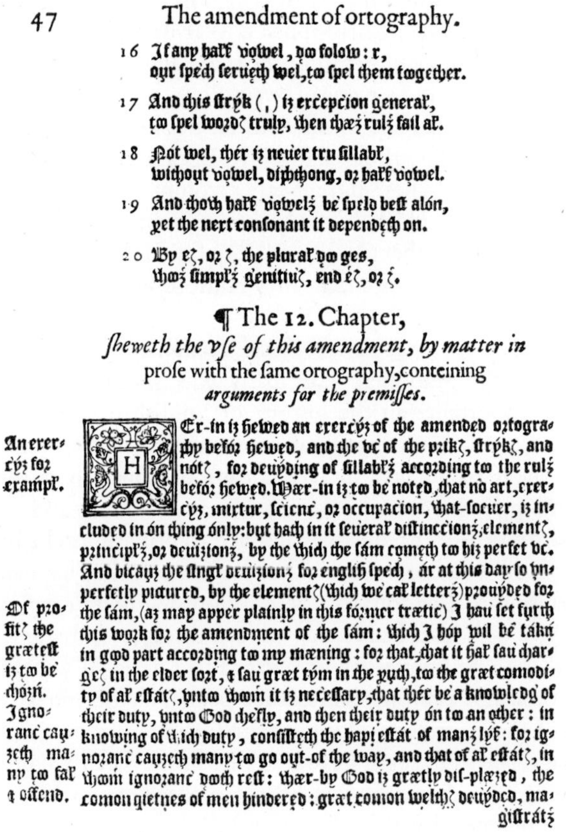

47   The amendment of ortography.

16 Jf any harf vowel, how folow: r,
our fpech feruëth wel, tw fpel them twgether.

17 And this ſtrýk (,) iz excepcion general,
tw fpel wordʒ trulý, then thæʒ rulʒ fail al.

18 Not wel, thér iz neuer tru fillabl,
without vowel, diphthong, oʒ harf vowel.

19 And thoth harf vowelʒ be fprld beſt alón,
yet the next confonant it dependeth on.

20 By eʒ, oʒ ʒ, the plural how geʒ,
thoʒ fimplʒ genitiuʒ, end éʒ, oʒ ʒ.

❡ The 12. Chapter,

ſheweth the vſe of this amendment, by matter in
proſe with the ſame ortography, conteining
arguments for the premiſſes.

An exer-
cýʒ foʒ
exampl.

Of pro-
fit? the
græteſt
iʒ tw be
chóʒn.

Jgno-
ranc cau-
ʒeth ma-
ny tw fal
& offend.

Er-in iʒ ſhewed an exercýʒ of the amended oʒtogra-
phy befóʒ ſhewed, and the vſe of the pʒikʒ, ſtrýkʒ, and
nótʒ, foʒ deuýding of fillablʒ accoʒding tw the rulʒ
befóʒ ſhewed. Thær-in iʒ tw be noted, that nó art, exercýʒ, mixtur, fcienc, oʒ occupacion, that-focuer, iʒ included in ón thing only: but hath in it feueral diſtinccionʒ, clementʒ,
pʒinciplʒ, oʒ deuiſionʒ, by the which the fám cometh tw hiʒ perfet vſe.
And bicauʒ the ſingl deuiſionʒ foʒ englih fpech, ár at this day fo vn-
perfetly pictured, by the clementʒ (which we cal letterʒ) pʒouýded foʒ
the fám, (aʒ may apper plainly in this fóʒmer trætic) J hau fet furth
this woʒk foʒ the amendment of the fám: which J hóp wil bé tákn
in gwd part accoʒding tw my mæning : foʒ that, that it hal fau char-
geʒ in the elder foʒt, & fau græt tým in the yuth, tw the græt comodi-
ty of al eſtátʒ, vntw whom it iʒ neceſſary, that thér be a knowlcdg of
their duty, vntw Gwd cheſly, and then their duty ón tw an other : in
knowing of which duty, confiſteth the hapi eſtát of manʒ lýf: foʒ ignoʒanc cauʒeth many tw go out-of the way, and that of al eſtátʒ, in
whom ignoʒanc wth reſt: thær-by Gwd iʒ grætly diſ-plæʒd, the
comon qietnes of men hindered : græt comon welthʒ deuýded, ma-
giſtrátʒ

FIGURE 63. A page from *Bullokars Booke at large, for the Amendment of Orthographie for English speech*. William Bullokar was a 16th-century teacher and phonetist who advocated a 40-letter alphabet.

recommendation of Anne Boleyn, but it was made a condition of his acceptance that he should take none but English apprentices.

Elizabethan regulation of the printing and publishing trades culminated in the famous Star Chamber decree of 1586, the provisions of which determined the course of the English book trade for the next half century. It put an end to all provincial printing, for no printer was allowed to practice 'but onelye in the cittie of London, or the suburbs thereof except one presse in the universitie of

Cambridge, and one other presse in the universitie of Oxforde, and no more'. But despite the rigours of the Star Chamber decrees, the authorities were quite unable to stop the flow of prohibited books, which came from clandestine presses, the best-known of which was run by the printer Robert Waldegrave who issued polemical tracts under the pseudonym of 'Martin Marprelate'. Waldegrave moved his press from place to place but after twice being put in prison he fled overseas to La Rochelle and thence, in 1590, to Edinburgh, where he was appointed royal printer to James VI of Scotland.

25

The Seventeenth Century

THE seventeenth century, so remarkable in literary history, has little to recommend it in the annals of printing. The contemporaries of Shakespeare, Cervantes, Corneille and La Fontaine, *inter alia*, never had the pleasure of reading them in worthily presented volumes. In fact it seemed almost an axiom in that century that the better printed the book the less the literary value of its contents.

In quality, speaking broadly, the books produced in Western Europe during the seventeenth century, with a few exceptions like the first productions of the Imprimerie Royale in France, cannot stand comparison with the typographical masterpieces of the preceding century. The handsomest books of the seventeenth century were generally large folios, such as Merian's *Theatrum Europaeum* or his *Topographia*, lavishly illustrated with copper-plate engravings. Nor was there anything outstanding in the matter of type design, and although during this century specimen books began to be more frequent, the types displayed were in the main those of a previous age with the exception of the faces cut by Jean Jannon. The script type of Pierre Moreau was no more than a novelty. But during the second half of the century we see the beginning of the great age of the Dutch founders ushering in the work of such men as Christoffel van Dijk and Reinhard Voskens.

The century saw the rise of the Elsevier and Bleau presses at Leyden and the continuation of the famous Plantin Press at Antwerp by several generations of Moretus. Printing in Sweden developed under Gustavus Adolphus and Christina, and, of significant importance, the century saw the beginnings of newspaper publication.

The first flowering of the art of the book had spent itself soon after the middle of the sixteenth century, and by the seventeenth century the standard of printing had declined everywhere in Europe. 'All over Europe,' wrote A. W. Pollard, 'printing at the beginning of the seventeenth century was bad; in England it was very bad indeed.' But not, one might think, as bad as in Germany, where the level of typography was probably the lowest of all. The impoverishment of the country after the battles of the Thirty Years War was followed by a long period of stagnation and decline, and when the country recovered from the effects of the war, little amelioration was possible in the field of printing owing to the rigid guild regulations which continued in force up to the end of the eighteenth century. The effects of continuous warfare engendered by religious and political hatreds brought economic hardships to many parts of Europe, and this was reflected in most trades, including printing.

Whereas up to the middle of the sixteenth century printers had kept their independence, by the seventeenth century they became the hirelings of the publishers who often exercised monopolistic privileges which exempted them from healthy competition and led them to place cheapness before quality. In France the newly founded Imprimerie Royale turned out some good work, but the restrictions placed upon the ordinary printer were many and onerous. In 1624 a royal censorship came into being with the appointment of four censors from the Faculty of Letters at the University of Paris.

In Flanders and Holland the state of affairs in the printing industry was brighter. Although literature reached a high level in England, Spain and France, 'only in Holland,' writes Margaret B. Stilwell, 'did a golden age of poetry and art run parallel to a creditable period in printing and in engravings.'*

When we turn our attention to what was printed and ignore how it was printed, we find considerable diversification in the categories of published works. True, the production of the humanists who had enriched printing during much of the sixteenth century had almost ceased. Religious tracts and pamphlets were as prolific as ever, but were characterised by an increasing spiritual poverty. In England, certainly, a great part of the output of the press during the first half of the seventeenth century was made up of political and religious tracts disseminated by opposing factions and denominations until the country was overrun with a flood of controversial tracts, vying with each other in the vehemence of their abuse. In workmanship slipshod, in typography vile, dressed up with ancient blocks and printed on the poorest of paper, these pamphlets demonstrated to what low levels the standards of the printing trade had sunk.

To turn to more heartening aspects of the printing trade, the 'age of scientific endeavour', as the seventeenth century has been termed, saw the first appearance in print of a large number of works by eminent scientists, while many important contributions to scientific knowledge were published in the numerous periodicals which came into being during this century.

The oldest scientific journal is the *Journal des Scavans* (as it was then spelt), which began publication at Paris in January 1665. Its first editor was Denis de Sallo, writing under the pen name of 'Sieur de Hédouville'. One hundred and eleven volumes were issued between 1665 and 1792, when the publication was supressed during the French Revolution. It resumed publication in 1816 under the auspices of the Institut de France.

* A History of the Printed Book ('The Dolphin' No. 3), New York, 1938.

In England the Royal Society (founded in 1600) began to publish its *Philosophical Transactions* on 6 March 1665, and thus became the first periodical publication of a learned society. In it have been published over the years many important contributions to human thought. Its first publisher was Henry Oldenburg, the secretary to the Society.

In Italy the Accademia dei Lincei was founded at Rome in 1603, and although it was closed soon afterwards, it was revived in 1609, in which year it began to publish its proceedings as *Gesta Lynceorum*. It came to an end through lack of support in 1657, but its name was restored in 1784 with the founding of the present Accademia Nazionale dei Lincei.

In Germany the Schweinfurt physician Johann Lorenz Bausch founded the Academia Naturae Curiosorum in 1652. Its publication *Miscellanea Curiosa*, which began to appear in 1670, did much to foster an interest in medical and allied sciences not only in Germany, but also in neighbouring countries.

Among the famous scientists whose works were published during the seventeenth century were Galileo, Huygens, Hevelius, Halley, Boyle, Leibniz, Van Leeuwenhoek, Lister, Blasius, and of course Sir Isaac Newton, whose *Philosophiae naturalis principia mathematica*, a work which established a conception of the universe unchallenged until Einstein, was printed by Joseph Streater for Samuel Smith, who published it in 1687.

GERMANY

Germany during the seventeenth century was more bedevilled by the upheavals of the time than most of the other large countries of Europe. Here religious differences were even greater than elsewhere. The Thirty Years' War ruined most trades, and not least the book trade. The end of that struggle left Germany in misery and despair; no longer was it a dominating influence in European politics. At the beginning of the sixteenth century Germany had been in the forefront of European civilisation – by the end of the war both art and literature had sunk to the lowest level.

This state of affairs was reflected in the dismal productions of the book trade. Particularly noticeable was the wretched quality of the paper. The German papermaking industry had been disrupted and the supremacy in this field now passed to Holland, whence came the best quality paper for printing.

Nevertheless the first years of the century saw the introduction of printing into several German towns: **Weimar** in 1601, **Goslar** in 1604, **Darmstadt** in 1605, and **Aachen** in 1620.

The seventeenth century also saw the introduction into Germany of those news-books which were the forerunners of our modern newspaper. In 1609 appeared the two first regular numbered and dated news-books to appear in Europe, both of which made their appearance in January of that year. They were: *Avisa, Relation oder Zeitung*, printed by Julius Adolph von Söhne, at Wolfenbüttel, and *Relation: aller Fürnemen und gedenkwürdigen Historien*, printed at Strassburg by Johann Carolus. The *Avisa*, which was edited in Prague and in part written by its founder, Duke Heinrich Julius, was produced as an instrument in the Duke's effort to reconcile the Protestant and Catholic factions. The third-oldest newspaper recorded is the *Gedenckwürdige Zeitung* which first appeared in May 1610, and was probably printed in Cologne. Berlin's earliest newspaper, *Bericht*, etc., came out for the first time on 29 December 1617.

At the beginning of the century, Leipzig was the most important city in Germany for book production, with Frankfurt and Cologne coming next, but as the century drew on the two last-named cities took the first places, whilst Leipzig dropped back to third. Nuremberg and Strassburg were the next most important centres of the book trade.

The news-sheets we have mentioned were often brought out at irregular intervals, and the earliest daily newspaper in Germany was the *Neueinlaufende Nachtricht von Kriegs- und Welthändeln*, printed and published at Leipzig by Timotheus Ritzsch, of which the first number appeared on 1 January 1660. This became in 1734 the *Leipziger Zeitung*, and eventually ceased publication in 1921 as a result of economic difficulties following the First World War. Other towns soon had their daily newspaper: Königsberg in 1661, and in the same year Vienna with the *Italienischen Zeitung*. Frankfurt-am-Main followed suit in or about 1665 with the *Journal*.

By this time typefounding had become a separate trade and there were now few firms which combined printing and publishing with the founding of type. One which did so was the Nuremberg printing house of Georg Leopold Führmann. In 1616 Führmann brought out a specimen book, the introduction to which gives an account of the origin of printing. The types shown are good examples of those used in an important German printing office at the beginning of the seventeenth century. A few of the types shown were cut by Führmann, but some of the romans are probably Garamonds and most of the italics were cut by Robert Granjon. Among the foundries which issued specimens during the seventeenth century in Germany was the famous Egenolff-Berners foundry, whose specimen of 1592 was important in that it showed the names of the designers of the types which figured on it. During the seventeenth century this firm issued several broadside specimens, as did the Frankfurt foundry of Philipp Fievet, established around 1632.

In Leipzig at the beginning of the century the most important printer was Abraham Lamberg, who was active in that city from 1587 until 1629. Publisher as well as printer, he produced altogether some 900 titles and his name is closely linked with the history of the Leipzig *Messkatalog*, over which he had a long-lasting quarrel with Henning Grosse I. He printed a number of books for the notorious publisher, Johann Francke of Magdeburg. He did not always carry on the business by himself. During the latter part of his career, in the seventeenth century, he rented out his printing office to Wolf Meissner, Hans Ulrich, Georg Liger and Hans Glück, and in 1624 he sold his bookselling business to Gottfried Grosse.

Other well-known Leipzig printers of this century included Gregor and Timotheus Ritzsch (1624–43; 1638–78), Henning Köhler and his son Johann (1633–56; 1665–1701), Johann Wittgau (1651–71), Johann Erich Hahn, who was also a type-founder (1656–*c*. 1678), and Elias Fiebig (1677–80). Fiebig was originally a bookseller and publisher, but in 1677 he bought the disused printing office of Christoph Cellarius, who had worked in Leipzig from 1652 until 1658. Fiebig's printed publications were mostly of an ephemeral nature – calendars, dissertations, and a variety of cheap tracts. Some sixty printers worked in Leipzig in the seventeenth century.

At Cologne Johann Gymnich IV, son of the third of that dynasty of bookseller–printers, was active from 1598 until 1634 at the sign of the Unicorn; at his death the business was continued until 1653 by his son Gerwin Gymnich. Hermann Mylius the son of Arnold Mylius (1585–1604) succeeded to his father's business, which he continued with success until his death in 1656. Hermann Mylius, who had a branch at Frankfurt-am-Main, became Burgermaster of Cologne in 1650.

Bertram Hilden (1620–*c*. 1650) printed theological and legal books for the University and was the founder of an important newspaper publishing house. His son Peter (1646–82) brought out in 1664 the Cologne news-book *Extraordinariae Relationes*, and his grandson, Peter Theodor Hilden (1687–1709) continued the family business.

At Frankfurt-am-Main the firm of Latomus spanned the entire century, for Sigmund Latomus worked there from 1599 until about 1625, and his heirs carried on the business until 1712. Sigmund had in 1599 inherited the printing office of his father-in-law, Johann Kolitz. He printed mainly periodical publications such as the *Messrelationen* (news of the Leipzig Fair), the official catalogue of the Fair, and he was also the printer of the *Mercurius Gallo-Belgicus*, a weekly news-sheet.

Balthasar Christoph Wust the Elder (1656–1702) was, like Hans Lufft in the sixteenth century, mainly noted as a printer of Bibles, of which he printed around 100,000. A son of the Wittenberg bookseller Christian Wust, he issued many of the sermons and biblical commentaries of the Wittenberg theologians.

Another well-known Frankfurt printer of this period was Johann Andreae the Younger who in 1666 received a printing press from his brother-in-law Daniel Fivet, as part of the inheritance of his wife Christine, who was a daughter of Phillipp Fivet I (see *infra*). He worked at Frankfurt until 1693, and was often employed by others, notably the heirs of Merian, Johann Zunner, and Caspar Wächtler. The Fievet family were prominent printers during the second half of the century. Philipp Fievet I printed from 1642 until his death in 1649, after which his widow carried on the business until 1656. Then their son Daniel ran the firm until 1673, and Philipp Fievet II prolonged its existence until almost the end of the century. The Fievet family had their own foundry, later transferred to J. A. Schmidt.

One of the most important printing dynasties in Germany was the Endter family of Nuremberg, which lasted from 1590 until 1740. The founder of the firm was Georg Endter the Elder, who began his career in 1590 as a bookbinder, and by his professional skill paved the way for his son Wolfgang's ensuing success as a printer–publisher. Wolfgang improved the printing office, to which he added a foundry, and then formed a publishing house which grew swiftly in importance. He died in 1659, leaving as his masterpiece the *Kurfurstenbibel*, printed in 1641, and so-called on account of its frontispiece showing portraits of the Electors of Saxony. His brother Georg Endter the Younger, died in 1629, but the numerous sons of the two brothers and their followers carried the firm along until well into the eighteenth century.

During the years 1680 to 1684 the business was run jointly by three members of the Endter family: Wolfgang Moritz Endter (1653–1723), Georg Andreas Endter (1654–1727) and Wolfgang Andreas Endter (1659–82). After the death of the last-named the business was divided between Georg Andreas, who took over the printing office, and Wolfgang Moritz who supervised the bookselling branch.

A landmark in the history of education was the publication in 1658 by the Endter firm of *Orbis sensualium pictus quadrilinguis* by Jan Komenskí (Johannes Comenius), Bishop of the Moravian Brethren, and one of the leading educationalists. He was the first to stress the value of visual aids in the education of young children, and this was the first picture-book designed to appeal to the intelligence of the young. It was reprinted by the same firm in 1666, and to date some 250 editions in many languages are recorded.

Another well-known Nuremberg printer was Wolfgang Felsecker, who worked there from 1658 until 1680. He is probably best known as the printer of Hans Jacob Christoffel von Grimmelshausen, *Abentheurliche Simplicissimus*, that novel of the Thirty Years' War which Professor Robertson acclaimed as 'the greatest German book of the seventeenth century'.* The author concealed his identity under the pseudonym of G. Schleifheim von Salsfort, and the book bore the fictitious imprint 'Mompelgart, bey Johann Fillion'. Two editions were printed in 1669, one by Georg Müller at Frankfurt-am-Main and the other by Wolfgang Felsecker at Nuremberg.

* J. G. Robertson, *The Literature of Germany*, 1913.

Other Nuremberg printers of the time included Johann Christoph Lochner the Elder (1632–76) and his son of the same name (1676–*c*. 1696), and Balthasar Scherf (1607–43) who in 1619 established a branch of his printing business at Altorf, where he became the University printer.

Books on theological subjects were still in great demand. Up to 1642 some 170,000 copies of the works of the Jesuit writer Hieronymus Drexel were put on the market, of which 107,000 came from the Munich publisher Cornelius Leysser (1625–43). The chief centres for the printing and distribution of Lutheran writings and song-books were Leipzig and Wittenberg, as well as Lüneburg, where the brothers Johann and Heinrich Stern were keenly active in this field. This famous firm had made its début in 1624 with *Cryptomenytices et Crypto-graphiae* by Gustavus Selenus, the pseudonym of Duke Augustus the Younger of Braunschweig-Wolfenbüttel. Nevertheless the influence of the Church on German life had waned considerably since the sixteenth century.

Exotic printing was carried out by the Lothringian Franz de Mesgnien Meninski, who, after spending some years in Constantinople, was invited by Leopold I to Vienna, where in 1661 he set up a printing office which produced a number of oriental works for which the exotic type came from the foundry of Johann Lobinger at Nuremberg. These works included *Linguarum orientalium turcicae, arabicae, persicae institutiones* (1680) and the three-volume *Thesaurus linguarum orientalium* (1680–87).

Earlier in the century three Jews from Frankfurt had obtained authorisation to set up at Hanau a press for printing Hebrew books. In 1609 the press was granted a privilege for ten years and received the name of Typographia Orientalis. One Hans Jakob Henne was engaged as printer and the press was set up in his house. After Henne's death in 1613 the press was transferred to the house of a certain Jakob Wentzel, and Abraham Leo, who seems to have learned his trade with Jean Aubry, was appointed printer. The press was active until about 1630.

Another name connected with oriental typography is that of the philologist Hiob Ludolf (1624–1704). Born at Erfurt, he studied at the university in that town, learning Greek, Latin, French, Italian, Spanish and Dutch. Then a professor of theology introduced him to the oriental tongues, and with his exceptional facility in learning languages he soon had a grounding in all the Semitic dialects with the exception of Ethiopian, for which he could not find a teacher. But with great difficulty, and even greater determination, he gathered material for an Ethiopian dictionary and a grammar of that language. He published *Historia Æthiopica* at Frankfurt-am-Main in 1681; a *Lexicon Amharico-Latinum* in 1698; and his *Grammatica Æthiopica* in 1702. He himself paid for the cutting of an Ethiopian fount, and the matrices, together with the Ethiopian books he had printed he bequeathed to the people of Abyssinia.

The year 1635 saw the publication at Frankfurt-am-Main of the first volume of the *Theatrum Europaeum* with illustrations by the engraver Matthäus Merian the Elder (1593–1650). This immense chronicle of contemporary events in thirty-one volumes was not completed until 1738. The complete work contains ninety-two maps and 1,486 copper-plate engravings as well as 2,142 separate views. It is worth remarking that the views of towns contained in this work – unlike the fanciful drawings found in, for example, the Nuremberg Chronicle – were for the first time actually drawn on the spot, and so provide an important and authentic testimony regarding the appearance of many towns at that time. In the first twenty-nine volumes of the first edition, completed in 1672, the towns represented were in the main those of France and Germany. Later, two volumes were added, dealing with Italy and Rome. After the death of the Basel engraver, the work was brought to a successful conclusion by his sons Matthäus (1621–87) and Kaspar. The publishing firm of Merian continued to flourish under the management of the grandson of the founder – Johannes Matthäus Merian (1659–1716). Maria Sibylla (1647–1717), daughter of Matthäus I, made a name for herself through her flower and insect books.

HOLLAND: THE ELSEVIERS AND OTHER DUTCH PRINTERS OF THE SEVENTEENTH CENTURY

One of the most famous names associated with Dutch printing in the seventeenth century is that of Elsevier. The founder of the firm, Louis Elsevier I, was born at Louvain and his father worked as a pressman for Plantin from 1567 until 1589. The young Louis had done some binding for Plantin between the years 1565 and 1567, but for religious reasons he found it prudent to leave Antwerp shortly before the arrival of the Duke of Alva, and sought refuge in Liège, his wife's home town. Later he went to Wesel, and after the amnesty proclaimed by Requesens in 1574, returned to the Netherlands, settling for a time at Douai. In 1580 he went to Leyden, where he opened a bookshop, but either he was a poor man of business or ill-luck dogged him, for he incurred debts which almost overwhelmed him. Fortunately he managed to secure a post as beadle to Leyden University which not only provided him with a regular salary, but also the opportunity of gaining influential clients. Louis Elsevier died in February 1617; he had seven sons and two daughters.

Of his sons, the eldest, Mathijs, and the youngest, Bonaventura, took over their father's business as booksellers in Leyden. Louis II Elsevier managed a branch of the business at the Hague, and Joost became a bookseller in Utrecht. Thus the Elsevier business was at first devoted exclusively to bookselling. It was not until 1620 that Louis I's grandson Isaac, who had opened a printing office following a rich marriage, became University printer and began the rise to European fame of the name of Elsevier.

In 1625 Isaac greatly increased the importance of his printing office by purchasing the printing material of the oriental press managed by the recently deceased Thomas Erpenius, professor in Oriental languages at the University of Leyden. But having thus enlarged his scope by the purchase of exotic types, Isaac unaccountably gave up his business, left Leyden and eventually became an official in the Dutch Admiralty. The contents of his printing office he turned over to his uncle Bonaventura and his cousin Abraham, whose partnership, begun in 1622, lasted thirty years. Bonaventura was, so to speak, the managing director of the business, while Abraham superintended the actual printing. 'During the thirty-year period,' writes Mr Davies,* 'they published nearly half the books issued by the Leyden Elseviers in the one hundred and thirty-two years of the firm's existence, and were easily the best typographers of the Elsevier dynasty.'

When Abraham and Bonaventura both died in the year 1652 the Leyden firm was continued by Johannes and Daniel Elsevier, the sons of Abraham and Bonaventura respectively. But they soon encountered difficulties brought about by plague, the war with England, and a general stagnation in industry. In 1655 Daniel left Leyden and joined the Amsterdam bookselling and publishing business of his cousin Louis Elsevier, who was active in that city from 1638 until 1664. Johannes continued in Leyden as University printer, and after his death in 1661 the business was carried on by his widow, Eva van Alphen, who was allowed to retain the status of University printer, continuing in that position until 1681, when she handed over the business to her son Abraham, a person of standing in the professional world as an advocate and doctor of laws, but an inept printer who incurred the displeasure of the University authorities on account of the high prices he charged for poor quality printing. A German named Dr Lämmerman, who visited Leyden in 1710, wrote: 'The Elsevier press, which was once so justly famous, has now greatly declined, and appears to fall lower every day.'

On the other hand, Louis and Daniel Elsevier in Amsterdam did much to restore the dimmed lustre of the name of Elsevier. Among the authors they printed were Descartes, Pascal (with a false Cologne imprint), Bacon, Hugo Grotius, Comenius, Milton and Thomas Hobbes – not forgetting Molière of whom they published twenty-four separate plays and two complete editions of his works.

In 1664 Louis retired from business, and from then until his death on 13 October 1680, Daniel Elsevier carried on the Amsterdam branch alone. His widow decided to give up the business after having published a few books remaining unfinished at her husband's death, and by March 1681 the Amsterdam firm closed. There remained only the Leyden business, which by the negligence

---

* David W. Davies, *The World of the Elseviers*. The Hague, 1954.

of Abraham was at a low ebb. When he died on 30 July 1712, the Elsevier story came to an end.

The reputation of the Elseviers as printers has waxed and waned. The garrulous Dibdin went into raptures over them; in the present century Daniel B. Updike was less than enthusiastic. Of their small classics he wrote: 'How ever anyone ever read with comfort pages so solidly set in such monotonous old style type passes understanding – or at least mine' (Updike, 1933). Nevertheless, the books from the Elsevier presses enjoyed a remarkable vogue during the greater part of the nineteenth century, fostered by romantic novelists for whom a book lover was always supposed to have a shelf full of 'priceless little Elseviers'.

In their day the Elsevier 12mo classics were so successful, being handy pocket editions, that they were extensively imitated. But the Elseviers themselves were not over-scrupulous in their trading methods; they were not above pirating works first printed by others, and many works were issued by them either without any imprint or with a fictitious one. Political works were often printed pseudonymously – from the Leyden house under the name of 'Jean Sambix' and from the Amsterdam branch under that of 'Jacques le Jeune'. 'Their editions of the contemporary French authors, now classics themselves,' wrote Andrew Lang, 'are lovely examples of practical enterprise. . . . They stole right and left, but no one complained much in these times of slack copyright.' *

The reputation of the Elseviers as printers has been exaggerated. In the words of the typographer S. L. Hartz, 'they only represent the average printing of their era, and in several of their productions do not even approach the best done by others'.†

Good printing in Holland was certainly not the exclusive prerogative of the Elseviers. As befitted the great maritime nation that Holland then was, some of the finest maps and atlases came from her printing presses. The three-volume folio *Atlas Novus* published at Amsterdam in 1638, printed by Henricus Hondius, the second son of the Amsterdam publisher Jodocus Hondius, is a handsomely printed work. But the great cartographic printers of the seventeenth century were the Blaeu family. The founder of the firm, Willem Janszoon Blaeu (1571–1638) had been in Denmark as a young man, and there studied under Tycho Brahe, from whom he got the idea of making maps and globes.

His first map, of Holland, appeared in 1604, and in the following year he brought out a map of the world. It was not the first complete world atlas to be published in Holland. That had come from the press of Cornelisz Claesz at Middelburgh, in 1598, with plates engraved by Jodocus Hondius. But Blaeu soon made his name as a map printer, and in 1633 was appointed cartographer to the Dutch East India Company. Although his fame rested mainly upon his maps and charts, he was also the publisher of some of the best poets of his day,

* *The Library*, 1881.
† *The Elseviers and their contemporaries*, Amsterdam, 1955.

FIGURE 64. Title-page of the Stettin edition (1628) of *De Magnete* by William Gilbert, a native of Colchester who became physician to Queen Elizabeth I. The first edition of this work was published at London, 1600, but was not translated into English until 1900.

such as his friend Roemer Visscher and the famous Josse van den Vondel.

On 13 September 1637 Blaeu opened a great new printing house in Amsterdam, which Evelyn visited in 1641. 'It is furnished,' he wrote, 'with nine type-presses, named after the nine Muses, six presses for copper-plate printing, and a type foundry.... Fronting on the canal is a room with cases in which the copper plates are kept, from which the Atlases, the Book of the Cities of the Netherlands and of foreign countries, also the Mariners' Atlases and other choice books are printed, and which must have cost a ton of gold.' He goes on to describe in detail this establishment, which was evidently one of the sights of the city. One of the first works to be printed in this new printing house was Vondel's *Gijsbrecht van Aemstel*.

Willem Jansz. Blaeu died on 21 October 1638 and was succeeded by his sons Joan and Cornelis Blaeu, but Cornelis died shortly afterwards. Joan added fresh lustre to the name of Blaeu, particularly with his *Atlas Major* in eleven volumes, which far surpassed anything which had been produced up to that time in the field of cartography. The edition with Latin text appeared between 1650 and 1662, and was closely followed by editions in French and Spanish.

Another dynasty of printers who contributed much to the fame of Dutch printing was that of Van Waesberghe. Jan van Waesberghe, the founder, was for many years a printer in Antwerp, and left that city for Rotterdam about 1589. Although he died about a year later, the business flourished so successfully during the seventeenth century that no fewer than sixteen Van Waesberghes followed each other as managers of the printing office. Other members of the family started branches in Amsterdam, Utrecht and Breda, and as far afield as Danzig. The Amsterdam printing office attained considerable importance under Johannes Janssonius van Waesberghe during the thirty years 1651–81. He printed all kind of books in competition with the Elseviers, and also dealt in maps and atlases which he had taken over from his father, Johannes Janssonius, whose name he added to his own. Many of his books were published in partnership with Elizeus Weyerstraeten, who had married one of the daughters of Janssonius.

At Leyden the University, founded 1575 by William of Orange, gave work to many printers, among whom the best-known were Franciscus Hackius, the Van Ravesteyns, Jean le Maire, the Van Gaesbeeks, Pieter van der Aa and the firm of Luchtmans, which was still in existence in the middle of the nineteenth century.

The Janson series of types is probably better known to the student of printing than is the name of their creator. At least, in England; in Hungary it is otherwise. Although the Janson types originated in Holland they were cut by the Hungarian Miklós Kis, born in 1650 at Alsö-Misztótfalu. After a few years as a school-master, Kis went to Holland to take a degree in theology, intending to be a preacher. However, he was eventually dissuaded from taking this course by a

FIGURE 65. Engraved title-page by William Hole for the *Polyolbion* of Michael Drayton. London, 1612.

friend, who managed to persuade him that he would serve both religion and his country better by becoming a printer rather than a preacher, of which there were more than enough.

Accordingly, in 1680 he entered the famous firm of Blaeu as a pupil, and there learned the craft of cutting and casting type. Two years earlier the Blaeu foundry had been taken over by Dirk Voskens and Johannes Adams, and it was probably Voskens himself who taught Kis his art. When Kis eventually set up in business on his own his work began to be noticed. After a time he felt himself sufficiently competent to print a Magyar Bible with his own types, and this was published at Amsterdam in 1685, with separate editions of the Psalms and the New Testament following in 1686 and 1687. At about this time he had a master-printer and twenty men doing the printing for him.

When the Bible was finished he is said to have melted down the types, which no longer satisfied him, and cut others, the sale of which financed his printing. In 1689 he left Holland to return to his homeland, where he set up a press and type-foundry at Kolozsvár. In 1698 he wrote and printed his autobiography, and when he died in 1702 his foundry was bought by the Church. A type specimen is said to have been issued in 1723, but no copy of it is now known.

The so-called Janson types are shown in two specimens of the Erhardt foundry at Leipzig printed during the first half of the eighteenth century. Both roman and italic are shown in various sizes, headed 'Verzeichniss der Holländischen Schrifften'. The modern name is an allusion to Anton Janson, a Leipzig type-founder of the late seventeenth century, whose business descended to the Erhardt family, but there are no valid grounds for associating these types with him.

A good linguist, like most Central Europeans, Kis cut a square Hebrew character for German and Polish Jews and was one of the first to cut Armenian and Georgian alphabets. Although he had received an offer to become printer to the Grand Duke of Tuscany he preferred to devote his services to his native Hungary, where he is honoured as patriot, reformer of the Magyar tongue, and one of the country's most famous printers.

Hungary suffered, like other European countries, from the general decline of printing in the seventeenth century, and the only other press of importance was that of Abraham Kertesz, who had learned his trade in Belgium. His press, which enjoyed the patronage of Count Stephen Bethlen, was situated in Grosswardein, and when that town was besieged by the Turks in 1660 he fled to Cluj, in Transsylvania, and there in the following year he printed his great Hungarian Bible. Later he moved to Nagy-Szeben (Hermanstadt), where he died in 1667.

ENGLAND

In most European countries the standard of printing showed marked deterioration during the seventeenth century, and in England it sank to a very low level,

FIGURE 66. William Hole's engraved title-page for the *Works of Ben Jonson*, printed by William Stansby in 1616.

especially when compared with the best seventeenth-century printing in France. It would be unfair to state that there was no fine printing at all in England during this century, but the good was unfortunately the exception.

The decline was especially marked during the first half of the century and was due to a variety of causes, chief among them being the increasingly severe restrictions placed upon printing by the Crown. The system of monopolies deprived the trade of beneficial competition, and hatred of the foreigner deprived it of much-needed technical stimulus. The severity of the restrictions placed on printed books was due largely to constant religious and political strife, for both Church and State feared the power of the printed word.

Fortunately there were certain works which saved English printing from the charge of being completely undistinguished. One was the *St John Chrysostom*, printed nominally by John Norton at Eton, but in reality by Melchisidec Bradwood* of the Eliot's Court Press, which appeared in eight folio volumes between 1610 and 1613. The work was undertaken at the expense of, and under the direction of, Sir Henry Savile, Provost of Eton. Reed called it 'one of the most splendid examples of Greek printing in this country'. The Great Primer Greek type used for the main text is a close copy of the famous 'grecs du Roi' and its origin is uncertain. It is a French type, purchased possibly at Frankfurt. The whole work is said to have cost Savile £8,000 – a tremendous sum of money in those days. The Greek type eventually came into the possession of the Oxford University Press.

John Norton, whose name appears as printer, had been appointed King's Printer in Hebrew, Greek and Latin in 1603. He was three times Master of the Stationers' Company, but it is doubtful if he was ever a working printer, any more than was Christopher Barker. They held their patents by purchase and were employers of labour to exploit that patent.

One of the most celebrated English books produced during the seventeenth century is the first collected edition of Shakespeare's plays, known today as the 'First Folio'. It appeared in 1623, and its printers, according to the title-page imprint, were Isaac Jaggard and Edward Blount, though the actual printer was Jaggard, Blount being a bookseller-publisher who joined in the venture some time after the printing had begun. One cannot help regretting that so famous a book should be so poorly printed; but as Sir Francis Meynell has remarked: 'It is a tragic fact that not one contemporary edition of Shakespeare, the Authorized Version, Donne, Herbert, Vaughan, Herrick, Marvell, was good to look upon as a piece of book-making.'†

* Although this printer's surname is written Bradwood in most reference books, in the Parish Register of St Giles, Cripplegate, it is given as 'Broadway' on nine occasions, and 'Bradwoode' only twice.
† *English Printed Books*, 1946.

Isaac Jaggard's father, William Jaggard, was a good printer, and in the opinion of that excellent designer of books, Bruce Rogers, his edition of *Nobilitas Politica vel Civilis*, issued in 1608, was one of the handsomest books of that period, and a 'compendious example for students of Elizabethan typography'.

Of the four great polyglot Bibles printed during the sixteenth and seventeenth centuries, one was printed in England, the *Biblia Sacra Polyglotta*, in six volumes, edited by Brian Walton and published between 1633 and 1657. Printed by Thomas Roycroft, it exemplifies seventeenth-century English printing at its best. The exotic founts employed (Hebrew, Latin, Greek, Aramaic, Syriac, Samaritan, Ethiopic, Arabic and Persian) appear to have been furnished by the four English type-founders nominated under the Star Chamber *Decree concerning Printing*, of July 1637. (They were John Grismand, Thomas Wright, Arthur Nichols and Alexander Fifield.) The work is therefore a landmark in the history of letter-founding in England, since never before had a work of importance been printed in England in any of the 'learned' characters except Latin and Greek.

The year 1611 saw the publication of the King James's Bible, commonly known as the 'Authorised Version'. The nominal printer was Robert Barker, the King's Printer, but so great was the expense of printing a complete folio Bible that Barker received financial help from three London stationers, the cousins John and Bonham Norton and John Bill, who advanced the money in return for a share in the profits. A quarto edition, in roman type, followed in 1612.

About the same time, although undated, was published the first music book in England to be printed from copper plates. This was an anthology of music for the virginals entitled *Parthenia*, and it contained twenty-one keyboard works by Byrd, Bull and Gibbons. It was engraved by William Hole, published at London by John Clarke, and was probably issued some time between November 1612 and February 1613, since it was published to celebrate the betrothal of Elisabeth, daughter of James I, to Frederick, Elector Palatine of the Rhine.

The best-known publishers of music in England during the second half of the seventeenth century were the Playfords, father and son. John Playford the elder (*c.* 1623–93) was a bookseller of the Inner Temple, London, who dealt chiefly in music books, of which the best-known is *The English Dancing Master*. First published in 1651, it had run into eighteen editions by 1728, and forms an invaluable record of English popular melodies of the period. Although the bulk of Playford's publications were printed from movable type, one or two of his later music books were engraved, such as the two-volume *Musick's Handmaid* of 1678 and Henry Purcell, *Sonnatas of III parts* (1683), the earliest known music engraved by Thomas Cross, who did much to popularise music engraving in England. John Playford's business was continued by his son Henry Playford (*c.* 1657–1710).

On 24 September 1621 appeared the first newspaper in English printed in England. Its title was *Corante, or newes from Italy, Germany, Hungarie, Spaine and France*, 1621. It was a small sheet 'printed for N.B.' which might stand for either Nicholas Bourne or Nathaniel Butter, both of whom were well-known London stationers. It is generally conceded that they stand for the latter. Butter, the son of the stationer Thomas Butter, was admitted to the Stationers' Company in 1604 and by 1620 was well established, publishing a number of books, usually in association with other booksellers. The seven corantos he published in 1621 are the oldest surviving periodical news-books in England, for although the stationer Thomas Archer is said to have issued news-sheets during the same year, no copy of them is known.

During the whole of the first half of the seventeenth century much of the output of the press in England was made up of political and religious tracts disseminated by opposing factions and denominations, for all parties, whether political or religious, hoped to gain their object by printed propaganda, and soon the country was over-run with a flood of controversial pamphlets, vying with each other in the vehemence of their abuse.

The Civil War, especially, brought in its train a spate of vituperative tracts, for the most part ill-printed, and this pamphlet warfare assumed such dimensions that an Act of 1649, which was a virtual reimposition of the former Star Chamber decrees, imposed also a fine of forty shillings on anyone found carrying or sending by post seditious books or pamphlets. In workmanship slipshod, in typography vile, dressed up with ancient blocks and printed on the poorest of paper, these pamphlets show to what low level the standards of the printing trade had fallen.

But repulsive as so many of them are to look at, these fugitive pieces are now of inestimable value to the historian, who has to thank the indefatigable George Thomason, a bookseller of that time, for having collected, over the period between 3 November 1640, and 23 April 1661, every small book, pamphlet or news-sheet he could acquire published in England – or abroad, if in English. This collection, now known as the 'Thomason Tracts', is today in the safe custody of the British Museum, a gift from George III in 1762. Altogether it contains 22,255 items.

A great name in the history of Oxford printing during the seventeenth century is that of Dr John Fell, Dean of Christchurch 1660–86, Vice-Chancellor of the University and one of the Delegates of the Press, in which capacity, both by his munificence and personal exertions, he set the 'Learned Press' once again on the road traced out by Laud. In 1671 he became the head of a partnership of four which rented the management of the University Press during the years

FIGURE 67. Frontispiece to the first edition of Bunyan's *The Pilgrim's Progress*, printed for the bookseller Nathaniel Ponder in 1678.

1672–90 and spent a considerable sum of money in equipping it with a foundry and a variety of matrices, punches and type. Much of this was purchased from type-foundries in Amsterdam with his own money, and bequeathed to the University of Oxford by his Will of 11 June 1686. For this reason the Oxford printing house holds the oldest punches and matrices surviving in England.

For long it was customary to describe these 'Fell Types' as Dutch, and certainly a number of faces are of Dutch origin, and may have been cut by Christoffel van Dijck and/or Dirck Voskens, both of whom were famous Dutch punch-cutters of the seventeenth century. But there are also some types of older date, among them italics which were almost certainly cut by Robert Granjon. 'The oldest founts,' wrote Stanley Morison, 'have survived the vicissitudes of four hundred years. The youngest are three hundred years old. The whole mass of the romans, italics, greeks, black-letters, and exotics, with initial letters and decorative material, has been acclimatized in Oxford by continuous use since the date of the bequest.'* These types are shown to advantage in the Clarendon Press edition of the *Poems of Richard Lovelace* (1925).

FRANCE

Nowhere was the curb applied to the printing trade more severely than in France, where the overriding authority was the royal one. The religious wars which had rent that country during the second half of the sixteenth century had failed to shake the absolute system of government which prevailed, and when they were over, the power of the French monarchy was even more comprehensive than before. Ordinances regulating printers and booksellers succeeded one another with dismal regularity. From 1612 onwards royal authority alone had the right to grant 'lettres de permission' without which no printing was legally possible. A regulation dated 30 March 1635, forbade the printing or selling of any written matter save with royal permission or a privilege under the Great Seal, under penalty of death. An edict of Louis XIV on the subject of printing promulgated in 1649 confirmed a host of previous regulations and in addition insisted that apprentices were to be of French birth and of the Roman Catholic religion. In 1686 an *Edit du Roy pour le Règlement des Imprimeurs et des Libraires de Paris* limited the number of printing offices in Paris to thirty-six, and jurisdiction over them passed from the University of Paris to the Government. No bookseller could apply for a printing office if he had not been registered as a printer before the edict was published, and printers were only allowed to have their shops or offices in the University quarter. Small wonder, then, that resentment occasionally vented itself in print, as in Blondel's anonymous *Mémoire sur les vexations qu'excerçent les Libraires et Imprimeurs de Paris* (1725).

Nevertheless, despite these vexations, French printers produced a respectable body of work during the whole of this century. But some of the great names in the typographic annals of the sixteenth century are missing. The religious wars were responsible for a sharp cleavage in the ranks of the leading dynasties of printers and publishers. Those who had taken the side of the Reform had been

---

* Stanley Morison, *The Fell Types*. Oxford University Press, 1950.

obliged to flee the country; their premises and goods were confiscated. The Estiennes and the De Tournes were by no means isolated examples.

One of the most prominent figures among Paris printers of the seventeenth century was Sébastien Cramoisy, who was active from 1601 until 1669 and was reputed to be the finest printer and publisher of his time for Greek and Latin works, and was himself responsible for a tenth part of all the books published in Paris during his working life. Not a year passed without his publishing at least thirty works, and with a controlling interest in several companies of booksellers he was responsible for an even larger part of the books issued on the Paris market.

The growth of these companies was due to the system of monopolies which was prevalent during the first half of the century. It was a system which met with the approval of the authorities since by suppressing competition it suppressed at the same time the tendency to seek the cheapest possible outlay, resulting in editions of poor quality and corrupt text. Collaboration between the more wealthy publishers enabled expensive undertakings to be attempted at a time when, as an aftermath of the wars, scarcity of money was hindering business.

Moreover the monarchy looked with favour upon the system, for by its power to withdraw its favours it ensured that no works harmful to the régime would be published by those to whom such monopolies had been granted.

Cramoisy was the accredited publisher of the Cistercians and especially of the Jesuits, and in addition held the appointment of King's Printer and Bookseller. Richelieu, whose personal bookseller he had been since 1614, appointed him Director of the Imprimerie Royale upon its foundation in 1640. After the death of Richelieu, Cramoisy found a protector in the Chancellor Séguier and later was on friendly terms with Colbert. Of his two brothers, Claude became works manager at the Imprimerie Royale in 1645, and Gabriel became Assistant-Director of the same establishment.

Distinction between printers and publishers became more clearly defined during this century. The most important bookseller-publishers seldom had a printing office, but employed printers to work for them. According to Georges Lepreux,* Cramoisy, in 1644, had seven Parisian printers working for him alone, and he often made use of the presses of the Imprimerie Royale, after he had become its Director, for his own personal publications.

On the other hand it was rare for a printer to become a publisher of any consequence, since more often than not he lacked the necessary capital. Thus the printer was to a large extent dependent on the publisher, who did not always settle the printer's bill promptly. Moreover, until the edict of 1686 limited the

* *Gallia Typographica.* Sér. Parisienne. Tome I. Paris, 1911.

number of printing offices in the capital, Paris had too many presses chasing too little work; in 1666 there were no fewer than 216. Printers were therefore, if not employed by one of the big publishing firms, often without work, except perhaps for a little jobbing. In 1644 Paris had 176 presses, shared between 75 printing offices and employing a total of 257 journeymen and 94 apprentices. The majority of the small printers had only one, or at most two presses. Antoine Vitré, King's Printer for Oriental languages, had five presses, and Mathurin Hénault, less well known, had seven.

The large illustrated volume became fashionable and the woodcut block was abandoned in favour of copper plate engraving, the vogue for which seems to have come from the Low Countries, where Plantin and others had popularised it during the preceding century. During the first three decades of the seventeenth century the most popular engravers were Thomas de Leu and Léonard Gaultier. They were followed by other excellent artists such as Michel Lasne, Grégoire Huret, Stefano Della Bella and François Chauveau, in addition to three outstanding illustrators: Claude Mellan, Abraham Bosse and Robert Nanteuil. All these men worked in Paris. Lyons made no attempt to compete with Paris in this field, and the only Lyons artist whose work could compare with the artists of the capital was Claude Audran.

One work in which Thomas de Leu and Léonard Gaultier collaborated was the *Images ou tableaux de plate peinture des deux Philostrate*, the first edition of which, with its ninety-five engraved plates, was published in 1614 by the widow of Abel Langelier. The plates, engraved after Caron, represent scenes from mythology and antiquity. Gaultier was one of the first engravers to work for Sébastien Cramoisy, and was employed also by Nicolas Buon, Charles Chatelain, François Huby, Thomas Blaise and Charles Morel among others.

If one were to examine those books which were somewhat above the typographical standard of current French production during the seventeenth century, one would find among them few of the great names of French literature. The contemporaries of Corneille and La Fontaine were unable to read them in decently printed editions, and the first editions of Molière and Racine were duodecimos printed carelessly and frequently full of faults. In fact few seventeenth-century books, apart from some of the early editions of the Imprimerie Royale, can compare with the typography of the sixteenth century.

The books which show to greatest advantage are those devoted to historical subjects, with especial reference to the splendours of the royal houses and of the nobility. We find, also, majestic volumes devoted to heraldry, such as the *Théâtre d'honneur* of Vulson de La Colombière enriched with plates by Grégoire Huret. This was published in 1648 in two folio volumes by the Parisian bookseller and publisher Antoine Courbé who specialised in the publication of magnificently illustrated books. One of his finest was *Les Délices de l'Esprit* by

Mr. WILLIAM
SHAKESPEARES
COMEDIES,
HISTORIES, &
TRAGEDIES.

Publiſhed according to the True Originall Copies.

LONDON
Printed by Iſaac Iaggard, and Ed. Blount. 1623.

FIGURE 68. Title-page, with the Droeshout portrait, of the first collected edition of Shakespeare's plays. It was printed in 1623 by Isaac Jaggard in conjunction with the bookseller Edward Blount.

Desmarets de Saint-Sorlin (1658), beautifully illustrated by François Chauveau. Chauveau (1613–76) was a prolific illustrator and his whole career was devoted almost exclusively to the decoration of books. Besides the book mentioned above, his talent is shown to advantage in his plates for Scudéry's *Alaric* (much better than the poem) and Desmarets' *Clovis* (1657). Most of the important publications of the second half of the seventeenth century embodied his work and altogether he engraved some three thousand plates.

Michel Lasne, who had studied at Antwerp, settled in Paris about 1620 and he, too, worked for a number of publishers. His work can be studied in the 1633 edition of H. d'Urfé, *L'Astrée*. An artist who introduced the Flemish style into French books was the Dutchman Crispin de Passe, who went to France for a time as a drawing master and illustrated a number of books, including the inevitable *Metamorphoses* of Ovid. Robert Nanteuil became 'dessinateur et graveur ordinaire du roi'. In 1662 Evelyn wrote in his *Sculptura* that 'the hand of Nanteuil renders one immortal'. Of the many portraitists of that time Nanteuil was certainly the greatest, his only rival being Gérard Edelinck. One of the finest illustrated books of the reign of Louis XIV appeared at the close of the century. This was the folio *Les hommes illustres qui ont paru en France pendant ce siècle* (1696–1700), by Charles Perrault with engravings by Edelinck and others. Sébastien Leclerc, a native of Lorraine, was particularly noted as a decorator of books and his lively invention can be seen to advantage in Le Laboureur, *La Promenade de Saint-Germain* (1669).

About half-way through the seventeenth century a change came over Parisian publishing. Under Louis XIII the output had been mainly religious and scholarly. After the accession of Louis XIV in 1643 new classes of society arose and a reading public for the classics developed. In addition, since few women read Latin, far more works were published in the vernacular.

But though there was more variety in the subject matter of books, the paper they were printed on declined steadily in quality, especially after 1640 when paper, which had hitherto been considered 'marchandise libre et franche' because its purposes were intellectual, was suddenly burdened with various taxes, and since most of the paper mills were situated in the region surrounding Troyes, these additional taxes, added to the constantly increasing cost of transport from the centre of France to the capital, made the price of paper almost prohibitive, at least as far as the better qualities were concerned. From a memorandum sent by Antoine Vitré to Colbert (*Bib. Nat. Ms. Fr.* 16746) we learn that Paris publishers could no longer afford to buy paper from Angoulême, despite its excellent quality. It cost at this time (*c.* 1670) 3 livres 5 sols a ream, to which freight and taxes added a further 46 sols. On the other hand the inferior paper known as 'petit papier commun' or 'papier du procureur' cost only 20 to 75 sols per ream, according to weight, plus 12 sols in tax.

Another factor which weighed to the detriment of the Paris publisher was that paper for export paid no duty, and when sent by sea from Bordeaux to Holland, it cost the Dutch publishers far less than was paid by their French competitors. The French paper trade declined even further after 1685, when the Revocation of the Edict of Nantes led many paper-makers to emigrate.

A landmark in the history of French printing during the seventeenth century was the completion in 1645 of the great Paris Polyglot Bible in ten folio volumes. It was printed by Antoine Vitré and published by Guy Michel Le Jay. Vitré, who was 'imprimeur ordinaire du roi pour les langues orientales' from 1630 until 1674, was one of the best printers in France. The languages employed in this Bible were Hebrew, Samaritan, Chaldaic, Greek, Syriac, Latin and Arabic. But, writes Margaret Stillwell,* 'this stupendous work nearly caused the financial ruin of Le Jay, its publisher, for Richelieu, who is reputed to have offered to defray the costs if his name might appear as publisher, apparently became cool to the venture when his suggestion was not adopted.'

The periodical press made its modest début in France largely owing to the initiative of one man, Théophraste Renaudot, a doctor by profession and businessman by inclination. He and his brothers Eusèbe and Isaac obtained a privilege from Louis XIII to found a news-sheet which they called simply the *Gazette* (later *Gazette de France*). The first number, under the editorship of Théophraste Renaudot, appeared in 1631. Published at first once or twice a week, from 1792 it appeared daily.

The success of this news-sheet, a small quarto of eight pages, led to a number of imitations many of which were short-lived. But in 1665 Denis de Sallo (under the pseudonym of Sieur d'Hédouville) started the *Journal des Savants*, a famous scientific and literary periodical which exists to this day. In 1672 appeared for the first time the *Mercure galant*, founded by Donneau de Vizé and which, later called the *Mercure françois*, continued to appear up to the time of the Revolution.

The published works of Molière made their first appearance as a two-volume edition of *Les Oeuvres de Monsieur Molière* in 1666. A seven-volume edition came out during the years 1674–75, but the first edition of the complete works was the eight-volume set published in 1682 by D. Thierry, C. Barbin and P. Trabouillet, which included the posthumous works. But as was the case with the seventeenth-century classics of English literature, the original editions of Molière, Corneille and Racine have nothing to recommend them typographically. The collected Corneille of 1669, issued in two folio volumes, has no illustration other than a frontispiece.

From the point of view of typography the seventeenth-century book in France offered little of interest to begin with. Ancient founts of large body, often badly battered and heavily leaded were in general use among those printers who had insufficient resources to renew their material. Some of the better printers made use for a time of Plantinian types, whilst the Imprimerie Royale was

---

* *A History of the Printed Book*: No. 3 of 'The Dolphin'. New York, 1938.

fortunate in having type which had been cut by the best punch-cutters of the preceding century, above all those of Claude Garamond in different sizes of roman, italic and Greek.

The only new type cut during the first quarter of the century which had any pretension to elegance was that cut by Jean Jannon, a former workman of Robert III Estienne, who in 1611 set up a printing office at Sedan. There he cut a small letter used for the first time in a Latin Virgil of 1625. The face became popular under the name of 'petite Sédanaise'. Until 1610 Jannon had been a master printer in Paris, but his Protestant sympathies caused him to move to Sedan, where the Calvinist Academy gave him work. He was, however, forbidden to print for anyone other than the Prince of Sedan★ or the Academy. He remained there for twenty years before eventually returning to Paris. In 1621 he published his *Espreuve de caractères nouvellement taillez*, which comprised eleven roman faces, eight italic, one Hebrew and a set of two-line initials. Apart from the specimen book of Le Bé in the Bibliothèque Nationale, this is probably the earliest French founder's book of type specimens. Jannon's types were used later by the Imprimerie Royale which acquired them in 1642 and called them 'caractères de l'université'.

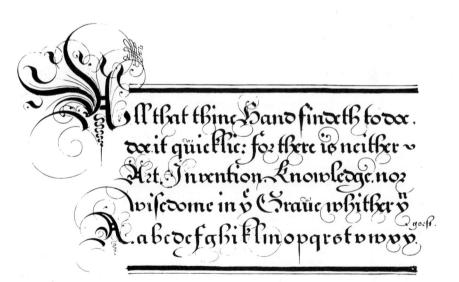

FIGURE 69. A leaf from the writing book of Martin Billingsley, called *The Pens Excellencie or the Secretaries Delight*. London, 1618.

★ Henri Robert, son of Robert IV, Duc de Bouillon, recognised as sovereign in Sedan. Henri Robert made of Sedan a Protestant centre.

In 1643 a Paris calligrapher named Pierre Moreau who specialised in Books of Hours, for which he engraved both type and illustrations, printed an edition of *L'Imitation de Jesus Christ* in a script type of his own design, one of a number of books which he printed in similar script types. These types, after passing through several hands, were eventually bought in 1787 by the Imprimerie Royale.

This same year, 1643, produced a specimen of types possessed by the Imprimerie Royale.* Only one copy of this important document, recently discovered at the Bibliothèque Nationale, is known to exist. It formed part of a collection of specimens which entered the Bibliothèque Royale (as it then was) during the decade 1740–50. Although this specimen does not bear the names of any punch-cutters, the types have been for the most part identified as the work of, *inter alia*, Garamond, Granjon, Guillaume I Le Bé, Jean Jannon, and possibly Sanlecque. From the recently published inventory of the Le Bé foundry there is evidence to show that it was from this foundry that the Imprimerie Royale received most of its founts.

While the century was drawing to its close Louis XIV, around 1692, ordered new characters to be cut for the Imprimerie Royale. They were engraved by the titular punch-cutter to the royal printing house, Philippe Grandjean, but the complete founts were not finished for half a century; further details will therefore be found in Chapter 27.

For the publication of important works necessitating a large outlay of capital, and with a view to minimising losses should a work prove less attractive to the public than had been estimated, there grew up in France various syndicates for publishing and marketing books at a cost shared by the members. In 1586 was founded the Company known as the *Grand Navire*, called thus because the books it published bore the device of the ship figuring in the arms of Lutetia, or Paris. The members of this company were Baptiste and Jacques Dupuis, Sébastien Nivelle and Michel Sonnius, all of whom were booksellers and publishers in a large way of business and able to put up considerable sums for the financing of this enterprise.

The beginning of the seventeenth century saw a wide development in this method of book-sharing, which may be compared with that of the Printer Conger in England, though this did not become common in England until a century later. Other similar companies formed in France during the seventeenth century were:

1608. *Bibliopola urbis Parisiensis consortes*, comprising Nicolas Buon, Claude Chapelet, Sébastien Cramoisy, Robert Fouet, Claude Morel and Marc Ory. This was followed in 1618 by a second company called the *Grand Navire*. In 1622 the *Compagnie des Libraires du Palais*; 1624 the *Societas Graecarum Editionum*;

---

* See André Jammes, *La Réforme de la typographie royale sous Louis XIV*. Paris, 1961.

1629, *Le Soleil*; 1631, a third version of the *Grand Navire*; 1633, the *Societas Typographica officiorum Ecclesiasticorum*; and in 1638, the *Compagnie des Libraires pour les S. S. Pères.*

In 1640 Louis XIII, on the recommendation of Cardinal Richelieu created the Imprimerie Royale. France had recovered from the religious wars of the preceding century and the Church sought to turn its activities eastwards. Politically, also, the country was interested in spreading its cultural activities in the direction of the Near East. Indeed Richelieu had founded in 1631 a society for printing and distributing Catholic writings among the peoples of the Levant, though its efforts had not been crowned with much success. Now the Cardinal had in mind, as its successor, a printing house which should be subservient to the orders of the State (in practice himself) and which should become an instrument of both religious and political propaganda.

Officially charged with publishing government ordinances and enactments, and with diffusing the most notable monuments of religion and letters, the Imprimerie Royale showed such zeal that during the first ten years of its existence it published nearly a hundred volumes in French, Greek, Latin, and Italian. The first Director of the new royal printing house was Sébastien Cramoisy, and the first-fruit of the new establishment was an edition of Thomas à Kempis, *De Imitatione Christi.* In 1642 was published Richelieu's own work, *Instruction du Chrestien*, and it is interesting to note that a commemorative facsimile edition of this work, published in 1942, just 300 years later, was printed with the help of the very punches and matrices which had served for the original edition.

Sébastien Cramoisy (1585–1669), the first Director of the Imprimerie Royale had been a printer in Paris since the beginning of the century and was reputed to be the best printer and publisher of books in the classical tongues. His brothers Claude and Gabriel were both distinguished printers; the former became 'chef des travaux' at the Imprimerie Royale in 1645, whilst Gabriel became assistant-director. Sébastien Cramoisy was succeeded in his functions, after the very brief interregnum of Antoine Vitré, by his grandson, Sébastien Mâbre, who adopted the surname of Mâbre-Cramoisy.

In 1624 an edition was begun of the writings of the Fathers of the Church printed with the once more available *Grecs du Roi* in ten folio volumes, and published by a consortium known as the 'Grand Navire'. Later these same types were used by the Imprimerie Royale for their comprehensive collection of Byzantine writers.

The first book printed at Paris in Syriac type was the Arabic Psalter of Gabriel Sionita, which Antoine Vitré, later to become Royal Printer in Oriental languages, printed in 1625, at Sionita's expense, with the types of Savary de Brèves. François Savary de Brèves was the French ambassador to the Sublime Porte during the reigns of Henri III and Henri IV. He had a series of exotic types designed after the finest manuscripts he could come across, and the punches were cut in France by Guillaume II Le Bé. Other oriental types were cut for him by Jacques de Sanlecque.

Sent to Rome in 1613, Savary de Brèves, with the help of the printer Etienne Paulin, brought out several works, including an Arabic Psalter and a Catechism of Bellarmini, which bear the colophon 'Romae, ex typographia Savariana, excudebat Stephanus Paulinus'. Towards the end of 1614, Savary de Brèves returned to Paris with his printer and two maronites, Gabriel Sionita and Jean Hesronita, whom he had engaged as translators and correctors; but Paulin soon went back to Rome after printing one work, in French and Arabic, in Paris. During the five following years the printer of the Tyographia Savariana was Jérome Blageart. De Brèves died in 1627 and his wife in 1631. In 1632 his heirs sold the oriental punches and matrices, which were bought for the French king by Antoine Vitré, and used for the Polyglot Bible of Le Jay (see p. 296), issued between 1628 and 1645.

The punch-cutter Jacques de Sanlecque, who acquired a reputation from the types he cut for Savary de Brèves, was born about 1573 either at Chaulnes [*Larousse & Nouvelle Bibliographie Générale*] or Clenleu [P. Hédouin in *Archives Hist. et Litt. du Nord de la France*]. As a young man he became interested in printing and especially in designing type and cutting punches. To acquire the necessary training he worked under Guillaume Le Bé II, who in addition to cutting many magnificent letters, also traded in matrices and strikes. Like his teacher, Jacques de Sanlecque specialised in Oriental founts, and was responsible for the Syriac, Chaldee, and Arabic founts which Vitré used in the Paris Polyglot of Guy Michel Le Jay, *maitre des requètes* and canon of Vézelay.

Sanlecque died on 20 November 1648, at the age of seventy-five, and not ninety, as Hédouin states. He was succeeded by one of his sons, Jacques II, who himself died in 1660, leaving his widow to carry on the business until their son Jean in turn took over the foundry. Jean died in 1716, leaving the business to his son Jean-Eustache Louis de Sanlecque, who died in 1778. In 1757 Lottin printed an *Epreuves des Caractères du fond des Sanlecques*, though the Sanlecque foundry had, in fact, been acquired by Haener of Nancy in 1734. This specimen contains much charming type which seems to date back to the first Sanlecque. It also contains some old music types, possibly those cut by Jacques II and used for some of the music books published by the Ballard family.

If Cardinal Richelieu was the guiding spirit behind the creation of the Imprimerie Royale in 1640 it was possibly due to his personal interest in the art of printing, for in the same year the Cardinal set up a private press in his château on the borders of Touraine and Poitou. Claudin remarked that the works which came from this press were noteworthy for the beauty of the press work and above all by the clarity of the small type. It was commonly believed that this came from the foundry of Jean Jannon at Sédan.

In 1691, after the death of the widow of Cramoisy, Jean Anisson, a printer from Lyons, who had established himself in Paris as 'libraire-imprimeur' was appointed Director of the Imprimerie Royale du Louvre, and with this appointment a movement was started which in a short space of time was to change the typography of Western Europe.

ITALY

In Italy, as elsewhere, printing suffered a decline during the seventeenth century. Venice continued to be a flourishing centre of printing and publishing, although the quality of its production deteriorated. But business does not seem to have suffered, for according to the *Cronaca Veneta* of P. A. Pacifico, published in 1697, this city of about 160,000 inhabitants had twenty-seven printing offices and some seventy bookshops. One of the best-known presses was that of the Pinelli family, started by Antonio Pinelli about 1610, and which, for almost two centuries, until the fall of the Republic, was run by the privileged 'stampatori ducali'. Also well known were Lorenzo and Nicolo Pezzana, father and son, who came from Trino and succeeded the Giunti, whose once prosperous business had failed. The firm of Pezzana surpassed all others in Italy during the seventeenth and eighteenth centuries for the production of Bibles and liturgical books.

Typographical decadence was also manifest in Florence, and really the only printing firm worth mentioning at this period was that run by the partners Signoretti and Nesti, to whom in 1643 the Grand Duke Ferdinand II extended his patronage. This was the origin of a press which later became the Stamperia Granducale, and which, after some vicissitudes, became the property of the state. It was later ceded to Gaetano Cambiagi, in whose family it remained for almost a century. Other printers working in Florence at this time include the German, Volkmar Timann, and Pietro Ceccarelli, who had a privilege for printing Gazettes.

In Naples the quality of printing was of equally poor standard, but there were a few important printers working there including one of the best printers of his time, Giacomo Raillard. There was also Ottavio Beltrano, a native of Calabria, who was himself the author of several books, including the *Descrizione del Regno di Napoli*, first published in 1640 and several times reprinted. Mention should also be made of Secondino Roncaglioli, who, during the revolt of Masaniello printed the decrees of the new government and added to his imprint 'Stampatore di questo fedelissimo popolo', later changed to 'Stampatore di questa Serenissima Repubblica'.

Turin, about the middle of the century, saw the first appearance of the

Fontana family, a dynasty of printers who were active in that city for several generations. The first of the line, Giovanni Battista Fontana worked as printer and bookseller in Turin for fifty-one years. The printing house flourished until the middle of the nineteenth century, its most active period being between 1838 and 1843 when the firm employed more than 160 workmen. Then it suddenly declined and came to an end in 1853.

At Rome, in 1618, Stefano Paolino printed *Rudimentum Syriacum*, a veritable specimen book of the Syriac characters which Savary de Brèves had had engraved at Constantinople (see p. 300). In 1622 the Congregatio de Propaganda Fide was founded at Rome, and it was decided that it should have its own polyglot printing office for missionary work. This was set up in 1626 and its first director was Paolino, who was himself a skilled punch-cutter. Some of the exotic founts came from the Vatican printing office and other characters were cut by Paolino. Within a very few years the press had founts in twenty-three different tongues, and in conjunction with its press the Congregatio established a type-foundry which eventually became the most complete polyglot foundry in Europe. The foundry began to issue specimens of these types produced for missionary presses, the first such catalogue, compiled by Giovanni Verusi, appearing in 1629 under the title *Elenchus librorum sive typis sive impensis S.C. de Propaganda Fide impressorum*. The foundry continued to issue these specimens until the latter half of the nineteenth century, some fifty in all.

Only a few isolated works bore witness to the fact that the former high standards of Italian printing had not been entirely forgotten. Among them were the *Historia Veneta* of Morsoni which Pinelli brought out at Venice in 1623, and the three-volume *Del Arcano del Mare* by Robert Dudley, son of the Earl of Leicester, which was published at Florence in 1646–7.

In the field of technology one should mention the poorly-printed but highly interesting work of Vittorio Zonca – *Novo Teatro di Machine ed Edificii* – published at Padua in 1607 by F. Bertelli. Among its plates is one showing a copper-engraving press.

SPAIN

The outstanding event in the history of Spanish printing at the beginning of the seventeenth century was undoubtedly the publication of the First Part of *El Ingenioso Hidalgo Don Quixote de la Mancha*, the masterpiece of Miguel de Cervantes Saavedra. It first saw the light at Madrid in 1605, and was printed by Juan de la Cuesta for the king's bookseller, Francisco de Robles. It is a quarto of 664 pages, of which 632 form the text. A rare book, it abounds in printers' errors, having apparently never been revised by the author. The second edition of this book, with an approbation dated 26 February 1605, a little more than two months later than that found in Cuesta's first edition, was printed at Lisbon by Jorge Rodriguez. Portugal, at this date, was under the Spanish crown. This was a pirated edition printed without the sanction of the author.

The text of the first edition of *Don Quixote* is indifferently printed in a large roman with headings in italics. The type is not particularly pleasing, but on the whole it is superior to that in common use in the Spanish book production of that period. The Second Part, also printed by Juan de la Cuesta, appeared in 1615, a quarto of 548 pages, similar in form to the First except for smaller chapter headings. The title-page of this part substitutes *Cavallero* for the *Hidalgo* of the first. A spurious Second Part, printed without any licence or approbation, was printed in 1614 at Tarragona under a fictitious publisher's name, Alonso Fernandez de Avellaneda.

Typical of the better class of book published in Spain during this century was the *Teatro de las grandezas de la Villa de Madrid* by G. Gonzalez de Avila (1623) issued at Madrid in 1623 by Tomas Junta, the royal printer. The type is passable, especially the rather handsome characters used for the dedication to the king, but the decorations and ornaments are used without discrimination. Antonio de Solis, *Historia de la Conquista de Nueva España* (Mexico) printed in 1684 at Madrid by Bernardo de Villa-Diego, has on the first page a headband almost identical with one in common use in England at that time. It is not uncommon to find, at this period, headpieces in Madrid books which are a close copy of those in use at London (see, for example, Figs. 322, 323 in Harold Bayley's *A New Light on the Renaissance*).

Engraved frontispieces appeared in many Spanish books of the seventeenth century, and as in France, were usually based on an architectural motive, an archway or portico which framed the actual title, with figures placed in convenient niches. As an example the *Historia de las Ordenes militares* of Fray Caro de Torres, publishes by Juan González at Madrid in 1621, has an elaborately engraved frontispiece of an arched gateway flanked by pedestals on which stand respectively the kings Carlos V and Philip IV. The engraving bears the signature of the Flemish artist Alardo de Popma.

Among the Spanish artists employed in this form of book illustration were Francisco de Herrera, Juan Villar, Pedro de Villafranca, Diego de Obregon, Francisco Navarro and Marcos de Orozco, but copper engraving was far less common in Spain at this time than it was in other countries. One outstanding opportunity for a good illustrator was missed, namely the masterpiece of Cervantes, for it was left to Holland to produce the first properly illustrated edition. Spain had to wait until the end of the eighteenth century for a decently illustrated edition of *Don Quixote*. The first illustrated edition was for the Dutch translation published at Dordrecht in 1657 and illustrated by Jacob Savry. The first illustrated edition of the Spanish text was published at Brussels by J. Mommarte in 1662 with illustrations by Boutatts.

All in all there is little of outstanding interest in Spanish printing during the seventeenth century. Just a few works towards the end of the century, such as Antonio de Solis, *Historia de la Conquista de Mexico*, which was published at Madrid by Bernard de Villa-Diego in 1684.

26

Around the Mediterranean

It may seem strange that Malta should have been without a printing press until almost the middle of the seventeenth century, considering how close the island lay to Italy with its long printing history. 1642 is the earliest ascertainable date for the introduction of the printing press into the island. In that year a certain Pompeo de Fiore, thought to have been a Sicilian, applied to Jean-Paul de Lascaris-Castellar, the Grand Master of the Order of Saint John of Jerusalem, for permission to start a printing office in Valetta, and with this end in view he had brought to the island the necessary equipment 'at great labour and expense'. The permission was granted on 17 June 1642, but Pompeo de Fiore did not receive any exclusive privilege for printing, as he had hoped.

Indeed the request may have suggested to the Grand Master the benefits which the Order might derive from having its own press, for in the same year he wrote to the Treasurer of the Order at Messina, Federico Gotho, asking that a printer should be sent to Valetta to take charge of the printing office which the Order intended to set up. Gotho despatched a printer from Calabria named Mario Villari, but for some reason his appointment seems to have fallen through, for nothing more is heard of him. The man who got the job was a certain Paolo Bonacota, of whose antecedents there is now no record.

As to Pompeo de Fiore, nothing has survived bearing his name. In May 1644, he was granted a privilege for a restricted category of books, such as ABCs, Donatuses, Catechisms, etc., but since the Order now had its official printer Pompeo de Fiore probably found himself confined to jobbing work. Parnis states that at his death one of his sons took over the management of the press,* which must have printed mainly ephemera, or surely something would have survived with his imprint.

For long it was thought that the earliest printed book in Malta was *Della Descrittione di Malta, Isola nel Mare Siciliano*, by Giovanni Francesco Abela, printed in 1647 by Paolo Bonacota. There is however, in the Library of Congress, Washington, D.C., a probably unique copy of *I Natali delle Religiose*

---

* Dr E. Parnis, *Notes on the first establishment, development, and actual state of the Printing Press in Malta*. Malta, 1916.

FIGURE 70. Title page of *Della Descrittione di Malta, Isola nel Mare Siciliano*, printed by Paolo Bonacota in 1647 and once thought to be the earliest book printed on the island.

Militie, etc., by Commendatore Geronimo Marulli. Below the arms of the Order on the title-page is the imprint 'In Malta, l'anno MDCXXXXIII'. There is no printer's name, but in view of the fact that the title-page bears the arms of the Order of St John it is more likely to have been the work of Bonacota rather than that of Pompeo de Fiore. The British Museum has a book called *Relatione del sanguinoso combattimento e presa d'un galeone e d'un de' Turchi* ... of which the title-page bears the words 'In Malta con licentia de Superiori' and the colophon states: 'In Malta & in Roma, per Lodovico Grignani. 1644.' This account was probably printed at Rome for sale in Malta, for we know that Grignani was printing at Rome for a number of years.

Paolo Bonacota did not print many books during his tenure of office. The most important was the *Descrittione di Malta* already mentioned. In that same year, 1647, he also printed Fabrizio Cagliola, *Elogio del Commendatore F. Rinaldo Bech La Buissière*. In 1648 he printed F. Carlo Michaleff, *L'Ismeria* (later reprinted at Venice and at Viterbo), but nothing else is known bearing his signature, though he may have been the printer of F. Don Juan de Galdiano, *Relatione della Festa celebrata in Malta ad honore di San Francesco Saverio*, which bears the imprint 'In Malta con permesso de' Superiori, 1649.'

Now comes a gap of some eighty years in the history of printing in Malta, for Bonacota left the island for Messina, and after his departure there is no trace of a printer in Malta until well into the eighteenth century. During the intervening period the volumes of statutes, laws, and rolls of the Order of St John were printed at Borgo Novo, near Novi in Italy, where in the castle of the Marchesato di Roccaforte there was a Stamperia Camerale.

TURKEY

Although a printing-office had been established in Constantinople as early as 1503, when David Nahmias, with his son Samuel, printed books in Hebrew, there was no Turkish press until 1726. This was due in part to religious scruples, but perhaps even more to the opposition of the scribes, of whom, according to Marsigli, there were at this time in Constantinople no fewer than ninety-thousand.

However, Ahmed III (1637–1736), who succeeded to the throne in 1703, showed a greater, if somewhat superficial, interest in matters pertaining to the arts and sciences. His Grand Vizier, Ibrahim Pacha, was responsible for the construction of the first public library in the Seraglio (1719), and we are told that he took a lively interest in European science; an interest which he cultivated by assiduously reading the *Journal des Scavans*. This was at a time when French influence was particularly strong in Turkey and the French ambassador, De Villeneuve, took an active interest in promoting scientific studies in that country.

When the idea of a Turkish press was first mooted there was strong opposition from the Mufti, who declared that writing was the foundation of faith, and that the sacred books would no longer be writing if they were printed. According to Arthur Davids,* the chief credit for the formation of a Turkish printing-office should go to Ibrahim Pacha, who by his perseverance gradually overcame the religious scruples of the Moslems. Also active in persuading

* *A Grammar of the Turkish Language*. London, 1832.

Ahmed III of the necessity for a press in Constantinople was Said Effendi, who in 1720 had accompanied his father Mohammed Effendi when the latter was sent by the Sublime Porte on a secret mission to ascertain the strength of the Christian armies opposed to the Turks in Europe, and who had returned to Constantinople impressed with certain aspects of Western culture.

At all events the *Gazette de France* published on 18 January 1727, a letter dated 17 November 1726, confirming that a press had indeed been set up in Constantinople, an announcement confirmed in vol. 81 of *Le Journal des Scavans* (1727). In establishing the press by royal decree Ahmed III had imposed two restrictions: each work was to be submitted to the censorship and correction of four 'judges and scholars'; furthermore, works which dealt with a religious theme were definitely ruled out, and of course works such as the Koran and its exegesis, and the utterances of the Prophet, were on no account to be printed.

The press was installed in a private house, and not in the Seraglio, as some European papers stated at the time, and was built at the cost of the State. Said Effendi and a certain Ibrahim Muteferrika were appointed managers. The latter, the more intellectual of the two men, was the technical director of the press, which he presided over until his death.

This man was a renegade Hungarian, or more correctly a Szekler, born at Kolozsvár (Klausenburg). His contemporary, César de Saussure, tells us that as a young man of eighteen or twenty the Hungarian, who had studied to become a Calvinist minister, had the misfortune to be taken prisoner by the Turks in 1692 or 1693 during the Transsylvanian campaigns. To better his lot he became a Muslim and took the name of Ibrahim; what his baptismal name was remains unknown. He learned Turkish, and applied himself with such good purpose to the study of Turkish classical culture that he was soon given employment in the government service with the title of Muteferrika, a Court servant charged with special missions, and in this way acquired some importance.

In 1715 he was sent with a missive from the Sublime Porte to Prince Eugene and stayed for four months near Vienna. In 1716 he took part in the campaign against Austria and during the following year he acted as interpreter in the Belgrade area, and after the treaty of Pozsarevàc (Passarowitz) in July 1718, he was appointed official interpreter to the famous Prince Franz Răkóczi II in Constantinople. The latter became very friendly with him, and recommended him highly to the Grand Vizier, Ibrahim Pacha, and it was not long after this that preparations went ahead for setting up this first Turkish press. Within two years of the imperial permission the first book appeared, but much had to be done in the meantime. In the first place the opposition of the orthodox was overcome by a *Fetva* or legal judgment issued by the Mufti Abdallah to the effect that the printing of books, provided it were done with skill and the text overseen by scholars, was in itself praiseworthy. Then there was the essential acquisition of type and presses. According to Kundmann, Said Effendi had Arabic and Turkish letters cast locally, but as these were not sufficient six Turks were sent to Leiden, there to have made between forty and fifty hundredweight of Arabic and Turkish characters, so that sufficient material should be available to make a start. The Turkish Aga in Vienna took several journeyman printers and compositors into his service and sent them to Constantinople where there were already eight master-printers, mostly Greeks who understood the language of the country thoroughly, and thirty-six apprentices working in the newly installed printing-office. Thus Kundmann; but he does not mention from whom the Turks acquired their oriental type at Leiden.

When two presses had been obtained from France work was ready to begin on the first production of the new press, which was issued in February, 1729. This was a translation into Turkish by Mohammed ben Mustafa, surnamed Vankuli, because he came from Van, in Armenia, of the famous Arabic Lexicon of Abu Nasr ben Hammad al-Gauhari. This work, in two folio volumes of 666 and 756 pages, was prefaced by a facsimile of the imperial *firman* authorising the establishment of the first Turkish printing office. This was soon followed by other works, including a geographical treatise of Hagi Khalifah, and Ibrahim's own work, the *Tarikhi Seiah* or 'Journal of a Traveller', which he translated into Turkish from the Latin of the Jesuit missionary Judas Krusinski.

In 1730 the press brought out the first book for which it made use of the Latin alphabet – *Grammaire Turque ou methode courte et facile pour apprendre la langue turque*. It bears no author's name but carries a dedication to Cardinal A. H. de Fleury. According to the Comte de Saussure, in a letter from Pera dated 21 February 1732, the author was one M. De Laria, who compiled it under the supervision of a Strassburg Jesuit, Johann Holdermann, a learned Orientalist.

During the period when Ibrahim Muteferrika was in charge of the printing office, from 1728 until 1742, seventeen works in twenty-three volumes were printed. The last work to come from the press during this period was a two-volume Persian–Turkish lexicon of 454,450 pages. At the end of this work, instead of the usual colophon mentioning Ibrahim Muteferrika as the printer, it is signed 'Through the handiwork of an inferior who was entrusted with the printing'. From this it would appear that Ibrahim was no longer engaged in practical work at the office.

He died in 1745 and the management of the establishment passed into the hands of his pupil Khadi Ibrahim, probably the 'inferior' of the last-mentioned book, who carried on for a further two years but was insufficiently talented to make a success of it. The press closed down, and for twenty-one years no further printing work was undertaken save for a reprinting in 1756 of the Gauhari Lexicon.

It was revived, however, by a decree of the Sultan Abdul-Hamid dated 11 March 1784. It seems that Khadi's zeal stagnated as a result of the wars which scattered his workmen, and finally he died, and the tools and material remained in the possession of his widow. During the ensuing twenty years no books were printed, and, states the decree, 'during these years a large part of the printed ones were lost or sent abroad'.

This time the patent was held by a syndicate of Turkish Civil Servants and scholars who were instructed to make available to lovers of science and the arts 'the memorials of imperial benificence'.

GREECE

Although books in the Greek language were published throughout the centuries which followed the invention of printing, Greece was one of the last countries in which printing found a home, for under the long domination by the Turks no printing was allowed there and most of the liturgical books in Greek came mainly from Venice.

In 1627 a press was in operation at Constantinople for the printing of Greek books. It was organised by Nicodemus Metaxas under the aegis of the Patriarch of Constantinople, Kyrillos Lukaris. During the eighteenth century numerous presses for the printing of Greek books were in existence. In 1730 the monk Gregorious Konstantinides worked a Greek press at Moschopolis, in Epirus. Nineteen works are known to have been printed there, the first dated 1731 and the last 1769, the year of the destruction of Moschopolis by the Albanians and Turks.

In 1759 the Archimandrite Kosmos from Epidauros set up a press at Athos, and three years later there was a Greek press operating at Smyrna under the direction of Markos Emmanuel from Rhodes. At Constantinople in 1756 yet another Greek press was established under the patronage of the Patriarch Kyrill V, and the same city harboured another Greek press in 1798, again sponsored by the Greek Church at the behest of the Patriarch Gregorios V.

At Corfu a Greek press was introduced into the island by the French in 1798, and in 1809 was founded at Xante the 'Pubblica Stamperia delle Isole Ionie liberate' following the establishment of a Republic of the Ionian Islands under British protection. The liberation of the Greeks was slowly approaching. In 1813 we find a Greek press at Kuklutza, not far from Smyrna, and another at Kydonia, run by Konstantin Domras until it was destroyed by the Turks during the Greek War of Liberation, which lasted from 1821 until 1829.

When Greece began to regain her freedom in 1821, Ambroise Firmin-Didot presented her with her first printing-office, which was established on the island of Chios. Earl Stanhope sent a press to Athens and within a short space of time Corinth, Patras and Hydra had presses of their own. It was also through the initiative of Firmin-Didot that the first native periodical, the *Athens Journal*, was printed at Hydra, but when the Turks temporarily recaptured the town the printing office was destroyed. However, by 1834 it was successfully reinstated by M. Koromelas, who had worked previously with the Didots.

In 1831 the President of the newly-liberated Greece, J. Kapodistrias, inaugurated a government printing-office under the title of the National Printing Office. At first it was divided into two sections, one in Ægina and the other at Nauplia. After the transference of the government to Athens the printing office was, in 1835, removed to the new capital.

After the arrival of King Otto in Greece the number of presses began to grow.

27

The Eighteenth Century

By the beginning of the eighteenth century the dissemination of printing throughout Europe was almost complete, and few regions were by now without a printing press. In England the so-called Press Restriction Act, in force in one form or another since the middle of the sixteenth century, came to an end in 1693, which meant that printing in England, hitherto restricted to London, York and the university presses of Oxford and Cambridge, could at last expand. Nor was the trade of type-founding confined any longer to four individuals. As a result of this freedom more than sixty towns in Britain introduced printing presses during the first half of the century.

The nadir of typography having been reached during the seventeenth century it would have been calamitous if no improvement had followed. De Vinne, himself a printer of merit, talks of 'the shabby type-printing of the seventeenth century . . . which had made general the belief that typography was an inferior art from which high merit could not be expected'.* Fortunately a gradual amelioration in standards of taste during the eighteenth century made amends for the printers fall from grace during the previous one.

One of the first manifestations of a change of style was to be found in a more attractive layout of the title-page which, particularly in England and Germany, had become increasingly verbose, crammed from head to foot with unnecessary verbiage set in a variety of types which were presumably supposed to provide a conspectus of what was available in the printer's office. The engraved title-page, a repulsive aberration according to Dr Steinberg, which spread all over Europe during the seventeenth century came to a timely end.

In typography it was a century of changing type forms brought about in England by Caslon and Baskerville; in France by Luce, following in the footsteps of Grandjean and Pierre-Simon Fournier; in Italy by Bodoni, and in Spain by Antonio de Sancha. And towards the end of the century came François-Ambroise Didot to leave an indelible mark on French typography.

Not only did the style change during the eighteenth century but so also did the content of the book. In France this was particularly noticeable. Books on

* T. De Vinne, *A Treatise on Title-pages*. New York, 1902.

religious subjects which had previously formed more than half the total production of the country showed a marked decline, whereas there was a considerable increase in the number of novels and collections of poetry, usually on
more or less erotic themes. It was above all the century of the *livre de luxe*,
richly ornamented and abounding in illustrations, of which an outstanding
example is the celebrated *fermiers-généraux* edition of La Fontaine's Contes et
Nouvelles with plates after Eisen and vignettes by Choffard.

Looking at French book production as a whole during the eighteenth century,
one cannot fail to notice the growth of the book trade by comparison with the
previous century in spite of such restrictive measures as the relatively high taxes
on book-selling and publishing and the drastic curtailment in the number of
printers. The reading public was larger and they read more. The reading matter
they sought was very different from that which formed the staple diet of their
seventeenth-century predecessors. During that century the great writers were
psychologists and moralists preoccupied with spiritual matters. There was a
tendency towards the *vie dévote* inspired by eminent theologians from Saint
François de Sales to the writers and preachers of Port-Royal. Moral values and
self-analysis were the order of the day. And under the surveillance of the pious
Madame de Maintenon even the courtiers of Versailles had to pretend to some
measure of piety while the ageing Racine wrote his biblical tragedies for the
young ladies of Saint-Cyr.

By contrast the eighteenth century sought pleasure. The production of books
of a devotional or meditative character which had formerly made up some
three-quarters of the total production, now gave way to volumes of poetry,
stories of romance, and a burgeoning of frivolous writings tinged with an aura
of eroticism enhanced by frequently scabrous but almost always delightful
illustrations. It was a time when there was an increasing vogue for luxury in
every department of life; for those, that is, who could afford it. And the wealthy
were prepared to pay handsomely for handsome books.

The outstanding characteristic of the French book during the eighteenth
century is the abundance of illustrations. No longer was it enough, as in the
previous century, to make do with a mere, and usually austere, frontispiece,
with perhaps a few *culs-de-lampe* as a concession to ornament. The vignettist and
the engraver come into their own as collaborators with the author. The great
French classics, so poorly treated in the seventeenth century, at last received a
worthy presentation. On the other hand minor writers often received a treatment out of all proportion to their merit. Dorat's *Fables* and his *Baisers*, the
Chansons of B. de Laborde, and the *Fables* of Houdart de la Motte would long
since have sunk into oblivion but for the outstanding talents of Claude Gillot,

Charles Eisen, Clément Marillier and Moreau le Jeune, among the finest of French illustrators. In fact, one wit maliciously remarked of Dorat, that he was fortunate 'de se sauver de planche en planche'.

Good book illustrators were in such demand that they could always get work. Many of the most celebrated among them had begun as painters but found that the illustration of books was more lucrative. Thus François Boucher illustrated the six-volume edition of Molière which Prault published in 1734 with thirty-three full-page designs engraved by Laurent Cars; Jean-Baptiste Oudry was responsible for the frontispiece and 275 plates of the four-volume *Fables* of La Fontaine, which were engraved after his designs by forty engravers (1759); and Fragonard illustrated the 1795 edition of the *Contes* by the same author. These painters often provided little more than a rough sketch, which it was left to the engravers to fill out, and right well they did their job.

The finest period of the *livre à gravures* was towards the end of the reign of Louis XV – roughly between 1760 and 1775. These were the years which saw the publication of a number of masterpieces. In 1762 Barbou published La Fontaine, *Contes et Nouvelles en Vers* in the famous edition produced at the expense of the Fermiers Généraux, with eighty plates after Charles Eisen and fifty-three *culs-de-lampe* by P. P. Choffard. Eisen was the drawing master of Madame de Pompadour who paid him a salary of 7,500 livres. Another sumptuous edition, of which the costs were defrayed by the Fermiers-Généraux, was the *Decameron* of 1757, in five volumes, with 110 plates and ninety-seven *culs-de-lampe* after Gravelot, Boucher, Cochin and Eisen. Possibly the finest French illustrated book of the century was B. de Laborde, *Choix de Chansons*, published by de Lormel in four volumes in 1773. The engraved title, the frontispiece to each volume, and most of the plates in the first volume are after J. M. Moreau le Jeune, a large number being actually engraved by him.* Even the text is engraved on copperplate. Moreau was one of the finest of the remarkable school of designers who brought such lustre to the French illustrated book of the eighteenth century. Vying with his illustrations for the Laborde was the *Monumens du costume* printed by Prault for Ebertz in 1777.

Charles-Nicolas Cochin was himself the son of an engraver, and worked for some fifteen years in England before returning to France to become a most accomplished illustrator and eventually designer to the Menus Plaisirs. The work which first made his name was the commemorative volume published for the coronation of Louis XV. He was a prolific engraver whose production included such things as fashion plates, ex-libris, and ornaments of various kinds.

Clément Pierre Marillier was an engraver whose vignettes rivalled in charm those of Eisen. Called 'le dessinateur de l'infiniment petit' he excelled in giving

---

* De Laborde quarrelled with Moreau, and the other three volumes were illustrated by Le Barbier, Saint-Quentin and Le Bouteux.

movement to his subjects even in the most confined space. His best work is generally considered to be his illustrations for the *Oeuvres Badines* of the Comte de Caylus, published by Visse, 1787, in twelve octavo volumes.

At the outbreak of the French Revolution the Paris publisher Defer de Maisonneuve began to issue a series of very fine books with colour plates by Nicolas André Monsiau and Jean Frédéric Schall, reproduced by stipple engraving. One of these was an edition of Milton, *Paradise Lost*, with text in English and French (two quarto vols., 1792). This has eleven plates, engraved and printed in colour by Clément Colibert, Demonchy and Gautier after the paintings by Schall.

TYPOGRAPHY

In 1702 there came from the Imprimerie Royale a magnificent folio, *Médailles sur les principaux événements du règne de Louis le Grand*, in which appeared for the first time the 'romain du roi' of Philippe Grandjean, officially 'premier graveur du roi pour son Imprimerie du Louvre'. As far back as 1675 Colbert had invited the assistance of the Académie des Sciences in the preparation of an eventual *Description des Métiers*. A team of specialists, consisting of Jacques Nicolas Jaugeon, Gilles Filleau des Billettes and Sébastien Truchet set to work in 1693, having decided to begin the series with 'l'art qui conservera tous les autres', namely printing.

These three men, together with the Abbé Bignon, set about designing new types and to this end not only did they examine all the most perfect incunables of Mainz, Venice, Paris, etc., and the best work of the Estiennes, the Wechsels, and the Elseviers, but also studied all the authors who had written on the subject of letter designing, such as Dürer and Tory. The subject was examined geometrically as well as historically and eventually a number of designs were engraved on copper by Louis Simonneau and later by Rochefort. The first of these plates is dated 1695, the last 1718. The plates, as completed, were handed over to the punch-cutter to follow.

Louis-Laurent Anisson, upon his appointment in 1723 as director of the Imprimerie Royale, brought the foundry – until then some distance away – under the same roof as the printing house. This done, the king ordered an inventory to be made of the royal punches and matrices which were still in the possession of the widow of Grandjean. This was carried out by the chief engraver, Alexandre, and M. de Foncemagne, of the Académie des Inscriptions, after which all the foundry material belonging officially to the king, was transported into that part of the Louvre which had been assigned to the Imprimerie Royale.

The fact that the royal punches and matrices were now placed under the sole charge of Anisson rather annoyed Alexandre, since his predecessors had been directly responsible for them, but nevertheless he remained royal engraver, an office which, as Bernard has shown, brought him in considerable emoluments.

Grandjean died in 1714, and his work was continued by N. Alexandre his friend and pupil, and by Louis Luce, Alexandre's son-in-law. When finally completed in 1745, the 'romains du roi' had been cut in twenty-one sizes of roman and italic, together with twenty bodies of roman and italic initials, making eighty-two complete founts in all. Although these types were exclusive to the Imprimerie Royale, they were closely imitated by other French typographers, as we can see from Pierre Cot's *Essais de Caractères d'Imprimerie*, a specimen of Oriental and Greek types, published five years after the *Médailles*. 'The descriptions of the types shown,' writes A. F. Johnson, 'are set in a roman which has all the characteristic features of the "romain du roi".' When, in 1783, Pierre François Didot le Jeune was accused of imitating these types he pointed out that several typefounders, among them Sanlecque and Gando, had for years shown designs very like the 'romains du roi'.

In addition to his work as royal engraver and punch-cutter, Louis Luce cut a number of types on his own account. Many of them are shown in his *Essai d'une Nouvelle Typographie*, which Barbou printed handsomely in 1771, and are accompanied by a splendid collection of ornaments and borders designed especially to marry with the types. 'No modern type-foundry', writes Updike, 'has produced a more magnificent suite of appropriate and *printable* ornaments.' (Updike, 1922.)

For the Imprimerie Royale Luce had cut a very small size of type shown in his eight-leaved specimen *Epreuve du premier Alphabeth droit et penché ornée de quadres et de cartouches* which he issued in 1740. He described it in his own words as 'le plus petit & le plus délicat qui se soit vû jusqua'à présent, étant d'un tiers de corps & d'oeil au dessous de la Sédanoise' – a fount which had first been used in a 32mo edition of *Phaedri Fabulae* in 1729. Luce died in 1773 and was succeeded by Fagnon, who was the last to bear the title 'graveur royal'.

One of the outstanding names in French typography during the eighteenth century is that of Fournier. Jean Claude Fournier, who had managed the Le Bé foundry for many years, had three sons who survived childhood: Jean Pierre, known as Fournier l'aîné; François, who became a printer at Auxerre, and Pierre Simon, commonly called Fournier le jeune. The eldest son acquired in 1730 the Le Bé foundry which his father had managed for so many years, and thus became the proprietor of a foundry renowned for its collection of types cut by the master punch-cutters of the preceding centuries. Fournier l'aîné, himself both a cutter and founder of types died in 1783, leaving the foundry in the hands of his three daughters.

Pierre Simon Fournier le jeune was born at Paris in 1712, and as a young man studied drawing under the miniaturist J. B. G. Colson. His first job was to cut blocks for his elder brother while he himself began to learn two crafts which particularly attracted him: the cutting of punches and the casting of letters. He became a prolific designer of type, who in the course of just over thirty years, until his death in 1768, cut some 60,000 punches for 147 complete alphabets of his own design, ranging from 5 to 84 point.

When he was only twenty-five he published, in 1737, his *Tables des proportions des différens caractères de l'imprimerie*, which was an attempt to standardize type sizes by a point system. He postulated a series of bodies approximating to those already in common use, but all multiples of a unit which he termed a 'point typographique', based on a scale of 144 points. In size this point equalled 0.955 of the later Didot system (see p. 398). His theories were amplified in a 1742 edition and given their final form in his most famous work, the *Manuel Typographique*.

Three years after his registration as punch-cutter and type-founder with the *Chambre Syndicale* in Paris (on 30 January 1739), he published two specimen books, of which the first, *Modéles de Caractères de l'imprimerie et des autres choses necessaires audit art*, shows a complete range of sizes of the new founts he had cut so rapidly. His industry enabled him to offer 'not one St. Augustin or Cicero roman, but a whole family, on the same body, all cut by himself'. This first

FIGURE 71. A specimen issued in 1773 by the Delacolonge foundry of Lyons, mentioned by Fournier as an ancient and respectable establishment.

edition of the *Modèles de Caractères* (1742) is one of Fournier's finest books; in fact, as a book, finer than the *Manual*. In the foreword Fournier draws attention to the difference between his own italic and those of previous designers, and, says A. F. Johnson, 'with the addition of the roman serifs, the absence of tied letters and the regularity of the inclination, Fournier carried the idea of conformity with roman further than any earlier designer'. Fournier's italics became very popular for a time, but did not survive their cutter's death for long, being superseded by the types of the Didot foundries.

Fournier's *Manuel Typographique, utile aux Gens de Lettres* . . . was published in two volumes, 1764 and 1766. The first volume bears the imprint 'Imprimé par l'Auteur, rue des Postes, & se vend chez Barbou, rue S. Jacques'; the second simply 'Chez l'Auteur, rue des Postes. J. Barbou, rue des Mathurins'. The fact is that although Fournier had applied for permission to print the book himself, he was not registered as a printer and the Syndics opposed his registration as a 'supernumerary printer'. The work was therefore printed by Barbou. It was a disappointment to Fournier who wrote' 'The said work has been held over for five years on account of the hope I always had of printing it myself.' The second volume was held up by its author's illness and did not appear until two years after the date on the title-page.

The first volume deals with the art of type-founding and contains sixteen engraved plates showing instruments used by the type-founder; the second shows a vast range of type specimens, each page being enclosed within a border. The work was never completed, for Fournier had intended to publish two further volumes, the third dealing with the history of printing, and the fourth with celebrated typefounders.

In 1756 Fournier issued a specimen of his music types entitled *Essai d'un nouveau caractère de fonte pour l'impression de la musique*, though unfortunately no copy of this specimen is now known. Fournier had been quick in adapting the new method of printing music invented by Breitkopf in 1755 (see p. 322) using a special mould of his own design. A few years later he improved his own system and brought out a complete fount of music type containing 147 different characters cast on five sizes of body and combinable so that notes and stave could be printed at one impression.

Naturally Fournier wanted to sell this improved music type to his customers, but he came up against strenuous opposition from Christophe-Jean François Ballard. Since the time of Henri II music printing in France had been the hereditary monopoly of the Ballard family, and their music types had hardly been improved during the two hundred years of the firm's existence. Fournier attacked this monopoly, and not unexpectedly met with considerable opposition from Ballard, who even sent bailiffs to try and seize Fournier's new characters. The latter replied with a *Traité historique et critique sur l'origine et le progrès des caractères de fonte pour l'impression de la musique* (1765) and his energetic opposition to Ballard led to a Royal Warrant enabling any type-founder to cast music type, though not every printer might use them.

In the same year, 1765, Barbou published, in three volumes, Monnet's collection of songs entitled *Anthologie Française*, in which Fournier's music type in conjunction with Gravelot's frontispiece and Caron's decorations combine to make a most charming work.

Although Fournier's work, both as punch-cutter and type-founder was technically brilliant he cannot be considered an innovator in the field of type design, in which his ideas were mainly adaptations of the work of others though clearly influenced by the new styles coming from the Imprimerie Royale. Nevertheless he was no servile copier but often carried out sensible modifications, such as aligning capitals with the tops of lower-case ascenders as well as squaring the angles of capitals and some of the lower case letters. But like Luce, Fournier was more advanced in his treatment of italic than in the roman, though his ordinary 12 pt roman is rather more condensed than had been the habit. He also engraved two founts of script type based on the hand of the writing master Rossignol.

One striking aspect of Fournier's specimens is the charm and variety of his ornaments – flowers, head-pieces, cul-de-lampes – and it is to him that we owe 'most of the finest cast ornament which throws such a distinctive glamour over the more pretentious eighteenth-century printing'. At the time of his death, in 1768 his establishment was the foremost of all the privately owned foundries in Europe.

THE ENCYCLOPÉDIE

The year 1751 saw the publication of that landmark in the history of European thought, the *Encyclopédie, ou Dictionnaire raisonné des Sciences, des Arts, et des Métiers*. The project was conceived, though on a vastly smaller scale, by the printer and bookseller Le Breton, who envisaged at first a mere translation of the English *Cyclopedia* published by Ephraim Chambers in 1727. However, realising that this work was already out of date in some respects, he considered it would be better to undertake a new work, to be produced and edited by Denis Diderot in association with d'Alembert, with contributions by some of the most brilliant scholars of the age.

Owing to the expense of the undertaking, Le Breton found three other booksellers, Briasson, David, and Durand, to share in the venture and in 1746 he obtained a privilege from the king to print and publish the *Encyclopédie*. In 1751 the first two volumes were published, but some of the theological articles by the abbé de Prades having been severely criticised by the archbishop of Paris, on 7 February 1752, the Conseil d'Etat suppressed both volumes. Thanks to the intervention of the comte d'Argenson the interdiction was lifted, but three censors were appointed to examine forthcoming articles in manuscript. This seems to have been arranged with a view to appeasing the Jesuits and other religious bodies.

Despite many difficulties, including the promulgation in 1759 of a Brief by Pope Clement XIII condemning the *Encyclopédie*, publication continued and the first edition was completed by 1780. It consisted of 35 volumes, subdivided as follows:

(1) 17 vols. of text and 11 vols. of plates were published, under Diderot's editorship, between 1751 and 1772.* (2) 4 vols. of text, one supplementary volume of plates, and 2 vols. of Index, were published between 1776 and 1780 by Charles-Joseph Panckoucke and his partners Stoupe and Brunet. A second edition, including the republication of the previously suppressed Vols. 1 and 2, was issued at Lucca by O. Diodati between 1758 and 1771, whilst the third edition made its appearance at Leghorn between 1770 and 1779.

After volumes 3 to 7 had been published there was a further crisis due to political events and polemics which arose over certain articles written by D'Alembert, who judged it prudent to withdraw from the enterprise. However, the government feared that the *Encyclopédie* might, after all, be printed abroad, and the subscribers, both numerous and influential were complaining at the non-appearance of the remaining volumes. So the authorities employed a face-saving strategy. It was understood that the volumes would continue to be printed in Paris, but the imprint would bear the address Neufchâtel, as if they had been printed in Switzerland, and they would then be despatched to the provinces, whence they would return to Paris. Thanks to this fiction, which deceived no one, the *Encyclopédie* managed to get printed in its entirety.

The many articles on arts and crafts contained in the *Encyclopédie* is evidence of a growing demand for vocational knowledge at the beginning of the Industrial Revolution. In Spain the president of the Council of Castile, Pedro de Campomanes, was so impressed that, interested as he was in the economic revival of his country he recommended that all the articles on arts and crafts in the *Encyclopédie* should be translated and circulated throughout Spain.

THE ANISSON FAMILY

For more than a century, from 1691 until 1794, the Imprimerie du Louvre was directed by members of the Anisson family. Before becoming head of the Imprimerie Royale, Jean Anisson (1642–1740) and his brother Jacques (d. 1714) were in charge of the largest and most influential publishing house in Lyons, with extensive business connections in Spain and Italy.

* Vols. 1–7 bear the imprint 'Paris: Briasson, David l'aîné, Le Breton, Durand'. Vols. 8–17 bear the imprint 'Neufchastel: S. Faulche et Cie'.

Jean Anisson was appointed director of the Imprimerie Royale on 15 January 1691, in place of the widow of Sébastien Marbre Cramoisy, despite protests from the Paris booksellers. He had Grandjean cut new types (see p. 315) and finally relinquished his .post in 1707 on his nomination as delegate to the Conseil du Commerce. He died in 1721.

He was replaced as director of the Imprimerie Royale on 16 February 1707, by his nephew Claude Rigaud, who held that office until 1725, when he was succeeded by Louis-Laurent Anisson, the son of Jacques, who retired from the post in 1733. He in turn was succeeded by his brother Jacques Anisson-Duperron, who had obtained the survivorship. He held the post nominally until his death in 1788. His son Etienne-Alexandre-Jacques Anisson-Duperron (1749–93) was associated with the Imprimerie Royale from an early age, and in 1765, when only 16, was appointed director in survivorship of his father. He invented a new kind of press (see p. 359) and continued to manage the Imprimerie du Louvre during the early years of the Revolution, but was arrested and guillotined in 1793.

(see p. 315)
(see p. 359)

GERMANY

Johann Gottlob Immanuel Breitkopf was the son of a printer, Bernhard Christoph Breitkopf. Born at Leipzig 23 November 1719, he was expected to carry on his father's business as a printer, though he had no inclination towards a business career and was more interested in literary pursuits. Nevertheless he entered on his apprenticeship to the craft in 1736. A study of the history of printing stimulated his interest and in 1745 he took over the management of the firm to whose reputation he was to devote himself exclusively.

His name is probably best known today for his inventions in the field of music printing. Himself a lover of music, he was keenly aware of the shortcomings of the methods then used for printing music. At the time he began his experiments it was still difficult to print chords or florid music otherwise than by engraving, which was an expensive method. After several years of research he devised a new method of printing music with movable and interchangeable characters. His solution was to divide the customary single type-unit into separate pieces for note-head and stem, whilst the stave was cast in segments of differing lengths. At the end of the stem could be fitted another portion with one, two, or three hooks for notes of different time-values. The types were thus made infinitely variable.

His first work printed by the new process, and issued in 1754, was an *Aria* which he presented to the Electress of Bavaria, who was so impressed that she encouraged him by allowing him to print her pastoral drama *Il Trionfo della Fedeltá* which was published in 1756.

It so happened that Pierre-Simon Fournier le Jeune was working in Paris on somewhat similar lines, and in 1756 he issued his specimen book called *Essai d'un nouveau Caractère de fonte pour l'Impression de la Musique*. His method, however, differed in practice from that of Breitkopf in that whereas all the characters in the latter's music were of one body size and could be made up into composite pieces as needed, the various parts of Fournier's music-type were 'adapted for casting on one of five bodies, varying in size in regular progression'. But Fournier was unable to overcome the monopoly for the printing of music held by the family of Ballard which dated from 1552. As a result Fournier did not print much music with his type, whereas Breitkopf's musical business prospered.

Immanuel Breitkopf also invented a new system for printing maps with movable type and in 1777 published his *Über den Druck der geographischen Charten*. A tireless worker, he managed not only the printing office, but also his typefoundry and bookshop, which between them employed some 130 workmen. He also set up branch bookshops in Dresden and Bautzen. His continued interest in everything connected with books led him to write *Über Bibliographie und Bibliophilie*, which he published in 1793, and a *Geschichte der Schreibkunst* which came out after his death in 1794.

Breitkopf was a man of strong character, reliable and honest in his dealings, and at his death he left his firm in full growth. From his foundry had come some 400 different alphabets, which were exported to many countries. In the printing office were twenty presses for book-work and four presses for music printing. After Breitkopf's death the business suffered a decline, for neither of his sons was capable of managing the inheritance. But the firm recovered when Gottlob Breitkopf, who had become the sole owner, took his friend Gottfried Christoph Härtel as partner at the end of 1795. In 1796 the name of the firm became, as it has ever since remained, *Breitkopf & Härtel*. Shortly before his death in 1800, Gottlob Breitkopf made Härtel his sole successor, and the firm has remained until the present day one of the most famous in the field of music publishing.

Georg Joachim Göschen (1752–1828) was born at Bremen and became apprenticed to the book trade in that city at the age of thirteen. Later he worked as assistant to the bookseller Crusius in Leipzig and about 1782 went to Dessau, where, a year previously, there had been founded a 'Buchhandlung der Gelehrten' which offered to print scholars' works at their own expense. In 1785 Göschen opened his own publishing house in Leipzig, and became the publisher of works by Schiller, Goethe, and Wieland. Between the years 1787 and 1791 he printed the first collected edition of Goethe's works.

In order to bring out a sumptuous edition of the works of Wieland he set up his own printing office, since the existing establishments could not meet his demands. While his publishing business remained in Leipzig, in July 1797 he moved the printing office to Grimma, where he died on 5 April 1828.

At about this time roman type (which the Germans call Antiqua) was temporarily gaining favour in that country. The reputation of the new Didot characters had induced Göschen to set his editions of the works of Wieland and of Klopstock in a Didot-style roman. It is interesting to note that Schiller, when he sent the text of his *Jungfrau von Orleans* to Johann Unger to be published, wrote to the publisher that he would be greatly obliged to him if he would print it in 'lateinische Schrift'. But the generally held opinion was that roman was admissible chiefly for works of a scientific character, the influence of which might extend beyond the borders of Germany, but that Fraktur was to be considered an essentially national form of letter. The result was that from then onwards most German scientific books and periodicals were printed in roman, which the non-German finds easier to read than Fraktur. One attempt was made in the nineteenth century to make the best of both worlds when the Berlin firm of C. G. Shoppe produced a hybrid character which they called *Centralschrift* in 1853 – a particularly revolting type which sought to combine a roman upper half with a Fraktur lower half. Dr Steinberg rightly calls it 'the most remarkable specimen of typographical folly ever thought of'. (Steinberg, 1955.)

An outstanding name in German printing at the end of the eighteenth century is that of Johann Friedrich Unger. The son of a printer and woodcutter, Johann Georg Unger, he was born in Berlin on 16 August 1753, and as a youth was apprenticed to the Berlin printer Rudolf Decker. In 1780 he received governmental permission to start his own printing office, which so quickly acquired a reputation that in 1788 Unger was appointed printer to the Prussian Academy of Arts and Crafts. In 1791 he added a typefoundry to his business.

Unger took a lively interest in typography, and entered into a friendly relationship with Firmin Didot, whose light roman letter he did much to popularise in Germany. But in view of the opposition to roman type from some quarters he decided to bring out a Fraktur designed to be more easily read by those unused to the gothic character of the Fraktur then commonly employed. At the beginning of 1793 he issued a specimen entitled *Probe einer neuen Art deutscher Lettern. Erfunden und in Stahl geschnitten von J. F. Unger.* Unger Fraktur has been resurrected from time to time, but although more easily read by the non-native than the normal Fraktur in German books of the eighteenth century, it is not a particularly pleasing type, for as is so often the case when an attempt is made to obtain the best of both possible worlds the result is unsatisfactory.

By the end of the century the firm of Unger had acquired a high reputation. It printed not only the works of Goethe and Schiller, but also books by the most promising of the early writers of the Romantic school. Nor should we forget that Unger published the first eight volumes of Schlegel's translation of Shakespeare. He died in 1804, before it could be completed, and the ninth volume was signed by his widow, the remainder coming from the press of Georg Reimer.

Towards the end of the century Johann Unger acquired a considerable part of the material of the old Luther foundry at Frankfurt-am-Main. His punch-cutter, responsible for engraving the final version of his new Fraktur, was Johann Christoph Gubitz.

That intellectual resurgence which took place in Germany in the last thirty years of the eighteenth century and was known as 'Sturm und Drang', from a drama of that name by Friedrich Maximilian von Klinger, received a certain impetus from abroad, notably from the works of Jean-Jacques Rousseau. It was the voice of youth freeing itself from the shackles of outworn traditions, and one of the heralds of the new intellectual freedom was Goethe with his *Götz von Berlichingen* (1773), which inspired directly or indirectly many of the plays of the 'Sturm und Drang' period, including Klinger's own play of that name, which appeared in 1777, though with the date 1776, and no mention of printer or place of printing. In fact it was printed in Berlin by Georg Jacob Decker.

The publication of *Götz* was undertaken by Goethe's friend Johann Friedrich Merk. Goethe procured the paper and Merck paid for the printing, which was done by Johann Wittich of Darmstadt. It was no easier then than now for an unknown author to find a publisher and the first edition of Schiller's *Die Räuber* was published at his own expense without any indication of author or publisher. Eight hundred copies were put on sale by the Stuttgart bookseller Benedikt Metzler in 1781. But so popular did Schiller's works become that in 1798 Metzler brought out a collected edition of the poet's works, which he prefaced by remarking that soon the name of Schiller would be uttered with as much patriotic pride and reverence as were those of Klopstock, Goethe and Wieland.

Through the intermediary of a mutual acquaintance the Leipzig publisher Georg Joachim Göschen sought to enter into business relations with Goethe and proposed to the latter that he should plan an edition of his collected works to be printed and published by the firm of Göschen. The contract drawn up on 2 September 1786, specified an eight-volume edition, for which the publisher was to give the author an honorarium of 2,000 gold Thalers.

Daniel Nikolaus Chodowiecki (1726–1801) was one of the most important and influential book illustrators of the eighteenth century. His outstanding ability to identify himself with the textual matter made him an author's artist *par excellence*, and he consistently remained true to the spirit of the book. He illustrated several of Goethe's works, including *Hermann und Dorothea*, first published in Berlin by Hans Friedrich Vieweg (where it appeared in the *Taschenbuch für Frauenzimmer von Bildung*), and especially the French edition of *Werther* published at Maastricht in 1776. He also illustrated a number of Almanachs, such as the *Berliner Genealogischer Kalender* (1770), the *Gothaischer Hofkalender*, and the *Göttinger Taschenkalender*.

For a special feature of German book production during the eighteenth century were the *Almanachs*. These Almanachs surveyed almost every sphere of activity. There were Almanachs for Doctors, merchants, soldiers, Freemasons, gourmets, wine-lovers, and for almost every profession and coterie one can think of; even a *Revolutionskalender* with gruesome copper plates. They were sometimes quite miniature affairs, and hardly ever larger than pocket size, frequently bound in coloured leather, and almost always enlivened with engravings by artists of the calibre of Chodowiecki, Karcher, Penzel, Bolt and so on. Among the almanachs, later to acquire world-wide fame, was the *Gothaischer Hofkalender* or *Almanach de Gotha*, which made its first appearance in 1763. The early numbers are now exceedingly rare and the earliest issue to be found in the British Museum is that for 1774. From 1780 until 1794 Chodowiecki was a regular contributor to the *Almanach de Gotha*, he illustrated Lessing's *Fables*, the *Gil Blas* of LeSage, Beaumarchais' *The Marriage of Figaro*, and also contributed some pages of anecdotes relating to Frederick the Great, which may be looked upon as an introduction to Menzel's illustrations for the *History of Frederick the Great* by Kugler.

An eminent figure in German publishing towards the end of the century was Johann Friedrich Cotta (1764–1832), later Freiherr von Cottendorf, who took over the declining business of his father at Tübingen and made it into one of the leading publishing houses in the country. He became friendly with Goethe, who stayed with him at Tübingen on his way to Switzerland. He became Goethe's publisher for the last thirty years of the poet's life and was the first to bring out a collected edition of Goethe in twenty volumes between 1815 and 1819, which was followed, 1827–42, by the complete edition in sixty volumes. Cotta also founded the well-known periodical the *Allgemeine Zeitung*.

In 1765 the naturalist Jacob Christian Schäffer (1718–90) published at Regensburg the first part of his *Versuche und Muster, ohne alle Lumpen Papier zu machen*, completed in six parts in 1762. The work is concerned with Schäffer's experiments in quest of new material for paper-making, and shows specimens of paper made from a wide range of natural substances, including varieties of wood, vines, hemp, moss, bark, straw, potatoes, reeds, and even wasps' nests! In 1768 the Royal Society of Arts awarded him a silver medal for his work.

Towards the middle of the century the very long and over-crowded title-pages which had for so long been characteristic of German publications tended to disappear, and in the last decades of the century rococo decoration, which had crept into German books following the vogue in France, was on the way out, to be replaced by unadorned typography. Like Unger, Göschen, whose type came mostly from the Prillwitz foundry at Jena, made the light roman of Didot popular in Germany.

ITALY

In the eighteenth century Italy, like Spain, lacked abundance of literature of the highest quality. In Venice especially, and in other parts of Italy publishers attempted to overcome this lack of first class material by falling back on the work of an earlier generation and cultivating anew the inheritance of previous centuries.

In 1724 Almoro Albrizzi, belonging to a distinguished Venetian family, founded the society called after him the Società Albrizziana to which in particular representatives of the learned professions and high dignitaries of the church belonged. On entering this society each of its members had to promise to buy books, specially printed for them, to the value of forty ducats. One of the finest of these publications was the edition of Tasso, *Gerusalemme Liberata*, which appeared in 1745, with illustrations and ornaments by J. B. Piazzetta, and printed by Giambattista Albrizzi, probably the brother of Almoro. This magnificent folio is preceded by a full page engraving by Felix Polanzani after Piazzetta of Maria Theresa of Austria. Type, paper and press-work are all of the highest quality, and at the end of the book the price is stated: 'Il suo prezzo è di Zecchini otto.' In somewhat similar style Zatta brought out a *Dante* in 1757.

Antonio Zatta was certainly one of the most important printers in Venice during the latter part of the century, and an enormous and varied production came from his presses. Among his outstanding publications were, in addition to the *Dante*, *Il Parnaso Italiano* in fifty-six volumes (1784–91); the *Commedie* of Goldoni in forty-seven volumes (1788–95) illustrated with some 400 vignettes; Ariosto (with nearly 2,000), and the *Orlando Furioso* with illustrations by P. A. Novelli. In 1797 Zatta was appointed 'stampatore municipale'.

A firm of European renown was that of Remondini at Bassano, founded by Giovanni Antonio Remondini, who started in business by purchasing the material of Francesco Vittorelli; but the most famous member of the family was Giovanni Battista Remondini (1713–73) under whose direction it prospered and attained its maximum importance, employing at one time more than 1,000 workers, including fifteen engravers and about 100 painters, for the firm specialised in popular coloured picture books of the kind later known in France as 'images d'Epinal'. He is said to have had eighteen printing presses and twenty-four engraving presses. Nevertheless the Remondini's fortune seems to have been based on the *Dictionariolum*, or Latin thesaurus, which was used in all the schools and regularly reprinted every few years for half a century. Most of the Venetian vignettists, whose work had an enormous vogue during a large part of the century, came from the flourishing workshop of the Remondini at Bassano, among them Luigi and Nicoló Schiavonetti, Antonio Verico, the Giampiccoli, Teodoro Viero and Giovanni Folo.

Among the Roman printers of the eighteenth century one of the most famous was Giovanni Francesco Cracas. From his press came on 5 August 1716, the first number of the *Diario di Roma*, which was for a time the official organ of the Court. The first issue bore the title *Diario ordinario d'Ungheria* since it appeared during the war with Hungary. This press also published the *Notizie annuali*, and these two publications were commonly called 'Cracas' (just as one alludes to the French railway timetable as the 'Chaix').

Florence numbered among her printers at this time Bernardo Paperini, Giuseppe Manni, Francesco Moucke and the Stamperia Gran' Ducale, which had its origins in the seventeenth century, when in 1643 the Grand Duke Ferdinand II granted a privilege to the partners Signoretii and Nesti.

Bologna boasted Lelio della Volpe, active from 1723, who printed, among other things, a celebrated edition of the romance of *Bertoldo* (1736) put into verse by twenty-six poets and illustrated with engravings by Mattioli. The printer's son Petronio carried on the business until 1782.

The eighteenth century saw some resurgence of printing in Milan. In 1721 the Società Palatina was founded for printing the *Scriptores Rerum Italicarum* of Muratori, which was issued in twenty-seven volumes, 1723–37. A posthumous twenty-eighth volume appeared in 1751. The society was founded from patriotic motives by certain Milanese notables, who did not want the work to be printed in Holland, at Leyden, as was at one time suggested. The printing was entrusted to the Court Printer, Giuseppi Richini. This press also issued other erudite works, such as the *Collezione degli Scrittori Milanesi*, but these were not issued at the expense of the Society, the name of which is found only on the Muratori *Scriptores*, and another work by the same author, *Antiquitates Italicae Medii Aevi*.

One of the most famous eighteenth-century presses in Italy was that established at Padua in 1717 by Giovanni Antonio Volpi and his brother the Abbé Gaetano, and which was situated in their own house. The technical director of the press was the printer Giuseppe Comino, and the first book off the press was Joannis Poleni, *De motu aquae mixto*, 1717. Most of the publications of the Tipografia Volpi-Cominiani bear the inscription 'Excudebat Josephus Cominus Volpiorum aere'. The press was a private press, which did not work for profit, and after the death of the brothers Volpi the business passed to Angelo Comino, the son of Giuseppe.

At Turin we may take note of the printing house of Antonio Francesco Mairesse which he and his heirs ran from 1714 until 1780. It was for this firm that the young Bodoni worked for a time. The year 1731 saw the founding at Turin of the Stamperia Reale, founded by a society of patricians, the leading light among whom was Count Ignacio Favetti de Bosse. Between 1799 and 1814 the Stamperia Reale declined in importance on account of the French domination, but sprang to life again in 1816 under Victor-Emmanuel I. It lasted until

1873 (after the capital of the kingdom had been moved from Turin to Florence and finally to Rome) when the press was taken over by an educational publisher named Paravia – a firm which is still in existence.

Until the advent of Bodoni, book production in Italy during the eighteenth century followed a traditional contemporary pattern, in so far as the production of de luxe editions rich in copper engravings followed the same fashion as elsewhere. Mindful of its illustrious past, Venice exhibited some excellent specimens of her artistic talents in the many engraved book illustrations carried out by the Zucchi, an important family of engravers, and by the brothers Schiavonetti. In addition there were to be found in Venice many skilful engravers from other parts of Italy and from abroad, including the German Joseph Wagner, who had his own publishing house. Many artists were also employed in the printing office of the Remondini at Bassano, a town not far from Venice and situated in Venetian territory.

According to Fumagalli both printers and publishers of Venice did good business during the eighteenth century. The Baglioni, printers and booksellers, amassed a fortune which enabled them, in return for a gift of 100,000 ducats to the Republic, to be admitted to the patrician nobility of Venice in 1716. Their printing office, founded in 1637, existed until 1850.

Architectural books were much in evidence around the middle of the century. In 1761 Zatta brought out a magnificent large folio devoted to Saint Mark's at Venice, and between 1776 and 1785 Francesco Modena published at Vicenza a fine edition in four volumes of the works of Andrea Palladio. In Rome the four volumes of G-B. Piranesi, *Antichità Romane* came from the firm of Angelo Rotili.

On 16 February 1740, was born at Saluzzo, in Piedmont, the greatest Italian typographer of the eighteenth century, Giambattista Bodoni. He learned to be a printer in his father's printing house, and when he was eighteen went to Rome, where he found employment at the press of the Propaganda Fide. Pope Sixtus V had had Oriental types cast for this press and these had for long remained unused. The director of the press, Ruggieri, gave Bodoni the task of renovating the types, and it was this that started his interest in exotic types which later bore fruit in his *Oratio Dominica*. It was while at Rome that Bodoni began his career as type designer and punch-cutter and by 1766 he had already acquired a fair measure of skill in this exacting profession.

After Ruggieri had committed suicide on 11 November 1782, Bodoni tired of Rome and on the advice of his friends left that city with the idea of seeking employment in England. He got no further than Turin when he fell ill with a fever. After convalescing in his home town of Saluzzo he returned to Turin and there he received an offer which was the turning point of his career. Du Tillot, chief minister to the young Duke of Parma, had the notion to form an official ducal press, and it was Paciaudi, librarian at the Court of Parma, who

RELAZIONE.

*Negozianti di Parma af-
frettaronsi anch' essi a se-
gnalare il loro giubilo, e
la viva loro gratitudine.
Memori, e penetrati da
quanto l' augusto Padre del R. Infante
aveva operato a favor loro, andavano rac-
cogliendo di giorno in giorno nuovi frutti
della bontà, e saggia provvidenza del
Principe. Protezione, eccitamento, molti-
plicati soccorsi, e quanti vantaggi possono
procacciare al commercio un Governo illu-
minato, e benefiche Leggi, godeanli tutti a
quel grado che la natura medesima dello
Stato ad essi prescrivea. Avevano già ve-
duto scaturire, e vedevano ora sempre più
diffondersi le sorgenti della loro prosperità.*

    *Chiesero, ed ottenero la permissione di
render solenni i sentimenti della divota, e*

RELATION.

*es négocians de Parme
s'empresserent de même
à signaler leur joie &
leur vive reconnoissan-
ce. Pénétrés de ce que
l'auguste pere de l'Infant avoit fait en
leur faveur, ils recueilloient chaque jour
de nouveaux fruits de la bonté & de la
sagesse du Prince. Protection, encouragement, secours multipliés, tous les
avantages qu'un gouvernement éclairé,
des lois bienfaisantes, peuvent procurer
au commerce, ils les éprouvoient autant
que le permettoit la nature même de l'é-
tat. Ils avoient vu naître, ils voyoient
s'étendre de plus en plus les sources de
leur prospérité.*

    *Ils demanderent & obtinrent la per-
mission de faire éclater leurs sentimens*

FIGURE 72. Page from one of Bodoni's earliest editions: *Descrizione delle Feste . . . per le auguste nozze di S.A.R. l'Infante Don Ferdinando colla R.Arcid. Maria Amalia.* Parma: La Reale Stamperia, 1769. The vignettes were by Ennemondo Petitot.

recommended Bodoni to him. In March 1768, Giambattista Bodoni became director of the new royal printing office at Parma.

    One of the first things Bodoni did in his new post was to import from Paris some of the best of Fournier's types, making use of them in his first work, the *I Voti* of 1768. But from the start his ambition was to cut his own types. He obtained permission from the Duke of Parma to set up a foundry, and in this he was assisted by one of his brothers. In 1771 appeared his first specimen,

Fregi e Maiuscole incise e fuse da Giambattista Bodoni. In this the influence of Fournier is manifest, even to the style and format of the title-page, which is closely modelled on that of Fournier's *Manuel Typographique* of 1766. The Frenchman's influence continued to make itself felt for a number of years. Bertieri remarks that up to this period Bodoni oscillated between the simple and the ornate, but gradually tended towards the simplicity which was later to be the outstanding trait of his work as punch-cutter.* Until 1790 his types were still definitely 'old-face'. Then came a sudden change.

In that year Bodoni was invited to take charge of a press which De Azara, Spanish minister to the Papal Court, intended to establish. The Duke of Parma, having no wish to lose the services of so excellent a printer, sought to soften his refusal to allow Bodoni to leave Parma by granting him permission to set up a press of his own, which he might work as a side-line to his management of the ducal printing-office. This enabled Bodoni to print for other people.

He now started to print, in addition to the usual Italian, Greek and Latin books, works in French, Russian, German and English. In 1791 he printed in English an edition of Walpole's *Castle of Otranto* for the bookseller J. Edwards of Pall Mall, London; and in 1793 the *Poems* of Thomas Gray. In fact he printed several English books on commission for London booksellers in de luxe editions aimed at the collectors' market.

Bodoni issued a number of specimen books, commencing with the *Fregi e Maiuscole* of 1771. In 1788 he brought out a folio showing roman, italic, Greek, Russian and Cancellereschi types, a splendidly printed work. In 1806 came his famous *Oratio Dominica*, displaying the Lord's Prayer in 155 different type faces all designed by himself. This work is said to have been printed at the instigation of Pope Pius VII when he visited Parma in 1805.

But his monument is undoubtedly formed by the two volumes of his *Manuale Tipografico* completed by his widow Paola Margherita Dall'Aglio in 1818, under the supervision of Luigi Orsi, Bodoni's foreman for many years.

An edition of the *Manuale Tipografico* had been published in 1788, but towards the end of his life Bodoni envisaged a new type specimen book which should surpass all others, and he had assembled nearly all the material for it before he died on 30 November 1813. The introduction to this vast and magnificent collection of types embodies Bodoni's ideas regarding the aesthetics as well as the technical aspects of printing. Updike described the work as 'probably the most elaborate specimen that the world has ever seen – an imposing *tour de force*', and H. V. Marrott says 'it sums up our printer's whole career, and is the confirmation and seal of his reputation.'

---

* R. Bertieri, *L'Arte di Giambattista Bodoni.* Milan, 1913.

SPAIN

Spain, during the eighteenth century was not rich in original literary work, and in the field of printing the beginning of the century showed no marked improvement upon the preceding one. The monopoly for the printing of liturgical books was held by the monastery of the Escorial, and these were still being imported from the Plantin-Moretus Press at Antwerp. Although in 1729 a printer from Valencia named Antonio Bordázar proposed the setting up of a printing office in Spain for the production of service books for the Church, and followed it up in 1732 with a printed document *Plantificación de la Imprenta de el Rezo Sagrado* setting out details and estimates of cost, nothing came of it during his lifetime. Implementation of this project had to wait until almost the end of the century, when such a printing office was established by the Compañía de Impresores y Libreros de Madrid in conjunction with the authorities of the Escorial (see *infra*).

An attempt was made to improve conditions in the printing industry during the reign of Carlos III, and in 1763 a decree was passed exempting from military service printers, typefounders and punch-cutters. Various other privileges were conceded to printers and the price of type metal was reduced in an endeavour to help the industry. Carlos III showed himself to be an enlightened patron of the arts and his royal printer, Perez de Soto, turned out some creditable work around the middle of the century. But the status of Spain in European book production was enhanced towards the end of the century by one great printer, Joaquin Ibarra.

Ibarra was born at Saragossa in 1726, and established himself as a printer in Madrid about 1749. Between that time and his death on 13 November 1785, more than 2,500 books came from his press. He himself was the son of a printer, and the wide range of books which he produced could hardly have been surpassed by any printer of his day.*

It was not by chance that the amelioration in Spanish printing took place during the reign of Carlos III, which lasted from 1759 to 1788. This Bourbon prince, half-brother to Ferdinand VI, strove to stimulate the languishing industries of a country bedevilled by lethargy and obscurantism. He expelled the Jesuits from the kingdom, restricted the power of the Inquisition, and encouraged both arts and crafts. The art of the book in particular claimed his attention and profited by his favourable privileges. It was not long before Ibarra was appointed 'Impresor de Cámara del Rey', in which position he was unflagging in his zeal to acquire the latest printing techniques. The Imprenta Real, under his direction became an exceptionally busy press turning out, in addition to the normal government documents, editions of the classics, liturgical works and a great variety of other books.

* His brother Manuel became director of the Tipografia Universitaria at Cervera.

One of the finest books from Ibarra's press was the folio edition, in Latin and Spanish, of Sallust, *La Conjuracion de Catalina*, published in 1772. The Spanish translation was made by one of the king's sons, Don Gabriel. The large italic was cut by Antonio Espinosa, and figures in his *Muestras de los Caracteres, etc.*, of 1771. Bodoni paid tribute to the work of Ibarra by alluding to the book as 'the stupendous Sallust'. Ibarra was also printer to the Royal Academy for which body he produced in 1780 an edition of *Don Quixote*, which the Chevalier de Bourgoing, secretary to the French embassy at Madrid, declared to be 'equally admirable for the quality of the ink, the beauty of the paper, and the clearness of the letter, and comparable with the finest productions of the kind in any other nation.'

One of the factors contributing to the renaissance of the printing art in Spain was the introduction of a flourishing native typefounding industry, started by Pradell and his pupils, which freed Spain from her dependence on foreign type. There was also a great amelioration in the quality of paper, and for his *Don Quixote* Ibarra used a special paper made in Cataluña by Joseph Llorens, agreeable both in aspect and to the touch.

The names of Ibarra and of Manuel Salvador Carmona usher in a period of typographic renaissance: Joaquín Ibarra, Antonio and Gabriel Sancha, Benito Cano, and the *Imprenta Real* in Madrid; Benito Monfort in Valencia and Madrid; the brothers José and Tomás Orga, in Valencia: these are the outstanding names in Spanish printing during the eighteenth century. Hardly less eminent were Tomás Piferrer and Francisco Suriá y Burgada who worked in Barcelona.

The *Imprenta Real* at Madrid was the result of an agreement made between the State and the heirs of Francisco Manuel de Mena, printer of the *Mercurio histórico y político* and the *Gaceta de Madrid*. Since Mena could not discharge his debts towards the government, the latter, at the printer's death in 1780, took over his equipment in compensation and continued the printing of Mena's various publications on its own account. Shortly before his death Mena had published an excellent edition of Tomás de Iriarte, *La Música.* (1779.)

From the printing office of Benito Cano came a number of well-printed editions of contemporary authors. Between 1794 and 1797 he brought out an edition of the Vulgate in Spanish in no fewer than seventeen volumes with 330 engravings by the most famous artists of the time.

Benito Montfort senior, after working for a time in the printing office of Antonio de Bordázar, set up in business for himself in 1751, and was appointed 'Impresor del Seminario de la Compañia de Jesús'. From 1771 he was printer to the University, and from 1773 printer to the City of Valencia. He died in 1785 and the business was carried on by his son Manuel, a famous engraver, until 1806, and afterwards by the grandson of the founder.

Another important Valencian press was that run by the brothers José and

Tomás Orga. They printed a Spanish translation of the Bible by Father Felipe Scio de San Miguel, issued between 1790 and 1793 in ten volumes, with many fine engravings.

When we consider the great advance that typography made in Spain during the eighteenth century manifested in the work turned out by Ibarra, Montfort, Sancha and others, we should bear in mind that those printers were greatly aided in what they did in the way of fine printing by an amelioration in the material of which they disposed. As an instance of the progress which Spanish printing had made at this time Updike compares Villa-Diego's edition of Solis, *Historia de la Conquista de Mexico*, issued at Madrid in 1684, with Gabriele de Sancha's beautiful quarto edition of the same work, printed at Madrid in 1783. (Updike, 1922.) This had 24 plates by Vergaz and José Xímeno.

During the second half of the eighteenth century, the work of a number of Spanish artists, punch-cutters and type-founders succeeded by their efforts in freeing Spanish printers from their dependence on the supply of matrices from other lands. The first Spaniard to endow Spanish printing with new types was Eudaldo Pradell, a Catalan born in 1723. At first apprenticed to an armourer, he went to Barcelona when he was about twenty years old, and there was encouraged by Pablo Barra, the head of the Imprenta Real to try his hand at cutting type.

The first founts he produced were four in number – Peticano, Lectura, Texto, and Entredos. They were cast by the printer and founder Felio Pons in Barcelona, and were issued between 1758 and 1762. They were well received by the trade and praised by the calligrapher Fray Luis Olod in his *Tratado del Origen y Arte de escribir bien* (Gerona, 1766). Carlos III, a patron of the graphic arts, sent for Pradell and allowed him 100 gold *doblones* a year to enable him to carry on his work, as appears from a notice in the *Gaceta* of 17 September 1764. The king was himself keenly interested in printing and had his own private press in the palace, managed for him by the Madrid printer Antonio Marin.

The work done by Pradell from 1764, when he settled in Madrid, until his death in 1788 was enormous. After his death, his widow and his son issued a specimen book of his types, published at Madrid by Benito Cano in 1793. The foundry which he had set up in Madrid was continued by his son, Eudaldo Pradell II.

In 1787 a specimen book of types cut by order of Carlos III to be used by the Real Biblioteca in Madrid showed a varied assortment of founts most of which were cut by Jerónimo Gil. Another specimen, this time from the foundry of Pedro Ifern, was issued in 1795 by the printer Fermin Thadeo Villalpando. A prefatory note explains that the characters were cast from the matrices of Eudaldo Pradell I, and passed to Pedro Ifern as part of the dowry of his wife, Margarita Pradell.

Then in 1799 appeared the specimen book of the Imprenta Real, Madrid, in which appears some of the material cut by Jerónimo Gil for the Royal Library among a considerable collection of excellent roman and italic types, and a few exotics. Most of the ornaments and flowers are based on various European models translated into typically Spanish designs.

There were, of course, type founders in Spain before Pradell, but they had made use of matrices imported from abroad. We know that Carlos II (1665–1700) procured matrices from Flanders which he gave to the Madrid founder Juan Gomez Morales. In 1683 Diego Dises established a foundry in Madrid, but for lack of support it eventually closed down. The types cut and cast by Dises can be best seen in *Burlas de la fortuna*, a Spanish translation of Giovanni Loredano, *Scherzi geniali*, published at Madrid in 1688.

But to Eudaldo Pradell goes the honour of being the first to cut the punches for a national type. On 27 November 1800, the Junta de Comercio granted to Eudaldo Pradell II and Pedro Isern licence to use the royal arms and the inscription 'Real fábrica de fundición de letras hechas por el primer inventor que ha habido en España, D. Eudaldo Pradell.'*

Another factor which helped to stimulate the book industry was the freeing of prices by a law of 1762 which abolished the rigid tariff imposed by Philip II. But even more important was the concession awarded to the Compañía de Impresores y Libreros of Madrid giving them the right to print liturgical books, a right which for two centuries had been the prerogative of the Plantin Press at Antwerp. Understandably, Spanish printers and publishers had for years been complaining about this monopoly, which deprived them of a very considerable source of income, and finally an agreement was reached between the Company and the monastery of the Escorial. In return for the privilege of printing *libros de rezado* as the service books were termed, the Company promised to use only paper and ink manufactured in Spain, and to employ only Spanish artists for their illustrations. The agreement was published in June 1764 and the printing of liturgical works began in 1765. In 1781 a catalogue was published showing the service books and other books of devotion printed and published by the Company, which consisted of the best of the Madrid printers and publishers.

Important also as an added stimulus to the renaissance of Spanish typography was the foundation in 1744 of the Academia de Bellas Artes de San Fernando in Madrid, which was responsible for the emergence of a number of good book illustrators.

GREAT BRITAIN

English printing at the beginning of the eighteenth century was not appreciably

---

* The name is sometimes spelt Paradell, both forms being found in the punch-cutter's own autograph.

better than it had been during most of the preceding century. There were exceptions to the general poor standard, notably at Oxford, where Doctor Fell not only provided the University Press with good founts of type, but also gave it his backing in the struggle with the Stationers' Company and the King's Printers over the privilege for printing Bibles and Prayer Books.

Although fewer books were printed at Oxford during the eighteenth century than during the second half of the previous century, numerical deficiency was compensated for by the good workmanship of the impressive folios, such as Clarendon's *History of the Rebellion* (1702–4), and the merits of the scholarly series edited by the antiquary Thomas Hearne, among which were Leland's *Itinerary* (1710–12) and the *Chronicles* of William of Newbridge, Alfred of Beverley, William Camden, Peter Langtoft, and others.

Edward Hyde, Earl of Clarendon, gave his name to the Clarendon Building in Broad Street to which the learned press moved in 1713, and which was built largely from the profits accruing from his *History of the Rebellion*, perpetual copyright in which was granted to the University by Clarendon's son, Lord Cornbury.

Among the Bibles which came from the Oxford Press at the beginning of the century was the magnificent folio printed by John Baskett, 1716–17. Though splendidly printed this Bible was marred by so many misprints that it came to be called 'a Baskett-full of errors'. It has also been termed the 'Vinegar' Bible from a misprint for 'vineyard' in Luke XX.

Baskett was a stationer for many years before he became a printer. A shrewd businessman, he eventually secured the patent of King's Printer and its reversion, as well as obtaining a lease of the Oxford privilege and a third share of the Scottish patent. In 1725 he set up a press in Edinburgh and printed some rather mediocre editions of the Bible. He also incurred the enmity of the Edinburgh printer James Watson, who in 1720 accused him of 'making the just privileges of his patent a scandalous cover for a notorious monopoly, thereby encroaching even upon trade itself, by engrossing the sole printing of Bibles, New Testaments, Common Prayer Books, etc., in England, putting what price he pleased upon the subject, raising the price fifty and sixty per cent upon them, by the mere power of his monopolizing press' (Watson, 1713). This was probably only too true, but Watson was not a disinterested party. He had obtained a share in the patent of Queen's Printer for Scotland in 1711 together with another Edinburgh printer, Robert Freebairn, and John Baskett. During the 1715 rebellion Freebairn threw in his lot with the Old Pretender and went to Perth as his official printer. This act cost him his patent, and in 1716 a new patent was granted to John Baskett and the widow of the Glasgow printer, Andrew Anderson. Watson lost his share of the patent, probably because of his family's known connection with the Jacobites.

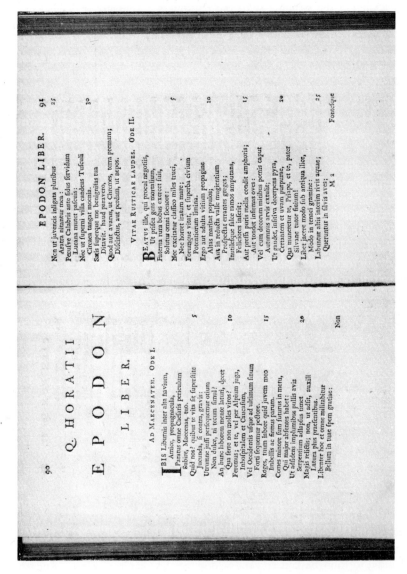

FIGURE 73. The edition of *Horace* published by Robert and Andrew Foulis at Glasgow in 1744 achieved a classical simplicity in its setting and was remarkable for its accuracy.

Two of the greatest names in Scottish printing during the eighteenth century were those of the brothers Robert and Andrew Foulis. Robert Foulis (1707–76) set up as a bookseller and publisher in 1741; his brother Andrew (1712–75) became his partner in 1748. The first books which Robert Foulis published were printed for him, and as at that time the state of printing in Glasgow was extremely poor the result was not satisfactory. So poor was it that the brothers, determined to improve the appearance of their books, 'attended a printing-house in town until they had gained a complete knowledge of the art'.*

Robert Foulis soon learned how to print, and to print well. Moreover, as both brothers were lovers of good literature, he knew what to print. In 1743 Robert produced his first Greek text, Demetrius Phalerus, *De Elocutione*, which he submitted with an application for the post of Printer to Glasgow University, a post to which he was nominated in the same year. In 1744 the type foundry of Wilson and Baine was moved from St Andrews to Camlachie, a village on the outskirts of Glasgow, and it was Wilson who thereafter not only supplied them with type, but cut special founts for them.

Alexander Wilson (1714–84) was at first intended for the medical profession, but through the patronage of Lord Isla (later Duke of Argyle) he was able to devote himself to scientific research, in which he was keenly interested. A chance visit to a letter foundry led to an interest in typography, and in partnership with a friend named Baine he started a foundry of his own in 1742, at St Andrews.

The Foulis partnership produced a steady stream of books, most of which were as good as any being produced at that time either in Britain or on the Continent, while some were outstanding in quality. The high watermark of their achievement is the four-volume folio *Homer* which was issued between 1756 and 1758 and has been termed 'one of the finest monuments of Greek typography which our nation possesses'. The double pica Greek was specially cut for it by Wilson, who was also responsible for many of the firm's roman founts, including a splendid double pica roman used for the quarto edition of Gray's *Poems* published in 1768.

Baine had left the firm in 1749, and from then on Wilson carried on the business himself. The Glasgow Letter-Foundry, as it was called, seems to have published no specimen until 1772, but was for many years a formidable rival of the London firms. In 1834 the Glasgow foundry was removed to London, but the business from that time gradually declined.

The classics produced by the Foulis brothers were noted not only for their appearance but also for their accuracy. The *Horace* which they published in 1744 was dubbed the 'immaculate' Horace. The twenty-volume *Cicero* of 1749 earned the commendation of Renouard, who preferred its type to that of the

* David Murray, *Robert and Andrew Foulis and the Glasgow Press*. 1913.

Elseviers, and their small folio edition of *Callimachus* (1755) was awarded a silver medal for the finest book of not fewer than ten sheets.

Andrew Foulis died in 1775 and his brother in the following year. The business was carried on for a while by Andrew Foulis, the son of Robert; and when he finally closed down the business in 1795 the firm had issued around 700 titles.

An important event at the beginning of the century was the passing of the Copyright Act of 1709, which took effect as from 1 April 1710, when for the first time in the history of printing in Britain, legal recognition was accorded to the rights of the author and the conception of permanent copyright was ended. No longer was an author compelled to sell his copy outright to a printer or publisher and thus lose control of it for what was often a derisory sum, or, in the case of a purloined or pirated copy, nothing at all.

In August 1712 the Government brought in the notorious Stamp Act which imposed a duty of a halfpenny on every paper contained in a half sheet or less, and a penny on every copy between a half sheet and a whole sheet (four pages). Pamphlets paid duty at the rate of two shillings for each edition, and every advertisement was taxed at one shilling. One result of this legislation was that publishers increased the size of periodicals to at least six pages, so that they might rank as pamphlets and thus pay two shillings on the whole edition instead of a halfpenny on each copy. To do this they introduced big mastheads, increased the size of the type and included features such as letters and essays, until they became more like magazines than newspapers. However, the Act was revised in 1725 to circumvent this ingenious dodge. The Stamp Duty was raised several times during the ensuing years and was not removed until 1855.

WILLIAM CASLON

Printing in Britain at the beginning of the eighteenth century was, as we have said, of wretched quality. It was a time of 'brown sheets and sorry letter'. The only English type founder with a respectable stock was Thomas James, and most of his type was cast from Dutch matrices. 'But,' says Reed, 'even these, in his hands, were so indifferently cast as to be often as bad as English type.' The decline in English printing was in the main the product of an excessively long period of restrictions, monopolies and privileges which had marked the Stuart régime. Even when the power of Star Chamber, with its stultifying decrees, had been broken, the apathy which it had bred through years of repression had left printers bereft of all incentive. Perhaps not all. Some were dissatisfied with the general standard of printing and sought to improve it. Such a man was William Bowyer who, like most of the better printers of his day, was obliged to depend for his types on the Dutch foundries. So was John Watts, in whose printing-house in Wild Court Benjamin Franklin worked as a journeyman in 1725.

A somewhat fortuitous circumstance led eventually to a radical change in English printing. One day Bowyer happened to notice in a bookseller's window, near Temple Bar, some volumes which had been lettered with uncommon neatness. He enquired by whom the dies for these bindings had been cut, and was introduced to William Caslon, a young man just out of his apprenticeship to an engraver and chaser of gun-locks and barrels. Caslon had started in business on his own and did various kinds of engraving to order. Bowyer felt that if he could cut book-binders' dies so efficiently he could possibly cut punches for type. Accordingly he took the young Caslon to Thomas James's foundry to show him the business. Though the process was entirely new to him, Caslon seemed to have no doubt that he could master the new craft, and said as much to Bowyer after having requested the printer to give him a day to think the matter over.

The upshot was that Bowyer, together with two other printers, Bettenham and Watts, agreed to lend Caslon £500 between them to enable him to start on a new career as a punch-cutter, with which purpose in view he took a room in Helmet Row, Old Street, London.

Caslon learned his new trade quickly and with such competence that in 1720 he was commissioned by the Society for Promoting Christian Knowledge to cut a fount of Arabic to be used in printing a New Testament and Psalter for distribution in Palestine and Syria. The fount was approved, and with it were printed first the Psalter (1725) and then the Arabic New Testament (1727).

Under the direction of his patron, William Bowyer, Caslon then cut a fount of pica Coptic for the *Pentateuch*, edited by Dr David Wilkins, of which 200 copies only were printed and published in 1731. From that time onwards his business grew as his reputation became solidly established.

In 1727 Caslon removed to Ironmonger Row, and by the time his first specimen appeared in 1734 his roman had become accepted as an outstanding book type. His pica roman first appeared, not in the *Opera* of John Selden (1726), as John Nichols stated, but in the notes at the end of the *Anacreon*, published by Bowyer in 1725. The Selden type is of Dutch origin. Caslon's specimen of 1734 shows examples of thirty-eight founts, including a pica black (a handsome specimen of traditional English black-letter), Greek, Saxon, Gothic, Coptic, Armenian, Samaritan, Hebrew, Syriac and Arabic.

Caslon's roman became one of the most widely used book types for the next two centuries, with but a brief eclipse from about 1810 to 1840 (the era of Bodoni and Didot). All but three of the founts shown on the 1734 specimen sheet were cut by Caslon himself – the fruits of fifteen years of tireless work. In 1728 he had seriously thought of buying the Grover foundry which came on the market, but negotiations fell through, fortunately perhaps for English printing, since Caslon was able to concentrate exclusively on his own types.

He did, however, join with John James in 1739 to purchase Robert Mitchell's foundry, the matrices including music type and some old black-letter. By then he had cut the best of his own types.

Caslon's skill and industry meant that the dominance of the Dutch foundries in supplying the English market with type was brought to an end. Nevertheless, Caslon was no innovator in the matter of letter-forms; he took Dutch models and improved upon them by giving them more character, for even the best Dutch types were apt to be monotonous. In some indescribable way he transformed what was typically Dutch into something essentially English – a type which reads easily, and though lacking in elegance has a warmth and humanity one misses in the types of Baskerville and Bodoni.

In one respect at least Caslon performed a great service to the printing trade in England. For the first time a printer could procure from one foundry a sound and well-cut letter in matching founts in a full range of sizes. In 1737 Caslon moved his foundry to Chiswell Street, where it continued in business on the same site until 1911, when it was transferred to the opposite side of the street; there it remained until 1936, when the stock was purchased by Stephenson, Blake and Company. The sites of both Chiswell Street premises were destroyed by air raids in 1940 and 1941.

William Caslon I, who was born at Cradley, near Halesowen in Shropshire, in 1692, died on 23 January 1766, and was buried in the churchyard of St Luke's, Old Street, the parish in which all three of his foundries had been situated. Caslon was married three times, and by his first wife, Sarah Pearman, he had a daughter, Mary, and two sons: William, who joined his father's business about 1740 and succeeded to it on his father's death, and Thomas, who was a bookseller of repute and became Master of the Stationers' Company in 1782.

On the death of William Caslon II in 1778 the foundry passed to his two sons William and Henry, the former of whom managed the business till 1792, when he sold his share for £3,000 to his mother and the widow of Henry, who had died in 1788. After his mother's death in 1795 the foundry was bought at auction by Mrs Henry Caslon for the very small figure of £520.

Mrs Henry Caslon had new founts cut by John Isaac Drury, and took as an active partner a distant relation, Nathaniel Catherwood. The business prospered during the lives of the partners, but Mrs Henry Caslon (who became Mrs Strong in 1799) died in March 1809, and Mr Catherwood three months later. The foundry remained a family business until 1873 when H. W. Caslon, the great-great-grandson of the founder of the firm, and the last of the family, retired.

Among the apprentices of William Caslon I had been Thomas Cottrell, who was employed as a dresser. In 1757, after a dispute about wages, Cottrell and a fellow apprentice, Joseph Jackson, were dismissed. Cottrell thereupon set up a foundry of his own in Nevil's Court, Fetter Lane. He issued a broadside specimen of his types in 1760 and others which are undated. In 1766 he issued the first of two specimen books. He died in 1785, and a curious note is included in the record of his death published by John Nichols,* It reads: 'Mr. Cottrell died, I am sorry to add, not in affluent circumstances, though to his profession of a letter-founder were superadded that of a doctor for the toothache, which he cured by burning the ear; and had also the honour of serving in the Troop of His Majesty's Life Guards.' In 1794 Cottrell's foundry was bought by his former apprentice, Robert Thorne, and removed to the Barbican.

JOHN BASKERVILLE

Eighteenth-century England was fortunate in possessing two outstanding figures whose letter-forms acquired a reputation which remains to this day. Yet they were as disparate in personality as were the characteristics of their types. Baskerville's work was appreciated perhaps even more abroad that it was at home, whereas Caslon remained comfortably English.

William Caslon was a man who spent practically the whole of his working life in the business of cutting and founding type. He was the thorough professional and limited his field of activity to the one thing he could do supremely well. He was not a printer or a designer of books. Baskerville, on the other hand, was an amateur who came to printing fairly late in his career, when he had made money and could afford to experiment and produce the books he wanted to in his own way and with his own types.

John Baskerville was born in 1706 of a family that had lived for generations at Wolverley, near Kidderminster. Of his early years we know little, though even as a lad it is said that 'he was ever to be found with a pen in his hands'. His love of letter-forms never left him.

In 1725 he went to Birmingham, where he taught writing and book-keeping. He was also, for a time, a stone cutter. Still preserved in the Birmingham Public Library is a piece of slate which he used as an advertisement; in five different kinds of letter it announced 'Gravestones cut in any of the hands by John Baskerville, writing master'.

For some ten years he worked at these trades with little financial reward. Then he went into business as a maker of japanned ware and by 1745 was rich enough to buy land and build himself a house, at the same time startling the staid burgesses of Birmingham with his gorgeous carriage and eccentricities of dress.

He now had money to spend on a hobby, and that this should be printing was only natural in view of his early training as a calligrapher and his business knowledge of metals and varnishes. 'Having been an early admirer of the beauty

---

* John Nichols, *Literary Anecdotes of the Eighteenth Century*. 1812–15.

of Letters,' he tells us, 'I became sensibly desirous of contributing to the perfection of them.' In 1750, at the age of forty-four, Baskerville began his new
career as a printer. Not that he had any ambition to make money as an ordinary
commercial printer, buying his types from the foundry and executing whatever
commission came his way. Money he now had; printing was to be his relaxation.
'It is not my desire,' he wrote, 'to print many books, but such only as are books
of consequence, of intrinsic merit or established reputation . . . at such a price
as will repay the extraordinary care and experience that must necessarily be
bestowed upon them.'

Determined that whatever he printed should be distinguished by the same
craftsmanship that marked his japanned wares, he set about building his own
presses, making his own ink, and designing his own type. His presses were no
different in design from those used by other printers, but they were built with
greater precision. His experience in flat-grinding and fashioning metal plates
enabled him to provide brass platens ground with extreme accuracy so as to
present a perfectly flat surface. His ink, the formula for which probably owed
much to his experience in mixing varnishes for his japanned wares, was blacker
and more velvety than that used by other printers of his day. Baskerville also
had paper specially made for him by James Whatman, though not primarily for
books, but writing paper which he marketed through the stationer Dodsley in
London. Some of it he may have used for his *Virgil*, the prospectus for which
announced that it would be printed 'on this writing royal paper'.

But before any books could be printed six years had to be spent in the lengthy
and laborious process of designing the type and the punches, which were cut for
him by John Handy, later employed by Myles Swinney, who set up a letter
foundry in Birmingham after that of Baskerville was dispersed. Baskerville
is said to have spent between £600 and £800 before he had produced a type
with which he was satisfied. Although, in order to relieve the impatience of
Dodsley, who was to publish Baskerville's first book, the latter sent him an
impression of the two-line great primer on 2 October 1752, it was not until 1757
that the *Virgil* was issued to subscribers. It is a squarish quarto set in great
primer leaded, with italic capitals for the running heads, and although it has
been described as the first book wholly to be printed on the new wove paper, it
seems that all the known copies are printed partly on wove and partly on laid
paper. The first book printed wholly on wove paper was either the *Paradise
Regain'd* of 1759, or Edward Capell, *Prolusions*, which was published in the
same year.

The *Virgil* at once established Baskerville's reputation as a printer, although
there was considerable divergence of opinion as to whether the book could be
considered an example of fine printing. The work showed originality, enough
in itself to ensure a mixed reception. The press-work was perfect but to give

his printing a high finish he calendered, or 'hot-pressed', the sheets, giving a gloss that many declared was dazzling and hurtful to the eye – what Mores alluded to as 'trim glossy paper to dim the sight'. Dibdin thought this *Virgil* was a beautiful production and 'one of the most finished specimens of typography'.

It is, as Updike says, easy to read, yet can we call it a beautiful book? The copy in the British Museum does not appear to have been unduly trimmed in the binding, but the page appears overloaded. Three lines less to the page and slightly more space between the running head and the text would, perhaps, have improved the appearance. As to the title-page, its widely-spaced capitals give it a monumental quality with a slightly repellent flavour, and then one remembers that Baskerville was at one period a cutter of inscriptions on tombstones.

In 1758 Baskerville printed the works of Milton in two quarto volumes, followed the same year by an edition in imperial octavo, the publishers being J. and R. Tonson. Another quarto edition was called for in the following year, but although the book can be said to have been successful, Baskerville's pains-taking methods were not likely to be commercially profitable, and only his thriving japanned goods business enabled him to indulge his hobby without going bankrupt.

Like many famous printers, Baskerville wanted to produce a folio Bible and a Book of Common Prayer, and with this end in view he entered into negotiations with the Cambridge University Press, which granted him permission on rather onerous terms, and in order to obtain the privilege he had to carry out the printing at Cambridge. The first edition of his Book of Common Prayer appeared in 1760 in a type of which he wrote that it was 'calculated for people who begin to want spectacles but are ashamed to use them at Church'. Four octavo editions were printed between 1760 and 1762, followed in the latter year by a 12 mo edition.

The Holy Bible was first issued in 1763 (bearing the date 1762), and was undoubtedly Baskerville's crowning achievement. This magnificent folio Bible, set in a handsome great primer, is one of the most beautiful printed in Britain; but it was a financial failure, for only half the edition of 1,250 copies was sold, and within two years the rest were remaindered to a London bookseller. This experience made Baskerville disenchanted with the profession of printer, and in 1762 he made an offer of his foundry to the Court of France for £8,000 through the intermediary of the French ambassador, the Duc de Nivernais. The offer was politely refused. Thereafter the printer more or less retired from business, leaving his printing house in the care of his former journeyman, Robert Martin, who printed five works, which included a 12 mo edition of Shakespeare in nine volumes (1768).

However, Baskerville's interest in printing revived about 1769, and between 1770 and the time of his death in January 1775, he printed a series of quarto editions of the classics – Horace; Lucretius; Catullus, Tibullus and Propertius; Terence; Sallust and Florus. The Horace alone was illustrated, but all are distinguished by excellent typography. In 1772 the brothers Pietro and Giovanni Molini, booksellers with branches in London, Paris and Florence, commissioned Baskerville to print an edition of Ariosto, *Orlando Furioso*, which was issued in 1773 in two formats.

But although the merits of Baskerville's roman and italic types were immediately recognised by competent authorities, no one had a good word to say for the Greek fount which he cut and cast in 1758 for the Delegates of the Oxford University Press. The quarto and octavo editions of the New Testament (1763) added nothing to the printer's reputation, and a proposed edition of Euripides in this fount was cancelled. The fount was never used again, but the punches, matrices and some of the type are still preserved at Oxford.

After Baskerville's death his widow carried on the letter foundry for a time, but eventually it was sold to the Duc de Nivernais, acting for Beaumarchais and the Société Littéraire Typographique of France. As is well known, Beaumarchais made use of Baskerville's types for printing the famous 'Kehl' edition of the works of Voltaire.

In the course of time the Baskerville punches and matrices were acquired by the French firm of Deberny and Peignot, who with notable generosity presented the punches to the Cambridge University Press in 1953. Baskerville's influence was greater in Europe than in his own country, though during the present century Baskerville type has gained in popularity as a book face since its recutting by the Monotype Corporation in 1924. Few type designs have given rise to greater divergence of opinion than has Baskerville's roman. Reed considered it 'one of the most beautiful we have had'; William Morris and Emery Walker both considered it poor and uninteresting. H. V. Marrot considered Baskerville's founts to be 'a definite advance on those of Caslon in finish, grace, and general suave attractiveness'. Many would dispute this and, while acknowledging the refinement of Baskerville's design, find his type completely lacking in charm.

To his credit he eliminated superfluous ornament in his books and relied on pure typography. His sober title-pages, clean and uncluttered, with their spaced capitals, gave an air of distinction to the books he printed, though possibly the effect is a little chilling in the larger formats.

Towards the end of the eighteenth century wood-engraving took on a new lease of life and had a vogue all over Europe which lasted until the arrival of photo-mechanical methods of illustration. The man chiefly responsible for this revival was Thomas Bewick, born in 1753 at Cherryburn, near Newcastle. Apprenticed to an engraver named Ralph Beilby, Bewick showed more aptitude for engraving on wood than for copperplate work. After he had ended his apprenticeship he went into partnership with his erstwhile master, and his younger brother John Bewick became in his turn their apprentice.

One reason for the earlier eclipse of the woodcut as a medium of illustration had been the difficulty, with the old technique of gouging out the whites with the knife on the side grain of a piece of soft wood, of obtaining good clear impressions once the woodcutter attempted to reproduce the fine detail which copper engraving had made possible. Bewick, by using the graver on the end grain of hard wood was able to produce lines as finely laid as those made by the burin on metal. And by employing a hard, smooth surface such as that provided by boxwood, it was found possible to make a wood block capable of giving a large number of satisfactory impressions. Whether or not he invented either the use of the graver on wood or the practice of working on the end grain of a hard wood, he undoubtedly made the process peculiarly his own, and the development of this technique by Bewick and his followers, both in England and on the Continent, made possible the copious illustration of books in the nineteenth century.

Bewick's first major work was the *General History of Quadrupeds* published in 1790, with illustrations both drawn and engraved by himself, but much of his best work is to be found in the vignettes and tail pieces with which he adorned many books of the period. Thomas Bewick died at Gateshead in 1828 and was buried at Ovingham. His younger brother John had died in 1795.

The careers of two excellent printers of fine books, William Bulmer and Thomas Bensley, overlap the eighteenth and nineteenth centuries. Bulmer was a native of Newcastle-upon-Tyne and served his apprenticeship with a local printer. He then went to London and entered the printing office of John Bell. His path to fame started when he became acquainted with the bookseller George Nicol who was looking for a printer good enough to be entrusted with the printing of his projected magnificent edition of Shakespeare, illustrated with plates in possession of the art publishers Messrs Boydell. For this work type had been cut by William Martin of Birmingham, brother of the Robert Martin who had been Baskerville's foreman. In 1790 the Shakespeare Printing Office was established under the firm of W. Bulmer and Co., and in January 1791, the first part of the Shakespeare was issued. It at once gained for Bulmer an enviable reputation, and set him at once among the ranks of the country's finest printers.

The Shakespeare was followed by Milton's works in three folio volumes (1793–97) and in 1795 Bulmer produced a beautiful specimen of the printer's art in the *Poems* of Oliver Goldsmith and Thomas Parnell, a quarto volume illustrated with wood engravings by Thomas and John Bewick. A companion volume, William Somervile's poem *The Chase*, appeared in 1796, again with vignettes by the Bewicks. Of William Martin, who cut the types for the

FIGURE 74. John Pine (1690–1756) was one of the ablest engravers in England during the 18th century. Between the years 1733 and 1737 he published the works of Horace in two vols., printed entirely from engraved copper-plates, text as well as ornament.

Shakespeare Printing Office, Reed writes: 'the productions of the Shakespeare Press justify his reputation as a worthy disciple of his great master Baskerville.' His foundry, which belonged to the Press, was in Duke Street, not far from the premises of the Press itself (Reed-Johnson, 1952).

So highly did Dibdin think of Bulmer that he chose him to print three of his own works at the Shakespeare Printing Office – the *Typographical Antiquities*, an enlarged edition of the Ames-Herbert work (four vols., 1810–19); the *Bibliotheca Spenceriana* (four vols., 1814–15); and the *Bibliographical Decameron* (three vols., 1817). In these volumes Martin's roman, a type much favoured by Bulmer, is shown to great advantage. Although Martin himself did not issue a specimen, his types were displayed in one issued in 1807 by the Liverpool printer G. F. Harris. Martin's typefaces, as might be expected, were at first strongly influenced by Baskerville, but his later types, following the fashion set by Bodoni, became increasingly 'modern' in face.

Much of Bulmer's work was done for learned societies, and he also became the first choice of publishers seeking a well-printed text to accompany fine illustrated books. That he and Bensley were recognised as being the best printers of their time for book-work is clear from the fact that they were chosen to print many of the publications of the Roxburghe Club, the oldest society of bibliophiles in Great Britain, though Bulmer printed the greater number.

Bulmer printed one or two enormous folio volumes, among which one stands out for its remarkable series of coloured portraits. This is *A Series of Portraits of the Emperors of Turkey* by John Young, published in 1816. This work was printed at the expense of the Sultan Selim, and according to Timperley the whole impression was sent to the Ottoman Court.

Although Bensley's career as an independent printer was longer than that of Bulmer – thirty-nine years as against Bulmer's twenty-eight – the latter was the more successful of the two financially, and in 1819 he retired with a considerable fortune. He died on 9 September 1830.

Thomas Bensley (d. 1835), the son of a printer, was first established in the Strand, London, but afterwards removed to Bolt Court, Fleet Street, where, like his rival, Bulmer, he specialised in fine printing. In 1797 Bensley printed a very handsome edition of James Thomson, *The Seasons*, with engravings by F. Bartolozzi and P. W. Tomkins after originals by W. Hamilton, R.A. This work has a fine title-page on which the name of Vincent Figgins features as designer of the type. This folio volume, wrote Reed, 'still remains one of the finest achievements of English typography'.

Figgins, who had been apprenticed to Joseph Jackson and was later manager of his foundry, set up a foundry of his own after Jackson's death in 1792. At the beginning of his career he was fortunate enough to obtain a commission from Bensley to cut a fount for Macklin's *Bible*, for which Jackson had already cut a two-line English roman fount just before his death. Figgins was required to match this and did so with uncommon dexterity. In a similar manner he completed the double pica fount for Hume's *History of England* upon which Jackson had also been engaged. These two works made the reputations both of Bensley and of Figgins. The Bible, in seven volumes, was completed in 1800. Hume's History did not appear until 1806.

Between the years 1804 and 1807 Bensley was busy with J. T. Smith's *Antiquities of Westminster*, which he printed for the author. This was the first book published in Britain with a lithographic illustration. After 300 impressions had been taken off, a failure to keep the lithographic stone sufficiently moist led to pieces of the drawing being torn in attempting to remove them from the stone. As a result, only the first 300 copies of the book had the lithograph; the remainder of the plates are aquatints and mezzotints together with a few wood engravings.

In 1796 Bensley printed Townshend's *Poems* in an edition which H. V. Marrot terms 'a marvel of fragile delicacy'. Marrot stresses Bensley's tendency towards extreme lightness, almost to tenuity of texture. 'He turned out the most adorable little books, employing a frail, light type, heavily leaded. Indeed, the only heavy thing about Bensley was his leading!'

Like William Bowyer I, Bensley saw his premises destroyed by fire. On 5 November 1807, they were badly damaged as a result of boys letting off fireworks. On 26 June 1819, they were almost totally destroyed – printing offices, warehouse, and part of the dwelling house in Bolt Court, formerly the residence of Dr Johnson. John Johnson, author of *Typographia, or the Printers' Instructor*, worked for a time with Bensley before setting up his own Apollo Press.

Soon after the destruction of his premises Bensley decided to retire, although he still retained the management of a smaller business in Crane Court. He died on 11 September 1835.

The beginning of the eighteenth century had found printing in Britain bogged down in a morass of mediocrity, but by the end of the century there had come about a remarkable change. Thanks to such punch-cutters and letter-founders as Caslon, Baskerville, Wilson, Martin, Austin and Figgins, England could at last hold her own typographically with the Continent, and the monopoly held by the Dutch as suppliers of type to Britain was broken. Thanks to James Whatman and William Balston, fine printing, writing and plate papers, all of which were used for letterpress printing, could be obtained on the home market; there was no longer any need to send to Genoa. Finally, thanks to printers like Bowyer, Bell, Bulmer and Bensley, book production had reached a high standard, and the half century from 1780 to 1830 may be looked upon as a high water mark in British book production.

HOLLAND

At the beginning of the eighteenth century Haarlem, although already an important business centre, had made little mark in printing history beyond being the home of Laurens Coster, once claimed by Holland as the inventor of printing in Europe. It was to be placed securely in its present position of eminence by the house of Enschedé, founded by Izaak Enschedé, who, after an apprenticeship with the city printer Gerard Casteleyn, was admitted to the Haarlem printers' guild on 21 June 1703.

It is not known with certainty when he began to print on his own account, but there is jobbing work in existence bearing his imprint from 1707 onwards. His first recorded book is a Dutch grammar dated 1710. His business was a modest one, but he was evidently a competent printer for in 1728 he became Master of the guild. His son Johannes, who was admitted a journeyman in 1726, was a shrewd businessman who greatly enhanced the reputation of the firm.

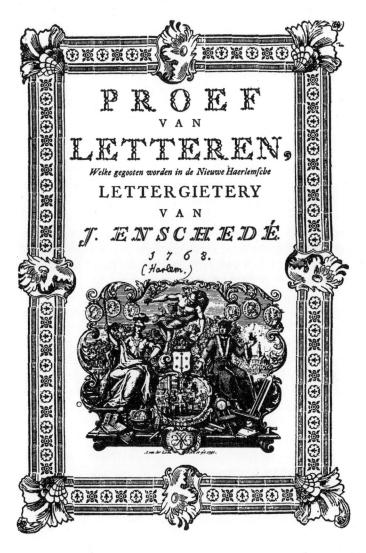

FIGURE 75. Title-page of *Proef van Letteren*, a type specimen printed at Haarlem in 1768 by J. Enschedé. It shows types by Fleischman, Rosart, and Christoffel van Dyck, as well as a black-letter attributed to Henric Lettersnyder. A supplement was issued in 1773.

In addition to working for his father, he set up as a paper-merchant, and it was Johannes who, in 1735, induced his father to join with him in purchasing the house formerly owned by Casteleyn, together with the goodwill of the business. After the widow's death in 1737, the Enschedés were granted the sole rights for twenty years of printing the *Haerlemsche Courant* and the municipal acts and ordinances.

In 1743 Johannes and his father bought up the material of the Amsterdam letter-founder Hendrik Floris Wetstein. Johannes also engaged the punch-cutter J. M. Fleischman, a Bavarian who had settled in Holland and who worked for the Enschedé firm from 1743 until his death in 1768. Thus the business now consisted of both printing office and type foundry, allied to the proprietorship of a newpaper and the lucrative work of city printer.

Izaak Enschedé died in 1761 at the ripe age of eighty, and Johannes was confirmed in his appointment as city printer and licensee for the *Courant* (by now one of the leading newspapers in the country) for a further twenty years. To meet the demands of his growing business Johannes Enschedé bought new premises in 1761, two houses in the square now called the Klokhuisplein. Here and hereabouts the firm of Enschedé remains to this day. During the time of the first Johannes Enschedé, in addition to books of local interest, his office printed many service books for the Protestant Church, such as the *Canticles* of the Dutch Mennonist Church (1756). From 1763 onwards the firm printed Bibles, at first in Dutch and later also in the Malay tongue for use in the Dutch East Indies.

The stock of the type foundry was greatly increased by purchases from the firm of Jan Roman and Company, and the growth of this part of the firm's business led to the issue of a new book of type specimens in 1768, which is of considerable interest to historians of printing on account of its notes regarding the provenance of the older founts. It also contained a foreword praising the punch-cutter J. M. Fleischman, who had died in that year. Fleischman, even though he did not quite match the brilliance of Christoffel van Dijck, was nevertheless an excellent craftsman, whose types were always in great demand. His music-type, exclusive to the firm of Enschedé, was used in 1766 for a Dutch edition of Leopold Mozart's *Violinschule*, first published in German at Augsburg ten years earlier. The composer confessed that the Dutch edition was 'uncommonly fine and superior to my own'.

In 1769 Johannes Enschedé purchased the foundry of Willem Cupy of Amsterdam, a printer who had specialised in Hebrew books, and thus the Haarlem firm acquired a splendid collection of Hebrew types, which have been put to use in quite recent times.

Johannes I Enschedé died in 1780, and was succeeded by the eldest of his three sons, Johannes II Enschedé, who, with his brother Jacobus, had been admitted as journeymen in the printers' guild in 1773, an occasion which was marked by styling the firm Johannes Enschedé en Zonen, a style it still bears. Jacobus took over the management of the printing-office, while Johannes looked after the newspaper and the foundry, the fame of which spread steadily.

To return to the beginning of the eighteenth century, it was in 1701 that a

FIGURE 76. Page from the type specimen printed at Haarlem in 1768 by J. Enschedé.

Lutheran minister named Johann Müller who, in conjunction with the Leyden firm of Van der Mey had invented a method of stereotyping, printed the first book making use of this process, a small prayer book. Müller then went into partnership with the Dutch bookseller Samuel Luchtmans, and several books bearing their joint imprint were printed from stereotype plates. One such plate, used for printing a Dutch Bible issued by Müller's sons and Luchtmans & Co. in 1718, is preserved in the British Museum.

The early years of the century also saw the production of a work of prime importance, the *Opera Omnia* of Holland's famous son Erasmus, issued by the Leyden publisher Peter van der Aa in ten folio volumes between 1703 and 1706. Peter van der Aa was also a printer and bookseller who made a name for himself with some excellent publications, the most important of which was *La Galérie agréable du Monde*, which appeared around 1729 in sixty-six volumes containing more than a thousand copper-plate engravings of views, towns, costumes and historical scenes from countries all over the known world.

The book production of the Netherlands during the eighteenth century was voluminous. Much of it was employed in printing books which had been banned by censorship in other countries, and also in the diffusion of pirated editions, particularly of French works, many of which appeared with the imprint 'Aux Dépens de la Compagnie'.

The Dutch still supplied type to England, as they had done in the seventeenth century, and some of them are shown in the specimen printed at the beginning of Watson's *History of the Art of Printing* (1713). But the importation of Dutch types came to an end with the rise of the English punch-cutter and founder William Caslon (see *supra*). The Dutch types, moreover, had, in the words of Daniel Updike, 'begun to assume a general uncouthness which helped the English to abandon their purchase for those more comfortable and "cheerful" roman letters designed by William Caslon' (Updike, 1922).

DENMARK

The development of printing in Denmark during the first half of the eighteenth century followed that of Germany in many respects. The type in general use was German Fraktur, and the quality of printing was for the most part poor, with old and battered cuts for illustrations. In the more expensive publications the German baroque style was favoured, but considerable amelioration took place after the middle of the century, when books became influenced by French fashions in typography.

This was particularly noticeable in the case of the Orphan House Press (Vajsenhuset), from which came in 1755 one of the most sumptuous of Danish publications – the *Voyage d'Egypte et de Nubie* by Friderik Ludvig Norden. The two folio volumes were published with French text, translated from the Danish by J. B. des Roches de Parthenay, with 150 copper plates and numerous vignettes. The artists were the Danish painter Peter Cramer and the German Marcus Tuscher.

In 1717 a Danish Bible was printed by the College of Missions, an institution founded in 1714 which had a privilege for printing and selling Bibles. When this press was destroyed by fire in 1728, the printing of Bibles was transferred to the Orphan House Press, founded in 1727, whose first Bible appeared in 1732.

A great fire ravaged Copenhagen in October 1728, when seven of the city's nine presses were burned and the University Library was destroyed.

During the second half of the century many good books came from the press of Andreas Hartvig Godiche. Among them was a magnificent though unfinished treatise on Shells, *Auserlesne Schnecken, Muschelen und andere Schaalthiere*, by the German engraver Franz Michel Regenfuss (1758). Only the first volume appeared, with text in German and French. Also from this press came the Danish Atlas of Pontoppidan, a fine quarto edition of Ludvig Holberg, *Peder Paars* (1772), and Laurids de Thurah, *Hafnia hodierna* (1748), a description of Copenhagen with some 110 copper engravings and text in Danish, French and German.

At the end of the century two more distinguished presses were established in Copenhagen: those of Thiele (founded 1770) and of Schultz (founded 1783).

On 3 January 1749 appeared the first issue of the Copenhagen newspaper *Berlingske Tidende* (Berling's Gazette), thus called after the name of its founder.

SWEDEN

The leading printer in Sweden for a long period was Peter Momme, who in 1738 had acquired the Stockholm printing house of Johann Hendrik Werner, and became Royal Printer. In 1768 the press descended to his son, but the privilege as Royal Printer was acquired by his son-in-law Henrik Fougt. In 1757 Peter Momme printed the *English and Swedish Dictionary* of Jacob Serenius.

Fougt, a Laplander by birth, was a great anglophile and much of his typographic work was based on ideas received during a stay in England around 1767. He received an English patent (24 December 1767) for his invention of 'certain new and curious types . . . for the printing of music notes', and while in England he published a considerable amount of music printed with his type, the first being Francesco Uttini, *Six sonatas for two violins and a bass* (1768). For many years the press was one of the best known in Sweden.

THE BEGINNING OF THE NEWSPAPER IN RUSSIA

The first of the Romanov Tsars, Michael Fedorovitch, in 1621 gave orders for handwritten 'corantos' to be produced for his personal information, and these, although not produced at regular intervals, did for a time enable the ruler of all the Russias to keep abreast of news from foreign countries which filtered through to government circles. But the better part of a century had still to elapse before a regular printed news-sheet was published in Russia. In any case the production of a regular newspaper at that time would hardly have been feasible since, apart from the clergy and a few high officials, most Russians could neither read nor write.

The press of Russia's first printer, Ivan Fedorov, was, as we have seen, a short-lived affair, and it was not until about 1700 that the vast Russian kingdom owned a single regular printing office, and it printed almost without exception nothing but religious books.

Even at the beginning of the eighteenth century there was no apparent desire for newspapers in Russia. It was Peter the Great who 'first opened the western window wide upon the Russian world' and gave the country, among other things, its first Russian newspaper, *Vedomosti* (News), which was born on 2 January 1703. The full title read 'News concerning military and other interesting and notable matters which have occurred in the province of Moscow and other neighbouring territories'. Peter the Great was not only the founder of the first Russian newspaper, but might well be called the first Russian editor and journalist, for he saw that his own articles were published and was often to be seen in the press room.

The first Russian newspaper did not appear regularly. There were frequent interruptions while the Tsar was travelling or commanding his troops in the field. In any case it was looked upon as a royal caprice. Nevertheless some 150 numbers appeared between 1703 and 1706. They did not contain very much material, nor could they be bought in the street or by subscription. They were posted up in government offices and almost their sole readers were government officials.

In October 1727 the St Petersburg printing house, where this journal was printed, became part of the recently founded Academy of Sciences. In place of the former news-sheet the Academy brought out the *St Petersburg Academy News*, which appeared for the first time on 2 January 1728. But already, a year previously on 6 January 1727, there had appeared the first Russian newspaper with text in German, the *St Petersburger Zeitung*, also a product of the Academy of Sciences and edited by their first President, Professor Laurent Blumentrost.

28

Dawn of the Machine Age

AN invention usually comes into being when there is an imperative demand for it and the conditions for its employment are favourable. Gutenberg's invention was the result of a demand for the rapid multiplication of texts, but it would have made little headway had the printer been forced to rely on expensive and limited supplies of vellum as a printing surface instead of the cheaper and replaceable product available since the recent introduction into Europe of the papermill.

Until the latter part of the eighteenth century there had been no spectacular growth in the demand for reading matter since the early days of printing. Population growth had been steady but not overwhelming. But between 1801 (date of the first census) and 1831 the population of England and Wales increased from nine million to 13,750,000. Similar large increases took place in most countries of Western Europe, especially in France, where during the first half of the nineteenth century the population rose from 26.9 million to 36.5 million.

The sudden growth of an industrialised society, eager for education, posed a problem. For 350 years the hand press had existed without much modification. Its production was extremely limited, but so was the demand for print. The era of widespread literacy did not arrive before the end of the eighteenth century. Even when, around 1800, the wooden press was superseded by Lord Stanhope's iron press it turned out no more than 200 impressions of a single side in an hour,* and twice that time was needed for perfected copies. Even if sufficient for book printing at the time, it was far from satisfying the needs of the newspaper, which demanded ever increasing operational speeds to meet the steadily growing demand for newspapers.

However, a solution to the problem was at hand. One result of the Industrial Revolution was the releasing and harnessing of an almost limitless form of energy in the shape of steam, which caused a greater revolution in the production of printed matter than anything that had happened since the days of Gutenberg. The printing machine came into being, for neither the wooden press which had endured for three and a half centuries, nor the iron press of Stanhope, could properly be termed a machine, since their operation was not automatic.

* *Manchester Guardian*, 6 May 1871.

It was not an unmixed blessing. The original aim of Gutenberg, the rapid and standardised multiplication of texts, was to be achieved in a manner which the inventor of printing would have considered quite incredible. But vastly increased productivity brought wealth only to the periodical printers; few book printers during the first half of the nineteenth century could afford expensive steam presses, and contented themselves with the new makes of iron presses such as the Columbian and the Albion. The book trade did not start to expand until William Clowes showed the way.

Although the coming of the steam press enabled the printing industry to cope with a rapidly expanding market, it led to a marked falling-off in typographical standards, especially after about 1840, when printers such as Bensley and Bulmer were no more and their example unemulated. For this there was a reason. During the preceding centuries the function of the press had been devoted more to the preservation of the world's literary heritage than to the dissemination of knowledge and, in the main, books were readily accessible only to the leisured and relatively wealthy classes. With the coming of the machine age and the growth of education the more intelligent of the artisan class began to demand books and at a price commensurate with their meagre wages.

And so with the availability of the steam press books started to pour out. For the first time there was a considerable demand for cheap periodicals devoted to popular instruction, and the penny magazines began to proliferate. In England the publisher Charles Knight (1791–1873) founded the Society for the Diffusion of Useful Knowledge in 1826 and in 1832 published the first number of the weekly *Penny Magazine*, printed by William Clowes on Applegath and Cowper presses – one of the first British periodicals to make use of woodcuts on a large scale. A year later the first German *Pfennigmagazin* made its appearance.

The market for the large quartos of the eighteenth century was superseded by an insatiable demand for cheap books in octavo or 12 mo editions and, in consequence, there was a noticeable falling-off in typographical standards, only redeemed by the work of a few printers, such as Charles Wittingham the Younger, who were convinced that machine printing need not necessarily be bad printing. But it was not until the end of the century that reformers like William Morris sought to introduce higher standards and rescue printing from the decadence into which it had fallen. If Morris himself carried his reforms to extremes, at least his ideals influenced others, both in England and abroad, and paved the way for a general amelioration in the standards of commercial printing.

THE PRINTING PRESS

The wooden press remained unchanged in its essentials for some 350 years, with only minor alterations which were not always of universal application.

A true & exact Representation of the Art of Casting & Preparing Letters for Printing.

FIGURE 77. A view of the Caslon Foundry, from *The Universal Magazine* (June 1750).

We know very little about the earliest presses. Karl Dieterichs, in his book *Die Buchdruckpresse*, thinks that the first printing press was modelled on the paper-makers' press with the difference that the platen was made to exert less pressure but with a greater steadiness in action. Others have suggested that since Mainz is situated in a wine-growing area a version of the wine press was more likely.

Unfortunately, although some thirty-four woodcuts of early presses appear in sixteenth-century books, they are not sufficiently detailed nor accurate enough to give more than a general idea. The first reproduction of a press, in the Lyons *Danse Macabre* of 1499, tells us little beyond the fact that the press was held to the ceiling by means of heavy beams, for the platen and bed of the press are barely visible. From 1507 onwards the printer Josse Bade made use of a series of devices incorporating a printing press, all of which show a straight bar and a rather small platen. Indeed, one of the great drawbacks of the early presses was that two pulls of the bar were needed to print one forme, and since the pressure needed was considerable the whole process was extremely arduous for the pressman. One of the first cuts to show the construction and working of the press appeared in 1548 at Zurich, in Stumpff's *Schweizer Chronik* printed by Froschauer, but a more realistic illustration of the wooden press appears in Samuel Ampsing's *Description of Haarlem* printed in 1628. Perhaps the best-known engraving of a seventeenth-century press is that dated 1676 by Abraham von Werdt, who worked at Nuremberg between 1640 and 1680. Here we see two pressmen at work – one laying on and taking off the sheets as well as pulling the bar, while the other is inking the forme with his two inking balls. The engraving shows the forme, the tympan and the frisket and, although the press is a better piece of furniture than those shown in earlier representations, in essentials it does not differ from Bade's press.

Improvement in the construction of presses came slowly. The forme of type had twice the area covered by the platen, so that to print a full-sized sheet necessitated two pulls of the bar for each side. The first reform of any note was made by Willem Jansen Blaeu about 1620, and this mainly concerned the 'hose', a sleeve which enclosed the screw which raised and lowered the platen. The Blaeu press, although praised by Moxon in his *Mechanick Exercises* (1683), was not taken up with any enthusiasm in England, where the 'Common' press, as the wooden press without Blaeu's reforms was called, continued to be employed throughout the eighteenth century.

And yet, despite the fact that printing was a slow process with the wooden press, greater productiveness does not seem to have been seriously envisaged until almost the end of the eighteenth century. In 1772 one Wilhelm Haas of Basel built a press in which both bed and platen were of iron; but in face of opposition from the printers' guilds he could not put his ideas into practice. In 1783 a detailed description of a new press which could print at one pull, the invention of Etienne Anisson-Duperron, later to be Director of the Imprimerie Royale, was read before the French Academy. A description of the press was published at Paris in 1785 in a quarto volume of forty pages, with four large copper-plate engravings explaining the mechanism. But the press was too complicated and too expensive to be adopted by the trade. But the time was now ripe for a press which would overcome the drawbacks of the customary wooden press.

An American named Adam Ramage made a press around 1800 with an iron bed and a spring mechanism which raised the platen after an impression had been taken, thus easing the pressman's work, but the first significant improvement took place at the beginning of the nineteenth century when the wooden press was at last superseded by Earl Stanhope's iron press, which combined an iron frame, compound lever action and a platen which covered the whole of the forme. The result was greater speed, and a whole battery of Stanhope presses was used to print *The Times* for the first fourteen years of the nineteenth century.

The first step towards faster printing was the substitution of cylindrical pressure for the flat weight of the platen. The idea of printing by means of an impression cylinder was not a new one, for it was used in the sixteenth century by printers of copper-plate engravings, though such presses were rudimentary in design.

On 29 April 1790 a Londoner named William Nicholson (1753–1815) took out a patent (No. 1748) in connection with various inventions relating to printing. Nicholson, who was a scientist, inventor, school teacher and patent agent, was editor of *Nicholson's Journal of Science*, and wrote the article on 'Printing' in the *British Encyclopaedia* (1809). His specifications embodied many of the essential features of later printing machines, such as the reciprocating table with geared impression cylinder; the inking of the forme by rollers instead of by ink balls; the distribution of ink upon the rollers by means of subsidiary rollers; an ink duct for supplying ink in pre-determined quantity at each revolution of the cylinder; and grippers for carrying round the sheet. Another part of his invention foreshadowed rotary printing in that he suggested the use of curved stereotype plates to fit the cylinders. His specification, in the words of Wilson and Grey, 'embraced more original ideas than any other single patent applicable to printing that was ever granted. . . . Let Nicholson go down to posterity as the inventor of the printing machine, even if it took twenty years more and an "ingenious foreigner" to apply his suggestions in a practicable manner.'*

Unfortunately Nicholson was one of those men teeming with original ideas and constantly engaged in scientific projects who seem unable to derive any

* Wilson, F. and Grey, D., *A practical treatise upon modern printing machinery and letterpress printing.* London, 1888.

material advantage from their labours. He was constantly in financial difficulties, and for lack of money his patent was never carried out in practice.

THE COMING OF THE PRINTING MACHINE

The credit for building the first practical printing machine belongs to Frederick König, born in Thuringia in 1774. At the age of fifteen he was apprenticed as trainee compositor and printer with the famous Leipzig firm of Breitkopf and Härtel. At the end of his apprenticeship he thought of giving up his trade as a printer to devote his time to scientific matters in which he was interested. About 1802 he first turned his attention to the construction of a printing machine, and having borrowed some capital set up a workshop in Suhl and there began to build a printing machine. This was simply a mechanised hand press, built of wood, and it aroused very little interest.

His greatest need, common to all inventors, was capital. A journey to St Petersburg, whence had come hopes in this respect, proved fruitless, and in 1806 König came to London, where he was at first employed in a printing office near Poland Street, and later found another job in a German library which had been founded by a compatriot named Weiss. On 12 March 1807 he was introduced to Thomas Bensley, one of the most eminent printers in Britain, to whom he out-lined his ideas for a powered printing machine. Bensley was a shrewd and practical man who grasped at once the significance of König's proposals and saw that their practical realisation would give him a tremendous advantage over his competitors. He agreed to purchase the invention if it bore out the claims of its inventor, but the amount of money needed to develop the machine being more than Bensley himself was prepared to risk, two other printers, George Woodfall and Richard Taylor, were induced to join him.

König's first English patent was taken out in 1810. This machine, built with the help of his compatriot, Andreas Bauer, was a platen screw-press driven by steam power, and although it was used in Bensley's printing office in April 1810 for printing part of the *Annual Register* for that year, there is no record of any other work being done by it, and it was eventually abandoned. It was an improved version of the Suhl press and was fully automatic, needing only manual laying-on and taking-off of the sheets.

Nevertheless, the machine must be reckoned a failure, probably because König had persisted with the platen principle. He recognised that he had been working on the wrong lines, trying, as Jacobi says, 'to make an improvement on what was hardly capable of improvement'.* For the design of his next machine he turned to the cylinder type of machine which Nicholson had already patented. It is very likely that König had seen Nicholson's specifications, but his own machine cannot be said to have been copied from this patent, from which it

* C. T. Jacobi, *Printing*. London (6th edn.), 1919.

FIGURE 78. Interior of an early press room showing the pressman, left, pulling the bar to press the platen on to the inked forme. Right, an assistant is inking a forme of type with ink balls. In the background we see compositors working at the case and correctors examining the proofs.

differed considerably. Nicholson, for instance, proposed having the type imposed upon the surface of a second cylinder, a method not feasible at that time. König fixed the forme to the flat bed of the press. This bed, a cast-iron plate, had a reciprocating movement designed to bring the type alternately under the action of the inking rollers and the impression cylinder, which was recessed to enable the reciprocating carriage to return. Since the inking of the type was carried out automatically as the table was being run in and out, the nine operations which had been necessary in hand printing were reduced to three: laying-on, impression and taking-off. The output of König's first cylinder printing machine, built in 1812, was 800 impressions an hour.

By his agreement with Bensley, König had retained the right to make other machines to this design, and when the prototype was exhibited publicly in König and Bauer's workshop in White Cross Street, John Walter, the proprietor of *The Times*, found it to be just what he had been looking for, except that this single-cylinder machine was intended only for book work. But the inventor assured him that a double-cylinder machine on the same principle could be built for the printing of newspapers; whereupon John Walter ordered two such presses. The first machine was erected at Printing House Square in secret, and on 29 November 1814 *The Times* was printed on the first practical printing machine. The rate of production was increased from the maximum 250 impressions an hour possible with the Stanhope to 1,100 an hour.

As is the case with most inventions which pose a threat to full employment, the advent of the printing machine was viewed with disapproval by the majority of printers. This did not deter William Clowes, founder of the present well-known firm, from using König's machine for book printing; nor did it deter the inventor from building, in conjunction with Bauer, their first perfecting machine, namely one which would print both sides of the paper. This was completed in 1816.

In 1817 König left England and returned to his native land, in despair at the many infringements of his patents and disgusted with the attitude of Bensley, who sought to oppose the sale of his machines to other printers and who tried all he knew to avoid paying König the money he owed him under their contract. 'Always shabby and overreaching' was the verdict passed by Richard Taylor, the other partner in the patent, upon Thomas Bensley.

König and Bauer decided to return to Germany for good. In 1817 König purchased the abandoned monastery of Premonstratensian monks at Oberzell near Würzburg, and there established a factory which was the forerunner of the famous König and Bauer A.G. He died in January 1833, but his partner Bauer lived until 1860 and carried on with great success a business which still exists.

After the departure of König, *The Times* appointed Augustus Applegath and Edward Cowper as their engineers. Cowper, who was Applegath's brother-in-law, was one of the first to experiment with Nicholson's idea of a curved printing surface. In 1816 he patented a process for curving stereotype plates made by the plaster process, and a machine employing them was used for printing banknotes at the Bank of England. But the rotary machine proper did not come into being until the middle of the century as a practical proposition (see *infra*). However, some mention should be made at this point of Bacon and Donkin's prismatic rotary of 1813, for although it was not a great success, it was the first machine on the rotary principle to be built and used. The type was arranged on four sides of a prism opposite an impression cylinder of similar shape. In this machine for the first time a composition of glue and treacle was used to cover the inking rollers. The Earl of Stanhope had attempted to replace the old ink balls by skin rollers, but the seam left a mark on the type. The glue and treacle composition is said to have been the discovery of a printer named Forster, who had seen it being used by china decorators for printing colours on biscuit ware.*

In 1827 Applegath and Cowper built a new machine for *The Times*, in which

---

* The French attribute this composition to the chemist J. N. Gannal in 1819.

they abandoned 'perfecting' but increased the speed of operation to 4,200 sheets an hour. It was a four-feeder requiring eight attendants, four to lay on and four to take off the sheets. The forme travelled the whole length of the machine, the cylinders rising and falling alternately, so that one pair printed as the carriage moved one way, and the other pair did the same on its return.

The search continued for higher speed and greater production capacity, for the circulation of *The Times* was constantly increasing. Between 1842 and 1852 it doubled. When Applegath learned that the demand for the paper could only be met by the building of an even faster machine, he then, to use his own words, 'determined upon changing the reciprocating motion of the forme into a circular one'. He built a machine with a great vertical cylinder, some 17 feet in circumference, around which were arranged eight impression cylinders each revolving on its own vertical axis, and to each of which paper could be fed. The type cylinder was not truly circular, but consisted of a number of flat surfaces, each the column width of the paper. The type itself was held in position by means of tapering column rules, and inking rollers were grouped between the impression cylinders. This machine, completed in 1848, is said to have produced 10,000 copies an hour, and later a nine-feeder was installed. But neither of these machines had really solved the problem of rotary printing.

At this period there was keen competition between *The Times* and R. Hoe and Company of New York, for both firms were searching for a still faster running press, and to the American company must go the credit of producing the first true rotary newspaper printing press, one of which was erected in the office of the Philadelphia *Ledger* in 1846. This was a four-feeder, and though in general conception the Hoe machine was similar to Applegath's, the horizontal arrangement of the cylinders was much more convenient. Grippers and tapes delivered the printed sheets without handling, and the machine was so compact when compared with the vertical rotary, that it eventually superseded the Applegath machine. In 1856 Lloyd's *Weekly Newspaper* installed a 'Hoe Type Revolving Machine', as it was called, with six cylinders, and later *The Times* installed a ten-feeder from the same company.

Meanwhile, in Germany, König and his partner Bauer found plenty of work for their newly-established factory at Oberzell. On 12 July 1824 the publisher Cotta installed a cylinder press for the *Allgemeine Zeitung* at Augsburg. König himself supervised its erection in conjunction with his nephew, Fritz Reichenbach, a mechanical engineer. A second nephew, Friedrich Helbig, later made a name for himself as a builder of presses in Vienna.

In 1826 König built eleven machines, the first two going to J. B. Metzler at Stuttgart and F. A. Brockhaus at Leipzig. Two were sent to Paris, the first for the firm of A. Guyot and Scribe and the second for E. Pochard. Two were also built for the firm of Enschedé at Haarlem.

FIGURE 79. The first Hoe Web Press used in England was installed in the printing office of "Lloyd's Weekly Newspaper" in 1871.
Courtesy of Messrs. R. Hoe & Crabtree Ltd.

When König died in 1833 he had exported some sixty steam presses, and the firm of König and Bauer completed its 2,000th machine on 6 September 1873. Of these 1,243 were bought in Germany, while no fewer than 392 were exported to Russia, of which 208 went to St Petersburg. After the founding of the König & Bauer Maschinenfabrik at Augsburg by König's nephew, Fritz Reichenbach, its expansion was remarkable.

In Austria the first makers of steam presses were Helbig and Müller. Helbig was a son of the first marriage of König's sister, Marie Rosine and had learnt his trade with König. Leo Müller was a native of Rieglern in Vorarlberg, whose mechanical bent had sent him to Oberzell as a youth.

The first mechanical press to be set up in France, in 1823, was a two-cylinder press built by Cowper and Applegath and exported to France for use in the printing office of the *Bulletin des Lois* at Paris. In the same year a single-cylinder machine was shown at the Paris exhibition by MM. Dupont, Gauthier-Laguionnie and Middentrop.

What the names of König and Bauer meant to Germany, that of Marinoni meant to France. Hippolyte Marinoni was born at Sivry-Courty on 8 September 1823. As a youth he was apprenticed to the engineer Gaveaux, who, after constructing a number of useful hand presses on the lines of the Stanhope, was the first in France to build a mechanical press for newspaper work – a two-cylinder perfector, built in 1831 for *La Nationale*. He eventually became foreman in Gaveaux' establishment and in 1848, in collaboration with his employer, he constructed the first four-cylinder flat-bed press made in France, for the newspaper *La Presse*. This embodied the principles of the two-cylinder press patented by Philippe Taylor in 1822.

In 1854 Marinoni set up in business on his own account and in partnership opened up as 'Marinoni et Chaudré', mechanical engineers, in the rue de Vaugirard, Paris. The firm quickly became 'Hippolyte Marinoni', and the business prospered to such an extent that its founder moved to larger premises in the rue d'Assas, still the head office of the 'Etablissements Marinoni' which in the course of time has taken over other noted construction firms such as Derriey, Voirin, and Pierre Alauzet.

Although Marinoni built all kinds of presses, lithographic as well as typographic, it was in the field of the rotary press that he showed himself pre-eminent. The rotary he built for *Le Petit Journal* in 1868 was the most rapid of all the sheet-fed presses of its time, since the sheet was perfected at one operation. In the same year the contract for printing the *Moniteur Universel* and *Moniteur du Soir* was given to Wittersheim & Co., who ordered five of Marinoni's new rotary perfecting presses. In 1872 Marinoni installed his first web-fed rotary in the premises of the Paris newspaper *La Liberté*. Eventually Marinoni became proprietor and director of the newspaper *Le Petit Journal*, and with an installation of twenty rotaries printed over a million copies daily.

Meanwhile the platen principle had been revived by David Napier for book-work, and his double-feeder power platen of 1830 was largely used for quality printing before the introduction of the Wharfedale.

In 1850 a London printer named Main patented a cylinder machine in which the cylinder did not rotate, but oscillated, making about three-quarters of a revolution. Instead of the paper being fed at the top, as hitherto, it was fed to the underside of the cylinder, where it was seized by grippers. This made possible the use of a smaller cylinder for a given sheet size. The cylinder was lifted clear of the forme on the reverse stroke by means of eccentric bearings.

Two years later a Frenchman named Dutartre patented a machine in which the cylinder made one complete revolution as the carriage moved forward and then stopped while the carriage returned. This was the origin of the so-called stop-cylinder machine (in French, *à arrêt de cylindre*), the principle of which was embodied in one of the most successful flat-bed cylinder machines for book-printing and general commercial work, known as the Wharfedale from its place of origin, the first model having been built around 1858 by William Dawson and his foreman, David Payne, at Otley in Wharfedale, Yorkshire. This machine, both efficient and economical, was never patented and became so popular that all machines of that type, wherever made, became known as Wharfedales. During the years since the original Wharfedale was introduced many improvements have been made, and Wharfedale machines can now be had for two-colour work.

Later came the two-revolution machines, so-called because the cylinder rotates once to print the sheet and again to deliver it, being lifted clear of the type-bed during the second revolution. This was the invention of the American Robert Miehle, after whom it is called. Machines of this type were built in many countries, and a high-speed Miehle will turn out on an average some 3,000 impressions per hour. In Britain the Harrild and Otley presses were also excellent two-revolution machines. The vertical Miehle resembles the platen press in so far as the forme and bed lie in the vertical plane, but it is nevertheless a cylinder machine, the cylinder making the impression as the bed, with the forme clamped to it, moves up and down. Another vertical press, the Harrison automatic, will give speeds up to about 4,000 impressions an hour, with a maximum type area of 45 cm. by 26 cm.

For many years experiments had been conducted with a view to making curved stereotype plates which could be affixed to cylinders. For newspaper work speed was the essential factor and whatever mechanical improvements might be made in flat-bed machines, the alternating motion of the bed constituted a delaying factor which limited considerably their speed. Eventually the problem was solved by the Italian founder James Dellagana (see p. 373) and the Hoe machines profited by the progress made in this direction. From 1846 onward the rotary press, in which the curved forme replaced the flat forme and the pressure necessary for the impression was carried out by two cylinders working one against the other, began its successful career.

The first rotaries were sheet-fed, but after the middle of the century, when the paper-making machine was able to turn out one continuous sheet, or 'web', these were replaced by rotaries fed from reels of paper. It was in 1865 that William Bullock of Philadelphia first successfully completed a web perfecting cylinder press which printed from a continuous roll of paper on both sides. The firm of William Bullock was later taken over by the Hoe Company. The web-fed rotary presses were rapidly developed and perfected until today they are capable of printing a sixteen-page periodical at a rate of some 30,000 copies an hour.

29

A Chapter of Inventions

With the coming of the printing machine there was an ever-increasing demand for more and cheaper paper. An effort had to be made to replace the slow hand process of paper-making, by constructing a machine for the purpose. The first one was invented around 1799 by Nicolas-Louis Robert at Essones in France, but financial difficulties, due to the unsettled state of France after the Revolution prevented Robert from developing his machine (a model of which may be seen in the Science Museum at South Kensington), and he sold the patent to St Léger Didot. It was soon afterwards taken up in England by the brothers Henry and Sealey Fourdrinier, stationers and paper-makers. Improvements led to the engineer Brian Donkin completing successfully the first Fourdrinier paper-making machine. Although the brothers lost almost all their private fortune in perfecting the machine, and ultimately became bankrupt, their name is immortalised in the paper industry, for the machines used today, based on the same essential principles, are still known as 'Fourdriniers' although the vast size and complexity of the present-day machines would undoubtedly astonish the original inventors. By 1840 there were 280 Fourdrinier machines at work in the United Kingdom alone. Whereas the hand-produced paper had been made sheet by sheet, the machine makes one continuous sheet or 'web', and with its coming the output of paper increased ten-fold.

One problem encountered soon after the introduction of the machine was a shortage of traditional material, namely the linen rags which had always been used for good quality paper.

Experiments were made with all sorts of fibrous materials, as various patents between 1801 and 1862 show. Straw was one of the first to be suggested, and other substances included the bark of various trees and shrubs, reeds, vegetable stalks and hop bine. Although the use of wood pulp had been suggested by Réaumur as early as 1719, the idea did not take practical shape until 1840, when mechanical or ground wood pulp was introduced, to be followed a decade later by first the soda, and then the sulphite process of treating wood until it is reduced to a mass of cellulose fibres. In 1856 Thomas Routledge introduced esparto grass as a suitable fibre, and though lacking strength, paper made from esparto grass readily absorbs dyes and pigments and so became extensively used for tinted papers.

In England Edward Lloyd, founder of *Lloyd's Weekly London Newspaper* (1843) did much to develop the paper trade during the latter part of the nineteenth century. In 1877 he built a large paper-mill at Sittingbourne, in Kent, which in its day had the largest output of any paper-mill in the world. He also leased over 100,000 acres of land in Algeria for the growing of esparto grass.

THE INVENTION OF STEREOTYPING

A most useful invention from the standpoint of the economics of the printing trade was that of stereotyping, a method of reproducing a relief printing surface so that the type can be returned to case. Storing pages of standing type calls for considerable space and constant attention, and the amount of type thus locked up can provide a serious problem to the small printer.

This problem of preserving pages of type for an eventual reprint exercised the minds of many printers in the eighteenth century, and the history of the solution to the problem is still rather obscure. Briefly, the process of stereotyping, shorn of its technical details is as follows. From the forme of 'matter' to be duplicated is taken a mould from which can be cast a plate in relief corresponding to the original. Since the duplicate is only about one-sixth of the thickness of the page of type it is easier to store, and furthermore the type is released for further use.

The oldest method of preparing stereotypes was by making the mould of gypsum (plaster of Paris), which was baked before a cast could be made. The plaster mould was broken in the process, so that only one plate could be made at a time, each additional duplicate necessitating a new mould. Later, a papier mâché mould (called a flong) was used, from which more than one plate could be made; moreover, it had the advantage of being flexible, so that from it could be cast curved plates ready for fixing to the cylinder of a rotary press. In fact it was the development of the papier mâché flong which enabled the newspaper press to reap the full advantage of the rotary method of printing.

The earliest stereotype plates are thought to have been the invention of a Lutheran minister named Johann Müller in conjunction with one Van der Mey, and together they are said to have printed a small prayer-book from stereotype plates about 1701. Müller later went into partnership with the Dutch bookseller Samuel Luchtmans and several books bearing their joint imprint were produced from stereotypes. The British Museum possesses a stereotype plate used for printing a Dutch Bible issued by Müller's sons and Luchtman and Co. in 1718, Müller himself having died in 1710. A letter from the firm of Luchtmans to the Paris bookseller A. Renouard dated 24 June 1801, accompanied a copy of a stereotyped Bible, of which the publisher remarked: 'The plates are all in our possession, and notwithstanding the fact that we have printed several thousand copies from them, they are still in excellent condition. . . . The plates were made by an artist named Van der Mey at the beginning of last century at the expense of my late grandfather, Samuel Luchtmans, bookseller. . . .' Although Lottin

TEN CYLINDER ROTARY TYPE-REVOLVING PRESS

FIGURE 80. Hoe Ten Cylinder Rotary Type Revolving Press, as used by "The Times" in 1857–58.
Courtesy of Messrs. R. Hoe & Crabtree Ltd.

claims that a Paris printer named Valleyre printed almanacs from stereotype plates about the year 1700, his statement is unsupported by any proof.

In Britain the first successful stereotype plates were made about 1727 by William Ged of Edinburgh, a goldsmith by profession. After two years of experiment and at the cost of all his available capital Ged produced a serviceable plate, but lacked money to exploit his invention. In 1729 a London stationer named William Fenner offered to finance him in return for one-half of the profits. Shortly afterwards a company was formed in which Ged and Fenner were joined by the letter-founder Thomas James and his brother John James, and by James Ged, the son of the inventor.

The partnership was not a happy one, as John Carter has shown in his masterly account of 'William Ged and the Invention of Stereotype'.* It was frequently bedevilled by disagreements and Ged had constant trouble with his workmen. In 1730 the partnership was granted a licence by the University Press at Cambridge to print Bibles and Prayer Books under the University's privilege, but whether any of the Prayer Books completed at Cambridge were actually printed from Ged's plates is still a debatable point. It is thought that the octavo Common Prayer, Cambridge, 1733, may have been printed in part from stereotype plates made by William Ged, but as Mr Carter points out 'the presswork of the only available copy of the 1733 Common Prayer is too bad to allow of a decisive verdict on technical grounds'. In 1733 Ged returned to Scotland, taking his invention with him. In 1739 he published an edition of Sallust in Edinburgh which bears on the title-page an announcement in Latin to the effect that it was printed 'by William Ged, goldsmith of Edinburgh, not with movable type, as is commonly done, but from cast plates'. This, and the reissue of 1744 were printed entirely from Ged's own plates. In 1742 two separate editions of Henry Scougal, *The Life of God in the Soul of Man*, were printed from Ged's plates by John White of Newcastle. Ged intended to enter into a fresh London partnership at the end of 1749, but died after a sudden illness on 19 October of that year. His son James went to Jamaica a few years later, and the plant, which was to have been sent out to him, was misappropriated by a friend and subsequently disappeared.

About 1779 another Scot, Alexander Tilloch, though unacquainted with Ged's work, which had been forgotten since his death, introduced, in conjunction with the printer Andrew Foulis, 'a method of making plates for the purpose of printing by or with plates, instead of movable types commonly used' for which they took out patents in 1784. Later the third Earl Stanhope purchased the rights from Tilloch and Foulis and further developed the process in association with the printer Andrew Wilson, who set up a Stereotype Office in Duke Street, London.

* *The Library*, September 1960.

In 1784 an Alsatian named François Hoffmann set up a workshop in Paris for making stereotype plates. He had seen Ged's *Sallust* and recognised the great possibilities inherent in the process. In partnership with his son he obtained exclusive rights 'de graver en creux et en relief par les procédés d'un art nouveau', and produced the *Journal polytype des Sciences et des Arts*. In place of plaster of Paris for his moulds he made use of a clay base into which he poured a composition of lead, tin and bismuth. As was the case with Ged, the Hoffmanns encountered hostility from other printers. In 1787, after they had printed several books by their method with success, intrigue by members of the 'Chambre Royale et Syndicale de la Librairie et Imprimerie de Paris' resulted in a prosecution on a charge of publishing dangerous writings, and the firm was obliged to close. Hoffmann went back to Alsace and transferred his business to his home town of Sélestat.

Hoffmann had his imitators in France. In 1787 Philippe Pierres published *Zélie dans le désert* from stereotype plates, but the finished product was poor in quality. In 1787 a printer of Toul, Joseph Carez, obtained a licence to print 'sur planches fondues' by a process which he called 'homotypie'. Neither of these attempts produced satisfactory results.

More important was the partnership between the inventor Louis-Etienne Herhan, the engraver Nicolas Gatteaux, and the printer Firmin Didot for the exploitation of three patents which they had registered separately, and which dealt with perfections in the process of stereotyping. All three published numerous stereotyped editions. Louis-Etienne Herhan (1768–1854) devised a new method of printing assignats, the paper money issued by the French revolutionary government, which it was hoped would foil the numerous counterfeiters. The method of stereotyping invented by Herhan differed radically from that used by previous experimenters, for it consisted in using copper matrices, carefully struck from punches and justified, which could be set in page form as with movable type. The page of matrices driven with force into molten type-metal gave a page in relief which could be printed from. This costly system was later abandoned, but not before it had produced a collection which rivalled for a time the stereotyped publications of Firmin Didot.

In 1844 J. M. Kronheim patented a method of making moulds for the casting of curved stereo plates in which he used alternate layers of paste and thin paper. Jean-Paptiste Genoux had experimented with a somewhat similar composition at Gap in 1808; details of this process have not been recorded, but his brother Claude, working at Lyons in 1829 made moulds of alternate layers of paper and clay.

In 1846 an Italian named Vanoni introduced into England moulds made of papier-mâché which were at that time in common use in France. At about the same time the brothers Dellagana came to England from Paris, where they had worked in the printing office of *Le Constitutionnel*, and set up a factory for making stereotype plates. James Dellagana became the most successful stereotyper of his time. In 1855 he perfected and patented a system for casting stereo plates type-high, but hollow inside, by making use of a core in the casting box. By 1863 the brothers had successfully made use of a curved casting box which enabled them to produce convex plates which could be fitted directly to the cylinder of a rotary press, thus enabling the full potentialities of this form of printing to be used for newspapers, where increased machine speed was of primary importance.

Later the Autoplate, invented by Henry Wise Wood of New York, saved both time and labour by eliminating the hot press and by forming from forty to fifty plates simultaneously.

LITHOGRAPHIC AND OFFSET PRINTING

The invention of the planographic method of printing known as lithography was due to a Bavarian named Aloys Senefelder. At first called simply 'Stein-druckerei' (Stone printing) or 'chemische Druckerei' (Chemical printing), it was when the new art was introduced into the Feiertagschule, Munich, in 1804, that the head of this school gave it the name of 'Lithographie'.

Senefelder, the son of an actor, was born at Prague on 6 November 1771. He began to study law at the University of Ingolstadt, but his father died in 1791, leaving Aloys without enough money to continue his studies at the university. He had to earn his living, and having failed both as actor and dramatic author, he sought other means of livelihood. He decided to try his luck as a printer. But he had not the money to buy the necessary materials; possibly if he had been able to do so he would have been an ordinary printer and not the inventor of lithography.

So he went his own way and had recourse to other methods, but with indifferent results, partly from want of skill, partly from lack of money. He tried etching his text on a copper plate, which entailed writing backwards, but as he said, 'the want of a sufficient number of copper plates, the tediousness of grinding and polishing those I had used, and the insufficiency of tin plates, which I tried as a substitute, soon put an end to my experiments in this way. It was at this period that my attention was accidentally directed to a fine piece of Kellheim stone, which I had purchased for the purpose of grinding my colours.' At first this stone attracted him merely as a more useful surface on which to practice his lettering, since the writing could easily be erased and the surface repolished.

By a process of trial and error which lasted several years Senefelder sought a satisfactory way of transferring lettering to the stone; the first step towards a solution came when he traced his letters in a greasy ink on to the stone and then etched the surface of the block with acid. The acid did not affect the letters for the greasy ink resisted its action; instead it ate away the surface of the stone, leaving the writing in relief. But although an impression could be taken from this relief surface, it was, after all, little different from ordinary letterpress printing, with the added difficulty that the text had to be drawn in reverse. It was not until 1798 that he stumbled across the final solution which turned this relief printing on stone into the planographic method which we now term lithography. The final stage in his quest he describes thus: 'I took a cleanly polished stone, inscribed it with a piece of soap, poured thin gum solution over it and passed over all a sponge dipped in oil colour. All the places marked with the fat became black at once, the rest remaining white. I could make as many impressions as I pleased; simply wetting the stone after each impression and treating it again with the sponge produced the same result each time. At this early period I could not guess that I was to invent a form of printing, a method which was based not on mechanical but purely chemical properties.' (Senefelder, 1819).

Lithography, therefore, is based on the power of certain kinds of minerals (such as the porous carboniferous limestone with which Senefelder experimented) to absorb fatty organic substances, and the antipathy of grease to water. The lettering, or design, drawn with a greasy pigment, is fixed in the pores of the stone by means of a slight acid bath. The stone is then damped and a roller charged with greasy printing ink is passed over it, whereupon the ink adheres to the design but is repelled by the remainder of the damp stone. If a sheet of paper is placed upon the stone and pressure exerted on it, a faithful reproduction of the design in reverse is secured.

Senefelder obtained the patent rights for his invention in Bavaria for fifteen years, and later went into partnership with a music-dealer from Offenbach named André. After a lithographic press had been established in that town, Senefelder patented his process in London in 1800 and Paris in 1801. In 1803 London saw the first book lithographed in England – a collection of prints by T. Stothard published under the title *Specimens of Polyautography*. One of the first major works to be produced wholly by lithography was a collection of drawings by Dürer redrawn on the stone by Johann Strixner, and published by Senefelder and Baron Aretin at Munich in 1808. Senefelder then wrote a manual of lithography in German,* which was translated into English and published in London by Rudolf Ackermann in 1819.

Before he died in 1834 Senefelder saw his invention develop into a flourishing branch of the printing industry in many European countries. But for many years after its introduction lithography was confined to hand presses and used

---

* *Vollständiges Lehrbuch der Steindruckerey.* Munich & Vienna, 1818.

chiefly as a means of illustration, particularly in France, where Delacroix, Daumier, Degas and Toulouse-Lautrec used the medium with great effect. In England lithography, though less popular than in France during the nineteenth century, found some excellent practitioners in Blake, Cotman, Prout, Whistler and others. Autolithography, as the process is sometimes termed, to distinguish it from photolithography, which came much later, has always made a special appeal to some artists because there is nothing to come between the artist's work on the stone and its immediate printing.

The best lithographic stone comes from German quarries located around Solenhofen. But stone is heavy, inconvenient to handle, and liable to fracture. Senefelder himself realised this fact and tried various other substances, but it was not until some time later that zinc was used in place of the cumbersome and fragile stone. The metal had to be grained to provide minute hollows which would retain the moisture necessary for the process.

The primitive press of Senefelder was replaced about the middle of the century by a mechanical press, which resembled in some ways the stop-cylinder press used for relief printing. The stone was placed on a horizontal bed in the same manner as the forme for letterpress printing, as this type of press was still used after zinc had emerged as a substitute for the weighty litho stone. In 1868 a two-cylinder machine was tried out by Marinoni in Paris, but the wear caused by a rotary machine of this sort outweighed its advantages. As a result direct lithography was for some decades little used except for illustrations.

The transition from the comparatively restricted field of direct lithography to the now widely used method of offset lithography was performed by interposing a third cylinder, clad in a rubber blanket, between the zinc plate and the impression cylinder. The paper is then pressed into contact with the impression on the rubber blanket and thus transferred, or 'offset' on to the paper. The precursor of the present-day 'offset' machine was invented and patented in France by Henri Voirin for printing on tin and metal plate by transfer on to a cylinder with a rubber overlay, and in 1884 Marinoni constructed a similar machine, called a 'Rotolitho', for printing on paper by this offset method. But he was ahead of his time and it was not until 1904 that Ira W. Rubel, a New York lithographer, commercially developed offset printing on paper. He designed a special press for the purpose which was built by the Potter Printing Press Co. of New York, and a similar type of machine was patented in England in 1906 and built by George Mann.

Zinc remained in use as the metal for litho work for many years, and in fact is still used. But aluminium has since come to the fore, especially in the form of anodised aluminium. The anodised layer used in lithography is extremely thin and is normally grained to provide a suitable surface.

The first commercial 'offset' machine to be used in Europe seems to have been built in 1906 by Maschinenfabrik Zweibrücken in Germany to the plans of Caspar Hermann, who was the first to patent (1908) a perfecting machine for offset litho, which made use of four cylinders, the paper passing between the two central cylinders, each of which was provided with an offset blanket.

One of the main advantages of lithography is the comparative simplicity of making an offset plate which, whether of zinc or aluminium, is thin enough to be curved around the press cylinder. After the press run, the plates can be stored for reprints. Size for size the cost of an offset plate is appreciably less than an equivalent letterpress engraving or gravure etching.

MECHANICAL TYPECASTING

As late as 1851 the hand mould was still being employed by founders, and the *Jury Reports* on the Great Exhibition of that year declared that 'since the invention of casting types by Peter Schöffer . . . this art has made little progress'. But another decade passed before the majority of founders were using typecasting machines.

The only improvement in the hand mould had been made in 1811 by a Scotsman named Archibald Binney, who patented in America a device consisting of a spring lever attached to the mould which gave a quicker release of the casting and increased the output from four to five hundred medium-sized castings an hour to around eight hundred.

One of the first typecasting machines was that invented by Dr William Church as part of his combined British patent of 1822 for a printing press, casting machine and composing machine. But the first really effective machine was that of David Bruce, of New York, who patented his invention in the U.S.A. in 1838. This was the forerunner of what are known as 'pivotal' casters, in which the mould is on the end of an arm which, by the action of a cam, is placed in the proper position to receive the molten type-metal, which is forced into the matrix by means of a pump. But the types still had to be dressed by hand after casting.

Britain lagged behind France and Germany in making use of machinery for casting, due, it is said to the reluctance of many founders, who feared trouble with their workmen if they introduced it. In 1823 Louis Jean Pouchée introduced a machine calculated to cast from 150 to 200 types at each operation, the operation being repeated twice or oftener in a minute. When Pouchée bought the patent rights for this machine, an invention of Henri Didot known as 'Polymatype', he could not market it in England owing to the opposition of certain type-founders, who bought one of the machines and destroyed it; a piece of vandalism reminiscent of the Luddites.

In 1828 Thomas Aspinwall patented an improved method of casting types by means of a 'Mechanical Type Caster'. None of these early machines were very successful, but in 1878 came Frederick Wick's rotary typecasting machine, patented in 1881, which in its later versions could cast and deliver 60,000 finished types per day. This was of great importance to *The Times*, by whom Wicks was employed, for it meant that when used in conjunction with the Kastenbein composing machine (p. 378) fresh type could be employed for the newspaper every day, and the labour of distribution was saved. It was eventually superseded by the Linotype, in which casting and composing were combined in a single machine, just as the 'Monotype' became the standard casting-composing machine for letterpress printing.

THE COMPOSING MACHINE

Setting type by hand is a slow process, however skilful the compositor, and although speed in setting is not inevitably vital for book and jobbing printing (though it often may be), for a newspaper it is of the utmost importance. Between 1816 and 1874 improvements to the newspaper printing press increased the speed of printing enormously. But as long as composing was done by hand these advantages could not be fully utilised. And so the search for a practical solution of the problem of speeding type-setting occupied the minds of inventors and produced a variety of devices during a large part of the nineteenth century.

The first known inventor of a type-composing machine was William Church of the Britannia Works, Birmingham, whose patent was dated 21 March 1822. Although he took out his patent in England (he lived for some time at Southwark, in London), he was a native of the United States. It was a triple patent for an improved printing-press, a casting machine, and a composing machine. The last named was a machine in which the type was stored in inclined grooves, each character being released by the operation of a keyboard and assembled in a continuous line. No provision was made for the justification of successive lines, which had to be carried out by a second operator. There is no evidence, however, that a machine to Church's patent was ever built.

The first practical composing machine, in principle similar to that proposed by Church, was designed by the engineer Sir Henry Bessemer in 1840, in conjunction with James Young and Adrien Delcambre, under whose names the patent was taken out. It was used to set the weekly magazine *The Family Herald*, raising the speed of composition to over 6,000 letters and spaces an hour – about six times the speed of the most skilful compositor. A description of the machine and an illustration is to be found in Bessemer's *Autobiography*.

The Family Herald was not, however, the first periodical to be set on this machine, which had earlier been used to compose *The London Phalanx*, an obscure monthly magazine. The first book to be mechanically set on the Young-Delcambre machine was Edward Binns, *The Anatomy of Sleep* (1841), which bore the imprint 'Printed by J. H. Young by the New Patent Composing Machine, 110 Chancery Lane'.*

As was to be expected, composing machines were bitterly attacked by the London compositors, who feared unemployment among their number as a result of the introduction of composing machines. It was opposed also because female, hence cheap, labour was employed on this machine, which nevertheless proved a failure in the long run and its use was abandoned. John Walter saw it at work, and the fact that he showed no interest in it was a sufficient condemnation of its effectiveness.

A much more effective composing machine was the one invented by Robert Hattersley in 1853 and patented in 1857 and 1859. It proved more successful than the Young-Delcambre machine, because its keyboard was more compact and the types were composed in a short line accessible to the compositor for justifying. It could set 7,500 letters an hour in the hands of a skilled operator and was used in a number of provincial newspaper offices. Some of these machines were still in use in 1914. The machine was later accompanied by the Hattersley justifying machine.

One great disadvantage of the early composing machines, in which the type was stacked in grooves, each containing supplies of one character, was that after the type was distributed it had to be once again set up in rows ready for insertion into the proper channels. This time-wasting process tended to minimise the advantage of having a composing machine.

Next came the Kastenbein typesetter of 1869, invented by Charles Kastenbein, which, although it made no radical departure from the principles embodied in its predecessors, had one advantage in that later models were provided with a distributing machine. This advantage, however, was to some extent discounted by the fact that the distributing machines supplied by the manufacturers were not altogether satisfactory and could only be worked economically by cheap juvenile labour, and this the London Society of Compositors would not countenance. Nevertheless the Kastenbein machine was used by *The Times* for many years. After 1880 it was combined with the Wicks typecasting machine, invented by Frederick Wicks about 1878. This machine was said to have been capable of casting 60,000 finished sorts in a day. Kastenbein was a Swiss living in Brussels, and a description of his machine appeared in the *Printers' Register* for March 1876.

The Thorne type-setting and distributing machine, worked on the rotary system, was patented by J. Thorne in the United States in 1887 and in Britain in 1888. This machine had two vertical grooved cylinders, placed one above the other, the lower one being the magazine and the upper one a receptacle

---

* Delcambre, who had an office in Paris, sold his machines in France, where one was used in 1855 to print *Paris chez soi*.

for used type ready for distribution. Each letter and space was distinguished by a particular combination of nicks on the rear edge, and the grooves in the lower cylinder were provided with wards corresponding with the nicks on the type allotted to that particular groove. When in use the upper cylinder revolved step by step, and as each type reached the groove with wards corresponding to the nicks, it was automatically dropped into its proper place in the magazine. The *Manchester Guardian* was one of the newspapers which used the Thorne machine. J. Southward praises the machine highly in his *Type-Composing Machines* (1891), though confessing that composing machines had, on the whole, proved a failure. Up to that time the increased speed of composing compared with hand-setting was not sufficiently great to compensate for the initial cost and the frequent breakdowns of the intricate mechanism.

THE LINOTYPE

In fact, mechanisation of type-setting was not satisfactorily solved until 1886, by which time Ottmar Mergenthaler had developed the Linotype, which composed lines of type in the form of slugs. It was an ingenious invention, for all the operations of casting, composing, justifying, and eventually distributing, were combined in one machine. Depression of a key on the keyboard releases from a magazine above a brass matrix corresponding to the character selected, which is carried by a travelling belt to an assembler box. After each word a spaceband, consisting of two opposing wedges is released. When there are sufficient matrices in the box to make a line they are conveyed to the face of the mould, where the wedge-shaped spacebands are forced upwards until the spacing is increased sufficiently to fill out the line to the required measure. Once justified, the line of matrices moves along until it forms the front of a horizontal mould, and there molten metal is pumped against and into the matrices, forming as it cools a solid line or 'slug' of metal with the letters in relief along one edge. The slug is automatically trimmed to the correct size and ejected from the mould on to a receiving galley, while the matrices are conveyed to the top of the magazine and distributed, to be used again.

One essential element in the success of Mergenthaler's invention was not his own, for the double-wedge spaceband used for justification had been patented by J. W. Schuckers of Philadelphia, and it cost nearly half a million dollars to secure the rights. Much of the success of the Linotype lay in the solving of the problem of distribution, for this was completely avoided by the remelting of the slugs after the forme had been printed. The first London newspaper to adopt the Linotype (first used by the *New York Tribune* in 1886) was the *Globe* in 1892, to be followed shortly afterwards by the *Financial News*. By 1895 at least 250 machines were in use by provincial papers, as against 32 Hattersleys and 14 Thornes.

FIGURE 81. A twentieth-century Linotype machine.

The first book composed on a Linotype, *The Tribune Book of Open Air Sports*, was published in New York in 1887. It bore the notice: 'This book is printed without type, being the first product in book form of the Mergenthaler machine which wholly supersedes the use of movable type.'

In that same year, 1887, Tolbert Lanston demonstrated the prototype of his 'Monotype' composing machine. Tolbert Lanston of Ohio was a man with no mechanical training but possessed of an enquiring and inventive mind. The punched card system used in the Hollerith tabulator interested him, and he considered it possible that the principle might be embodied in a composing machine. The idea had been foreshadowed by Alexander Mackie who in 1867 had invented a composing machine which was used in the printing office of the *Warrington Guardian*. He anticipated Lanston in being the first to use a perforated ribbon to actuate his machine.

Lanston's prototype proved a failure, and it was not until 1897 that the first successful 'Monotype' machine was built. In that same year a syndicate bought the British rights for £220,000, and from then on the development of the 'Monotype' keyboard and caster was in the hands of two independent companies – the Lanston Monotype Machine Company in the United States, and in England the Monotype Corporation Ltd.

The machine, now an indispensable adjunct to every important letterpress printing firm, is divided into two main components: a keyboard and a caster, the former punching a ribbon with perforations which control the caster by passing over air vents. Stop-pins rise by the action of compressed air as the perforations for a particular letter pass over the vents, and stops the matrix case at the required position over the mould for just that fraction of time necessary for the selected character to be cast from the molten metal and ejected.

The machines mentioned above were the most successful, but there was no lack of inventors who hopefully brought out composing machines which were unable to make the grade. To name but a few there was Benjamin Foster of London in 1815; Ballanches at Lyons in 1835; Bidet's 'Compositeur Typographe' made its appearance in 1837; Napoléon Chaix produced a machine in 1844; the following year Gaubert demonstrated a 'Gérautype'; Lefas' 'Pianotype' came out in 1850, a year after Leblond had invented the 'Balistotype'. In 1855 there appeared the 'Composeuse', and in 1863 the 'Compositeur typographe mécanique'.

The Russian Petr Pavlovich Kniaghininsky preceded Mackie by a few months in patenting (24 August 1867) a perforated tape system, of which a prototype was built and exhibited at St Petersburg in 1870, but the inventor failed to obtain financial backing and died soon afterwards. In 1885 Ernesto Codignola invented his 'Compofonditrice', while in 1899 another Italian named Lamonica produced his 'Elettrostenotipo'.

These are only a few of the attempts made to mechanise composition during the nineteenth century, and most of them became monuments to misdirected zeal. Only the Linotype and the 'Monotype' are still with us today, although the machines of Kastenbein and Hattersley had a long run.

PHOTOGRAVURE

Photogravure is a photo-mechanical method of etching a plate or cylinder in intaglio – a modern adaptation of a very old process, as exemplified in the copper-plate engraving, in which by means of a tool or with acid the image to be reproduced is hollowed out in the surface of the metal plate. The plate was inked, the surface was wiped, and the ink remained localised in the recesses.

This method of illustration could only produce a limited number of reproductions, for not only was the inking and wiping, which had to be recommenced for each new sheet of paper, a matter of skill, but the copper plate had a relatively short life owing to the pressure which had to be applied to it.

About the middle of the eighteenth century certain industrialists conceived the idea of using the technique of copper engraving for printing designs on fabric, which was already being manufactured in continuous lengths wound onto bobbins, whereas paper was still being made in single sheets. The woven material was drawn over a copper cylinder on which had been engraved by hand with the artist's designs. The recesses were filled with pigment by a roller, the excess being removed by a scraper.

As soon as paper became available in the reel, a Frenchman named Auguste Godchaux, who had worked for many years at the plant which wove the famous 'toiles de Jouy', turned his experience to account by inventing a machine on similar principles for printing covers to school exercise books. His machine, constructed in 1860, was still functioning in Paris some eighty years later.

However, engraving a cylinder by hand would be a long and costly operation and for anything less simple than a school book cover would be most uneconomical. Trials were made with plates engraved or etched in the traditional manner and curved to fix on a cylindrical support, but the results were not encouraging.

The first break-through came about in 1864 when the Englishman, J. W. Swan, made use of carbon tissue, a sensitised paper upon which a photographic image can be printed and by means of which the copper can be etched. The process stemmed from developments which were being made in photography, and for this reason rotary intaglio printing is referred to as photogravure.

The first really practical developments in this process were made by the Czech Karl Klić (1841–1926) around 1879, although it was not until 1895 that he made his first successful prints. He was assisted in his work by Samuel Fawcett, who had himself been pursuing the same line of research, and the perfected process was marketed by the Rembrandt Intaglio Printing Company, although for some years it was limited to the production of prints.

About 1910 a German, Dr Mertens, applied the process to the printing of newspapers, and the *Freiburger Zeitung* became the first newspaper to be illustrated throughout in photogravure printed on normal newsprint. This achievement was carried out on a rotary press built by the Mulhouse firm Société Alsacienne de Constructions Mécaniques. In Britain one weekly newspaper, the *Southend Standard*, adopted the process shortly afterwards.

Today an enormous number of cheap illustrated periodicals are printed in photogravure. At first printing was from a flat plate, but nowadays it is mainly carried out on reel-fed rotary presses, for by and large sheet-fed gravure has almost disappeared. Colour gravure was attempted in the early days of the Rembrandt Co., but the expense at that time proved prohibitive. The idea was later revived by F. Thevoz and J. Frey in Geneva, but the First World War temporarily ended their researches; however, in 1923 work was resumed and good results obtained.

With the development of modern panchromatic emulsions and improvements in web printing colour-gravure has become a commonplace. Today colour work can be printed on multiple-unit rotaries for the former technical difficulties of ensuring correct registration have been largely overcome by the use of electronic devices.

In addition to its widespread use for the mass production of colour magazines, photogravure is employed for the printing of postage stamps and packaging: in fact for any work where identical copies of a design are required in very large numbers. Because of the complicated procedures which go to make the printing cylinder, gravure is economically unsuitable for short runs. On the other hand, for runs from 100,000 upwards it can work out cheaper than other printing processes. The time needed for cylinder production has been somewhat curtailed of recent years by the use of electronic engraving machines. At all events, for photogravure it's a case of the longer the run the better.

30

Nineteenth Century Printing in Europe

ON 28 May 1796, Ernst Kircher, printer to the City Council of Goslar, sought permission to set up a type foundry. His request was granted, when suddenly Kircher abandoned his plan of starting a foundry, and ceded his privilege to Justus Erich Walbaum. It was probably a prearranged affair.

The son of a clergyman, Walbaum was apprenticed to a grocer and confectioner at Brunswick, and there served out his time. But in the meantime he had discovered his own talents as an engraver and decided that life as a shop-assistant held but poor prospects in comparison with the art of engraving; instead he began a new career by engraving music plates for the firm of Spehr. In this he was completely self-taught for previously he had known nothing about music. Johann Peter Spehr owned a flourishing music printing and publishing firm in Brunswick, which was carried on by his widow after Spehr's death in 1825.

On 18 July 1796, the city fathers agreed to the transfer to Walbaum of Kircher's privilege, and the former started on his successful career as a type-founder. But he did not remain long in Goslar, which was too small a town for a man of his ambition. In 1803, with the permission of the Duke of Saxe-Weimar and Eisenach, he moved to Weimar, which, if not a great city in size, had become the intellectual centre of Germany.

Walbaum's foundry in Weimar became one of the most famous in Germany. In 1836, saddened by the death of his only son Theodore, who had taken over the management of the firm in 1828, Justus Walbaum sold the business to F. A. Brockhaus, the Leipzig printer and publisher, and the foundry was removed to Leipzig. Walbaum did not long survive his son, and died in Weimar on 21 June 1837. In 1918 the foundry was acquired by the firm of H. Berthold, in whose possession remain the original punches and matrices of J. E. Walbaum. Walbaum is not mentioned in Updike, but Walbaum's types have recently come back into favour and his *Antiqua*, which has been described as 'the most *human* of the neo-classic faces', was recut in 1959 for machine composition by the Monotype Corporation.

In 1796, the same year that Walbaum had started his career as a type founder, Karl Christoph Traugott Tauchnitz (1761–1836) bought a small printing office in Leipzig and founded the famous firm which still bears his name. During the decades which followed it grew into one of Germany's largest businesses. In 1798 he added a bookselling and publishing house and in 1800 added a type foundry.

Around 1816 he was bringing out excellent cheap editions of the Greek and Latin classics by means of the stereotype process, which he was the first to use in Germany. He also had cut for him Hebrew and Arabic founts which he used for his publications, among which was an edition of the Koran, as well as Bibles. His son Karl Christian Philipp Tauchnitz disposed of the publishing side of the business after a few years, and in 1854, sold printing office and foundry to Friedrich Metzger, who in 1868 made over the foundry to W. E. Drugulin. In 1841 another son, Christian Bernhard Tauchnitz founded his own publishing firm at Leipzig, which became renowned for its 'Collection of British and American Authors'. He was accorded many distinctions and was eventually ennobled as Freiherr.

Another well-known Leipzig printer of this period was Benediktus Gotthelf Teubner (1784–1856) who in 1806 took over a small printing office in which he worked for a time on his own, as compositor, pressman and corrector. With great industry he built up his business until it became one of the best-known printing houses, to which he later added a foundry and stereotyping plant. In 1840, as part of the Gutenberg celebrations he issued Karl Falkenstein, *Geschichte der Buchdruckerkunst*, a very handsome book. He also printed philologic and mathematical works as well as Greek and Latin classics. After his death the business was carried on by his sons-in-law A. Rossbach and Albin Ackermann who retained the name of Teubner.

The name of Brockhaus is associated in most minds with that celebrated publication the *Konversationslexicon*, one of the most successful of European encyclopaedic dictionaries – a German equivalent of the French *Larousse*. Friedrich Arnold Brockhaus, a native of Dortmund (1772–1823), was in 1805 part proprietor of a bookselling business in Amsterdam, but left that city for Altenburg in 1811, and in 1817 went to Leipzig. There, since he had not learned printing under the supervision of the Guild, he had to conduct his printing-office under the firm of Teubner. He made very much his own the *Konversariionslexicon*, which had been begun in 1796 by Dr Löbel in Leipzig. He completed it and with his edition of 1812 placed it on its way to become an essential educational work, since when it has gone into innumerable editions, both large and small.

Upon the death of Friedrich Brockhaus the business was carried on by his sons Friedrich and Heinrich, the former of whom – printer, publisher and type founder – greatly developed the firm. He had learned the trade with Vieweg in Brunswick and later had worked in Paris under Crapelet. He introduced the iron press, in 1833 he built a stereotyping plant, and in 1836 he purchased the famous Walbaum foundry. After Friedrich's retirement in 1850, Heinrich Brockhaus managed the firm, at first on his own, and later with his sons Eduard and Rudolf.

In Brunswick one of the most flourishing bookselling businesses was that of Vieweg, founded by Hans Friedrich Vieweg (1761–1835), a native of Halle who settled in Brunswick in 1801. His son Eduard greatly enlarged the scope of the business, adding to the printing-house a type foundry and stereotyping plant. The firm became noted for the publication of books on natural history, and after the death of Eduard in 1869 was continued by his son Heinrich.

Johann Christian Bauer (1802–67), the founder of the well-known Bauersche Giesserei at Frankfurt-am-Main, worked for a time at the Edinburgh branch of the Wilson Foundry, and for a while had his own foundry in that city, under the style of Bauer, Ferguson and Hill – later, on Bauer's return to Germany, Ferguson Brothers. On his return to Germany this native of Hanau set himself to improve on the available founts of Fraktur, and during the course of his career he brought out a number of new types, including Russian. At the time of his death he left some 10,000 punches which he himself had cut, and it was from his workshop and materials that the famous Bauersche Giesserei developed. At about the same time as Bauer started up in Germany, another well-known foundry came into being – that of Dresler and Rost-Fingerlin at Frankfurt-am-Main. This was the old Schleussnersche foundry started by the punch-cutter F. W. Schröter in 1757 and which in 1827 was carried on under the style of Firma F. Dresler & Rost-Fingerlin. In 1859 this foundry was acquired by Heinrich Friedrich Gottlob Flinsch and under the direction of Ferdinand Flinsch grew into one of the largest type-foundries in Europe. In 1916 it was bought by the Bauer foundry at Frankfurt-am-Main with which it was merged.

A significant name in German printing of the nineteenth century is that of Baedeker, of guide-book fame. It was in 1828 that Karl Baedeker (1801–59) bought from the Coblenz firm of Fr. Röhling their *Reisehandbuch für den Rhein* for his own publishing business and with it inaugurated the famous series of guide books which bear his name.

The history of the machine press was continued in 1840 by the foundation of two firms of printing machine constructors by nephews of Frederic König. One was the firm started by Frederic Helbig (partnered by Leo Müller) at Mödling, near Vienna; the other was that of Louis Sander at Augsburg, that city where printing had flourished since 1468. This latter firm was taken over, four years later, by Charles Reichenbach and Charles Buz, and eventually became the present M.A.N. (Maschinenfabrik Augsburg-Nürnberg).

The nineteenth century in Germany saw the founding and subsequent expansion of many famous printing houses. For instance in 1847 Franz Otto Spamer

(1829–86) founded a publishing firm in Leipzig. As a development of the existing business came the Spamer Bindery in 1868 and the Spamersche Buchdruckerei in 1877. By 1898 it had become one of the most important printing businesses in Germany, and was formed into a limited liability company run by members of the family in 1933.

Wilhelm Drugulin (1822–79) was a printer who learned his craft with the firm of Nies at Leipzig and then turned to art publishing. In 1869 he purchased the old printing house of Nies, and acquired material of the Tauchnitz foundry including some of the exotic founts. His son-in-law Johannes Baensch-Drugulin won for the firm a considerable reputation for its printing in oriental languages, adding a vast number of new founts to the firm's repertory. His greatest achievement in this line was the publication in 1902, to mark the 500th anniversary of the birth of Gutenberg, of *Marksteine aus der Weltlitteratur in Originalschriften*, a large folio decorated by L. Sütterlin and containing text in thirty-four different languages. In 1919 the foundry passed to Stempel A.G. in Frankfurt but the printing house came in 1930, after a merger with the Druckerei Haag in 1928, as the Offizin Haag-Drugulin, into the possession of the firm of Koehler & Volckmar.

Oscar Brandstetter (1846–1915), son of Friedrich Brandstetter founder of the Leipzig publishing firm of that name, acquired in 1880 the Garbrecht printing house founded in 1862. In conjunction with Otto Säublicher, Brandstetter introduced many technical innovations.

GREAT BRITAIN

As we have seen, the eighteenth century had been a good period for printing in Britain, especially the second half. And the three outstanding printers of the end of the century, Bulmer, Bensley and Charles Whittingham the Elder, continued to produce impeccably printed books during the opening decades of the new century.

But with the appearance of the steam press and the replacement of monied collectors of expensive quartos and folios by a new industrialised society eager to buy educational works at a price within their less than modest means, quality was rapidly submerged by quantity and standards of printing went by the board. There were, of course, individual printers, as we shall see, who did not find machine methods incompatible with good printing, but obsessed with the profits to be made from the rapid multiplication of books through the new medium of the steam press, many printers let good printing go hang.

Yet when all is said and done the man whom Samuel Smiles called 'the greatest multiplier of books in his day', William Clowes, never descended to slipshod work while building up one of the most extensive printing establishments in the country. Clowes, born at Chichester on 1 January 1779, was apprenticed to

FIGURE 82. An illustration from *Pine's Costumes*, published by William Miller in 1805. It depicts a fire brigade of the period, when the fire-fighting services were provided by the assurance companies.

a printer of that town named Joseph Seagrave, the printer of William Hayley's *Life of Cowper*, with engravings by Blake. His apprenticeship over, Clowes went to London and worked for a time as compositor with the printer Henry Teape. But being ambitious he managed with the help of friends and what money he had been able to save, to set up as a master printer on his own. Towards the end of 1803 he started printing in Villiers Street, Strand, with the help of one assistant, a man named Pardoe, and his stock of type was so small that at first he was compelled to work at night to print off what he had set so that the type could be distributed ready for the next day's work. But Clowes was industrious and he had come into the printing trade at a time when it was expanding rapidly. He was also a forward-looking man and since power print-ing had begun to replace the old hand press Clowes installed the newly patented perfecting machine of Applegath and Cowper, becoming, by so doing, the first book printer to make regular use of the steam press.

In 1825 he moved to Duke Street, Blackfriars and there his business grew rapidly, for his move into more extensive premises coincided with the remark-able growth in public demand for works of popular information. In the course of a few years Clowes had installed no fewer than twenty Applegath and Cow-per machines and was busy printing the numerous publications of the Society for the Diffusion of Useful Knowledge, which included the *Penny Magazine*, edited by Charles Knight (which had a circulation of 200,000) and the *Penny Cyclopaedia*.

By 1839 Clowes was casting his own types at a time when type-founding was still considered as a separate trade, and he also made use of stereotyping on a large scale. When he died in 1847 he was the owner of an establishment which, for the period, was gigantic indeed, and he left behind him a firm which, as William Clowes and Sons Ltd., is still one of the largest in the country.

Another interesting figure appeared on the printing scene at the beginning of the century in the person of William Savage (1770–1843) who arrived in Lon-don from Yorkshire in 1797 and about two years later was appointed printer to the Royal Institution. He was particularly interested in the problems of colour printing, then in its infancy, and demonstrated his theories on the use of coloured inks in his *Practical Hints on Decorative Printing*, completed in 1823, and in his *Preparations in Printing Ink in Various Colours*, 1832. Savage's work had no immediate influence and no further attempts were made to develop his process until George Baxter (1804–67) turned his attention to it. Basically his method did not differ greatly from that of Savage, except for the use of metal key plates in addition to wood blocks, and the use of oil colours in place of Savage's ink, which had no oil in its constituents.

Baxter called his process Polychromatic printing, and Robert Mudie, in the preface to his *The Feathered Tribes of the British Islands* (2 vols. 1834), the plates of which were by Baxter, says:

'By this method every shade of colour, every breadth of tint, every deli-cacy of hatching, and every degree of evanescence in the outline can be obtained. . . . In carrying this very beautiful branch of the typographic art successfully into effect, Baxter has, I believe, completed what was the last project of the great Bewick, but which that truly original and admirable genius did not live to accomplish.'

In 1837 Chapman & Hall published *Pictorial Album, or Cabinet of Paintings* with eleven colour reproductions of paintings printed by Baxter, and in 1842 came Sir Harris Nicolas, *History of the Orders of Knighthood of the British Empire*,

Elizabeth Regina.

2 PARALIPOM. 6.

¶ *Domine Deus Iſrael, non eſt ſimilis tui Deus in cælo & in terra, qui cuſtodis paĉtum & miſericordiam cum ſeruis tuis, qui ambulant coram te in toto corde ſuo.*

FIGURE 83. Frontispiece to *The Book of Common Prayer* printed by Charles Wittingham, and published in 1853 by William Pickering. The illustrations are based on those in *A Booke of Christian Prayers* first printed by John Day in 1569.

in four volumes, published by William Pickering and printed by Charles Whittingham with twenty-one plates in colour by Baxter as well as a magnificent double-spread title-page in colour.

Charles Knight (1791–1873) patented in 1838 a process of colour printing which he termed 'Patent Illuminated Printing', by which a colour print could be made from wood or metal blocks in any number of colours from four to sixteen by means of a press fitted with a revolving polygonal frame to which the blocks were fitted, each one being brought into position as required. The process was used in two popular educational works: *Old England*, published in ninety-six parts, 1844–45, and *Old England's Worthies*, 1847. These were the first books with colour plates meant to cater for the popular market, and the result, as far as the colour plates were concerned, was highly successful. But possibly the method proved uneconomic, for Knight made no further use of colour in his succeeding publications.

For a century and a half the name of the Chiswick Press stood for good printing and book design. The imprint was first used by its founder, Charles Whittingham the Elder (1767–1840) who in 1809 left his London press in the hands of his partner Robert Rowland and went to live at Chiswick, where he set up a press at High House, and there continued to work until his death in 1840, when the business passed into the hands of his nephew, Charles Whittingham the Younger, who had started his own printing office in 1828 at 21 Took's Court, off Chancery Lane. From 1840 he carried on both businesses until 1848.

His style of printing appealed to the publisher William Pickering (1796–1854) for whom he printed many works. In 1843 Pickering commissioned Whittingham to print for him a *Juvenal* to be given as a prize at Eton. The latter asked the type-founding firm of Caslon to cast from the matrices of their predecessor William Caslon I, a small fount of roman in Great Primer body. This led in 1844 to the use of a smaller size of the same letter for George Herbert's *The Temple*, printed for Pickering, and *The Diary of Lady Willoughby* (anon., but by Mrs Richard Rathbone) for Longmans; though which was the earlier is still a matter of conjecture. The *Diary* met with such success that it was several times reprinted, and as a result the Edinburgh founders Miller & Richard cut a series of punches in a somewhat similar style, which were named 'Old Style' and were at once widely copied.

In 1853 the Chiswick Press printed for Pickering a *Book of Common Prayer* with woodcuts based on those in the so-called 'Queen Elizabeth's Prayer Book' printed by John Day in 1569. The hundred-odd blocks for the Pickering edition were cut by Mary Byfield, who worked nearly all her life for the Chiswick Press, and they harmonise perfectly with the Caslon type in which the book is set.

'The world of printing, after the Whittingham-Pickering period,' wrote the authors of *A Survey of Printing*, 'passed into something worse than the meanness and squalor of the late seventeenth and eighteenth centuries'; but that stricture never applied to the Chiswick Press at any time in its history.

BULGARIA

Less than 150 years ago it was forbidden in Bulgaria to read, much less to print a book in the vernacular, under penalty of death. Such was the decree of the Turkish overlords. As we have seen, books in Cyrillic characters had been printed during the sixteenth century at various places, some in Venice others at Cetinje, Targowitce, Belgrade and elsewhere. But most of these were service books printed in a mixture of Slavonic tongues. Many have now disappeared; even the *Abagar* of Stanislavov, which was printed at Rome in 1651 and must have been in the Bulgarian tongue, together with the Venice-printed *Life of the holy Dyonisius* by Nikola Glika, are no longer extant.

It was not until 1828 that the first Bulgarian press came into existence. It was, as it had to be, a clandestine press, set up secretly in a cellar at Samokov by Nikola Karastojanov. He had bought an old hand-press in Belgrade and transported it to its destination by ox wagon. On this press he at first printed woodcuts of scriptural subjects, which he obtained from Serbia, and later, having bought secretly from Budapest 150 Oka characters, printed his first prayer books.

It is difficult today to realise that the very existence of a Bulgarian race was almost unknown at the beginning of the nineteenth century. For more than four centuries since the last vestige of Bulgarian independence vanished with the fall of Vidin in 1396 the country was subjected to the harsh rule of the Turkish invaders. Neither the Turks nor the Greek Church would allow the establishment of a Bulgarian press, and although books in Bulgarian came into the country, they were all printed abroad, mostly by the University Press at Budapest.

But the time came, at the beginning of the nineteenth century, when the Bulgarians were allowed to maintain their own schools, and now and again religious services were held in the Bulgarian tongue, so that the need for printed service books necessitated the establishment sooner or later of a Bulgarian press. When the first Bulgarian High School was founded at Gabrowo in 1835 permission was sought for the establishment of a printing office, but repeated requests to the authorities remained unanswered. Despite all efforts the fulfilment of this project was made more difficult not only through the intransigence of the Turks, but also the difficulty in obtaining type suitable for printing in a language which lacked a uniform orthography at that time.

We have seen how the daring of Karastojanov sought to apply some remedy to this situation. In order not to betray his secret activities he pretended that the books he printed came from Serbian and Hungarian presses. At length, in 1847, after many petitions, permission was finally granted to print books for churches and schools. At last Karastojanov's press could emerge into the light of day, and the first book he printed in freedom was a Prayer Book decorated with initials by his son Athanas, a gifted woodcutter, engraver and printer, who was himself the author of a book on the art of printing. Later he brought out a number of church service books and what is perhaps his best effort, a Life of Saint George.

The successful development of their press encouraged father and son to acquire further material for their printing house, and in 1862 Athanas went to Belgrade for this purpose. A popular uprising took place during the course of which his newly acquired goods were stolen, and he had to remain in Belgrade. This was a great blow to his father, but in 1866 his youngest sons, Sotir and Dimiter, whom their father had trained, took over the business. Karastojanov died in September 1874 at the age of ninety-six, after an indefatigable career as Bulgaria's first printer.

GREENLAND

In 1793 appeared the first book printed in Greenland – *Tuksiautit Akioreeksautikset* (*lit.* 'Songs for several persons'). This book of choral songs was the work of an amateur printer, a missionary named Jesper Brodersen, who, after studying theology at Copenhagen, was sent in 1786 to Neu Herrnhut, near Godthaab in Greenland. A unique copy of this book is now in the Royal Library at Copenhagen. No further printing seems to have taken place in Greenland until 1855.

Towards the end of that year a few small publications were printed in Godthaab, the first of which, a small handbill of news items, was dated 21 October 1855. These small Godthaab pamphlets, four in all, were printed by a Greenlander, Rasmus Berthelsen, under the direction of Hinrich Rink, a government administrator who had discovered the material belonging to Brodersen's press. He later obtained a small grant from the Danish authorities and bought from a Copenhagen printer a small printing press as well as a lithographic press. These he took with him to Greenland in 1857 and started a Greenlandic printing office at Godthaab, which began to produce the first real printed publications in Greenland.

The first substantial work to come from Rink's press was a book about the travels of a Greenlander, Pok, who visited Denmark with his friend Qiperoq. It was printed at Rink's press (known as the Inspector's Press) by Rasmus Berthelsen and his assistant, Lars Møller in 1857.

Rink, who had always wanted to print a newspaper for the Greenlanders, began publication on 1 January 1861, of *Atuagagdliutit*, which was at first published irregularly, some forty-five numbers appearing between 1861 and 1865. It was not until 1874 that regular monthly issues began to be printed. From that year onwards the periodical was edited by Lars Møller (known as Arqaluk) who only retired in 1922, after he had reached the age of eighty.

At about the same time as Rink's press was established at Godthaab, another press began to work at nearby Neu Herrnhut. It was run by a gifted missionary

393

KALADLIT ASSILIALIAIT

GRØNLANDSKE TRÆSNIT.

KIRKEN, SEMINARIET OG INSPEKTEURBOLIGEN
VED KOLONIEN GODTHAAB.

GODTHAAB.

TRYKT I INSPEKTORATETS BOGTRYKKERI AF L: MØLLER
OG R: BERTHELSEN.
1860.

FIGURE 84. Title page of *Greenland Woodcuts*, published by Hinrich Rink in 1860.

named Samuel Kleinschmidt, to whom the press was sent by the community of Zeist in Holland. Kleinschmidt's press produced its first book *nunalerutit* (a geography) in 1858, and heralded a long series of books all written, set and printed by Kleinschmidt himself, who may be said to have created the written Greenlandic language, which up to then had no hard and fast rules for spelling.

In 1859 he left the Moravian Mission and entered the Danish educational service, becoming a teacher at the Danish seminary in Godthaab. In 1861 he printed a little book on the Augsburg Confession, and gave his press the title of the Missionaries' Press to distinguish it from the Inspector's Press of Rink. Among the works he printed was a history of the missionary movement, the first edition of which was published in 1867 and a second enlarged edition in 1877. This book contained a large folding map of the world which was not printed or lithographed, but hand drawn and coloured by Kleinschmidt himself, and since both editions were of 800 copies, this meant that the author had himself, incredible as it may seem, produced 1,600 copies of the map by hand.

FRANCE

From a typographical point of view the nineteenth century in France might well be termed the century of the Didots, a dynasty of printers, punch-cutters, founders, and publishers, which dominated the book world of France for many decades. The founder of this celebrated family was François Didot (1689–1757), who set up as a bookseller in Paris at the sign of the *Bible d'Or* in 1713, having been received that year as a member of the *corporation des libraires*. He is said to have been licensed as a printer late in life: in 1754 according to Lottin.

François Didot had himself been apprenticed to André Pralard, printer and bookseller, in 1669, and was the son-in-law of the bookseller Sébastien Revenel. Two noted booksellers, Guillaume de Bure and Jacques Barrois, became his sons-in-law, whilst his aunt Françoise Didot had married a bookseller, Jean-Nicolas Nyon.

François Didot's eldest son, François-Ambroise (1730–1804), the first to bring the family name into European repute, was admitted bookseller in 1753 and printer in 1757.

It was about the year 1775 when François-Ambroise Didot turned his attention to cutting new types. For the books he had published he had hitherto made use mainly of Garamond types. His edition of Louis Dutens, *Des pierres précieuses et des pierres fines*, set in Garamond, and published in conjunction with De Bure aîné, 1776, had been highly praised but it did not entirely satisfy him. He had, he said, tried to produce a handsome book, but had only succeeded in printing a rather pretty one.

About 1777, in an endeavour to improve his press work he constructed a new single-pull press, on which in November of that year he began to print Longus, *Daphnis et Chloe*, which was published in 1778. Meanwhile his younger brother Pierre-François Didot (1732–95) acquired a printing office in 1777, becoming printer to the Comte de Provence (the future Louis XVIII). The two brothers soon started their own foundries, and Pierre-François, in addition to printing in 1789 took over the important paper-mill at Essonnes, which contributed as much to the renown of the family as did the typographic prowess of its other members.

François-Ambroise set up his foundry in his own house at Paris in the rue Pavée Saint-André-des-Arcs, and employed a punch-cutter who worked under his direction – one Pierre-Louis Wafflard, of Flemish origin, who had been a pupil of Joseph Gillé.* A. F. Johnson states that 'there seems to be no record of any actual type cut by him, and possibly this man has been given too much prominence in the history of the Didot types' (Johnson, 1932). Nevertheless Wafflard is known to have lodged in Didot's house and lived there until 1785 as a salaried workman.

In December 1781, F. A. Didot received from the paper-mill at Annonay the first batch of wove paper. This was the first use in France of wove paper, modelled on that used by Baskerville in England. Upon it, and with the first series of types in which he had collaborated with Wafflard, F. A. Didot printed a *Conte allégorique* of the Marquise de Montesson; followed a few months later by an extract from *Poème des jardins*, by the Abbé de Lille, which he described as *Epreuve d'un nouveau caractère de Didot l'Aîné sur un essai de papier vélin de France de la fabrique de Matthieu Johannot d'Annonay.*

With this fount, which shows some relationship with the types of Grandjean, Didot printed in 1782 a magnificent two-volume limited edition of the *Peintures antiques de Bartoli* for the Paris booksellers Molini and Lamy.

The fount of Petit-Parangon, with which this book had been printed was succeeded by a Gros-Romain, also due to the collaboration of Wafflard and Didot, which showed an evolution in the direction of a more modern style. As a specimen, Didot reprinted an Edict of Louis XVI.

In 1783 Didot was violently attacked in an anonymous letter which appeared in the *Courrier de l'Europe*, and in which the new types were savagely criticised. The writer, who hid his identity under the pseudonym of 'Un Amateur', was in reality, Etienne Anisson-Duperron, the director of the Imprimerie Royale, and for many years an embittered rival of François-Ambroise Didot. Didot's reply was to bring out a splendid edition of Corneille which, said *L'Année littéraire*, 'reduced his enemies to silence'. It did not, for the controversy continued for some time.

It was with François-Ambroise that Franklin placed his grandson, Benjamin Franklin Bache in 1785, so that he might learn something of punch-cutting and type founding, for he looked upon François-Ambroise as the greatest printer of his time. Another pupil of Didot's was the punch-cutter Vibert, who later worked for his son Pierre.

One of François-Ambroise's ambitions was to produce a series of French and Latin classics unsurpassed by any European printer and to this end he secured the patronage of Louis XVI and issued these works with the imprint: 'Imprimé par ordre du Roi pour l'éducation de Monseigneur le Dauphin.' And almost at the same time Monsieur, the king's brother, who wanted to have a fine edition of Tasso's *Gerusalemme liberata*, with illustrations by Cochin and Tilliard, confided the printing of it to Didot l'aîné.

* Gillé's specimens describe him as 'Graveur et Fondeur du Roi'.

FIGURE 85. From the chromo-lithograph frontispiece to *The History of Printing*, published by the S.P.C.K. The artist was William Dickes (1815–92) a well-known engraver and colour printer of Victorian books.

The first volume of the quarto classics appeared in 1783. The work chosen to inaugurate the series was *Les Aventures de Télémaque* by Fénélon, set in Didot's *gros romain* and printed, in a limited edition of 200 copies, on Matthieu Johannot's wove paper. It was followed shortly afterwards by a three-volume edition of Racine.

When in 1784 the two volumes of *La Gerusalemme liberata* came from the press it introduced Didot's new *gros romain*, in which the thin flat serifs and the vertical stress of the letters make of this fount what is generally accepted as the first modern face. The titling capitals for this work were cut by Firmin, the young son, then aged twenty, of François-Ambroise, who cut four sizes of capitals under the supervision of Wafflard.

But the old names for type sizes, the *gros romain*, *cicero*, *parangon*, and the rest, which had been in use since the early days of printing were soon to disappear in France, for in 1784 François-Ambroise Didot (who for a time was director of the Imprimerie Nationale), revised the point system of Fournier le Jeune, and related it to the legal standard of measurement then in force, the *pied du roi*, and established an authoritative point system, the Didot point, which became generally adopted in France.

From 1785 onwards most of the books from the presses of François-Ambroise were cut by Firmin Didot, for Wafflard had by then set up his own foundry. François-Ambroise Didot died in 1804, the year which ushered in the Empire.

In 1797 he had handed over his printing office to his elder son Pierre (1761–1853) and his foundry to his younger son Firmin (1764–1836). One of the first projects conceived by the two brothers was a new collection of literary masterpieces, handsomely printed and illustrated by the finest artists of the time. The three authors chosen to inaugurate this series were Virgil, Horace and Racine. So highly were the Didots considered by this time that the Ministry of the Interior put at the disposal of Pierre Didot the rooms in the Louvre formerly occupied by the Imprimerie Royale, which in 1792, under the name of Imprimerie Nationale, had been transferred to the rue de la Vrillière.

There he printed the celebrated collection called the 'Editions du Louvre'. The *Virgil* appeared in 1798, with illustrations by the famous painter David and his pupils Gérard and Girodet. The *Horace* came out the following year, and the first volume of the *Racine* in 1801. Indeed the *Racine*, set in type cut and cast by Firmin, is a magnificent example of typography; but the illustrations cannot be said to be inspired, despite the array of talented names.

The French Revolution had introduced into the art of the country the sterner virtues of a Cornelian classicism. Banished were the rococo delights of the eighteenth century. In the words of Henri Bouchot: 'Le livre à vignettes documentaires plaisant et gracieux était immolé aux mânes du vertueux Brutus.'* It was largely the influence of the painter David which drove the graces of a former age from both canvas and the printed book.

* H. Bouchot, *Le Livre*. Paris, 1886.

Apart from such books as these Didot classics it must be said that generally speaking French book production at the outset of the nineteenth century, and indeed for some thirty years after the Revolution was mediocre when not frankly deplorable. The Revolution had not made life any easier for the book trade. In times fraught with danger few are inclined for the peaceful joys of the bibliophile; nor was there money to spare. Perhaps that was why Didot limited his de-luxe classics to 250 copies, for there cannot have been many people who could afford to pay, at that time, 1,200 francs or 1,800 francs for an edition with proofs of the illustrations 'avant la lettre'.

By 1816 the vogue of the toga had passed. David, the austere Jacobin, who had reached the height of his fame under the Empire, bowed out under the Restoration. Perhaps the first sign of a new spirit abroad was Géricault's famous canvas *Le Radeau de la Méduse* exhibited in 1819. Within a few years there arrived that 'nouvelle vague' to which the name Romantic has fastened itself. David had foreseen it. In 1808 he wrote 'In ten years' time the study of the classics will be laid aside. All these gods, these heroes, will be replaced by knights-at-arms, by troubadours singing under the windows of their lady-loves, at the foot of some ancient dungeon.' He was absolutely right.

Meanwhile, Pierre Didot began in 1809 to design type for a foundry of his own, the first specimen from which appeared in 1819, entitled: *Specimen des nouveaux caractères de la Fonderie et de l'Imprimerie de P. Didot, l'Ainé*. The types were cut under his supervision by the punch-cutter Vibert, with whom he worked regularly for three hours a day for some ten years running, and whom he termed 'one of our most skilful punch-cutters'. Vibert *fils* was himself the son of a punch-cutter and in 1798 was running his own foundry in partnership with M. Luy. In 1809 he left the business to work for Pierre Didot, and Luy took over sole control of the Vibert & Luy foundry, which was eventually merged in the Fonderie Générale. Vibert stayed with Didot for a number of years, and in 1823 is found working for J. Carez, who established a short-lived foundry in that year.

Pierre Didot followed his father's reform of the system of type measurement, and tells us in his specimen that he has followed the point system for the de-nomination of his types 'instead of meaningless and often bizarre names which offer no clue to their actual proportions'. Names which he had held up to ridicule in his *Epitre sur les progrès de l'imprimerie* (1784) when he wrote:

> Tous ces grotesques mots, Gaillarde, Trismégiste,
> Gros texte, Gros canon . . . fastidieuse liste
> Des vains noms qu'ont porté tant de types divers.

Whatever we may think of the Didot types today, and many, like Thibau-deau, consider them 'of extreme dryness and absolutely glacial rigidity of line', they were in keeping with the neo-classicism of the period. 'Because the Didot,' writes Albert J. George, 'had long specialized in publishing the ancient masters, the age came to associate their types with antiquity itself, reading into the rigid,

clean, restrained characters their own understanding of a past they admired.'*
At all events, the Didots succeeded in imposing their types throughout France
and in many other European countries as well. The name of Didot became
almost synonymous with printing and the enormous success of the firm owed
much to the close and fruitful collaboration between the two brothers Firmin
and Pierre.

Firmin Didot (1764–1836) worthily upheld the fame of his father and of his
elder brother. Printer, punch-cutter and founder, he cut the types used in
Pierre's 'Editions du Louvre' and was one of the first in France to make use of
stereotyping, a process he employed for the logarithmic tables of Jean François
Callet (1795). Appointed Printer to the Institut Français in 1811, and Royal
Printer in 1814, he retired from the printing business in 1827 to devote himself
to public affairs as Deputy for Nogent-le-Rotrou, leaving the business in the
capable hands of his sons Ambroise-Firmin Didot (b. 1790) and Hyacinthe
Didot (b. 1794). Firmin Didot had, as his *violon d'Ingres* a predilection for
writing, and from his pen came two tragedies: *La Mort d'Annibal* and *La Reine
de Portugal*, the latter reaching the stage. He also made French verse translations
of Virgil's *Bucolics* and the *Idylls* of Theocritus.

The three sons of Pierre-François Didot (1732–95), the brother of François-
Ambroise, who had founded the paper-mill at Essonnes and had been printer
to Monsieur (later Louis XVIII) followed in the steps of their father and uncle.
The eldest, Henri Didot (1765–1852) was a type-founder and punch-cutter,
best remembered in the latter capacity for the microscopic types which he cut
when well past middle age for editions of *Horace* (1828) and *La Rochefoucauld*
(1832). The second son, Didot Saint-Léger (1767–1829), managed the paper
mill at Essonnes, and introduced into France the paper-making machine. A
third son, known as Didot jeune, succeeded his brother Henri as a successful type-
founder. One of Pierre-François' daughters, Félicie, married the author Bernardin de Saint-Pierre, who was for a time associated with the Essonnes mill.

The roman type of Firmin Didot dominated French typography for over half
the century. But from the time of the Restoration the vogue of the Romantics
brought about a revival of the gothic letter, though only for titles and running
heads. Fournier's gothic was rather neglected in favour of that of Didot (1825)
and latterly that from the Mayeur foundry. The disappearance of the school of
David was followed by the *entrée en scène* of the vignettists, led by Alexandre
Desenne (1785–1827) whose light and happy touch is shown at its best in
L'Hermite de la Chausée d'Antin by Etienne de Jouy (1814). In 1817 Charles
Thompson, a pupil of Bewick, settled in Paris, where he founded a school of
engravers on wood, among them Porret and Best. This school served as an

---

* George, A. J., *The Didot family and the Progress of Printing*. Syracuse U.P., 1961.

'atelier de clicherie' (*polytypage*) for cutting vignettes from the drawings of well-known artists. In 1828 Pinard published a *Recueil de vignettes gravées sur bois et polytypée par Thompson*.

In 1826 the famous novelist Honoré de Balzac set up as a printer in partnership with A. Barbier at 17 rue des Marais-Saint-Germain (now rue Visconti), but he

FIGURE 86. A fearful example of the typographic excesses of English printing during the nineteenth century. By no means an isolated example.

abandoned the craft two years later. One of his last efforts as a printer was a specimen book of the Laurent & De Berny foundry, which is historically interesting in that it shows examples of the typographical material used by the general run of printers at that time. Balzac made use of his experience in his novel *Illusions Perdues*, which opens with the words: 'At the period when this story begins, the Stanhope press and inking rollers were not yet employed in the small provincial printing offices.'

Lithography was introduced into France during the first years of the Empire, but the vogue for this method of printing did not come until after the Restoration. An outstanding work in this field was begun in 1820 when Charles Nodier and Baron Taylor started to publish *Voyages pittoresques et romantiques de l'ancienne France*, the twenty-five volumes of which were not completed until 1878. This vast, though towards the end very unequal, work had illustrations by Horace Vernet, Ingres, Isabey, Bonington, Coignet, Géricault and Célestin Nanteuil.

The lithograph lent itself best to large scale work, and was invariably used *hors texte* for folios of travel and for botanical works and collections of costumes, such as that of Lanté. (Incidentally the largest botanical book to be illustrated with lithographic plates was an English publication, James Bateman's *The Orchidaceae of Mexico and Guatemala* (1837–41).) Pancrace Bessa made a great deal of money out of flower books with his illustrations to Charles Malo, *Guirlande de Flore* (1815) and *Parterre de Flore* (1820) and Charlotte de Latour, *Le Langage des Fleurs* (1833).

A landmark in the history of Romantic book illustration was the appearance in 1828 of Albert Stapfer's translation into French of Goethe's *Faust*, superbly illustrated with seventeen lithographs by Delacroix. It was published in Paris by Motte and Sautelet, and the lithographs were pulled on china paper, pasted down. It was issued in brown wrappers designed by Devéria.

Goethe himself was greatly impressed by these lithographs and declared 'the artist has assimilated from this dark work all the sombre quality it contained in its original conception'. But perhaps because they had captured the Germanic mood so thoroughly, the lithographs met with a cool reception in France, except by the *enfants terribles* of the new era, for whom Delacroix was the protagonist of the new Romantic school.

In the same year appeared the *Chansons* of Béranger, with illustrations by Henri Monnier and Charles Devéria, a work which, though in a completely different style, pointed to the new tendencies in book illustration.

As soon as Bewick's technique of engraving on the end-grain of hardwood was adopted in France wood engraving became widespread largely because publishers welcomed the economy effected by printing the illustrations at the same time as the text. Among the illustrators who made good use of the process were Jean Gérard (known as Grandville), the brothers Johannot, Sulpice Guillaume Chevalier (called Gavarni), Henri Monnier, Raffet, Bertall, Jean Gigoux and Devéria. At first the wood engraving was printed *hors texte*, but Jean Gigoux made it a part of the printed page, a juxtaposed commentary on the text, as shown in his 600 engravings for Le Sage, *Gil Blas*, published by the firm of Paulin in 1835. This was an example which was speedily followed.

One of the finest illustrated books of the Romantic period is L. Curmer's edition, issued in thirty parts, of Bernardin de Saint Pierre, *Paul et Virginie* and *La Chaumière Indienne* (1838). It contains 450 vignettes in the text engraved on wood after Tony Johannot, Meisonnier, Jean-Baptiste Isabey, Steinheil, Paul Huet and others, as well as twenty-nine plates engraved on wood and seven steel-engraved portraits.

In the decade between 1816 and 1826 the French book trade witnessed a flood of cheap editions of the French classics in collected form, since stereotyping had considerably reduced the cost of reprinting. Against the advice of his colleagues the publisher Théodore Desoer decided in 1816 to launch an edition of the complete works of Voltaire in twelve large octavo volumes. It proved a success, whereupon every publisher felt bound to follow suit, flooding the market with a succession of *oeuvres complètes* in anything from thirty to seventy volumes. It was a fashion which came to an end almost as suddenly as it began owing to the saturation of the market.

After 1840 the 'romantic' style began to decline when the public had become weary of historical reconstitutions tailored after the fashion of Sir Walter Scott, or witches' Sabbaths in the gothic manner. The last of the great romantics among the French illustrators was Gustave Doré, born at Strassburg in 1833. He was also the last important wood engraver before wood gave place to metal. Among the many works which he illustrated were the Bible, Balzac's *Contes Drolatiques*, *Don Quixote*, Dante's *Divine Comedy* and La Fontaine's *Fables*. He was as well known in England as in France, for he worked a good deal for English publishers. At first he drew on wood and the designs were cut by professional engravers, but after 1862, when photography had come into its own his drawings were photographed onto the wood and then engraved.

In his illustrations for the Bible and for La Fontaine's *Fables* Doré made use of pure line, but in his best works he made use of wash, which posed problems for the engravers who had to adopt a new technique which, by differentiating the depths of cut, sought to approximate the tints of the original – a difficult task in which the engraver Pisan was unsurpassed.

From 1840 onwards Gavarni and Daumier made of the illustrated French book a real document of social history. That dauntless publisher J. L. Curmer brought out in 422 parts (8 vols.) *Les Français peints par eux-mêmes* in which each part was devoted to a certain professional or social type. The writers included

Balzac, Jules Janin, Alphonse Karr, and Charles Nodier, and among the illustrators were Gavarni, Daumier, Charlet, Eugène Lami, Tony Johannot and Meissonier. The first three volumes were almost entirely illustrated by Gavarni. The success of this work inspired a number of social satires and documentary books.

Gavarni's outstanding trait was elegance, and he found in the magazine *La Mode* an ideal field for his talent. Honoré Daumier, though equally prolific, was more powerful and vigorous in style; he was essentially a lithographic artist, and to the famous periodical *Charivari*, founded in 1832 by Charles Philipon, he contributed no fewer than 3,958 lithographs, many of them bitter political caricatures. He was even sent to prison for daring to depict Louis XVIII as Gargantua. Some of his best caricatures are to be found in *Les Représentans Représentés*.

With the intervention of photography the character of the illustrated book changed. The first French book to be illustrated with actual photographic prints was the *Paris photographié* of Renard, which appeared in 1853, but direct photographic illustration of books was not yet practicable, though several inventors were searching for a solution. Nevertheless in 1852 the lithographer Rose-Joseph Lemercier, together with the optician Noël Lerebours, published *Lithophotographie*, the first successful example of photo-lithographic printing. Two years earlier Firmin Gillot had taken out patents for a process of line engraving on zinc, which he termed *paniconographie*, a method which soon became known in France as 'gillotage' after its inventor. It was later improved by Beslay and others, and in 1859 the *Gazette des Beaux-Arts* published in its first number two line engravings on copper made by Beslay's process. But the protests of the engravers on wood hindered any progress in this direction for many years. Nevertheless wood engraving was doomed, for photography had dealt it a mortal blow.

After a temporary slowing down of all printing and publishing due to the Franco-Prussian war, the number of books produced rapidly increased, partly on account of increased mechanisation in the printing offices, partly owing to the new methods of making paper from wood pulp by chemical means.

In 1872 the new technique of transferring photographs on to the surface of the wood block came into use in France, where it rapidly spread owing to the saving of time which it effected. Many engravers specialised in converting these photo transfers into line blocks, notably Frédéric Florian. Photography, indeed, began more and more to invade the printing office, especially after the invention, patented at Munich by Georg Meisenbach in 1882, of the first practicable photographic half-tone process for letterpress printing.

But although wood engraving was no longer in such demand as formerly, it was still needed while process engraving was in its infancy. One of the finest book illustrators of the '70s and '80s was Daniel Vierge, born in 1851 at Madrid and son of the artist Vincente Urrabieta Ortiz. Vierge was his mother's name. He came to Paris just before the outbreak of the Franco-Prussian war. When it was over he was engaged by Charles Yriarte, then director of the *Monde illustré*, and began a brilliant career, working incessantly both for his journal and for book publishers. When his right side was paralysed in 1882 he learned to draw with his left hand and in less than two years regained his former virtuosity. His output was prodigious. He illustrated books by Victor Hugo, Michelet, Châteaubriand and Zola, in which he remained faithful to wood engraving. He died, aged fifty-three, just when he was about to change his medium and illustrate *Carmen* with etchings.

There was during this period a renewal of interest in etching, but although illustrators in this medium were numerous, few were outstanding. One of the greatest was Félicien Rops, as is shown by his illustrations to Barbey d'Aurevilly, *Les Diaboliques* (1886).

In 1876 Jean-Claude Motteroz printed the first volume of the *Librairie du Victor Hugo Illustré*. This was *Les Travailleurs de la Mer*, illustrated by Victor Hugo himself and Daniel Vierge. After a varied career as compositor, pressman, lithographer and machine-minder, Motteroz started his own printing firm in Paris. In 1897 he became managing director of the Librairies-Imprimeries Réunies. One of his pupils was F. Thibaudeau, printer and author of *La Lettre d'Imprimerie*.

Another printer, Albert Quantin, published in 1877 his own book *Les Origines de l'Imprimerie et son introduction en Angleterre*. In 1876 he acquired the Imprimerie Claye, in which he had worked as a foreman, and began business as publisher, one of his publications being the magazine *Monde Moderne*.

In 1896 Edouard Pelletan established his publishing firm and issued his first book, *Les Nuits & Souvenir* by Alfred de Musset, with wood engravings by Florian from designs by A. Gérardin. The book was printed on hand presses by the Maison Lahure in two separate editions, quarto and octavo, with different typography for each. Pelletan was dissatisfied with the standards of book printing in France and in 1896 published a manifesto addressed to booklovers in which he put forward the principle that typography must be the fundamental element of the book, and that therefore it must be appropriate to the individual character of each book and realise a harmony between the typographic style and the ideas of the writer. Pelletan also considered that wood engraving should be employed for illustration in preference to any other method. 'The book,' he wrote, 'is black upon white; colour should only be used with moderation.' He also stated categorically 'there can be no good book without a good text' and he showed this by publishing the works of writers like De Musset, Alfred de Vigny, Hugo, Chateaubriand and Renan.

31

Some Private Presses

PRIVATE presses of one kind or another have existed throughout most of the five centuries following the introduction of printing. Cardinal Richelieu set up a private press at his château in Touraine in 1640. Almost a century before that Archbishop Matthew Parker is said to have had a private press at Lambeth Palace. Frederick the Great set up a private press in 1749 in his palace of Sans-Souci at Potsdam, on which Christian Friedrich Henning printed a number of fine books with the address 'Au donjon du Château'. In 1757 the first work came from Horace Walpole's private press at Strawberry Hill, Twickenham. Sir Egerton Brydges founded the Lee Priory Press at Ickham, near Canterbury, in 1813, and in 1845 the Rev C. H. O. Daniel, later to become Provost of Worcester College, Oxford, began the Daniel Press.

These early presses were not primarily concerned with problems of typography. In the case of Daniel printing was a hobby, undertaken for pleasure. Frederick the Great wanted to see his own work in print. Walpole's private press was begun as the whim of a rich dilettante, but managed to last for thirty-two years. But towards the end of the nineteenth century the private press heralded a revolt against the debased standards of commercial printing.

With William Morris we come to a man for whom the private printing-press became not merely a hobby, but an all-consuming passion. Yet, like Baskerville, he came to printing late in life. Although his interest in fine books was life-long, his practical participation in the craft was determined by a lantern lecture given by Emery Walker to the Arts and Crafts Exhibition Society on 15 November 1888. Walker (later Sir Emery) (1851–1933) was by profession a typographer and process engraver who in 1886, in partnership with Walter Boutall, founded the firm of Walker and Boutall, process and general engravers.

Walker, of whom Sir Sydney Cockerell wrote: 'It is scarcely too much to say that his influence direct or indirect can be discerned in nearly every well-designed page of type that now appears', was directly responsible for Morris's active interest in the production of printed books. In December 1889, Morris asked Walker to go into partnership with him as a printer, and although the latter was unable to accept the offer, the founding of a press was decided upon.

In that same month Morris began to design his first type, for none of the founts available from the type-founders would suit his special needs. Medieval-ist enthusiasm was contagious among the Pre-Raphaelists and their associates. Morris, ever since his Oxford days, kept his passionate interest in medieval art and architecture and it is therefore not surprising that for his type he sought his models from the cradle days of printing. Two books which he studied especially in making designs for his first type were Jenson's *Pliny* of 1476 and a *History of Florence* printed at Venice by Jacobus Rubeus in the same year. The roman types used in both these books were very similar. At first he called the type, the punches of which were cut by Edward Prince of Islington, the Jenson-Morris, but later he named it the Golden type since it was to be used (but wasn't) in an edition of *The Golden Legend* which Morris had set his heart on printing, and which was eventually printed in a gothic type to which he gave the name of Troy. The Golden type, cast at the Fann Street foundry of Sir Charles Reed, was the first fount used at Morris's press, which he called the Kelmscott Press. It was located in a cottage near his house on the Upper Mall, Hammersmith. The first book to come from the Kelmscott Press was Morris's own *The Story of the Glittering Plain*, completed in April 1891. Morris was then fifty-eight.

The crowning achievement of the Kelmscott Press was beyond doubt the *Works of Geoffrey Chaucer*, on which Morris laboured for nearly four years. It was printed in black and red, double column, in Morris's Chaucer type, with headings to the longer poems in Troy type. These two founts were black-letter, based on early German models as shown in the books of Mentelin and Gunther Zainer. The Chaucer was a smaller version of the Troy, which was found to be too large for the body-text of the Chaucer. The latter face derived its name from its first use in Morris's reprint of Caxton's *The Recuyell of the Historyes of Troye* (1893).

Four hundred and twenty-five copies of the *Chaucer* were printed on hand-made paper supplied by Joseph Batchelor of Little Chart, Kent, and thirteen on vellum, by Henry Band of Brentford, containing eighty-seven illustrations designed by Sir Edward Burne-Jones and engraved on wood by W. H. Hooper, as well as fourteen large borders, eighteen frames and twenty-six initials designed by Morris. The book was completed on 8 May 1896, and Morris died on 3 October that same year.

Most of the books Morris turned out were printed on the 'Super Royal genuine Albion Press' which he had bought for £42.10.0 from Hopkinson & Cope of 103 Farringdon Road. During the printing of the Chaucer another press was added and the two were almost continuously at work. After Morris's death, the Kelmscott Press was continued for a while by Sydney Cockerell and F. S. Ellis, ceasing publication in 1898 with the founder's *Note on his aims in founding the Kelmscott Press*. The total number of books issued by the Press was fifty-two, in sixty-six volumes. The press had occupied Morris for the last five years of his life; in that short space of time he exerted an influence on printing that was widespread, though on the nature of that influence opinions vary.

The Kelmscott books were beautiful, of their kind. 'It was the essence of my undertaking,' wrote Morris, 'to produce books which it would be a pleasure to look upon as pieces of printing and arrangement of type.' But their kind is alien to our modern preference for simplicity; they are heavy in appearance and over-ornate. The supreme virtue of Morris's 'typographical adventure' was his insistence on good workmanship, fine materials and careful press-work.

Morris's Kelmscott Press did not, perhaps fortunately, have any direct influence on the twentieth century book as far as type and illustration were concerned. Nevertheless, despite his revivalist outlook and medieval mannerisms, and the fact that his typographical ideas were retrograde rather than progressive, Morris's general conception of the book as an organic whole in which press-work, paper, type and binding should be nothing less than the best, provided the impetus to others who, equally imbued with the spirit of fine craftsmanship, nevertheless felt that Morris's deliberate archaisms had left him marooned in a backwater, and that a handsome book could be produced without the need for excessive decoration, or by harking back to the cradle days of the art.

During the forty years which followed the closing down of the Kelmscott Press and the outbreak of the Second World War a number of distinguished private presses were functioning, notably in England and Germany. They showed how beautiful a book could be when good taste was allied to fine workmanship. But in general their productions were limited in number, costly, and laboriously printed by methods of the past. But it is not easy to define exactly what is meant by a private press. A. W. Pollard wrote: 'For a press to be private a double qualification seems necessary: the books it prints must not be obtainable by any chance purchaser who offers a price for them and the owner must print for his own pleasure and not work for hire for other people.'

This definition could well apply to such a press as that of the Rev C. H. O. Daniel at Oxford, which was run entirely for the pleasure its owner got out of it. But the line of demarcation which separates private enterprise presses from commercial ventures is not always clearly marked. C. R. Ashbee, the founder of the Essex House Press took the definition a step further when he wrote that a private press 'caters for a limited market and is not concerned with the question of the commercial development of printing by machinery'. Bernard Newdigate goes a little further and states that the private press printers show 'a zeal in the pursuit of their art which has been inspired by something more than mere money-making, and in many cases by the attainment of a degree of excellence which invests their work with a peculiar interest for all those who study printing'.

In England, following Morris, came a number of private presses which sprang

FIGURE 87. A page from *The Glittering Plain*, by William Morris. This was the first book issued by the Kelmscott Press, 1891. The illustration is by Walter Crane.

up at the turn of the century. Among them were the Ashendene Press founded by C. H. St John Hornby in 1894; the Eragny Press founded by Lucien Pissarro in the same year; the Vale Press of Charles Ricketts; the Essex House Press of C. R. Ashbee; and the Doves Press run by Emery Walker, the former colleague of Morris at the Kelmscott Press, in conjunction with the well-known bookbinder T. J. Cobden-Sanderson. The work done by the Doves Press was the very antithesis of that which came from the Kelmscott Press, for the typography was plain almost to the point of severity and illustration completely absent.

The most famous work issued from the Doves Press was the folio Bible of 1905 in five volumes. It was entirely set by hand on one hand press and the sole compositor, J. H. Mason, later became Head of the London School of Printing, where his influence had a good effect on the printing industry at large. The splendid initial letters of the Doves Press Bible were drawn by one of the finest of modern calligraphers, Edward Johnston.

The Doves Press had its own typeface, based on Jenson. But whereas Morris had sought to thicken his Jenson so that, in his own words, it tended rather more to the gothic than did the original, the Doves Press face, the punches for which were cut by Edward Prince, was Jenson fined down. Unfortunately the Doves Press books, although they achieved great beauty in their simplicity, showed no variation in the style of successive books. Some fifty books in all were issued by the Doves Press before it closed down in 1916.

The Ashendene Press was founded in 1894 by C. H. St John Hornby, inspired by the example of William Morris. In 1901 he had a special fount cut for his press, based on the Subiaco type used by Sweynhein and Pannartz, and again the punches were cut by E. B. Prince. It is in its way a handsome type, but very black, and though suitable perhaps for reprints of Latin poetry would be unacceptable as a modern book face.

Founded by Lucien Pissarro in 1894, the Eragny Press was so called after the village in Normandy where Lucien had worked with his father Camille Pissarro. A friend of Charles Ricketts, whose Vale Press was founded in 1896, Pissarro obtained permission to print with the Vale type, designed by Ricketts himself, on condition that the books printed with this type were issued through the Vale Press and the first sixteen Eragny Press books were issued to Vale Press subscribers. However, the Vale Press closed down in 1903 and in the following year Pissarro, who had removed his press to Hammersmith, London, in 1900, designed a roman letter which he designated the Brook type. Thirty-two books were printed at the Eragny Press, mostly small volumes, many of which contained coloured wood engravings drawn by Pissarro and cut either by himself or by his English wife, Esther.

The Essex House Press, founded by C. R. Ashbee, brought out its first issues in Caslon type, and these were typographically superior to the books produced in Ashbee's own Endeavour type and Prayer Book type, neither of which proved satisfactory.

In Germany the private presses turned out some excellent work between the early years of the twentieth century and the outbreak of the Hitler War. The first of these was the Januspresse, founded at Leipzig in 1907 by Carl Ernst Poeschel (1874–1944) in conjunction with his friend Walter Tiemann (1876–1951) who designed the types and initials. This was followed by a number of other private presses, among them the Ernst-Ludwig-Presse, which also dates from 1907 and took its name from the Grand Duke Ernst Ludwig of Hesse, who was its patron. The press, situated in Darmstadt, was directed until 1914 by F. W. Kleukens (1878–1956) and his brother Ch. H. Kleukens (1880–1955) who was in charge from 1918 until 1937. Friedrich Wilhelm Kleukens himself founded the Ratio Presse in 1919, and his brother Christian Heinrich founded the Mainzer Presse about 1927.

At Bremen in 1911 Dr Willi Wiegand (1886–1961) and his friend Dr Ludwig Wolde founded the Bremer Presse which lasted until 1939. Until its closure it was one of the finest private presses in Germany. All its books were printed in roman types designed by Wiegand, and Wolde was responsible for the literary direction of the press until his retirement in 1922. The punches were cut by Louis Hoell (d. 1935) in close collaboration with the designer. Hoell worked for the Flinsch foundry before the First World War, and from 1916 he worked for the Bauer foundry, with which the Flinsch business had been merged. He cut the later designs of Lucian Bernhard and Emil Rudolf Weiss. Many of the initials and much of the title-page lettering for the productions of the Bremer Presse were drawn by Anna Simons, a pupil of the calligrapher Edward Johnston, and cut on wood by Joseph Lehnacker. The Bremer Presse was moved to Tölz during the years 1919–21, and from 1921 until the outbreak of the Second World War was situated in Munich.

In 1913 Count Harry Kessler (1868–1937) founded the Cranach Presse at Weimar (once the home of the famous artist Lucas Cranach). Among the various illustrators employed by this press were Eric Gill, Aristide Maillol, E. Gordon Craig and Marcus Behmer. The rise of the Nazis forced Kessler to leave Germany, and his work was disrupted. Among the outstanding books from the Cranach Presse were Shakespeare's *Hamlet* with woodcuts by Edward Gordon Craig, the *Song of Solomon* illustrated by Eric Gill, and Virgil's *Eclogues*, with woodcuts by Maillol. This last work was printed in a Jenson-style roman cut by Edward Prince and an italic designed by Edward Johnston. The *Hamlet* which had appeared in 1928, translated into German by Gerhardt Hauptmann, appeared in an English edition in 1930, edited by J. Dover Wilson.

Also in 1913 the Rupprecht Presse was founded at Munich by F. H. Ehmcke, who for many years was a professor at the Kunstgewerbeschule (now the Akademie) at Munich. This press was active until 1934, and in the course of its existence issued fifty-seven hand-printed works set in Ehmcke's own type-faces.

The Ratio Presse founded at Darmstadt in 1919 by F. W. Kleukens issued as its first publication a *Vogel-ABC*, with fifty-two illustrations lithographed by Kleukens and hand coloured. Meanwhile in the same year his brother founded the Kleukens Presse at Frankfurt-am-Main.

The year 1921 saw the founding of yet another private press, the Juniperus

Presse at Stuttgart. Its founder was the illustrator and book designer Ernst Schneidler (1882–1956) who was the designer of a number of type faces, including Schneidler-Mediaeval, Zentenar-Fraktur, and a cursive named Legende. Schneidler was a professor at the State School for Arts and Crafts at Stuttgart.

In Holland Jan Greshoff and Jacques Bloem, later joined by P. N. van Eyck, founded the Dutch private press known as De Zilverdistel (The Silver Thistle). Its first publication, in 1910, was Van Eyck's *Worstelingen*, printed at Haarlem by Joh. Enschedé en Zonen in an eighteenth-century type face cut by J. M. Fleischman. In 1913 the press was run by P. N. van Eyck and J. F. van Royen, and in 1915 came under the direction of J. E. van Royen alone. In van Royen the press had a printer whose ideals were those which had imbued the minds of men like Morris in the 'nineties of the previous century, and from 1913 onwards he took over most of the work of the Zilverdistel. From 1916 onwards he printed himself on a hand press. In 1923 he renamed the press the Kunera Press and ran it entirely on his own. Its first publication was *Oostersch*, verses after Persian and Arabic poets by J. H. Leopold, printed by van Royen in the Disteltype designed for the press by Lucien Pissarro. In 1942, on 10 June, Jean François van Royen, born at Arnhem 27 June 1878, died in the concentration camp at Amersfoort. Most of his work had been produced on the Albion press sent out to him from England in 1914 by his friends the Pissarros. Some of his books were set in the Silvertype designed for his press by the eminent Dutch typographer S. H. de Roos (1877–1962).

Sjoerd Hendrik de Roos, who was by profession an industrial designer as well as typographer, founded the Heuvelpers (Hill Press) at Hilversum in 1926, and the first book from this press, the *Tractatus Politicus* of Spinoza, appeared in June 1928, set in Roos's own Meidoorn type. De Roos had designed his first book in 1903, and appropriately enough, considering his own aims, it was a translation into Dutch of lectures by William Morris, published under the title *Kunst en Maatschappij*. In 1942, A. A. M. Stols published a tribute to De Roos, *Het Werk van S. H. de Roos*, set in Roos's Hollandsche Mediaeval. Stols himself founded the Halcyon Press in 1927.

Most of the private presses in Europe which had been working during the twenty years following the First World War, were forced to close by 1940. One famous press, however, is still active – the Officina Bodoni run by the distinguished scholar-printer Giovanni Mardersteig, born in Weimar, but now a naturalised Italian. In 1917, after a short period as a schoolmaster, Mardersteig joined the publishing house of Kurt Wolff in Leipzig, and later in Munich. Ill health drove him to seek a milder climate, and in 1922 he went to Montagnola di Lugano where he produced his first book. He was fortunate enough to obtain permission from the Italian government to cast type from Bodoni's original matrices, still preserved at Parma.

From the large range of faces available he chose about a dozen text founts, including italics, as well as a few sets of titling. In the next four years he produced a number of distinguished books which immediately attracted the attention of lovers of fine printing. But for certain works which Mardersteig envisaged Bodoni's types were not really suitable, and following a visit to Montagnola by Stanley Morison he began to extend his range of types, aided in this project by the American printer and type designer Frederic Warde. One of the results of this collaboration was the production of a facsimile of Vicentino's writing books of 1522 and 1523 (see p. 155) set in Warde's Arrighi types cut by the Paris punch cutter Charles Plumet.

In 1926, as the result of a competition organised by the National Institute of Italy, Mardersteig was chosen to print a complete edition of the works of Gabriele d'Annunzio. To facilitate his work on this project Mardersteig decided to move his printing office to Verona, where, with the help of his friend the publisher Arnoldo Mondadori, he found new premises and the additional staff needed for the production of the forty-nine volumes of d'Annunzio's works, all of which had to be set by hand and took some five years to complete. Two hundred and nine sets were printed on vellum on hand presses while 2,000 were printed on paper by machine.

When the vast d'Annunzio project had been successfully concluded, Mardersteig installed his hand press in his private house at Valdonega, on the outskirts of Verona, and there continued to print and publish a variety of fine books. After the Second World War he decided that, after all, a hand press was something of an anachronism and in 1949 he started the Stamperia Valdònega for machine production. Nevertheless, in view of the demand from discriminating collectors, and in order to continue his own editions, Mardersteig kept the Officina Bodoni alive as well as the new mechanised plant.

In addition to being his own printer and publisher, Giovanni Mardersteig is also a designer of type. As a result of a sojourn in Glasgow during 1932 with the Collins Cleartype Press, he designed for that firm the face known as Fontana, which was made under Mardersteig's direction by the Monotype Corporation for the exclusive use of Collins – though it was later released by them for general use. Mardersteig used it himself for an edition of Landor's *Imaginary Conversations* which he designed and printed for the Limited Editions Club of New York. He also designed the fount known as Dante, which was first used in Boccaccio, *Trattatello in laude di Dante*, 1954. This was cut for him by the French punch cutter Charles Malin (1883–1956) who had cut the punches for Eric Gill's well-known Perpetua. This Dante type was subsequently issued for mechanical composition by the Monotype Corporation.

At the time of writing Giovanni Mardersteig, is as busy as ever. His *apologia pro vita sua* is to be found in his autobiographical *Ein Leben den Büchern gewidmet*, issued in 1968 by the Verlag der Gutenberg-Gesellschaft at Mainz and printed in Verona by the Stamperia Valdònega, set in his own Dante type. For many years now, Giovanni Mardersteig has been ably assisted by his son Martino, who has charge of the mechanised plant.

32

Art Nouveau (Jugendstil) and After

THE stylistic phenomenon known as *Art Nouveau* (in Germany as *Jugendstil*) affected all the arts and crafts, including the art of the book. A revolt against the traditionalism of the nineteenth century, it took the form of a relatively short-lived but very significant style of decoration in which the ornamental element is always dominant and sinuous patterns, especially in the long curving lines of botanical growth, usually highly stylised, fill an important ornamental role. Even the human form is also adapted to ornamental needs. The naturalistic representational shape gave way to a stylised linear conception.

The movement was not known as Art Nouveau at its inception in the 1880s, but the name caught on after an art dealer named Samuel Bing had opened a shop which he called 'L'Art Nouveau' in the rue de Provence, Paris in 1895. The interiors were designed by one of the apostles of the new style, the Belgian Henry Van de Velde (1863–1957). As far as book illustration is concerned, the first work in which Art Nouveau makes its appearance seems to be the cover and title-page of *Wren's City Churches*, designed by its author, Arthur Heygate Mackmurdo and published at Orpington, Kent, in 1883. Mackmurdo (1851–1942) was an architect, and one of the founders, in 1882, of the Century Guild. He was joint-editor with Herbert P. Horne, of the Guild's periodical, *The Hobby Horse*, started in 1884, in which the illustration formed an integral part of the layout. It is significant, in view of the subsequent development of the style, that *The Hobby Horse* abandoned the traditional three-dimensional form of book illustration in favour of a two-dimensional effect emphasising the decorative value of line, one of the hallmarks of Art Nouveau style.

Walter Crane, whose book *Claims of Decorative Art* (1892) was translated into Dutch,* wrote: 'The revival in England of decorative art of all kinds culminat-ing, as it appears to be doing, in book design, has not escaped the eyes of ob-servant and sympathetic artists and writers on the Continent.'

Brussels was the city where English examples of Art Nouveau made their initial impact, though in architecture and painting rather than in the arts of the book. During the 1880s and 90s Brussels was always receptive to the latest

* *Kunst en samenleving.* Amsterdam, 1894.

FIGURE 88. Alphonse Mucha (1860–1939), the Czech artist, notable exponent of the Art Nouveau style, designed a number of posters for the actress Sarah Bernhardt, the one above showing her as Lorenzaccio in De Musset's play of that name.

avant-garde ideas, and one of the most important promoters was Octave Maus, who founded the review *L'Art Moderne* in 1881. He was also the founder of the 'Société des Vingt' which at one of its first exhibitions showed books illustrated by Herbert Horne (1864–1916) and Selwyn Image (1849–1930), both of whom were connected with the Arts and Crafts Movement in England.

Art Nouveau even made its impact felt in bookbinding, and in many countries experiments along these lines were being carried out both in lettering and binding, one of the chief exponents being the artist René Wiener of Nancy, who treated the whole of the book, both text and cover, as a decorative entity.

In Germany two important periodicals made their first appearance at Munich in 1896. They were *Simplicissimus* and *Jugend*, the latter giving its name to the Art Nouveau style known in Germany as Der Jugendstil. The breeze which blew from Schwabing, the Chelsea of Munich, cast many a ripple over the surface of German book illustration, and affected German type forms as well. In Berlin, just a year before, had appeared the first issue of the art and literary magazine *Pan*, which heralded a renaissance in German printing. In October 1899, a monthly periodical *Die Insel* made its appearance, printed by the Offizin W. Drugulin at Leipzig.

One contributor to all these various periodicals who deserves special mention is Otto Theodor Eckmann (1865–1902), a talented and many-sided craftsman whose work in the field of applied arts embraced designs for furniture and ceramics, and who was well-known as painter, book illustrator and type designer. Five title-pages of *Jugend* were decorated with coloured designs by Eckmann, and in Darmstadt Alexander Koch commissioned Eckmann to do the cover for his new magazine *Deutsche Kunst und Dekoration* (October 1897).

A master of Jugendstil decoration, Eckmann was also a type designer who worked for Karl Klingspor. His *Eckmann Schrift* appeared in 1900 and was first shown in Max Martersteig, *Der Schauspieler*, published at Leipzig in 1900 by Breitkopf & Härtel for Eugen Diederichs, who had founded a publishing firm at Florence in 1896, and was one of the founders, in 1907, of the Deutsche Werkbund, which, the times having changed, came to reject the Jugendstil decoration. Another of Eckmann's type faces, very much in the style of 1900, was used for the prospectus of the Steglitzer Werkstatt, in the Autumn of 1901.

Somewhat akin to Eckmann was the sensitive and rather precious illustrator Heinrich Vogeler, though some of his bookwork, such as the title-page for Maeterlinck's *Sister Beatrice*, published by *Die Insel*, betrays the very worst mannerisms of Art Nouveau.

Another instigator of the 'Neue Kunst' in Germany was Peter Behrens (1869–1940), painter, illustrator, type designer and architect. He studied at the Karlsruhe School of Art and later at Düsseldorf, but his artistic career was spent mainly at Munich. He soon gave up painting and under the influence of Jugendstil devoted himself to graphics and the applied arts. But after a period when he was influenced by Henry van de Velde he gradually moved away from this style.

In 1902 appeared *Die neue Buchkunst*, by Rudolf Kautzsch, published by the Weimar Gesellschaft der Bibliophilen, and set in a new type designed by Peter Behrens. In 1913 came another type design from his pen, the *Behrens Mediaeval*.

By the end of the first decade of the twentieth century the vogue of Art Nouveau–Jugendstil had passed and its mannerisms were discarded. But it had served its purpose, and now the revolt against traditional styles was channelled into a stronger style reflecting the new age. In October 1907 the Deutscher Werkbund was founded at Munich by, among others, the designer F. H. Ehmcke, the publisher Eugen Diederichs, and the architect Hermann Muthesius. Although primarily concerned with industrial design and architecture, the Werkbund exerted considerable influence on the arts of the book. Its aim was to secure co-operation between industry and the arts and crafts, and was to all intents and purposes based on the axiom of William Morris that 'essential beauty . . . arises out of the fitness of a piece of craftsmanship for the use for which it is made'.

The Werkbund had a considerable influence on typography in Germany. Whereas in England experiments in this field were confined to individuals and private presses, in Germany they permeated the whole printing industry, and an immense variety of new types were brought out by the Klingspor and other German foundries. The first incentive to the Germans to produce new type designs for the world market had been the great Paris Exhibition of 1900, a year which also coincided with the commemoration of the 500th anniversary of the birth of Gutenberg and the publication of the notable *Festschrift der Stadt Mainz* edited by Heinrich Wallau. It was the year which saw the appearance of Heinz König's *Walthari* fount, issued by the Klingspor Brothers, whose foundry was the first in Germany to employ well-known artist-calligraphers as type designers. And 1900 also saw the new *Eckmann Schrift* from Klingspor. In fact three German foundries – Genzsch & Heyse of Hamburg, the Reichsdruckerei, and the Brothers Klingspor of Offenbach (which had incorporated the former Rudhard foundry) brought out new type designs by famous artists in 1900.

The Reichsdruckerei was not to be outdone by the private foundries. In 1898 it issued a folio edition of *Die Niebelungen* printed in a type-face designed by Joseph Sattler based on manuscript hands of the early Middle Ages, and called *Niebelungen-Schrift*; and in 1900 it brought out a *Neudeutsch* designed and cut by Georg Schiller. This was a very readable type, very German in character though far removed from Fraktur. It was first used in the official catalogue of the German section at the Paris Exhibition.

Genzch & Heyse also brought out a type-face called 'Neudeutsch', which was the work of Ootto Hupp (1859–1949) a talented designer who was responsible for a series of type-faces for the Klingspor foundry. Hupp's special field was heraldry, and for many years, beginning in 1885, he produced the heraldic annual known as the *Münchener Kalender*. Hupp's 'Neudeutsch', unlike that of Schiller, was more closely related to the conventional Fraktur and in style predictably inspired by Hupp's heraldic work.

At a time when, in England, attempts to raise the standard of typography were confined mainly to the efforts of individuals, in Germany the commercial printers, thanks to the enlightened attitude of type-founders such as those we have mentioned, were provided with a great variety of types which were used, on the whole, with commendable style.

One man who wielded considerable influence on German typography was Rudolf Koch (1876–1934). Born at Nuremberg on 20 November 1876, son of the sculptor Paul Koch, he started work in 1892 at a metallurgical factory at Hanau, where he learned metal chasing. His spare time he spent at the local art school and he soon came to the conclusion that the trade of 'Ziseleur' was not the right calling for him. He moved to Munich, entered the Polytechnic and decided to become a calligrapher, and did indeed become one of the most eminent in Europe. For a time he worked as a litho draughtsman in the fashionable Jugendstil, which he soon abandoned. In the autumn of 1903 he had the idea of designing type, and in this he was encouraged by Eugen Diederichs. But his real career began in 1906 when he joined the staff of the Klingspor foundry at Offenbach-am-Main where he worked until his death, the only interruption being during the First World War. He quickly became one of the most remarkable type designers and punch cutters of modern times. Among the typefaces he designed were *Maximilian* (1914), *Koch Antiqua* (1922), *Neuland* (1923), *Jessen* (1924–30), *Prisma* (1928–31) and *Claudius* (1931–37). He left a short autobiographical sketch in the magazine *Das Plakat*, September 1921.

In that same year the Felix Krais Verlag of Stuttgart published Hans Loubier, *Die Neue Deutsche Buchkunst*, with 157 reproductions of title- and text-pages from works of the leading German publishers and book designers of the first two decades of the twentieth century, and of specimens of type faces by Koch, Behrens, Tiemann, Ehmcke, Kleukens and others.

Strangely enough, when all these new types were being produced, one well-known publisher, Hans von Weber, who had founded his publishing house at Munich in 1906, was singularly addicted to the older types, such as those of Drugulin in Leipzig and of the Dutch firm of Enschedé, or earlier still, those of Unger and Didot. Weber is remembered mainly for his 'Drucke für die Hundert', a series of hand-printed works in small editions published between 1909 and 1923, and his 'Hyperion-Drucke', with texts of European classics finely printed by Poeschel and by Enschedé (1908–13). In 1913 the rights in the Hyperion-Drucke were acquired by Ernst Rowohlt and Julius Schröder, and they were continued until 1923 as 'Dreiangeldrucke'.

Soon after the First World War new life was infused into German typography by the theories of Gropius and the Bauhaus, which from its seat at Weimar was the focal point of post-war revolutionary ideas concerning art and design, with the concept of 'function' as the over-riding principle, and in the realm of typography a break with traditional arrangement in the layout of the book. Experimenters like Lazlo Moholy-Nagy and Jan Tschichold discarded the

FIGURE 89. This lithograph, published in 1896, is by George de Feure (1868–1928) a painter, lithographer and illustrator who played an important part in the dissemination of the style known as Art Nouveau.

accepted rules and evolved new styles. Tschichold, who had worked for some years with the publisher Georg Müller, gave expression to his ideas in a manual called *Typographie als Kunst*, 1922 (renamed, in subsequent editions, *Die Kunst der Typographie*), and his later *Typographische Gestaltung* (1935). In 1926 he was engaged to teach typography and calligraphy at the Munich Meisterschule für Deutschlands Buchdrucker. As a type designer Tschichold is known for his *Furura* (1925) and the sans serif italic *Saskia* which he created for the Schelter & Giesecke foundry in 1935.

After Rudolf Koch, the most important, and certainly one of the most prolific type designers who worked for the Klingspor foundry was Walter Tiemann (1876–1951), for many years the head of the State Academy for Graphic Arts at Leipzig. Painter, illustrator, book and type designer, he designed the types and initials used by the Janus-Presse of his friend Carl Poeschel, and did much work for Insel-Verlag, the publishing firm founded at Leipzig in 1899, and which, after it had been taken over about 1905 by Anton Kippenberg, became one of the best known houses in Germany, famous both for the literary quality of the books it published and for its typography and book design.

The Second World War was responsible for the destruction of many German foundries, including those of Klingspor and Ludwig & Mayer. The Bauer foundry and Stempel A.G. were also damaged, but most of the punches and matrices had been safely stored away. After the war German type founding continued in its pre-war manner, with new designers among whom were Paul Renner, Rudolf Wolf, Heinrich Jost and Imre Reiner.

Of special importance with regard to exotic types was the firm of Drugulin, founded at Leipzig by Wilhelm Drugulin, who had been apprenticed to Johann Nies of that town. In 1869 he bought Nies's business, which included a type foundry, acquired matrices from the Tauchnitz foundry, and also from Karl Tauchnitz' former agent Metzger, including several Oriental founts. Drugulin's son-in-law Johannes Baensch, who became a partner about 1882, gave the firm its reputation for printing in exotic scripts and had a large series of such types cut for the Offizin Drugulin. His most remarkable achievement in this field was the book which he brought out in 1902 as a souvenir of the 500th birthday celebrations in honour of Gutenberg. Its title was *Marksteine aus der Weltliteratur in Originalschriften*, printed in thirty-four languages with colourful ornamentation by Ludwig Sütterlin. The Drugulin foundry was taken over in 1919 by the firm of D. Stempel in Frankfurt-am-Main. The printing house was in 1930 merged with the Haag printing office under the style of Offizin Haag-Drugulin and run by the firm of Köhler & Volckmar.

Another famous printing house which bridged the nineteenth and twentieth centuries was that of Poeschel & Trepte, founded in 1870 by Heinrich Ernst Poeschel, Justus Naumann and Emil Trepte. The firm was especially successful under the management of Carl Ernst Poeschel, the son of the founder, who in 1906 became a partner in the business, which had perhaps more influence on German commercial printing than any other printing and publishing firm of that time. Carl Ernst Peeschel (b. 1874) died on 19 May 1944, six months after his premises and their important archives had been destroyed in an air raid. One of the later specialities of the firm was the printing of astronomical works in conjunction with the German Astronomical Society.

The resurgence of German book-printing, foreshadowed in the 1890s with the appearance of the magazine *Pan*, began in earnest at the very beginning of

FIGURE 90. This drawing by Robert Burns called *Natura Naturans*, published in *The Evergreen*, 1895, shows all the qualities of Art Nouveau illustration, with its swirling lines and two-dimensional conception.

the new century with Heinz König's *Walthari* fount and the *Eckmann Schrift* of Otto Eckmann.

The old Rudhard foundry, a small provincial business situated at Offenbach, and which had existed since 1841, was eventually acquired by the father of the brothers Karl and Wilhelm Klingspor. It was still a small and relatively obscure foundry when in 1892, at the age of twenty-four, Karl Klingspor first entered it, after an apprenticeship to a very different profession – the tobacco trade. His brother Wilhelm joined him as partner three years later, and in 1906 the name

Rudhardsche Giesserei was changed to that of Schriftgiesserei Gebrüder Klingspor.

As with William Morris in England, Karl Klingspor was actuated by motives other than commercialism and he sought to make his foundry play an effective part in the development of a new style in German book printing by getting some of the country's best artists and designers to work for the Klingspor foundry; men like Otto Eckmann, Peter Behrens, Otto Hupp, Rudolf Koch and Walter Tiemann. A conspectus of the new style in German bookwork was to be seen in the examples shown at the Leipzig BUGRA, an exhibition of the book and graphic arts held in February 1914.

After the war German book design entered into a second and most interesting phase of development in which not only that of the Klingspor Brothers, but several other German type foundries played a substantial part by commissioning new founts from leading designers, among whom where Emil Rudolf Weiss, F. H. Ehmcke and C. H. Kleukens.

Eckmannschrift was an attempt to overcome the dichotomy of German type by seeking a mean between roman and gothic, although, like the earlier attempts by Unger, the effect is not entirely satisfactory. Unhappily Otto Eckmann died in 1902 at the early age of thirty-seven. In addition to his *Eckmann Schrift*, he had also designed a number of experimental letter forms, including an ornamented alphabet. During his short but busy life he designed catalogues, letter-headings, business cards, book jackets and ornamental borders, a selection of which are reproduced in *Das Plakat* for July-August 1921. A master of the *Jugenstil* decoration, he was a man of many talents, a painter, metalworker and industrial designer.

Peter Behrens, who designed a series of founts for the Klingspor foundry between 1901 and 1913, was an architect by profession. He designed, *inter alia*, the German Embassy at St Petersburg. His own approach to letter forms was conditioned by his early training. His 1901 *Behrens Schrift* is very four-square and the characters convey just a hint of posts and lintels. He was a member of the Darmstadt 'Artists' Colony' (founded in 1899) and his type was used for the first time in the Festschrift of that body.

CZECHOSLOVAKIA

Ever since its inception as a sovereign state in 1918 Czechoslovakia has been a centre of activity in the arts of the book. Since the 1920s a considerable number of Czech type designers and graphic artists have established their reputation, not only in their own country but also abroad – among them Vojtěch Preissig, Method Kaláb, Karel Dyrynk, Slavoboj Tusar, Josef Týfa and others.

But the most famous among modern Czech type designers is undoubtedly Oldřich Menhart (1897–1962), who in 1948 won the Czechoslovak State Prize for calligraphy, lettering, typography and book design. From 1930 onwards he designed many typefaces, including 'Parlament', a special type commissioned by the government for use in official documents, 'Figural' (1940), 'Manuscript' (1944), 'Uncial' (1945), 'Triga' for Linotype (1951), Grazáanka' (1952), 'Azbuka' (1955) and 'Standard' (1959), named after his friend the New-York calligrapher Paul Standard. One of his designs, bearing his own name, was cut by the Monotype Corporation in 1933/34. He also wrote a number of works treating of the various aspects of his craft.

Jana Žižky z Kalichu

nevynímajíce, jakožto k zloději božímu
a obecnému, jakož se jest stalo Acha-
noví pro čepicí dcer královských a pro
plášť; nebo-li jinou smrtí, buďto kníže,
pán, rytíř, nebo panoše, měštěnín, řemeslník, nebo sedlák, nižádného nevy-
mlúvajíce, ani k osobám hledíce a zříce,
s pomocí boží takovým činiti nad nimi
pomstu dali. Sváruov, křikuov a potrž-
hání aby žádných nebylo u vojště, aní
mezi námi. Jest-li žeby kdo koho byl
ranil, ochromil, nebo zabil, buď nad
ním pomstěno podlé zákona božího,
jako pán Buoh dopustí, žádného ne-
vymieňujíce, ani k osobám zříce. Dále
věžte, že kdoby se kolivěk kradl, nebo
šel, nebo jel, nebo vezl od nás z vojsky,
když bychom polem táhli nebo leželi,
bez dopuštění starších jmenovaných
svrchu, a znamení jistého nebude míti,

[12]

Vojenský řád husitský

buď kníže, pán, rytíř, panoše, měštěnín,
řemeslník, nebo robotěz, nebo kterýž
kolivěk člověk, a bylby popaden, že chtí
k jeho hrdlu i k statku popravit, jakožto nad zlodějem nevěrným, jenž se

[13]

FIGURE 91. Oldrich Menhart (1897–1962) was the most famous of modern Czech type designers, and this illustration shows one of his types as used in a book on the Military Orders of the Hussites.

33

Modern Trends in Printing

THIS process is, in its present state, a comparative newcomer to the printing industry, and the name 'flexography' was given to it as recently as 1952. It is, in fact, an updated version of a process formerly known as analine printing, and was then used in the packaging industry which needed quick-drying inks. Normal drying by oxidation had to be replaced by the quicker process of evaporation, and for this purpose the ink was made by dissolving a coal-tar dye in alcohol. It was from these aniline dyes that the process derived its name.

The first attempts, made in Britain around 1890 by Bibby, Baron and Sons, were not very successful, and the first really practical machine seems to have been built by the Alsatian firm of Holweg in 1905, and was employed mainly in the printing of paper bags.

But the quality of the inks used at that time was poor, and it was not until the development of better pigments, resins and solvents (the three main ingredients of flexographic ink) that aniline printing began to find more general use. The name by which the process is now known comes from the fact that the very fluid but quick-drying ink is nowadays used in connection with flexible rubber relief plates mounted on the cylinder of a web-fed rotary. Although still mainly used in the now vast field of packaging, it can also be used for book printing, but because of the fluidity of the ink highly absorbent paper tends to consume too great a quantity and so is not economical. Hard-surfaced materials are ideal, such as the cellophane which plays so large a part in modern packaging. Flexography is used especially in food wrappings, for which special odour-free inks have been prepared.

PLATES

One of the greatest changes in the nature of letterpress printing has been the replacement of the hard-surfaced metal plate by more resilient and flexible ones made of rubber or plastic. Although a patent was taken out as long ago as 1853 for making printing plates of rubber, the moulded plate did not become commercially feasible until thermosetting phenolic resins such as Bakelite became available as a moulding material.

During the 1930s natural rubber plate compounds were supplemented by various synthetic materials. Then came the development of the thermoplastic plate, and new materials are constantly cropping up in an endeavour to supply the right kind of plate for particular purposes. For rotary printing it has been found that a hard-faced and soft-backed plate is most suitable. One such plate, which has a facing of hard plastic bonded to a flexible rubber backing, is known as a 'Cambridge' plate because it was developed by the University Press at Cambridge. Although made and finished flat, it will wrap round the press cylinder easily, which is an essential requirement of any flexible plate.

For offset litho two types of plate are in general use: the direct-image plate and the pre-sensitised plate. The former is used mainly for hand-lettering, typing or drawings. Pre-sensitised plates are usually of aluminium or plastic, coated with a material sensitive to light, and a negative is printed down photographically onto the plate. The exposed part becomes hard and insoluble, whereas where no light passes through that area remains soluble. The plate is washed after exposure to remove the soluble part of the coating, and then a lacquer is wiped on to make the printing area ink-retaining. For long runs of good quality work bi-metallic plates are often used.

In short, the tendency has been to replace wherever possible the old-fashioned stereotype, which raised immense storage problems, by plastics substitutes which are easily transportable.

The ultimate aim has been to eliminate stereotyping, whether performed with metal, rubber or plastic plates, and replace it by an entirely different method of printing, in which composing machines should deliver, in place of lines of metal, transparent films, either negative or positive, which could be used directly without having recourse to the intermediate stages of plates. In other words, to replace mechanical setting by photocomposition or filmsetting.

FILMSETTING: A TECHNICAL REVOLUTION

Filmsetting is the most fundamental change in the printing industry since the introduction of movable type in the middle of the fifteenth century, for it probably foreshadows the eventual end of printing from metal type. This form of composition, the application of photography to typesetting, dates experimentally from the end of the nineteenth century. W. Friese-Greene, an early pioneer of the cinema, patented a device for reproducing text by photographic means in 1895, but apparently no prototype was ever built, the inventor's interests having shifted to other fields. Although many experiments in photocomposing were made during the early part of the present century, and a number of systems were hailed as providing a solution to the problem, most of them fell by the wayside.

In 1896 E. Porzholt patented a keyboard-controlled machine which photographed single characters by reflected light onto a sensitised plate, and three years later Richards's single-alphabet machine was patented, which specified the use of transmitted light for the formation of images.

During the period between the two world wars various filmsetting machines were tried out, one of the most promising being the Uhertype, an invention of the Hungarian engineer Edmond Uher, which was developed in Augsburg from 1931 onwards. But, as the editor of *Penrose's Annual* for 1933 wrote:

> 'It must not be expected that the practice of photocomposing will come quickly.... Just as it was difficult at first to introduce type-composing machines, so it will be no easier to persuade the trade to accept photo-composing; in fact it will be harder, because it will be necessary to bring about changes in printing methods.'

As if to justify his words, at the last International Printing Exhibition to be held before the war, in 1936, not a single photocomposing machine was to be seen on any of the stands.

The war halted further progress in this field for some years, and after the war the scene had changed. For the time being no more was heard of the Uhertype, and the patents for another photocomposing machine taken out by Scheffer in 1937 in Switzerland had been acquired by the Intertype Corporation of America, and used in their Fotosetter. In England Arthur Duncan's promised Flickertype had apparently given its final flicker.

The post-war years saw rapid progress, for after years of experimenting photocomposition had got over most of its teething troubles. Developments in electronics solved many of the initial problems, and machines for photo-composition became less of a rarity. These machines can be divided into two categories. The first comprises those machines which derive naturally from metal composing machines already in existence. Thus the Fotosetter of the Intertype Corporation of America is an adaptation of their Intertype in which the caster of the latter is replaced by a camera which photographs in rotation the matrices selected by the keyboard operator.

In Europe one of the most successful machines in this category is the 'Mono-photo' Filmsetter. This is in effect a 'Monotype' machine with a photographic unit substituted for the caster. Instead of producing columns of single type from molten metal, it produces exposed photographic film or paper which can be developed to give negatives or positives, which are used mainly for offset lithography or photogravure. With one or two minor modifications the keyboard of the 'Monophoto' is similar to that used for the 'Monotype' and the perforated ribbon controls the positioning of the film matrix case of the 'Monophoto'. Each character selected is projected onto the film through the optical system, the positions of the lens and prisms being adjustable to give whatever degree of magnification is required for the point size selected.

The second category of photocomposing machines departs entirely from the conception of previous type-composing machines and works on a different system. The Lumitype (called Photon in the United States) has a keyboard resembling that of an electric typewriter which operates electronic devices for the selection of the character and its size, and both spacing and justification are automatic. The codified information is turned into electrical impulses which control the photographic unit, which is a revolving glass disc bearing the characters for a number of founts, arranged in concentric rings. The selected character is photographed by a beam of light at the precise moment when it passes the lens of the photographic unit.

The Mergenthaler Company was experimenting as early as 1946 with a cathode ray tube, similar to that used for television, but at that time it was not found practicable. Later, however, resolution and illumination had ameliorated sufficiently to make the project commercially viable. The system used employs two cathode ray tubes, one to generate images of the selected characters and the other to ensure correct alignment and positioning on the page.

The Linotron is among the fastest operating filmsetter machines at the time of writing, and the tube can generate characters at a phenomenal speed in eight different point sizes from a special charactered grid containing 256 typographic symbols. The Lumizip is another high-speed filmsetter, which has 264 characters assembled in eleven horizontal lines of twenty-four characters, each backed by a separate flash tube so that any one of them can be illuminated by flash according to an electronic memory control. The lens moves at speed over the lines, a flash exposing each selected character the instant its image reaches its allotted place in the line.

The 1960s saw the printing industry making use of transistor circuitry for many operations and the impact of the cathode ray tube on filmsetting is shown by the increasing number of machines available, including the Mergenthaler models already mentioned, the RCA system known as 'Videocomp' and Harris-Intertype's 'Fototronic'. Even the computer is now used as an adjunct to photocomposition, and is particularly suitable for matter in tabular form, such as time-tables, especially when the format remains constant for each succeeding edition and can be re-set from the same master computer programme.

The first book in Britain to be entirely film-set was the Penguin edition of Eric Linklater's *Private Angelo* (1957), which was issued in a special privately printed edition of 2,000 copies prior to the trade edition. This special edition was printed by deep-etch offset on Bible paper, and the colophon reads: 'The book was composed entirely without metal type; it is the first to have been produced in Great Britain by means of photo-composition on the Intertype Fotosetter.'

But this may have been preceded (according to James Moran) by *A Child's Book of Horses* and *A Child's Book of Dogs*, set on a Hadego machine in July 1952, although this machine was not primarily intended for printing text, but, like the Ludlow, for titling.

In France the first film-set book seems to have been *Le Mariage de Figaro* (1957), set on the Photon-Lumitype in a type called Méridien, specially designed by Adrian Frutiger, art director of the Deberny & Peignot foundry, and responsible, among other type designs, for the very popular Univers, a sans-serif of which over a score of varieties are available.

The first book to be computer-typeset in England was Dylan Thomas, *Selected Poems* 1934–1952, published by J. M. Dent and Sons Ltd. in their 'Everyman Library'. It was computer-typeset by Rocappi Ltd. Otford, Kent, and printed by the Aldine Press, Letchworth.

At present filmsetting is used mainly for offset and gravure workings, providing a photographic original to print down direct on the gravure or litho plates, thus doing away with the necessity of making a proof from metal composition. The film can, however, be reversed from positive to negative and used for making wrap-around letterpress printing plates by the powderless etch process.

It is not without interest today to recall the words written by William Gamble in *Penrose's Annual* for 1933. He wrote then:

> 'Printers have become so accustomed to printing from metal that the possibility of utilising any other materials as printing surfaces is barely thought of. . . . But when one comes to think of it, type metal is a clumsy material to handle. It locks up an enormous amount of capital and requires considerable space for its storage and use. Moreover, while the type matter must be nearly an inch in height for its effective handling, perhaps not more than one-sixteenth of that height is necessary to form the actual printing surface.'

Although filmsetting today may show no saving over the use of metal, there is little doubt that developments in the field of electronics will ultimately make possible a much wider use of filmsetting techniques. Apart from inertia and the traditional conservatism of the printing industry, one factor which ensures the continuance for some time of the hot metal system is the size of the investment in letterpress printing by the trade, coupled with the fact of a very large labour force trained in the use of metal type. But as someone recently wrote (the source escapes me): 'ultimately the change may be wrought by newcomers who will object to carrying heavy trays of metal in a dirty shop'.

Appendix I

Establishment of Early Presses in Europe — 15th Century

Germany

1468	Augsburg
1460/61	Bamberg
1475	Blaubeuren
1475	Breslau
1465/66	Cologne
1498	Danzig
1484	Eichstatt
1467	Eltville
1473	Erfurt
c. 1472	Esslingen
c. 1491	Freiburg
1487	Freising
1488/89	Hagenau
1491	Hamburg
1484/85	Heidelberg
1484	Ingolstadt
1489	Kirchheim
1472/73	Lauingen
1481	Leipzig
1474	Lübeck
1493	Lüneburg
1479/80	Magdeburg
1450	Mainz
1492	Marienburg
1474	Marienthal im Rheingau
1483	Meissen
1480	Memmingen
1473	Merseburg

1482	Metz
1482	Munich
1485	Münster
1470	Nuremberg
1496	Offenburg
1480	Passau
1495	Pforzheim
1485	Regensburg
c. 1478	Reutlingen
1476	Rostock
1486	Schleswig
1478	Schussenried
1471	Speyer
1487/88	Stendal
1458	Strassburg
1486	Stuttgart
1481	Trier
1498	Tübingen
1472/73	Ulm
c. 1479	Urach
1482	Vienna
1479	Würzburg
c. 1495	Zinna
1487	Zweibrücken

Italy

1482	Aquila
1477	Ascoli
1496	Barco
1471	Bologna

Italy *cont.*

1473	Brescia
1475	Cagli
1493	Cagliari
1489	Capua
1481	Casale
1486	Casalmaggiore
1475	Caselle
1495	Cesena
1486	Chivasso
1480	Cividale del Friuli
1478	Colle di Valdelsa
1474	Como
1478	Cosenza
1472/73	Cremona
1476	Faenza
1471	Ferrara
1472	Fivizzano
1471	Florence
1495	Forlí
1470	Foligno
1487	Gaeta
1471/72	Genoa
1472/73	Jesi
1477	Lucca
1471	Milan
1472	Mantua
1473	Matelica
1478	Messina
1474/75	Modena
1472	Mondoví
1471	Naples
1480	Nonantola
1484	Novi
1491	Nozzano
1471	Padua
1478	Palermo
1472	Parma
1473	Pavia
1471	Perugia
1485/86	Pescia

1475	Piacenza
1479	Pinerolo
1475	Piove de Sacco
1482/83	Pisa
1476	Pogliano
1489/90	Portese
1475	Reggio (Calabria)
1480	Reggio (Emilia)
1467	Rome
1481	Saluzzo
1499	San Cesario
1484	San Germano
1474	Sant' Orso
1473/74	Savigliano
1474	Savona
1494/95	Scandiano
1484	Siena
1483	Soncino
1464/65	Subiaco
1478	Torrebelvicino
1478/79	Toscolano
1470	Trevi
1471	Treviso
1475	Trento
1474	Turin
1484	Udine
1493	Urbino
1469	Venice
1485	Vercelli
1472	Verona
1474	Vicenza
1478	Viterbo
1486	Voghera

Belgium

c. 1475	Alost
1481	Antwerp
1473/4	Bruges
1475	Brussels
1483	Ghent
1474	Louvain

Belgium *cont.*

1480	Oudenaard

Holland

1476/77	Delft
1477	Deventer
1477	Gouda
1483	Haarlem
1480	Hasselt
1484	s'Hertogenbos
1483	Kuilenburg
1483	Leiden
1479	Nijmegen
1478	Sint Maartensdijk
1498	Schiedam
1494/95	Schoonhoven
1469/70	Utrecht
1478	Zwolle

Switzerland

c. 1470	Basel
1470	Beromünster
1475	Burgdorf
1478	Geneva
1493	Lausanne
1482	Promenthoux
1481	Rougemont
1500	Sursee

Denmark

1490	Copenhagen
1482	Odense

Spain

1473? 1475?	Barcelona
1485	Burgos
1489	Coria
1483	Gerona
1496	Granada
1482	Guadalajara
1485	Hijar

1483/84	Huete
1479	Lerida
1485	Mallorca
1494	Monterrey
1499	Montserrat
1487	Murcia
1489/90	Pamplona
1480/81	Salamanca
1489	San Cucufate (Cugat)
1483	Santiago de Compostela
1477	Seville
1484	Tarragona
1484	Toledo
1477	Tortosa
1473	Valencia
1481	Valladolid
1481/82	Zamora

Portugal

1494	Braga
1487	Faro
1492	Leiria
1489	Lisbon
1496/97	Oporto

Sweden

1498	Gripsholm (Mariefred monastery)
1483	Stockholm
1495	Vadstena

France

1486	Abbeville
c. 1475	Albi
1476/77	Angers
1491	Angoulême
1497	Avignon
1487	Besançon
1484	Bréhan-Loudéac
1480	Caen

France *cont.*

1478	Chablis
1503?	Châlons-sur-Marne
1484	Chambéry
1482	Chartres
1492	Cluny
1491	Dijon
1490	Dôle
1489/90	Embrun
1490	Grenoble
1487/88	Lantenac
1495/96	Limoges
1473	Lyons
1493/94	Mâcon
1486	Moûtiers en Tarantaise
1493	Nantes
1491	Narbonne
1490/91	Orléans
1470	Paris
1498	Périgueux
1500	Perpignan
1479	Poitiers
1496	Provins
1484/85	Rennes

c. 1485	Rouen
1483	Salins
1476	Toulouse
1493/94	Tours
1485	Tréguier
1483	Troyes
1493	Uzès
1500	Valenciennes
1478	Vienne
1496	Valence

Bohemia & Moravia

1486	Brno
1489	Kuttenberg
1499	Olomouc
1476	Pilsen
1487	Prague
1484	Winterberg

Poland

1474	Cracow

Hungary

1473	Buda

Appendix II

WHEN AND WHERE THE FIRST BOOKS WERE PRINTED

PLACE	DATE OF FIRST PRINTING	PRINTER	FIRST BOOK
ABBEVILLE	1486	Pierre Gérard	Jean Boutillier: *La somme rurale*
ALBI	c. 1475	Anon.	Aeneas Silvius: *Epistola de amoris remedio*
ALOST	1475	John of Paderborn & Thierry Martens	Aeneas Silvius: *De duobus amantibus*
ANGERS	5 Feb. 1476/77	Johannes de Turre (& Johannes Morelli)	Cicero: *Rhetorica Nova*
ANGOULÊME	17 May 1491	Petrus Alanus & Andreas Calvinus	*Auctores octo*
ANTWERP	8 June 1481	Matthias van der Goes	*Boexken van der officien ofte dienst der Missen*
AQUILA	16 Sept. 1482	Adam von Rottweil	Plutarch: *Vitae parallelae* [Italian]
ASCOLI PICENO	1477	Gulielmo de Linis	Isodorus Hispalensis: *Chronica* [Italian]
AUGSBURG	12 Mar. 1468	Günther Zainer	Bonaventura: *Meditationes vitae Christi*
AVIGNON	1497	Pierre Rohault	Lucian: *Palinurus, Scipio Romanus, etc.*
BAMBERG	1459/60	Unknown (Gutenberg?)	*36-line Bible* (begun at Mainz.)
BARCELONA	1473? 1475?	Heinrich Botel, Georg vom Holtz & Johannes Planck	Aristotle: *Ethica, Oeconomica, Politica* (Undated
BARCO	15 Sept. 1496	Gershom Ben Moses of Soncino	*Prayers for the remission of sins* [Hebrew]
BASEL	c. 1470	Berthold Ruppel	*Biblia Latina*
BERGAMO	1555	Gallo de' Galli	*Libro de l'origine ... della città di Bergamo*
BEROMÜNSTER	10 Nov. 1470	Helias Heliae	Joh. Marchesinus: *Mammotrectus super Bibliam*
BESANÇON	1487	Pierre Metlinger	*Regimen sanitatis cum tractatu epidemiae*
BLAUBEUREN	1475	Konrad Mancz	Albrecht von Eyb: *Ehebüchlein*
BOLOGNA	1471	Balthasar Azzoguido	Ovid: *Opera*
BRAGA	12 Dec. 1494	Johann Gherlinc	*Breviarium Braccarense*
BRATISLAVA (see PRESSBURG)			
BRÉHAN-LOUDÉAC	Dec. 1484	Robin Foucquet & Jean Crès	*Le Trépassement de Notre-Dame*

PLACE	DATE OF FIRST PRINTING	PRINTER	FIRST BOOK
BRESCIA	21 Apr. 1473	(Georg of Butzbach?) For Pietro Villa	Virgil: Opera
BRESLAU	9 Oct. 1475	Caspar Elyan	Statuta Synodalia Vratislav
BRNO (BRUNN)	7 Oct. 1486	Konrad Stahel & Matthias Preinlein	Agenda Olomucensis
BRUGES	c. 1473/74	William Caxton	Raoul Le Fèvre: The Recuyell of the Histories of Troy
BRUSSELS	3 Mar. 1475	Brothers of the Common Life	Johannes Gerson: Opuscula
BUDA	5 June 1473	Andreas Hess	Chronica Hungarorum
BURGDORF	not after 1475	Printer of Jacobus de Clusa	Bernardus: Sermo de humana miseria
BURGOS	12 Mar. 1485	Friedrich Biel	A. Guttierez: Grammatica
CAEN	6 June 1480	J. Durand & Gilles Quijoue	Horace: Epistolae
CAGLI	29 June 1475	Robertus de Fano & Bernardinus de Bergamo	Maphaeus Vegius: De morte Astyanactis
CAGLIARI	1 Oct. 1493	Salvador de Bologna	Hugo de Sancto Caro: Speculum ecclesiae [Catalan]
CAPUA	10 Mar. 1489	Christian Preller	Breviarium Capuanum
CASALE MONFERRATO	6 Sept. 1481	Gulielmo de Canepanova de' Campanili & Ant. de Corsiono	Hubertinus Clericus: Commentum in Heroidas Ovidii
CASALMAGGIORE	21 Aug. 1486	Josua Salomon of Soncino	Mahzor. Part 2. [Hebrew]
CASELLE	30 Aug. 1475	Johannes Fabri	Vitas Patrum
CESENA	26 Mar. 1495	Paulus Guarinus & Johannes Jacobus de Benedictis	Antonio Manilio: Prognosticon dialogale
CETINJE	1493–4	The monk Makarije	Oktoich
CHABLIS	1 Apr. 1478	Pierre Le Rouge	Jacques Legrand: Le livre de bonnes moeurs
CHÂLONS-s-MARNE	1503?	Arnauld Bocquillon	Diurnale Catalaunense [dated wrongly '1403'; 1503?]
CHAMBÉRY	5 May 1484	Antoine Neyret	Le Doctrinal de sapience
CHARTRES	31 July 1482	Jean Du Pré	Missale Carnotense
CHIVASSO	13 May 1486	Jacobinus Suigus	Angelo Carletti: Summa angelica de casibus conscientiae

PLACE	DATE OF FIRST PRINTING	PRINTER	FIRST BOOK
CIVIDALE	24 Oct. 1480	Gerardus de Lisa	Bartholomaeus Platina: *De honesta voluptate*
CLUNY	1492	Michael Wenssler	*Breviarium Cluniacense*
COLLE DI VALDELSA	July 1478	Johannes de Medemblik	Dioscurides: *De materia media*
COLOGNE, *see* KÖLN			
COMO	9 Aug. 1474	Ambrosio de Orco & Dionysius Paravisinus	Joh. Ant. de Sancto Georgio: *Tractatus appellationum*
CONSTANCE	1470?	Anon.	*Breviarium Constantiense*
COPENHAGEN	Mar. 1490	Govaert van Ghemen	Donatus: *Ars minor* (now lost)
CORIA	1489	Bartolomé de Lila	Petrus Gratia Dei: *Blasón general*
COSENZA	1478	Octaviano Salamon	Giacomo Campora: *Dell' immortalità dell'anima* (or other 1478)
CREMONA	26 Jan. 1473	Dionysius Paravisinus & Stephanus Merlinis	Angelus de Ubaldis: *Lectura super . . . Digesti Novi*
CULEMBURG	6 Mar. 1483	Joh. Veldener	*Historia Sanctae Crucis* [Dutch]
DANZIG	before 10 June 1499	Konrad Baumgarten	Donatus: *Ars minor*
DELFT	10 Jan. 1477	Jakob van der Meer & Mauritius Yemantszoon	Old Testament [Dutch]
DEVENTER	1477	Richard Paffraet	Petrus Berchorius: *Liber Bibliae moralis* [or other 1477]
DIJON	4 July 1491	Pierre Metlinger	*Privilegia ordinis Cisterciensis*
DILLINGEN(?)	1488/89	Johann Sensenschmidt	*Missale Augustanum*
DÔLE	31 May 1490	Pierre Metlinger	*Coutumes du comté et du duché de Bourgogne*
EICHSTÄTT	1484	Michael Reyser (Types of Georg Reyser)	*Statuta Synodalia Eystettensia*
ELTVILLE	4 Nov. 1467	Heinrich & Nikolaus Bechtermünze	*Vocabularius Ex quo.*
EMBRUN	March 1489	Jacques Le Rouge	*Breviarium Eburodunense*
ERFURT	end of 1473	Anon.	*Almanac for Erfurt for year 1474*

437

PLACE	DATE OF FIRST PRINTING	PRINTER	FIRST BOOK
ESSLINGEN	not after 1473	Konrad Fyner	First extensive work: *Petrus Lombardus, Glossa in Ep^a. Pauli*
FAENZA	31 Dec. 1476	Kilian Fer & Heinrich Kandler	Alex. de Villa Dei: *Doctrinale*
FARO	30 June 1487	Samuel Porteira	*Pentateuch* [Hebrew]
FERRARA	12 Mar. 1471	Andreas Belfortis	Augustinus Datus: *Elegantiolae*
FIVIZZANO	1472	Jacobus de Fivizano	Virgil: *Opera* (or *Cicero*, or *Juvenal*)
FLORENCE	7 Nov. 1471	Bernardo & Dominico Cennini	Servius: *Comment. in Vergilii Bucolica*
FOLIGNO	1470	Johann Neumeister	L. B. Aretino: *De bello Italico adv. Gothos*
FORLÌ	16 Apr. 1495	Paulus Guarinus & Johannes Jacobus de Benedictis	Nic. Ferettus: *Commentariola isagogica . . .*
FREIBERG IN SACHSEN	9 Nov. 1495	Konrad Kachelofen	*Missale Misnense*
FREIBURG im BREISGAU	c. 1490	Kilian Fischer	Guillermus: *Rhetorica divina* OR the *Ephrem*
FREISING	31 Aug. 1487	Johann Sensenschmidt	*Missale Frisingense*
GAETA	1487	Andreas Freitag	Chris. Landino: *Formolario di epistole*
GENEVA	24 Mar. 1478	Adam Steinschaber	Francisco Jiménez: *Livre des saints anges*
GENOA	20 Feb. 1471	Lambertus Laurenszoon & Antonius Mathias	[Not known]
GERONA	17 Nov. 1483	Printer for Mateo Vendrell	Felipe de Malla: *Memorial del pecador remut*
GHENT	8 Apr. 1483	Arend de Keysere	*Traité d'Arras*
GOUDA	24 May 1477	Gerard Leeu	*Epistelen en evangelien*
GOUPILLIÈRES	8 May 1491	Michel Andrieu	*Heures*
GRANADA	30 Apr. 1496	Meinard Ungut & Joh. Pegnitzer	Francisco Jiménez: *Vita Christi*
GRENOBLE	29 Apr. 1490	Etienne Foret	Guido Papa, *Decisiones Parlamenti Dalphinalis*
GRIPSHOLM	24 Mar. 1498	Kloster Mariefred	Alanus de Rupe: *De utilitate Psalterii Mariae*
GUADALAJARA	1482	Salomo Ibn-Alkabez	David Qimhi: *Comment. on later Prophets* [Hebrew]

PLACE	DATE OF FIRST PRINTING	PRINTER	FIRST BOOK
HAARLEM	10 Dec. 1483	Jacob Bellaert	Lijden en passie ons heeren Jesu Christi
HAGENAU	1489	Heinrich Gran	Joh. de Garlandia: Cornutus
HAMBURG	14 Nov. 1491	Joh. & Thomas Borchard	Laudes B.M.V.
HASSELT	1480	Peregrinus Bermendo	Epistelen en evangelien
HEIDELBERG	21 Jan 1485	(Heinrich Knoblochtzer?)	Hugo de Prato Florido; Sermones
's HERTOGENBOSCH	1484	Gerard Leempt	Tondalus visioen
HIJAR	Aug./Sept. 1485	Elieser Ben Alantansi	Jacob Ben Aser: [Hebrew]
HUETE	11 Nov. 1484	Alvaro de Castro	Diaz de Montalvo: Ordenanzas reales [first dated book]
INGOLSTADT	1484?	Printer of the Lescherius	3 Decrees of Bishop Barth. de Marascis
JESI	4 Oct. 1473	Federico de' Conti	Constitutiones Marchiae Anconitanae
KIRCHEIM in Alsace	End of 1489	Marcus Reinhard	Hans Schrotbanck: Practica for 1490
KÖLN	c. 1465	Ulrich Zell	Cicero: De Officiis
KRAKOW	end of 1473	Kaspar Straube?	Almanach for 1474
KUILENBURG see CULEMBURG			
KUTTENBERG	14 Nov. 1489	Martin von Tischnowitz	Biblia Bohemica
LANTENAC	26 Mar. 1487	Jean Crès	Mandeville: Voyage en terre sainte
LAUINGEN	9 Nov. 1472	Anon.	Augustine: De anima et spiritu
LAUSANNE	1 Dec. 1493	Jean Bellot	Missale Lausannense
LEIDEN	9 July 1483	Heynricus Heynrici	Cronike van Hollant
LEIPZIG	28 Sept 1481	Marcus Brandis	Joh. Annius: De futuris Christianorum triumphis in Saracenos
LEIRIA	25 July 1492	Abraham Ben Samuel Dortas	Proverbs of Solomon [Hebrew]
LÉRIDA	16 Aug. 1479	Heinrich Botel	Breviarium Ilerdense

PLACE	DATE OF FIRST PRINTING	PRINTER	FIRST BOOK
LIMOGES	21 Jan. 1495/6	Jean Berton	*Breviarium Lenovicense*
LISBON	1489	Rabbi Elieser	*Comment. on Pentateuch* [Hebrew]
LONDON (City)	1480	John Lettou	Ant. Andreae: *Quaestiones super . . . Aristotelis*
LOUVAIN	after 7 Aug. 1474	Johann Veldener	Jacobus de Theramo: *Belial*
LÜBECK	5 Aug. 1475	Lucas Brandis	*Rudimentum novitiorum* [some undated works earlier?]
LUCCA	17 May 1477	Bartholomaeus de Civitali	Petrarch: *Trionfi*
LÜNEBURG	22 May 1493	Johann Lucae	*Imitatio Christi*
LYONS	17 Sept. 1473	Guillaume Le Roy	Innocent III: *Compendium breve*
MÂCON	10 Mar. 1493	Michael Wenssler	*Diurnale Matisconense*
MAGDEBURG	end of 1479	Bartholomaeus Ghotan	*Almanach for 1480* (*Missale Magdeburgense 1480*)
MAINZ	1453/1456	Joh. Gutenberg, Fust, Schöffer	*Biblia Latina* [first actual book]
MAJORCA	20 June 1485	Nicolaus Calafat	Gerson: *De regula mandatorum*
MANTUA	1472	Georg & Paul von Butzbach & Petrus Adam de Michaelibus	A. de Gambilionibus: *Tractatus maleficiorum*
MARIENBURG	13 Mar. 1492	Jacob Karweysse	Joh. von Marienwerder: *Das Leben . . . Dorothea*
MARIENTHAL	12 Mar. 1474	Brothers of the Common Life	*Breviarium Moguntinum*
MATELICA	1473	Barth. de Columnis (Simon Koch?)	Ant. Cornazzano: *La vita della Vergine Maria*
MEISSEN	16 July 1483	Albrecht Kunne	*Breviarium Misnense*
MEMMINGEN	c. 1480	Lucas Brandis	Rudolf von Werdenberg: *Ablassbrief*
MERSEBURG	3 Aug. 1473	Gabriele di Pietro	Augustinus: *De quaestionibus Orosii*
MESSAGA	1478	Heinrich Alding	Donatus: *Ars minor, etc.* (no copy extant)
MESSINA	15 April 1478	Joh. Colini & Gerardus de Nova Civitate	*Life of St. Jerome* [Italian]
METZ	1482	Pamfilo Castaldi (& Zarotus bros.)	*Imitatio Christi* (P.I)
MILAN	3 Aug. 1471		Sextus P. Festus: *De verborum significationibus*
MODENA	23 Jan. 1475	Johannes Vurster	Virgil: *Opera*
MONDOVÌ	24 Oct. 1472	Ant. Mathiae & Balt. Corderius	Antoninus Florentinus: *Confessionale*
MONTERREY	3 Feb. 1494	Gonzalo Rodriguez de la Passera	*Missale Aurense*

PLACE	DATE OF FIRST PRINTING	PRINTER	FIRST BOOK
MONTSERRAT	16 Apr. 1499	Johann Luschner	Bonaventura: *Meditationes vitae Christi*
MOUTIERS	18 Mar. 1486	Johann Walther	*Breviarium Tarentasiense*
MUNICH	28 June 1482	Johann Schaur	*Mirabilia Romae* [German]
MÜNSTER (Westphalia)	31 Oct. 1485	Johann Limburg	Joh. Kerckmeister: *Comoedia Codri*
MURCIA	12 Jan. 1484	Alfonso de Cordoba	Breviary for Cartagena
NANTES	15 Apr. 1493	Etienne Larcher	Jean Meschinot: *Les lunettes des princes*
NARBONNE	31 Oct. 1491	(In Claustro S. Justi. Types of Jean Du Pré, Lyons)	*Breviarium Narbonense*
NAPLES	1471	Sixtus Riessinger	Bart. de Saxoferrato: *Lectura super ... Codicis*
NEUCHATEL	22 Aug. 1533	Pierre de Vingle	*Le livre des marchans*
NIJMEGEN	1479	Anon.	Engelbertus Cultrificis: *Defensorium privilegiorum ...*
NONANTOLA	May 1480	Giorgio & Antonio Miscomini	*Breviarium Romanum*
NOVI LIGURE	1484	Nicolaus Girardengus	Baptista de Salis: *Summa casuum conscientiae*
NOZZANO	1491	Heinrich von Köln & Heinrich von Haarlem	Paulus Turretinus: *Disputatio de dote*
NUREMBERG	1470	Johann Sensenschmidt & Heinrich Keffer	Franciscus de Retza: *Comestorium vitiorum* (or undated)
ODENSE	1482	Johann Snell	Guil. Caoursin: *Obsidionis Rhodiae ... descriptio*
OFFENBURG	5 Jan. 1496	(Kilian Fischer)	Robertus Caracciolus: *Sermones ...*
OLMÜTZ	1499	Matthias Preinlein	Joh. Fabri: *Planctus ruinae ecclesiae.*
OPORTO	4 Jan. 1497	Rodrigo Alvarez	*Constituíçoes do sinodo do Porto de 1496*
OPPENHEIM	1499	Jakob Köbel	Joh. Virdung: *Praktika* for 1500
ORLEANS	31 Mar. 1490	Mathieu Vivian	Guido de Monte Rotherii: *Manipulus curatorum* [French]
OUDENAARDE	1480	Arend de Keysere	Hermannus de Petra: *Sermones ...*
OXFORD	17 Dec. 1478	(Theodoric Rood?)	Hieronymus: *Expositio in symbolum apostolorum*

PLACE	DATE OF FIRST PRINTING	PRINTER	FIRST BOOK
PADUA	9 June 1471	Laurentius Canozius	Mesue: Opera
PALERMO	1478	Andreas Vyel	Consuetudines urbis Panormi.
PALMA de MALLORCA	20 June 1485	Nicolaus Calafat	Joh. Gerson: De regulis mandatorum
PAMPLONA	15 Dec. 1489 (1490?)	Arnão Guillén de Brocar	Manuale Pampilonense
PARIS	(1470)	Gering, Friburger & Krantz	Gasparinus Barzizius: Epistolae
PARMA	23 Sept. 1472	Andreas Portilia	Plutarch: De liberis educandis
PASSALI	(end of 1480)	Benedict Mayr	Appellation des Domkapitels Passau an Papst . . .
PASSAU	6 Aug. 1481	B. Mayr & C. Stahel	Passau Breviary
PAVIA	30 Oct. 1473	Johannes de Sidriano	Angelus de Gambilionibus: Lectura super institutionum
PÉRIGUEUX	1498	Jean Carant	Joh. de Lapide: Resolutorium dubiorum
PERPIGNAN	31 Oct. 1500	Johann Rosenbach	Breviarium Elnense
PERUGIA	(after 1 May, 1471)	Petrus Petri & Joh. Nicolai	Philippus de Franchis: Lectura super titulo . . .
PESCIA	28 Feb. 1485[86]	Franciscus de Cennis	Bernardinus Senensis: Della confessione
PFORZHEIM	(end of 1495)	Thomas Anshelm	Almanac for 1496
PIACENZA	1475	Johannes Petrus de Ferratis	Biblia Latina
PILSEN	26 Apr. 1476	Anon.	Statuta provincialia Arnesti (First dated printing in Bohemia)
PINERLO	1479	Jacobus Rubens	Guarinus Veronensis: Regulae Grammaticales
PIOVE DI SACCO	5 July 1475	Mešulla Kôzi	Jacob Ben Aser: [Hebrew]
PISA	23 Mar. 1482[83]	Anon.	Franciscus de Accoltis: Consilia
POITIERS	14 Aug. 1479	Jean Bouyer	Landulphus de Columna: Breviarium historiale
POJANO (nr. VERONA)	1 Oct. 1476	Felix Antiquarius & Innocens Ziletus	Petrarch: De Viris illustribus [Italian]
PORTESE	20 Aug. 1490	Bartholomaeus de Zanis	Statuta commun. Ripariae Benacensis
PRAGUE	1487 (1478?)	(Johann von Hohennauth?)	Psalterium Bohemicum
PRESSBURG (BRATISLAVA)	after 11 May 1480	Anon.	Johannes Han: Litterae indulgentiarum
PROMENTHOUX	2 Aug. 1482	Louis Cruse (Guerbin)	Le Doctrinal de sapience
PROVINS	1 Oct. 1496	Guillaume Tavernier	Joh. Friburgensis: La Règle des marchands

PLACE	DATE OF FIRST PRINTING	PRINTER	FIRST BOOK
REGENSBURG	5 Mar. 1485	Johann Sensenschmidt	*Missale Ratisponense*
REGGIO di CALABRIA	Feb. 1475	Abraham Ben Garton Ben Isaac	*Comment. on Pentateuch* [Hebrew]
REGGIO nell'EMILIA	29 July 1480	Barth. & Laurentius de Bruschis	Nic. Perottus: *Rudimenta Grammaticae*
REICHENSTEIN	1477	Erwin. von Stege (types of Nikolaus Götz)	Heinrich Urdermann: *Dialogus de libertate*
RENNES	26 Mar. 1484	Pierre Bellescullée	*Coutumes de Bretagne*
REUTLINGEN	not before 18 Oct. 1476	Michael Greyff	Eberhard of Württemberg: *Brief an Herzog Sigmund*
ROME	1467	Sweynheim & Pannartz	Cicero: *Epistolae ad familiares*
ROSTOCK	9 Apr. 1476	Brothers of the Common Life	Lactantuis: *Opera* (perhaps earlier books?)
ROUEN	c. 1485	Guillaume Le Talleur	*Entrée du roi Charles VIII à Rouen* [April 1485]
ROUGEMONT	1481	Heinrich Wirczburg	Werner Rolevinck: *Fasciculus temporum*
ST. ALBANS	1480	Schoolmaster printer	Thomas de Erfordia: *De modus significandi*
SALAMANCA	(1480)	Anon.	*Leyes de las Cortes de Toledo* or A. Nebrissensis: *Introductiones Latinae*
SALINS-LES-BAINS	1483	Jean du Pré	Claudius Ewrardi: *Indulgence*
SALUZZO	10 Feb. 1481	Martinus de Lavalle	Persius: *Satyrae*
SAN CESARIO	1499	Ugo Rugerius	Bernardus: *De meditatione passionis Christi* [Italian]
SAN CUGAT DE VALLES	29 Nov. 1489	Hans Hurus	Isaac: *De religione* [Catalan]
SAN GERMANO	21 Oct. 1484	Jacobinus Suigus	*Breviarium Cisterciense*
SANTIAGO DE COMPOSTELA (?)	1483/4	Juan de Bobadilla & Alvaro de Castro	*Breviarium Compostellanum* [no copy now known]
SANT' ORSO	1474	Leonardus Achates de Basilia	*Vitae Patrum* [Italian]
SAVIGLIANO	c. 1473/4	Christoph Beyamus & Joh. Glim	Guido de Monte Rotherii: *Manipulus curatorum*
SAVONA	(1474)	Johannes Bonus	Alex. de Villa Dei: *Doctrinale*
SCANDIANO	10 Jan. 1495	Peregrino Pasquale	Appianus: *Historia Ronana. Pars I*
SCHIEDAM	1498	(Otgier Nachtegael)	Joh. Brugman: *Vita S. Liduinae*
SCHLESWIG	1486	Steffan Arndes	*Missale Slesviense*

PLACE	DATE OF FIRST PRINTING	PRINTER	FIRST BOOK
SCHOONHOVEN	28 Feb. 1495	Brothers of S. Michael in den Hem	Breviarium Traiectense
SCHUSSENRIED	1478	Abbey of the Praemonstraten	Leonardus Brunus Aretinus: Gracchus et Poliscena
SEGOVIA?	not before 10.6.1472	Johann Parix of Heidelberg	Synodal de Segovia
SEVILLE	1477	Antonio Martinez, Alfonso del Puerto & Bartolomé Segura	Alonso Díaz de Montalvo: Repertorium
SIENA	21 July 1484	Heinrich of Cologne	Paulus de Castro: Super VI. Codicis
SINT MAARTENSDIJK	Nov. 1478	Pieter Werrecoren	Der zyelen troeste
SONCINO	19 Dec. 1483	Josua Salomon Soncino	Talmud – Comment. [Hebrew]
SPEYER	1471	Anon.	Postilla scholastica super apocalypsin
STENDAL	(1488)	Joachim Westral	Joh. Gerson: Donatus moralisatus
STOCKHOLM	20 Dec. 1483	Johann Snell	Maynus de Mayneris: Dialogus creaturarum
STRASSBURG	c. 1460 (1458?)	Johann Mentelin	49-line Latin Bible
STUTTGART	(1486)	(material of Konrad Fyner)	Election of Maximilian (16 Feb. 1486)
SUBIACO	1465	Sweynheym & Pannartz	1st Donatus [missing]; Lactantius 29.10.1465
SURSEE	14 Jan. 1500	Anon.	Schradin: Chronicle of the Swiss Wars
TARRAGONA	3 Aug. 1484	Nicolaus Spindeler	Guido de Monte Rotherii: Manipulus curatorum
TOLEDO	before 20 Feb. 1484	Juan Vazquez	Letter of Indulgence
TORINO (TURIN)	not before 1474	Joh. Fabri & Johanninus de Petro	Breviarium Romanum
TORRE BELVICINO	19 Sept. 1478	Giovanni Leonardo Longo	Johannes Climachus: Scala Paradisi [Italian]
TORTOSA	16 June 1477	Peter Brun & Nicolaus Spindeler	Nicolas Perottus: Rudimenta grammaticae
TOSCOLANO	12 Jan. 1479	Gabriele di Pietro	Guarinus Veronensis: Regulae grammaticales
TOULOUSE	20 June 1476	Heinrich Turner	Andreas Barbatia: Repetitio rubricae . . .
TOURS	10 Feb. 1493/4	Simon Pourcelet	Breviarium Turonense
TRÉGUIER	17 May 1485	Ia. P. [Initials only known]	Coutumes de Bretagne [only recorded signed book]
TREVI	1470	Johann Reinhard	Historia quomodo beatus Franciscus petivit a Christo . . .

444

PLACE	DATE OF FIRST PRINTING	PRINTER	FIRST BOOK
TRENT	6 Sept. 1475	Albrecht Kunne	*Historia de passione pueri Simonis* [German]
TREVISO	1471	Gerardus de Lisa	Augustinus: *Manuale*
TRIER (TREVES)	c. 15 Aug. 1481	Anon. (J. Colini & G. de N. Civitate?)	Hermann von Schilditz: *Speculum sacerdotum*
TROYES	25 Sept. 1483	Jean Le Rouge	*Breviarium Trecense*
TÜBINGEN	24 Mar. 1498	Johann Otmar	Paulus Scriptor: *Lectura in Joh. Duns Scotum* . . .
UDINE	31 July 1484	Gerardus de Lisa	*Constituzioni della patria di Friuli*
ULM	11 Jan. 1473	Johann Zainer	H. Steinhöwel: *Ordnung wider die Pestilenz*
URACH	1 Feb. 1481	Konrad Fyner	*Plenarium* [German] [possibly preceded by others undated]
URBINO	15 May 1493	Heinrich of Cologne	Tancredus de Corneto: *Summa quaestionum*
UTRECHT	c. 1470?	Anon.	*Speculum humanae salvationis*
UZÈS	2 Oct. 1493	Jean Du Pré	*Breviarium Uticense*
VADSTENA	not after 1495	[Birgittenkloster]	*Officium B.M.V.*
VALENCE?	1496	Jean Belon?	*Missale Valentinense*
VALENCIA	towards end 1473	Lambert Palmart	Aristotle: *Ethica, Oeconomica, Politica*
VALENCIENNES	1500?	Jean de Liège	Georges Chastelain: *Les chansons georgines*
VALLADOLID	not after 1481	Abbey of N. Señora del Prado	Alfonso, Bp. of Avila: *Indulgence*
VENICE	1469	Johann von Speyer	Cicero: *Epistulae ad familiares*
VERCELLI	27 Oct. 1485	Jacobinus Suigus	Nicolas de Ausmo: *Suppl. Summae Pisanellae*
VERONA	1472	Johannes de Verona	Robertus Valturius: *De re militari*
VICENZA	25 Nov. 1474	Leonardus Achates de Basilia	Fazio degli Uberti: *Dittamondo*
VIENNA	1482	(Stephan Koblinger?)	*Vocabulista* [Italian–German]
VIENNE	1478	Johann Schilling (Solidi)	Bartolus de Saxoferrato: *Litigatio Satanae*
VIMPERK (see WINTERBERG)			
VITERBO	12 Jan. 1488 [1478?]	Anon.	Servius: *De ultimis syllabis*
VOGHERA	1 June 1486	Jacobus de Sancto Nazario	Alexander Tartagnus: *Apostillae ad Bartolum*

PLACE	DATE OF FIRST PRINTING	PRINTER	FIRST BOOK
WESTMINSTER	before 13 Dec. 1476	William Caxton	John Sant, Bp. of Abingdon: *Indulgence*
WINTERBERG (VIMPERK)	1484	Johann Alacraw	Augustinus: *Soliloquia animae*
WÜRZBURG	after 20 Sept. 1479	Georg Reyser (with S. Dold & J. Beckenhub)	*Breviarium Herbipolense*
ZAMORA	25 Jan. 1482	Antonio de Centenera	Iñigo Lopez de Mendoza: *Vita Christi per coplas*
ZARAGOZA	15 Oct. 1475	Mattheus Flander	Guido de Monte Rocherii: *Manipulus curatorum*
ZENGG	7 Aug. 1494	Blaž Baromić	*Missale Glagoliticum*
ZINNA	c. 1495	Cistercian Abbey	Hermann Nitzschewitz: *Psalterium B.M.V.*
ZÜRICH	c. 1479	Anon. (Sigmund Rot?)	Albertus de Albo Lapide: *Laus cantici 'Salve Regina'*
ZWEIBRÜCKEN	1487	Jörg Gessler	*Missale Tullense*
ZWOLLE	after 6 June 1478		*Overijsselsche Landbrief.*

Bibliography

GENERAL HISTORIES OF PRINTING

Barge, Hermann. *Geschichte der Buchdruckerkunst.* Leipzig. 1940.

Bauer, Konrad. *Aventur und Kunst.* Frankfurt. 1940.

Berry, W. T. & Poole, H. E. *Annals of Printing.* London. 1966.

Billoux, R. *Encyclopédie des arts graphiques.* Paris. 1943.

Binns, Norman. *An Introduction to Historical Bibliography.* London. 1962.

Bloy, C. H. *A History of Printing Ink, Balls and Rollers, 1440–1850.* London. 1967.

Bogeng, G. A. *Geschichte der Buchdruckerkunst.* Three vols. Hellerau. 1928.

Bohigas, Pedro. *El libro español.* Barcelona. 1962.

Bouchot, Henri. *Le Livre.* Paris. 1886.

Brun, R. *Le Livre Français.* Paris. 1969.

Calot, Michon, & Angoulevent. *L'art du livre en France.* Paris. 1931.

Carter, J. & Muir, P. (Eds.). *Printing and the Mind of Man.* London. 1967.

Clair, Colin. *A Chronology of Printing.* London. 1969.

Dahl, S. *History of the Book.* New York. 1959.

Faulmann, Karl. *Illustrierte Geschichte der Buchdruckerkunst.* Vienna. 1882.

Flocon, A. *L'Univers des Livres.* Paris. 1961.

Handbuch der Bibliothekswissenschaft. Four vols. 1952–61.

Kirchner, J. & Löffler, K. (Eds.) *Lexikon des gesamten Buchwesens.* 3 vols. Leipzig. 1935–37.

Lechêne, Robert. *L'Imprimerie de Gutenberg à l'électron.* Paris. 1972.

Le Livre. Catalogue of an exhibition at the Bibliothèque Nationale, Paris. 1972.

Lorck, C. B. *Geschichte der Buchdruckerkunst.* Leipzig. 1882–83.

McMurtrie, Douglas C. *The Book.* New York. 1937.

Morison, Stanley. *Four Centuries of Fine Printing.* London. 1924.

Néret, J. A. *Histoire de la librairie française.* Paris. 1953.

Orcutt, W. Dana. *Master Makers of the Book.* New York. 1928.

Oswald, John Clyde. *A History of Printing.* New York. 1928.

Palmer, Samuel. *The General History of Printing.* London. 1732.

Pollard, A. W. *Fine Books.* London. 1912.

Rodenberg, Julius. *Die Druckkunst als Spiegel der Kultur.* Berlin. 1942.

Schottenloher, Karl. *Bücher bewegten die Welt.* 2 vols. Stuttgart. 1951.

Steinberg, S. H. *Five Hundred Years of Printing.* London. 1955.

Trevisani, Piero. *Storia della Stampa.* Rome. 1953.

Twyman, M. *Printing 1770–1970 . . . in England.* London. 1970.

Vervliet, D. (Ed.) *The Book through 5000 years.* London. 1972.

Vingtrinier, M. *L'Imprimerie à Lyon.* Lyons. 1894.

Wroth, L. C. *A History of the Printed Book* ('The Dolphin' No. 3). New York. 1938.

TYPOGRAPHY

Audin, Marius. *Les Livrets typographiques des fonderies françaises*. Amsterdam. 1965.

Avis, F. C. *Edward Philip Prince: Type Punchcutter*. London. 1967.

Balsamo, L. & Tinto, A. *Origini del corsivo nella tipografia italiana del Cinquecento*. Milan. 1967.

Bauer, F. *Chronik der Schriftgiessereien in Deutschland*. 2nd edn. Offenbach.a.M. 1928.

Bengtsson, Bengt. *Svensk stilgjuterei*. Stockholm. 1956.

Bodoni, G-B. *Oratio Dominica in CLV linguas*. Facsimile edition, Parma. 1966. (Displaying 155 different type faces).

Carter, Harry. *A View of Early Typography*. Oxford. 1969.

— *Plantin's types and their makers* in 'Gedenkboek der Plantin-Dagen'. Antwerp. 1955.

— Carter, H. & Vervliet, H. D. L. *Civilité Types*. (Oxford Bibliographical Soc. Pubns.) Oxford. 1966.

Dowding, Geoffrey. *An Introduction to the History of Printing Types*. London. 1961.

Enschedé, C. *Fonderies de caractères et leur matériel dans les Pays-Bas du XVe au XIXe siècle*. Haarlem. 1908.

Hart, Horace. *Notes on a century of typography at the University Press, Oxford, 1693–1794*. Oxford. 1900.

Hellinga, W. (Ed.) *Copy and Print in the Netherlands*. Amsterdam. 1962.

— & L. *The Fifteenth-century Printing Types of the Low Countries*. 2 vols. Amsterdam. 1966.

Isaac, Frank. *English & Scottish Printing Types, 1501–35; 1508–41*. London. 1930.

— *English and Scottish Printing Types, 1535–58; 1552–58*. London. 1932.

Javet, A. & Matthew, H. *Typographie*. Lausanne. 1956.

Johnson, A. F. *Type Designs*. 2nd edn. London. 1959.

Jolles, O. *Die deutsche Schriftgiesserei*. Frankfurt. A.M. 1923.

Letouzey, V. *La Typographie*. Paris. 1964.

Mores, E. Rowe. *A Dissertation upon English Typographical Founders and Foundries*. (1778). Edited by Harry Carter and Christopher Ricks. Oxford. 1961.

Mori, Gustav. *Die Egenolff-Lutherische Schriftgiesserei in Frankfurt-am-Main*. Frankfurt-a-M. 1926.

Morison, Stanley. *Type Designs of the Past and Present*. London. 1926.

— *A tally of types*. Cambridge. 1953.

— *L'Inventaire de la fonderie Le Bé*. 'Documents Typographiques Français.' Vol. I. Paris. 1957.

Reed, Talbot Baines. *A History of the Old English Letter Foundries*. (1887) revised and enlarged by A. F. Johnson. London. 1952.

Rodenberg, J. *In der Schmiede der Schrift. Karl Klingspor und sein Werk*. Berlin. 1940.

Simon, Oliver. *Introduction to Typography*. London. 1947.

Sixteenth Century French Typefounders. The Le Bé Memorandum edited by Harry Carter. 'Documents Typographiques Français' Vol. III. Paris. 1967.

Thibaudeau, F. *La Lettre d'Imprimerie*. 2 vols. Paris. 1921.

Updike, D. B. *Printing Types: their History, Forms and Use*. 2nd edn. 2 vols. Cambridge (Mass.) 1937.

Van Krimpen, J. *On Designing and Devising Type*. London. 1957.

Bibliography

Veröffentlichungen der Gesellschaft für Typenkunde des XVn Jahrhunderts. 9 vols. Halle. 1907–22 (1,350 facs. reproductions).

Vervliet, H. *Type Specimens of the Vatican Press.* Amsterdam. 1967.

— *Sixteenth-century Printing Types of the Low Countries.* Amsterdam. 1968.

Veyrin-Forrer, J. & Jammes, A. *Les premiers caractères de l'Imprimerie Royale.* 'Documents Typographiques Français'. Vol. II. Paris. 1958.

Wolf, R. *Fraktur und Antiqua.* Frankfurt-a-M. 1934.

Zapf, H. & Stauffacher, J. W. *Hunt Roman: The birth of a type.* Pittsburgh. 1965.

THE INFANCY OF PRINTING

Bernard, Auguste. *De l'origine et des débuts de l'imprimerie en Europe.* Paris. 1853.

Blume, André. *Les origines de la gravure en France.* Paris. 1927.

Bogeng, G. *Geschichte der Buchdruckerkunst.* (Vol. I. Der Frühdruck). Dresden. 1939.

British Museum Catalogue of Incunabula. London. 1908.

Butler, P. *The origin of printing in Europe.* Chicago. 1940.

Conway, W. M. *The Woodcutters of the Netherlands in the fifteenth century.* Cambridge. 1884.

Cundall, Joseph. *A Brief History of Wood Engraving.* London. 1895.

De Vinne, T. *The Invention of Printing.* London. 1877.

Duff, E. G. *Early Printed Books.* London. 1893.

Febvre, L. & Martin, H-J. *L'Apparition du Livre.* Paris. 1958.

Geldner, F. *Buchdruckerkunst im Bamberg.* Bamberg. 1964.

— *Die deutschen Inkunabel-Drucker.* Stuttgart. 1969.

Häbler, Konrad. *Die Erfindung der Druckkunst . . .* Mainz. 1930.

— *The Study of Incunabula.* New York. 1933.

Hind, A. M. *An Introduction to a history of woodcuts.* London. 2 vols. 1936.

Hodnett, Edward. *English Woodcuts, 1480–1535.* London. 1935. Rev. edn. 1973.

Jackson, J. *A treatise on wood engraving.* London. 1839.

McMurtrie, D. C. *The Gutenberg Documents.* Toronto. 1941.

Mortet, Charles. *Les origines et les débuts de l'imprimerie d'après les recherches les plus récentes.* Paris. 1922.

Pilinski, Adam (Ed.) *Monuments de la Xylographie.* 8 vols. Paris. 1882–86.

Publications of the *Gutenberg Gesellschaft.* Mainz.

Requin, Abbé H. *L'Imprimerie à Avignon en 1444.* Paris. 1890.

Rosenthal, Léon. *La Gravure.* 2nd edn. Paris. 1939.

Sotheby, S. L. *Principia Typographica – The Block Books.* London. 3 vols. 1858.

Winship, G. P. *Printing in the 15th Century.* New York. 1940.

FIRST FRUITS OF THE INVENTION

Bernard, Auguste. *De l'origine et des débuts de l'imprimerie en Europe.* 2 vols. Paris. 1853.

Blum, Rudolf. *Der Prozess Fust gegen Gutenberg.* Wiesbaden. 1954.

Butler, Pierce. *The Origin of Printing in Europe.* Chicago. 1940.

De Vinne, T. *The Invention of Printing.* London. 1877.

Febvre, L. & Martin, H-J. *L'Apparition du Livre.* Paris. 1958.

Festschrift zum fünfhundertjährigen Geburtstage von Johann Gutenberg. Mainz. 1900.
Fuhrmann, Otto W. *Gutenberg and the Strasbourg documents of 1439.* New York. 1940.
Guignard, Jacques. *Gutenberg et son oeuvre.* Paris. 1960.
Gutenberg Jahrbuch. Mainz. 1926 onwards.
Holtrop, J. W. *Monuments typographiques des Pays Bas au XVe siècle.* The Hague. 1868.
Lehmann-Haupt, Hellmut. *Peter Schoeffer.* New York. 1950.
Meisner, H. & Luther, J. *Die Erfindung der Buchdruckerkunst.* Leipzig. 1900.
Menn, Walter. *Das Helmaspergersche Notariatsinstrument.* Greifswald. 1941.
Painter, George D. *Gutenberg and the B36 Group: a Re-consideration.* In 'Essays in Honour of Victor Scholderer'. Mainz. 1970.
Presser, Helmut. *Johannes Gutenberg.* Reinbek bei Hamburg. 1967.
Ruppel, Aloys. *Johannes Gutenberg, sein Leben und sein Werk.* Berlin. 1941.
— *Die Technik Gutenbergs und ihre Vorstufen.* Düsseldorf. 1961.
Scholderer, Victor. *The Invention of Printing.* (In 'The Library', Vol. XXI, 1940).
— *Johann Gutenberg, the inventor of printing.* London. 1963.
Van der Linde, A. *Geschichte der Erfindung der Buchdruckerkunst.* Berlin. 1886.
Voullième, E. *Die deutschen Drucker des fünfzehnten Jahrhunderts.* Berlin. 1922.
Wehmer, Carl. *Mainzer Probedrucke in der Type des sogennanten Astronomischen Kalenders für 1448.* Munich. 1948.
Winship, G. P. *Printing in the fifteenth century.* Philadelphia. 1940.

SPREAD OF PRINTING IN GERMANY

Geldner, F. *Buchdruckerkunst im Bamberg.* Bamberg. 1964.
Hase, Oskar von. *Die Koberger.* 2nd edn. Leipzig. 1885.
— *Die Entwicklung des Buchgewerbes in Leipzig.* Leipzig. 1887.
Kapp, F. & Goldfriedrich, J. *Geschichte des deutschen Buchhandels.* 4 vols. Leipzig. 1886–1913.
Lorck, C. *Druckkunst in Leipzig.* Leipzig. 1879.
Lübbecke, F. *500 Jahre Buch und Druck in Frankfurt.* Frankfurt. 1948.
Rodenberg, J. *Die Druckkunst als Spiegel der Kultur.* Berlin. 1942.
Scholderer, Victor. *50 Essays in 15th and 16th century bibliography.* Amsterdam. 1966.
Schottenloher, C. *Das Alte Buch.* 2nd edn. Berlin. 1921.
Steiff, Karl. *Der erste Buchdruck in Tübingen, 1498–1534.* Tübingen. 1881.
Voullième, Ernst. *Die deutschen Drucker des fünfzehnten Jahrhunderts.* 2nd edn. Berlin. 1922.
Zedler, G. *Die Bamberger Pfisterdrucke.* Mainz. 1911.

EARLY PRINTING IN ITALY

Barzon, A. *Stampatori in Padova.* Padua. 1959.
Bühler, Curt F. *University and Press in Bologna.* Notre Dame. 1958.
— *The Fifteenth Century Book.* Philadelphia. 1960.
De Vinne, T. *Notable Printers of Italy.* New York. 1910.
Duff, E. Gordon. *Early Printed Books.* London. 1893.
Essling, Victor Masséna, Prince of. *Les livres à figures vénitiens.* 5 vols. Paris. 1907–9.
Fava, M. & Besciano, G. *Stampa à Napoli nel XV secolo.* 1911–13.

Bibliography

Fumagalli, G. *Lexicon typographicum Italiae*. Florence, 1905.

Goldschmidt, E. P. *The Printed Book of the Renaissance*. Cambridge. 1950.

Hind, A. M. *An Introduction to a History of Woodcut*. 2 vols. London. 1935.

Nesi, E. *Diario della stamperia di Ripoli*. Florence. 1903.

Orcutt, W. D. *The Book in Italy*. New York. 1928.

Painter, George D. *The Hypnerotomachia Poliphili of 1499*. (An Introduction to the Eugrammia Press edition of the work. London. 1963.)

Parisi, G. A. *Jacottino de Rubeis*. Pinerolo. 1953.

Pastorello, E. *Bibliografia storico-analitica dell'arte della stampa in Venezia*. Venice. 1933.

Pollard, A.W. *Early Illustrated Books*. London. 1893.

Poppelreuter, J. *Der anonyme Meister des Polyfilo*. Strassburg. 1904.

Pulega, D. *Tipografia bolognese*. (Bib. de l'Archiginnasio. Ser. 2. No. 54.)

Sander, Max. *Le livre à figures italien 1467–1530*. Milan. 1942. 6 vols.

Santoro, C. *Libri illustrati milanesi di Rinascimento*. Milan. 1956.

— *L'Arte della stampa à Milano*. Milan. 1960.

Scholderer, Victor. *50 Essays in 15th and 16th century bibliography*. Amsterdam. 1966.

THE FIRST PRINTERS IN SWITZERLAND

Binz, Gustav. *Die Anfänge des Buchdrucks in Basel*. Mainz. 1925.

Büchler, Eduard. *Die Anfänge des Buchdrucks in der Schweiz*. Bern. 1951.

Harrisse, Henry. *Les premiers incunables bâlois, et leurs dérivés*. Paris. 1902.

Hartmann, Alfred. *Die Amerbachkorrespondenz*. 2 vols. Basel. 1942–45.

Heckethorn, C. W. *The printers of Basle in the XVth and XVIth Centuries*. London. 1897.

Kleinschmidt, J. *Les imprimeurs de Genève*. Geneva. 1948.

Leeman van Elck, P. *Die Offizin Froschauer*. Zürich. 1939.

Pache, Constant. *L'Imprimerie. Son invention: Histoire et Légende*. Lausanne. 1898.

Rudolphi, E. C. *Die Buchdruckerfamilie Froschauer in Zürich*. Zürich. 1869.

Scholderer, Victor. *50 Essays*. Amsterdam. 1966.

Staedtke, J. *Anfange und erste Blütezeit des Zürcher Buchdrucks*. Zürich. 1967.

Steinmann, M. *Johannes Oporinus*. Basel & Stuttgart. 1967.

Stevenson, A. *The Problem of the Missale Speciale*. London. 1967.

Vögelin, Salomon. *Die Entwicklung der schweizerischen Typographie*. Zürich. 1884.

PRINTING IN HOLLAND AND BELGIUM

[*Bibliotheca Belgica*]. 6 vols. Brussels. 1964–70.

Diederich, J. *Vijf eeuwen boek in Nederland*. Haarlem. 1940.

Campbell, M. F. *Annales de la typographie néerlandaise au XVe siècle*. The Hague. 1874. With 4 vols. Supplements 1878–1890.

Catalogue of the Exhibition 'The Development of Printing in the Netherlands'. Haarlem. 1923.

Delen, A. J. J. *Histoire de la gravure dans les anciens Pays-Bas et dans les provinces belges*, etc. 3 vols. Paris. 1924–35.

Denucé, J. *Oud-Nederlansche Kaartmakers in betrekking mit Plantijn.* 2 vols. Antwerp: The Hague. 1912–13.

Dermul, A. & Bouchery, H. F. *Bibliographie betreffende de Antwerpsche Drukkers.* Antwerp. 1938.

Duff, E. Gordon. *Early Printed Books.* London. 1893.

Febvre, L. & Martin, H-J. *L'Apparition du Livre.* Paris. 1958.

Funck, M. *Le Livre Belge à gravures.* Paris: Brussels. 1925.

Nijhoff, W. *L'Art typographique dans les Pays-Bas pendant les années 1500 à 1540.* 3 vols. The Hague. 1926–35.

Pollard, A. W. *Early Illustrated Books.* London. 1893.

Putnam, G. H. *Books and their makers during the Middle Ages.* 2 vols. New York. 1897.

Scholderer, Victor. *50 Essays in 15th and 16th century bibliography.* Amsterdam. 1966.

Van Ortroy, F. *L'Ecole cartographique belge au 16e siècle.* Louvain. 1910.

Vincent, J-B. *Essai sur l'histoire de l'imprimerie en Belgique.* Brussels. 1867.

EARLY PRINTING IN FRANCE

Blum, André. *Les origines du livre à gravures en France.* Paris & Brussels. 1928.

Brun, Robert. *Le livre français.* Paris. 1948.

Calot, F., Michon, L-M., & Angoulvent, P-J. *L'Art du Livre en France.* Paris. 1931.

Claudin, A. *Antiquités typographiques.* 3 vols. Paris. 1880–97.

Claudin, A. *Histoire de l'imprimerie en France.* 4 vols. Paris. 1900–05.

Comet, J. *L'Imprimerie à Perpignan. Rosembach, 1493–1530.* Perpignan. 1896.

Congrès des Bibliothécaires. *Le Livre français.* Paris. 1924.

Duff, E. Gordon. *Early printed books.* London. 1893.

Febvre, Lucien & Martin, H-J. *L'Apparition du livre.* Paris. 1958.

La Caille, J. *Histoire de l'imprimerie.* Paris, 1689.

Lepreux, Georges. *Gallia Typographica.* Paris. 1921.

Martin, André. *Le livre illustré en France au XVe siècle.* Paris. 1931.

Pansier, P. *Histoire du livre . . . à Avignon.* Avignon. 1922.

Pollard, A. W. *Early illustrated books.* London. 1893.

— *French Book of Hours.* London. 1897.

— *Fine Books.* London. 1912.

Pottinger, D. *The French book trade, 1500–1791.* Cambridge, Mass. 1958.

Renouvier, J. *Antoine Vérard.* Paris. 1859.

— *Simon Vostre.* Paris. 1862.

Ritter, F. *L'Imprimerie alsacienne.* (Hautes Etudes Alsaciennes. Tome 14.) Strasbourg. 1955.

Vingtrinier, M. *L'Imprimerie à Lyon.* Lyons. 1894.

PRINTING COMES TO ENGLAND

Bennett, H. S. *English Books & Readers, 1475 to 1557.* Cambridge. 1952.

Blades, W. *The biography and typography of William Caxton.* 2 vols. Revised edn. London. 1882.

Blake, N. F. *Caxton and his world.* London. 1969.

Bibliography

Bradshaw, H. *Collected papers*. Cambridge. 1889.

Clair, Colin. *History of Printing in Britain*. London. 1965.

Crotch, W. J. B. *The Prologues and Epilogues of William Caxton*. London. (Early English Text Soc. Pub. 176.) 1928.

Dibdin, T. F. *Typographical Antiquities*. 4 vols. London. 1810–19.

Duff, E. Gordon. *Early English Printing*. London. 1896.

— *The Printers, Stationers and Bookbinders of Westminster and London from 1476 to 1535*. Cambridge. 1906.

— *The English Provincial Printers*, etc. Cambridge. 1912.

— *Fifteenth century English books*. Oxford. 1917.

Gray, G. J. *John Siberch. The first Cambridge Printer*. Cambridge. 1921.

Hodnett, E. *English Woodcuts, 1480–1535*. Oxford. 1935. Rev. edn. 1973.

Plomer, H. *A Short History of English Printing, 1476–1898*. London. 1900.

Plomer, H. R. *Wynkyn de Worde and his Contemporaries*. London. 1925.

Pollard, A. W. & Redgrave, G. R. (Eds.) *A Short-title catalogue of Books printed in England, Scotland and Ireland and of English Books printed abroad, 1475–1642*. Oxford. 1926.

Reed, A. W. *Early Tudor Drama*. London. 1926.

Roberts, S. C. *The evolution of Cambridge publishing*. 1956.

Worman, E. J. *Alien members of the book trade during the Tudor period*. Oxford. 1906.

EARLY PRINTING IN THE IBERIAN PENINSULA

Bohigas, Pedro. *El Libro Español*. Barcelona. 1962.

Burger, Konrad. *Die Drucker und Verleger in Spanien und Portugal von 1501 bis 1536*. Leipzig. 1913.

Castañeda y Alcober, V. *La Imprenta*. Madrid. 1927.

Cortez Pinto. *Da famosa arte de imprimissao*. Lisbon. 1948.

del Arco, A. *La imprenta en Tarragona*. Tarragona. 1916.

Häbler, Konrad. *The early printers of Spain and Portugal*. London. 1897.

Lyell, J. P. R. *Cardinal Ximenes*. London. 1917.

— *Early book illustration in Spain*. London. 1926.

Madurell, J. & Rubrió, J. *Documentos para la historia de la imprenta y librería en Barcelona*. Barcelona. 1955.

Manuel II of Portugal. *Early Portuguese Books in the Library of the King of Portugal*. 3 vols. 1929–35.

Mendez, F. *Typographia Española*.

Miquel y Planas, R. *El libro en España*. Madrid. 1933.

Norton, F. J. *Printing in Spain, 1501–1520*. Cambridge. 1966.

Pereira Forjaz de Sampaio. *A Tipografia portuguesa no seculo XVä*. Lisbon. 1932.

Pinto de Oliveira. *O primeiro impressor portugues*. Lisbon. 1942.

Thomas, H. *The printer George Coci of Saragossa*. Mainz. 1925.

— *Spanish sixteenth-century printing*. London. 1926.

Vindel, F. *Origen de la imprenta en España*. 1935.

SCANDINAVIA

Benedikz, Benedikt S. *Iceland* (The Spread of Printing). Amsterdam. 1969.

Bring, E. S. (Ed.) *Svenskt Boxlexicon, 1700–1829.* 2 vols. Uppsala. 1958. 1961.

Collijn, I. G. A. *Det Svenska boktryckets utveckling, 1438–1850.* (Catalogue). Uppsala. 1936.

Dahl, S. *Bogens historie.* Copenhagen. 1927. Translated as *History of the Book.* New York. 1968.

Dansten & Nielsen. *Nordisk Lexikon for Bogvaesen.* 1951.

Haugsted, Mogens. *AEldre danske bogtrykker.* (Fund of forskning. Nos. 2, 3.) 1955 etc.

Hermannson, H. *Icelandic Books of the 16th Century.*

— *Icelandic Books of the 17th century.*

Klemming & Nordin. *Svensk boktrykerihistoria, 1483–1883.* Stockholm. 1883–1885.

Lagerström, H. *Svensk Bokkonst.* Stockholm. 1920.

Möller, Bert. *Svensk bokhistoria.* Stockholm. 1931.

Nielsen, Lauritz. *Dansk Bibliografi, 1482–1600.* 2 vols. Copenhagen. 1919, 1933.

Nielsen, L. M. *Dansk typografisk Atlas, 1482–1600.* Copenhagen. 1934.

Nordal, S. *Monumenta typographica Islandica.* Copenhagen. 1933, etc.

Oldendow, Knud. *Bogtrykkerkunsten i Grønland, etc.* Copenhagen. 1957.

— *Greenland* (The Spread of Printing). Amsterdam. 1969.

Pedersen, V. *Dansk bogtypografi.* Copenhagen. 1959.

Pettersen, Hjalmar. *Norsk Boglexicon, 1643–1813.* 3 vols. Christiana. 1899–1908.

— *Norsk Boglexicon (after 1814).* Christiania. 1913–24.

Vasenius, V. *Outlines of the history of printing in Finland,* translated from the Finnish by E. D. Butler. London. 1898.

Vingedal, S. E. *Den Svarta Konsten. Tidig svensk boktryckarkonst. Inkunabelperioden, 1483–1500.* Holmis. 1958.

EARLY MUSIC PRINTING

Cohen, P. *Musikdruck und -Drucker zu Nürnberg.* Nuremberg. 1927.

Die Musik en Geschichte und Gegenwart. 14 vols. Kassal & Basel. 1949–68.

Eitner, Robert. *Quellen Lexikon der Musiker.* 11 vols. Graz. 1959–60.

Fétis, F. J. *Biographie Universelle des Musiciens.* 2nd edn. 10 vols. Paris. 1860–80.

Gamble, W. *Music Engraving and Printing.* London. 1923.

Goovaerts, A. *Histoire et Bibliographie de la typographie musicale dans les Pays-Bas.* Antwerp. 1880.

Grove, George. *Dictionary of Music and Musicians.* 10 vols. London. 1954–61.

Heartz, Daniel. *Pierre Attaignant, Royal Printer of Music.* Berkeley, 1969.

Kidson, Frank. *British Music Publishers, Printers and Engravers.* New edn. 1966.

King, A. Hyatt. *Four Hundred Years of Music Printing.* London. 1964.

— *The Significance of John Rastell in Early Music Printing.* (In 'The Library' Sept. 1971.)

Kinkeldey, O. *Music and Music Printing in Incunabula.* (In 'Papers of the Bibliographical Soc. of America'. 1932.)

Marksdale, A. B. *The Printed Note.* Toledo, Ohio. 1957.

Meyer-Baer, Kathi. *Liturgical Music Icunabula.* London. 1962.

Bibliography

Riemann, Hugo. *Musik Lexikon*. 2 vols. Mainz. 1959–61.

Sartoria, C. *Bibliografia delle opere musicali stampata de Ottaviano Petrucci*. Florence. 1948.

Steele, R. *The Earliest English Music Printing*. London. 1903.

Stellfeld, J. A. *Bibliographie des éditions musicales plantiniennes*. Brussels. 1949.

PRINTING IN CENTRAL EUROPE

Badalić, J. *Jugoslavica* (Bibliotecha bibliographica aureliana. No. 2.) 1959.

Borsa, Gedeon. *Die Buchdrucker des 15 und 16 Jahrhundert in Ungarn*. (In 'Bibliothek und Wissenschaft. Bd. 2, 1965).

Borsa, G. & Köves, B. *A magyar könyv* (Das ungarische Buch.) Budapest. 1961.

Csapodi, K. & Soltesz, –. *Aus der Geschichte des ungarischen Buches*. (In 'Marginalien'. Aug. 1960. Budapest.)

Gardonyi, A. *Buchdruck und Buchhandel Ungarns am Ausgang des Mittelalters* (in 'Gutenberg Jahrbuch' Mainz.)

Gulyás Pal. *A Könyvnyomtatas Magyarorszagon a VX es XVI szazadban*. 2 vols. Budapest. 1929/31.

Horák, František. *Five Hundred years of Czech printing*. Prague. 1968.

Juhász, J. *A magyarorszagi könyvdiszites*. Budapest. 1961.

Lam, Stanislaw. *Le livre polonais au XV er XVI siècle*. Warsaw. 1923.

Novak, A. (Ed.) *Das tschechische Buch*. Prague. 1926.

Painter, George D. & Chrástek D. B. *Printing in Czechoslovakia in the fifteenth century*. London. 1969.

Petkov, P. *La Presse en Bulgarie*. Paris. 1910.

Piekarski, K. *Polonia typographica*. 1936.

Slavische Rundschau (1940). Prague.

Tobolka, Z. *Český slovnik bibliografický*. Prague. 1910.

— *Dějiny československeho knihtisku v dobé nejstaeší*. Prague. 1930 (with a summary in German).

Turdeanu, E. *Le livre roumain*. Paris. 1959.

Various. *Res Litteraria Hungariae Vetus Operum Impressorum, 1473–1600*. Academy Press. Budapest. 1971.

Volf, J. *Geschichte des Buchdrucks in Böhmen und Mähren*. Weimar. 1928.

MALTA & TURKEY

Chauvin, V. *Notes pour l'histoire de l'imprimerie à Constantinople*.

Clair, Colin. *Malta* (in the 'Spread of Printing' series.) Amsterdam. 1969.

Davids, A. L. *Grammar of the Turkish language*. London. 1838.

Gauci, Alberto. *Origine e sviluppo della stampa in Malta*. Rome. 1937.

Layton, E. *Nikodemos Metaxas* (in 'Harvard Library Bulletin', Vol. XV, No. 2. 1967.)

McMurtrie, D. C. *A Malta imprint of 1643*. Chicago. 1939.

Omont, H. *Documents sur l'imprimerie à Constantinople au XVIIIe siecle*.

Parnis, E. *Notes on the first establishment . . . of the printing press in Malta*. Malta. 1916.

Reinaud, V. *Notice des ouvrages arabes, persans, turcs, et francais imprimes a Constantinople*. (In 'Bulletin Univ. des Sciences', Nov. 1831.)

Saussure, C. de. *Lettres et Voyages.* Lausanne. 1903.

Von Murr. *Journal zur Kunstgeschichte* (pp. 323–332: 'Von der türkischen Buchdruckerey zu Constantinopel.' 1787.

Weil, Gotthold. *Die ersten Drucke der Türken* (in 'Zentralblatt für Bibliothekswesen.' Feb. 1907.) Leipzig.

Wilson, Rev. S. S. *A Narrative of the Greek Mission Press.* London. 1845.

EASTERN EUROPE

Bas, I. *Ivan Fedorov* (in Russian.) Moscow. 1940.

Bosnjak, M. *A Study of Slavic incunabula.* Zagreb-Munich. 1968.

British Museum. *Examples of Slavonic printing.* (A collection under press-mark 1803. *c.* 31.)

Christian, R. F., Sullivan, J., & Simmons, J. S. G. *Early-printed Russian books at Saint Andrews* (in 'The Bibliotheck', Vol. 5, Nos. 7–8, Aberdeen. 1970.)

Estreichera, K. *Bigliografia Polska.* 33 vols. Cracow. 1906–1939.

Grasshoff, H. & Simmons (J.S.G.) *Ivan Fedorovs griechisch-russich kirchenslavisches Lesebuch von 1578.* (Abhandlungen der deutschen Akademie der Wissenschaften. Klasse für Sprachen, Literatur und Kunst, 1969, No. 2.) Berlin.

Jakobson, R. *Ivan Fedorov's Primer* (Harvard Library Bulletin, IX 1955 6.)

Kameneva, T. N. *Chernigovskaya tipografiya . . .* in 'Trudy', III. 1959.

Luppov, S. P. *Kniga v Rossii v XVII veke.* Leningrad. 1970.

Nadson, A. *Skaryna's Prayer Book.* Journal of Byelorussian Studies, 1972. London.

Nemirovskii, E. L. *The Rise of printing in Moscow* (in Russian.) Moscow. 1964.

Niesiecki, Kaspar. *Korona Polska.* 4 vols. Lwow. 1728–43.

Orlov, S. A. *Ivan Fedorov* (in Russian.) Leningrad. 1935.

Piekarski, K. *Pierwsza drukarnia Floriana Unglera.* Cracow. 1926.

— *Polonia typographica.* Warsaw. 1936–

Rochlin, R. *Die Anfänge der russischen Presse.* (In 'Zeitungswissenschaft', No. 6, June, 1935. Berlin.)

Sopikov, Vasili. *Russian Bibliography* (in Russian.) Six parts. St. Petersburg. 1904–08.

Slavische Rundschau. Prague, 1902–40. The last volume published, Jahrg. 12, Bd. 4, 1940, has some excellent articles on printing in Eastern Europe.

Titov, F. I. *Tipografiya Kievo-Pecherskoi Iavry.* 2 vols. Kiev. 1916–18.

16TH CENTURY GERMANY

Barge, Hermann. *Geschichte der Buchdrucker Kunst.* Leipzig. 1940.

Benzing, Josef. *Die Buchdrucker des 16 und 17 Jahrhunderts im deutschen Sprachgebiet.* Wiesbaden. 1963.

Butsch, A. *Die Bücher Ornamentik der Renaissance.* 2 vols. Leipzig. 1878, 1881.

Crous, E. *Die gotischen Schriftarten.* Leipzig. 1928.

Crous, E. *Die Schriftgiessereien in Berlin.* Berlin. 1928.

Davies, H. W. *Devices of the early printers, 1457–1560.* London. 1935.

Euler, A. *Die Geschichte der Buchdrucker und Verleger Ingolstats.* Ingolstat. 1957.

Grotefend, H. *C. Egenolff.* Frankfurt-a-M. 1881.

Hase, Oskar von. *Die Koberger*. Leipzig. 1885; reprinted 1967.

Johnson, A. F. *Germain Renaissance Title Borders*. Oxford. 1929.

Mejer, W. *Der Buchdrucker Hans Lufft zu Wittenberg*. Leipzig. 1923.

Muther, R. *Die deutsche Bücherillustration der Gothik und Frührenaissance (1460–1530)*. 2 vols. Munich & Leipzig. 1884.

Redgrave, G. *Erhard Ratdolt* (Bibliographical Soc. Monographs, No. 1.) London. 1894.

Schottenloher, C. *Das Regensburger Buchgewerbe im XV und XVI Jahrhunderts*. Mainz. 1920.

— *Das Alte Buch*. 2nd edn. Berlin. 1921.

— *Hans Schobser*. Munich. 1925.

Steinberg, S. H. *Five Hundred Years of Printing*. Rev. edn. 1959.

Von Dommer, A. *Die ältesten Drucke aus Marburg, 1552–1566*. Marburg. 1892.

ITALIAN PRINTERS OF THE XVI CENTURY

Ascarelli, F. *La tipografia cinquecentina italiana*. Florence. 1953.

— *Annali tipografici di Giacomo Mazzochi*. Florence. 1961.

Bandini, Angelo. *La stamperia Mediceo-Orientale*. Florence. 1878.

Barson, A. *Libri e Stampatori in Padova*. Padua. 1959.

Bernoni, D. *Dei Torresani*. Milan. 1890.

Bongi, S. *Annali di Gabriel Giolito*. 2 vols. Rome. 1890–1895.

Brown, H. R. *The Venetian Printing Press*. London. 1891.

Casali, S. *Annali . . . di Marcolini*. Bologna. 1953.

Donati, Lamberto. *Bibliografia Aldina*. ('Bibliofilia', LII. 1950.)

Evola, N. D. *Ricerche sulla tipografia*. (Bib. di bibliografia italiana. No. 15.)

Firmin-Didot, Ambroise. *Alde Manuce et l'hellénisme à Venise*. Paris. 1875.

Fumagalli, G. *Antonio Blado*. Milan. 1893.

—. *Lexicon typographicum Italiae*. Florence. 1905.

Gregori, L. de. *La Stampa a Roma nel secolo XV*. Rome. 1933.

Kristeller, P. *Early Florentine Woodcuts*. 2 vols. London. 1897.

Levi, A. *Le origine della stampa a Soncino*. Cremona. 1931.

Norton, F. J. *Italian Printers, 1501–1520*. London. 1958.

Parenti, Marino (Ed.) *Biblioteca bibliografica italiana*. 1951. Florence.

Pastorello, Ester. *L'Epistolario Manunziano*. Venice & Rome. 1957.

Renouard, A. A. *Annales de l'imprimerie des Alde*. 3rd. edn. Paris. 1834.

Sacchi, Federico. *Dei Soncino, celebri tipografi italiani*. Venice. 1878.

Trevisani, P. *Storia della Stampa* (Enciclopedia poligrafica, Ser. A. Vol. 1.) 1953.

Vervliet, H. D. *Type Specimens of the Vatican Press*. Amsterdam. 1967.

— *Robert Granjon à Rome, 1578–1589*. Amsterdam. 1967.

HOLLAND & BELGIUM: 16TH CENTURY

Anvers, Ville de Plantin et de Rubens. (Catalogue of an exhibition held at the Bibliothèque Nationale, Paris, 1954.)

Carter, H. *Plantin's types and their makers*. (In 'Gedenkboek der Plantin-Dagen'. 1956.) Antwerp.

Clair, Colin. *Willem Silvius*. (In 'The Library'. Sept. 1959.)
— *Christopher Plantin*. London. 1960.
Correspondance de Christophe Plantin. 9 vols. Antwerp–Gent–The Hague. 1883–1918.
'De Gulden Passer.' Antwerp. 1923–
Delen, A. J. J. *Christophe Plantin, imprimeur de l'Humanisme*. Brussels. 1944.
Dermul, A. & Bouchery, H. F. *Bibliografie betreffende de Antwerpsche drukkers*. Antwerp. 1938.
'Het Boek.' The Hague. 1912–66.
Rooses, Max. *Christophe Plantin, imprimeur anversois*. Antwerp. 1882.
Sabbe, Maurice. *La Typographie Anversoise au XVIe siècle*. Brussels. 1924/25.
— *De Meesters van den Gulden Passer*. Brussels. 1937.
Schneider, Maarten. *De Voorgeschiedenis van de 'Algemeene Lansdrukkerij'*. The Hague. 1948.
'Tijdschift voor Boek- en Bibliotheekwezen'. Antwerp. 1903–1911.
Van Durme, M. (Ed.) *Supplément à la correspondance de Christophe Plantin*. Antwerp. 1955.
Vincent, Auguste. *La Typographie en Belgique (sauf Anvers) au XVIe siècle*. Brussels. 1924–25.
Vincent, J-B. *Essai sur l'histoire de l'imprimerie en Belgique*. Brussels. 1867.
Voet, Léon. *The Golden Compasses*. 2 vols. Amsterdam. 1969, 1972.

16TH CENTURY FRANCE

Armstrong, Elizabeth. *Robert Estienne*. Cambridge. 1954.
Baudrier, J. *Bibliographie lyonnaise*. Lyons. 12 vols. 1895–1921.
Bernard, Auguste. *Geoffrey Tory*. 2nd edn. Paris. 1865.
Bouchot, H. *Le Livre*. Paris. 1886.
Brun, Robert. *Le Livre Français*. Paris. 1969.
Cartier, Alfred. *Bibliographie des éditions des de Tournes*. 2 vols. Paris. 1938.
Chassaigne, Marc. *Etienne Dolet*. Paris. 1930.
Christie, R. C. *Etienne Dolet*. London. 1899.
Dupont, P. *Histoire de l'imprimerie*. 2 vols. Paris. 1854.
Johnson, A. F. *French sixteenth-century printing*. London. 1922.
Léjard, André. *The Art of the French Book*. London. 1947.
Lepreux, G. *Gallia typographica*. 6 vols. Paris. 1909–13.
Lieure, J. *La gravure en France au XVIe siècle dans le livre et l'ornement*. Paris. 1927.
Lyon: Cercle des Relations Intellectuelles. *Le livre à Lyon des origines jusqu' à nos jours*. Lyons. 1933.
Mornand, Pierre. *L'Art du Livre et son illustration du XVe au XVIIIe siècle*. Paris. 1947.
Mortimer, Ruth (Compiler). *Harvard Catalogue of French 16th-century books*. 2 vols. Cambridge (Mass.). 1964.
O'Day, E. F. *Claude Garamond*. Eugene. 1940.
Renouard, A. A. *Annales de l'imprimerie des Estienne*. Paris. 1837.
Renouard, Philippe. *Imprimeurs et Libraires parisiens du XVIe siècle*. Paris. 1964, etc.
Vingtrinier, M. *L'imprimerie à Lyon*. Lyons. 1894.
Veyrin-Forrer, J. *Antoine Augereau*. ('Paris et Ile-de-France'. Tom. 8. Paris. 1956.)

Bibliography

NETHERLANDS. 17TH & 18TH CENTURIES

Berghman, G. S. *Etudes sur la bibliographie Elzevirienne, basées sur l'ouvrange 'Les Elzevier' de M. Alphonse Willems.* Stockholm. 1885.

Catalogus der Tentoonstelling van de ontwikkeling der Boekdrukkunst in Nederland. Haarlem 1923.

Copinger, H. B. *The Elzevier Press.* London. 1927.

Davies, D. W. *The World of the Elseviers.* The Hague. 1954.

Enschedé, Ch. *Fonderies de caractères . . . dans les Pays Bas.* Haarlem. 1908.

— *Die Druckerei der Elsevier und ihre Beziehung zu der Lutherschen Schriftgiesserei.* Haarlem. 1919.

Hartz, S. *The Elseviers and their contemporaries.* Amsterdam. 1955.

Lederboer, A. M. *Het Geslacht Van Waesberghe.* The Hague & Utrecht. 1869.

McMurtrie, D. C. *The Brothers Voskens and their Successors.* Chicago. 1932.

Mori, Gustav. *Die Schriftgiesser B. und R. Voskens.* Frankfurt. 1923.

Officina Joannis Blaeu. Amsterdam. 1961.

Sabbe, Maurice. *La Vie des Livres à Anvers aux XVIe, XVIIe et XVIIIe siècles.* Brussels. 1926.

The House of Enschedé 1703–1953. Haarlem. 1953.

Verwey, H. de la Fontaine. *Het werk van de Blaeu's* (in *'In Officina Joannis Blaeu.'* Amsterdam. 1961.)

Vincent, J-B. *Essai sur l'Histoire de l'Imprimerie en Belgique.* Brussels. 1867.

Willems, A. *Les Elzevier.* Brussels. 1880. (Reprint 1962.)

FRANCE: XVIITH & XVIIITH CENTURIES

Audin, M. *Les livrets typographiques des fonderies francaises.* Amsterdam. 1965.

Bernard, A. *Histoire de l'Imprimerie royale du Louvre.* Paris. 1867.

Billioud, J. *Le livre en Provence du 16e au 17e siècle.* Marseille. 1962.

Boissais, M. & Deleplanque, J. *Le Livre à gravures au XVIIIe siècle.* Paris. 1948.

Bouchot, Henri. *The Book.* London. 1890.

Brun, R. *Le livre français.* Paris. 1969.

Calot, F., Michon, L-M., & Angoulevent, P. *L'Art du Livre en France des origines à nos jours.* Paris. 1931.

Delalain, P. *Les Libraires et Imprimeurs de l'Académie Française de 1634 à 1792.* Paris. 1907.

Flocon, A. *L'Univers des Livres.* Paris. 1961.

Maignien, E. *L'Imprimerie . . . à Grenoble du XVe au XVIIIe siècle.* Grenoble. 1884.

Mornand, P. *Les beaux livres d'autrefois. Le XVIIe siècle.* Paris. 1931.

Pingrenon, R. *Les livres ornés et illustrés en couleur.* Paris. 1903.

Portalis, R. *Les dessinateurs d'illustrations au XVIIIe siècle.* 2 vols. Paris. 1877.

Réau, Louis. *La gravure en France au XVIIIe siècle.* Paris & Brussels. 1928.

Sander, M. *Les livres illustrés francais du XVIIIe siècle.* Paris. 1926.

Tchemerzine, A. *Répertoire de livres à figures . . . edités en France au XVIIe siècle.* 3 vols. Paris. 1933.

Various. *La Bibliothèque Nationale.* Paris. 1907.

ENGLAND: 17TH & 18TH CENTURIES

Benton, J. H. *John Baskerville*. New York. 1944.

Clair, Colin. *A History of Printing in Britain*. London. 1965.

Cochrane, J. A. *Dr. Johnson's Printer. The Life of William Strahan*. London. 1964.

Freeman, R. *English Emblem Books*. New edn. London. 1967.

Gibson, Strickland. *English Printing, 1700–1925*. London. 1925.

Handover, P. M. *Printing in London*. London. 1960.

Jay, Leonard (Ed.) *Letters of John Baskerville*. London. 1932.

Journal of the Printing Office at Strawberry Hill (with notes by Paget Toynbee). London. 1923.

Morison, Stanley. *John Bell. 1745–1831*. Cambridge. 1930.

— *The English Newspaper*. Cambridge. 1932.

— *John Fell. The University Press and the 'Fell' types*. Oxford. 1967.

Moxon, Joseph. *Mechanick Exercises on the whole art of printing*. (Edited, with introduction and notes by Herbert Davis and Harry Carter.) 2nd rev. edn. London. 1962.

Plant, Marjorie. *The English Book Trade*. 2nd rev. edn. London. 1965.

Plomer, H. R. *A Short History of English Printing from 1476 to 1898*. London. 1900.

Twyman, M. *Printing, 1770–1970*. London. 1970.

18TH CENTURY SPAIN

Alvarez Calvo, J. *Homenaje a Pradell, 1721–1788*. Barcelona. 1942.

Bohigas, Pedro. *El Libro Español*. Barcelona. 1962.

Campo, J. del. *Historia de la imprenta in Madrid*. Madrid. 1935.

Casa Gans. *El Maestro Ibarra*. Madrid. 1931.

Castañeda y Alcober, V. *La Imprenta*. Madrid. 1927.

Esplendor del arte tipografico espanol en el siglo XVIII. (In 'Bibliografia Hisp. No. 4. 1942.)

Gonzalez Palencia. *Eruditos y libreros des siglo XVIII*. Madrid. 1948.

Ruiz Lasala, I. *Joaquin Ibarra y Marin, 1725–1785*. Saragossa. 1968.

Various. *Homenaje à Joaquin Ibarra*. Madrid. 1923.

ITALY: 18TH CENTURY

Aliprandi, G. *G. B. Bodoni e l'opera sua*. Padua. 1940.

Bertieri, R. *L'Arte di Giambattista Bodoni*. Milan.

Cosenza, M. E. *Biographical and Bibliographical Dictionary of the Italian Printers and of foreign printers in Italy*. Boston, Mass. 1968.

Donati, L. *Contributi alla storia del libro italiano*. Florence. 1969.

Hadl, R. *Druckwerke des Giambattista Bodoni und der Parmenser Staatsdruckerei*. Leipzig. 1926.

Kalab, Method. *Giambattista Bodoni*. Prague. 1922.

Olschki, L. S. *Le Livre en Italie à travers les siècles*. Florence. 1914.

Publicazione d'Arte Grafica. (Issue dedicated to Bodoni.) Parma. 1940–41.

Servolini, Luigi. *Autobiografia di G. B. Bodoni in duecento lettere inedite all'incisore Francesco Rosaspina*. Parma. 1958.

Bibliography

Silomon, K. H. *Giambattista Bodoni*. [Frankfurt-a-M.] [1941.]
Trevisani, P. *Bodoni: Epoca, vita, arte*. Milan. 1951.
Various. *Bodoni celebrato a Parma*. Biblioteca Palatina. 1963.

FRANCE. 1789–1914

Brunet, Gustave. *Firmin Didot et sa famille*. Paris. 1870.
Camus, A. G. *Histoire du polytypage*. Paris. 1801.
Carteret, L. *Le Trésor du bibliophile, romantique et moderne, 1801–1875*. 4 vols. Paris. 1924–28.
— *Le Trésor du bibliophile. Livres illustrés modernes (1875–1945)*. 3 vols. Paris. 1946–47.
Champfleury. *Les vignettes romantiques*. Paris. 1883.
Crapelet, G. *Etudes sur la typographie*. Paris. 1837.
Didot, Firmin. *L'imprimerie à l'Exposition*. Paris. 1854.
Didot, Pierre. *Epître sur les progrès de l'imprimerie*. Paris. 1784.
George, Albert J. *The Didot Family*. Syracuse. 1961.
Gillot, F. *Paniconographie*. Paris. 1852.
Girard, H. & Moncel, H. *Les Beaux Livres d'autrefois. Le XIXe siècle*. Paris. 1930.
Hesse, R. *Histoire du livre d'art du XIXe siècle à nos jours*. Paris. 1927.
Lyons – *Exposition Louis Perrin*. Lyons. 1923.
Néret, J. *Histoire de la Librairie*. Paris. 1953.
Sander, M. *Les livres illustrés francais du XIXe siècle*. Paris. 1924.

PRIVATE PRESSES

Catalogue of an Exhibition of English Private Presses, 1757–1961. London. 1961.
Cave, R. *The Private Press*. London. 1970.
Davies, J. M. *The Private Press at Gregynog*. Leicester. 1959.
Descriptive Bibliography of Books published at the Ashendene Press, 1895–1935. London. 1935.
Forman, H. Buxton. *The Books of William Morris described*. London. 1897.
Franklin, Colin. *The Private Presses*. London. 1969.
Kautzsh, R. *Die neue Buchkunst*. Weimar. 1902.
Kessler, Graf H. *Tagebücher 1918–1937*. Franfurt-a-M. 1961.
Lehnacker, J. *Die Bremer-Presse*. Munich. 1964.
Mardersteig, G. *Die Officina Bodoni*. Paris. 1929.
Müller-Krumbach, R. *Harry Graf Kessler und die Cranach-Presse in Weimar*. Hamburg. 1969.
Ransom, Will. *Private Presses and their Books*. New York. 1929.
Rodenberg, J. *Deutsche Pressen*. Zürich. 1925.
Royen, J. van & Eyck, P. van. *Over Boekkunst en de Zilverdistel*. The Hague. 1916.
Sparling, H. H. *The Kelmscott Press and William Morris*. London. 1924.
The typographical adventure of William Morris. (Catalogue of an Exhibition arranged by the William Morris Society.) London. 1957.

A CHAPTER OF INVENTIONS

Bolza, A. *Friedrich Koenig, der Erfinder der Schnellpresse*. Würzburg. 1922.
Burch, R. M. *Colour Printing and Colour Printers*. London. 1910.

Chiappino, L. *Dal torchio alla rotolito*. Turnin. 1947.

Corrigan, A. J. *A printer and his world*. London. 1944.

Curwen, Harold. *Processes of Graphic Reproduction in Printing*. London. 1934.

Gamble, C. W. *Modern Illustration Processes*. London. 1935.

Gibson, Peter. *Modern Trends in letterpress printing*. London. 1966.

Gill, Eric. *An Essay on Typography*. London. 1936.

Goebel, Theodor. *Friedrich Koenig und die Erfindung der Schnellpresse*. 2nd edn. Stuttgart. 1906.

Höhne, Otto. *Geschichte der Setzmachinen*. Berlin. 1935.

Isaacs, G. A. *The Story of the Newspaper Printing Press*. London. 1931.

Jennett, S. *The making of Books*. London. 1951.

Legros, L. A. & Grant, J. C. *Typographical Printing Surfaces*. London. 1916.

Lewis, C. C. *The Story of Picture Printing*. London.

Lewis, John & Brinkley, John. *Graphic Design*. London. 1954.

McLean, Ruari. *Modern Book Design*. London. 1958.

— *Victorian Book Design and Colour Printing*. London. 1963.

Renner, Paul. *Mechanisierte Grafik*. Berlin. 1931.

Southward, J. *Progress in Printing and the Graphic Arts during the Victorian era*. London. 1897.

Tarr, John C. *Printing today*. London. 1945.

Various. *L'Imprimerie et les Métiers Graphiques*. Paris. 1947.

Willy, C. M. *Practical Photo-Lithography*. London. 1938.

Wilson & Grey. *Modern Printing Machinery*. London. 1888.

THE TWENTIETH CENTURY

Alphabet and Image. 1946–

Ammonds, C. C. *Photoengraving: Principles and Practice*. London. 1966.

Cannon, R. V. & Wallis, F. G. *Graphic Reproduction*. London. 1963.

Coupe, R. R. *Science of Printing Technology*. London. 1966.

Curwen, H. *Processes of Graphic Reproduction in Printing*. 4th edn., revised by Charles Mayo. London. 1966.

Day, Kenneth (Ed.) *Book Typography, 1815–1965*. London. 1966.

Engelmann, A. & Schwend, K. *Der Offsetdruck*. Stuttgart. 1962.

Gibson, Peter. *Modern Trends in Letterpress Printing*. London. 1966.

Gross, A. *Etching, Engraving and Intaglio Printing*. London. 1970.

Hamilton, E. A. *Graphic Design for the Computer Age*. London. 1970.

Hutchings, E. A. D. *Printing by Letterpress*. London. 1964.

Hutchins, Michael. *Typographics*. London. 1969.

Hutt, Allen. *Newspaper Design*. London. 1960.

Lawson, L. E. *Offset Lithography*. London. 1963.

Lewis, John. *Typography: Basic Principles*. 2nd end. London. 1967.

McLean, Ruari. *Modern Book Design*. London. 1958.

Mertle, J. S. & Monsen, J. L. *Photomechanics and Printing*. Chicago. 1957.

Moran, James. *Stanley Morison*. London. 1971.

Polygraph Jahrbuch.

Printing Review. 1931–

Rosner, C. *Printer's Progress (1851–1951).* London. 1951.

Schauer, G. K. *Deutsche Buchkunst, 1890 bis 1960.* 2 vols. Hamburg. 1963.

Tarr, J. C. *Printing Today.* Rev. edn. London. 1949.

The Penrose Annual. 1896–

Various. *L'Imprimerie et les Métiers Graphiques.* Paris. 1947.

Wallis, F. G. & Howitt, H. *Photo-Litho in Monochrome and Colour.* London. 1963.

Whetton, H. (Ed.) *Practical Printing and Binding.* London. 1946.

Williamson, Hugh. *Methods of Book Design.* London. 1956.

Index

A

A.B.C., 202

Aa, Pieter van der, 283, 351–2

Aachen, 274 *see also* Aix-la-Chapelle

Aanau, 276

Abagan: Stanislavov, 392

Abbeville, 64–6

Abckiria Michael Agricolo Christiano Salutem: Agricola, 229

Abdallah, Mufti, 307, 308

Abdul-Hamid, Sultan of Turkey, 310

Abela, Giovanni Fransesco, 305

Abentheurliche Simplicissimus: Grimmelhausen, 277

Ablassbrief: von Werdenberg, 440

Äbo, 229

Academia de Bellas Artes de San Fernando, 334

Academia Naturae Curiosum, 274

Académie des Inscriptions, 315

Académie des Sciences, 315

Acate, Leonardo, 56

Accademia dei Lincei, 274

Accademia Nazionale dei Lincei, 274

Accedens of Armory: Legh, 260

Accoltis, Fransiscus de, 442

Achates de Basilea, Leonardus *see* Acate, Leonardo *and* Basilia, Leonardo Achates de

Achilleis: Statius, 54

Aciato, –, 167

Ackermann, Albin, 385

Ackermann von Böhmen: von Schüttwa, 25

Ackermann, Rudolf, 374

Acquaviva, Belisario, 151

Acte whereby cetayne offences be made Treason, 257

Acts and Monuments of these latter & perilous days see *Book of Martyrs*

Adagia: Erasmus, 123

Adams, Johannes, 285

Adelkind, Cornelius, 205

Adelkind, Daniel, 206

Adelkind, Giovanni ben Baruch, 206

Adrian VI, Pope, 149

Adventures de Telemaque, les: Fenelon, 398

Advertisements, 115–16, 117 (Fig 30), 118–19

Aelfredi regis res gestae: Asser, 260

Aesop, 25, 34, 49, 71, 95 (Fig 14), 97, 234

Aesop: Zucco, 57

Aetna, De: Bembo, 144 (Fig 36)

Afrique au 16e siècle et le Commerce anversois: Denoucé, 122n

Agenda, 235

Agenda Olomucensis, 436

Agenda Pragensis, 233

Aglio, Paola Margherita Dall', 330

Agnés, Juan Battista, 192

Agricola, Georgius, 181

Agricola, Martin, 210

Agricola, Mikael, Bishop of Äbo, 225, 229

Agrippa, Camillo, 148, 149 (Fig 38)

Ahmed III of Turkey, 397, 308

Aix-la-Chapelle, 8

Aix-en-Provence, 173

Alakraw, Johann, 233, 446

Alamanni, Luigi, 170

Alanasov, P., 242 and n

Alanus, Petrus, 435

Alaric: Scudéry, 295
Alauzet, Pierre, 365
Albion Iron Press, 356, 412
Albo Lapide, Albertus de, 446 *see also* Weissen-
    stein, Albert von
Albrecht V, Duke of Bavaria, 140
Albrecht, Laurentz, 138
Albrizzi, Alonso, 326
Albrizzi, Giambattista, 326
Alcalá de Henares, 187–8
Alciato, Andrea, 169
Alcobaza, Fr Bernardo de, 85
Aldine Greek type, 47, 144
Aldine italic type, 146, 147, 148, 248
Aldine Press, 143–7, 158
Aldine roman type, 144 (Fig 36)
Alding, Heinrich, 440
Aleksnadrovskaya sloboda, 252
Aleksei Mikhailovich of Russia, 252
Alemán, Fadriqué, 83 and n, 188–9 *see also* Biel,
    Friedrich
Alemanus, Franck *see* Silber, Eucharius
Alemanus, Leonardus, 82
Alembert, J, d', 319, 320
Aleria, Bishop of, 38
Alexandre, N., 315, 316
Alfonsi, Petrus, 25
Algemeine Zeitung, 325, 363
Algorithmus: de Sacrobusto, 248
Allen paden, von: Gruz, 236
Allen, Cardinal William, 166
Alliaco, Petrus de, 75
Almanac for Erfurt for 1474, 437
Almanac for 1496, 442
Almanach for 1474, 439
Almanach for 1480, 440
Almanach de Gotha see *Gothaischer Hofkalender*
Almanach fur Munchen auf das Jahr 1491:
    Mansfeld, 140
Almanach perpetuum coelestium motum: Zacuto, 86
Almanaches, 248, 324–5
Almela, Diego Rodriguez de, 191
Alost, 73
Alpen, Eva van, 280
Alphabeth ornee de Quatres et de Cartouches: Luce,
    316
Alphabetum Graecum, 174
Alphabetum hebraicum, 183
Alphabetum seu Instructio Sacerdotum, 173
Alt, Georg, 31

Alvares, Rodrigo, 86, 441
Alvearie: Baret, 264
Alvise, Albeeto, 57
Alvise, Giovanni, 57
Amadis de Gaule, 172
Amerbach, Johann: 31, 88–9, 126, 180
    Frankfurt Fair, 220
    Opera of St Augustine, 90 (Fig 13), 122
Amman, Jost, 14, 132 (Fig 33), 133
Amoris remedio, De: Silvius, 64
Amoros, Carlos, 191
Amphiareo, Vespasiano, 157
Ampsing, Samuel, 358
Amsterdam, 281, 283
Amyot, –, 165
Analine printing *see* Flexography
Anatome Blefkeniana: Jónsson, 230 (Fig 51)
Anatomy of Sleep Binns, 377–8
Anderson, Mrs, 335
André, –, 374
Andreae, Ant., 440
Andreae, Hieronymus, 134
Andreae, Johann the Younger, 276–7
Andreae, Nicolaus, 91
Andrieu, Michel, 438
Aneau, B., 172
Angelus, Jacobus, 34
Angermann, –, 251
Angers, 64
Anglicanus, Bartholomaeus, 101
Anglo-Saxon type, 260
Angulo, Andrés de, 187, 189
Anima Mia, 49
Anima et Spiritu, De: St Augustine, 439
Anisson, Jacques I, 320, 321
Anisson, Jean 301, 320, 321
Anisson, Louis-Laurent, 315, 321
Anisson-Duperron, Etienne-Alexandre-Jacques,
    321, 359, 396
Anisson-Duperron, Jacques, 321
Annales Ecclesiastica, 158
Année Litteraire, L', 396
Annius, Johannes, 35, 439
Annual Register (1810), 360
Annunzio, Gabriele d', 413
*Annus tertius saecularis inventae Artis Typographi-
    cae:* Seiz, 78
Anshelm, Thomas, 131, 442
Anshelm, Valerius, 179
Anthologie Françoise, 319

Antichita Romane: Piranesi, 328
Antico, Andrea, 209
Antiqua type, 37, 322–3, 384, 419
Antiquarius, Felix, 442
Antiquitates Italicae Medii Aevi: Muratori, 327
Antiquities of Westminster: Smith, 347
Antoine Augereau: Veyrin-Forrer, 164 and n
Antoine Verard: Macfarlane, 67n
Antoni, Antonio degli, 153
Antwerp, 195–6, 200, 214–15
Antwerp Fair, 219
Apffel, Michael, 142
Aphorisms: Hippocrates, 167
Apiarius, Mathias, 138, 179, 210
Apiarius, Samuel, 179
Apiarius, Sigfrid, 179
Apocalypse, 5, 32
Apocrypha, the, 181
Apologia: Agnés, 192
Apologia: Jewel, 263
Apologie for Poetrie: Sidney, 266 (Fig 60)
Apollo Press, 348
Apostol, 243, 250–1
Appellation des Domkapitels Passau an Papst . . ., 442
Appentegger, Wolf, 188
Appian, A., 43 (Fig 6), 443
Appiani Alexandrini Romanarum Historiarum, 174
Applegath, Augustus, 362–3
Applegath and Cowper perfecting machines, 389
Applegath Press, 356
Aquinus, St Thomas, 21, 27, 32, 73, 88, 347
Arabic Lexicon, 309
Arabic New Testament, 339
Arabic Psalter, 299, 300
Arabic type, 177, 288
Aramaic type, 288
Arason, Jón, Bishop of Hólar, 230
Arbor duorum mandatorum, 6
Arcano del Mare, Del: Dudley, 302
Archer, Thomas, 289
Archives Hist. et Litt. du Nord de la France: Hedouin, 300
Aretin, Baron, 374
Aretino, Leonard, 53, 438, 444
Aretino, Pietro, 149, 150
Aretio, Angelus de, 56 *see also* Gambilionibus, Angelus de
Argenson, Comte d', 320
Arinyo, Gabriel Luis de, 83, 84

Ariosto, Ludovico, 123, 150, 326, 344
Aristophanes, 143
Aristotle:
 France, 174
 Italy, 40, 45, 144
 Spain, 78, 79, 80 (Fig 11), 435, 445
Arithmetica: Calandri, 49
Armenian alphabet, 285
Armenian type, 177
Armillers, Huber d', 175
Armorial, 29
Armstrong, Mrs Elizabeth, 183
Arndes, Stephen (Steffan), 57, 225, 443
Arnoullet, Balthazar, 167, 172
Arnoullet, François, 167
Arnoullet, Jacques, 167, 172
Arnoullet, Olivier, 167, 172
Arquluk *see* Moller, Lars
Arras, Jean d', 71
Arras, Pierre d', 92
Arrighi, Lodovico degli, 146, 148, 155, 156
Arrighi types, 148–9 (Fig 38), 155 (Fig 40), 156 (Fig 41), 413
Arrivabene, Giorgio, 47
Ars minor: Donatus, 437, 440
Ars Moriendi, 3, 4 (Fig 1), 5, 6, 35–6
Art de bien vivre et de bien mourir, 67
Art of Good Lyvyng and Good Dyeing, 68 (Fig 8)
Art Moderne, L', 416
Art Nouveau, 415–16 (Fig 88), 417–18, 420 (Fig 89), 422 (Fig 90)
Art de Venerie, L': Twici, 104
Arte di Giambattista bodoni, L': Bertiere, 330
Arthur, Prince of Wales, 70
Arte subtilissima por la qual se ensener a escrivir perfectamente: de Yciar, 188
Arts and Crafts Exhibition Society, 406
Arundel, Earl of, 97
Asbuka type, 424
Ascensius, Jodocus Badius *see* Bade Josse
Ascham, Roger, 261
Ashbee, C. R., 408, 409, 410
Ashendene Press, 34, 37, 409
Ashkenazi, Joseph ben Jacob, 206
Aspinwall, Thomas, 376
Aspra crudelità del Turco a quagli di Caffa, L', 142
Asser, –, Bishop of Sherborne, 260
Ast, Astesanus de, 116
Astrée, L': d'Urfe, 295
Astromiae instauratae mechanica, 228

Astronomical Calendar, 16
Athens Journal, 311
Athos, 310
Atlas Major, 283
Atlas-Novus, 281
Attaignant, Pierre, 211, 212–13
Atuagagdliutit, 393
Aubrey, Jean, 133, 278
Auctores octo, 435
Audenarde, 77
Audran, Claude, 293
Augereau, Antoine, 163–4, 168, 173
Augereau, Guy, 164
Augereau, Michel, 164
Augsburg, 28–30, 133–7
Augustinus, 73, 440, 445, 446
Augustus, Duke of Braunschweig-Wolfenbüttel
  see Selenus, Gustavus
Aureri, Francesco, 157
Aureum opus regalium priviligiorum et regni Valen-
  tiae, 191, 192
Aurevilly, Barbey de, 405
Auserlesne Schnecken, Muschelen und andere Schaal-
  thiere: Regenfuss, 353
Ausmo, Nocolas de, 445
Ausonius, 160
Ausoult, Jean, 171
Austin, Richard, 348
Authorised Bible, 288
Autobiography: Bessemer, 377
Auto plate, 373
Ave Maria: Verdonck, 216
Avellaneda, Alonso Fernandez de, 303
Averroes, –, 55
Avian, –, 25
Avicenna, –, 52, 62
Avila, Alfonso, Bishop of, 445
Avila, G. Gonzalez de, 303
Avisa, Relation oder Zeitung, 275
Ayala, Juan do, 191
Ayrer, Marcus, 23, 26
Azzoguidi, Alberto, 51
Azzoguidi, Baldassare, 50, 51, 435
Azzoguidi, Pietro, 51

B

Babst, Valentin, 210
Babylonian Talmud, 205
Bac, Govaert, 77
Bache, Benjamin Franklin, 396

Bacon, –, 280, 362
Badalić, Josip, 244
Bade, Catherine, later Vascosan, 164
Bade, Josse, 62, 160, 358
Badius, Conrad, 183
Badius, Hermann, 183
Baedeker, Karl, 385
Baensch, Johannes, 421
Baensch-Drugulin, Johannes, 387
Baglioni, Braccio de, 57
Baglioni, the, 328
Baildon, John, 263 (Fig 58)
Baisers: Dorat, 313
Bakalář, Mikuláš, 235
Baland, Etienne, 167
Balbus, Johannes, 20
Baldini, Baccio, 48
Baldovino, Juan, 192
Balet comique de la Royne, 213
Balhorn, Johann I, 137
Balhorn, Johann II, 137–8
Balhornsche Druckerei, 138
Balistotype, 381
Ballances, –, 381
Ballard, Christophe-Jean François, 318
Ballard, Pierre, 213
Ballard, Robert, 211, 213
Balston, William, 348
Balzac, Honoré de, 401–2, 403, 404
Bamberg, 18, 25–6
Bamberg Missal, 26
Bamberg, Prince-Bishop of, 18
Bämler, Johann, 28–9, 118
Band, Harry, 407
Bandello, Matteo, 153
Bang, Christen, 228
Bang, Bishop Petrus, 229
Baňská Bystrica, 237–8
Baranovich, Lazar, Bishop of Chernigov, 253
Barbata, Andreas, 63, 144
Barbero, Gil, 185
Barbier, A., 401
Barbier, Nicholas, 183, 184
Barbin, C., 296
Barbou, Denise, later Arnoullet, 172
Barbou, Jean. 171, 172, 314, 316, 318, 319
Barbour, John, 105
Barcelona, 78, 79
Bardejov, 237
Baret, John, 264

Barker, Christopher, 268–9, 287
Barker, Robert, 288
Barley, William, 218
Barnes, Joseph, 268 (Fig 62)
Baromić, Blaž, 45, 244, 446
Baronius, –, 158
Barra, Pablo, 333
Barrois, Jacques, 395
Barth, Hans, 226–7
Bartolozzi, F., 347
Barzizus, Gasparinus, 59, 87, 442
Basa, Domenico, 158, 177
Basel, 87–91, 180–1
Basel Missal, 89
Basel type, 190, 225
Basel University Library, 89
Basilia, Leonardus Achates de, 443, 445
    see also Acate, Leonardo
Bask, Bishop Hans, 226
Baskerville, John, 312, 341–4, 348, 406
Baskerville types, 342, 343, 344, 346
Baskerville's Bible, 343
Baskett, John, 335
Bassano, 326
Bastard types, 75, 101, 163, 234 see also Lettre
    Batarde and named bastards
Batchelor, Joseph, 407
Bateman, James, 402
Batrachomyomachia, 125
Baudrier, –, 171
Bauer, Andreas, 360
Bauer, Friedrich Andreas, 361, 362, 363
Bauer, Johann Christian, 386
Bauer, Ferguson and Hill, 385
Bauersche Giesserei, 385
Bauhaus, the, 419
Baumann, Georg, 137, 248
Baumann, Georg II, 248
Baumgarten, Konrad, 236, 437
Bausch, Johann Lorenz, 274
Bavaria, Electress of, 321
Baxter, George, 389, 390
Bayerischen Staatsbibliothek, 140
Bayley, Harold, 303
Bazaleni, Caligula de, 51
Beaufort, André, 54, 55, 438
Beaufort, Margaret Countess of, 97
Beaujon, Alexandre, 201
Beaujoyeulx, Baltasar, 213
Beaulieu, –, 213

Beaumarchais, –, 325, 344
Beauvais, Vincent de, 88
Bechtermünstze, Heinrich, 21, 437
Bechtermüntze, Nicholas, 21, 437
Beck, Leonhard, 134
Beckerhyb, Johann, 24, 26, 446 see also Dold and
    Beckerhub
Bedričić, Silvester, 45
Begna-Kozicic, Simon, Bishop of Modrus, 245
Beham, Hans Sebald, 138
Behem, Franz, 128
Behem, Kaspar, 128
Behmer, Marcus, 411
Behrens Mediaeval type, 417
Berhens, Peter, 417, 423
Behrens schrift, 423
Beilby, Ralph, 344
Beitragezur Inkunabelkunde, 76n
Belfort, Andrea see Beaufort, André
Belfortis, Andreas see Beaufort, André
Belial: de Theramo, 25, 26, 74, 440
Bell, John, 345
Bella, Stefano Della, 293
Bellaert, Jacob, 77, 439
Bellarmini Catechism, 300
Bellère, Jean, 193, 215
Bellère, Lucas, 223
Bellescullée, Pierre, 72, 443
Bello Italico adversus Gothos, De: Aretino, 53, 438
Bellone, Antonio, 151, 153
Bellone, Marcantonio, 153
Bellum grammaticale: Guarna, 264
Belon, Jean, 445
Belot, Jean, 92, 93, 439
Beltrano, Ottavio, 301
Bembo, Pietro, 144 (Fig 36), 150
Ben Alantansi, Elieser, 439
Ben Aser, Jacob, 439, 442
Ben David, Chiyyah Meir, 205
Ben Garton Ben Isaac, Abraham, 443
Ben Moses, Gershom, 435
Benchorius, Petrus, 437
Beneda, –, 234
Benedetti, Francesco dei, 51
Benedicht, Lorenz, 227, 228
Benedictine Breviary, 43
Benedictis, Franciscus de, 50
Benedictis, Jacobus de 436
Benedictis, Johannes Jacobus de, 438
Benedictis, Nicolaus de, 55

Ben edikz, B enedikt S., 231
Bengtsson, Bengt, 225
Benkner, Johann (Hans), 240, 243
Bennett, H. S., 121
Bensley, Thomas, 345, 347–8, 356, 360, 387
Bentivoglio, Giovanni II, 50
Bentivoglio, –, 150
Benzing, Josef, 133
Beplin, Joannes, 150
Béranger, Jean Pierre, 402
Berg, Adam, the Elder, 140, 210
Berg, Johann, 210
Bergamo, Bernardinus de, 436
Bergher, Adrien van, 195, 196
Bergmann von Olpe, Johann, 91
Bericht, 275
Berlin, 137
Berlin Observatory, 16
Berliner Genealogischer Kalender, 324
Berling's Gazette, 353
Berlingske Tidende, 353
Bermentlo, Peregrinus, 439
Bermudo, Juan, 218
Bern, 179–80
Bernard, Auguste, 21, 163, 316
Bernardus, –, 436, 443
Berner, Carl, 133
Berner, Conrad, 132, 133
Berner, Johann, 133
Berner, Katharina, 133
Berners, Dame Juliana, 104
Bernersche Schriftgiesserei, 133
Bernhard, Lucien, 411
Bernhardt, Sarah, 416 (Fig 88)
Bernoni, –, 45
Bernuz, Pedro, 188
Berny, – De *see* Laurent and De Berny
Beroaldo, Filippo, 162
Berokot, 204
Berquin, Louis de, 169
Bertall, –, 403
Bertelli, F., 302
Berthelet, Thomas, 254, 255, 257
Berthelsen, Rasmus, 393
Bartholdus, –, 32
Bertieri, R., 330
Bertin, Dominique, 173
Bertocchi, Donnino, 51
Bertoldo, 327
Berton, Jean, 440

Beschreibung Wilhelms Hetzogs und der Renata gehaltenen hochzeitlichen ehrenfestes: Wagner, 140
Besicken, Johann (Joannes), 89, 150
Beslay, –, 404
Bessa, Pancrace, 402
Bessarion, Cardinal, 60
Bessemer, Sir Henry, 377
Best, –, 400
Bethlen, Count Stephen, 285
Bettenham, –, 339
Bettini, Antonio, 48
Beuter, P. A., 189
Beverley, Alfred of, 335
Bevilacqua, Giovanni Battista, 153
Bevilacqua, Nicoló, 153
Bewick, John, 345
Bewick, Thomas, 344–5, 400, 402
Beyamus Christoph, 443
Bèze, Theodore de, 183
Bibby, Baron and Sons, 426
Bibel in't Corte, 196
Bible de Serrières, 184
Bibles see individual bibles, *Gutenberg, 36-line* etc.
Biblia Bohemica, 234, 439
Bibliae Latinae, 435, 440, 442 *see also Latin Bibles*
Biblia Neerlandica, 75
Biblia Pauperum, 3, 5, 25–6
Biblia Sacra, 174
Biblia Sacra Polyglotta, 288
Bibliande, Theodor, 181
Biblicae Historiae, 140
Bibliographical Decameron: Dibdin, 197n, 346
Bibliographie und Bibliophilie, Über: Breitkopf, 322
Bibliographie des editions musicales: Lesure & Thibault, 214n
Bibliographie des Impressions Espagnols des Pays-Bas: Peeters-Fontaines, 193n
Bibliopola Urbis Parisiensis Consrtes, 298
Bibliotheca Apostolica Vaticana: Roccha, 177
Bibliotheca Spenceriana: Dibdin, 346
Bibliotheca universalis: Gesner, 181
Bibliothèque de l'Arsenal, Paris, 59
Bibliothèque Mazarine, Paris, 173
Bibliothèque Nationale, 298
Bibliothèque Royale, 298
Bidet, –, 381
Bidpai, the Brahmin, 34
Biel, Friedrich, 87, 436 *see also* Alemán de Basilea, Fadrique

Biener, Matthias *see* Apiarius, Matthias

Bignon, Abbé, 315

Bill, John, 288

Billettes, Gilles Filleau des, 315

Billingsley, Martin 297 (Fig 69)

Bing, Samuel, 415

Binney, Archibald, 376

Binns, Edward, 377

Biographie Universelle: Weiss, 163

Birckmann, Arnold the Elder, 128

Birckmann, Arnold II, 128

Birckmann, Francis, 128, 214

Birckmann and Gymnich, 128

Birckmann and Quentel, 128

Birgettenkloster, 445

Biringuccio, Vannoccio, 14

Birth of Mankynde: Raynalde, 260

Bishops' Bible, 133 and n, 228, 257–8, 262 (Fig 57)

Bisticci, Vespasiano da, 50, 109

Black-letter type:
England, 291, 339, 407; Germany, 108 (Fig 22); Netherlands, 201, 349 (Fig 75); Spain, 185, 194

Blado, Antonio, 147–9 (Fig 38), 157, 158

Blado, Paolo, 157

Blaeu, Cornelis, 283

Blaeu, Jean, 283

Blaeu Press, 272

Blaeu, William Janszoon, 281, 358

Blageart, Jérome, 300

Blaise, Thomas, 293

Blake, William, 375, 388

Blanc, Antoine, 183

Blanchardyn and Eglantine, 97

Blanchot, Raymond, 175n

Blandin, Richard, 61

Blasius, –, 274

Blasón general: Gratia Dei, 437

Blason de la Perle: Merchadier, 173

Blastus, Nicolaus, 47

Blavis, Bartholmaeus de, 45

Bleeding and bloodletting calendars, 18, 28, 234, 239

Block books, 3, 4 (Figs 1, 2), 5–6

Bloem, Jacques, 412

Blount, Edward, 287, 294 (Fig 68)

Blumentrost, Laurent, 354

Bobadilla, Juan de, 84, 443

Boccaccio, Giovanni, 33–4, 41, 47, 58, 104 (Fig 20), 413

Bocquillon, Arnauld, 64, 436

Bodoni, Giambattista, 312, 327, 328, 329 (Fig 72), 330, 332

Bodoni types, 329–30, 346, 412–13

Boethius, –, 97

Boexken van dem hemelschen Wyngaert: St Bernard, 195

Boexken van der officien ofte dienst der Missen, 435

Boexken van verduldich Lyden: St Bernard, 195

Bogard, Jacques, 197

Bogbinder, Hans Missenheim, 250

Bogdan, Prof., 242

Bohemian Brethren, the, 237

Bohemian New Testament, 233

Boke named the Governour: Elyot, 254

Boleyn, Anne, 270

Bollifant, Edmund, 264

Bologna, 50–1, 327

Bologna, Salvador de, 436

Bolt, –, 325

Bomberg, Cornelius, 205

Bomberg, Daniel, 205, 206

Bomberg, David, 205

Bomberghen, Cornelius van *see* Bomberg, Cornelius

Bonaccorsi, Francesco, 49, 53

Bonacota, Paolo, 305, 306 (Fig 70)

Bonaventura *see* St Bonaventure

Boner, Ulrich, 25

Bonetus, –, 78

Bonfadini, –, 177

Bonhomme, Jean, 71

Bonhomme, Macé, 167

Bon homme, Pasquier, 61, 71

Bonington, –, 402

Boninus, Bonino de, 46, 57, 243

Bonnefoy, Jean, 183

Bonnin, –, 166

Bonus, Johannes, 443

Book of Christian Prayers, 390 (Fig 83), 391

Book of Common Order, 266

Book of Common Praier noted, 216

Book of Common Prayer, 390 (Fig 83), 391

Book containg divers sortes of hands: Chesne and Baildon, 263 (Fig 58)

Book of Martyrs: Foxe

Book of Nurture, 67

Book of St Albans, 100 (Fig 17), 102

Book-hand, 251

Books of Hours:
England, 105; France, 66, 67, 69 (Fig 9), 70,

Books of Hours: (contd)
  126, 163, 298; Jugoslavia, 245; Poland, 247;
  Russia, 251, 252
Borchard, Johann, 439
Borchard, Thomas, 439
Bordázar, Antonio de, 331, 332
Bordeaux, 172–3
Borgia, Alonso, *see* Calixtus III
Borsdorf, Rudolf, 247
Bosse, Abraham, 293
Bosse, Count Ignacio Favetti de, 327
Botanicum: Dorstenius, 131
Botel, Heinrich, 79, 84, 435, 439
Böttiger, Gregorius, 36
Boucher, François, 314
Bouchot, Henri, 398 and n.
Boudeville, Guyon, 173
Boulonois, Edmé de, 199 (Fig 47)
Bourne, Nicholas, 289
Boutall, Walter, 406 *see also* Walder and Boutall
Boutatts, –, 303
Boutellier, Jean, 435
Bouyer, Jean, 442
Bowyer, William, 338, 339, 348
Boydell, Messrs, 345
Boyle, Robert, 274
Bracciolini, Poggio, 109
Bradwood, Melchisidec, 287 and N.
Braga Missal, 86
Brahe, Tycho, 228, 281
Brandenburg, Johann Georg, Elector of, 137
Brandis, Lucas, 36, 65, 440
Brandis, Marcus, 34, 439
Brandis, Matthaeus, 226
Brandis, Moritz, 36
Brandstetter, Friedrich, 387
Brandstetter, Oscar, 387
Brant, Sebastian, 91
Brask, Bishop Johann, 225
Brasov *see* Brassó
Brassó, 239–40, 241, 242, 243
Bratislava, 237, 238, 239
Braunschweig, Hieronymus, 24, 139 (Fig 35)
Breda, Jacobus de, 75
Bréhan-Loudeac, 72
Breitkopf, Bernhard Christoph, 321
Breitkopf, Gottlob, 318, 321, 322
Breitkopf and Härtel, 322, 360, 417
Breitkopf, Gottlob Immanuel, 321, 322
Bremer Press, 411

Brescia, 56
Brescia, Bartolomeo da, 245
Breslau, 137, 236, 248
Bressani, Luigi, 157
Brest-Litovsk, 248
Breve y mas compendiosa doctrina christiana, 186
Brèves, Francois Savary de, 300, 302
Breviarium Braccarense, 435
Breviarium Capuanum, 436
Breviarium Cisterciense, 443
Breviarium Cluniacense, 64, 437
Breviarium Compostellanum, 84, 443
Breviarium Constantiense, 437
Breviarium Eburodunense, 437
Breviarium Elnense, 442
Breviarium, Geneva, 92
Breviarium Herbipolense, 446
Breviarium historiale: de Columna, 442
Breviarium Holense, 230
Breviarium Ilerdense, 439
Breviarium Lemoviense, 440
Breviarium Misnense, 440
Breviarium Moguntinense (Moguntinum), 21, 440
Breviarium Narbonense, 441
Breviarium Ottoniense, 226
Breviarium Romanum, 441, 444
Breviarium Tarentasiense, 441
Breviarium Traiectense, 444
Breviarium Trecense, 64, 445
Breviarium Turonense, 444
Breviarium Uticense, 445
Breviaries, 30, 43, 45, 55, 244, 441 *see also Bre-*
  viarium and named *Breviaries*
Breydenbach, Bernhard von, 29, 82, 235
Breyn, Jacob, 249
Briard, Etienne, 211
Briasson, –, 319, 320n
Brief an Herzog Sigmund: Eberhard of W., 443
Brito, Jean, 75
Britannia Works, Birmingham, 377
Britannicus, Angelus de, 56
Britannicus, Jacobus de, 44, 56, 244
British Encyclopaedia, 359
British Museum, 5, 69, 70n., 116, 351
Brno, 235–6
Brocar, Arnão Guillén de, 82, 125, 187–8, 442
Brockhaus, Eduard, 385
Brockhaus, Friedrich, 385–6
Brockhaus, F. A., 363, 385
Brockhaus, Heinrich, 385–6

Index

Brockhaus, Rudolf, 385
Brodersen, Jesper, 393
Brook type, 410
Brothers of the Common Life, 21, 77, 123, 138, 436, 440, 443
Brothers Klingspor, the, 418
Brothers of St Michael in dem Hem, 444
Brotherton Collection, 124 (Fig 32)
Brucioli, Francesco, 206
Bruges, 74–5
Bruggen, Henrik ter, 214
Brugman, Johann, 443
Brun, Peter (Pedro), 78, 84, 444
Brunet, 69, 320
Brünn *see* Brno
Bruschis, Barth. de, 443
Bruschis, Laurentius de, 443
Brussels, 77
Brvijal po zakonu rimskoga dvora, 45
Brydges, Sir Egerton, 406
Brześć Litewski *see* Brest Litovsk
B–36 type, 15, 16
Bucer, Martin, 183
Buch zu distillieren, Das: Braunschweig, 139
Buch der Natur: von Megenberg, 28–9
Buch der vier Historien, 25
Buch de Weisheit der alten Weisen, 34
Buchdruckpresse: Dieterichs, 358
Buchpinder, Benedict, 140
Buckinck, Arnold, 38
Bucolics: Virgil, 400
Buda, 238–9
Budapest University Press, 392
Budé, Guillaume, 160, 167
Bühler, Dr Curt F., 2 and n., 50
Buinichi, 253
Bula de indulgencies de la Santa Cruzada, 81
Bulla anna jubilei: Paul II, 55 *see also Bulls Papal*
Bulletin des Lois, 365
Bullock, William, 367
Bullokar, William, 264, 270 (Fig 63)
Bullokars Boke . . . . . for the amendment of Orthographie for English Speech, 264, 270 (Fig 63)
Bulls Papal, 18, 55, 99, 115, 157, 158
Bulmer, William, 345–7, 348, 387
Bulmer, William, and Co., 345
Bungart, Hermann, 128
Bunney, Edmund, 265
Bunyan, John, 290 (Fig 67)
Buon, Nicolas, 293, 298

Burdin der Zyt, 88
Bure, ainé de, 395
Bure, Guillaume de, 395
Bureus, Johannes, 225
Burgkmair, Hans, 134, 135, 136
Burgo de Castilliono, Pietro Antonio de, 52
Burgos, 83, 188–9
Burgundy, Grand Bastard Antoine of, 65
Burlas de la fortuna, 334
Burne-Jones, Sir Edward, 407
Burnhart, Joost, 107
Burns, Robert, 422 (Fig 90)
Burtsov-Protopopov, Vasili Fedorov, 252
Bury, Richard de, 268 (Fig 62)
Busdraghi, Vincenzo, 153
Butter, Nathaniel, 289
Butter, Thomas, 289
Büttner *see* Victor, Hieronymus
Butzbach, Georg von, 56, 436, 440
Butzbach, Paul von, 440
Bawar, Florian *see* Ungler, Florian
Buyer, Barthélemy, 62
Buz, Charles, 386
Byddell, John, 254, 255–6
Byfield, Mary, 391
Bynneman, Henry, 263, 264
Byrd, William, 216, 218, 288

C

Cadeaulx type, 163
Caderousse, Davin de, 9
Cagliola, Fabrizio, 307
Caillaut, –, 65
Calafat, Nicolaus, 440, 442
Calandri, Filippo, 49
Calcar, John of, 181
Calderini, Domizio, 143
Calendar: Regiomontanus, 115
Calepinus, –, 150
Calixtus III, Pope, 18
Callet, Jean François, 400
Callimachus, 338
Callierges, Zacharias, 47
Calvin, Jean, 172, 183, 184, 264–5
Calvinus, Andreas, 435
Calvo, Francesco Minicio, 148
Cambiagi, Gaetano, 301
Cambridge Plate, 427
Cambridge University Press: 269, 270–1, 312, 427

Cambridge University Press (*contd*)
  Baskerville punches, 344
  Prayer books, 343, 371
Camden, William, 335
Camera Apostolica, 148
Campanili, Gulielmo de Canepanovade de', 436
Campomanes, Pedro de, 320
Campora, Giacomo, 437
Cancionero general: del Castillo, 189
Canizarius, Laurentius, 55
Cano, Benito, 332, 333
Canon de medicina: Avicenna, 52
Canones et decreta Concilii Tridentini, 154
Canozio da Lendinara, Cristoforo, 58
Canozo da Lendinara, Laurenzo (Lorenzo), 56, 57–8, 442
Canterbury Tales: Chaucer, 94, 101, 103 (Fig 19)
Canticum Canticorum, 3, 5
Cantiones, 216
Canzone, sonetti, strambotti et frottole, 209
Canzoniere et triomphi: Petrarch, 151
Caorsin, Gulielmus, 226, 441
Capcasa, Matteo, 46
Capell, Edwards, 342
Caracciolus, Robertus, 87, 441
Caractères de l'université *see* Jannon types
Caraffa, Cardinal, later Pope Paul IV, 158, 238
Carant, Jean, 442
Carbo, Johannes *see* Kohl, Hans
Cardon, Horace, 171
Carez, Joseph, 372, 399
Carletti, Angelo, 436
Carlos II of Spain, 334
Carlos III of Spain, 331, 333
Carlovingian script, 108
Carmen, Merrimé, 405
Carmona, Manuel Salvador, 332
Carnerio, Agostino, 55
Carnerio, Bernardo, 55
Carolingian miniscule, 109 (Fig 23)
Carolus, Johann, 275
Caron, –, 293, 319
Carpintras, Elzéar *see* Genet, Elzéar
Cars, Laurent, 314
Carter, Harry, 13 and n., 14, 107, 129, 147, 176
Carter, John, 371
Carter and Ricks, 260
Carthusiensis, Adrianus, 112
Carthusiensis, Dionysius, 73
Carzel de amor: de San Pedro, 81

Casas, Fr Bartolomé de las, 192
Caslon Foundry, 357 (Fig 77)
Caslon, Henry, 340
Caslon, Mrs Henry, later Strong, 340
Caslon, H. W., 340
Caslon, Thomas, 340
Caslon types, 312, 339, 391, 410
Caslon, William I, 312, 339–40, 341, 348, 352, 391
Caslon, William II, 340, 391
Caslon, Mrs William II, 340
Caslon, William III, 340
Časoslovec, 247
Cassolis, Jacobus de, 49
Castaldi, Pamfilo, 52, 440
Castel of helth: 255
Casteleyn, Gerard, 348, 349
Casteleyn, Mathias de, 216
Castiglione, –, 264
Castillo, Fernando del, 189
Castle of Otranto: Walpole, 330
Castro, Alvaro de, 84, 439, 443
Castro, Alvar Gomez de, 189
Castro, Paulus de, 444
Castro, Pedro de, 191–2
Catalogue chronologique des Libraires: Lottin, 173
Catalogues of censored books, 158
Catalogus: Anshelm, 179
Catechism: Luther, 237, 240
Catena aurea: Aquinas, 32
Catherwood, Nathaniel, 340
Catholicon, 13, 21, 115
Catholicon type, 118
Catholycke Epistelen, 196
Cato Christianus, 168
Catharensis, Andreas de Paltasichis *see* Paltasic, Andrija
Catullus, 125, 151, 344
Cauteret, Jean, 167
Cavalcanti, –, 150
Cavallis, Vas, 173
Cavazzoni, Marco Antonio, 209
Cawood, John, 257, 258 (Fig 54)
Caxton types, 99–100, 101–2
Caxton, William:
  Bruges, 49, 74
  Cologne, 28
  Westminster, 94–5 (Fig 14), 97, 99–100, 446
Caylus, Comte de, 315
Cebes, –, 161 (Fig 42)

Ceccarelli, Pietro, 301
Celestina, 82, 83, 192
Cellarius, Chrisyoph, 276
Celtis, Conrad, 30, 114 (Fig 28), 209
Cenni del Fora, Bernardo di, 47
Cenni del Fora, Domenico di, 47
Cennini, Bernardo, 438
Cennini, Dominico, 438
Cennini *see also* Cenni del Fora
Cennis, Franciscus de, 442
Cent histoires de Troie, Les: de Pisan, 69
Cent Nouvelles Nouvelles, Les, 67
Centenera, Antonio de, 83, 84, 446
Centralschrift, 323
Century Guild, 415
Cerdonis, Matthaeus, 57, 58, 243
Cervantes Saavedra, Miguel de, 302, 403
Cervicornus, Eucharius, 128, 129, 256
Cervini, Cardinal Marcello, 148
César, Pierre *see* Kaiser, Peter
Cetinje, 244
Cetveroblago vestije (four Gospels), 245
Chablis, 66
Chaix, Napoléon, 381
Chalcondylas, Demetrius, 48, 49, 53 *see also*
　Damilas, Demetrius
Châlons-sur-Marne, 64
Chambers, Ephraim, 319
Chambre Royale et Syndicate de Pa Libraine et
　Imprinerie de paris, 372
Chambre Syndicale, 317
Champ Fleury: Tory, 163
Champs, Janot des, 167
Chancery italic, 155, 156 (Fig 41)
Channay, Jean de, 211
Chansons: Beranger, 402
Chansons: Jannequin, 211
Chansons: de Laborde, 313
Chansons georgiennes, Les: Chasteain, 445
Chansons Nouvelles: Beaulaigue, 177
Chansons nouvelles en musique, 211
Chapelet, Claude, 298
Chapman, Walter, 71
Chapman & Hall, 389
Chardella, Simon Nicolai, 38
Charivari, 404
Charlemagne, 108
Charles V of Spain, 188, 196, 214
Charles VII of France, 40, 59–60
Charles IX of France, 165

Charlet, Nicolas, 404
Charlier de Gerson, J., 34
Chartres, 64
Chase: Somerville, 345
Chasovnik, 251
Chastelain, Georges, 445
Chastysing of goddes chyldern, 98 (Fig 16), 100
Chateau de labeur, Le: Gringoire, 69
Chateaubriand, François René, Vicomte de, 405
Chatelain, Charles, 293
Chaucer, Geoffrey, 94, 103 (Fig 19), 105, 122
Chaucer type, 407
Chaucer, Works of, 407
Chaudré *see* Marinoni et Chaudré
Chauliac, –, 70
Chaumiere Indienne, La: de Saint Pierre, 403
Chauvet, –, 59
Chauveau, Francois, 293, 294
Chemin, Nicolas du, 211, 212 and n., 214
Chemische Druckerei, 373
Chernigov, 253
Chesne, John de Beau, 263 (Fig 58)
Chevalier Chrestien, Le: de Berquin, 169
Chevalier, Sulpice Guillaume, 403
Child's Book of Dogs, 429
Child's Book of Horses, 429
Chios, 310
Chiswick Press, 391
Chodowiescki, Daniel Nikolaus, 324, 325
Choffard, P. P., 313, 314
Choix de Chansons: de Laborde, 314
Cholin, Materne, 128, 223
Choralbuchlein: Spangenberg, 210
Christian III of Denmark, 250
Christian III's Bible, 228
Christianiae religionis institutio: Calvin, 184
Christianismi Restitutio: Servetus, 172
Christina of Sweden, 229, 272
Christlichen Adel deutscher Nation, An den: Luther,
　123, 130
Chromo-lithograph frontispiece, 397 (Fig 85)
Chronica: Hispalensis, 435
Chronica Hungarorum: Kezai, 238, 239, 436
Chronica Hungarorum: de Thwrocz, 30, 235, 236
　(Fig 52)
Chronicle at Large: Grafton, 261 (Fig 56)
Chronicle of the Swiss Wars: Schradin, 444
Chronicles: Franck, 179
Chronicles: Holinshed, 264
Chronicles: Newbridge et al., 335

Chronicles of England, 102
Chronicon Budense see Chronica Hungarorum: Kezai
Chroniques des Empereurs: Gueroult, 172
Chroniques de France, 71
Chroniques de Normandie, Les, 71
Chrysander, Friedrich, 209
Chrysostomus see St John Chrysostom
Church music, 207
Church, Dr William, 376, 377
Cicero:
  Epistolae ad Brutum, 40
  Epistolae ad familiares, 37–8, 40, 52, 443, 445
  Finibus, De, 41
  Officiis, De, 21, 55, 439
  Oratore, De, 37, 60n.
  Rhetorica Nova, 435
  Tusculanae quaestiones, 38
  works of, 125, 337, 438
Cicéro type, 174, 175, 398
Ciolek, Erasmus, 248
Cistercian Abbey, 446
Cite de Dieu, La: St Augustine, 64
Cividale, 57
Civelitate morum puerorum libellus, De: Erasmus, 175, 202
Civilité type, 175 (Fig 43) 176, 202
Civitale, Bartholomaeus de, 440
Civitate Dei, De: St Augustine, 37, 40, 89, 90 (Fig 13)
Civitate G. de N., 445
Claesz, Cornelisz, 281, 283
Claims of Decorative Art: Crane, 415 and n.
Clair, Colin, 133n.
Clarenden, Edward Hyde, Earl of, 335
Clarenden Press, 291
Claris Mulieribus, De: Boccaccio, 33–4
Claris Mulieribus, De: Foresti, 55
Clarke, John, 288
Claudin, –, 300–1
Claudius type, 419
Clebat, Esteban, 71
Clement V, Pope, 112
Clement VII, Pope, 158
Clement VIII, Pope, 158
Clementine Bible, 158
Clementine Index, 158
Clericus, Hubertinus, 436
Clichtove, Josse, 160
Climachus, Johannes, 444

Clovis: Desmaret, 295
Clowes, William, 356, 362, 387–9
Clowes, William and Sons Ltd, 389
Cluj see Kolozsvár
Cluny, 64
Clusa, Jacobus de, 436
Cobden-Sanderson, Thomas James, 44, 409
Cochin, Charles-Nicolas, 314
Coci, Jorge, 186, 188, 218
Cock, Symon, 214
Cockerell, Sir Sydney, 406
Codex egregius comestoris viciorum, 20
Codignola, Ernesto, 381
Cohen, Gershom ben Solomon, 204
Coignet, –, 402
Colbert, Jean Baptiste, 292, 295
Colibert, Clément, 315
Colines, Simon de, 126, 161–2, 164, 165, 173, 221
Colini, Joh., 440, 445
Collana degli istorici grecie latini, 150
Collected edition: St Augustine, 89
Collectorium sper Magnificat: de Gerson, 34, 207
Colleget: Averroes, 55
Collezione degli Scrittori Milanese, 327
Collins Cleartype Press, 413
Cologne, 26–8, 275, 276
Cologne, Heinrich, 444, 445
Cologne, John of, 41, 43 see also Colonia, Johannes de
Columnis, Barth., de, 440
Colon, Giovanni da, Nicoló Jenson e Compagni, 43–4
Colonia, Arnoldus de, 36
Colonia, Henricus de see Dalen, Heinrich
Colonia, Johannes de 88 see also Cologne, John of
Colonia, Pablo de, 81
Colonia y Socios, Paulo de, 81
Colonna, Egidio, 81
Colonna, Francesco, 145 (Fig 37), 146
Colonna, Guido della, 232
Colonna, Marco, Bishop of Salerno, 177
Colophons and Printers Device from Latin Bible, 122 (Fig 26)
Colophons (definition), 114–15
Colour plates, 315
Colour printing, 104, 389
Colour-gravure, 383
Colson, J. B. G., 316
Columbian iron press, 356

Columbus, Christopher, 86, 91
Columna, Aegidius, 83
Coumna, Landulphus de, 442
Combattim ento e presa d'un galeone . . ., 306
Comenius, Johannes, 280 *see also* Komenskí, Jan
Comestor, Petrus, 73, 196
Comestorium vitiorum: de Retza, 20, 30, 441
Comino, Angelo, 327
Commedie: Goldoni, 326
Comment of later Prophets (Hebrew): Qimhi, 438
Comment on Pentateuch (Hebrew): 440, 443
Comment in Vergilii Bucolica: Servius, 438
Commentaries: Caesar, 82
Commentariola isagogica . . .: Ferettus, 438
Commentary on the Pentateuch: Nachmanides, 206
Commentary on Vergil: Honoratus, 47
Commentum in Heroidas Ovidii: Clericus, 436
Commin, Vincent, 65
Commino, Giuseppe, 327
Comoedia Codri: Kerckmeister, 441
Comoediae: Terence, 63 (Fig 7), 125
Compagnia della Stampa, 153
Compgnie des Libraires lyonnais, 171
Compgnie des Libraires du Palais, 298
Compagnie des Libraires pour les S. S. Peres, 299
Compañeros Alemanes, 82
Compañia de Impresores y Libreros, 334
Compendium breve: Innocent III, 62, 440
Compendium Musices: Lampadius, 179
Complutensian Bible, 125
Complutensian Polyglot Bible, 82
'Compofonditrice', 381
'Composeuse', 381
Composing Machines, 377–9
'Compositeur Typographe', 381
'Composieur typographe mecanique', 381
Compost et Kalendrier des Bergiers (Bergers), 65
Comprehensorium: Johannes, 79
Computer-typesetting, 430
Confectbuch und Houss Apotek: Ryff, 132 (Fig 33)
Confesio verae religionis: Melcer, 238
Confessionale: Florentus, 239, 440
Confessione, Delle: Senensis, 442
Confutatorium errorum: de Prexamo, 81
Congregatio de Propaganda Fide, 302
Conis, De: Pergeus, 154
Conjuracion de Catalina, La: Sallust, 332
Conquista da Mexico, La: de Solis, 304, 333
Conquista de Nueva España: de Solis, 303
Consilia: de Accoltis, 442

Consolácion of Philosophie: Boethius, 97
Constance Breviary, 39n., 207–8
Constantia, Paulus de, 79
Constantin, Mes., 164
Constantinople, 307–9, 310
Constituiçoes do sinodo do Porto de 1496, 441
Constitutiones: Clement V, 112
Constitutiones Marchiae Anconitanae, 439
Constitutionnel, Le, 373
Constitutions of Oporto bishopric, 86
Constitutions synodales de l'Eglise de Genève, 92
Consiituzione della patria di Friuli, 445
Consuetudines urbis Panormi, 442
Conte Allegorique: de Montesson, 396
Contes Drolatiques: Balzac, 403
Contes et Nouvelles en Vers: La Fontaine, 313, 314
Conti, Federico de', 439
Cope *see* Hopkinson and Cope
Copenhagen, 226, 352–3
Copenhagen Royal Library, 393
Copper-plate engraving, 283, 259, 381–2
Copper-plate engravings:
   France, 172, 173, 272, 293, 314, 404
   Italy, 48
   Spain, 303
Copie of certen orders concerning printing:
   Stationers Co., 121 and n.
Copyright Act, 338
Coralle, Etienns, 54
Corante, newes from Italy etc, 289
Corderius, Balt., 440
Cordiale quattuor novissimorum, 74
Cordoba, Alfonso Fernández de, 84, 441
Cordova, Hernandez de, 218
Coresi, –, 240, 242, 243
Coresi, Serban, 240
Corfu, 310
Corinth, 310
Cornatus: de Garlandia, 439
Cornazzano, Antonio, 440
Cornbury, Lord, 335
Corneille, Claude, 172, 293, 296, 396
Corneto, Tancredus de, 445
Cornil, S., 86n.
Cornucopia: Perottus, 144
Correspondence de Plantin, 223n.
Corsellis, Frederick, 99
Corte instruccye ende onderwys: van der Heyden,
   13, 201
Leyes de las Cortes de Toledo, 443

Cortigiana, La: Aretino, 149
Corvinus, Antonius, 230
Corvinus, Matthias, 239
Corvus, Andreas, 235
Coryciana, 156
Cosimo de' Medici, Piero di, 57
Cosín, Pierres, 187
Cosman, Cristóbal, 189
Cosmographia: Ptolomy, 34, 56
Cosmographicall Glasse: Cunningham, 260
Cosmography: Münster, 180
Coster, Laurens, 13, 348
Cot, Pierre, 316
Cotman, –, 375
Cotta, Johann Friedrich, 325, 363
Cottendorf, Freiherr von see Cotta Johann Friedrich
Cottrell, Thomas, 340–1
Council of Trent, 196
Courbé, Antoine, 293
Courrier de l'Europe, 396
Courteau, Thomas, 183, 184
Courtier: Castiglione, 264
Coutumes de Bretagne, 72, 443, 444
Coutumes de comté et du duché Bourgogne, 437
Coverdale Bible, 129, 259 (Fig 55)
Coverdale and his Bibles: Mozley, 256n.
Coverdale, Myles (Miles), 129, 256
Cowper and Applegath, 356
Cowper, Edward, 362–3
Cowper Press, 356
Cracas, Giovanni Francesco, 326
Cracovia, Mattheus de, 21
Cracow, 246–9
Craig, E. Gordon, 411
Cramer, Peter, 352
Cramoisy, Claude, 292, 299
Cramoisy, Gabriel, 292, 299
Cramoisy, Sébastien, 292, 298, 299
Cramoisy, Sébastien Mâbre- see Mâbre-Cramoisy, Sébastien
Cranach, Lucas, 130, 411
Cranach Presse, 411
Crane, Walter, 409 (Fig 87), 415
Cranmer, Archbishop, 256
Crantz, Martin, 59
Crapelet, –, 385
Crato, Johann Heinrich, 241
Cravato, Martino, 150, 153
Cremer, Hentry, 115

Crès, Jean, 72, 435, 439
Cresci, Giovanni Francesco, 157
Crespin, Jean, 167, 183, 184, 216
Creussner, Friedrich, 32, 114 (Fig 28), 118
Crivelli, Galeazzo de, 52
Crom, Matthew, 256
Cromberger, Jacobo, 185, 189
Crovberger, Juan, 185, 186
Cromberger, Juan y Jacomo, 186
Cromwell, Thomas, 256, 257
Cronaca Venetá: Pacifico, 301
Cronica: Tinódi, 240
Cronica van der Hilliger Stat van Coellen: 11, 27
Cronica del Rey Juan el Segundo: Guzman, 188
Cronike van Hollant, 439
Cronycles of the londe of Englōd, 77
Cross, Thomas, 288–9
Cruse, Aloys (Louis), 92, 442
Crusius, –, 322
Cryptomenytices et Cryptographiae: Selenus, 278
Csaszmai, Stephen, 243
Cuatro Compañeros Alemanes, 81
Cuesta, Juan de la, 193 (Fig 46), 302, 303
Culs-de-lampe, 313, 314
Cultrificus, Engelbertus, 441
Cultura veche romina: Bogdan, 242n.
Cunningham, William, 260
Cupy, Willem, 350
Curia, the, 38
Curmer, J. L., 403
Curmer, L., 403
Cursive types, 146, 150 see also Italic types
Curteus, Thomas see Courteau, Thomas
Cusi, Meshullam, 204
Cuspidus, –, 167
Cyclopedia, 319
Cylinder press, 359, 360 see also rotary presses
Cyrillic alphabet, 177
Cyrillic type: 392: Brassö, 240, 241: Cracow, 242, 247, 249: Vienna, 142: Vilna, 251
Czech Bible, 238

D

Dale, Henrik vanden, 77
Dalen, Heinrich, 55–6
Dalmatin, Grgur, 243, 244
Dalza, Joan Ambrosio, 208
Damilas, Demetrius, 49, 125 see also Chalcondyles Demetrius
Dance of Death, 5, 171–2 see also Danse Macabre

Daniel, Rev. C. H. O., 406, 408
Daniel Press, 406
Danish Bible, 138
Danse Macabre, 65, 358 *see also Dance of Death*
Danse Macabre des femmes, 65
Dansk Musikhistorie: Hammerich, 228
Dansk Rimkronike, 226
Danske Salmebog: Thomeses, 228
Dante Alighieri: 149, 326
   Divina Commedia, La, 48, 53, 403
   Inferno, 37, 189
Dante: Marcolini, 148
Dante type, 413, 414
Danvillier, Anthony, 175
Danvillier, Hubertus *see* Armilliers, Hubert d'
Daphnis et Chloe: Longus, 395
Darlow and Moule, 233, 234, 237, 240
Darmstadt, 274
Dathenus, Pierre, 216
Dati, Leonardo, 49
Datus, Augustinus, 101, 438
Daumier, Honoré, 375, 403, 404
David, l'ainé, 319, 320n.
David, Jacques Louis, 398, 399
Davids, Arthur, 307
Davies, David W., 280
Davies, R., 264
Dawson, William, 366
Day, John, 201, 260, 390 (Fig 83), 391
Day, Richard, 262
Daye, John, 216
Debermy and Peignot, 344, 430
Debrecen, 241
Decades: Aneau, 172
Decalogus de Sancto Paulo primo heremita, 5, 147
Decameron, 67, 148, 150, 314
Decisiones Parlamenti Dalphinales: Papa 438
Decker, Georg Jacob 324
Decker, Rudolf, 323
Decree concerning printing, 288
Decrees of Bishop Barth. de Marascis, 439
Defensiones sancte Thomas Aquinatis: de Deza, 81
Defensiorum privilegiorum: Cultrificis 441
Deffense de M. le Duc et Mme la Duchesse
   d' Austriche et de Bourgogne, 75
Degas, Edgar, 375
Delacolonge foundry, 317 (Fig 71)
Delacroix, –, 375, 402
Delcambre, Adrien, 377, 378n.
Delft, 75

Delices de l'Esprit, Les: de Saint-Sorlin, 293–4
Dellagana, James, 366, 372–3
Demonchy, –, 315
Denicker, David, 142
Denecker, Hercules, 142
Denham, Henry, 263, 264
Dent, J. M. and Sons Ltd, 430
Denti di Bellano, Battista, 46
Denuce, J., 122n.
Derriey, firm of, 365
Descates, –, 280
Description of Haarlem: Ampsing, 358
Description of the Low Countries: Giucciardini, 198
Description des Métiers, 315
Descrittione di Malta . . . .: Abela, 305, 306 (Fig
   70), 307
Descrizione delle Feste . . . . per le nozze di . . . .
   Ferdinando colla . . . Maria Amalia
Descrizione del Regno di Napoli: Beltrano, 301
Desenne, Alexandre, 400
Desmaret, –, 295
Desoer, Théodore, 403
De Somme type *see* Lettre de Somme
Destruction de Troye, La, 71
Deutsch, Hans Rudolf, 181
Deutsche Kunst und Dekoration, 417
Deutsche Werkbund, 417, 418
Deventer, 75
Deveria, Charles, 402, 403
Devilliers, –, 167
De Vinne, T. L., 12 and n., 13, 75, 312 and n.
Devoot en profitelijck boexken, Een, 214
Deza, Didacus de, 81
Diaboliques, Les: d'Aurevilly, 405
Dialect Bibles, 27
Dialogue de la vie et de la mort: Ringhieri, 175
   (Fig 43)
Dialogus creatorasum: de Mayneriis, 444
Dialogus de libertate: Urdermann, 443
Diario ordinario d'Ungheria, 327
Diario di Roma, 327
Diario della stamperia di Ripoli: Nessi, 48n.
Diary: Machyn, 255
Diary of Lady Willoughby: 'Anon', 391
Dibdin, Rev. T. F., 197, 281, 343, 346
Dichtung und Wahrheit: Goethe, 222
Dickes, William, 397 (Fig 85)
Dictes or Sayengs of the philosophres, 94
Dictionariolum, 326
Dictionarium: Calepinus, 150

Dictionary: Elyot, 255
Didactic Gospels, 251
Diderot, Denis, 319
Didot, Ambroise Firmin, 400
Didot family and the Progress of Printing: George, 400n.
Didot, Felicie, later de Saint-Pierre, 400
Didot, Firmin, 323, 372, 398, 400
Didot, François, 395
Didot, François-Ambroise, 312, 395, 396, 398
Didot, Françoise, later Nyon, 395
Didot, Henri, 376, 400
Didot, Hyacithe, 400
Didot, Pierre, 396, 398, 400
Didot, Pierre-François, 395
Didot, Pierre François le jeune, 316, 400
Didot, St Léger, 368, 400
Didot types, 317, 323, 395–6, 398, 399, 400, 419
Diederichs, Eugen, 417, 418, 419
Diest, Gillis Coppens van, 197
Dieterichs, Karl, 358
Dietz, Ludwig, 138, 227
Dijck, Christoffel van, 272, 291, 340 (Fig 75), 350
Dijon, 64
Dimitrović, Radiša, 245
Dinckmus, Conrad, 6, 33
Dino, Francesco di, 48
Diodati, O., 320
Dioscurides, 437
Directorium Chori ad usum sacrosanctae Basilice Vaticanae, 177
Discepolo, Gerolamo, 155
Discursus politicus de prudentia: Wexonius, 229
Dises, Diego, 334
Disputatio de dote: Turretinus, 441
Dissertation: Mores, 260
Distel type, 412
Dittamondo: Uberti, 445
Diurnale Basiliense, 91
Diurnale Catalaunense, 64, 436
Diurnale Matisconense, 88, 440
Diversche Liedekens: Castelyn, 216
Dives and Pauper: Parker, 102 (Fig 18), 166 (Fig 29)
Divina commedia, La (Divine Comedy): Dante, 48, 53, 403
Divinis institutionibus, De: Lactantius, 37
Divinus Laudibus, Da: Pontanus, 83
Dobrić, Dobruško *see* Boninus, Bonino
Dbbrowsky, –, 233

Doctrinal de Sapience, Le, 92, 442
Doctrinale: Gallus, 73
Doctrinale: Grammaticus, 101
Doctrinale: de Villa Dei, 123, 438, 443
Dodo, Augustinus, 89
Dodoens, Rembert, 198
Dodsley, –, 342
Dolarius *see* Victor, Hieronymus
Dold, S., 446
Dôle, 64
Dolet, Etienne, 167–8
Domras, Konstantin, 310
Don Quixote de la Mancha: Cervantes, 193 (Fig 46), 302, 303, 332, 403
Donatus, Aelius: 37, 47, 444
  Ars Minor, 437, 440
  Latin Grammar, 3, 4 (Fig 2), 6, 16, 73
  Table of Planets, 17
Donatus moralisatus: Gerson, 444
Donatus de Octibus Partibus Orationis: Donatus, 16, 122
Doni, Antonfrancesco, 149, 151
Donkin, Brian, 362, 368
Donne, Sebastiano dalle, 154
Dorat, –, 313, 314
Doré, Gustave, 403
Dorice, Valerio, 157
Dorp, Martin, 91
Dorstenius, –, 131
Dortas, Abraham Ben Samuel, 439
Douai Bible, 166
Double pica type, 174, 337
Doves Press, 409–10
Doves Press Bible, 410
Doves Press type, 44
Dowland, John, 218, 267
Doze Trabajos de Hercules: de Villena, 83
Drach, Peter, 12
Drayton, Michael, 284 (Fig 65)
Dreiangeldrucke, 419
Dresler and Rost-Fingerlin, 386
Dresseler, Jan, 220, 223
Drexel, Hieronymus, 278
Dritzehen, Andreas, 8, 9
Dritzehen, Georg, 8
Dritzehen, Klaus, 8, 9
Droeshout, Martin, 294 (Fig 68)
Druck der geographischen Charten, Über den: Breitkopf, 322
Drucke für die Hundert, 419

Druckerei Haag, 387
Drugulin types, 419
Drugulin, Wilhelm, 387, 417, 421
Drugulin, W. E., 385
Drury, John Isaac, 340
Dubčansky, John, 237
Dubois, Jacques *see* Sylvius Jacques
Duchess of Malfi: Webster, 153
Dudley, Robert, 302
Duff, –, 47, 71, 75
Dufour, Piotr, 249
Dugué, Jean, 213
Dugué, Lucrèce, later Ballard, 213
Duncan, Arthur, 428
Dünne, Hans, 9
Duobus amantibus, De: Sylvius, 73, 435
Dupont, Gautier-Laguionnie and Middentrop,
  365
Du Prés types, 65
Dupuis, Baptiste, 298
Dupuis, Jacques, 298
Durán, Domingo Marcos, 81
Durand, J., 319, 320n. 436
Durandus type, 19, 118
Duranti, Gulielmus, 19
Dürer, Albrecht, 32, 134, 135, 136, 315, 374
Dürer, Hans, 136
Dutartre, –, 366
Dutens, Louis, 395
Dutch East India Company, 281
Dutch handwriting type, 2
Dyrynk, Karel, 423

E

Earliest Books printed in Spain: Written, 79
Early and Later Prophets, 206
East, Thomas, 217, 218, 263, 266–8
Ebertz, –, 314
Ecclesiae Londino-Batavae Archivum: Hessels,
  223n.
Ecclesiastes (Polish), 248
Eckmann, Otto, 417, 422, 423
Eckmann Schrift: Eckmann, 417, 423
Eckmannschrift, 418, 422, 423
Eclogues: Virgil, 411
Ecluse, Charles de l', 198
Economica: Aristotle, 80 (Fig 11)
Edelinck, Gérard, 295
Edelstein, Der: Boner, 25
Edict of Charles IX, 165

Edict of Louis XVI, 396
Edicts of Louis XIV, 291
Edinburgh, 266, 335
*Edit du Roy pour le Règlement des Imprimeurs et des
  Libraires de Paris,* 291
Éditions du Louvre, 398, 400
Edwards, James, 330
Egenolff, Christian, 131, 140, 210, 220
Egenolff, Paulus, 133
Egenolff-Berners foundry, 275
Eggestein, Heinrich, 24, 117 (Fig 30)
Ehebuchlein: von Eyb, 435
Ehmcke, F. H. 411, 418, 419, 423
Ehmcke type, 411
Ehrismann, Gustav, 25
Eisen, Charles, 313, 314
Election of Maximilian, 444
Eleganciis Tullianis, Super: Datus, 101–2
Elegantiolae: Datus, 438
*Elenchus Librorum. . . . de Propaganda Fide
  impressorum,* 302
'Elettrostenotipo', 381
Elieser, Rabbi, 440
Eliot's Court Press, 264, 287
Elizabeth I of England, 216
Ellis, Frederick Startridge, 407
Elocutione, De: Phalerus, 337
*Elogio del Aommendatore F. Rinaldo Bech La
  Buissière:* Cagliola, 307
Elsevier, Abraham I, 280
Elsevier, Abraham II, 280
Elsevier, Bonaventura, 279, 280
Elsevier, Daniel, 280
Elsevier, Isaac, 279
Elsevier, Johannes, 280
Elsevier, Joost, 279
Elsevier, Louis I, 279
Elsevier, Louis II, 279
Elsevier, Louis III, 280
Elsevier, Mathijs, 279
Elsevier Press, 272
Elseviers, the, 281
Elseviers and their contemporaries: Hartz, 281 and n.
Eltvil, 21
Elyan, Caspar, 248, 436
Elyot, Sir Thomas, 254
Emanuele Filiberto, Duke of Savoy and
  Piedmont, 55
Emblems: Alciate, 169
Emerico, Giovanni, 46

Emmanuel, Markos, 310
Enchiridion militis christiani: Erasmus, 169
Encyclopédie, 13, 319, 320
Endeavour type, 410
Endter, Georg Andreas, 277
Endter, Georg the Elder, 277
Endter, Georg the Younger, 277
Endter, Endter, Wolfgang, 277
Endter, Wolfgang Andreas, 277
Endter, Wolfgang Moritz, 277
English Catechisms, 262
English Dancing Master, 288
English New Testament, 256
English Printed Books: Maynell, 287 and n.
English-Swedish Dictionary: Serenus, 353
Engravings see Copper-plate engravings and
    Woodcuts
Enschedé, firm of, 363
Enschedé, Izaak, 348, 350
Enschedé, Jacobus, 351
Enschedé, Johannes I, 348, 349 (Fig 75), 350
Enschedé, Johannes II, 350
Enschedé, Johannes en Zonen, 350, 412, 419
Enschedé types, 348, 349 (Fig 75), 351 (Fig 76),
    419
Entredos type, 333
Entrée du roi Charles VIII à Rouen, 71, 443
Ephrem: Guillermus, 438
Epeuvres des Caractères du fond des Sanlecques, 300
Epistelen en Evangeien, 74, 438, 439
Epistelen van Paulus, 196
Epistola de amoris remedio: Silvius, 435
Epistola de insulis nuper inventis: Columbus, 91
Epistolae: Barzizius, 87, 442
Epistolae: Horace, 436
Epistolae: Phalaris, 79
Epistolae ad Brutum: Cicero, 40
Epistolae Erasmi, 201
Epistolae ad familiares: Cicero, 37–8, 40, 52, 443,
    445
Epistolae Hieronymi, 112
Epistole e Evangelii, 49
Epistre envoyee au Tigre de France: L'Homme, 168
Epitome de la Corographie d'Europe, 172
Epitome . . . . des dix livres de Vitruve: Gardet, 173
Epitome of Institutes: de Lawne, 265
Epitome Rei Militaris: Vegetius, 97
Epitome trium terrae partium, 221
Epitomes des Rois France, 172
Epitre sur les progres de l'imprimerie: Didot, 399

Eragny Press, 409, 410
Erasmus: 167, 196
    Civilitate, 175, 202
    Duplici Copia Verborum, 169
    Enchiridion, 169
    Goede manierlikje seden, 202
    Klag des Frydens, 181
    Medallion head, 169
    Moriae encomium, 121, 123
    New Testament, 180
    Nutzliche Ynderwysung, 181
    Opera omnia, 351
Ercole I, Duke of Ferrara, 54
Erdösi, János, 240
Erfordia, Thomas de, 443
Erhardt foundry, 285
Erlangen University Library, 30
Ernst-Ludwig-Presse, 411
Erotemata see Greek Grammar, Lascaris
Erpenius, Thomas, 280
Eschenbach, Wolfram von, 24
Espinosa, Antonio de, 186, 332
Espreuve de caractères nouvellement taillez, 297
Essai d'une Nouvelle Typographie: Luce, 316
Essais de Caractère d'Imprimerie: Cot, 316
Essay on Colophons: Pollard, 54
Essayes of a Prentise in . . . . . Poesie: James VI and
    I, 266
Essemplare di piu sorti Lettere: Cresci, 157
Essemplare . . . di tutti le sorti di lettere cancellaresche:
    Hercolani, 157
Essex House Press, 408, 409, 410
Esslingen, 34
Este, T., 67
Estienne, Charles, 160
Estienne, François, 160
Estienne, Guyone, later Colines, 161
Estienne, Henri I, 160, 161
Estienne, Henri II, 162, 183, 184, 220
Estienne, Robert 1, 126, 160–1, 162, 164, 174, 183
Estienne, Robert III, 297
Estiennes, the, 197, 292
Establissements Marinoni, 365
Ethica, Oeconomica et Politica: Aristotle, 79, 435,
    445
Ethiopic type, 278, 288
Ettore, Benedetto di, 51
Etymologiae: Isidore, 28
Etymologicum, 47
Euclid, 43, 261

Eusebius, –, 44, 175
Eustazio, –
Evangelica praepatione, De ,44
Evangelische peerlen, 195
Evangheliar, 242
Evelyn, John, 283, 295
Évènement bibliographique, Un: Cornil, 86n.
Evergreen, 422 (Fig 90)
Everyman Library, 430
Ewrardi, Claudius, 443
Exodus, 243
Exotic types, 177, 288, 291, 296, 300 *see also* Oriental types
Exoticarum plantarum centuria prima: Breyn, 249
Explanatio in Psalterium: Turrecremata, 246
Exposicio Sancti Ieronimi Apostolorum: Rufinus, 99
Exposicion Historico del Libro, 78
Expositio Psalterii: Turrecremata, 112, 246
Expositio in Symbolum apostolorum: Hieronymus, 441
Extraordinariae Relationes, 276
Eyb, Albrecht von, 435
Eyck, P. N. van, 412
Eygentliche Beschreibung aller Stande see Standebuch, Das

F

Fables: Aesop, 25, 34, 49, 71, 95 (Fig 14), 97
Fables: Dorat, 313
Fables: La Fontaine, 314, 403
Fables: Lessing, 325
Fables: de la Motte, 313
Fabre *see* Fabri
Fabri, Bartholomaeus, 225
Fabri, Johann(es) (Giovanni, Jean), 55, 71, 224, 225, 436, 441, 444
Fabritius, Johann, 241
Fabritius, Walther, 128
Facta et Dicta memorabilia, 44
Falkenstein, Karl, 385
Fall of Princis: Lydgate, 260
Fall of Princis: Boccaccio, 104 (Fig 20)
Family Herald, 377
Fano, Roberto de, 436
Farri Brothers, Dei, 206
Fasciculus Temporum: Rolewinck, 27, 74, 81, 88, 443
Faust: Goethe, 402
Favole de Aganippe, Le: Mariconda, 151
Fawcett, Samuel, 382

Faytts of Arms, 97
Feathered Tribes of the British Islands: Mudie, 389
Febvre and Martin, 122
Fedorov, Ivan, 251, 353
Fell, Dr John, 289, 335
Fell types, 290–1
Fell Types: Morison, 291 and n.
Felsecker, Wolfgang, 277
Fenig, Georg, 246
Fenner, William, 371
Fenollar, Bernardo, 78
Ferdinand of Spain, 187
Ferdinand I of Naples, 55
Ferdinand II Grand Duke of Florence, 301
Ferehumanistica type, 28, 60
Ferettus, Nic., 438
Ferguson Brothers *see* Bauer, Ferguson and Hill
Fermiers généraux, 313, 314
Fernandez, Valentin, 85 (Fig 12), 86
Ferrara, 54–5
Ferrabosco, –
Ferrando, Tommaso, 56, 125
Ferratis, Johannes Petrus de, 442
Ferrose, Girard, 9, 10
Festa in Malta di San Francesca Saverio: de Galdiano, 307
Frestschrift: Hartwig, 19
Festschrift zum 500 jahrigen Geburstag Gutenbergs, 8n.
Festschift der Stadt Mainz, 418
Festus, Sextus P., 52, 440
Feure, George de, 420 (Fig 89)
Feyerabend, Sigmund, 127, 133
Fezendat, Michel, 175
Fiammetta: Boccaccio, 58
Fichet, Guillaume, 59, 60
Fiebig, Elias, 276
Field, Richard, 264, 265 (Fig 59)
Fieol, Szwaipolt *see* Fiol Swietopec
Fierabras, 92
Fiesole Library, 50
Fievet, Christine, later Andreae, 276
Fievet, Daniel, 276, 277
Fievet, Philipp I, 275, 276, 277
Fievet, Philipp II, 277
Fifield, Alexander, 288
Fifteenth-Century Book, 2n.
Fifty Essays: Scholderer, 39
Figgins, Vincent, 318, 347
'Figurial' type, 424

Filmsetting, 427–8
Filocolo, 47
Financial News, 379
Fine Books: Pollard, 18
Fine, Oronce, 162, 165
Finibus, De, 41
Finnish Bible, 229
Finnish Primer: Agricola, 225
Fiol, Swietopec (Schweipolt), 242, 247, 249
Fiore, Pompeo de, 305
Firmin-Didot, Ambroise, 310, 311
First Book of Ballets to Five Voices: Morley, 218, 267
First Folio Shakespeare, 287
First Press at Barcelona: Painter, 79
Fischer, Kilian, 438, 441
Fisher, H. A. L., 234 and n.
Fiume (Rijeka), 245
Five Hundred Years of Printing: Steinberg, 10
Fivizanno, Jacob de, 46, 238, 243
Flach, Martin, 24, 88, 89
Flander, Mattheus, 446 *see also* Flandro Mateo
Flanders, Matthew of *see* Flandro Mateo
Flandria, Gerardi de, 57
Flandro, Mateo, 79 *see also* Flander, Mattheus
Fleischman, –, 349 (Fig 75), 350, 412
Fleischman types, 350
Fletcher, Giles the Elder, 251
Flexography, 426
Flickertype, 428
Flinsch, Ferdinand, 386
Flinsch foundry, 411
Flinsch, Heinrich Friedrich Gottlob, 386
Florence, 47–50, 301, 327
Florentus, Antonius, 239, 440
Flores S. Augustini, 74
Floretus, 189
Florian, Frédéric, 404, 405
Florus, 344
Fluminibus, De: Sequester 150
Foa, Tomaso, 206
Fofanov, Nikita Fedorov, 252
Foigny, Jean de, 166
Foix, Gaston, Comte de, 104
Folger Library, Washington D.C., 201
Foligno, 53
Folo, Giovanni, 326
Folz, Hans, 236
Foncemagne, M. de, 315
Fonderie Générale, 399

Fontana, Giovanni Battista, 302
Fontana type, 413
Foresti, Jacobus, 55
Foret, Etienne, 438
Fori regni Valentiae, 192
Forme type, 163
Formica, Leonhard, 142
Formolario di epistole: Landino, 438
Fors et Costumas de Bearn; Los, 173
Forster, –, 362
42-line Bible, 15, 17, 18, 24, 107
49-line Latin Bible, 444
Fossombrone, Bartolomeo, 208
Foster, Benjamin, 381
Fotosetter, 428
Fototronic filmsetter, 429
Foucquet, Robin, 72, 435
Fouet, Robert, 298
Fougt, Henrick, 353
Foulis, Andrew I, 336 (Fig 73), 337, 338
Foulis, Andrew II, 338, 371
Foulis, Robert, 336 (Fig 73), 337, 338
Four Gospels – Romanian, 243
Four Hundred Years of Music Printing: King, 209n.
Fourdrinier, Henry, 368
Fourdrinier paper-making machine, 368
Fourdrinier, Sealey, 368
Fournier, l'ainé, Jean Pierre, 316
Fournier, François, 316
Fournier, Jean Claude, 316
Fournier, Pierre-Simon: 316–17, 319
   Delacolonge foundry, 317 (Fig 71)
   Manual Typographique, 317, 318, 330
   Music type, 211, 319, 321–2
   Point system, 317, 398
   Type formes, 312
Fournier Types, 317–18, 329, 398, 400
1462 Bible type, 118
Foxe, John, 257, 260
Fragonard, –, 314
Fraktur type:
   Denmark, 228, 352; Germany, 33, 38, 323, 386; *Maximilian's Prayer Book*, 134; Petri specimens, 129; Sweden, 225
Frakturlein Sabon Type, 132
Français peints par eux-mêmes, Les, 403
Francesco, Baldassare di, 157
Franchis, Philippus de, 442
Franck, Andreas, 142
Franck, Sebastian, 179

Francke, Johann, 276
Francofordiense Emporium sive Francofordienses Nundinae: Estienne, 220n.
François I of France, 162, 165, 174, 211
'Francoys de lettergieter' *see* Guyot, François
Frank, Melchior, 246
Frankfurt-am-Main, 131–2, 275, 276–7, 278–9
Frankfurt Fair, 128, 181, 219–22
Frankfurt, Nicolas of, 247
Franklin, Benjamin, 338, 396
Frederick II Bible, 228
Frederick II of Denmark, 231
Frederick the Great of Prussia, 406
Freebairn, Robert, 335
Fregi e Maiuscole: Bodoni, 330
Freiburger Zeitung, 382
Frein, Berthélemy, 171
Freitag, Andreas, 438
Frellon, François, 167, 171
Frellon, Jean, 167, 171
French Littleton: de Sainliens, 264
Frey, J., 383
Freydahl, 135
Friburgensis, Joh., 442
Friburger, Michael, 59, 441
Fridolin, Stefan, 31
Friedrich III of Holy Roman Empire, 134
Friese-Greene, W., 427
Frisner, Andreas, 30
Froben, Johann, 88, 89, 91, 121, 126, 180
Frontispieces, 290 (Fig 67), 303, 314, 390 (Fig 83), 397 (Fig 85)
Froschauer, Christoph I, 121, 181, 182 (Fig 44), 221, 358
Froschauer, Christoph II, 181
Froschauer, Eusebius I, 181
Froschauer, Eusebius II, 181
Froschauer, Johann (Hans), 181, 210
Frottole, 208
Frutiger, Adrian, 430
Fuchs, Leonhard, 172, 181
Fuenllama, Miguel de, 217 (Fig 49), 218
Fugger, firm of, 127
Führmann, Georg Leopold, 275
Fuhrmann, O. W., 8n.
Fumagalli, –, 150, 328
Furter, Michael, 89
Fust, Johann, 10–11, 20, 59, 440
Fust, Margarete (later Henkis), 20
Fust and Schöffer: 11

Bible, 17
Catholicon, 20
De Officiis, 21
Printers mark, 27, 111, 112 (Fig 26)
Psalter, 18–10, 115
Futura type, 420
Futuris Christianorum triumphis in Saracenos, De: Annuis, 439
Fyner, Conrad, 34, 207, 438, 444, 445

G

Gabiano, Balthazar, 147
Gabrani, the, 219
Gabriel, Prince of Spain, 332
Gaceta de Madrid, 332, 333
Gacon, Samuel, 85
Gaddi, Cardinal, 148
Gaesbeek, van *see* Van Gaesbeek
Gafurius, –, 207
Gaguin, Robert, 60
Galdiano, Juan de, 307
Galeomyomachia: prodromus, 143
Galerie agréable du Monde, 352
Galileo, 274
Galletti, Fabrizio, 154
Galli, Gallo di, 435
Gallia Typographica: Lepreux, 292
Gallus, Alexander, 73
Gambilionibus, Angelus de, 440, 442
Gamble, William, 430
Game and Playe of the Chesse: de Cassolis, 49
Gannal, J. N., 362n.
Gara, Giovanni di, 206
Garamond, Claude, 162, 164, 173–5
Garamond types:
    Berner specimens, 133; Bibliotheque Royal specimens, 298; Didot's *Pierres Precieuses*, 395; Furhmann's specimens, 275; Greek, 125, 174; Imprimerie Royale, 297; roman, 164, 165, 174, 178
Garbrecht printing house, 387
Gardet, Jean, 173
Gargantua: Rabelais, 123n.
Garlandia, Joh. de, 439
Garton, Abraham, 204
Gascoigne, –, 211
Gaspard of Bavaria *see* Hochfeder, Caspar
Gasparino, –, 60
Gast, Matthieu, 194
Gate of Honour woodcut, 135

Gatteaux, Nicolas, 372
Gaubert, –, 381
Gauhari, Abu Nasr ben Hammad al, 309
Gauhari lexicon, 309
Gaultier, Guillemette, later Garamond, 174
Gaultier, Léonard, 173, 293
Gaultier, Piere, 174
Gautier, –, 315
Gaveaux, –, 365
Gavarni, Sulpice Guillaum, 403–4
Gazeau, Guillaume, 169
Gazette, 296
Gazette des Beaux-Arts, 404
Gazette de France, 296, 308
Gazini, Nicolas, 191
Gebet-buch: Maximilian, 134
Ged, James, 371
Ged, William, 371
Gedaliah, Judah, 204
Gedenckwurdige Zeitung, 275
Geiler, –, 136
Geilhoven, Arnoldus de, 77
Geldner, Dr Ferdinand, 18
General History of Printing: Palmer, 100
General History of Quadrapeds, 345
Genesis, 243, 262 (Fig 57)
Genêt, Elzéar, 211
Geneva, 91–2, 183–4
Geneva Bible, 183, 269
Genoux, Claude, 372
Genoux, Jean-Baptiste, 372
Gensfleisch zur Laden, Johann 7 see also Guten-
   berg, Johann
Gent see Ghent
Gent University Library, 216
Genzach and Heyse, 418
George, Albert J., 399–400 and n.
Georgian alphabet, 285
Geography: Ptolomy, 38
Gérard, Jean, 398, 403
Gérard, Pierre, 64, 435
Gérardin, A., 405
'Gérautype', 381
Gericault, –, 399, 402
Gering, Ulrich, 59, 442
German Bible, 24, 32
German type, 133
Germanus, Nicolaus, 34
Germonia, Jacobus, 55
Gerona, 78, 83

Gerson, Jean Charlier de, 195
Gerson, Johannes, 77, 207, 436, 440, 442, 444
Gerusalemme Liberata, La: Tasso, 326, 396, 398
Geschichte der Buchdruckerkunst: Falkenstein, 385
Geschichte der Schreibkunst: Breitkopf, 322
Geschichte des zu Trient ermordeten kindes, 142
Gesner, Conrad, 181, 182 (Fig 44)
Gessler, Jörg, 446
Gesta Lynceorum, 274
Gesta Romanorum, 73
Geyer, Nikolaus, 128
Geystliche Lieder: Luther, 210
Gezelius, Bishop Johann, 229
Gheestelicke boomgaard, 195
Ghelen, Jan van
Ghemen, Gotfred of, 226
Ghemen, Govaert van, 437
Ghent (Gent), 77, 215–16
Gherlinc, Johann, 86, 435
Ghotan, Bartholomaeus, 36, 224, 225, 249, 440
Giampiccoli, the, 326
Giannotti, Donato, 148
Gibbons, Orlando, 288
Gigoux, Jean, 403
Gijsbrecht van Aemstel: Vondel, 283
Gil Blas: Le Sage, 325, 403
Gil, Jerónimo, 333, 334
Gilbert, William, 282 (Fig 64)
Gill, Eric, 411, 413
Gille, Joseph, 396 and n.
Gillot, Claude, 313
Gillot, Firmin, 404
Gillotage, 404
Ginami, –, 245
Gioliti de' Ferrari, the, 149–50
Giolito, Bernardino see Stagnino, Bernardino
Giolito, Giovanni il Vecchio, 150, 153
Giolito, Giovanni Gabriele, 150, 157
Girardengus, Nicolaus, 441
Girodet, –, 398
Giunta, Barbardo de, 151
Giunta, Bernardo, 148
Giunta, filippo, 141, 148
Giunta Giacomo (Jacques) de, 151, 171
Giunta, Lucantonio de, 46, 47, 149, 151, 171
Giunta, Tommaso, 148
Giunta see also Junta
Giuntas, the, 126, 151, 219, 301
Giuccardini, –, 198
Giustiniano, Agostino, Bishop of Nebbio, 151

Giustiniani, Marcantonio, 206
Glagolitic type, 45, 243–4
Glagolitic Missal, 244 and n.
Glasgow, 337
Glasgow Letter-Foundry, 337
Glika, Nikola, 392
Glim, Joh., 443
Globe, 379
Glockner, Tomas, 81
Glossa super Apocalypsim: Annius, 35
Glück, Hans, 275
Gnotosolitos: de Geilhoven, 77
Godchaux, Augusta, 382
Godiche, Andreas Hartvig, 352
Goede manierlikje seden: Erasmas, 202
Goes, Matthias van der, 77, 107, 435
Goethe, Johann Wolfgang, 222, 322, 324, 325, 402
Goetz (Götz), 12, 27–8, 443
'Golden Compasses', 197, 199
Golden Legend: de Voragine, 28, 97, 407
'Golden type', 44, 407
Goldini, –, 326
Goldschmidt, E. P., 146n.
Goldsmith, Oliver, 345
Golz, Hubert, 220
Gombert, –, 211
Gómez, Alonso, 187
González, Juan, 303
Gorricio, Melchior, 82
Göschen, Georg Joachim, 322, 323, 324
Goslar, 274
Gothaischer Hofkalender, 324, 325
Gothic Bastard type, 109, 110 (Fig 24) *see also* Lettres batarde and named bastards
Gothic notation, 208
Gothic types:
    France, 126, 159, 400; Germany, 28, 108 (Fig 22), 138; Monk matrices, 225; Moravia, 235; Portugal, 86; Spain, 186, 194; *see also* Named types
Gotho, Frederico, 305
Gotico-antiqua type, 37, 109
Göttinger-Taschenkalender, 324
Götz von Berlichingen: Goethe, 324
Gonda, 76–7
Gourmont, Gilles de, 123, 163
Gourmont, Jean de, 160
Gracchus et Poliscena: Aretinus, 444
Gradual of Constance Breviary, 39n.

Gradual: Jespersen, 228
Graduale, 231
Graf, Urs, 180
Grafton, Richard, 216, 256, 257, 261 (Fig 56)
Gramática: Maturini, 186
Grammaire Turque, 309
Grammar of the Turkish Language: Davids, 307n.
Grammatica: Guttierez, 83, 436
Grammatica: Niger, 208
Grammatica Aethiopica, 278
Grammatica Hungarolatina: Erdösi, 240
Grammaticus, Alexander, 101
Gran, Heinrich, 439
Grand Navire I, II, and III, 298 299
Grandes Chroniques de France, 61
Grandjean, Philippe, 298, 312, 315, 316, 321, 396
Grandville, *see* Gerard, Jean
Granelli, Dr Francesco, 57
Granjon, Jean, 175
Granjon Robert:
    France, 173, 175, 176 (Fig 43), 178; Italy, 154; Netherlands, 177, 212
Granjon types, 133, 177, 178, 275, 291, 298
Granvelle, Cardinal, 197
Grasshof, H. and J. S. G. Simmons, 251n.
Grāt danse macabre, La, 70
Gratia Dei, Petrus, 437
Grave, Claes de, 195, 196
Gravelot, Hubert, 314, 319
Graveur de Haarlem, the, 77
Gray, Thomas, 330, 337
Graz, 142
Graz, Clement von, 236
'Grazdanka' type, 424
Great Bible, 257 and n.
Great Primer types, 174, 287, 391
Grecs du Roi' type, 125, 174, 287, 299 *see also* Royal Greek type
Greek Grammar: Lascaris, 125, 143
Greek type:
    England, 263, 291; France, 316; Germany, 129, 133; Italy, 37n., 47, 125; Scotland, 337; Spain, 192
Greenland Woodcuts, 394 (Fig 84)
Gregori, Gregorio de, 46
Gregori, Giovanni de, 46
Gregorii, Gregorius, 46
Gregorii, Joannes, 44
Gregorii *see also* Gregori
Gregorios V, Patriarch, 310

Gregorius, –, 87
Gregory IX, Pope, 118
Gregory XIII, Pope, 177
Greiff (Greyff) Michel, 34, 167, 443 *see also* Gryphe
Grenville Library, British Museum, 129
Greshoff, Jan, 412
Greus, Georg, 240
Griffo, Francesco, 107, 144, 146, 150–1
Grignani, Lodovico, 307
Grijs, Pawel, 224
Grimm, Sigismund, 210
Grimmelshausen, Hans Jacob Christoffel, 277
Gringoire, Pierre, 69
Grismand, John, 288
Grisone, Frederico, 151
Gröll, Michal, 249
Gropius, Walter, 419
Gros parangon type, 174, 175
Gros romain type, 174, 175, 396, 398
Gross, Henning, 223, 275–6
Grosse, Gottfried, 276
Grosse Kompagnie, 128
Grotius, Hugo, 280
Groulleau, E., 32
Ground of Artes: Record, 255 (Fig 53)
Grunenberg, Johann *see* Rhau Johann
Gruner, –, 34
Grüninger, Johann (Hans), 25, 88, 138, 139 (Fig 35), 210
Gruyer, Gustave, 48n.
Gryphe, François, 167
Gryphe, Sebastien, 162, 167, 168, 175, 221
Gryphus, Petrus, 113 (Fig 27)
Guarin, Thomas, 184
Guarino, Battista, 143
Guarinus, Paulus, 436, 438
Gubitz, Johann Christoph, 324
Gudspjallabók, 230
Guerbin, Louis *see* Cruse, Aloys (Louis)
Guerin, Thomas, 167
Gueroult, Guillaume, 172 177
Guidon, Le: Chauliac, 70
Guillermus, –, 438
Guirlande de Flore: Malo, 402
Gumiel, Diego de, 84, 191
Gunther, Johann, 236–7
Gustav I of Sweden, 224
Gustav Vasa's Bible, 225
Gustavus Adolphus of Sweden, 272

Gute Lehre von allen Wildbädern: Folz, 236
Gutenburg and the B-36 Group: Painter, 10n., 16
Gutenburg – Ein Census, Die: Lazare, 17
Gutenburg, Fust and Schöffer, 15, 440
Gutenberg, Johann: 2–6, 7 (Fig 3), 87, 122, 356
  B-46 type, 21n.
  Fichet document, 60
  500th anniversary, 418, 421
  Helmasperger Instrument, 8, 10–11
  Strassburg Documents, 8–9
  36-line Bible, 11, 17–18
Gutenburg Museum, Mainz, 15
Gutenberg and the Strasbourg Documents, 8
Gutenberg-Jahrbuch, 79, 175n.
Gutgesel, David, 237
Gutterwitz, Andreas, 225
Guttierez, A., 83, 436
Guyart, Johan, 173
Guyot, A., 363
Guyot, Christoffel, 201
Guyot, François, 201, 261
Guyot, François II, 201
Guyot, Gabriel, 201
Guyot and Scribe, 363
Guzmán, Fernando (Fernán) Peréz de, 188
Gymnich, Gerwin, 276
Gymnich, Johann, 128
Gymnich, Johann II, 128
Gymnich, Johann III, 128
Gymnich, Johann IV, 276
Gymnich, Martin, 128
Gysser, Hans, 82
Gyulafehérvár, 241

H

Haarlem, 77, 348–50
Haarlem, Heinrich von, 441
Haarlem, Henricus de, 51, 56
Haarlemsche Courant, 350
Haas, Wilhelm, 358
Haebler (Häbler), –, 81, 82, 85
Hackius, Francescus, 283
Hadego filmsetter, 429
Haener, 300
Hafnia Lodierna: de Thurah, 353
Hagenbach, Peter, 82, 186
Hahn, Johann Erich, 276
Hahn, Ulrich, 140
Hakluyt Society, 257n.
Halcyon Press, 412

Hale, J. R., 135 and n.
Hall, Rowland, 183
Haller, Johann, 115, 246–7, 248, 249
Halley, Edmund, 274
Hamill, Richard, 72
Hamilton, W., 347
Hamlet: Shakespeare, 411
Hamman, Johannes, 46, 205 *see also* Hertzog, Johannes
Hammerich, A., 228
Han, Johannes, 442
Han, Ulric, 5, 38, 111, 112, 208
Handy, John, 342
Hänler, –, 86
Hannauwe, Bertolff *see* Rupell, Berthold
Han's Missal, 39, 208
Harmonice Musices Odhecaton, 208
Harrild Press, 366
Harris, G. F., 346
Harris–Intertype, 429
Harrison automatic Press, 366
Harrison, William, 264
Harsy, Antoine de, 172
Harsy, Denis de, 167, 172
Härtel, Gottfried Christoph, 322
Hartlieb, Johann, 6
Hartwig, Otto, 19
Hartz, S. L., 281
Hassia, Johannes de, 57
Hatfield, Arnold, 264
Hattersley justifying machine, 378
Hattersley, Robert, 378
Haultin, Pierre, 133, 173, 210, 211, 212–13, 214
Hauptmann, Gerhardt, 411
Haürteur, –, 211
Hayley, William, 388
Hazanas y la Rúa, Don Joaquín, 185
Hearne, Thomas, 335
Hebrew Bible, 121, 204
Hebrew type:
    England, 288; Germany, 129, 133; Italy, 177, 205, 206; Netherlands, 350; Spain, 192
Hectoris, Benedictus, 50
Hédouin, P., 300
Hédouville, Sieur de *see* Sallo, Denis de
Heere, Lucas d', 216
Heilmann, Andreas, 8
Heinrich, Julius, Duke of, 275
Heirs of Samuel Apiarius, 179
Helbig, Friedrich (Frederic), 363, 365, 386

Hèle, Georges de la, 215
Heliae, Helias, 435
Hellinga, L. and W., 76 and n.
Helmasperger, –, 10
'*Helmasperger Notorial Instrument*', 8, 10, 11
Heltai, Gaspar I, 240, 241
Heltai, Gaspar II, 240
Helyae, Canon Helyas, 91
Hénault, Mathurin, 293
Henkis, Conrad, 20
Henkis, Margarete, formerly Fust, 20
Henne, Hans Jakob, 278
Hennibg, Christian Friedrich, 406
Henri II of France, 213
Henri III of France, 165
Henri IV of France, 166
Henricpetri *see* Petri Heinrich
Henry VII of England, 97
Hentzke, Michael, 137
Herbarium: Juhász, 241
Herbert, George, 391
Herbipolensis, Martinus *see* Landsberg, Martin
Herbort, Hans, 44
Herbst, Magno, 81
Hercolani, Giuliantonio, 157
Herford, John, 104
Herhan, Louis-Etienne, 372
Hermann, Caspar, 376
Hermann und Dorothea: Goethe, 324
Hermite de la Chausee d'Antin: de Jouy, 400
Hero and Leander, Musaeus, 143
Herolt, Georg, 55
Herrera, Antonio de, 187
Herrera, Francisco de, 303
Hertzog (Herzog) Johannes, 106, 254 *see also* Hamman Johann
Hesronita, Jean, 300
Hess, Andreas, 238, 436
Hessels, J., 223n.
Hester, Andrew, 259 (Fig 55)
Heures, 438 see also *Books of Hours*: France
Heuvelpers, 412
Hevelius, Jan, 249, 274
Heyden, Cornelius (Cornelis), 13, 201
Heyden, Sebaldus, 248
Heylin, 88
Heynlin, Jean, 59
Heynrici, Heynricus, 77, 439
Hieronymite Breviary, 188
Hieronymus *see* Victor Hieronymus

Hiesse, Jehan, 177
Higden, Ranulph, 207
High German Bible, 27
Hilden, Bertram, 276
Hilden, Peter, 276
Hilden, Peter Theodo, 276
Hill see Bauer, Ferguson and Hill
Hind, Arthur, 49, 65, 83, 146
Hippocrates, 167
Hirtzhorn, Eucharius see Cervicornus, Eucharius
Hispalensis, Isodorus, 435
Hispanus, Petrus, 73, 76
Histoire de la Belle Melusine see Melusine
Histoire tolosaine: Noguier, 173
Historia Aethiopica, 278
Historia animalium: Gesner, 182 (Fig 44)
Historia de la bendita Magdalene, 189
Historia Davidis, 5
Historia Griselidis: Petrarch, 117
Historia literario-typographica Midiolanensii: Sassi, 52n.
Historia Major: Paris, 263
Historia de las Ordenes militares: de Torres, 303
Historia de passione pueri Simonis: Tuberinus, 142, 445
Historia quomodo beatus Franciscus petivit a Christo, 444
Historia Romana. Pars I: Appianus 43 (Fig 6), 443
Historia Sanctae Crucis, 437
Historia S. Nicolai Lincopensis, 225
Historia scholastica super Novum Testamentum: Comesta, 73, 196
Historia stirpium commentarii, De: Fuchs, 172, 181
Historia de le sucedido. . . . Maria Estuarda, Reyna de Escocia: de Herrera, 187
Historia de Valencia: Beuter, 189
Historia Veneta: Morsoni, 302
Historiae: Orosius, 56
Historias e conquestas dels. . . . . . Reys de Arago: Tomich, 191
Historie of Jason, 97
History of the Art of Printing: Watson, 352
History of England: Hume, 347
History of Europe: Fisher, 234 and n.
History of Florence, 407
History of Frederick the Great: Kugler, 325
History of the Orders of Knighthood of the British Empire: Nicolas, 389-90
History of the Printed Book: Stillwell, 273 and n., 296

History of Printing, 397 (Fig 85)
History of the Rebellion: Clarenden, 335
Hlaváč, Jan see Olovetsky, Jan
Hlohovce, 237
Hobbes, Thomas, 280
Hobby Horse, 415
Hochfeder, Caspar, 33, 246
Hochstetter, firm of, 127
Hoe Company presses, 366
Hoe, R. and Company, 363
Hoe, R. and Crabtree Ltd, 364 (Fig 79), 370 (Fig 80)
Hoe Rotary Press, 370 (Fig 80)
Hoe Type Revolving Machine, 363
Hoe Web Press, 364 (Fig 79)
Hoell, Louis, 411
Hoernen, Arnold ther, 21, 27, 112
Hof, Vinzenz Im, 180
Hoffhalter, Raphael, 141-2, 241, 243
Hoffhalter, Rudolf, 241
Hoffgreff, György, 240
Hoffmann, François, 372
Hohenmauth, Johann von, 442
Hohenmauth, Jonathan von, 233
Hohenzollern, Friedrich von, Bishop of Augsburg, 29
Hólar, 229-31
Holbein, Hans, 172, 180, 240
Holberg, Ludvig, 353
Holdermann, Johann, 309
Hole, William, 284 (Fig 65), 286 (Fig 66), 288
Holinshed, Raphael, 264
Hollandsche Mediaeval type, 412
Holle, Lienhart, 33, 34
Hollerith tabulator, 380
Holtz (Holz), Georg von, 79, 84, 435
Holtzel, Hieronymus, 129
Holweg, firm of, 426
Holyband, Claudius see Sainliens, Claude de
Holz see Holtz
Homberch, Eckert van, 195
Homer, 48, 49, 191
Homer: Eustazo, 148, 337
Homilies: Chrysostom, 263
Homm es illustré qui ont paru en France pendant ce siècle: Perrault, 295
Honate, Giovanni Antonio de, 53
Hondius, Henricus, 281
Hondius, Judocus, 203, 281
Honesta volupate, De: Platina, 57, 437

Index

Honoratus, Servius Maurus, 47
Honter, Johann, 239
Hoochstraten, Johann (Jan), 226
Hoochstraten, Michel Hillen van, 195
Hooftman, Gilles, 121–2
Hooper, W. H., 407
Hoover, Herbert, 181
Hopfer, Daniel, 138
Hopkins, –, 216
Hopkinson and Cope, 407
Hopyl, Wolfgang, 160
Horace:
    France, 162, 344, 398, 400, 436; Germany, 210;
    Italy, 125; Scotland, 336 (Fig 73)
Horae B. V. M., 66
Horák, František, 233
Hornby, St John, 34, 37, 409
Horne, Herbert P., 415, 416
Horologium Devotionis: Bertholdus, 32
'Horse-shoe nail' *see* Gothic notation
Hortus Sanitatis, 29, 138
Hotyulus animae, 195, 248
Hruby, Zikmund, 238
Huby, François, 293
Huet, Paul, 403
Huete, 84
Hufnagelschrift *see* Gothic notation
Hugo, Victor, 405
Huguetan, –, 166
Humani corporis fabrica, De: Vesalius, 180
Humanistic script, 109, 111 (Fig 25)
Humery, Dr Konrad, 20
Hummelberger, Michael, 131
Hundred good poyntes of Husbandrie: Tusser, 260
Hungarian Protestant Bible, 240
Hunte, Thomas, 99
Hupfuff, M., 6
Hupp, Otto, 418, 423
Hupsch Lied vom Ursprung der Eydgnoschafft, Ein,
    179
Huret, Grégoire, 293
Hurus, Juan (Hans), 82, 443
Hurus, Pablo (Paul), 79, 82, 84, 188
Hus, Jan, 234
Husner, Georg, 12, 24
Huss, Martin, 70
Huss, Matthias, 70, 88
Hussites, military orders of, 425 (Fig 91)
Huszár, David, 241
Huszár, Gál, 241

Hutz, Leonhard, 188
Huvin, Jean, 105
Huygens, –, 274
Huym, Didier, 64
Hyde, Edward *see* Clarenden, Earl of
Hydra, 310–11
Hydragiologia: Colonna, 177
Hygman, Johann, 160
Hyperion-Drucke, 419
Hypnerotomachia Poliphile: Colonna, 144, 145
    (Fig 37)

I

Ibarra, Joaquin, 331, 332, 333
Ibarra, Manuel, 331n.
Ibraham, Muteferrika, 308–9
Ibraham, Pacha, 307
Icelandic Bible, 231
Icelandic New Testament, 227
Idylls: Theocritus, 400
Ifern, Pedro, 333
Illuminated manuscripts, 66
Illusions Perdues: de Balzac, 402
Illustrated books:
    France, 66, 70, 293, 313–15; Germany, 25, 28;
    Italy, 49, 145; Russia, 252; *see also* Woodcuts
    and Copperplate engravings
Illustratione degli epitaffi et medaglie antiche:
    Symeoni, 169
Illustrations des ecrits de Savanarole, Les, 48
Image, Selwyn, 416
Images ou tableaux des deux philostrate, 293
Imaginary Conversations: Landor, 412
Imagines Mortis, 240
Imitation de Jesus Christ, L': à Kempis, 298
Imitatione Christi, De: à Kempis, 123, 299, 440
Immortalita dell' anima, Dell': Campora, 437
Imperial Book Commission, 222
Imprenta Real, 187, 331, 332, 334
Imprimerie Claye, l', 405
Imprimerie du Louvre, l', 301, 315, 321
Imprimerie Nationale, l', 174, 398
Imprimerie en Roumanie, L': Alanasov, 24n.
Imprimerie Royale:
    17th C., 272, 273, 296–7, 298, 299–301
    18th C., 315, 316, 321, 398
Imprimerie Royal du Louvre *see* Imprimerie du
    Louvre l'
In this Boke ar côteynyd xx sôges, 216
Inchoationes quinternorum, 112

Index Expuratorius, 149
Index Librorum Prohibitorum, 158
Index, sive Specimen Characterum Christophori Plantini, 201
Indexes, 112–13
Indulgence: Bishop of Avila, 445
Indulgence: Ewrardi, 443
Indulgence of Nicolas V, 15, 17
Indulgence: Sant, Bishop of Abington, 446
Indulgence: Sixtus IV, 94
Indulgences against Turks, 15, 17, 99
Inferno: Dante, 37, 189
Ingenioso Hidalgo Don Quixote . . . . see *Don Quixote*
Ingres, Jean, 402
Initials:
 Bulgaria, 392; England, 258 (Fig 54), 259, 261, 291; France, 66, 70, 159, 169; Germany, 18–19, 28, 42, 111; Italy, 149
Innocent III, Pope, 62, 440
Innocent VIII, Pope, 99, 158
Insel, Die, 417
Insel-Verlag, firm of, 421
Inspectors Press, 393
Institutes: Calvin, 265
Institutes: Justinian, 55
Institution of a Christian Man, 255
Institutiones: Justinian, 74
Instructio Visitationis Saxonicae: Melanchthon, 227
Instruction du Chrestien: Richelieu, 299
Instructione novitiorum: Bonaventura, 83
Intabulatura de Lauto: Dalza, 149, 208
Intertype Corporation, 428
Introductiones Latinae: Nebrissensis, 443
Invention of Printing: De Vinne, 12 and n.
Iriarte, Tomás de, 332
Iron Presses, 355, 356, 358–9, 412 *see also* Stanhope press
Isaac, –, 150, 443
Isabella of Spain, 81, 187, 189
Isabey, Jean-Baptiste, 402, 403
Isadore, –, 28
Isagwge: Sylvius, 164
Isenburg, Diether von, 8, 23
Isengrin, Michael, 181, 184
Isern, Pedro, 334
Ismeria: Michaleff, 307
Istomin, Karion, 253
Italic type:
 Denmark, 226; England, 291; France, 159;

Germany, 129, 133; Italy, 147, 149 (Fig 38); Spain, 191; *see also* named types
Italic Types of Robert Granjon: Johnson, 177
Italienischen Zeitung, 275
Itinerary: Leland, 335
Ivan Federov's Primer: Jakobson, 251n.
Ivan Federovs . . . . . Lesebuch, 251
Ivan IV of Russia, 250
Iverskii Monastry, 253

J

Jackson, John, 264
Jackson, Joseph. 340, 347
Jacobi, C. T., 360 and n.
Jacobszoon van der Meer, Jacob, 75
Jacques le Jeune, 281 *see also* Elseviers, the
Jaggard, Isaac, 287, 288, 294 (Fig 68)
Jaggard, William, 288
Jakob, 245
Jakobson R., 251n.
James, John, 340, 371
James VI and I, 266, 271
James, Thomas, 268 (Fig 62), 338, 339, 371
James, Andre, 298n.
Jangeon, Jacques Nicolas, 315
Janin, Jules, 404
Jannequin, Clément, 211
Jannon, Jean, 272, 297, 298, 301
Jannon types, 297
Janson, Anton, 285
Janson types, 283, 285
Jansz, Willem, 283
Janusowski, Jan, 249
Januspresse, 410, 421
Jardin de dévotion, Le: de Alliaco, 75
Jardin musixual, 215
Jardin, Simon du, 92
Jenson and De Colonia, 55
Jenson, Nicolas, (Nicholas):
 France, 12; Germany, 59, 60; Italy, 40, 41, 43–4, 60, 88
Jenson, Nicolas and Partners, 41
Jenson, Nicolaus et Socii, 41
Jenson, Nicoló *see* Colon, Giovanni de, Nicolo Jenson e Compagni
Jenson types, 44, 45, 197, 407, 410
Jerusalem libertata: Tasso, 187
Jerusalem Talmud, 205
Jespersen, Nils, 228
Jessen type, 419

Jesuits, 142
Jewel, Bishop, 263
Jimenez, Francisco, 81, 82, 91, 438 *see also*
  Ximenez de Cisneros
Joffre, Juan, 189, 192
Johann Gutenberg: Scholderer, 9
Johannot, Matthieu, 398, 403
Johannot, Tony, 403, 404
John Rylands Library, Manchester, 19
Johnson, A. F.:
  Aldine italic type, 148
  Arrighi type, 156
  Didot-Wafflard type, 396
  French 16th C. printing, 162, 166, 176, 177
  German Renaissance title borders, 131, 138,
  Grandjean type, 316
Johnson, John, 348
Johnston, Edward, 410, 411
Jones, William, 264
Jónsson, Arngrimur, 230 (Fig 51)
Jónsson, Jón, 230 (Fig 51)
Josephus, 57, 186
Josquin, –, 210
Jost, Heinrich, 421
Journal (Frankfurt-am-Main), 275
Journal polytype des Sciences et des Arts, 372
Journal des Scavans, 273, 296, 307, 308
Jouy, Etienne de, 400
Juda, Leo, 181
Jugend, 417
Jugendstil, 417, 423 *see also* Art Nouveau
Jugge, Richard, 133, 257, 258 (Fig 55), 262
  (Fig 57)
Juhász, Peter, 241
Julius Caesar, 82, 125
Julius II, Pope, 147
Jullet, Germaine, later Attaignant, 211
Jullet, Hubert, 211
Jungfrau von Orleans: Schiller, 323
Juniperus Presse, 411–12
Junta, Juan de, 189, 190 (Fig 45)
Junta, Tomas, 187, 303
Junta *see also* Giunta
Jury Reports, 1851, 376
Justi, François, 167, 171
Justinian, 55, 74
Juvenal: Virgil, 391, 438

K

Kachelofen, Conrad (Konrad), 35–6, 438

Kaetz, Peter, 214
Kaiser, Peter, 61
Kaláb, Method, 423
Kalendarium, 42
Kalendrier des Bergiers (Bergers), 65
Kalila Wa-Dimna: Bidpai, 34
Kammermeister, Sebastian, 31
Kamp, Jan, 233, 234
Kamp-Severýn Press, 234
Kandler, Heinrich, 438
Kapodistrias, J., 311
Karai, Ladislaus, 238
Karastojanov, Athanas, 392–3
Karastojanov, Dimiter, 393
Karastojanov, Nikola, 392–3
Karastojanov, Sotir, 393
Karcher, –, 325
Karlsburg, 241
Károlyi, Gáspár, 240
Karr, Alphonse, 404
Karweysse, Jacob, 440
Kassa, 241
Kastenbein, Charles, 378
Kastenbein composing machine, 377
Kastenbein typesetter, 378
Kautzsch, Rudolf, 417
Keere, Hendrik I van den, 202
Keere, Hendrik II van den, 202, 203, 215
Keere, Peter van den, 202
Kefer, Heinrich, 11, 20, 30, 441
Kehl edition of Voltaire, 344
Keinspeck, Michael, 89
Keisarilda, Henrich, 229
Kellam, Laurence, 166
Kelmscott Press, 407, 408, 409 (Fig 87)
Kempen, Gottfried von, 128
Kempis, Thomas à, 123, 195, 299
Kerckmeister, Johann, 441
Kerle, – de, 215
Kertesz, Abraham, 285
Kerver, Thielmann, 70
Kervers, the, 160
Kesler, Nicolaus, 89, 111
Kessler, Count Harry, 411
Ketelaer, Nicolaus, 73
Keyere, Arend de, 77, 438, 441
Kezai, Simon, 238
Khadi Ibraham, 309, 310
Khalifah, Hagi, 309
Khodkevich, Prince Georgii, 251

Kiev, 253
King Edward's Grammar, 255
King, Hyatt, 208
King James's Bible, 288
Kings Printers, 335
Kippenberg, Anton, 421
Kircher, Ernst, 384
Kis, Miklós, 283
Klag des Frydens, Ein: Erasmus, 181
Kleinschmidt, Samuel, 394
Kleukens, Christian Heirich, 411, 423
Kleukens Friedrich Wilhelm, 411, 419
Kleukens Presse, 411
Klič, Karl, 382
Klingspor foundry, 418, 421
Klingspor, Wilhelm, 422–3
Klopstock, –, 323
Kniaghininsky, Petre Pavlovich, 381
Knight, Charles, 356, 389, 390
Knoblochtzer, Heinrich, 24, 439
Köbel, Jakob, 441
Koberger, Anton: 12, 30–2, 88, 89
    advertisements, 119
    Frankfurt Fair, 220
    High German Bible, 27
    international publisher, 121, 126
Koberger, Anthoni, 239
Koberger, firm of, 129
Koblinger, Stephan (Steffan), 56, 141, 445
Koch, Alexander, 417
Koch, Georg see Coci, Jorge
Koch, Paul, 419
Koch, Rudolf, 419, 420–1, 423
Koch, Simon, 36, 440
Koch type, 419
Kochanowski, Jan, 249
Koehler and Volckmar, 387, 421
Kofman, Cristóbal, 192
Kohl, Hans, 142
Kohlen, Johann, 210
Köhler, Henning, 276
Köhler, Johann, 276
Kölhoff, Johann I, 27
Kölhoff, Johann II, 11, 27
Kolitz, Johann, 276
Köln, Heinrich von, 441
Kolozsvár (Cluj), 240, 285
Komedia česká, 237
Komedia nová o vdově, 237
Komenskí, Jan, Bishop, 277

Komjati, 241
Komjati, Benedek, 239
Konáč, Mikuláš, 234
König and Bauer A. G., 362, 365
Konig and Bauer Maschinenfabrik, 365
König, Frederick, 360–2, 363, 365, 385
König, Heinz, 418, 422
König, Marie Rosine, later Helbig, 365
Königsberg, 275
Konstantinides, Gregorius, 310
Konversationslexicon, 385
Köpfel, Wolfgang, 131
Koran, the, 181
Korand, Václav, 234
Koromelas, M., 311
Kosinj, 244
Kosmos, Archimandrite, 310
Kosorsky, Jan, 234
Kōzi, Mešullà, 442
Kraffts, the, 241
Kraft, Kaspar, 141, 142
Kralice, 237
Kralice Bible, 237
Krantz, –, 442
Kreussner, Friedrich, 138
Kreuzer, Stephan, 141, 142
Kriegskunst zu Fuss: Wallhausen, 252
Kronheim, J. M., 372
Kröger, Aswer, 138
Krusinski, Judas, 309
Kruydtboeck: de l'Obel, 200
Küchenmeisterei, 32–3
Kugler, –, 325
Kuhn, Valentin, 228
Kuilenberg, 77
Kuklutza, 310
Kulezar, –, 237
Kulundzić, Zvonimir, 244
Kundmann, –, 309
Kunera Press, 412 see also Zilverdistel de
Kunne, Albrecht, 142, 440, 445
Kunst Chiromantia, Die, 6
Kunst en Maatschappij, 412
Kunst en Samenleving, 415n.
Kunst der Typographie, Die: Müller
Kurfurstenbibel, 277
Kuteino, 253
Kutnáttora, 234
Kuttenberg, 234
Kydonia, 310

Index

Kyrill V, Patriarch of Constantinople, 310
Kyrmezet, Pavel, 237

L

Laborde, B. de, 313, 314
La Caille, –, 164
La Cruse, Guerbin de, 92, *see also* Cruse, Aloys
Lactantius, 37, 444
La Colombière, Vulson de, 293
Laet, Jan (Hans) de, 197, 215
La Fontaine, Jean de, 293, 313, 314, 403
La Haye, Corneille de *see* Corneille, Claude
Lamberg, Abraham, 223, 275
Lambillion, Antoine, 71
Lambrecht, Joos, 13, 201, 202
Lami, Eugène, 404
Lamiis, De, 34
Lämmerman, 280
Lamonica, –, 381
La Motte, Houdart de, 313
Lampadius, –, 179
Lancelot du Lac, 65
Landino, Chris., 438
Landor, Walter Savage, 413
Landry, La Tour, 89
Landsberg, Martin, 36, 111
Lang, Andrew, 281
Langage des Fleurs, Le: de Latour, 402
Langelier, Mme Abel, 293
Langland, William, 122
Langtoft, Peter, 335
Lansberg, Dietrich von, 222
Lanston Monotype Machine Company, 381
Lanston, Tolbert, 380–1
Lantenac, 72
Lapi, Domenico de', 51
Lapide, Joh. de, 442
La Porte, Hughes de, 172
La Rue, Pierre de, 210
Larcher, Étienne, 441
Laria, M. D., 309
Lascaris, Constantine, 49, 53, 125, 143
Lascaris-Catellar, Jean-Paul de, 305
Lasne, Michel, 293, 295
Lasso, Orlando di, 210, 218
Lasius, B., 184
Latin Bible:
  Gutenberg's, 11, 17
  Koberger's illustrated, 31–2
  Mentelin's, 24

Switzerland, 87, 91
  see also *Biblia Latina* and named Bibles – King James's, Mazarin etc.
Latin Compendium, 265
Latin Grammar: Donatus, 16, 73
Latin Grammar: Lily, 225
Latin Grammar: de Nebrija, 82, 188
Latin Psalter, 18, 19, 35
Latin thesaurus, 326
Latin type, 192, 288 *see also* Roman type
Latomus, Sigmund, 276
Latour, Charlotte de, 402
La Tour, Jean de, 46
Lattre, Jehan de, 215
Laudes B. M. V., 439
Lauer, Georg, 38, 39, 238–9
Lauffen, Canon Helyas Helyae von *see* Helyae, Canon Helyas
Laurenszoon, Lambertus, 438
Laurent and De Berny, 402
Laurentsson, Amund, 225, 229
Laus cantici 'Salve Regina': de Albo Lapide, 446
Laus et commendatio. . . . cantici Salve regina: von Weissenstein, 92
Lausanne, 92–3
Lavagne, Philippus de, 52, 53
Laalle, Martinus de, 443
Lawne, Gideon de, 215
Lawne, William de, 265
Laxurkalender, 18
Lazare, Edward, 17
Le Barbier, 314n.
Le Bé foundry, 316
Le Bé, Guillaume I, 174, 298
Le Bé, Guillaume II, 162n., 164, 173, 213 and n., 297, 300
Leben den Büchern gewidmet, Ein: Mardersteig, 413–14
Leben. . . . Dorothea, Das: Marienwerder, 440
Leben der Heiligen, 28
Leblond, –, 381
Le Bourgeois, Jean, 64
Le Bouteux, –, 314n.
Le Breton, –, 319, 320n.
Le Caron, Pierre, 67
Le Caron, Josquin, 191
Leclerc, Sébastien, 295
Lectura: Tartagnus, 51
Lectura super. . . . Codicis: Saxoferrato, 44

Lectura super institutionum: de Gambilionibus (Aretio), 442
Lectura in Joh. Duns Scotum. . . Scriptor, 445
Lectura super primam partem digesti novi: de Ubaldus (Perugia), 57, 437
Lectura super primam partem Infortiati: Saxaferrato, 53
Lectura super titulo: de Franchis, 442
Lectura type, 333
Leeds University Library, 124 (Fig 32)
Leempt, Gerardus de, 73, 439
Lee Priory Press, 406
Leeu, Gerard (Gheraert):
  Antwerp, 76–7, 195, 200
  books in English, 77, 106
  Gouda, 97, 438
  printer's mark, 111
Leeuwenhoek, – van, 274
Lefas, –, 381
Le Fèvre, Raoul, 436
Lefèvre d'Étaples, Jacques, 160
Legenda aurea: de Voragine, 70, 97
Legenda di S. Catarina, 48
Legende cursive type, 412
Legende sanctorum Henrici imperatoris et Kunigundus imperatricis, 77
Legendis poetis, De: Magnus, 238
Legh, Gerard, 260
Lename, Giovanni Filippo di, 39
Legrant, Jacques, 66, 436
Lehmann-Haupt, Hellmut, 20
Lehnacker, Joseph, 411
Leibnitz, Gottfried Wilhelm, 274
Leiden (Leyden), 77, 279–81, 351–2
Leipzig, 34–5, 275–6, 321–2, 384–6, 387
Leipzig BUGRA, 423
Leipzig Fair, 219, 222–3, 276
Leipzig University Library, 35
Leipziger Zeitung, 275
Leira, 86
Le Jay, Guy Michel, 296, 300
Le Jeune, Moreau, 314
Le Laboureur, –, 295
Leland, –, 335
Le Maire, Jean, 283
Lemberger, Georg, 138
Lemercier, Rose-Joseph, 404
'Le Normand' *see* Barbou, Jean
Leo, Abraham, 278
Leo X, Pope, 125, 147, 205

León, Juan de, 218
Leopold, Alexander, 142
Le Petit, Laurens, 67
Le Prest, Jean, 72
Le Preux, François, 183
Le Preux, Georges, 292 and n.
Le Preux, Jean, 183
Le Preux, Poncet, 211
'Le Prince' *see* Nourry, Claude
Lerebours, Noël, 404
Lerida, 78
Lern, Wolfgang, 248
Le Rouge, Guillaume, 66
Le Rouge, Jacques, 437 *see also* Rubeus, Jacobeus
Le Rouge, Jean, 64, 66, 445
Le Rouge, Nicholas, 66
Le Rouge, Pierre, 65, 66, 67, 436
Le Roux, Nicolas, 72
Le Roy, Adrian, 211, 213
Le Roy, Guillaume, 62, 70, 166, 440
Le Sage, Alain René, 325, 403
Lescherius, printer of, 439
Lessing, Gotthold Ephraim, 325
Lesure and Thibault, 213, 214n.
Le Talleur, Guillaume, 71, 101, 443
Letra grifa, 146
Letter of Indulgence, 444
Letters: St Jerome, 20, 38, 39, 117
Letters of St Paul, 239
Lettersnijder, Henric, 349 (Fig 75) *see also* Pieterszoon, Henric
Lettou, Johannes (John), 97, 99, 440
Lettou's type, 99
Lettre de forme *see* Textura type
Lettre françoise *see* Civilité type
Lettre d' Imprimerie, La: Thibaudeau, 405
Lettre de Somme, 109, 163
Lettre Batarde, 61, 67, 159, 224 *see also* Bastard type
Leu, Thomas, 293
Leuschner, Johann, 83
Levet, Pierre, 67
Lexicon Amharici-Latinum, 278
Leyden *see* Leiden
Leye, Gerard van der, 57
Leysser, Cornelius, 278
L'Homme, Martin, 168
Libellus de re herbaria novus: Turner, 256
Liber Bibliae moralis: Berchorius, 437

Index

Liber Chronicarum: Schedel, 23, 31
Liber Festivalis: Mirk, 99, 100
Liber Missarum, 211, 214
Liber de rege et regno: Aquinas, 73
Liber Selectarum Cantionum, 210
Liberis educandis, De: Plutarch, 53, 442
Liberte, La, 365
Librairie du Victor Hugo Illustré, 405
Librairies–Imprimeries Réunies, 405
Library: Long, 281 and n.
Library of Congress, Washington D.C., 305
Libri, Bartolommeo di, 49
Libri de re rustica, 150
Libro del delphin de musica para tañer vihuela, 218
Libro di Giuocho delli scacchi: de Cassolis, 49
Libro llamado declaración de instrumentos musicales, El: Bermudo, 218
Libro de Marco Polo veneciano, El, 185
Libro de musica de vihuela: Milan, 191, 218
Libro de musica para Vihuela, intitulado Orphenica lyra: Fuenllama, 218
Libro nuovo d'imparare a Scrivere Tutte Sorte Lettere: Palatino, 157
Libro de l'origine . . . della citta di Bergamo, 435
Libros Decretalium, Super: Panormitanus, 87, 88
Liechtenstein, Hermann, 56
Lied von der Schlacht beschähen vor Sempach, Das, 179
Liège, Jean de, 445
Liesvelt, Jacob van, 196
Life of Cowper: Hayley, 388
Life of God in the Soul of Man: Scougal, 371
Life of the holy Dyonisius: Glika, 392
Life of St Amaro: de Osma, 190 (Fig 45)
Life of St George, 393
Life of St Jerome (Italian), 440
Liger, Georg, 275
Lignano, the brothers de, 153
Lijden en passie ons heeren Jesu Christi, 439
Lila, Bartolomé de, 437
Liluim musicae planae: Keinspeck, 89
Lille, Abbé de, 396
Lily, William, 255
Limburg, Johann, 441
Limited Editions Club, New York, 413
Linguarum orientalium 278
Linis, Gulielmode, 435
Linklater, Eric, 429
Linotron filmsetter, 429
Linotype, 377, 381

Linotype machines, 379, 380 (Fig. 81)
Lisa, Gerardus de, 57, 437, 445
Lisbon, 86, 303
Lister, –, 274
Literature of Germany: Robertson, 277n.
Literary Anecdotes of the Eighteenth Century: Nichols, 341 and n.
Lithographic Illustrations, 402
Lithographs, 347, 420 (Fig 89)
Lithography, 373–6, 402
Lithophotographie, 404
Litigatio Satanae: Saxoferrato, 445
Litterae indulgentiarum: Han, 442
Liturgiarion, 244
Liturghier, 242
Lives: Plutarch, 165
Lives of the Fathers, 97
Livre, Le: Bouchot, 398 and n.
Livre de bonnes moeurs, Le: Legrant, 66, 436
Livres de Chasse: Foix, Comte de, 104
Livredes marchans, Le: Marcour, 183, 441
Livre du Roy Modus, 64
Livre des ruraulx prouffitz, Le, 71
Livre des saints anges: Jiminez, 91, 438
Livy, 125
Ljubavić, Božidar, 244
Ljubavić, Djuradi, 244
Ljubavić, Theodor, 244
Llorens, Joseph, 332
Lloyd, Edward, 369
Lloyd's Weekly London Newspaper, 369
Lloyd's Weekly Newspaper, 363, 364 (Fig 79)
Löbel, Dr –, 385
Lobinger, Johann, 278
Locatelli, Boneto, 44, 46
Lochner, Johann Christoph, the Elder, 278
Lochner, Johann Christoph, the son, 278
Logofetul, Dmitri, 243
Logofatul, Oprea, 240
London:
   City, 97, 99, 101, 106
   Westminster, 94–5, 97, 101, 105–6
London Phalanx, 377
London School of Printing, 410
London Society of Compositors, 378
Long Primer type, 174
Longmans, firm of, 391
Longo, Giovanni Leonardo, 142, 444
Longus, –, 395
López, Fransisco, 187

López de Mendoza, Iñigo, 187, 446
Loredano, Giovanni, 334
Lorenzaccio: 416 (Fig 88)
Lorenzo, Nicoló di, 48
Lorint, –, 241
Lormel, –, de, 314
Lorraine, Cardinal de, 168
Löslein, Peter, 41–2
Lotter, Melchior I, 36, 118 (Fig 31), 130, 138, 225
Lotter, Melchior II, 130
Lotter, Michael, 130
Lottin, A. M., 174 and n., 300, 369, 395
Loubier, Hans, 419
Louis XI of France, 60, 219
Louis XII of France, 219
Louis XIII of France, 299
Louis XIV of France, 291, 298
Louis XVI of France, 396
Louvain, 73–4
Love and complaints between Mars and Venus:
    Chaucer, 105
Love's Labours Lost, 51
Low German Bible, 228
Lübeck, 137–8, 224
Lublin, Biernet of, 248
Lucae, Johann, 440
Luce, Louis, 312 ,316
Luchtman, Samuel, 351, 369
Luchtman and Co., 369
Luchtmans, the, 283
Lucian, 435
Lucii Apulii Platonice et Aristotelici philosophi
    Epitoma, 141
Lucretius, 344
Luculentum theatrum musicum, 215
Ludlow filmsetter, 430
Ludo Scaccorum, De: de Cassolis, 49
Ludolf, Hiob, 278
Ludolphus, –, 77
Ludwig, Mayer, 421
Lufft, Hans, 130, 138
Lukaris, Kyrillos, 310
Luminario di authmetica: Tagliente, 157
Lumitype filmsetter, 429
Lumizip filmsetter, 429
Lüneburg, 276
Lunettes des Princes, Les: Meschinot, 441
Luppov, S. P., 252
Luschner, Johann, 441
Luther foundry, 133, 324

Luther, Johann, 133
Luther, Johann Nikolaus, 133
Luther, Martin, 129, 130, 180, 210
Lutheran Bibles, 133, 136
Luther's Bible, 122, 181, 196
Luther's Catechism, 237,240
Luther's New Testament, 123, 130, 180
Lute music, 208–9
Lutz, Thibaus, 221
Lutzelburger, Hans, 171–2
Lux Bella: Durán, 81
Luy, M., 399
Lvov, 251
Lydgate, John, 260
Lyons, 62, 70–1, 166–72, 213–14
Lyons Fair, 62, 219
Lyra, Nicolaus de, 31, 38, 87

M

Mâbre, Sebastien, 299
Mâbre-Cramoisy, Sebastien 299, 321
Mabre-Cramoisy, Mme Sebastien, 301, 321
Macarius, Metropolitan of Moscow, 250
Macfarlane, J. 67n.
Macé II, Robert, 197
Machiavelli, 148
Machlinia, William de, 75, 99, 101
Macho, Julian, 70
Machyn, Henry, 255
Mackie, Alexander, 381
Macklin's Bible, 347
Mackmurdo, Arthur Heygate, 415
Madrid, 186–7, 331–2
Madrigal, Pedro, 187
Madrigals, 217–18
Madrigals: Wilbye, 218, 267
Maeterlinck, Maurice, 417
Magdeburg, 36
Magdeburg Missal, 36
Magnete, De: Gilbert, 282 (Fig 64)
Magni, Jacobus, 60
Magnificat: de Gerson, 34
Magnus, Albertus, 233
Magnus, Basilus, 238
Magyar Bible, 285
Magyar New Testament, 240
Mahzor part 2, (Hebrew), 436
Maillet, Jacques, 70
Maillol, Aristide, 411
Main, –, 366

Mainz: 7–8, 9, 12, 21, 23
  archives, 18
  museum, 15
  see also Gutenberg
Mainz Psalters, 18, 107, 127
Mainz type, 117
Mainzer Catholicon, Das: Zedler, 20
Mainzer Presse, 411
Mainzer Probedrucke, 16n.
Mairesse, Antonio Francesco, 327
Maison Lahure, 405
Maisonneuve, Defer de, 315
Maiuscole *see* Fregi and Maiuscole
Makarije (Makarie) the monk, 242, 244, 436
Malaiapodoroznaia Knizica, 234
Malay Bibles, 350
Maler, Bernhard, 41–2, 43
Malin, Charles, 413
Malla, Felipe de, 82, 438
Malmö, 226
Malo, Charles, 402
Malpigli, Annibale, 50–1
Malpigli, Scipione, 51
Mammotrectus super Bibliam: Marchesinus, 91, 435
Mamonich, Kuzma, 251
Mamonich, Luke, 251
Manaila, –, 241
Manchecourt, –, 211
Manchester Guardian, 355n., 379
Mancz, Konrad, 435
Mandeville, John de, 29, 72, 97, 101, 439
Manilio, Antonio, 436
Manilius, Corneille, 215
Manilius, Gislain, 215, 216
Manipulus Curatorum: de Monrocher (Monte Rocherii):
  France, 60, 61, 441; Germany, 141; Italy, 443; Spain, 79, 444, 446
Manlius, Johannes, 241
Mann, George, 375
Manni, Giuseppe, 327
Mansfeld, Balthasar, 140
Mansion, Colard, 74, 75
Manthen, Johann, 41, 88
Mantskovit, Bálint, 240
Mantuanus, Baptista, 51
Manual de Adultos, 185
Manual for Pamplona, 82
Manuale: Augustinus, 445
Manuale Pamplonense, 442

Manuale Tipografico: Bodoni, 330
Manuel Typographique: Fourni, 317, 318, 330
Manuscript type, 185, 233, 424
Manuzio, Aldo I: 45, 46, 149
  Aetna, De, 144 (Fig 36)
  Catalogues, 221
  Greek printing, 125, 144
  House of, 107
  Hypnerotomachia Poliphili, 145, (Fig 37)
  see also Aldine Press
Manuzio, Aldo II, 153
Manuzio, Antonio, 147
Manuzio, Paolo, 147, 153–4, 177, 197–8
Manzolo, Michele, 57
Map printing, 56, 281, 283, 322
Marchant, Guy, 65, 70
Marchesinus, Joannes, 91, 435
Marcolini, Francesco, 148, 149
Marcour, Antoine, 183
Marcus Aurelius, 186
Mardersteig, Giovanni, 412
Mardersteig, Martino, 414
Mareschal, Jacques, 173
Mareschal, Pierre, 71
Margarita Philosophica: Reisch, 210
Marian exiles, 183
Mariconda, Antonio, 151
Marie of Burgundy, 134
Mariefred, Kloster, 438
Marienwerder, Joh. von, 440
Marillier, Clément Pierre, 314–15
Marin, Antonio, 333
Marinoni et Chaudré, 365
Marinoni, Hippolyte, 365, 375
Markham, Gervase, 267 (Fig 61)
Marksteine aus der Weltlitteratur in Original-schriften, 387, 421
Marmi, I: Doni, 149
Marne, Claude de, 133
Marnefs, the, 160
Marot, Clément, 167, 171, 215
Marprelate, Martin *see* Waldegrave, Robert
Marriage of Figaro: Beaumarchais, 325, 430
Marrot, H. V., 330, 344, 348
Marschalk, Nikolaus, 129
Marsigli, –, 307
Martens, Thierry, 73, 77, 435
Martersteig, Max, 417
Martial, 162
Martin, Robert, 343

Martinz Tišňova press, 234
Martin William, 345–6, 348
Martínez, Anton, 79, 81, 444
Martini, Antonius, *see* Martínez, Anton
Martinis, Lucas de, 55
Martin's types, 346
Martorelli, Juan, 84
Martzan, Melchior, 228
Marulli, Geronimo, 306
Maschinenfabrik Augsburg-Nürnberg, 386
Maschinenfabrik Zweibrücken, 376
Mason, J. H., 410
Massimi, Francesco de', 37
Massimi, Piero de', 37
Materia medica, De: Dioscurides, 437
Mathias, Antonius, 438, 440
Matthew Bible, 256, 257
Matthias Corvinus, King of Hungary, 238
Matthiasson, Brandur, 231
Matthiasson, Jón, 230
Matthiasson, Jón Jónsson, 230, 231
Mattioli, 327
Mattsson, Eskil, 225
Maturini, –, 186
Maufer, Petrus, 57
Maurus, Hrabanus, 24
Maus, Octave, 416
Maximilian I of H.R. Empire, 133–4, 135
   (Fig 34)
Maximilian type, 419
May, Juan, 192
May, Pedro Patricio, 192
Mayeur type, 400
Mayneriis, Maynus de, 444
Mayr, Benedict, 235, 442
Mayr, Sigismund, 151
Mazarin Bible, 17, 115
Mazzocchi, Giacomo (Jacopo), 148, 150
Mechanick Exercises: Moxon, 358
Meckenem, Israhel van, 251
Meda, Gerolamo de, 153
Medaille sur les événements du régne de Louis le
   Grand, 315, 316
Medelplan, Daniel, 229
Medemblik, Johannes de, 437
Meder, Johannes, 89
Medici, Cosimo de', 50
Medici, Cardinal Ferdinando de', 154
Meditatione passionis Christi, De: Bernardus, 443
Meditationes: Turrecremata, 38, 39

Meditationes Vitae Christi: Bonaventura, 83, 435,
   441
Meer, Jacob van der, 196, 437
Megenberg, Konrad von, 28–9
Meidoorn type, 412
Meisenbach, Georg, 404
Meissen Missal, 36
Meisonnier, Ernest, 403, 404
Meissner, Wolf, 276
Melanchthon, Philip, 131, 227
Melantrich, Jiří, 238 *see also* Rozdalovsky, Jirí
   Cerny
Melcer, Rehor, 238
Melgar, Alonso de, 189
Mellan, Claude, 293
Melopoeiae: Titonius, 209
Melusine: d'Arras, 71, 92
Memmingen, Albrecht de, 221
Memoire sur les vexations. . . . . : Blondel, 291
Memoires pour servir à l'Histoire des Hommes
   Illustrés: Niceron, 168n.
Memorandum: Le Be, 162n.
Memorial del pecador remut: de Malla, 83, 438
Mena, Francisco Manuel de, 332
Menard, Jean, 67
Mendoza, Iñigo Lopez de, 83, 84
Menhart, Oldřich, 423–4, 425 (Fig 91)
Menhart types, 425 (Fig 91)
Meninski, Franz de Mesgnien, 278
Mennonist Canticles, 350
Mennonites, 127
Mensural music, 207, 208
Mensural notation, 208–9
Mentelin, Johann, 24, 116, 221, 444
Menus Plaisirs, the, 314
Menzel, –, 325
Mer des Hystoires, La, 65, 66
Merbecke, John, 216
Merchadier, Pierre, 173
Merck, Johann Friedrich, 324
Merckel, Henrik Christofer, 229
Mercure françois, 296
Mercure galant, 296
Mercurio historico y politico, 332
Mercurius Gallo-Belgicus, 276
Mergenthaler Company, 429
Mergenthaler, Ottmar, 379
Merian, the heirs of, 277
Merian, Johannes Matthäus, 279
Merian, Kaspar, 279

Index

Merian, Maria Sibylla, 279
Merian, Matthäus, the Elder, 272, 279
Merian, Matthäus II, 279
Méridien type, 430
Merlini, Stefano dei, 57, 437
Mertens, Dr, –, 382
Meschinot, Jean, 441
Meslier, Denis, 65
Messkatalog (Leipzig), 275
Messrelationen, 276 see also *Relationes historicae*
Mesue, –, 56–7, 442
Metal blocks in music printing, 209
Metamorphoses: Ovid, 169, 295
Metaphysica: Bonetus, 78
Metaxas, Nicodemus, 310
Metlinger, Pierre, 64, 435, 437
Metric Psalms, 262
Mettayer, Jamet, 165–6
Metzger, Friedrich, 385, 421
Metzler, Benedikt, 324
Metzler, J. B., 363
Mexico, 185–6
Meyenberger, Friedrich, 131
Meyer, Dr W. J., 92
Meynell, Sir Francis, 287 and n.
Meynial, Guillaume, 61
Mezzotints, 347
Michael Fedorovitch of Russia, 353
Michaelibus, Petrus Adam de, 440
Micheleff, Carlo, 307
Michelet, Jules, 405
Mickiewicz, Adam, 249
Middelburgo, Paulus de, Bishop of Fossombrone,
    152
Miehle Press, 366
Miehle, Robert, 366
Mierdman, Steven, 260, 263
Milan, 51–3, 327
Milan, Luys, 218
Military Orders of the Hussites, 425 (Fig 91)
Miller and Richard, 391
Miller, William, 388 (Fig 82)
Milton, John, 280, 315, 345
Miquel, Pere, 78, 84
Mirabilia Urbis Romae, 5, 140, 147, 441
Mirabilibus Sacrae Scripturae, De: Augustinus, 73
Mirk, John, 99
Miriouer dela Redemption, 70
Mirror or Portrait of an upright man: Rej, 249
Mirrour of the World, 97

Misal Hrvacki, 245
Misceelanea Curiosa, 274
Miscomini, Antonio, 49, 441
Miscomini, Giorgio, 441
Misintis, Bernardinus de, 56
Missale Augustanum, 437
Missale Aurense, 440
Missale Carnotense, 64, 436
Missale Frisingense, 438
Missale Glagoliticum, 446
Missale Hafniense, 225
Missale H. spalense, 192
Missale Lausannense, 93, 439
Missale Magdeburgense, 440
Missale Misnense, 438
Missale mixtum, 82
Missale Nidrosiense, 226
Missale Ordinis S. Benedicti, 26
Missale Pragense, 36
Missale Ratisponense, 443
Missale Romanum, 186
Missale Slesvicense, 443
Missale Strigoniense, 235
Missale Tullense, 446
Missale Valentinense, 445
Missals, 30, 36, 39 *see also* named missals, Bam-
    berg etc
Missel de Paris, 64
Missel de Verdun, 64
Missionaries' Press, 394
Mitchell, Robert, 340
Mode, La, 404
Modéles de Caractères de l'Imprimerie: Fournier,
    317
Modena, 56
Modena, Francesco, 328
Modern plates, 426–7
Modern Printing machinery and letterpress printing:
    Wilson and Grey, 359n.
Moderne, Jacques, 167, 213–14
Modestus, Publius, 153
Modo di temperare le penne, Il, 155 (Fig 41)
Modros, 244
Modus significandi, De: de Erfordia, 443
Moerentorf, Jan, 200, 220, 223 *see also* Moretus,
    Jan
Mogilev, 253
Mohammed Effendi, 308
Moholy-Nagy, Laxlo, 419–20
Molière, Jean Baptiste, 280, 293, 314

Molini, Giovanni, 344
Molini, Pietro, 344
Molitor, Heinrich, 28
Molitoris, Ulricus, 34
Molitvennik, 243
Molitvoslov (Horologeum), 245
Möllemann, Stephan, 138
Moller, Lars, 393
Molner, Diederich, 27
Mommarte, J., 303
Momme, Peter, 353
Mondadori, Arnoldo, 413
Monde illustré, 405
Monde Moderne, 405
Moniteur du Soir, 365
Moniteur Universal, 365
Monnet, –, 319
Monnier, Henri, 402, 403
'Monophoto' filmsetter, 428
'Monotype,' 377, 381
Monotype composing machines, 380–1
Monotype Corporation Ltd, 344, 381, 413, 424
Monsiau, Nicolas André, 315
'Montaigne' type, 44
Montalvo, Alfonso (Alonso) Diaz de, 84, 444
Montalvo, Diaz de, 80, 82, 439
Montana, Cola, 52
Monte, Filippo di, 215
Monte Rocherii, Guido de, 441, 443, 444, 446
Monte Sancto di Dio: Bettini, 48
Montefeltro, Federigo da, 50
Montesdoca, Martin de, 217 (Fig 49), 218
Montesino, –, 85, 187
Montesson, Marquise de, 396
Montfort, Benito, 332, 333
Montrocher, Guy de, 60 *see also* Monte Rocherii, Guido de
Montserrat, –, 83
Monumens du costume, 314
Morales, Juan Gomez, 334
Moralia in Job: Gregorius, 87
Moran, James, 429
Moravia, Valentinus **de** *see* Fernandez, Valentim
Moravus, Mathias, 239
More, Thomas, 120, 123, 260
Moreau le Jeune, J. M., 314
Moreau, Pierre, 272, 298
Morel, Charles, 293
Morel, Claude, 165, 298
Morel, Fédéric I, 164, 165

Morel, Fédéric II, 165
Morel, Jean, 64
Morelli, Johannes, 435
Mores, Edward Rowe, 260 and n., 343
Moreto, Antonio, 47
Moretus, Jan, 200, 272 *see also* Moerentorf, Jan
Morgante Maggiore: Pulci, 48
Morgiani, Lorenzo, 49
Moriae enconium: Erasmus, 121, 123
Morin, Martin, 72
Morison, Stanley, 144, 291 and n., 413
Morley, Thomas, 218, 267
Morrhé, Gerhard, 165
Morris types, 44, 406–7
Morris, William, 344, 356, 408, 409 (Fig 87), 412, 418
Morsoni, –, 302
Mort d'Annibal, La: Didot, 400
Morte Astyanactus, De: Veguis, 436
Morton, Cardinal John, 101
Moscheni, Francesco, 153
Moscheni, Simone, 153
Moscow, 250–3
Moscow Printing House, 252, 253
Moscow type, 251
Motets: Beaulaigue, 177
Motley, John, 195–6
Motte and Sautelet, 402
Motteroz, Jean-Claude, 405
Motu Aquae mixto, De: Poleni, 327
Moule *see* Darlow and Moule
Moucke, Fracesco, 327
Mouton, –, 211
Moxon, Joseph, 358
Mozarabic Breviary, 186
Mozarabic Missal, 82, 186
Mozart, Leopold, 350
Mozley, J. F., 256
Mstislavets, Petr Timofeev, 251
Much Ado: Shakespeare, 153
Mucha, Alphonse, 416 (Fig 88)
Mudie, Robert, 389
Muestras de los Caracteres: Espinosa, 332
Muhlbach, 240
Müller, Georg, 277, 420
Müller, Johann, Bishop, 32, 42 (Fig 5), 42n., 351, 369
Müller, Leo, 365, 386
Müller, Nicolaus, 62, 112
Müller, Philip, 62

Münchener Kalender, 418
Muncka matrizer, 225
Munich, 16, 140
Munich Meisterschule für Deutschlands Buch drucker, 420
Munich State Library, 134
Munster, Sebastian, 180
Muratori, –, 327
Murcia, 83
Muret, –, 223
Murner, Beatus, 131
Murner, Thomas, 131
Murray, David, 337n.
Musaeus, –, 143
Music:
    engraved, 216
    notation, 33, 208, 216
Music printing:
    Denmark, 228; England, 216–18, 266–7, 288–9; France, 211–14; Germany, 34, 321; Italy, 39 and n., 46; Spain, 81; Switzerland, 89, 179; *see also* Chap. 19, 207–18
Music type, 177, 300, 318, 321–2, 353
Música, La: Iriarte, 332
Musica instrumentalis: Agricola, 210
Musica Transalpina: Yonge, 217
Musick's Handmaid, 288
Musset, Alfred de, 405, 416 (Fig 88)
Mustafa, Mohammed ben, 309
Musurus, Marais, 144
Muthesius, Hermann, 418
Muzio, –, 150
Mylius, Arnol, 276
Mylius, Hermann, 276
Myller, Andrew, 71
Mýto, Jonata z Vysoké *see* Hohenmauth, Jona-than von

N

Nachmanides, Moses, 205
Nachrichten: Neudörffer, 129
Nachtegael, Otgier, 443
Nádasdy, Tamás, 240
Nadler, Jörg, 209
Nadson, Alexander, 234
Nagera, Bartolomé de, 188
Nagra christeliga boot predikniger: Rothovius, 229
Nagyzombat *see* Trnava
Nahmias, David, 204, 307
Nahmias, Samuel, 204, 307

Nani, Ercole, 51
Nanteuil, Célestin, 402
Nanteuil, Robert, 293, 295
Napier, David, 365
Naples, 301
Nasier, Alcofribas *see* Rabelais, Francois
Nassau, Adolf von, 8, 23
Nassinger, Leonhard, 142
Natali delle Religiose Militie, I: Marulli, 305–6
National Printing Office, Athens, 311
Nationale, La, 365
Natura Naturans: Burns, 422 (Fig 90)
Natura Stirpium, De: Ruel, 162
Natural History: Pliny, 32, 38
Naumann, Justus, 421
Navarro, Francisco, 303
Navarro, Juan, 192
Nebrija, Antonio de, 82, 188, 189
Nebrija, Sancho de, 189
Nebrissensis, A., 443
Nedêle, Kaspar, 237
Nederlansche Spellijnghe: Lambrecht, 201
Nefedev, Marusha, 250
Neger, Joost de, 134
Néobar, Conrad, 162, 174
Neo-Caroline script, 109
Nerlii, Bernardo, 48
Nerlii, Nero, 48
Nessi, E., 48
Netolicky, Bartholomew, 234, 238
Neuber, Ulrich, 210
Neudeutsch type, 418
Neudörffer, Johann, 129, 134
Neue Buchhaus, Die: Kautzsch, 417
Neue Deutsche Buchkunst, Die: Loubier, 419
Neueinlaufende Nachtricht von Kriegs und Welthändeln, 275
Neuf Preux, Les, 6
Neuland type, 419
Neumeister, Johann, 18, 53, 63, 438
Nevezha, Andronik Timofeev, 252
Nevezhin, Ivan Andronikov, 252
New Interlude and a mery of the Nature of the IIII Elements, 216
New Light on Caxton and Colard Mansion: Sheppard, 74n.
New Light on the Renaissance: Bayley, 303
New York Tribune, 379
Newbridge, William of, 335
Newdigate, Bernard, 408

Newsbooks *see* Newspaper printing in Germany

Newspaper printing: 266–7, 272, 355, 373
Denmark, 353; England, 289, 362–3 *see also*
Times, the; France, 365; Germany, 274–5;
Greenland, 393; Russia, 353–4

Newton, Sir Isaac, 274

Newton, Ninian, 264

Neyret, Antoine, 64, 436

Niceron, the Abbé, 168

Niccoli, Niccoló, 109

Nicholas the Bachelor *see* Bakalář Mikuláš

Nichols, Arthur, 288

Nichols, John, 339, 341 and n.

Nicholson, William, 359–60, 360–1

Nicholson's Journal of Science, 359

Nicol, George, 345

Nicola, Abbot, 244

Nicolai, Arnold, 258 (Fig 54)

Nicolai, Johannes, 57, 442

Nicolas V, Pope, 15

Nicolas, Sir Harris, 389–90

Nider Johannes, 27

Niebelungen, Die: 418

Niebelungen-Schrift, 418

Nielson, Tyge, 228

Nies, Johann, 421

Nies Printing House, 387

Nifo, Agostino, 151

Niger, Franciscus, 208

Nikoforov, Vasyuk, 250

Nikon, Patriarch of Moscow, 252, 253

Nitzchewitz, Hermann, 446

Nivelle, Sébastien, 298

Nizhnii Novgorod, 252

Nobilitas Politica vel Civilis, 288

Nodier, Charles, 402, 404

Noguier, Antoine, 173

Nonceaux, Henry, 44n.

Norden, Friderik Ludvig, 352

Nördlingen, Johannes de, 51

Norton, Bonham, 288

Norton, F. J., 82

Norton, John, 287, 288

Norton, Thomas, 265

N. Señora del Prado Abbey, 445

Notary, Julian, 104, 105

Note on his aims in founding the Kelmscott Press:
Morris, 407

Notizie annuale, 327

Nourry, Catherine, later Vingle, 183

Nourry, Claude, 167, 171, 183

Nouveau Caractère de fonte pour la Musique:
Fournier, 322

Nouvelle Biographie Generale, 165, 170n.

Nova Civitate, Gerardus de, 440

Novo Modo a Scrivere, Uno: Amphiareo, 157

Novelli, P. A., 326

Novelliere: Bandello, 153

Novgorod-Severskii, 253

Noviomagus, Hermannus Hortenbergus, 223

Novo Teatro di Machine ed Edificii: Zonca, 302

Novy karakter polski, 249

Nucio, Martin, 193

Nuits et Souvenir: Les: de Musset, 405

Numerals, Arabic, 42

Nunalerutit, 394

Nuremberg, 14, 23, 30–3, 275, 277–8

Nuremberg Chronicle, 31, 117

Nutzliche ynderwysung, Ein: Erasmus, 181

Nuyts, Martin, 197

Nyevelt, Willem van Zuylen van, 214

Nyhoff, –, 196

Nyirö, János, 240

Nyon, Jean-Nicolas, 395

O

Obel, Matthias de l', 198, 200

Obod, 244

Obras de Bosán y Garcilaso, Las, 191

Obregon, Diego de, 303

Obres e trobes. . . de la. . . . Verge Maria: Fenollar,
78, 79

Obsequials, 29, 30, 33

Obsidionis Rhodiae. . . . descriptio: Caoursin, 226,
441

Oces, Juan de *see* Navarro, Juan

Ochsenkuhn, Sebastian, 210

Octo Missae: de la Hèle, 215

Octa partibus orationis, De: Donatus, 16

Octoich, 243

Odes: Horace, 210

Odyssey: Homer, 190, 192

Oeconomica: Aristotle, 435

Oeuvres de Monsieur Moliere, Les, 296

Oeuvres morales et meslées de Plutarque, Les, 165

Officii Missae sacrique Canonis expositio: Gruner,
34

Officiis, De: Cicero, 21, 55, 439

Officina Bodoni, 412, 413

Officio missae, De: Andreae, 91

Index

Officium B.M.V., 445
Offizin Drugulin, 417, 421
Offizin Haag-Drugulin, 387, 421
Oficii blazenie devi marie, 245
Offset lithography (litho), 375, 376, 427
Ogerolles, Jean d', 167
Öglin, Erhard, 136, 209, 216
Ohly, Dr Kurt, 87
Oka type, 392
Oktoich (choral book), 244, 247, 436
Old England, 391
Old England's Worthies, 391
Old Style type, 391
Old Testament (Dutch), 437
Oldenborch, Niclaes van, 196
Olivetan, Pierre Robert, 184
Olivetsky, Jan, 236
Olivetsky, Sebastian, 236
Olivier, Pierre, 72
Olney, Henry, 266 (Fig 60)
Olod, Fray Luis, 333
Olomouc, 235-6
Olpe, Johann Bergmann von *see* Bergmann von
Olpe, Johann
Onser Liever Vrouwen Souter: St Bernard, 195
Oostersch: Leopold, 412
Opéc, Baltasar, 248
Opera: Lactantius, 443
Opera: Mesue, 56-7, 442
Opera: Ovid, 435
Opera: St Augustine, 122, 180, 246
Opera: Selden, 339
Opera: Virgil, 436, 438, 440
Opera nova contemplativa, 5
Opera Omnia: Erasmus, 351
Opere Toscane: Alamanni, 170
*Operina . . . . da imparare di scrivere lettera can-
cellarescha, La*, 155-6
Oporin (Oporinus), Johann, 179, 180, 183
Oporto, bishopric of, 86
Opuscula: Gerson 77, 436
Oracional: de Guzman, 83
Oracula Sybellina, 5
Oradea, 241
Oratio: Gryphus, 113 (Fig 27)
Oratio Dominica: Bodoni, 328, 330
Oratore, De: Cicero, 37, 60n.
Orbis sensualium pictus quadrilinguis: Komenski,
277
Orchi Ambrogio degli, 53

Orchidaceae of Mexico and Guatamala: Bateman,
402
Orco, Ambrosio de, 437
Ordenanzes Reales: de Montalvo, 82, 84, 439
Ordini di Cavalcare, Gli: Grisone, 151
Ordnung wider die Pestilenz: Steinhowel, 445
Ordonnances royales, Les, 173
Orga, José, 332-3
Orga, Tomás, 332, 333
Organ tablature, 209
Ory, Marc, 298
Oriental types 137, 177, 309, 316, 328, *see also*
Exotic types
Origen y Arte de escribir bien: Olod 333
Origin and Development of Humanistic Script:
Ullman, 109n.
*Origine et le progrès des caractères de fonte pour la
musique, l':* Fournier, 318-19
*Origines de l'Imprimerie et son introduction en
Angleterre:* Quantin, 405
Orlando Furioso: Ariosto, 123, 150, 326, 344
Orosius, –, 56
Orozco, Marcos de, 303
Orphan House Press *see* Vajsenhuset
Orphenica lyra: de Fuenllana, 217 (Fig 49)
Orsi, Luigi, 330
Orsini, Emiliano de', 53
Orsoni, Gabriel, 52
Ortas, Abraham ben Samuel D', 86
Ortelius, Abraham, 198, 223
Orthodox Missal, 242
Orthographia: Gasparino, 60
Ortiz, Vincenté Urrabieta, 405
Ortuin, Gaspard and Peter Schenck, 70
Os, Pieter van, 75-6 (Fig 10)
Osma, Alfonso Diaz de, 190 (Fig 45)
Ostrog, 251
Ostrog Bible, 251, 252
Otley Press, 366
Otmar, Johann (Hans), 34, 131, 136, 209, 445
Otmar, Sylvan, 136, 138
Otmar, Valentin, 136, 241
Otto, Hans, 210
Oude en Nieuwe Testament, 196
Oudry, Jean-Baptiste, 314
Oujezdsky, Alexander, 237
Outline of Veronese Bibliography: Rhodes, 154n.
Ouvres Badines: de Caylus, 215
Ovar, 241
Overijsselsche Landbrief, 446

Ovid, 50, 169, 295, 435
Oxford, 97, 99
Oxford University Press, 271, 287, 289, 312, 335

P

P. Ia, 444
Pablos, Juan, 185, 186
Pachel, Leonhard, 53
Paciaudi, –, 328–9
Pacifico, P. A., 301
Pacini da Pescia, Piero, 49
Paderborn, Johann (John) of, 435 see also West-
    phalia, John of
Padua, 56–7, 327
Padua, Clement of, 39, 41
Paffraet, Richard, 75, 437
Painter, George D., 10 and n., 11, 16, 79
Painter, William, 153, 264
Palace of Pleasure: Painter, 153, 264
Palatino, Giovanni Battista, 157
Palazzolo, Marc' Antonio, 155
Palestrina, 218
Palinurus, Scipio Romanus etc: Lucian, 435
Palladio, Andrea, 328
Palladius, Peder, 226
Palmart, Lambert, 78, 79, 84, 445
Palmer, Samuel, 100
Paltašíc, Andrija, 46, 244
Paltascichi, Andrea de see Paltašíc, Andrija
Pamplona, 82–3
Pan, 417, 421
Panckoucke, Charles-Joseph, 320
Pandette 151
'Paniconographie', 404
Pannartz, Arnold and Sweynheim, Conrad:
    Rome, 37–8, 111, 118, 121, 443
    Subiaco, 22, 24, 37, 444
Pannartz and Sweynheim types, 22, 24, 37–8, 111
Panormitanus, Nicolaus, 87, 88, 118
Pantagruel, roi des Dipsodes: Rabelais, 167, 171
Pantheologia: de Pisis, 30, 31
Paoli, Giovanni see Pablos, Juan
Paolino, Stefano, 302
Papa, 241
Papa, Guido, 438
Paper Mills, 246, 247, 369
Paperini, Bernardo, 327
Paper-making machines, 368–9, 400
Papers of the Bibliographical Society of America, 79
Parabosco, –, 150

Paradell see Pradell
Paradise Lost: Milton, 315
Paradise Regain'd: Milton, 342
Parangon des Chansons, Le, 214
Parangon type, 398
Paravacino, Dionigi da, 52, 53, 57, 125
Paravia, – , 328
Paravisinus, Dionysius, 437 see also Paravicino
    Dionigi da
Pardoe, –, 388
Parente, Giorgio see Arrivabene, Giorgio
Parenza, Mazo dei, 206
Paris, 59–62, 159–66, 211–13, 291–3, 395–6,
    398–400
Paris chez soi, 378n.
Paris Hours, 69 see also Books of Hours
Paris, Matthew, 263
Paris Photographié: Renard, 404
Parix, Johann, 71, 444
Parker, Henry, 116 (Fig 29)
Parker, Archbishop Matthew, 260, 406
Parliament type, 424
Parma, 53–4, 329–30
Parmensio, Caesar, 56
Parnaso Italiano, Il, 326
Parnell, Thomas, 345
Parnis, Dr E., 305n.
Pars secunda super librum secundum decretalium:
    Gregory IX, 118
Parsifal: Eschenbach, 24
Parthenia, 288
Pascal, Blaise, 280
Pasquale, Peregrino, 443
Pasquet, Jean, 151
Passau Breviary, 442
Passe, Crispin de, 295
Passera, Gonzalo Rodriguez de la, 440
Passional: de Voragine, 110 (Fig 24)
Passiones quas beatissimi apostoli, 185
Pasti, Matteo de', 57
Pastyme of people: Rastell, 105 (Fig 21)
'Patent Illuminated Printing', 390–1
Paterbonus, Maphaeus de, 45
Patisson, Mamert, 213
Patras, 310
Pau, 173
Paul II, Pope, 55, 112, 134
Paul IV, Pope, 153, 158 see also Caraffa, Cardinal
Paul et Virginie, 403
Paulin, Etienne, 300

Paulin, firm of, 403

Paveri-Fontana, Gabriel, 52

Pavia, 36

Payen, Thibaud, 167

Payne, David, 366

Paypus, Friedrich, 138

Peder Paars: Holberg, 353

Pedersen, Christiern, 226

Peeters-Fontainas, J., 193n.

Pegnitzer, Johann (Hans) 81, 84, 189

Peintures antiques de Bartoli, 396

Pelicano type 333

Pelletan, Edouard, 405

Penguin edition, 429

Penny Cyclopaedia, 389

Penny magazines, 356, 389

Penrose's Annual, 428, 430

Pens Excellence or Secretaries Delight, 297 (Fig 69)

Pentateuch:

Coptic, 339

Czech, 237

Hebrew, 204, 205, 206, 438

'Perdono d' Assisi', 53

Peregrinationes: Breydenbach, 82, 235

Perfecting machines, 362

Perfetto Scrittore, II: Cresci, 157

Perfite platforme of a Hoppe Garden: Scot, 264

Pergeus, Apollonius, 154

Periodical Press, 296

Periodicals, 327

Perottus, Nicolas, 38, 443, 444

Perpetua type, 413

Perrault, Charles, 295

Perrin, François, 183

Persian type, 288

Persian-Turkish lexicon, 309

Persius, 125, 443

Perugia, 57

Perugia, Angelola da, 57

Perusino, Lautizio *see* Rotelli, Lautizio di Bartolomeo dei

Peter the Great of Russia, 353-4

Peter Schoeffer of Gernsheim and Mainz: Lehmann-Haupt, 20

Petit, Jean, 160, 161 (Fig 42), 257

Petit Journal, Le, 365

Petit Parangon type, 396

Petite Sédanaise type, 297

Petitot, Ennemondo, 329 (Fig 72)

Petits, the, 160

Petra, Hermannus de, 441

Petrarch, 117, 150, 151, 170, 440, 442

Petreius, Johann, 216, 218

Petri, Adam, 180

Petri, Heinrich, 180

Petri, Johann:

Germany, 32, 129, 141, 210; Italy, 47, 49

Switzerland, 91, 180

Petri, Petrus, 57, 442

Petro, Johanninus de, 444

Petrucci, Ottaviano, 46, 152 (Fig 39), 208

Petrus Lobardus, Glossa in Ep^a. Pauli, 438

Petzenheimer, Heinrich, 26

Peypus, Friedrich, 129

Pezzana, Lorenzo, 301

Pezzana, Nicolo, 301

Pfennegmagazin, 356

Pfeyl, Johann, 26

Pfinzing, Melchio, 134, 135 (Fig 34)

Pfister, Albrecht, 17, 18, 21n., 25-6

Pfister Bible, 26

Pfister, Sebastian, 26

Pflugel, Leonhard, 39

Pforzheim, Jakob von, 91

Phaedri Fabulae, 316

Phalaris, -, 52, 79

Phaleris, Demetrius, 337

Phalèse, Corneille, 215

Phalese, Pierre, 214-15

Phalese, Pierre II, 215

Phalizen, Pieter vander *see* Phalèse, Pierre

Philadelphia *Ledger,* 363

Philip II of Spain, 186, 198, 217, (Fig 49)

Philipon, Charles, 404

Philipp, Johann, 123

Philippe, Gaspard, 173

Philippe, Gillette, later Guyart, 173

Philippe, Jean, 70

Philippi, Nicolaus *see* Müller, Nicolaus

Philobiblon: de Bury, 268 (Fig 62)

Philocolo, 41

Philosophiae naturalis principia mathematica: Newton, 274

Philosophical Transaction, 274

Philovallis *see* Victor, Hieronymus

Photo composition *see* Filmsetting

Photography, 404

Photogravure, 382-3

Photo-lithography, 404

Photo-mechanical illustration, 344

Photon filmsetter, 429
Photon-lumitype filmsetter, 430
'Pianotype', 381
Piazzetta, J. B., 326
Pica types, 132, 339 *see also* named picas
Pico, –, 143
Pickering, William, 390 (Fig 83), 391
Pictorial Album or Cabinet of Paintings, 389
Pied du roi type, 398
Piero, Filippo, 41
Piero, Gabriele, 41
Pierres, Philippe, 372
Pierres precieuses et fines: Dutens, 395
Pieterszoon, Cornelius, 201
Pieterszoon, Henric, 107, 200
Pietro, Gabriele di, 440 444
Pietro, Giovannino di, 55
Piferrer, Tomás, 332
Pigouchet, Philippe, 67, 69, 211
Pilgrim's Progress: Bunyan, 290 (Fig 67)
Pilsen, 232–3, 235
Pinard, –, 401
Pine, John, 346 (Fig 74)
Pinelli, Antonio, 301, 302
Pine's Costumes, 388 (Fig 82)
Pio, Alberto, 143, 144
Pio, Caterina, 143
Pio, Leonello, 143
Piove di Sacco, 204
Piranesi, G-B., 328
Pirckheimer, Willibald, 30
'Pirot Picard' *see* Vingle, Pierre de
Pirotechnia: Biringuccio, 14
Pisa, Fra Piero da, 47
Pisador, 191
Pisan, Christine de, 69, 97, 403
Pisis, Rainerius de, 30
Pissaro, Camille, 410
Pissarro, Esther, 410
Pissarro, Lucien, 409, 410, 412
Pistoia, Fra Domenico da, 47
Pius II, Pope, 73, 115 *see also* Sylvius Aeneas
Pius IV, Pope, 153
Plainsong, 207
Plakat, Das, 419, 423
Planck, Johann, 79, 84, 435
Planctus ruinae ecclesiae: Fabri, 441
Planella, Antonio, 52
Plannck, Stephan, 39
Plantificación de la Imprenta de el Rezo Sagrado, 331

Plantin, Christopher: 197–202, 199 (Fig 47)
Frankfurt fair, 128, 220, 221, 223
illustrated books, 293
liturgical books, 215
Polyglot Bible, 122 and n.
Spanish books, 193
type metal, 14
Virgil, 121
Plantin Press, 126, 272, 334
Plantinian types, 201, 296
Plantin-Moretus Museum, 198, 202
Plantin-Moretus Press, 331
Plasirs, P. de, 45
Platea, Franciscus de, 246
Platina, Bartholomaeus, 57, 437
Platter, Thomas, 184
Plavecky Stvrtek, 237
Playford, Henry, 289
Playford, John, 288–9
Playing cards, 28, 33
Plenarium, 445
Pleydenwurff, Hans, 32
Pleydenwurff, Wilhelm, 31, 32
Pliny, 32, 38
Pliny: Jenson, 407
Plomer, Henry, 263
Plumet, Charles, 413
Plutarch, 53–4, 165, 435, 442
Pochard, E., 363
Poème des jardins: de Lille, 396
Poems: Goldsmith, 345
Poems: Gray, 330, 337
Poems: Parnell, 345
Poems: Townshend, 348
Poems of Lovelace, 291
Poeschel, Carl, 421
Poeschel, Carl Ernst, 410, 419, 421
Poeschel, Heinrich Ernst, 421
Poeschel and Trepte, 421
Poitevin, J., 70
Poivre, Pierre, 173
Polanzani, Felix, 326
Poleni, Joannis, 327
Polish Bible, 248
Politica: Aristotle, 40, 80 (Fig 11), 174, 435
Pollard, A. W., 18, 49, 54, 67, 272, 408
Polono, Ladislas, 185
Polono, Stanislao, 81, 187, 218
Polotskii, Simeon, 252
Polychromatic printing, 389

Polycronicon: Higden, 207

Polyglot Bibles:

England, 288; France, 296, 300; Netherlands, 198, 200; Plantin's 8-volume, 122n; Spain, 82, 188

Polyglot Psalter, 151

Polymatype, 376

Polyolbion: Drayton, 284 (Fig 65)

Polytypage, 401

Ponder, Nathaniel, 290 (Fig 67)

Pons, Felio, 333

Pontano, Caterina, 151

Pontano, Giovanno, 151

Pontanus, Ludovicus, 73, 83

Ponte, Gotardus de, 153

Pontoppidan Atlas, 353

Popma, Alardo de, 303

Porrus, Petrus, 151

Porteira, Samuel, 85, 438

Portila, Andreas, 51, 53, 442

Portonariis, Andrea de, 190, 191, 192

Portonariis, Domenico de, 170

Portonariis, Madeleine de, later Rouille (Roville), 170

Portonariis, Vicento de, 170

Portonariis's, the, 219

Portonbach, Johann, 221

Portraits of the Emperors of Turkey: Young, 347

Portu, Alphonsus de *see* Puerto, Alfonso del

Porzholt, E., 427

Posa, Pedro (Pere I), 78, 84

Posa, Pere II, 84

Posèn *see* Poznan

Poster 416 (Fig 88)

Postilla catechetica: Band, 228

Postilla super Evangela: de Lyra, 87

Postilla scholastica super apocalypsim, 444

Postillae super Biblia: de Lyra, 31, 38

Postille: Kulczar, 237

Potter Printing Press Co,. New York, 375

Pouchée, Louis Jean, 376

Pourcelet, Simon, 444

Powell, Thomas, 254

Poyntz, Sir Thomas, 70

Poznan, 246, 248

Pozsony *see* Bratislava

Pozzo, Francesco del, 50, 51

Practica for 1490: Schrotbanck, 439

Practical Hints on Decorative Printing: Clowes, 389

Pradell, Eudaldo I, 332, 333, 334 and n.

Pradell, Eudaldo II, 333, 334

Pradell, Margarita, 333

Pradnik Czerwony, 247

Prades, the Abbé de, 319

Praeceptorium, divinae legis: Nider, 27

Praelum Ascensianum, 160

Praemonstraten Abbey, 444

Praeparatio Evangelica: Eusebius, 175

Prague, 233–5, 238

Praktika for 1500: Virdung, 441

Pralard, Andre, 395

Prato, Felix de, 204, 205

Prato Florida, Hugo de, 439

Prault, –, 314

Prayer Book type, 410

Prayers for the remission of sins, 435

Pré, Jean de:

Breviaries, 441, 445

Chartres Missal, 64, 436

Decameron, 67

Indulgence, 443

Lancelot, 65

Roman de la Rose, 70 and n.

Pregnitza Joh., 438

Preinlein, Matthias, 436, 441

Preissig, Vojtěch, 423

Preller, Christian, 436

Premier Livre, contenant XXVIII Pseaulmes de David, 214

Premier Live de Tablature de Guiterre, 213

Premier Livre de Tabulature de Luth: Le Roy, 213

Premier Trophee de Musique, 177

Preparations in Printing Ink in Various Colours: Clowes, 389

Presente libro insegna la arte delo scrivere. . . . . . de litere, Lo: Tagliente, 157

Presles, Raoul de, 64

Presov, 237

Press *see* various types – iron, Stanhope, etc. and named presses

Press room interior, 361 (Fig 78)

Pressburg *see* Bratislava

Presse, La, 365

Preuss, Gerhard, 83

Prexamo, Pedro Jiménez de, 81

Prince, Edward, 407, 410, 411

Printed Book of the Renaissance: Goldschmidt, 146n.

Printer Conger, 298

Printers marks, 27, 111, 112 (Fig 26)
Printers' Register, 378
Printing: Jacobi, 360n.
Printing machines, 355–6
Printing Press in Malta: Parnis, 305n.
Printing Types: Updike, 174, 189–90
Prisma type, 419
Private Angelo: Linklater, 429
Privilegia ordinis Cisterciensis, 64, 437
Probe einer neuen Art deutscher Lettern: Unger, 323
Processional, 218
Procter, Robert, 45, 49
Prodromus, –, 143
Proef van Letteren, 349 (Fig 75)
Prognosticon dialogale: Manilio, 436
Programme music, 211
Prolusions: Capell, 342
Promenade de Saint-Germain, La: Le Laboureur, 295
Promptuarum latinae linguae, 198
Propaganda Fide Press, 328
Propertius, 125, 151, 344
Proportions des caracteres de l'Imprimerie: Fournier, 317
Proprietatibus rerum, De: Anglicanus, 101
Proseuticum ad divum Fridericum III: Celtes, 144 (Fig 28)
Prostějov, 237
Prostejovsky, Kaspar see Nedele, Kaspar
Protestant hymn book, 210
Protomathesis: Vascosan, 165
Prout, 375
Proverbios y Sentencieas: de Mendoza, 187
Proverbs of Solomon (Hebrew), 439
Provinciale Romanum, 16
Prünlein, Matthias, 235, 236 (Fig 52)
Prüss, Johann, 24
Psalms, 216
Psalms, Sonets and songs of sadness and pietie: Byrd, 217
Psalters, 115, 247 see also Latin psalters etc.
Psalter type, 117–18
Psalterium B.M.V.: Nitzschowitz, 446
Psalterium Bohemicum, 233, 442
Psaumes: Marot, 215
Ptolomy, 34, 38, 56
Ptolomy type, 34
Pubblica Stamperia delle Isole Ionie liberate, 310
Püchlin wie Rom gepaut war, 140
Puerilium Colloquiorum: Heyden, 248

Puerto, Alfonso del, 79–80, 81, 444
Pulci, Luigi, 48
Purcell, Henry, 288
Purging Calendar, 18
Putanic, Valentin, 244
Putelletto, Antonio, 154
Puys, Jacques du, 175
Pynson, Richard: 71
    Canterbury Tales, 103 (Fig 19)
    Dives and Pauper, 102 (Fig 18), 116 (Fig 29)
    Fall of Princes, 104 (Fig 20)
    Mandeville's Travels, 101
    Oratio, 113 (Fig 27)

Q

Qimhi, David, 438
Quadragesimale: Caracciolus, 87
Quadragesimale: Meder, 89
Quadragesimale: Warn, 140
Quadrins historiques de la Bible, 169
Quaestiones Alberti de modis significandi, 104
Quaestiones super Aristotelis: Andreae, 99, 440
Quaestionibus Orosii, De: St Augustine, 440
Quantin, Albert, 405
Quatre derrenieres choses, Les, 74
Queen Elizabeth's Prayer Book, 391 see also Book of Christian Prayers
Quentel, Heinrich, 27, 129
Quentel, Peter, 128, 129
Quentel see also Birckmann and Quentel
Question de amor, 191
Quijoue, Gilles, 436
Quintilian, 165
Quire signatures, 99

R

RCA system, 429
R-printer, the, 24
Rabelais, François, 123, 167
Rabinnic Bible, 205
Racine, Jean, 293, 296, 313, 398
Radeau de la Meduse, Le: Géricault, 399
Rademaker, Jan, 121
Radishevskii, Anisim Mikhailov, 252
Raeff, Canon Paul, 226
Raffet, –, 403
Raillard, Giacomo, 301
Raimondi, Giovanni Battista (Giambattista), 154, 177
Raison d'architecture antique: Vitruvius, 162

Raj duszny, 248
Ramage, Adam, 359
Rampazetto, –, 245
Raphelenghian office, 203
Raphelenghien, François, 200
Rasch, Johann, 133
Rastell, John, 105 (Fig 21), 216
Ratdolt, Erhardt:
  Germany, 29–30, 235; Italy, 41, 42 (Fig 5), 43
  (Fig 6), 115, 239
Rathbone, Mrs Richard, 391
Ratio Presse, 411
Rationale divinorum officiorum: Duranti, 19
Rauber, Die: Schiller, 324
Rauchfas, Johannes, 41, 43
Ravenstein, Albert, 36
Ravesteyns, the van, 283
Raynalde, Thomas, 260
Re metallica, De: Agricola, 181
Re Militari, De: Valturus, 57, 445
Real Bibliotica, Madrid, 333
Reale Stamperia, La, Parma, 329 (Fig 72)
Réaumur, René Antoine, 368
Recopilacion . . . intitulada Orthographia practica:
  de Yciar, 188
Record, Robert, 255 (Fig 53)
Recta Paschae celebratione, De: de Middelburgo,
  152 (Fig 39)
Recuyell of the Historyes of Troye: Le Fèvre, 74,
  407, 436
Redman, –, 257
Reed, Charles, 287, 338, 344, 346, 347, 407
Reflections upon Learning, Ancient and Modern:
  Wotton, 172
Réformation de l'Imprimerie, Sur la: Charles IX
  (Edict), 165
Reforme de la typographie royale: Jammes, 298n.
Reger, Johann, 33, 134
Regimen wider die Pestilenz: Steinhöwel, 33
Regimen sanitatis cum tractatu epidemiae, 435
Regimine principum, De: Columna, 81, 83
Regiomontanus, Johannes, 115 *see also* Müller,
  Johann
Registrum see Indexes
Regle des marchands, La: Friburgenses, 442
Regnault, François, 160, 257
Regulae cancellariae apostolicae: Paul II, 112
Regulae Grammaticales: Veronesnis, 442, 444
Regulus mandatorum, De: Gerson, 440, 442
Reichenbach, Charles, 386

Reichenbach, Fritz, 363, 365
Reichenthal, Ulrich von, 29
Reichsdruckerei, 418
Reiglement des advocats, 173
Reimer, Georg, 323
Reine de Portugal, La: Didot, 400
Reineke Fuchs, 97
Reiner, Imre, 421
Reinhard, Marcus, 62, 439
Reinhard (i), Johann *see* Reynhard, Johann
Reisch, Gregorius, 210
Reise in das gelobte Land: Tucher, 29
Reise ins heilige Land: Breydenbach, 29
Reisenhandbuch für den Rhein, 386
Reismoller, Peter, 245
Rej, Mikoloj, 249
Relation: aller Fürnemen und gedenkwürdigen
  Historien, 275
Relationes historicae, 128
Religione, De: Isaac, 443
Rembolt, Berthold, 61
Rembrandt Intaglio Printing Company, 382, 383
Remediis utriusque fortunae, De: Carthusiensis, 112
Remondini, Giovanni Antonio, 326
Remondini, Giovanni Battista, 326
Remondinis, the, 328
Remunde, Cristoffel van, 214
Renaissance Europe: Hale, 135
Renaissance types, 138
Renan, Ernst, 405
Renard, –, 404
Renaudot, Eusèbe, 296
Renaudot, Isaac, 296
Renaudot, Théophraste, 296
Renchen, Ludwig, 110 (Fig 24)
Renner, Paul, 421
Rennes, 72
Renouard, A., 369
Renouard, Ph., 175 and n., 211, 213n., 337
Repertorium quaestionum super Nicolaeum de Tude-
  schis: Montalvo, 80, 444
Repetitio rubricae: Barbatia, 62, 444
Représentans Représentés, Les, 404
Repubblica dei Veneziani: Giannotti, 148
Republicas del Mundo: Roman, 188
Rerum Musicarum: Frosch, 210
Rerum Venetarum Decades IV, 45
Resolutorium dubiorum: de Lapide, 442
Retza, Franciscus de, 30, 441
Reuchlin, Johann, 89, 91, 131, 210–11

Reutlingen, 34
Revenel, Sébastien, 395
Revolutionskalender, 325
Reynard the Fox, 97, 227 (Fig 50)
Reynhard (Reinhardi), Johann, 53, 444
Reyser, Georg, 437, 446
Reyser, Michael, 437
Rhau, Georg, 210
Rhau, Johann, 129
Rheims, 166
Rhetorica divina: Guillermus, 438
Rhetorica Nova: Cicero, 435
Rhetorica Nova: de Savona, 102
Rhodes, Dr D. R., 154 and n.
Rhymed Psalms, 214
Ricerchari, Motetti e Canzoni: Cavazzoni, 209
Richard, –, 428
Richel, Bernhard, 70, 87–8, 89, 107, 111
Richelieu, Cardinal Armand Jean, 123, 291, 292, 299, 300, 406
Richini, Giuseppi, 327
Richolff, Georg the Elder, 137, 224
Richolff, Georg II (Jurgen), 137, 138, 224–5, 227 (Fig 50)
Ricketts, Charles, 409, 410
Riessinger, Sixtus, 39, 112, 441
Riffe, Hans, 8
Rigaud, Benoît (Benoist), 167, 172
Rigaud, Claude, 172, 321
Rigaud, Pierre, 172
Rigaud, Simon, 172
Rijeka, 245
Rime: Petrarch, 150
Ringhieri, Innocenzio, 175 (Fig 43)
Rink, Hinrich, 393, 394 (Fig 84)
Ripariae Benacensis: Statuta commun.
Ripoli Press, 47–8
Rise of the Dutch Republic: Motley, 195–6
Ritter romane, 134
Ritter von Thurn, Der: Landry, 89
Ritzch, Gregor, 276
Ritzch, Timotheus, 275, 276
Rivers, Anthony Woodville, Earl, 94
Riverside Press, 44
Rivery, Abel, 183
Rivière, Jeanne, later Plantin, 197
Robert and Andrew Foulis and the Glasgow Press: Murray, 337n.
Robert IV, Duc de Buillon, 297n.
Robert, Nicola Louis, 368

Robertis, Domenico de, 192
Roberts, James, 266 (Fig 60), 267 (Fig 61)
Robertson, J. G., 277 and n.
Robi, Francesco, 150
Robles, Francisco de, 302
Roca, Lope de la, 83
Rocappi Ltd., 430
Rochefort, –, 315
Rochefoucauld, La, 400
Roches de Parthenay, J. B. Des, 352
Rocho and Da Valle Brothers, 153
Rockner, Vincenz, 134
Rococciola, Antonio, 56
Rococciola, Domenico, 56
Rodriguez, Jorge, 303
Roffinello, Venturino, 14
Rogers, Bruce, 44, 288
Rogers, John, 257
Rohault, Pierre, 435
Röhling, Fr, 386
Rollet, Philibert, 167
Rollet, Philippe, 171
Rolewinck, Werner, 27, 74, 81, 88, 443
'Romains du roi' type, 315, 316
Roman Catholic English New Testament, 166
Roman Curia, 40
Roman, Hieronymus, 188
Roman, Jan and Company, 350
Roman notation, 208
Roman de la Rose, 70
Roman type:
   Denmark, 226; England, 113 (Fig 27), 291; France, 126, 159, 316; Germany, 24, 28, 129, 133, 323; Italy, 22, 37, 38, 44, 109; Sweden, 225; *see also* named types
Romanian Gospels, 242
Romano, Diáz, 218
Romano, Francisco Diáz, 189, 192
Rome, 37–40, 302, 326–7
Roncaglioli, Secondino, 301
Rood, Theodoric (Theodor), 28, 96 (Fig 15), 97, 99, 441
Roos, Sjoerd Hendrik de', 412
Rooses, Max, 122
Rops, Felicien, 405
Rosarium mysticum, 195
Rosart, Jacques, 349 (Fig 75)
Rosenbach, Johann (Hans), 83, 84, 191, 442
Roskilde, 226
Rossbach, A., 385

Rossi, Lorenzo de', 55
Rossignol, –, 319
Rosso, Albertino, 46
Rost-Fingerlin *see* Dresler and Rost-Fingerlin
Rostock, 138
Rot, Sigmund, 96, 446
Rotary intaglio *see* photogravure
Rotary newspaper presses, 363, 365 *see also* Newspaper printing
Rotary presses, 362 *see also* Cylinder press
Rotelli, Lautizio di Bartolomeo dei, 155 (Fig 41)
Rothovius, Isak, 229
Rotili, Angelo, 328
Rotolitho machine, 375
Rottweil, Adam von, 345
Rotunda type, 41, 138, 233
Rouen, 71–2
Rouillé (Roville), Guillaume de, 126, 167, 170–1
Round-headed music notes, 211
Roussin, Jean-Jacques, 324
Roussin, Etienne, 171
Roussin, Jacques, 167
Roussin, Pierre, 167
Routledge, Thomas, 368
Rowland, Robert, 391
Rowohlt, Ernst, 419
Roxburghe Club, 347
Royal Antiphoner, 215
Royal Greek type, 174, 175n. *see also* Grecs du Roi type
Royal Printing House, Sweden, 224
Royal Society, The, 274
Roycroft, Thomas, 288
Royen, Jean François van, 412
Roydalovsky, Jiří Cerny, 234 *see also* Melantrich, Jiří
Ruano, Ferdinando, 157
Rubel, Ira W., 375
Rubens, Jacobus, 442
Rubeis, Laurentius de *see* Rossi, Lorenzo de'
Rubeis, Jacobeus, 407 *see also* Le Rouge, Jacques
Rubió, Prof. Jordi, 79
Rubricators, 114
Rudhard foundry, 418
Rudhardsche Giesserei, 422–3
Rudimenta grammaticae: Perottus, 38, 443, 444
Rudimentum Novitiorum, 65, 440
Rudimentum Syriacum, 302
Ruel, Jean, 162
Rufindus, –, 99

Rugerius, Ugo, 50, 51, 328, 443
Rumel, Heinrich, 30
Runa A. B. C. Boken: Bureus, 225
Runic types, 225
Rupe, Alanus de, 438
Ruppel, Dr Aloys, 15, 20
Ruppel, Berthold (Berchtold), 11, 87, 88, 91, 435
Rupprecht presse, 411
Ruremond, Christopher, 254
Ruremonde, Hans van, 196
Rusch, Adolf, 24, 89
Russe Common Wealth: Hakluyt Society, 251n.
Russian Gospels, 252
Ruyne des nobles hommes et femmes, De la: Boccaccio, 75
Ryff, Walther Hermann, 132 (Fig 33)
Rymann, Johann, 12
Rymann, Hans, 126

S

S.P.C.K., 339, 397 (Fig 85)
Sabbio, Stephano de, 156
Sabbio, Stefano Nicolini da, 154
Sabellico, –, 45
Sabon, Jacques (Jacob), 131, 132, 133, 173, 174
Sachsenspiegel, 88
Sachs, Hans, 133
Sacrae canziones, 215
Sacramental: de Vercial, 81
Sacrobusto, Johann de, 248
Sadeler, Jan, 216
Sadolet, Bishop of Carpentras, 167
Said Effendi, 308, 309
Sainliens, Claude de, 264
St Albans, 101–2, 104
St Albans Press, 101–2
St Ambrose, 98
St Augustine:
    Anima et Spiritu, 439
    De civitate Dei, 37, 40, 64, 89, 90 (Fig 13)
    Opera, 122, 180, 246
St-Augustine type, 164
St Bernard, 76 (Fig 10) 195
St Bonaventure, 83, 158, 195, 435, 441
St Jerome, 20, 38, 39, 117 *see also Life of St Jerome*
St John Chrysostom, 91, 263, 287
St Paul, 147
St Petersburg, 354
St Petersburg Academy News, 354

St Petersburger Zeitung, 354
St Scholastica Monastery, 37
St Thomas Aquinas *see* Aquinas, Thomas
Saint-Pierre, Bernardin de, 400, 403
Saint-Quentin, –, 314n.
Saint-Sorlin, Desmarets de, 294
Salado, Ottaviano, 54
Salamanca, 82, 192
Salamon, Octaviano, 437
Salesbury, William, 264
Saliceto, Gulielmus de, 73
Salis, Baptista de, 441
Sallo, Denis de, 273, 296
Sallust, 125, 332, 344, 371, 372
Salmon, –, 213
Salomo, Ibn-Alkabez, 438
Salomon, Antoinette, later Granjon, 175
Salomon, Bernard, 169
Salomon, Josua, 436
Salsburga, Johannes (Juan) de, 79, 84
Salsfort, G. Schleifheim von *see* Grimmelshausen
   H. J. C.
Salutari, Coluccio, 109
Salute corporis, De: de Salicato, 73
Samariton type, 288
Sambiz, Jean *see* Elseviers, the
Sambonettus, Petrus, 209
San Pedro, Diego de, 81
Sancha, Antonio de, 312, 332
Sancha, Gabriel, 332, 333
Sancto Caro, Hugo de, 436
Sancto Georgio, Joh. Ant. de, 437
Sancto Nazario, Jacobus, 445
Sancto Remigio, R. de, 29
Sander, Louis, 386
Sanlecque, Jacques de, 213, 298, 300
Sanlecque, Jacques II de, 300
Sanlecque, Jean de, 300
Sanlecque, Jean-Eustache de, 300
Sanlecque type, 300
Sant, John, Bishop of Abingdon, 446
Sanz, Lupus, 82
Saragossa, 78, 79, 188
Sarum Book of Hours, 69 (Fig 9), 70, 105
Sarum Manual and Processional, 214
Sarum Missal, 101, 105
Sarum Ordinale, 95
Sárvás-Újsziget, 240
Saskia italic type, 240
Saspach, Konrad, 9

Sassi, –, 52n.
Sattler, Joseph, 418
Satyrae: Persius, 443
Satyre Menuppee, 166
Säublicher, Otto, 387
Saussure, Cesar, Comte de, 308, 309
Sautelet, *see* Motte and Sautelet
Sautroiber, Wilhelmum, 116
Savage, William, 389
Savile, Sir Henry, 287
Savoie, Bishop Jean de, 92
Savona, Laurentius de, 102
Savonarola, Girolamo, 48
Savary de Brèves types, 300
Savry, Jacob, 303
Saxoferrato, Bartholus de, 53, 441, 445
Saxonia, Henricus de *see* Botel Heinrich
Saxonia, Ludolphus de, 85 (Fig 12), 187, 195
Saxonia, Nicolau de, 85 (Fig 12), 86
Saxony, George, Elector (Duke) of, 130
Scala Paradisi: Climachus, 444
Scenica progymnasmata: Reuchlin, 91, 210–11
Scève, Guillaume, 167
Scève, Maurice, 167
Schäffer, Jacob-Christian, 325
Schall, Jean Frédéric, 315
Scharffenberg, Crispin, 137, 248
Scharffenberg, Johann, 137, 248
Scharffenberg Marcus, 247
Scharffenberg, Matthäus, 248
Schatzbehalter: Fridoling, 31
Schäufelein, Hans, 134
Schaumberg, Georg von, Prince Bishop of
   Bamberg, 25
Schaur, Johann (Hans), 140, 441
Schauspieler, Der: Martersteig, 417
Schedel, Hartmann, 23, 31, 117
Scheffer, –, 428
Schelter and Giesecke, 420
Schenck, Peter *see* Ortuin, Gaspard Peter
   Schenck
Scherf, Balthasar, 278
Scherzi geniali: Loredano, 334
Schiavonetti, Luigi, 326
Schiavonetti, Nicoló, 326
Schiavonetti brothers, the, 328
Schilditz, Hermann von, 445
Schiller, Georg, 418
Schiller, Johann Christoph von, 322, 324
Schilling, Frederic, 246, 247

Schilling, Johann (Hans) 28, 445

Schindeleyp, Hermann, 142

Schlegel, August Wilhelm, 323

Schleinitz, H. von, 118 (Fig 31)

Schlick, Arnold, 210

Schlitte, Hans, 250

Schmidt, J. A., 277

Schneidler, Ernst, 412

Schneidler mediaeval type, 412

Schobser, Andreas, 140

Schobser, Hans, 140

Schöffer Christina, formerly Fust, 20

Schöffer, Gratian, 20, 127

Schöffer, Peter I: 19, 21, 23, 24, 107, 376
  Biblia Latina, 440
  Frankfurt Fair, 220
  Letters of St Jerome, 117 and n.
  Mainz Psalter, 18, 127
  Mammotrectus super Bibliam, 91
  Paris, 60–1
  Tyndale's New Testament, 256
  see also Fust and Schöffer

Schöffer, Peter, junior, 20, 107n., 127, 129, 179, 210

Scholderer, Dr Victor, 9, 17, 39, 45, 54, 92

Scholemaster: Ascham, 261

Scholtz, Kristofer, 238

Schön, Erhard, 138, 251

Schonsperger, Hans the Elder, 29, 133–4, 135 (Fig 34), 136

Schonsperger, Hans the Younger, 136

Schoolmaster printer, 443

Schorbach, K., 8n.

Schott, Johann, 210

Schott, Martin, 24

Schradin, –, 444

Schreyer, Sebald, 31

Schriftgiesserei Gebrüder Klingspor, 423

Schröder, Julius, 419

Schrotbanck, Hans, 439

Schrötter, F. W., 386

Schuchers, J. W., 379

Schultz Press, 353

Schüttwa, Johannes von, 25

Schwabacher type:
  Czechoslovakia, 234, 235; Denmark, 228; Germany, 28, 33, 114 (Fig 28) 138; Iceland, 230; Poland, 249; Sweden, 224–5

Schwabischer Chronik, 34

Schwartz, Hayyim ben David, 204

Schweizer Bibliophilen Gesellschaft, 92

Schweizer Chronik: Stumpff, 358

Scinzenzeler, Johannes Angelus, 53

Scinzenzeler, Ulrich, 53

Scio, Fr Felipe, 333

Scipio Romanus: Lucian, 435

Scolar, John, 99

Scot, Reynold, 264

Scotto, Amadeo, 47

Scotto, Bernardino, 47

Scotto, Giovanni Battista, 47

Scotto, Ottaviano, 44, 46–7

Scotto, Ottaviano junior, 47

Scotto, Paolo, 47

Scougal, Henry, 371

Scribe, –, *see* Guyot and Scribe

Script type, 202, 298, 319

Scriptor, Paulus, 445

Scriptores Rerum Italicarum: Muratori, 327

Scrittor' Utile: Hercolani, 157

Scudery, –, 295

Sculptura: Evelyn, 295

Seagrave, Joseph, 388

Seasons: Thomson, 347

Second Trophee de Musique, 177

Secretary type, 264

Secunda pars operum Baptistae Mantuani, 160

Sedan, Henri Robert Prince of, 297 and n.

Seguier, Chancellor –, 292

Segura, Bartolome (Bartolomeus), 79, 444

Seiz, Juan Cristiano, 78

Selden, John, 339

Selden type, 339

Selected Poems: Thomas, 430

Selenographia: Hevelius, 249

Selenus, Gustavus, 278

Selim, Sultan of Turkey, 347

Semi-gothic type *see* Subiaco type

Seneca, 71

Senefelder, Aloys, 373–5

Senensis, Bernardinus, 442

Senfli, Ludwig, 210

Sensenschmidt, Johann:
  Comestorium, 20, 30, 441
  Missals, 26, 437, 438, 443

Sensenschmidt, Laurentius, 26

September Testament, 130

Septimia Poenalis, 5

Sequester, Vibius, 150

Serban, Deacon, 243

Serenuis, Jacob, 353
Seres, William, 260
Serepando, Cardinal, –, 153
Serlio, –, 149
Sermisy, –, 211
Sermo de umana miseria, 436
Sermo ad populum predicabilis, 27
Sermones: Caracciolus, 441
Sermones: de Petra, 441
Sermones: de Prato Florido, 439
Sermones: St Bernard, 76 (Fig 10)
Servetus, Michael, 172
Servius, 438, 445
Sette Alphabeti: Ruano, 157
Seuse, –, 136
Severyn, Jan, 233, 234
Severyn, Jan the Younger, 235
Severýn, Pavel, 234
Seville, 79–81, 185, 192
Sfera, La: Dati, 49
Sforza, Duke Galeazzo Maria, 51
Shakespeare, William, 153, 265 (Fig 59), 294
   (Fig 68), 323, 411
Shakespeare Printing Office, 345–46
Sheppard, L. A., 74 and n.
Shoppe, C. G., 323
Short, Peter, 218
Shuckburgh, Evelyn, 188
Shuckburgh-Scribner, 17
Sibiu, 239, 241
Sibiu Catechism, 242, 243
Sibyllenbuch, 15
Sidney, Sir Philip, 266 (Fig 60)
Sidriano, Giovanni (Joannes) de, 52, 56, 442
Siebenbäumen, Martin von, 58
Siena, 55–6
Sieur d'Hedouville *see* Sallo, Denis de
Signoretti and Nesti, 301
Silber, Eucharius, 39–40
Silber, Marcello, 148, 157
Silva, Francesco de, 55
Silvertype, 412
Silvius, Willem, 177, 197, 200
Simons, Anna, 411
Simonneau, Louis, 315
Simplicissionus, 417
Simulachres et historiees faces de la mort, Les, 171–2
Singriener, Hans, 141
Singriener, Johann II, 141
Singriener, Matthaeus, 141

Singularia Juris: Pontanus, 73
Šintava, 237
Sionita, Gabriel, 299, 300
Sister Beatrice: Maeterlinck, 417
Sistine Bible, 158
Sittich, Hans, 6
VI Codices, Super: de Castro, 444
Six sonatas for two violins and bass: Utti, 353
*Sixteenth century printing types of the Low
   Countries:* Vervliet, 202n.
Sixtus LV, Pope, 38, 92, 94
Sixtus V, Pope, 157, 158, 328
Skarya's Prayer Book: Nadson, 234
Skorina, Franciska, 234, 235
Skrzetuski, Raphael *see* Hoffhalter, Raphael
Slavonic Bible, 252
Slavonic Prayer Book, 243
Smiles, Samuel, 387
Smith, Samuel, 274, 347
Smyrna, 310
Snell, Johann, 224, 226, 441, 444
Sobol, Spiridon, 253
Società Albrizziana, 326
Società Palati, 327
Societas Graecarum Editonum, 298
Societas Typographica officirum
   Ecclesiasticorum, 299
Societé Alsacienne de Constructions Mécaniques,
   382
Societé Géographique, 32
Societé Littéraire Typographique, 344
Societé des Vingt, 416
Society for the Diffusion of Useful Knowledge,
   356, 389
Söderköping, 225
Söhne, Julius Adolph von, 275
Soleil, Le, 299
Solidi, Johannes *see* Schilling, Johannes
Soliloquia animae: Augustinus, 233, 446
Solis, Antonio de, 303, 304, 333
Solis, Virgil, 133, 258
Somerville, William, 345
Somme rurale, La: Boutellier, 435
Soncino, Eleazar, 204
Soncino, Gershon, 204
Soncino, Girolamo, 153
Soncino, Israel Nathan, 204
Soncino, Joshua, 204
Soncino, Josua Salomon, 444
Song of Solomon, 411

Songes and Sonettes, written by the. . . . Earle of Surrey, and other, 260
Sonnatas of III parts: Purcel, 288
Sonnius, Michel, 298
Sophologium: Magni, 60
Sophonisba: Trissino, 156
Sorbonne Press, 60 and n., 61
Sorg, Anton, 14, 29, 140
Soter, Johann, 128, 129, 256
Soto, Perez de, 331
Souter Liedekens, 214
Southend Standard, 382
Southward, J., 379
Spamer, Franz Otto, 386–7
Spamer Bindery, 387
Spamersche Buchdruckerei, 387
Specimen, Delacolange foundry, 317 (Fig 71)
Specimen book, Führmann, 275
Specimen sheets, Luce, 316
Specimens of Polyautography, 374
Speculum Conversionis peccatorum: Carthusiensis, 73
Speculum ecclesiae: de Sancto Caro, 436
Speculum Humanae Salvationis, 5, 73, 74, 88, 445
Speculum Sacerdotum: von Schilditz, 445
Speculum vitae humanae: Zamorensis (Zamora), 61, 89
Spehr, Johann Peter, 384
Spengel, Theobald, 128
Speyer, Johann von, 445 *see also* Spira Johannes de
Spiegel menschlicher Behältnis, 88
Spiess, Wygand, 21
Spinaccino, Francesco, 208
Spindeler, Nicolaus, 84, 444
Spira, Johannes de, 40 *see also* Speyer, Johann von
Spira, Wendelin de, 40, 41, 118
Spoleto, Jacobus of Theramo, Bishop of *see* Theramo, Jacobus de
Sporer, Hans, 26
Spread of Printing: Iceland: Benedikz, 231
Springinklee, Hans, 136, 138
Squires, Henry, 101
Stabius, Hans, 136
Stadtbuchdruckerei, Breslau, 137
Stagnino, Bernardino, 150, 151
Stahel, Conrad, 235 (Fig 52), 236, 436, 442
Stainhofer, Kaspar, 142
Stamp Duty, 338
Stamperia Gran' Ducale, 301, 327

Stamperia Medicea, 154, 177
Stamperia del Popolo Romano, 154
Stamperia Reale, 327
Stamperia Valdònega, 413, 414
Stamperia Vaticana, 177
Standard, Paul, 424
'Standard' type, 424
Ständebuch, Das: Sachs, 14, 133
Stanhope, Philip Henry, Earl of, 310, 371
Stanhope's press, 355, 359, 362, 402
Stansby, William, 286 (Fig 66)
Stapfer, Albert, 402
Star Chamber decree, 288
Statboen, Hermann, 60
States-General, 199–200
Stationers' Company, 121, 269–70, 289, 335
Statius, –, 54
Statuta Communis Brixiae, 56, 442
Statuta provinciala Arnesti, 233, 442
Statuta Synodalia, 236
Statuta Synodalia Eystettensia, 437
Statuta Synodalia Vratislava, 248, 436
Statutes, Laws and Constitutions of the Polish Kingdom, 249
Statuum utraquistorum articuli, 233
Stazionari libraries, Bologna, 50
Steam presses, 356, 365, 388, 389
Steels, Jan, 193, 197
Stege, Erwin von, 443
Steglitzer Werkstatt, 417
Steinberg, Dr S. H., 10 and n., 322
Steindruckerei, 373
Steinheil, –, 403
Steinhöwell, H., 33, 445
Steinschaber, Adam, 91–2, 438
Stempel, A. G., 387, 421
Stempel, D., 421
Stencils, 29
Stephanus, Henricus *see* Estienne, Henri
Stephen III of Moldavia, 242–3
Stephenson, Blake and Company, 340
Stereotype, 351, 369–73, 385, 400, 427
Stereotyped Bible, 369
Stern, Heinrich, 278
Stern, Johann, 278
Sternhold, –, 216
Stevenson, Dr Allan, 5
Stillwell, Margaret B., 273, 296
Stimmer, Tobias, 184
Stipple engraving, 315

Stöckel, Wolfgang, 115, 129–31
Stockholm, 224, 225
Stoer, Jacon, 183
Stoll, Johann, 61
Stols, A. A. M., 412
Story of the Glittering Plain: Morris, 407, 409
    (Fig 87)
Stothard, Thomas, 374
Stoupe, –, 320
Strassburg, 7–8, 21, 23–4, 275
Strassburg Documents, 8
Straube, Kaspar, 246, 439
Streater, Joseph, 274
Strixner, Johann, 374
Struzzi, Baltassare, 56
Stuchs, Georg, 33, 246
Stultifera navis: Brant, 91
Stumpf, Hans, 181, 358
Sturm und Drang: Klinger, 324
Subiaco, 22, 37
Subiaco type, 22, 37, 38, 111
Suetonius, 125, 170
Suhl press, 360
Suigus, Jacobinus (Suigo, Jacopo), 55, 436, 443,
    445
Summa: Aquinas, 21, 88
Summa angelica de casibus conscientiae: Carletti,
    436
Summa Astexana, 221
Summa de Casibus: de Ast, 116
Summa casuum conscientiae: de Salis 441
Summa confessorum, 28
Summa de ecclesia contra impugnatores. ·. . . 40
Summa quaestionum: de Corneto, 445
Summulae logicales: Hispanus, 76
Super Royal genuine Albion Press, 407
Suppl. Summae Pisanellae: de Ausmo, 445
Suriá y Burgada, Francisco, 332
Surrey, Earl of, 260
Survey of Printing, 391
Susanneau, Hubert, 167
Susato, Tielman, 214
Sütterlin, Ludwig, 387, 421
'Svenski' *see* Matthiasson, Jón
Swan, Joseph Wilson, 382
Swash capitals, 156
Swedish New Testament, 224
Sweynheim, Conrad *see* Pannartz, Arnold and
    Sweynheim
Swinney, Myles, 342

Swiss Chronicle: Stumpf, 181
Syber, Jean, 70
Sylvester *see* Erdösi, János
Sylvius (Silvius), Aeneas, 23, 31, 63, 73, 224, 435
Sylvius, Jacques, 164
Sylvius type, 164
Symeoni, Gabriele, 169
Symmen, Henric van, 77, 200
Symonel, Louis, 61
Symphonia Angelica: Waelrant, 215
Synodal Constitutions of Pamplona, 82
Synodal de Segovia, 444
Syracuse University Press, 400n.
Syriac Catechism, 177
Syriac type, 142, 177, 288, 299, 302
Szás fabula: Heltai, 240
Szászváros, 240
Szeben *see* Sibiu
Szyling *see* Schilling, Frederic

T

Table, La: Cebes, 161 (Fig 42)
Table of Town name variation in Central
    Europe, 232
Tabulaturbuch: Ochsenkuhn, 210
*Tabulaturen etlicher Lobgesang, und Liedlein auf die
    Orgel und Lauten:* Schlick, 210
Tacitus, 125
Tagliente, Giovantonio, 155, 156, 157
Talavera, Fernando, Archbishop of Granada, 85
Tallis, Thomas, 216
Talmud, the, 205
Talmud-Comment (Hebrew), 444
Tanner, Lawrence, 94
Tarasiev, Nikifor, 252
Tardif, Guillaume, 61
Tarikhi Seiah: Ibrahim, 309
Tarague, Gabriel, 172
Tarragona, 78
Tartagnus, Alexander, 51, 445
Taschenbuch für Frauenzimmer von Bildung: 324
Tasso, Torquato, 150, 187, 326, 396
Tate, John, 101
Tauchnitz, Christian Bernhard, 385
Tauchnitz Collection, 385
Tauchnitz foundry, 387
Tauchnitz, Karl, 421
Tauchnitz, Karl Christian Philipp, 385
Tauchnitz, Karl Christian Traugott, 384–5
Tauler, –, 136

Index

Tavernier, Ameet, 197, 202
Tavernier, Guillaume, 442
Taylor, Baron, 402
Taylor, Philippe, 365
Taylor, Richard, 360, 362
Teape, Henry, 388
Teatro de las grandezas de Madrid: de Avila, 303
Technik Gutenbergs und ihr vorstufen, Die: Rupell, 20
Tedesco, Nicoló *see* Lorenzo, Nicoló di
Telegdi, Nikolaus (Miklós), 142, 241
Tellez, Antonio, 81
Temple: Herbert, 391
Temptations Vitae, 6
Tenores Novelli, 99
Terence, –, 62, 63 (Fig 7), 125, 344
Testimonie of Antiquitie, 260
Teubner, Benediktus Gotthelf, 385
Teuerdank, Der, 29, 134, 135 (Fig 34), 136
Text Hand, 263 (Fig 58)
Texto type, 333
Textura type, 28, 108 (Fig 22), 109, 138, 224
Textus ethicorum Aristoteles: Rood, 96 (Fig 15)
Textus Summularum: Hispanus, 73
Textus Summularum Petri Hispani, 115
Thanner, Jacobus, 36
Théâtre d'honneur: de la Colombière, 293
Theatrum Europaeum: Merian, 272, 279
Theocritus, 53, 143, 400
Theologica Germanica, 136
Theoricum opus: Gafurius, 207
Theramo, Jacobus de, 26, 74, 440
Thesaurus linguae graecae, 183
Thesaurus linguarum orientalium, 278
Thesaurus theutonicae linguae, 198
Thevoz, F., 383
Thibaudeau, F., 399, 405
Thiele Press, 353
Thierry, D., 296
36-line Bible, 15, 17–18, 435
Thomas, Dylan, 430
Thomas, H., 70
Thomas Wallensis Expositiones super Psalterium, 99
Thomason, George, 289
Thomason Tracts, 289
Thomesen, Hans, 228
Thompson, Charles, 400
Thomson, James, 347
Thorláksson, Gudbrandur, Bishop of Hólar, 230
Thorne, J., 378

Thorne, Robert, 341
Thorne typesetting and distributing machine, 378
Thurah, Laurids de, 353
Thurneysser, Leonhard, 137
Thwrocz, Johannes de, 30, 235–6 (Fig 52)
Tibullus, 125, 151, 344
Tidemansson, Torbjörn, 225
Tiemann, Walter, 410, 419, 423
Timann, Volkmar, 301
Tilloch, Alexander, 371
Tillot, –, 328
Times, The, 359, 361–3, 370 (Fig 80), 377, 378
Timperley, C. H., 347
Tinódi, –, 240
Tipografia Camerale *see* Vatican Press
Tipografia Volpi-Cominiani, 327
Tipographia Vaticana, 158 *see also* Vatican Press
Tirant lo Blanch: Martorell, 84
Tirgoviste, 242, 243
Tischnowitz, Martin von (Tišňova, Martinz), 234, 439
Title-page borders, 115, 138, 140 *see also* Woodcuts, 115, 138, 140
Title-pages: 113–15
  Denmark, 227
  England:
    16th C. 259 (Fig 55), 261 (Fig 56), 265 (Fig 59), 266 (Fig 60), 267 (Fig 61), 268 (Fig 62)
    17th C. 282 (Fig 64), 284 (Fig 65), 294 (Fig 68)
    18th C. 312
  France, 169, 176 (Fig 43), 314
  Germany, 34, 35 (Fig 4), 312, 325, 419
  Greenland woodcuts, 394 (Fig 84)
  Holland, 349 (Fig 75)
  Iceland, 230 (Fig 51)
  Italy, 42 and n. (Fig 5), 155 (Fig 40)
  Malta, 306 (Fig 70)
  Russia, 252
  Spain, 187, 190 (Fig 45), 191, 192, 193 (Fig 46)
  Switzerland, 179
Titonius, Petrus, 209
Tobias, 237
Toledo, 81–2, 191
Tomich, Fr., 191
Tomkins, P. W., 347
Tondalus visioen, 439
Tonson, Jacob and Richard, 343
Topographia: Merian, 272

519

Tornieri, Giacomo, 158
Torquemada *see* Turrecremata
Torre, Alfonso de la, 71
Torrentino, Laurentio, 151
Torres, Fray Caro de, 303
Torresano, Andrea, 45, 143, 147, 209, 244
Torresano, Maria, later Manuzio, 147
Torstenson, Anders, 225
Torti, Battista, 47
Torti, Silvester, 47
Tortosa, 78
Torún, 248
Tory, Geoffrey, 126, 161 (Fig 42), 162–3, 169–70, 315
Tottel, Richard, 260, 264
Tottel's Miscellany: Surrey and Wyatt, 260
Toulouse, 62–3
Toulouse-Lautrec, Henri de, 375
Tourneaure letter, 163
Tournes, Jacques de, 170
Tournes, Jean de, 167, 169–70, 171, 175
Tournes, Jean II de, 169, 170
Tournes, Jean-Jacques de, 170
Tournes, Nicole de, later Gazeau, 169
Tournes's, the, 291
Tournon, Cardinal de, 171
Townshend, –, 348
Toy, Humphrey, 264
Trabouillet, P., 296
Tractatus appellationum: de Sancto Georgio, 437
Tractatus contra Cremonensia: Müller, 32
Tractatus malificiorum: Gambilionibus, 440
Tractatus Politicus: Spinoza, 412
Tractatus rationis, 20–1
Tractatus restitutionum, 246
Tragedie of Sir Richard Grinvile: Markham, 267 (Fig 61)
Tragicomedia de Calisto y Melibea, 192
Traité d'Arras, 438
Traité de l'imprimerie musicale: Fournier, 211
Traité contre la peste. . . . . , 172
Transitional type, 71, 91
Trapoldner, Lucas, 239
Trattatello in laude di Dante: Boccaccio, 413
Trattato de scientia d'arme: Agrippa, 148, 149 (Fig 38)
Travailleurs de la Mer, Les: Hugo, 405
Travelling Library, 124 (Fig 32)
Travels: Mandeville, 97, 101
Travels of Marco Polo, 32

Treatise on Title pages: de Vinne, 312n.
Trebizond, George of, 52
Trechsel, Gaspard, 167, 172
Trechsel, Johann, 62, 63 (Fig 7), 125, 160, 172
Trechsel, Melchior, 167, 172
Trechsel, Thalia, 160
Tremann, Walter, 421
Trepassement de Notre-Dame, Le, 72, 435
Treperel, Jean, 65, 67
Trepte, Emil *see* Poeschel and Trepte
Tres Compañeros Alemanes, 81
Trevi, 53
Treviso, 57
Treviso, John of, 101
Triangulis, De: Müller, 32
Tribune Book of Open Air Sports, 380
Tridentine Index, 158, 216
'Triga' type, 424
Triod' Cvetnaja, 247
Triod' Postnaja, 247
Trionfò della Fedelta: Electress of Bavaria, 321
Trionfi: Petrarch, 440 see also *Triumphs: Petrarch*
Trissino, Gian Giorgio, 156
Triumphes of Oriana: Morley, 218, 267
Triumphs: Petrarch, 57, 170
Triumps of Maximilian, 134
Triumphwagen Kaiser Maximilians, 134
Trnava, 237, 241
Trojánská Kronika: Colonna, 232–3
Troost der Siele, 195
Trot, Barthélemy, 147
Troy type, 407
Troyes, 64
Truchet, Sebastien, 315
Trujillo, Sebastian, 192
Trukhmenskii, Afanasii, 252
Tryumphes of Fraunces Petrarcke, 258 (Fig 54)
Tschichold, Jan, 419–20
Tuberinus, Johann Mathias, 142
Tübingen, 131, 325
Tucher, Hans, 29
Tuerdank, 135 see also *Theuerdanck, Der*
Tuksiautit Akioreeksautikset, 393
Turčić, Gaspar, 45
Turin, 150, 153, 301–2, 327–8
Turin, Marguerite, Duchess of, 153
Turkenkalender, 16
Turner, Heinrich, 62, 71, 444
Turner, William, 256

Turoczi, John, 239 *see also* Thwrocz Johann
Turre, Johannes de, 435
Turrecremata, Cardinal (Torquemada), 37, 38, 39, 112, 246
Turretinus, Paulus, 441
Tusar, Slavoboj, 423
Tuscher, Marcus, 352
Tusculanae Quaestiones: Cicero, 38
Tusser, Thomas, 260
Twelfth Night: Shakespeare, 153
Twici, –, 104
Týfa, Josef, 423
Tyndale, William, 127, 129, 180, 256, 257
Tyndale's New Testament, 127, 129
Type used in Appian's *Historia Romana,* 43 (Fig 6)
Typecasting machines, 376–7
Type-Composing Machines: Southward, 379
Types *see* named types, Black-letter etc.
Typographia Honteriana, 239–40
Typographia Orientalis, 278
Typographia, or the Printers' Instructor: Johnson, 348
Typographia Savarinia, 300
Typographia Telegdiniana, 241
Typographic excesses, 401 (Fig 86)
Typographic printing, 3
Typographical Antiquities: Dibdin, 346
Typographie als Kunst: Müller, 420
Typographische Gestaltung: Müller, 420

·U

Ubaldi, Baldo degli, 57
Ubaldi, Matteo degli, 57
Ubaldis, Angelus de, 437
Uberti, Fazio degli, 445
Uglheimer, Peter, 41
Ugoleto, Angelo, 54
Ugoleto, Francesco, 54
Uher, Edmond, 428
Uhertype filmsetting machine, 428
Ullman, Prof. B. L., 109
Ulm, 6, 33–4
Ulman, Bendicht, 180
Ulozhenie: Aleksei Mikhailovich of Russia, 252
Ulrich, Hans, 276
Ulrici, Olaus, 225
Ulrickson, Oluf, 226
Ulyxea XIII libros, De la: Homer, 191
'Uncial' type, 424

Unger, Johann, 323
Unger, Johann Friedrich, 323
Unger, Johann Georg, 323–4
Unger types, 323, 419
Ungler, Florian, 246, 247–8
Ungut, Meinard (Meinhardt), 81, 84, 187, 189, 218, 438
Unholden oder Hexen, Von den: Molitoris, 34
Unio dissidentium: Badius, 183
Univers type, 430
Universal Magazine, 357 (Fig 77)
University Library, Copenhagen, 230
University Library, Gent, 216
University Library, Zagreb, 245
Universo, De: Maurus, 24
Unkel, Bartholomaeus von, 28
Updike, Daniel B., on:
 Dutch printing, 352
 English printing, 260–1, 342–3
 French printing, 162, 174, 281, 316
 Italian printing, 330
 Spanish printing, 194, 333
Upper-Rhine type, 110 (Fig 24)
Uppsala, 137, 224–5
Urdermann, Heinrich, 443
Urfé, H. d', 295
Usatges de Barcelona e Constitucions de Catalunya, 84
Ushakov, Simon, 252–3
Utilitate Psalterii Mariae, De: de Rupe, 438
Utrecht, 73, 214
Utrecht Missal, 214
Uttini, Francesco, 353

V

Vajsenhuset, 352
Valdarfer, Christopher, 41, 52–3
Valdezoccho, Bartolommeo de, 58
Vale Press, 409, 410
Valencia, 79, 189n., 192, 332–3
Valentin, Florent, 72
Valentin et Orson, 70
Valentin, Robert, 72
Valerio, Dorico, 157
Valerio de las istorias escolasticas: de Almela, 191
Valerius Maximus, 44, 60n., 125
Valetta, 305–7
Valkendorf, Archbishop Erik, 226
Valleyre, –, 371
Valturius, Robertus, 57, 445

Van Gaebeeks, the, 283
Van der May, –, 369
Van der May, the firm of, 351
Van de Velde, Henry, 415, 417
Vandrell, Mateo, 438
Vankuli, Mahommed ben Mustafa, 309
Vanconi, –, 372
Várad, 241
Varela, Juan, 192
Variarium Lectionem, 223
Vasa Bible, 137
Vascosan, Jeanne, later Morel, 164
Vascosan, Michel de, 164–5
Vazquez, Juan, 81, 444
Vatican Library, 148
Vatican Press, 157–8
Vautrollier, Thomas, 216, 263 (Fig 58), 264–5
Vechter, Thomas de, 202–3
Vedomosti, 354
Vegetius, 97
Vegius, Maphaeus, 436
Veldener, Johann (Jan), 73–4, 77, 437, 440
Vendrell, Matthew (Mateo), 79, 83 *see also* Flander, Mattheus
Venetias: Modestus, 153
Venice, 40–7, 205–6, 301, 326, 328
Venice Signoria, 40, 46
Venus and Adonis: Shakespeare, 265 (Fig 59)
Verard, Antoine, 65, 66, 68 (Fig 8), 70, 158
Verborum significatione, De: Festus, 52, 440
Vercellensis, Albertinus, 45
Vercellensis, Bernardinus, 209
Vercellensis, Joannes, 45
Vercial, Clemente Sanchez de, 81
Verdonck, Corneille, 216
Vergaz, –, 333
Vergetios, Angelos, 174
Vergier spirituel, 195
Verico, Antonio, 326
Verlag Felix Krais, 419
Verlag der Gutenberg-Gesellschaft, 414
Vernacular Bibles, 27
Vernet, Horace, 402
Verona, 57
Verona, Gaspare de, 143
Verona, Johannes (John) de, 57, 445
Veronensis (Veronese), Guarinus, 143, 442, 444
Verovio, Simon, 216
Versuch und Muster, ohne all Lumpen Papier zu machen: Schöffer, 325

Verusi, Giovanni, 302
Vervliet, H. D. L., 176, 177, 202
Vesalius, Andreas, 180
Vestenberger, Franz, 30
Veyl, Sweybold *see* Fiol, Swietopek
Veyrin-Forrer, Mme, 164 and n.
Viaje de la tierra sancta: Breydenbach, 82
Viart, Guyone, 160
Vibert, –, 396, 399
Vibert and Luy Foundry, 399
Viborg, 226, 229
Vicentino, Lodovico *see* Arrighi, Lodovico
Vicentino type, 146, 413 *see also* Arrighi types
Vicenza, 56
Victor, Hieronymus, 141, 246, 247, 248, 441
Victoria, Johann, S. J., 142
Victoria Public Library, Australia, 105
'Videocomp' filmsetter, 429
Vieillard, Nicolas, 173
Vieira, Fr Nicolau, 85
Vienna, 140–2, 275
Vienna State Library, 19, 136
Vierge, Daniel, 405
Viero, Teodoro, 326
View of Early Typography: Carter, 13n.
Vieweg, Eduard, 386
Vieweg, Hans Friedrich, 324, 385
Vieweg, Heinrich, 386
Vigils, 30
Vignay, Jean de, 49, 70
Vignettes:
   Denmark, 352; England, 345; France, 313, 314, 400–1, 403; Italy, 326, 329 (Fig 72)
Vignettes gravées sur bois et polytypée par Thompson, 401
Vignon, Eustace, 183
Vigny, Alfred de, 405
Villa, Pietro, 436
Villa Dei, Alexander de, 123, 438, 443
Villa-Diego, Bernardo de, 303, 304, 333
Villafranca, Pedro de, 303
Villalpando, Fermin Thadeo, 333
Villanueva, Juan de, 187
Villar, Juan, 303
Villari, Mario, 305
Villegas, Archdeacon Pedro Fernandez de, 189
Villena, Enrique de, 83
Vilna, 251
Vimperk, 233
Vincent, Antoine, 184

Index

Vincent, Barthélemy, 167
Vinegar Bible, 335
Vingaard, Hans, 226
Vingaard, Matz, 227, 228
Vingle, Jean de, 173, 188
Vingle, Pierre de, 183, 184, 441
Violette, Pierre, 72
Violinschule: L. Mozart, 350
Virdung, Johann, 441
Virgil:
    England, 342, 343; France, 71, 121, 398, 400; Germany, 411; Italy, 56, 125, 146, 436, 438, 440
Viris illustribus, De: Petrarch, 442
Visagier, –, 162
Visio delectable, La: de la Torre, 71
Vischer, Roemer, 283
Vissenaecken, Willem van, 214
Vita Christi: Jinénez (Ximinez), 81, 84, 438
Vita Christi: Ludolphus, 77
Vita Christi: de Saxonia, 85 (Fig 12), 86, 187
Vita Christi per coplas: de Mendoza, 83, 84, 446
Vita S. Lidwinae: Brugman, 443
Vita della Vergine Maria, La: Cornazzano, 440
Vitae imperatorum imagines, 220
Vitae parallelae: Plutarch, 435
Vitae Patrum (Italian), 443
Vitae sanctorum patrum, 112
Vitale, Bernardino, 153
Vitalis Manaud, 9, 10
Vitas Patrum, 100, 436
Vitré, Antoine, 293, 295, 299–300
Vittorelli, Francesco, 326
Vivian, Methieu, 441
Vizé, Donneau de, 296
Vizimbo, José, 86
Vizsoly, 240
Vocabulario universal en latin y en romance, 81
Vocabularius Ex Quo, 21, 437
Vocabulista, 445
Vocabulista Italico-Tedesco, 140
Vogel-ABC, 411
Vogeler, Heinrich, 417
Voirin, Henri, 365, 375
Volckmar *see* Kohler and Volckmar
Vollenhoe, Johannes de, 76
Vollstandiges Lehrbuch der Steindruckerey, 374n.
Volpe, Lelio della, 327
Volpe, Petronio della, 327
Volpi, Gaetano, 327

Volpi Giovanni Antonio, 327
Voltaire, 344, 403
Voltz, Nikolaus, 137
Vondel, Josse van den, 283
Voraine, Jacobus de, 70, 97, 110 (Fig 24), 195
Vos, Martin de, 216
Voskens, Dirk, 285, 291
Voskens, Reinhard, 272
Vostre, Simon, 66, 69, 70
Voti, I, 329
Voyage d'Egypte et de Nubie: Norden, 352
Voyage en terre sainte: Mandeville, 72, 439
Voyages pittoesques . . . . . de l'ancienne France, 402
Vuković, Božidar, 244, 245 and n.
Vuković, Vinzenz, 245 and n.
Vulgate Bible, 196, 332
Vulteius *see* Visagier
Vurster, Johannes, 440
Vydenast, Johannes, 57
Vyel, Andreas, 442

W

Wächtler, Caspar, 277
Wadham College Library, Oxford, 89
Waelrant, Hubert, 215
Waesberghe, Jan van, 193, 283
Waesberghe, Johannes Janssonius I, Van, 283
Waesberghe, Johannes Janssonius II, Van, 283
Wafflard, Pierre-Louis, 395–6, 398
Wagner, Gregor, 243
Wagner, Hans, 140
Wagner, Joseph, 328
Wagner, Leonhard, 134
Wagner, Peter, 32–3
Wagner, Valentin, 240
Walbaum, Justus Erich, 384
Walbaum, Theodore, 384
Walbeck, Johannes, 56
Walch, Georg, 81
Waldegrave, Robert, 271
Waldfoghel, Anna, 9
Waldfoghel, Procope, 9–10
Walker and Boutall, 406
Walker, Emery, 344, 406, 409
Wallau, Heinrich, 19, 418
Wallhausen, Jacobi von, 252
Walpole, Horace, 330, 406
Walt, Peder Eriksson, 229
Walter, John, 361–2
Walthari type, 418, 422

Walther, Johann, 441
Walton, Brian, 288
Wann, Paulus, 140
Warde, Frederic, 413
Warrington Guardian, 381
Watson, James, 335, 352
Watts, John, 338, 339
Weber, Hans von, 419
Web-fed rotary press, 365, 367
Webster, –, 153
Wechel, Andreas (André), 133, 168
Wechel, Chrestien, 133
Weelkes, Thomas, 218, 267
Wehmer, Dr Carl, 16
Weiditz, Hans, 138
Weigere, Hermen, 227 (Fig 50)
Weimar, 274, 384
Weimar Gesellschaft der Bibliophilen, 417
Weiss, –, 163
Weiss, –, 360
Weiss, Emil Rudolf, 411, 423
Weiss, Hans, 137
Weissenstein, Albert von, 92
Welker, Conrad, 27
Welser, the firm of, 127
Welsh Bible, 264
Wenssler, Michael:
   France, 64, 437, 440; Frankfurt Fair, 220;
   Switzerland, 83, 87, 88, 112, 254
Wentzel, Jakob, 278
Werdenberg, Rudolf von, 440
Werk van S. H. de Roos, Het: Stols, 412
Werner, Johann Hendrik, 353
Werrecoren, Pieter, 444
Werther: Goethe, 324
Westphalia (Westfalia), Johann of, 73, 74, 112
Westral, Joachim, 444
Westval, Joachim, 36
Wetstein, Hendrik Floris, 350
Wetter, Bernhard, 32
Wexonius, Michael, 229
Weyerstraeten, Elizeus, 283
Wharfedale Press, 366
Whatman, James, 342, 348
Whistler, –, 375
White, John, 371
Whitchurch, Edward, 256, 257
Whittingham, Charles the Elder, 387, 391
Whittingham, Charles the Younger, 356, 390
   (Fig 83), 391

Whittingham, William, 183
Wicks, Frederick, 377, 378
Wicks' typecasting machine, 378
Widmanstetter, Georg, 142
Wie Rome Gepauet ward, 5
Wie die Turken die christlichen Kirchen angefochten:
   de Sancto Remigio, 29
Wiegand, Willi, 411
Wiegand types, 411
Wieland, Cristoph, 322
Wielun, Hieronymus of, 248
Wiener, Johann *see* Petri, Johann
Wiener, René, 416
Wijnman, –, 203
Wilbye, John, 267
Wilkins, David, 339
Willer Catalogue, 221
Willer, Georg, 221
William Caxton's houses at Westminster: Tanner,
   94
William Ged and the Invention of Stereotype:
   Carter, 371
Williaert, Adrian, 149
Wilno, 234–5, 248
Wilson, Alexander, 337, 348
Wilson, Andrew, 371
Wilson and Baine, 337
Wilson foundry, 385
Wilson and Grey, 359 and n.
Wilson, J. Dover, 411
Wimpheling, –, 89
Winkler, Andreas, 137
Winsberg, Erhard, 60
Winter, Johann, 229
Winter, Rupprecht, 179
Winterburg, Hans, 141
Winters, Conrad, 28, 111
Wirczburg, Heinrich, 443
Wirsung, Marcus, 210
Wirzbieta, Maciej, 249
Wisdom Books, 206
Withage, Jan, 197
Witten, Laurence, 79
Wittenberg, 129–30, 276
Wittenberg letter (type), 118 (Fig 31)
Wittersheim and Co., 365
Wittgau, Johann, 276
Wittich, Johann, 324
Wohlgemuth, Michel, 31, 32
Wolde, Dr Ludwig, 411

Wolf, Jan, 234
Wolf, Johann, 181
Wolf, Rudolf, 421
Wolfe, Reyner, 255 (Fig 53), 263, 269–70
Wolfenbüttel Library, 25
Wolff, Jakob *see* Pforzheim, Jakob von
Wolff, Kurt, 412
Wood, Henry Wise, 373
Wood blocks:
  in music printing, 207, 208, 210, 214
  see also Woodcuts
Wood engravings *see* Woodcuts
Woodcuts:
  early title pages, 115
  England:
    Bensley, 347
    Caxton, 95 (Fig 14), 97
    Clowes, 356
    Day, 260–1
    Jugge, 257
    Pynson, 103 (Fig 19)
    de Worde, 100 (Fig 17)
    see also Bewicke, Thomas
  France, 63, 65, 68 (Fig 8), 70, 404
  Germany, 25, 28, 29, 138, 139 (Fig 35) *see also*
    Dürer, Albrecht
  Holland, 76 (Fig 10)
  Italy, 42 (Fig 5), 48
  Moravia, 235 (Fig 52)
  Netherland, 74 *see also* Holland
  Portugal, 85 (Fig 12), 86
  Russia, 250, 251
  Spain, 185, 186, 191, 192, 193
  Switzerland, 89, 90 (Fig 13)
Woodfall, George, 360
Worde, Wynkyn de, 74, 97–8 (Fig 16), 99–100
  (Fig 17), 101, 105, 207, 216, 255–6
Works of Geoffrey Chaucer, 407
Works of Ben Jonson, 286 (Fig 66)
World of the Elseviers: Davies, 280n.
Worstelingen: van Eyck, 412
Wotton, Dr William, 172
Wren's City Churches: Mackmurdo, 415
Wright, Thomas, 288
Wrocslaw *see* Breslau
Wurden die ersten Pressen in Barcelona und Zara-
  goza von einem Mann geleitet?: Rubio, 79
Wurm, Hans, 5
Wurster, Hans, 55
Württemberg, Eberhard of, 443

Würzburg, Theodor of, 208
Wust, Balthasar Christoph the Elder, 276
Wust, Christien, 276

X

Xante, 310
Xaravia, Antonio Martinez de *see* Nebrija,
  Antonio de
Ximeno, José, 333
Ximenez de Cisneros, Cardinal Francisco, 84,
  125, 187–8, 189 *see also* Jiménez, Francisco
Xylography *see* Woodcuts

Y

Yciar, Juan de, 188
Yemantszoon van Middelborch, Mauritz
  (Maurizius), 75, 196, 237
Ylimmaisen Keisaren Jesuxen Christuxen, 229
Yonge, Nicolas 217
York, 312
York, Alcuin of, 108
Young, James, 377, 378
Young, John, 347
Yriarte, Charles, 405

Z

Zabludov, 251
Zacuto, Abraham ben Samuel, 86
Zagurovic, Hieronymus (Jerolim), 244, 245
Zainer, Günther, 28, 33, 118, 123, 435
Zainer, Johann, 33–4, 95 (Fig 14), 445
Zamora, 83
Zamorensis, Rodericus, 61, 89
Zamość, 248
Zanetti, Bartolomeo, 151
Zanetti, Christoforo, 206
Zanetti, Luigi, 158
Zanis (Zanus) de Portesio, Bartolomeo de, 46,
  442
Zapolya, Jan Sigismund, 243
Zapolya, Rudolf, 243
Zarotto, Antonio, 52, 53
Zarotto, Fortunato, 52
Zarotus brothers, 440
Zatta, Antonio, 326, 328
Zayas, Gabriel de, 197
Zedler, Prof., 15, 16, 18, 20, 21, 25
Zeis, Gerardo de, 150
Zell, Ulrich, 12, 26–7, 117n., 439
Zelie dans le desert, 372

Zeninger, Conrad, 30, 32
Zentenar-Fraktur, type, 412
Zerotin, Jan of, 237
Ziletus, Innocens, 442
Zilverdistel, de, 412 *see also* Kunera Press
Zimmermann, Michael, 142
Zola, Emile, 405
Zonca, Vittorio, 302

Zöpfel, David, 133
Zucco, Accio, 57
Zucchi, the, 328
Zunner, Johann, 277
Zurich, 92, 181–2
Zwolle, 75–6
Zyelen troeste, Der, 444
Zywot pana Jezusa Krysta, 248